AF664342

Main Currents in Indian History

Main Currents in Indian History

Ancient, Medieval and Modern

(From the Beginnings to 1964)

K.S. Kameswara Rao

RAWAT PUBLICATIONS

Jaipur • New Delhi • Bangalore • Hyderabad • Guwahati

ISBN 978-81-316-0422-9

Published by
Prem Rawat for **Rawat Publications**
Satyam Apts., Sector 3, Jawahar Nagar, Jaipur 302 004 (India)
Phone: 0141 265 1748/7006 Fax: 0141 265 1748
E-mail: info@rawatbooks.com
Website: www.rawatbooks.com

New Delhi Office
4858/24, Ansari Road, Daryaganj, New Delhi 110 002
Phone: 011 2326 3290

Also at *Bangalore, Hyderabad* and *Guwahati*

Typeset by Rawat Computers, Jaipur
Printed at Chaman Enterprises, New Delhi

For

Vasanthi and Dr Satyarani

who inspired me

Contents

Part III
Modern and Post-Independent India

Prologue

Initiation to the study of the society and culture of the old world, Indian subcontinent as an academic discipline was started in the 18th century by European scholars. These scholars are influenced by European Enlightenment in their approach to the study. Perspectives of orientalism, utilitarianism evangelicalism and mercantilism influenced their studies. These studies led to the discovery of the past cultural legacy of India as a land of 'fabulous' and 'untold wealth' of 'mystical happenings' of 'gold digging ants', of naked wanderers in deep forests and also a 'wonder'. Utilitarian philosopher, James Mill, in 1818 published his work entitled *History of British India* and since then historiography of India witnessed the appearance of innumerable books based on the perspectives of traditional, colonial and imperialist, nationalist, Marxists, subaltern, annals, interdisciplinary and post-modern in disguising the process of history of India. Consequently, the scope of the subject enlarged from purely chronological framework of political power structure, society, economy and culture as independent entities to that of understanding the linkages between polity, economy, society and culture in shaping the course of historical development. As a result, the study includes all aspects of human life and relations in time and space. The great savants of pre-independent India delved deep into the original sources and prepared a solid foundation to reconstruct the historical edifice; the post-independent scholars were engaged in studying the process of history at local, regional and national levels from the different perspectives mentioned above. While traditional scholars reconstructed the dynastic, political and cultural history at national and regional levels, starting from D.D. Kosambi to Vijaya Ramaswamy, by their rigorous research based on authenticated sources add new dimensions to the existing images of India's past. All this new dimensional information has not percolated to the student community at bachelor level but remained as a valuable asset of the scholars of universities and articles published in international research journals.

As a teacher of history at the bachelor level, I always felt that there is definite necessity to introduce these new dimensions of recent advances in the areas of social formation, state formation and cultural formations of our pluralistic society to enable the student to understand the process by himself in an open-ended way to arrive at a meaningful appreciation of the historical development. The book *Main Currents in Indian History* placed before you is result of deep sense of urge experienced by me in the last four decades. I do not claim any originality in approach or new content, as my objective is to present in simple terms the synthesis of the last half a century of historical research to understand our past history as a process to the students and laymen.

By process I mean that transition of Indian people in time and space was the sum total effort and effect of man's quest to manipulate nature for advantage by his conscious and unconscious effort to suit his needs of time and space. In this endeavour, man has become a 'Social Animal', 'Tool Maker', 'Maker of History' by using the agencies of change – technology and ideology. We notice an evolution from hunting to food producing, from nomadism to settled life, rural to urban, agrarian to industrial, illiterate to literate and faith-based to rational outlook. In this process, by inventing new technological devices and institutions based on internal and external stimuli, man grew from primitive stage to the contemporary space age. What we notice is constant, continuous self-effort on the part of the people to face the challenges and respond to evolve an Indian view of life as part of universal heritage.

The title of the book signifies the 'Journey of the Indians' from the stone-age life of subsistence to the contemporary idea of a people living in definite geographical area with equity and social justice in a democratic environment within the republican set-up. It is to be noted with agony that still more of a cave culture and less of republican culture exists side by side and the transition in real sense is miles and miles away. It is for the younger generation to accept the challenge and respond positively to accomplish this ideal transition in near future. It is my dream and wish that a knowledge, based on historical awareness will usher in a new mind-set of looking towards the future. Thus, a study of this book enables a student to understand the continuous process of transition of material and cultural milieu of our country and create an awareness that history is not unconnected series of events of significance moulded and shaped by a few great philosopher saints, seers and rulers. The accumulated knowledge that a student gains must make the student practical and pragmatic, ethical and social, altruistic and humanitarian, fuelled by practical idealism for all-round betterment of our pluralistic society. The study should foster a spirit that "Indian culture is neither Hindu, Islamic nor any other wholly. It is a fusion of all." Further it is to be emphasized that a blind reverence for the past is bad and so also is contempt for it, for no future can be founded on either of these. The present and the future inevitably grow out of the past and bear its stamp, and forget this is to build without foundations and cut off the rules of national growth. A time has come when we have to agree with Vivekananda's remark "When, O Lord, shall our land been free from this eternal building upon the past." In the last 100 years and more, we were witnesses to the damage caused to our unified conceptual idea of India by too much concern for the revival and condemnation of the past by a determined few to the non-vocal silence of majority. Time has come for us to realize "we are made wise not by the recollection of the past, but by the responsibility for our future." Discipline of history should be a beacon of life rather than a divider of human beings on the grounds of race, religion, caste and language. Let us make our future to everybody secure, stable, vibrant and meaningful by learning the lesson, that history is a process and we have to avoid the past misdeeds by our collective wisdom.

This is my sincere wish. I am greatly obliged to my wife, Jyothirmayi who has been my constant source of inspiration and encouraged me to complete this book and also to my student friends and to my daughters. I am also grateful to my young friend T. Sashi Sekhar who has read the entire manuscript and offered constructive criticism and made necessary modifications wherever required and made this work presentable to younger generation. I also thank Srinu Chikatla who has typed competently and neatly by sitting with me hours and hours and days and days. I thank Pranit Rawat of Rawat Publications, Jaipur for bringing out the book neatly and attractively.

K.S. Kameswara Rao

Introduction to History as an Academic Discipline

History as an academic discipline is the study of the evolution of humankind in space and time, assiduously constructed by a historian with the help of authenticated sources, primary, secondary, of archaeology, and literary. As such, history becomes a record of man's endeavour in all aspects from times immemorial to the present. A historian, while recording man's efforts in totality chooses such facts, as he finds to be significant landmarks in political, social, economic and cultural spheres that determine the journey of man. Consequently, though the facts are sacred and can speak for themselves, it is the historian while recording and interpreting them speaks from his perception. Though a totally objective holistic construction of historical process is desirable, it cannot always be so, due to subjective perception of the historian and inadequacy of sources. Resultantly, there are different versions of historical explanations depending on the focus of the aspect chosen by a historian. As such, for some, the political aspect of historical process is more important than the other aspects such as society, economy and culture, while some give primacy to society, or economy or culture, it is to be realized that all these aspects are interrelated and complementary but sometimes they may conflict with the interests of the multitude of human beings of the society. An observation of the historiographical trends of reconstructing the history of any country reveals the same process with all its merits and demerits. As human beings are the subject and the object of the historical process, history is not the study of a single individual of however extraordinary qualities of leadership and charisma, but the sum total of activities of the people based on their aspirations, needs, values, grit, determination, and the course charted to achieve the world of their choice. As such, history is a collective memory of the victors and the vanquished, the achievers and the non-achievers, small and big, literate and non-literate, in their pursuit of a cherished goal. Thereby, history becomes a social science, where primacy is given to social group activity, as man can never live and exist in isolation. A study of history from that perceptive will be instructive, illuminating, interesting, and exhilarating as it makes one understand how social groups overcame the obstacles thrown up by nature and became successful or unsuccessful, developed or underdeveloped, exclusive or inclusive in outlook, that decided the historical process experienced by them in achieving their desired goal. It thus enables one to understand the process of history, accept what is desirable, and leave out the excess baggage of undesirable attributes and attitudes that stand in the way of progress from one stage to another. History thus provides one who properly understands the historical process, opportunities to be a benefit of such study and can become essential for human progress. In a country like Bharatavarsha or Bharatakhanda of ancient lore, having a continuous unbroken culture, in spite of cultural and political intrusions or encounters of other countries at regular intervals, makes one wonder at its resilience, its ability to meet the critical situations that threatened its roots of existence. But wonder and admiration are not enough; one requires a critical and judicious inquiry into the historical assumptions or conclusions or explanations of the process of historical change, if the study of history is to be meaningful and relevant one should learn the lessons of history and enable people to make future India vibrant, stable, secure and egalitarian in spirit and practice.

There are two perceptions of history – academic and popular. The academic discipline of history backed by rigorous research methodology of collating and scrutinizing the available different sources, proves that Bharatakhanda or Bharatavarsha of ancient lore is a vast country, whose history and culture are known from nearly more than five thousand years. Justifiably, the erstwhile Indian subcontinent is regarded as one of world's important great early centres of culture, along with Egypt, West Asia and China. Contrasting with the academic perception of the longevity of Indian culture is the popular belief that the Indian civilization is timeless; stretching the four *Yugas* of *Krita*, *Dwapara*, *Treta* and *Kali* (the present age). Rajesh Kocchar writing about the concept of time in his book *The Vedic People* (1995) summarizes the problem thus, "Our interpretation of the past depends upon our perception of the present. That is why history cannot provide proof; it can only provide illustrations. This, however, does not mean that history is a free-for-all and can never be definitive. Uncertainty in history lies at the level of the significance of events, not at the level of events themselves. If there are only two points marked on a graph paper, any number of curves can be made to pass through them. But if the number of points is large then the connecting curve suggests itself. When two historians disagree, they should not be telling each other: 'These are my facts and those are your facts, let us use them as brickbats'. Instead, they should be saying: 'These are the facts, not your facts or my facts but the facts. And this is my interpretation and that is yours'."

For a century and a half, scholars of various disciplines have studied the Indian culture with different perceptions, focussing their attentions on minute aspects of culture in space and time. Almost all the facets of life of the Indians have been thoroughly studied, receiving appreciation as well as criticism. Each scholar produced an image of India in space and time basing on his or her comprehension. The images vary from being 'wonderful', 'unique', to 'oppressive', 'stratified', 'stagnant and unchanging'. As a result, what we have today before us are partisan images but not holistic images of India. Efforts to arrive at possible holistic images are a desideratum in the long-term interests of the future of Indian socio-cultural mosaic. To quote Kocchar (1995) again, "All research is open-ended. At any given time, there are questions, which cannot be answered with certainty. To answer them new data are needed. The new data answers old questions but in turn raises new questions which, however, are more intricate than the earlier ones. In this manner the frontier of ignorance is pushed to more and more subtle levels."

Part I
Early India

1

A Survey of the Sources

Influence of Geography on Indian History

History is agreed upon as an uninterrupted process in time and space. Yet knowledge of the period is essential to understand and appreciate the nature of the historical changes that take place in time and space. Periodization of Indian history is a tricky and controversial concept. There is no unanimity among the historians about the periodization of Indian history. Broadly, there are two types of periodization in vogue, one on the religious and ethnic nature of rulers which divides it as Hindu, Muslim and the British periods and the other, borrowed from European historiography – Ancient, Medieval and Modern.

Initially, the British historian, James Mill proposed the tripartite division of Indian history on religious and ethnic nature of rulers as Hindu, Muslim and British. Even this division is not precise as all the rulers in the Hindu period were not Hindus and we have a number of rulers who migrated to India from other countries and ruled side by side with the Hindu rulers and the Hindus were not culturally a homogenous entity either. Further, this division is not acceptable to modern historians as it has communal tinge which is not desirable for a pluralistic country like India. But there are still some historians who believe in that division. The second type of division – Ancient, Medieval and Modern – is also regarded as inadequate as the terms are imprecise and vague and fail to explain the nature of changes that took place from time to time.

In the last few decades, there is a revisiting of periodization by the historians because new questions are asked and new sources are consulted and collated to arrive at conclusions regarding the factors of change that necessitated new socio-economic formations that led to new cultural and political patterns that shaped the course of our historical process.

Keeping the latest trends in periodization in mind an attempt is made in this book to give primacy to the nature of change propelled by factors of change – technology, material milieu and ideology – in the creation of new socio-economic formation linking it to political and cultural formation in time and space. As there is so far no new nomenclature acceptable to all, in this book too I followed the broad periodization of ancient, medieval and modern as that format is still popular.

In this book the ancient period begins with prehistory and ends with the Gupta age. The medieval period begins with the post-Gupta age and ends with the advent of Europeans. The medieval period witnessed the emergence and assertion of regional polities and cultures and the arrival of two separate nationalities, the Muslims with belief in Islam and the westerners believing in Christianity who played a crucial role in integrating politically and creating a crucible of culturally diverse India. The modern period begins with colonialism introduced by the new political masters, the British. The modern period witnessed the growth and spread of new ideas and ideals of democracy, equality, social justice, consequent to the introduction of western model of educational system. The introduction of colonial power structure which led to ruination of Indian populace led to non-violent and sometimes to violent mass upsurge that resulted in the declaration of Indian independence and division of India on the principle of separate nationalities in 1947. The book ends with 1964, the year in which our first democratically elected Prime Minister, Jawaharlal Nehru breathed his last after successfully building a vibrant India based on republican ideals.

Generally, the historian with the help of available primary and secondary sources reconstructs the history of any country. As history is not a simple narration of events in a chronological and spatial order, the historian has to choose the sources that are authentic and can be corroborated by other sources before arriving at a historical generalization. As the contemporary approach to history is to understand the historical process and attempt to explain it in the present times, a historian should be knowledgeable about theories of historical method as well as of other social sciences. It is essential to develop the needed analytical skills of source materials objectively before the historical process is constructed.

Primary sources are those, which are contemporaneous with an event or happening, and secondary sources are those, which belong to a later time. For instance, the Asokan edicts are the primary sources to understand Asoka's *Dhamma*. The Allahabad Pillar *Prasasthi* and the Aihole epigraph of Samudragupta and Pulakesin II are respectively the primary sources for understanding the conquests of Samudragupta and Pulakesin II. Romila Thapar's *Asoka and the Decline of the Mauryas* belongs to the category of secondary sources as she wrote that book after a thorough examination of the entire published and original sources.

Broadly, the sources of Indian history are divided as: (1) literary, and (2) archaeological. Literary sources are further divided into as sacred and secular, indigenous and foreign accounts, dramas, and Kavyas written in Sanskrit, Prakrit, Pali and different vernacular languages. Archaeological sources are divided into monuments, epigraphs and coins. The archaeological sources are very useful to reconstruct the history of the people who were not literate or whose script is yet to be understood satisfactorily as also of the early and medieval periods of Indian history. Besides the above mentioned conventional sources non-conventional sources like legends, myths, memories, beliefs, practices, language, proverbs, idioms, personal names, surnames and names of places are also used by a historian to obtain a comprehensive image of the society studied and analysed by him. Coming to modern and contemporary periods of study, sources like oral tradition, diaries, biographies, autobiographies, print media, visual media, photographs and cinema are also used by the historians.

Literary Sources

The Vedic literature consisting of the four Vedas, called the Samhitas, the Brahmanas the Aranyakas, the Upanishads, the Sutras and Sastric literature, the two great epics (the *Ramayana* and the *Mahabharata*), the eighteen Puranas, the Buddhist literature consisting of the three Pitakas (the *Vinaya*, the *Sutta* and the *Abhidamma*), the *Dhammapada*, the *Theragatha*, the *Buddha Vamsa*. *Dipa Vamsa* and *Mahavamsa,* the Ceylonese chronicles the works of Acharya Nagarjuna, *Prajna Paramita* and *Madhyamika Sutras* constitute literary sources; *Buddhacharita* of Asvaghosha and the Jatakas are some of the important sacred texts. Jaina literature also contains useful information about the Jaina faith and other aspects. Secular literature is enormous of which, *Mudrarakshasa* of Visakhadatta, *Arthasastra* of Kautilya, *Nitisara* of Kamandaka, Patanjali's *Mahabhashya* and Panini's *Asthadhyayi* the dramas of Kalidasa; *Malavikagnimitram, Abhijnana Sakuntalam* and his Kavya *Meghasandesa,* Bhasa's *Svapnavasavadatta* and *Pratijna Yaugandharayana,* Harshavardhana's *Nagananda*, *Ratnavali* and *Priyadarsika*. Bana's *Harshacharita*, Bilhana's *Vikramarkadevacharita*, Hemachandra's *Kumara Palacharita; Hammirakavya,* of Navachandra, *Navasahasankacharita* of Padmagupta and *Prithviraj Raso* of Chandbardai and Kalhana's *Rajatarangani* are important indigenous literary sources, which help a historian in reconstructing the history of India of their time. R.C. Majumdar observes, "One of the gravest defects of Indian culture, which defies rational explanation is the aversion of Indians to writing history that they never seriously took to the writing of history". Majumdar further notices that *Rajatarangini* can be regarded as a historical text in the true sense of the word as Kalhana followed the techniques of verifying the earlier literature on the subject and looked into the orders of the former kings relating to religious foundations and epigraphs. Further, the chronicles of Gujarat like the *Ras Mala* and *Kirti Kaumudi* of Someswara, *Sukritasamkirtana* of Arosimha, *Prabhandha Chintamani* of Merutunga and *Prabandha Kosha* of Rajasekhara are very useful. The Tamil Sangam literary works; *Tolkappiyam, Kural* or *Tirukkural*. *Silappadikaram* of Ilango Adigal, *Manimekhalai* of Cattanar, *Aggatiyam* of Saint Agathyar are some useful sources for the study of Tamilham in ancient times. Literary sources cannot be accepted as the sole source to reconstruct the historical edifice of a particular time as there is every possibility of the other eulogizing the patron of the literary piece and the purpose of the work may not be to record faithfully like a mirror the condition of the area and times. A historian should be skeptic of the information obtained from literature and corroborate the evidence with other sources.

Foreign Literary Accounts

K.A. Nilakanta Sastri observes that the accounts of any country and its people by foreign observers are of great interest to the historian of the country, for they enable him to know what impression it made upon the minds of such observers, and to estimate with greater confidence the part played by it in the general history of the world. Whereas in the case of India, the native sources of history fail him, partly or altogether, the writings of foreigners gain great value in his eyes.

Herodotus in his *Histories* provides us much useful information about the Indo-Persian relations. Skylark's work gives a good deal of information about India. The Greek author of the *Periplus of the Erythrean Sea* gives a list of Indian ports, harbours and merchandise along with the maritime activities of the ancient Indians. Though defective, Ptolemy's *Geography* gives valuable information about India. Pliny gives an account of the animals, plants and minerals of India of the 1st century AD and about Roman trade in general. Latin documents, accounts of Chinese travellers, the Tibetan historical texts of Taranath and the Arab historians, travellers, and geographers provide much useful information about India.

Archaeological Sources

Archaeology is another primary source for a historian. The most important source for an archaeologist is the excavation method. When a modern field archaeologist comes across an ancient site that needs to be explored he or she chooses a small area and digs vertically down until the natural soil is reached, below which no human habitation is possible. Human occupation of a site results in the accumulation of material in various kinds, which in course of time becomes debris for the next phase of settlement. An archaeologist's task is to identify strata or layers which represent successive phases of occupation. Thus, the history of such occupation is broken into periods, I, II, III and so on, with I denoting the deepest and the oldest. If necessary, the periods are divided into sub-periods: Ia, Ib, Ic. This periodization defines a site's relative chronology. Artifacts (mostly pottery fragments) from different sites are then intercompared to define a material culture on a cultural phase, often named after one of the sites. The next step is to try to establish an absolute chronology. Towards this end, suitable samples are collected from well-defined strata and taken to a laboratory where they are assigned absolute dates using techniques of Calibrated Radio Carbon Dating or Thermoluminescence. Strictly speaking, the laboratory date is applicable to the specific sample. However, by extrapolation, it is applied to the whole assemblage. The extrapolation however, can be problematic. Although each date in itself is accurate, very often a large number of samples from the same layer yield widely different dates. One must then 'select' a date, which represents the whole assemblage, keeping in mind the stratigraphy of the site and synchronism with the other sites. This method is uniformly applied to any archaeological site irrespective of its age and extent: right from the earliest layers of the Indus cultures to the Vijayanagar period.

Archaeological sources are further divided into epigraphs, coins and monuments. Epigraphs are commonly called inscriptions. The importance of epigraphs have been explained by E.J. Rapson as follows, "The inscriptions supply the most valuable evidence as to the political, social and economic conditions of the period and the country to which they belong. They testify on one hand to the restless activity of the military caste and on the other to the stability of institutions which were as a rule, unaffected by military conquest". Generally, the epigraphs are inscribed on stone and metals. The epigraphs of early India are in either Brahmi or Kharosti script. The epigraphs can be divided into commercial, donative, commemorative, literary, and eulogistic. The Hatigumpha epigraph of Kharavela of Kalinga is of pure eulogistic type. Allahabad Prasasti of Samudra Gupta is also of the same category. The Nasik Cave inscription of Usavadatta and the Nasik Cave inscription of Gautami Balasri belong to the mixed type. The Rumindei epigraph of Asoka belongs to the commemorative category because it reads as follows, "King Priyadarsi, beloved of the Gods, when he had been consecrated many years ago, came in person and did worship. Because here the Sakya sage, the Buddha, was born, he caused a stone wall to be made and a stone pillar to be erected". Copper epigraphs became numerous after the sixth century AD and they read like books. The historian has to ascertain the genuineness of the epigraph, as spurious epigraphs have become known.

Numismatics or Coins

Coins are useful in many ways to reconstruct the history of our country. They provide the names of the rulers, fix the chronology, and help to decide the extent of the kingdom of the period. The discovery of the Roman coins confirmed that there was brisk trading activity between Rome and India and proved the economic prosperity and the sea-going activities of the people of India. From the figures of the kings on the coins, we can know the headdress worn by the rulers. Coins indicate the general economic condition of the region at that juncture. Thus, a critical contextual analysis of the coins along with epigraphs and literary evidence yields very useful information to reconstruct the history of the period.

Monuments

Next to epigraphs and coins, monuments, serve a very useful purpose in reconstructing history. Archaeological excavations conducted at Harappa and Mohenjodaro brought to light the first urban civilization of India that helped trace the beginnings of Indian civilization to five or six thousand BC. The excavations at Taxila throw fresh light on the Kushans. The Stupas, Viharas, Chaityas, the earliest temple structures, sculptural embellishments of Barhut, Sanchi Amaravati and Nagarjunakonda, the paintings in Ajanta and Ellora Caves, and the rock-cut temples of the Pallavas are helpful in gaining knowledge of the evolution of Indian art. Along with the monuments, the available pottery and artifacts made of beads, ivory, iron, and copper found in excavations also throw valuable light on the life patterns of early and medieval India.

A survey of the sources for the reconstruction of the history of India can be concluded with a cautious observation that a historian has to be extremely careful while picking what he considers authentic and valuable, by skilful analysis of all available sources by corroborating them from different angles. Only then will a historian be able to make a valid historical generalization that can be useful in the reconstruction of history. Like any profession, history writing, analysis and interpretation is a specialist's craft, requiring special skills to understand the process of history unbiasedly.

Influence of Geography on Indian History

To form a holistic image of India, an attempt to understand and appreciate the role of geography and ecology in moulding the character and psyche of Indians is necessary. What we observe is a harmonious adjustment of physical and cultural environments. Further, we notice that the physical features of the subcontinent facilitating the coexistence of different levels of cultures in different regions is due to ecological and geographical conditions. We also notice the absence of a uniform pattern of culture throughout India at any given time. We come across the phenomenon of very complex cultures coexisting with others in various stages of evolution throughout different parts of India, all through its history, depending on their ecological set-up. Another noticeable feature is that the physical features also regulate the communication system, as are cultural levels. Based on the physical features of the subcontinent and the communication system, it is to be noted that while the main river basins constituted the areas of attraction, the tribal regions constitute the areas of retardation. The areas of relative isolation lay between the areas of attraction and retardation. Though it is agreed that the history of any nation and its environment are mutually complementary, it should be borne in mind that geographical determinism alone cannot explain the historical process of any nation. It can be agreed that geographical features play a significant role, though they are not the prime movers of historical process. The prime mover of historical process is man; the social animal and the toolmaker, or the collective conscious effort of all humans desirous of needed change to make their lives better, more peaceful and happier. In spite of this fact, knowledge of the basic physiographical features of India is essential to comprehend the historical process.

The Indian subcontinent is divided into (a) Himalayan uplands, (b) Indo-Gangetic plains, and (c) Peninsular India. These three divisions are further subdivided for better understanding of the historical process. The Himalayas perennially supply water to the three great systems – Indus, Ganga and Brahmaputra and provide large quantities of alluvium to the plains. Therefore, from the mouth of the Indus to the mouth of the Ganges, we have an alluvial plain spread over an area of, about 3,200 kms with a width of 320 kms. It is no exaggeration to suggest that while the Indus plains witnessed the flowering of the first urban civilization of the subcontinent, the Gangetic plains played a crucial role in sustaining and nurturing urban life, state and imperial power structure. The Indo-Gangetic plains and peninsular India are separated by central India, covering 1,600 kms extending from Gujarat to western Orissa. The Aravali hills in Rajasthan separate the Indus plain from the peninsula. This zone comprises the Vindhyan and Satpura ranges and the Chota Nagpur plateau. Peninsular India forms the southern edge of central India. It was a stable rocky ancient land mass. It gently slopes from west to east. Four major rivers, Mahanadi, Godavari, Krishna and Kaveri flow into the Bay of Bengal. By creating alluvial plains, these rivers created nuclear areas in plains and deltas that continuously sustained cultural growth throughout the course of history.

The rivers, Narmada and Tapti flow westward and join the Arabian Sea in Gujarat after traversing a long distance in the hilly central India. The Deccan plateau is starting here and extends from the Vindhyas in the north to the southern limits of Karnataka. The black soil of Maharashtra and the adjoining parts of central India is suitable for plough agriculture. It is very interesting to note that despite inadequate rainfall and irrigation facilities, early farming began in the Chalcolithic period in the Deccan plateau. The Deccan plateau ends with the Western Ghats on the west and in the east, it is separated from the eastern coastal plains by the Eastern Ghats. The eastern coastal plains are wider than the western coastal plains. The basic peninsular offshoots of the Eastern Ghats are the Nilgiris and the cardamom hills. These geographical divisions are roughly coterminous with the present day linguistic regions. Owing to the ecological and geographical variation, what we notice is biodiversity as well as diversity of lifestyles throughout the subcontinent of India. It is no wonder that Indian character and attitude in general are influenced by the vagaries of nature. It is thus an accepted fact that the pattern of the development of material cultures in India is influenced largely by geographical and ecological factors. It is because of the geographical location of the subcontinent. As the Indian subcontinent is peripheral to the Orient, the oriental influences are clearly visible in the pattern of development of culture and in course of time, those influences were absorbed into a synthetic culture of India.

Until 1922, it was believed that the roots and the beginnings of Indian civilization lay in the handiwork of the Aryans, who were not natives of India and who came to India as migrants. However, the sudden discovery of the Indus civilization or Harappa culture in 1922 revealed that the beginnings of the civilized life could be traced to 5000 years BC. Since then debate has been going on among foreign and Indian scholars regarding who could be the original or indigenous builders of this flourishing urban Indian culture. It has become a contentious issue leading to a sharp division among the scholars. While many believe that the builders of Harappa civilization are non-Aryan and pre-Aryan, or Dravidian, in recent decades the Aryan problem has reopened and now a view is prevalent that the Aryans were natives of India and the so-called invasion of the Aryans is a myth and that Harappans are also Aryans. Efforts are being made to take the antiquity of the Harappan culture back to 8,000 years or so. Unfortunately, it has become such a hotly contested issue, that scholars and people in general are divided into warring camps, throwing insinuation against each other, causing enormous damage to the unity and solidarity, which is essential for the survival of a feeling of oneness. It cannot be proved beyond doubt, that in the distant past, there existed either a pure Aryan or a pure Dravidian race and the culture of that time cannot be labelled either as purely Aryan or purely Dravidian. We are forgetting that this Aryan and Dravidian divide based on racial features and language, custom and tradition, is a colonial construct invented for strategic needs. Knowingly or unknowingly, we have become a prey to the selfish and narrow construct of the colonial masters and are making ourselves a laughing stock for our failure to free ourselves from mental slavey to the west. This is one of the major hurdles standing in the way of India becoming a nation for a century and more. This divide has created an unbridgeable gulf between Indians. As if this contentious issue is not sufficient to destabilize society, another view has gained currency that the original inhabitants of Indian subcontinent are the Adivasis, who have been marginalized in the historical process by the tradition of Brahmanical hegemony. A construct is in circulation that the Brahmanical dominance is responsible for keeping away the Adivasis, the original builders of Indian culture, from the mainstream, for treating them as outcastes or marginalized. This belief also created a stereotype of Indian society as a hierarchical and pyramidical in substance and shape.

2

Prehistoric Cultures of India

In this backdrop, let us attempt to construct the beginning of the process of cultures in India from the prehistoric period to the beginnings of the historical period. Human existence on the Indian soil is known from about the Pleistocene or the last Ice Age which goes back to two million years. Though we have not yet recovered a human skeleton of the early man, a paleolith or a stone tool used by the earliest Indian was discovered in 1863. Since then large quantities of artefacts have been discovered in different parts of India. Today, we are not in a position to satisfactorily determine the size and distribution of demographic pattern and the pattern and sequence of ecological adaptations in that distant past. B.B. Lal is of the view that in comparison to Africa, India was settled at a later period. A comparative study of the African and Indian settlements and tool patterns indicates that the stone technology of the subcontinent passed through the same broad evolutionary stages as that of Africa. Hand axe, cleaver, chopper, flake, side scraper, and burin were some of the paleolithic tools made by the early inhabitants of India. These tools make us believe that their makers led a hunter-gatherer life on a subsistence pattern. It is very likely that the habitants of India of this period subsisted on animals such as ox, bison, nilgai, chinkara, gazelle, black buck, antelope, sambar, spotted deer, wild boar, tortoise and fish, honey and plant foods like roots, seeds, fruits and leaves. Their subsistence pattern of living and social life can be inferred from the rock paintings and carvings. The general time-frame for Paleolithic cultures in India can be bracketed between 40,000 BC to 10,000 BC. The cultural sequences from 10,000 BC to the start of the proto-historic phase are again geographically divided and from roughly 5000 BC they can be subdivided from sporadic findings into specific ecological zones with typical use of tool-technologies and distributive patterns resulting in stratified assemblages. The cave paintings at Bhimbetka located on the Vindhyan range are a good means to infer the pattern of life of the earliest inhabitants. These paintings also reveal that they lived in small bands or groups, moving like nomads hunting and gathering food. We notice that as the climate and temperature became warm and dry, there were changes in fauna and flora, as also the pattern of life. The tools they made became small. This phase, called Mesolithic is said to have started around 8,000 BC. In this phase, man in India lived by hunting, fishing and fowling. Rock paintings reflect the ecological and material changes that took place during this age. We also come across both Paleolithic tools, like scraper, burin and choppers along with microliths ranging from one to eight cms like the blade, core, point, triangle, lunate and trapeze. In this phase, people led a life of subsistence. Their diet included meat and vegetables. Rock paintings found in sites like Bhimbetka, Adamgarh, Pratapagarh and Mirjapur reflect the ecological and material changes. Another factor of significance is that besides animals known to them, they painted what interested them – childbirth, child-rearing, burial ceremonies and sexual union. These evidences prove that by this time, social organization was taking stable shape and their religious beliefs started taking shape, influenced by ecological and material changes. Further, the wide distribution and location of Mesolithic sites in different parts of India clearly indicate that they exploited varied environments such as sparsely wooded territories, sandy areas, and Vindhyan and Kaimur sandstone ranges, riverbanks and seacoasts. This suggests that they were adept in adapting themselves to changing ecological and material conditions, due to the need of the times. B.K. Thapar is of the view that the climatic changes and the shifting of floral and faunal boundaries that occurred at the end of the Pleistocene period are not related to the origin of agriculture in the following stage of the Neolithic phase. For him, "The environment and the exploitative technology, combined with adaptability, were largely responsible for the transition from the food gathering to the food producing economy". Sir John Lubbock, in *Prehistoric Times* (1865) coined the term Neolithic. Sir John used the term Neolithic to describe an age where the lithic artefacts were more skilfully made, more varied in form and were polished. Later V. Gordon Childe explained the Neolithic-Chalcolothic culture as a revolution that heralded a self-sufficient food producing economy. Miles Burkitt described the practice of agriculture, domestication of animals, grinding and polishing of stone tools and the manufacture of pottery as the characteristics of the Neolithic age. In recent times, the term is used to denote a pre-metal age where there was an assured supply of food by producing cereals and domestication of animals, and where people led a settled life. In spite of these changes, the most essential characteristics of Neolithic culture are the groundstone tools. Domestication of plants and animals led to other features like the emergence of village societies based on settled life, the beginnings of agricultural techniques, and man's control over nature and exploitation of natural resources for the sustenance of life. The beginning of agricultural technology throughout the world was not uniform. It is suggested that the domestication of animals and plants by human beings began approximately in the Nile valley in 12,500 BC, in Western Asia from 8500 BC onwards, in Baluchistan from 6000 BC, in Belan valley in U.P. between 5440–4530 BC and in South India between 2500–1500 BC. It is to be noticed that while in some places cultivation of cereals preceded domestication of animals and plants, in some other areas domestication of animals and plants was followed by agricultural operations. Thus, prehistoric Indian society also evolved from hunting-gathering stage to food producing or a rudimentary agricultural society. An animated debate is going on in India regarding the stimuli for the beginning of the food producing society.

While Sankalia and Alchin attribute it to Western Asian or Iranian impact, A.V. Schchetenko, a Russian archaeologist, holds the view that the Chalcolithic culture of India is purely indigenous in origin and development. Contradicting the above two views, Wilhelm G. Solheim II and Saway opine that South-East Asia provided the necessary stimulus. I.K. Sarma, while accepting the above view with certain reservation, thinks that it cannot be established specifically. Further, I.K. Sarma is of the view that in the very process of evolution of man from the era of transition, from food collection to food producing, there were two distinct movements. The first group, who used groundstone axe, of central, eastern and peninsular India cleared forests, occupied rock shelters, caves and open sides in river valleys and hilly areas started the incipient cultivation. The second group of pastoralists who were by nature sedentary with herding of cattle as their main occupation, started incipient shifting cultivation besides food collection. From this observation, a hypothesis may be postulated that a long period of herding activity appears to have preceded the beginning of farming as we notice ashmounds in remote forest areas as well as near the settlements. We may agree with Shereen Ratnagar's opinion, "there was no particular period in south Asia when hunters and gatherers took to agriculture and animal rearing. The Neolithic stage appeared in different regions at different times, in each case with a unique stone and ceramic technology and range of domestication". Shereen Ratnagar's statement that not all Neolithic economies were based on species locally domesticated is also a valid explanation that needs to be noted. As noticed by Pande, Narain and Dikshit, the Neolithic cultures in the Jhelum valley and in the Garo and north Chachar hills exhibit a frontier character, with artefactual links with cultures outside the subcontinent. In Orissa, we observe the mingling of traditions from the Indian north-east and the Deccan plateau. Until the detailed stratigraphical levels with artefacts are recorded of all sites and detailed accounts of the role of the fauna or flora of the economy are available, nothing conclusive can be said about the regional distribution of the Neolithic society of the subcontinent. One more aspect to be noticed is that the flaked stone technology of the late hunter-gatherers persisted in the subcontinent not only among Neolithic and early farming cultures, but also in the Bronze age, in the cities of the Indus valley.

The archaeologist's spade has brought to light neolithic cultures in all the below regions; in the Kashmir Valley of Northern region, the Vindhyan region, covering the Belan Valley and the Vindhyan plateau in the districts of Allahabad, Mirjapur, Rewa and Sidhhi in the mid-eastern region, covering the northern Bihar district of Saran, the north-eastern region covering Assam and adjacent sub-Himalayan regions, the central eastern region comprising Bengal, Bihar and Orissa complex, covering the Chota Nagpur plateau and the southern region, covering Peninsular India. B.K. Thapar writes, "it must be admitted that except for the Belan Valley, none of the other five regions have the details of the transition from the stage of food-gathering to that of food producing and primary or settled village farming 'be worked out'". As such, our understanding of the origins and early spread of farming in India is still fragmentary.

3

Harappan Culture

Origin, Extent, Urban Planning, Nature of Polity and Economic Organization

In course of time, we notice a gradual transition to urbanization and the emergence of the city as an indicator of the new process of development. The Indus civilization or Harappa cultures were the first urban civilization of the Indian subcontinent. In recent times, these cultures are being commonly referred to as "Saraswati-Sindhu civilization". Harappa and Mohenjodaro are the two very important urban centres of this civilization, besides a number of other centres that have become known in the last eight decades. These changes in the extreme north-west of the Indian subcontinent were by no means sudden. The roots of this culture can be traced to about 7000 BC at Mehergarh. Mehergarh is situated 250 kms north-west of Mohenjodaro in the Kachi Plain between the Indus and the Baluchistan hills. It lies at the foot of the Bolan Pass on river Bolan, a tributary of the Indus. It is located on the historical route that connects the fertile Indus valley, via Quetta and Khandahar, to the Iranian plateau that in turn leads one to Central and West Asia. This culture is divided into 'Pre', 'Early', 'Mature', 'Late' and 'Post' Harappan phases corresponding to BC 5500–3500, BC 3500 to 2650, BC 2650–1800 and BC 1800 onwards. The basis for this division is the pattern of life inferred from the available artefacts unearthed in excavations. These phases clearly exhibit a transition from pastoralism, limited cultivation, seasonal and temporary occupation of villages and later emergence of permanent village settlements to the of use of copper, wheel and plough, and surplus production which enabled the people to undertake long-distance trade. Potteries of both of utilitarian and decorative patterns with motifs such as pepal, humped bull, cobra and horned deity have been discovered in excavations. An interesting feature that deserves notice is the standarization of pottery traditions, along with other material cultural finds belonging to the 'mature' phase despite the existence of regional variations. It may be postulated that the need for regional variations is as old as the Harappan cultures, yet exhibiting a uniform pattern. We also notice the existence of a large number of villages as well as defensive walls, and granaries to store surplus produce. This phase was followed by the growth of large cities with well-laid-out town planning with uniform burnt bricks, weights, seals, and beads along with pottery. The last phase is characterized by the abandonment of the previous Harappan sites and decline of inter-regional exchange. In the crafts and pottery tradition, we notice the impact of village cultures of Punjab, Sutlej, the Jamuna divide and Gujarat.

In the last eight decades, nearly eleven hundred settlements with the characteristic features of Harappa have become known. It is estimated that out of the 1,100 sites so far discovered, nearly 931 are located in the dried up Saraswati-Drishadvati rivers, locally called Hakra in the Bahwalpur sector of Pakistan. The geographical extent of this cultures covers the present-day Rajasthan, Punjab, Gujarat, Pakistan and some nearby regions. There is a debate regarding the core area of this civilization. While the earlier scholars considered the present-day Pakistan and north-western India as its core, recent scholars suggest that it spread from Rajasthan to north-western India and to Pakistan. The important centres or settlements of Harappan culture are Harappa, Mohenjodaro, Kalibangan, Lothal, Suktagendor, Banwali, Chanhudaro, Rangapur, Rojdi, Alamgirpur, and Dholavira. N.N. Bhattacharya (1988) observes: "Remains of Harappa cultures are scattered over an area no less than about a half million square miles and containing more than seventy centres. This area extends up to Suktagendor to the west on Makran coast near the border of Iran, Lothal on the gulf of Cambay and Bhagatrai on the Narmada to the south, the Himalayan foothills as far as Manda in Jammu to the north and Ganga-Yamuna region beyond Delhi to the east."

In spite of the abundant structural material and innumerable artefacts unearthed in excavations at different sites, nothing conclusive can be said about the way a state was formed or what the nature of such a state could have been. Generally, it is assumed that the rise of a highly evolved urban civilization extending over a vast area is associated with the emergence of a centralized "decision-making system" called the state. There are many surmises: (a) oligarchic commercial republics, (b) a single centralized state, (c) a theocratic state, (d) five independent political units, and (e) the first major empire in southern Asia. Until the Indus script is deciphered satisfactorily, and accepted by the majority; we can say that whatever be the form of the government, no coercive methods involving weapons were used since no defensive armour was found among the artifacts.

The economy of this civilization appears to be based on plough agriculture. They knew the cultivation of wheat club, Indian dwarf barley, lentil, horsegram, jawar, millets, rice, urad dal, ragi, sorghum-bicodor, pearl millet, dates, mustard, beans and sesamum. The people also produced cotton. The evidence of granaries at Harappa and Mohenjodaro reveals that there was surplus production and this surplus was collected through organized labour and stored in granaries. They supplemented their farming economy by domesticating animals like sheep, goats, Indian humped bulls, buffaloes, dogs, cats, pigs and fowls.

There are opposing views, one advocating that there was no evidence of horse and the other arguing that they knew horses. Besides agriculture and cattle rearing, their economy appears to be based on a highly organized system of craft-production as known from artifacts available. By this time, the needs of the people appear to have multiplied, which led to the creation of a number of professions that can sustain urbanism in a vast area. Naturally, this must have led to the creation of social groups engaged in specialized professions like priesthood, administration, trade, caravan leadership, farming, cattle keeping, manufacture and service-oriented groups like sweepers, washermen and labourers. There is no direct evidence to let us know whether the Indus society was divided based on rich and poor, clean and unclean professions or high and low. As there is proof of long-distance coastal trade between Mesopotomia and west Asian sites like Tell Asmar, Ur, Kish, Lagash and Susa, we can say that besides the sea route, they also knew a land route. The land routes were two: (a) the northern route linking north Iran, Oxus, Kabul and central reaches of Indus; and (b) the southern route linking central and southern Iran with Kandahar, Baluchistan and the more southern regions of Indus or Makran.

One interesting aspect to be noticed is that in spite of the flourishing sea and land-route trade and commerce, the non-availability of metallic coins makes us infer that trade was carried on by barter. Seals recently discovered might have been used by them to indicate the owner or the receiver of merchandise. They knew weaving and spinning. They used both wool and cotton. Pottery making also appears to be a widespread industry. Different kinds of pottery – plain and painted with designs were found in abundance. They made tools, weapons and implements with stone, copper and bronze. The Harappans knew how to make bronze by mixing copper with tin. It is suggested that they imported copper from Khetri of Rajasthan and tin from Afghanistan. Among artisans, bronze smiths might have occupied better positions because of their newly acquired skill. The Harappans wore ornaments made of gold, silver, copper, shell, beads and precious stones and undoubtedly, artisanship of jewellery reached its highest excellence. It is interesting to note that all the above metals, shells, beads and precious stones were imported from different places. If they could import these, it implies: (a) they were affluent, and (b) they all loved ornaments and used affordable ornaments of their choice and liking. The Harapppan people showed interest in the fun of children by providing them different types of toys; Chanhudaro appears to have been centre of toy manufacturing.

An attempt could be made to trace the transition of society of the Harappan culture with the help of artefacts found there. In the absence of corroborative evidence of literature, with the help of artefacts and structural monuments, it can be said that the Harappan social system and Harappan social structure consisted of different social groups that evolved because of the increasing needs of the urban social set-up. It can be argued that there existed different skilled professional groups catering to various needs of society. There is also no conclusive evidence to prove the existence of a warrior group nor any convincing proof of the dominance of the commercial group in the social set-up. We can only propose that while some led an affluent and luxurious life, the rest led a simple life. Thus, it can be considered that the social set-up of the Harappan times was based on economic rather than social status. The people of the Harappan culture led a comfortable life and appear to have been beauty conscious. The Harappans were not artistic by nature and temperament. All their material creations lack any traces of ornamentation, and exhibit only utilitarian outlook. The Harappans knew both music and dance.

There is proof to show that they created a stringed instrument, which seems like the prototype of the Veena, and the drum, the possible prototype of the Mridangam. The bronze female figure found in Mohenjodaro and a statue of a dancer found at Harappa suggests that dancing was also cultivated.

An attempt could be made to construct the religious beliefs and faith of the Harappans based on the identification of structures, relics, figures and engravings on seals. Some of the structures have been identified as temples. The Great bath and its adjacent structure have been identified as a sacred ritual place and the residence of a high priest or a group of priests. A figure found on a seal has been identified as proto-Siva, and based on other seals the figure surrounded by animals as *Pasupati*. The worship of mother goddess and the cult of fertility were also in vogue. Several seals with Pipal on them have led tree scholars to suggest that the Harappans worshipped trees. Some seals found with bull, some composite animals, and unicorn, have led to speculation that animal worship was also in vogue. Interestingly at Lothal and Kalibangan, fire altars have been discovered in the citadel area and lower town. This evidence encouraged some to identify the authors of this civilization as Aryans. The worship at fire altars could be a regional variation and it need not be of Aryan origin, or could have been a later time practice, a possible result of contact with the Aryans.

Though the Harappans knew burial practices, we do not come across anything like the pyramids of Egypt or the Royal cemetery of the Mesopotamian city of Ur. We also come across different types of earthen pots for burial, ornaments made of shell bangles, necklaces, earrings, and in some places collections of bones were found. At Lothal, we notice a pair of skeletons, which are identified as male and female found to be buried together. These evidences make us postulate that cremation was unknown to them. Harappan people appear to have believed in life after death. We may conclude by observing that different regions of Harappan culture appear to have retained their social roots and religious customs, in spite of apparent uniformity in many respects.

Harappans knew the art of writing and had a script but it is still a mystery, in spite of the claims made by innumerable scholars that they unlocked the mystery. So far, universally acceptable decipherment of the script has not been made. A number of seals or seal amulets of rectangular or square, cylindrical and cubic shape have script on them on one side and a number of animals on the other. While Fr. Heras and T. Burrow suggest that the language is proto-Dravidian, S.R. Rao believes it to be proto-Vedic or old Indo-Aryan.

No single explanation can be offered for the decline and final collapse of the Harappan culture. Several causes are suggested: (1) destruction by massive floods, (2) the shift in the course of rivers and gradual drying up of the Ghagga-Hakra river system, (3) invasion by barbarians, and (4) the growing demands of population disturbing the ecology of the region leading to the failure of area to support them any more. The gradual decline and collapse of this flourishing first urban civilization may be due to one or more reasons offered above.

Though the Harappan culture collapsed and became a part of history, certainly this culture continued. The inhabitants of the abandoned Indus town moved to small cluster in the Punjab region along with Rigvedic Aryans. Exchange between the Rigvedic Aryans and the post-Harrapans is manifested in the form of painted grey ware pottery that archaeologists refer to as the PGW culture. The surviving practices of the worship of Pasupati or Siva, the worship of the mother goddess and phallic worship, the cults of sacred places, rivers, trees and animals show the continuity of the Harappan cultural beliefs. Further, some aspects of the domestic life like the house-plan, attention to bathing, the traditional weights and currency system, the technique of pottery-making, their legacy of engineering skill as pioneers of artificial dock with water locking arrangements also remain. The circular saw, and the compass are still in use. Thus both in religious and secular spheres, we observe continuity as well as change. Wheeler and Allchin, initially assumed that Harappan cultures declined into a 'dark age' with an absence of urban centres and of the same pattern of complex socio-political organization in the Indus and upper Gangetic region. Nevertheless, in recent times, Jarrige and Enault, Schaffer, Allchin, Keyonar, Mughal and others express the view based recent excavations that instead of a decline in urbanism it may be better to characterize the change as localization of socio-economic and political interaction. Kenoyar further writes, "the complex process of change after the Harappan period begins with the late-Harappan to PGW transition (1900–800 BCE) during which the social and political order of the Indus cities was transformed but not clearly obliterated". Multiple factors such as changing river patterns, periodic floods perhaps disrupted the socio-economic base and led to significant change of localization of these cultures. This process is contextualized in the following chapters.

Non-Harappan Cultures

The gradual movement of the PGW culture from the regions of Punjab and further west gradually moved into the Gangetic plains. They merged with several other cultures bringing about the Iron Age in North India. However, this trend is specifically contained between the lands east of the Indus in Pakistan to the eastern ends of the Gangetic plain where, cultures other than the ones that show signs of integration were encountered. By 800 BC the entire region of North India mentioned in the above geographical context show levels of higher integration manifesting in the use of Northern Black Polished Ware

(NBPW). Peninsular India, including western India and the deep south has its own peculiarities in their integrative processes towards the proto-historical phase. Here we need to carefully skim through at least some of the non-Harappan cultures within northern India and their contemporaries in Peninsular India to have an understanding of the mosaic of cultures that made their respective contributions when some of these areas show signs of early interaction.

The usual model for social evolution in any given historical culture transits from rural to urban centres. The distinctive feature in India follows a reversal of the above-mentioned phenomena and has throughout its history oscillated between the rural and urban ends. Though the Harappan culture was the most widespread with urban and non-urban settlements, different cultural patterns also existed side by side in other parts of the subcontinent. These patterns had contacts with the Harappan cultures and vice versa. Between the second millennium BC and the first millennium BC, agriculture-based rural cultures existed in all the major regions of the subcontinent. These are classified as Chalcolithic cultures. From the beginning of the first millennium BC, besides stone and copper, iron began to be used for manufacturing tools both by the people of the Painted Grey Ware (PGW) culture of the upper Ganga valley as well as by the builders of the Megalithic culture of peninsular India. During this phase, life patterns were dependent on farming, hunting and food gathering along with pastoralism. A factor that deserves our notice is the quickening of historical change in the Ganga valley, which is attributed to the civilizing influence of the Aryans, who migrated to India. Nevertheless, this hypothesis has been questioned by historians in recent decades. Modern historians argue that there was neither large-scale migration of Aryans nor displacement of local population by ruthless conquest. The historians of recent times hold that the Aryan society was essentially pastoral and not substantially agrarian. The geographical knowledge of the early Aryans was limited to the Sapthasindu valley and historians are skeptical of the knowledge of the Ganga valley of the early Aryans. A cultural profile and life pattern of this period can be reconstructed from both the archaeological and the earliest literary texts.

During this phase, several regional cultures like the Banas, the Kayatha; the Malwa and the Jorwe have become known. Nearly more than a hundred sites excavated in the Ganga-Yamuna doab brought to light a sequence of ochre coloured pottery followed by black and red ware and painted grey ware. It is suggested that iron made its appearance in the above PGW period and the use of iron became widespread during the phase of Northern Black Polished Ware (NBPW). However, nearly 1570 sites of NBPW have come to be noticed; only 74 have been excavated. This culture sequence is to be noticed from Taxila and Udgaram in the north-west to Talmuk in East Bengal and Amaravathi of Andhra Pradesh in the south. This northern black polished ware culture is distinguished by two phases: (1) the absence of punch-marked coins and burnt-brick structures, and (2) the presence of the punch-marked coins and burnt-bricks.

Excavations at Kausambi and Hastinapur prove the emergence of well laid out cities along with large-scale building activity. At Kausambi, we come across lanes and by-lanes with brick floorings, and the use of burnt-bricks and timber in the construction of houses. Rooms are of square and rectangular shape, while roofs are covered. Interestingly, an elaborate drainage system was found at Hastinapur. These settlements were also fortified with mud or brick walls. The forts appear to be encircled by moats. The Kausambi fortification wall had guardrooms, towers and gates at regular intervals. All these evidences well-established political authority regulated show that the society had become complex and social relations. As the most important feature of this (NBPW) pottery is its glossy surface, it is suggested that it is a luxury item rather than a common one. Therefore, it is inferred by some that there existed some type of social divisions. Whether this division is based on economic or social criteria cannot be established beyond doubt. Discovery of several types of tools made of stone, glass, copper and iron indicates not only their technological development but also the levels of their material culture. Buddhist Jataka tales refer to 18 guilds or *Srenis*. The existence of guilds of both artisans and mercantile groups indicates that they produced goods for both consumption and trade. This is further attested by the availability of silver punch-marked coins, which indicate a system of exchange of goods through metallic currency. Ornaments of different metals, beads, horn and clay indicate that they too like Harappans loved ornaments and we can surmise the existence of a group of skilled specialist artisans who were in the business of manufacturing ornaments. These people knew the cultivation of rice, wheat, barley, millet, beans and black gram.

The economy appears to be of subsistence level for the majority who did not produce surplus. Nevertheless, evidence of internal and external trade indicates that at least some produced surplus. Until recently, scholars used to consider the Mauryan age as the benchmark for North India's entrance into the early historic phase. Now, it has been proved beyond doubt that the NBPW is the sign of social and economic integration amongst the various subcultures. State formation itself is now being seen as a process which, started with smaller kingdoms or chiefdoms in North India that culminated in the Mauryan Era, which is now seen as an early North Indian experiment in establishing an imperial lineage. Based on the *Arthasastra*, the core of which was written during the Mauryan phase, while it was rearranged and redacted in later ages and came to its final shape during the Gupta period, it is suggested that the state had a monopoly over industries using gold, silver, copper, iron, lead, tin and precious stones.

In South India, we do not have any definitive information to understand material culture, settlement pattern and social organization, which is a gradual evolution from food gathering economy to food producing economy. Early farming communities seem to make a sudden appearance. In third millennium BC, evidence suggests that this area was colonized in the favourable habitations of the river valleys of Godavari, Krishna, Thungabhadra, Penna and Kaveri. The settlements are scattered in the semi-arid, low rainfall and sandy-loamy regions that are suitable for dry farming and pastoralism. Almost all the settlements are sedentary with semi-permanent structures of wattle and daub. They used polished stone tools made of chert, jasper, chalcedony and agate with sheen on the cutting edge. It is suggested that these tools could have been used for harvesting of crops. They knew of hand-made as well as wheel-turned pottery. The use of pottery indicates settled village life. They were agro-pastoralists. Their daily food was supplemented by wild game.

Thus, based on the available evidence, we notice three broad phases in the evolutionary pattern of the early farming communities of South India. They are: (a) Period 1: 2500–1800 BC (b) Period 2: 1800–1500 BC, and (c) Period 3: 1500 to 1050 BC. The second and the third periods are characterized as Neolithic and Chalcolithic. The excavated ash-mound sites at Utnur, Kupgal, Kolekal, Palavoy, Piklihal, Maski and Brahmagiri belong to the first period. In the second period, we come across circular hutments of wattle and daub on wooden frames with mud floors and a kind of perforated and spotted vessels. This suggests that these people had contacts with regions in the north. They also used copper and bronze objects in this phase. The representative sites of the second phase are Nagarjunakonda, Paiyampalli, Veerapuram, Brahmagiri and Sanganakallu. In the third period besides stone axe and blade, copper and bronze tools were also in use. The commonly found pottery is of grey and buff ware with comparatively hard surface. In this period, we come across wheel-turned unburnished pottery with purple paint. The people of these times preferred low hill ranges which are close to streams. They appear to have preferred tropical black land, dry, tropical red and black sandy-loamy lands, sandy and deltaic alluvial soils. The rainfall annually was 600–1200 mm in the places of their habitation. Based on certain similarities and features, there is a view that the Neolithic people of South India had links with some points on the Indo-Iranian border.

In the time around 1100 BC three very important things were taking place in Peninsular India; Iron was being smelted in large quantities, exchange was happening between various communities scattered from the Vidarbha region to Tamil Nadu and most importantly, a new ritual culture was emerging in the form of building Megaliths and other assorted burial sites. There is a tendency amongst scholars to merge all the three above-mentioned features into one cultural complex to the point of suggesting homogeneity. Although it would be impertinent to categorize all these characteristics in calling it Megalithic culture, at least in the earlier stages of this important age, it is however, quite tempting to at least think of a probable link between iron, trade or exchange and lithical monuments for the deceased. Towards the end of the last millennium Before the Common Era (BCE), the three features define and distinguish the cultural spread of South Indian history way into the early Medieval period. Therefore, in many ways, the Megalithic phase or the South Indian Iron Age marks a watershed like in the case of NBPW to the Gangetic plains. A lack of internal chronology and other regional inconsistencies emanating from the lack of comprehensive archaeological data hampers the historian to speculate not only on the Megalithic phase but also on the Early Historic Period. Even the basis for a date in fixing the earliest extant iron tool comes from an artifact found at Hallur, proved by Carbon 14 test. We notice the overlapping of Neolithic and Chalcolithic culture traits into the Iron Age culture sites also. Excavations at Piklihal, Hallur and at the burial pits of Brahmagiri exhibit the evidence of the earliest phase of Iron Age in South India. Similarities between these cultures and that of Jorwe and Takawada are also noticed. The red or black ware and burnish-unpainted black and red ware characterize the succeeding phases of Iron Age settlements.

Megaliths have been found in Maharashtra, Karnataka, Andhra Pradesh, Tamil Nadu and Kerala. The most important sites are Nagpur, Maski, Nagarjunakonda and Adichallanur. Arrowheads, daggers, swords, spearheads, tridents, battle-axe, hoes, ploughshares, sickles, stirrups, ladders, tripod and lamp made of iron were found in most of the Megalithic graves. As pointed before, the phrase Megalithic is rather inadequate in explaining the whole assortment of lithical monuments raised for the dead during the time between the 1000 BC and the 3rd century of the Common Era. Basing on information so far gleaned from archaeological excavations, these Iron Age burials could be divided into four or five distinct categories. The largest numbers of burial sites come under Cairn circles, which resemble the letter 'C' under which, single or multiple urns containing bones or ashes of the dead are recovered. The next most common category is the Cromlech or Kistavaen, which are large free-standing stones, set in rows or following a geometrical alignment. In some regions, especially in the Deep South comprising southern parts of Andhra Pradesh, Karnataka and Tamil Nadu, burial chambers of stone in which there may be two or even three tiers to accommodate the remains of the deceased are called Dolmens or Dolmeniod Cists, depending on typology. In Kerala, rock-cut caves with underground carvings are also noticed, while the most pervading form is in form of dressed hood-stones aligned to dressed-hemispherical slabs, which are typified as 'Megaliths'. Attempts are made to identify this culture with either Aryan or Dravidian. The origin of this culture is traced either to central Asia, Iran or Caucasus or also to the indigenous neolithic and chalcolithic burial customs of the Deccan. The archaeological record of the South Indian Iron Age is still to be interpreted and interconnected to arrive at any meaningful chronology.

4

Vedic Cultures

In the evolution of the Indian society and its cultural and socio-economic tradition, the Vedic phase is very significant one. A prolonged debate is going on about the meaning of the term 'Aryan' and the original home of the Aryans. In spite of more than two centuries of study by different scholars from different perspectives, nothing conclusive could be said about the original homeland of the Aryans and meaning of the term Aryan. Though the predominant popular view among right-wing Indian scholars is that the Aryans are natives of India, the academic historians question this view and they are of the opinion that the Aryans are not indigenous. The myth of the large-scale migration of Aryans into India indulging in extensive destruction of the culture and civilization of the natives is no longer valid. The concept of the superiority of the Aryan race with better skill in warfare and technical expertise in comparison to the natives of the subcontinent of India is also not accepted as historical reality. The division of population of Indian subcontinent as Aryans and Dravidians is a construct of the colonial rulers to justify and perpetuate their rule in India. Unfortunately, our scholars as well as ordinary public could not understand the strategy of the colonial masters.

An image of the society of the Indian subcontinent of this phase could be constructed with the available information culled from Vedic literature. It is considered as the earliest literary tradition of the entire world. Based on changes witnessed in the course of time this phase is divided into early Vedic, Rigvedic and later Vedic periods. As it is very difficult to fix the exact date of the composition of this vast corpus of literature and establish the authorship of this literary tradition, we can only approximately date them. Though many Indians believe the Vedas as 'Revelation', dating back to lakhs of years, the scholars assign the earliest portion of the Rigveda to the period from 1800 BC, the rest of it from 1600 BC to 1000 BC and the later Vedas to a period from 1000 BC to 800 BC the remaining body of the Vedic literature is considered to be anterior to 6th century BC. Archaeologically, the Rigvedic phase seems to coincide with the pre-iron phase of the painted grey ware culture. The recently excavated sites at

Bhagawanpura in Haryana and three sites in Punjab, where painted grey ware culture has become known, was assigned to 1600 BC to 1000 BC, which is approximately the period of the composition of the later parts of the Rigveda.

Before we attempt to delineate the image of the early Vedic society, let us know about the Vedic literature. The word 'Veda' is derived from the Sanskrit word '*Vid*', which means 'to know'. The Vedic literature consists of 50 texts. These are divided into four principal categories: (a) Samhitas, (b) Brahmanas, (c) Aranyakas, and (d) Upanishads. Besides these categories, Vedangas and Upavedas also constitute the corpus of the Vedic literature. The Samhitas are a collection of hymns and verses that refer to particular rituals observed and the various aspects of life of those times in general. The texts of the Samhitas are Rigveda, Samaveda, Yajurveda and Atharvaveda. The Brahmanas is a group of interpretative texts and are associated with the particular Samhitas. For example, Aitereya and Kausitaki Brahmanas are associated with the Rigveda. Likewise, Pancavimsa, Sadavimsa and Jaimineya are associated with Samaveda. Katha, Taittiriya and Satapatha Brahmanas are associated with Yajurveda and Gopatha with Atharvanaveda. It is generally accepted in academic circles that the later Samhitas and the earlier Brahmanas could have been composed between 1000–800 BC, the later Brahmanas, and the earlier Aranyakas Upanishads between 700 as 500 BC. The content of Vedic literature is demarcated by assigning the Samhitas as a nomadic and an open period that incorporated an egalitarian hymn-tradition while the Brahmanas are texts of a settled people who rigidly formulated an interpretive grid to the rituals of the Samhitas. The Aranyakas again are a liberal delineation from the Brahmanas where the stress is more upon speculation or *Gyanavichara*. The last of the Aranyakas overlap with the earliest Upanishads that seem to be an even more sustained effort towards ontological discourse. There is a difference of opinion regarding the importance given to ritual and speculation. The whole corpus of Vedic literature had been rearranged and reconstituted throughout the Early Historic Period and the Early Medieval Period, when it was given the final form that exists today. Rigveda is the oldest of the four Vedas. It is a compilation of hymns chanted by priestly families at the time of sacrifices to gods. There are five recensions of the Rigveda. Out of the five, the Sakala recension consisting of 1,017 or 1,028 hymns has come down to us totally. The rest of the corpus is considered lost. Rigveda is not the work of one individual or family but a collective work of many families spanning over a considerable time. As a result, we notice considerable variation in style and in metres. Rigveda is divided into 10 mandalas or sections. Out of these six mandalas form the kernel of the Rigveda. The above six mandalas are also known as family mandalams. The authors of these six mandalas belong to the families of Gristsmada, Viswamitra, Vamadeva, Atri, Bharadwaja and Vasistha. Of the ten mandalas, the first, the eighth and the tenth mandalas are later additions; Yaska was the first one who attempted to arrange the verses in accordance with their contents. He refers to 17 commentaries that existed before his time. Sayana's commentary, written during the Vijayanagara period in the early 14th century AD, is the primary basis for the understanding of Rigveda in modern times. Puranas claim that Samaveda has a thousand Samhitas but only one Samhita has been left to us with three recensions – the Kanthama, Jaiminiya and the Ramayania. Samaveda contains 1,800 hymns and of them 261 are repetitions. Therefore, it is concluded that it has only 1,549 hymns. Even among 1,549 of these, except 75, the rest variations are from the Rigveda. Even these 75 hymns are repeated in other Samhitas and Brahmanas.

Samaveda is of immense value to a student of Indian music. It has three Brahmanas – the Tandya, the Shadvimsa and the Jaiminiya Brahmana of these three, the first the Tandya Mahabrahmana refers to a ceremony of *Vratyasoma* by which non-Aryans could be admitted into the Aryan fold. The mention of this ceremony indicates a process of acculturation that took place between the Aryans and non-Aryans and refers to the accommodative process of the society of that time. Atharvaveda is also called Atharvangirasa. It has two branches: Samnaka and Paippataka. This has 731 Suktas. These are grouped into 20 chapters. While all the other chapters are in verse, the 15th and the 16th chapters are in prose. The composers of this Atharvaveda appear to have a wider geographical knowledge than the authors of Rigveda. Further, social life as reflected in Rigveda is different from that of the Atharvanaveda. This Veda refers to charms, magic and spells by which one can overcome enemies and gain success in worldly matters. The Yajurveda is divided into two parts – Sukla or white and Krishna or black. While Sukla Yajurveda has only one branch – the Vajasaneya Samhita, the latter has four branches – Kautaka, Kapisthada, Katha, Taittariya and Maitrayani Samhitas. Vajasaneya Samhita has two recensions, the Kanva and the Madhyandina. It has 40 chapters. Yajurveda has two Brahmanas – Taittariya and Satapatha. While Taittariya belongs to Krishna (black) Yajurveda, Satapatha belongs to Sukla (white) Yajurveda.

Next in importance to the Samhitas are the Brahmanas. The Brahmanas are the texts of the rituals to be performed at various ceremonies. It is believed that, the objective of the Brahmanas is to mystify the sacrifices. Aranyakas are the concluding portions of the Brahmanas, which deal with mysticism and symbolism. Aranyakas may also be regarded as the natural transition to the Upanishads. The Upanishads are taught at the end of Vedic learning as they contain the ultimate philosophy of Vedic knowledge. The word *Upanishad* means sitting at the feet of the guru and acquiring knowledge through question and answer method or clearing of doubts of the Sishya by the guru.

Besides the above texts forming part of the Vedic tradition, we have 'sutras' texts closely associated with the Vedic tradition: Srauta, Dharma and Grihya sutra literature. Srauta means sacrifices. These texts describe the rituals involving the services of the Purohits. Rigveda has two Srauta sutras – Asvalayana and Samkhyayana. These describe the ritual duties of the Hotri or priest in a systematic fashion. While Asvalayana sutra is associated with Aitareya Brahmana, Sakhyayana sutra is affiliated to Kaushithaki Brahmana. Samaveda has two Srauta sutras: Latyayana and Drahyayana. Interestingly, while the Vedic tradition looks down on the Sudras, Nishadas and Vratyas as cursed; Latyayana Srautasutra differs in its treatment of these social groups from the Vedic tradition. Even if it is a solitary reference or instance, it needs to be noticed, as it happens to record a dissenting voice from the existing Vedic tradition. Krishna Yajurveda has two Srauta sutras: Apasthambha and Baudhyayana. Sukla Yajurveda has Katyayana Srauta sutras. Sometime after the composition of Srauta sutras, Grihya and Dharma sutras were composed. While Grihya sutras relate to domestic religious ritual or Karmakanda to be performed by an individual in his four stages of life (Chaturasrama), the Dharma sutras stipulate social relations. These Dharma sutras are the earliest sources of the later day Hindu law. Gautama, Vasista and Apastambha are some of the most important writers of the Dharma sutras. Besides these three; Srauta, Grihya and Dharma, we come across another category: Sulva sutras: attached to Srauta sutras. They deal with the rules and regulations regarding the measurement and construction of fire altars, which occupy an important place in the Vedic ritual. Generally, all these four sutras are known as Kalpa sutras. The composition of these sutras is assigned from 6th century to 2nd century BC. As a part of Vedic literature, we have a separate category called Vedanga literature. Siksha or phonetics, Kalpa or Vyakarana or grammar, Nirukta or etymology, Chandas or metres and Jyothisha or astrology are called Vedangas.

Along with Vedangas, there also exist Upavedas-Ayurveda, Dhanurveda, Gandharvaveda and Arthasastra. While the Vedas are considered to be of divine origin, the rest of the literature is agreed to have been composed and interpreted by human beings. A detailed survey of the Vedic literature is necessary because even today the Vedic literature has significant impact on the minds of the Indians. Whatever new philosophy or new instrument is invented anywhere in the world, there is a tendency among Hindus to believe that it has its origin in the Vedas. The Vedic tradition was so deep rooted, that it has become a way of life, knowingly or unknowingly of a large section of the populace. What is needed is not a blind admiration of the Vedic literature and thought; but a proper understanding and critical appreciation of the Vedic knowledge by all those who are concerned with the value of the Vedas. No doubt, the Vedic literature is the repository of all forms of early knowledge, skills, and speculations of the people of India from that of brewing wine to the highest abstract cosmological theories. In course of time, the basic content of the Vedic knowledge became spiritual in outlook. This knowledge in turn paved way for emergence of the Indian way of life. Even today, the Vedic concepts of transmigration of soul, karma and rebirth continue to retain their strong hold on the minds of many Indians. To sum up, every aspect of our social, cultural and legal system is influenced by Vedic thought and tradition.

Rigveda provides some information regarding the geographical knowledge of the Vedic people and this helps us to ascertain the area known to them. Rigveda refers to the Mujavant peak of the Himalayas and twenty-four rivers. Of these, Rigveda frequently refers to the Sarsavati river, which they worshipped. It has Nadistuti, a chapter devoted to praise of rivers. The Ganges does not appear to be an important river at that time. Their knowledge of sea is debatable. While A.B. Keith is of the view that they were not aware of the sea, Max Muller believes that they had a definite knowledge of the sea. We may safely conclude that they knew the present areas of Afghanistan, the Punjab, parts of Sindh and Rajputana, the north-western frontier province, Kashmir and eastern India up to the Sarayu river.

The data available from the archaeological sources and Rigveda provides the necessary clues to paint a picture of the society. The Rigvedic society can be characterized as simple with small settlements of cultivators and cattle raisers. They lived in wattle and daub huts with rammed earth floors, which gradually gave way to brick structures. As Rigveda refers to a number of tribes living in specific regions by name, it is inferred that their society was based on tribal organizational set-up. This phase appears to be a transitory period, from tribe to lineage. Rigveda refers to non-Vedic tribes also like Kikatas, Kiratas and Dasyus. It was a period of constant skirmishes among the Vedic tribes and the Vedic and the non-Vedic tribes for economic gains. The most important politically significant event appears to be a battle between ten kings or *Dasaraja Yuddha*. Trutsu-Bharata tribes fought against a confederacy of tribes comprising forces of Puru, Yadu, Turvasu, Anu and Drhyu and many others and defeated them. The fight between the tribes was for cattle, as it was considered wealth and conferred power and prestige. Each tribe attempted to enhance its cattle holding by raiding the other tribes besides cattle breeding. Even today in Srikakulam district of Andhra Pradesh, cattle is called *Sommulu* meaning wealth. A study of Nuer and Dinka tribes of East Africa proves that cattle raids are a common feature of pastoral society. Naturally, in such a society, the winner is considered as hero and in the Indian context, such hero is called *Gojit*. Rigveda refers to the head of the tribes as *Gopa*, *Gopat* and *Janasya Gopti*. These terms appear to be synonymous with *raja*, the common term we come across as head of a tribe or a small kingdom. In later times only, the Raja was also called Nripati and Naresvara the head of people or controller of the people. In course of time, the winner of cattle raids, who was called 'Gojit' or 'Gopa' or 'Gopati' later became 'Nripati' and 'Naresvara' and thereby established his right, which became a family right. The members of the tribe showed respect and loyalty to such an individual and family for increasing the wealth of the tribe as well as protecting them from the other tribal attacks. Most probably, the tribe out of gratitude or fear, agreed to make this heredity in the hero's family. We do not know whether the law of primogeniture was accepted or not, and can only suggest that we notice a gradual and slow transition from lineage to the state in the first millennium BC.

The Rigvedic society was, though primarily pastoral, dependent on agriculture to sustain itself as pastoralism and agriculture are complementary to each other. In the promotion of agriculture, we notice both Vedic and non-Vedic people cooperating and helping each other. This process of understanding, either on a small or large scale can be established by references to plough cultivation in the Rigveda and references to the agricultural implement *Langula*, a non-Vedic term, according to Burrow. It must have taken considerable time for agriculture to become an accepted profession by all. This gradual transition from pastoralism to agriculture must have influenced the social formation. The tribal society appears to have been divided into two groups: (i) Vis or ordinary members of tribe who took to the profession of cattle raising and cultivation, and (ii) Rajanya, men who were engaged in increasing and protecting the wealth and safety of the tribe. The gradual spread of agriculture required not only new areas of land but also control over water resources and thereby, it increased the role of the chief of the tribe and the persons involved in this process of protecting the tribe. We may surmise, in the beginning for some time the chief of the tribe depended on his kith and kin to discharge his new duties. In this process, the new social group of Rajanya based on blood relationship and lineage began to take shape. Acceptance of the superior social and political status of 'Rajanyas' by Vis was further legitimized by the custodian of Dharma, i.e., the priest in course of time. The evolution of the Vedic chief 'Gopati' or 'Nripati' involved the evolution or transformation of the Rajanya group into Kshatriya varna, a term that has its root in Kohatra or power which occurs frequently in later Vedic society. The *Varnasrama* model makes its appearance in the *Purushasukta* section of Rigveda. It is believed to be an interpolation by scholars and as such, the social group Rajanya could have become Kshatriya not in the early Vedic age, but in the later Vedic age. It is generally believed that hereditary monarchy existed in the Rigvedic phase, but as the evidence is not convincing it cannot be accepted with certainty. As Rigveda refers to 'Ganapati' or 'Jyeshta', scholars are of the opinion that there existed Gana rajya concept or a sort of republican form of government as well as elected monarchical system. Rajan or the head of the tribe who may be an elected or a hereditary functionary empowered with ruling authority is believed to be assisted by a number of functionaries and among them the Purohit, the Senapati and the Duta appear to be important. It indicates increase in the functions of the ruler as well as distribution of functions between different categories of functionaries. The title Senani indicates the emergence of a warrior group under the leadership of a Senani. The term Duta refers, perhaps, to a person who acted as a representative of the ruler or who looked after the relation between one tribe or kingdom and another. The term Purohita refers to a person who advised the king on auspicious dates and occasions as well as one who propitiated Gods through worship or prayer for the well-being of the whole of the tribe or state, rather than the ruler alone. The Rigveda refers to the pompous and luxurious lifestyle of the Rajan. Compared to the simple life of the ordinary people, the Rajan, perhaps, led a different life that made the seers imagine the position of Rajan to be pompous and luxurious. Rigveda refers to the bodies Sabha, Samiti, Gana, Vidhata and Parishad. It is not possible now to explain the nature and functions of these assemblies in detail with any certainty.

We can only surmise. It is generally believed that they acted as checks over the authoritarianism of the Rajan. The Samiti may be the representative body of the Vedic tribes and the Sabha a body of the elected or chosen representatives of the tribes. R.S. Sarma is of the opinion that these assemblies performed both civil and military functions. It is not easy to explain or define what those civil and military functions were. The Rigvedic Rajan appears to be a warrior, who was empowered to protect people as well as cattle. In return, the people offered him, 'Bali' or tribute to show their gratitude, loyalty and obedience for making their lives secure. We do not know whether Bali was offered voluntarily or fixed by the Rajan. We do not know how the Rajan and other functionaries maintained themselves. Rigveda refers to chariots drawn by horses and these chariots may have been used by Rajan. Bows and arrows, swords, spears, lances and axes are the weapons known to them. Rigveda refers to moving forts and *Purapatis* are said to be heads of these forts. It is also suggested that the army was divided into *Sardhavaha*, *Vrata* and *Gana*. It is very difficult to believe the above view as the maintenance of army with division involves vast resources. The exact extent of the territorial hold of the Rajan is not known. Rigveda refers to the term Jana 275 times and to Vis 170 times. These numerous references indicate their importance. Rigveda also refers to terms Kula and Grama. The head of Vis was known as Vispati, the head of Kula as Kulapati and the head of Grama as Gramapati or Gramani. More details are not available to indicate the relationship between Jana, Vis, Kula and Grama as well as the junctions and powers of Rajan, Vispati, Kulapati and Gramani.

Patriarchy, which is the basis of the social system even today, was the basis of the society at that time. The father appears to have had absolute control over the children's life. The family was the basic unit of society and the basis of family was the institution of marriage. Early marriages were unknown and as today, marriages took place in the bride's house. Girls were married after they attained marriageable age of 16 or 17. Dowry and bride price appears to have been socially acceptable in those days. Common people practised monogamy, but polyandry and polygamy were common among Rajanyas. Marriages with blood relations were prohibited. Childless widows were allowed to have a male child by their brothers-in-law, as the hymns of the Rigveda strongly indicate desire for male progeny. Like today, in most families, the girl child was not welcome and as such, we do not come across any hymns praying for the birth of a female child. Rigvedic society does not appear to have favoured the adoption of a child, though such practice was accepted. This society did not know the cruel practice of *Sati* but a symbolic act of asking the dead man's wife to lie on the pyre and to ask her to get down from the pyre is known from a Rigvedic hymn. No doubt, the Rigvedic society was male-oriented and dominated by men, yet women were not looked down upon as useless objects or as dolls to be petted. They appear to have enjoyed equal status with men because we have reference to women sages and authors of hymns. From this, we can infer that though a girl child was not welcome to a common person, the sages and the seers did not show discrimination. The hymns of Rigveda pray for perfect harmonious conjugal bliss for a hundred years. In addition, this makes us believe that the Vedic people were optimistic by nature and temperament and they wished to spend a whole life enjoying their togetherness. Generally, people lived in houses built of wood or reed. Every house invariably had a separate place for the fire altar because they worshipped fire. Every house had more than two or three rooms, with a separate room for women. The Rigvedic people wore dress of three parts: undergarment (nivi), a lower garment (vasa) and an upper garment 'adhivasa'. Both men and women wore turbans. They wore clothes made of cotton and wool. Like today, women combed their long hair into broad plaits. People favoured gold ornaments and both men and women wore floral wreaths on festive days.

The food habits of the Rigvedic people were very simple. Generally, they ate parched grain, apupa or cakes, milk products, fruits and vegetables. They also ate meat and on celebrations, beef. They knew Sura and Soma as drinks. Their favourite pastime was hunting and they hunted wild animals as well as deer and birds. The other pastimes were dancing and chariot racing. Women also took active part in dancing and music.

The Aryan society was lineage and kinship based. The Varnasrama model did not take shape yet. The conquered indigenous people were referred to as Dasas or Dasyus and there is reason to believe that the victorious Vedic people felt themselves superior. Though there was no caste system as such in that society, it witnessed social and economic inequalities due to the special place given to Rajanya and Purohita groups in the social, political and cultural spheres. The social inequity was not so deep as to create hierarchy and tensions between groups. The Rigvedic society was divided on occupational basis. We come across skilled specialist groups such as those of weavers, smiths, carpenters, leather workers and chariot makers apart from priests and rajanyas. This type of specialization took place due to the increase in people's needs and it necessitated the growth of various occupational specialist groups necessary for serving an agrarian society. The occupations were not divided into superior or inferior occupations, as all were needed for happy living. Yet we notice the beginnings of stratification in society based on the importance assigned to some occupations by the social system. For example, chariot-makers appear to have enjoyed better economic and social status, as the ruling group required their services.

The hymns of the Rigveda reflect religious ideology, rituals and practices. Religion, no doubt played a crucial role in their lives. Like all primitive societies, they too venerated nature and its elements. They invested nature with divinity and conceived the elements of the nature as masculine human forms. They worshipped a few female deities like Ushas or dawn, Dharithri or earth. Their religious ideology was primitive animism. As the Aryan society revolved around war, they created an image of Indra as the god of strength, who could destroy enemies. As their Chief was more of a warlord, they conceived of Indra as a warlord. Indra was also conceived as god of thunder and the rainmaker. It could be so because rain provided water that is essential for the survival of men, cattle, the plant and animal kingdom, and for agriculture. There appears to be hierarchical grading of the divine elements. Next in importance to Indra was Agni. Each family had a separate *Agnistuti*. Agni was considered very pure, the destroyer of dirt and germs that created diseases. The ritual of marriage was solemnized in the presence of Agni. Agni was also given primacy in the performance of the ritual of Yajna or sacrifice. Next in order, they worshipped Varuna, the water god. Next came Yama, the god of death, Surya, Soma, Savitru, Rudra and 100 Maruts were worshipped. They also worshipped weapons of war, drums and mortar. The Rigvedic worship centred on sacrificial rites. Hymns to various deities were recited, and animals were offered at the sacrificial altar – calling gods to bless them and provide all the material benefits that will enable them to lead a comfortable life on earth. The Rigvedic ritual of sacrifice was conducted by a social group of Purohits who acted as intermediaries between the worshippers and the gods. This enabled the priestly class group to become a crucial element of society, as they were capable of performing an act that made life sustainable on this earth. It is also suggested that animal sacrifice was a way for this pastoral society to get rid of old and useless cattle by endowing it with a religious significance and gave them ostensible justification on religious ground. At the time of sacrifice, the Rigvedic religion appears to be a patriarchal reflection of the pastoral warrior society. The Rigvedic religious philosophy never advocated devotees to surrender themselves to God as in the later *Bhaktimarga* or the path of devotion. An examination and study of the Vedic religious philosophical thought reveals a kind of progress from crude to more refined ideas and broader views. They also reflect the first principles of abstract, ritualistic, theistic, physiological and psychological foundations of the Rigvedic culture. Studies of the Rigvedic religious practices make us think of people who blended spiritual and materialistic approaches to life.

The Rigveda does not refer to *Nagara* or city but refers to *Pura* or seasonal fortification. This society was more or less pastoral and tribal with rudimentary agriculture not producing the surplus necessary for the growth of cities. These people domesticated the horse, the draught ox, the goat, the sheep and the dog. An interesting feature of this society was that the grasslands were held in common and this established the fact that the society was definitely pastoral and not agrarian. The *Panis* or non-Aryans controlled trade that was based on barter. The standard unit of exchange was the cow. The Rigveda refers to a gold coin Nishka and golden Mana, which has been identified with the old Babylonian weight. Chariots or Rathas and wagons or Ahas were the chief means of transport. Horses drew the Rathas and oxen drew the wagons. Thus, a study of the Rigvedic society and culture reveals that it was a dynamic society constantly evolving and willing to adapt to changes in socio-economic cultural spheres.

5

Post-Vedic Age

We notice a significant transition from Rigvedic or early Vedic society to that of later Vedic age. Chronologically, this transition is assigned to the period corresponding to 1000 BC to 600 BC. Both Vedic literature and archaeological sources provide sufficient material to reconstruct the history and culture of the people of the post-Vedic period. The literary evidences relate primarily to the territories of the upper and middle Ganga basin and somewhat peripherally to other region too. The archaeological spade found the existence of agricultural communities in the same geographical region; roughly corresponding to the same time span. Their culture is called Painted Grey Ware (PGW) culture and nearly 700 sites of this culture are found along the upper Ganga basin. These sites extend from the dry beds of river Ghaggar in Bahawalpur in Pakistan and northern Rajasthan, to the watershed of the Indus and the Ganges and the Ganga-Yamuna doab. The evidence of Sravasti site indicates that the eastern limit of the area of the PGW culture is restricted to the northern plains of the Ganges. It is also suggested that the Banas culture of southern Rajasthan reached the Ganges valley at around 800 BC and consequently black and red pottery users were said to belong to this period. While literary texts speak of the eastward shift of the Vedic Aryans, the archaeological excavations do not corroborate that view. Though there is discrepancy between the archaeological and literary sources in this period, they are in agreement regarding the use of iron by these people of PGW culture of the Gangetic basin. This can be confirmed by the Carbon 14 test conducted on the artefacts found in that region. The word *Ayas* referred to in the Rigveda is translated as 'iron'. We come across the term 'Syama Ayas' in the Yajurveda and 'Krishna Ayas' in the Brahmanas. Megalithic burials of southern India also reveal that they too were familiar with iron and its use. It is a prevalent view is that iron technology was indigenous rather than the consequence of foreign contacts.

A debate is going on among historians regarding the impact of iron technology on the material cultural base of the post-Vedic society. Two views prevail. One group holds the opinion that the iron technology was not an important factor, the other holds that the iron-socketed axes, iron tipped ploughshares, and nobs helped to clear the forests of the Gangetic 'doab' and improved the efficiency of the agricultural implements. The second view is questioned on the ground that the technology of smelting iron was at its primitive stage then. It is further pointed that the iron ore mines of Bihar were not fully exploited in this phase and was not very agrarian. Further, the artefacts that became known are only offensive weapons like iron-tipped arrowheads and spearheads and not agricultural implements like sickles, hoes and axes. It is now generally believed that iron technology did not influence the material cultural base till the second half of the first millennium BC as a ploughshare came into use only during this period. Further, the literary evidence of the Mahabharata refers to the mechanism of *Khandavadahana* to clear the forests by burning them rather than by iron implements.

In this phase, there was definite growth of agricultural operations as vast areas of fertile alluvial lands of the Ganga-Yamuna doab and the middle Ganga valley were available. No doubt, the later Vedic texts recognize pastoralism as an important occupation. We conclude that the mixed farming that included cultivation and herding continued to be the main occupation of the people. The people produced rice, wheat, and barley. Rice is referred to as *Vrihi*, *Tandula* and *Sali* in later Vedic texts, and excavated sites of PGW and Banas cultures yielded charred grains. Sathapatha Brahmana mentions agricultural operations like ploughing, sowing, reaping and threshing. Hesterman points out that in the major sacrificial rituals such as *Rajasuya*, the offerings of dairy products were less, compared to agricultural products. There is also a view that the economic pattern varied from region to region. From indirect evidences, it is suggested that the region around Mathura continued to be substantially pastoral for many centuries, while the middle Ganga plain shows limited evidence of pastoralism. This deduction was made based on specific reference to the amounts of grain and cattle in their offerings at the sacrificial ritual. A significant feature of this age was the emerging importance of land as an important commodity. Initially, the *Vis* or the clan owned the land collectively. In course of time, land became the property of a family. Consequently, cultivation of land became a family activity with the assistance sometimes of domestic servants and slaves. The reference to eight, twelve and twenty-four oxen yoked to the plough makes us speculate that the land holding varied in size leading to the emergence of hierarchy of landed families. The plough, an important agricultural implement was endowed with divinity and venerated as *Sita* by them. Besides the plough, the cow also became a sacred object as *Gomata*. We notice prayer to gods to protect the cow. We also come across reference to various occupations that were needed by the people. Sukla Yajurveda refers to a variety of occupations of this time. Weaving appears to have been in an advanced stage. We come across four types of pottery: (i) black and red ware, (ii) black striped ware, (iii) painted grey ware, and (iv) red ware. Coins like Satamana, Suvarna, Pedo and Krishnala besides Nishka are referred to in the Vedic texts of this period. We may postulate a hypothesis that surplus products produced by them enabled them to carry on trade both internally and externally, and coins might have been used as exchange medium in trade transactions. Trade facilitated the growth of towns and cities as we have literary references to Hastinapura and Kausambi.

A significant change also took place in the polity during this period. First, instead of tribal identity, territorial identity began to take shape. The word *Janapada* in the sense of a settled tribe became frequent along with the words '*rashtra*' and '*desa*'. The words 'Rashtra' and 'Desa' are not used in the sense of a 'state' as we understand, with fixed territorial boundaries. We have reference to Pancaladesa, where the Pancalas lived. Thus, instead of tribal identity, we now notice territorial identity and Rajan the warrior chieftain of the early Vedic phase becomes the protector of the territory where his tribesman lived a settled life. Further, Rajanya of the Vedic times becomes Kshatriya, whose literal meaning is the one who holds power over dominions. This Kshatriya began to receive presentations from 'Vis' for protecting the people. Bali and Bhaga, which were voluntary in the earlier period, became compulsory by this time. This shows that the Kshatriya was feared, respected and honoured. The status of the Kshatriya was not based on birth but on the act of legitimization by the ceremonial sacrifices like Rajasuya, Asvamedha and Vajapeya. Thus, during this phase, the Khsatriya lineage gained superior status and territory became the physical indication of the ruler's power. In this phase, the nature of conflict underwent a change. Conflicts arose for the acquisition and expansion of new territories, as territory became a physical manifestation of the greatness of the ruler. In these conflicts, iron weapons and light-wheeled chariots drawn by horses played a crucial role in gaining victories. The epic Mahabharata is nothing but intra-clan warfare between the tribes of Kauravas and Pandavas. The epic Ramayana also indirectly reflects the wish of Kaikeyi that her son Bharata should be the ruler of entire Bharatavarsha ruled by the Ikshvaku lineage.

Another important feature to be recorded during this phase is the ascendancy of the priest in his capacity to legitimize the power of the Kshatriya ruler. We also notice the feature of redistribution of wealth through the concept of *Dana* or *Dakshina* to the priests who performed the necessary consecratory rituals, and in course of time, the priests became the gods of earth demanding obedience from the other sections of the society.

The Rigvedic society became a society of hierarchically arranged social groups as the status of 'Vis' or 'Jana' declined and the priests and the Kshatriyas claimed a superior status in the social ladder. The *Purushasukta* of Rigveda narrates the origin of the four Varnas for the first time. In course of time, unequal status was assigned to these Varnas. The concept of superior and inferior, pure and impure, distant and nearness took shape and led to the division based on inequality. The Varna-based social order had the following features: (i) status fixed by birth (ii) a hierarchy-based social order in descending fashion, and (iii) rules of endogamy and ritual purity. Though later this Varna model was referred to in the Vedic literature, it appears to be only a theoretical framework but not practised rigorously. We do not come across the concept of untouchability in this phase. Owing to the fusion of Vedic and non-Vedic customs and traditions, the composite society based on composite culture began to take shape. The institution of Gotra, Gotra exogamy and abhorrence of Sagotra marriages began in this phase. Gotra literally means cow pen and as cows became sacred objects and worshipped during this period and the owners of the cow pens became the ancestors of a group, they were identified as belonging to one Gotra.

Patriarchal family was the basis of this society. *Grihapati* was the head of the family. Land-based household economy became the order of the day, thereby the position of the householder became predominant, and industrial arts provided the necessary wealth to the householders. These individual householders performed sacrifices to gain merit or Punya by giving Dana or Dakshina to the priestly group. This practice of Dana or Dakshina is said to be a redistribution of wealth accumulated by the householder. Though some women philosopher-scholars like Gargi and Maitreyi were known, in general the women occupied a secondary position without any role in decision-making. Women were allowed an equal place with husband in the practice of religious rituals and were called *Griharagni* but their activity was limited to the four walls of the house. The institution of 'Caturasramas' – *Brahmacharya*, *Grihasta, Vanaprasta* and *Sanyasa* appeared – to have been in vouge among Vedic people. However, we are not sure whether these caturasrmas were applicable to all social groups in their strict sense of observance or not. The post-Vedic texts record the existence of Vedic and non-Vedic traditions. While the Sama and Yajurveda and the Brahmanas record Vedic tradition, Atharvanaveda records the non-Vedic as well as folk traditions. This could be, as already explained, due to the fusion of Vedic and non-Vedic cultures, traditions and way of life. In this phase, religious beliefs centred on long-drawn out sacrifices, personal as opposed to State or royal sacrifices are recorded in the Vedic tradition. The rulers appear to have performed Aswamedha, Rajas Suya and Vajapeya sacrifices to exhibit their prowess and prestige and for the welfare of their people. The sacrifices became complex requiring specialists to perform them to be endowed with mystical power. During this period, Indra and Agni, the two powerful early Vedic deities lost their prominence and the Trinity of Brahma, Vishnu, Maheswara began to dominate and thus nature worship gave way to divine ordained deities. Worship of the Trinity and sacrifice-centred worship was referred to in Sama and Yajur Vedas. The hymns of Atharvanaveda refer to domestic and household problems faced by the individual Grihastas in their day-to-day life and included prayers for the cure of diseases, for improved health, more cattle and fields, and charms to produce harmony and love, and blissful conjugal life. The Upanishads, a genre of the Vedic tradition which are assignable to this period record a change that took place in the philosophical foundational process of this phase and revolve around the questions of the process of creation and destruction. The contribution to science, in particular to astronomy and mathematics appears to be significant.

By the 6th century BC, we find a transition to lineage-based territorial chieftainship; from Janapada to Mahajanapada, from pastoralism to settled farming, from nature worship to Trinity worship, from sacrifice centred ritual to Jnana-centred ritual. It may be rightly observed that the Vedic tradition gave rise to many later ideas, dealing with questions concerning the origin, nature and purpose of the world. The Vedic texts drew upon a variety of sources; including pre-Vedic and non-Vedic, ones, to reveal different world views based on material, divine, ritualistic and abstract principles. Even non-Vedic systems like Buddhism and Jainism and atheistic philosophies drew inspiration from the Vedic tradition. For example, the theistic school of Indian philosophy, the Purvamimamsa that has certain features in common with Buddhism and Jainism claims Vedic origin and it is committed to the Vedas. Purvamimamsa subordinates divine beings to human beings and propagates that by performing rituals the divine beings can be produced for the sake of human welfare. The ritualism is replaced by an ethical code of conduct by Buddhists and Jains to attain *Nirvana* or release from rebirth after death. We thus witness the society of India being dynamic and not static, taking cognizance of changes in material and spiritual outlook of the Vedic and non-Vedic people. The most obvious and visible development was the emergence of Varna-based social order. Varna etymologically signifies colour. However, in the historical context it refers to a specific connotation of 'social order' based on ritual purity and hierarchy. The origin of Varna is attributed to divinity as Purushasukta of the Rigveda and Aitreya Brahmana refer to the birth of the system, but the Purushasukta is now established to be a later interpolation, although the time of the interpolation is itself a debate among historians. This system comes into vogue from the time of the post-Vedic age, wherein we find references to the four Varnas: Brahmins, Kshatriyas, Vaisyas and Sudras. From them functions of individual Varnas and their hierarchy in social order took shape and got entrenched. Dipankar Gupta is of the view: "the Varna system came into being only after the Aryans settled in vast Indo-Gangetic plains. In the historical context of time and space, we notice a transition from Varna to Jati and reality is that there are thousands of Jatis and not just four Varnas". There is a view that Varna framework is only theoretical and not practised in the societal milieu. In the colonial period, Varna and Jati were identified with the Portugese word 'caste' and Indian society is characterized as a caste-based society. Romila Thapar is of the view that there is no unanimity regarding the precise social role of Varna and Jati. A protracted debate is going on among scholars of history, sociology and anthropology regarding the origin, definition and the nature of caste as an institution in the transition of Indian society. Our present goal is to create a casteless society where discrimination based on birth is absent.

6

Early Historic Period

The Sixteen Mahajanapadas – Rise and Expansion of Magadha

The period spanning from the 6th century BC to the 4th century BC is an important landmark in the evolution of Indian society and culture. The changes we noticed in the earlier period matured and these developments influenced the course of the evolution of Indian society later. Historians labelled this period as the beginning of the early historic period. Literary and archaeological sources provide valuable data to understand the historical process and construct the nature of society that evolved during this phase. While Vedic texts refer to *Janapadas*, the Buddhist and Jaina literatures refer to *Mahajanapadas*. For the first time geographical regions with different types of human settlements began to acquire specific territorial identity. The conflicts between various Janapadas led to the annexation of the vanquished Janapadas by the victors. Thus emerged the larger territorial and political entity of Mahajanapada. This process led to the decline of the power of the *Ganasanghas* and to the strengthening of the institution of kingship or monarchy, which is an important development in the sphere of the polity of early historic India. In each Mahajanapada, we come across human settlements designated as village, market-town, town and city. Thus, this period witnessed the beginnings of the second urbanization. It implies that people were following different professions besides food production on a larger scale now, more than in the early phase. The dichotomy between rural and urban areas began at this time. The concentration of food-producing groups by following agriculture, and cattle herding in a particular region led to the demarcations of rural areas. In urban areas, we find the professionals engaged in non-food producing activities living as separate communities. Both rural and urban areas were supplementing each other. It suggests that the rural areas were producing surplus food to meet the demand from the non-food producing specialist professional groups. This new development required a new mechanism to regulate and control effectively both these groups. The mechanism devised was the strengthening of royalty by making *Danda* or coercion as an essential feature along with protection and expansion of territorial unit. Consequently, taxes were imposed and collected by force to appropriate the surplus. Besides the already existing two social groups the priests and the Kshatriyas, a new social group of 'Settis' or Sreshtis, who acted as middle men and merchants supplying food grains to the non-food producing social groups was encouraged. In these new circumstances, in order to maintain equilibrium between different social groups, the theoretical framework of the Varna model was brought to the forefront, where the functions and privileges of the existing social groups were clearly demarcated. The Varna model appears to have served the purpose for which it was divised, and that may be the reason why even Buddha could not deviate from the Varna-based division of society though he strongly opposed the Vedic tradition and Brahmanical rituals.

The Buddhist literary tradition refers to the sixteen Mahajanapadas as a new politico-territorial unit that depended on the king equipped with Danda or coercive apparatus. The Buddhist text, *Anguttaranikaya* of *Suttapitaka* mentions the following 16 Mahajanapadas: (1) Kasi, (2) Kosala, (3) Aparanta, (4) Magadha, (5) Vajji (6) Malla, (7) Chedi, (8) Vatsa, (9) Kuru, (10) Panchala, (11) Matsya, (12) Surasena, (13) Assaka (14) Avanti, (15) Gandhara, and (16) Kambhoja. However, the *Mahavastu* another Buddhist text excludes Gandhara and Kamboja and substitutes Sibi and Dasarna in the Punjab and central India respectively. The Jaina texts also gave a different list as both the Buddhists and the Jains included only those areas known to them or those important to them. We may say that the figure 16 is only conventional. These sixteen Mahajanapadas extended from north-west Pakistan to East Bihar and from the regions of the Himalayas in the north to the river Godavari in the south.

Among the sixteen Mahajanapadas, Kasi appears to be the most powerful and Varanasi, its capital is located at the confluence of the rivers Ganga and Gomati in fertile agricultural zone. By 450 BC, Varanasi appears to have become a major town and a centre of cloth manufacturing, in particular *Kashaya* cloth worn by the Buddhist monks. By the time of the Buddha, the Mahajanapada of Kashi was annexed by Kosala, which led to a war between Magadha and Kosala. In due course, next to Kashi, the Mahajanapada of Kosala became a large principality, having four important towns – Ayodhya, Saketa, Kapilavastu and Sravasti. Hiranyanabha, Mahakosala Prasenajit and Suddhodhana are the known rules of Kosala. The Mahajanapada of Anga, which included the present-day districts of Bhagalpur and Munger in Bihar, had its capital at Champa. Anga was annexed by Magadha in the 6th century BC because of its flourishing trade and commerce. The Mahajanapada of Magadha included the present-day area around Patna and Gaya in South Bihar. It was protected in the north and west by rivers Son and Ganga. Its capital was Girivraja or Rajagriha. The name Girivraja signifies that it was protected by hills and the name Rajagriha testifies to the fact that it was the palace of Raja or king. The capital was shifted to Pataliputra in the 5th century BC and the Brahmanical texts give low status to Magadha as its population is said to be 'non-believers of Vedic Dharma and rituals'. However, the Buddhist tradition accords a great place to Magadha because its rulers Bimbisara and Ajatasatru were the disciples of the Buddha. Magadha became an important centre because of its fertile land that was the most suitable for wet-land rice cultivation, its control over iron ore of South Bihar, and its control over the routes of Ganga, Gandaki and Son rivers. Magadha gained further importance by occupying the territory of the Vajjis or pastoral nomads, who lived in the north of Ganga the Vaisali District of Bihar. This was a confederacy of eight different Ganas, of which Videhas, Lichchavis and Jnatrikas were the most powerful. The celebrated Jaina Thirthankara, Mahavira was born in this Gana. In this Mahajanapada, Vaisali and Mithila were important centres. Malla was another Gana Sangha, which had its headquarters at Kusinagara and Pawa. Kusinagara was the place where the 'enlightened one' breathed his last, and Mallas probably performed the last rites. The Chedi ruler Sisupala is said to be a contemporary of Lord Krishna. The territory of the Chedis corresponds to the eastern part of modern Bundelkhand and its capital was Suktimati, which is identified to be in the Banda district of Madhya Pradesh.

Vatsa with its capital at Kausambi was another powerful Mahajanapada, annexed by Magadha. The Kuru Mahajanapada is centred round the Delhi-Meerut region. Hastinapura, Indraprastha and Isukara are referred to as its capitals. The epic Mahabharata throws valuable light on the Kurus. The Panchalas appear to have been divided as northern and southern Panchalas according to literary tradition. Ahichchatra and Kampilya were the capitals of the northern and southern divisions respectively. They had close contact with the Kurus and became obsolete by the 6th century BC. Matsya Mahajanapada comprised the present-day Jaipur-Bharatapur-Alwar area of Rajasthan and Viratnagara was the capital. The Mahabharatha refers to the fact of Pandavas hiding in their court, and their being looted by the Kauravas. Bairat of modern times has been identified as Viratnagar and this was finally won by Magadha. The Mahajanapada of Surasena had its capital at Madhura, ruled by the Yadus, according to the epic Mahabharata and the Puranas. The Yadus were divided into a number of small clans and Lord Krishna, the central figure of the Mahabharata and an Avatara of Vishnu or Narayana belonged to the Yadus of Mathura. The Surasena Mahajanapada failed to create a strong kingdom because of its ecology. Assaka Mahajanapada had its capital at Paithan or Pratisthana about which we have very scant informulation. Besides Magadha, Avanti was one of the most important ones and its core area comprises the present-day Ujjain district of Madhya Pradesh. Pradyota was one of the powerful rulers of this Mahajanapada of the 6th century BC. Gandhara and Kambhoja Mahajanapadas existed very near to each other. The Brahmanical literary tradition considers the people of Kambhoja as 'uncultured' and Kautilya in his *Arthasastra* classified them as a confederation of agriculturists, herdsmen, traders and warriors.

A review of the newly emerged territorial entity called Mahajanapada reveals that seven out of sixteen – Anga, Magadha, Vajji, Malla, Kasi, Kosala and

Vatsa – were of the middle Gangetic valley, which was a rice producing, densely populated area. Magadha's access to important metal ores and the other factors made the middle Gangetic valley a politico-economic power centre. The fact that all these Mahajanapadas are contiguous to each other made it easy for Magadha to conquer them all and create a large kingdom. The event of the Magadhan ascendancy was completed by 400 BC by Bimbisara and Ajatasatru of the Haryanka clan, who successfully exterminated the Vajjiyan tribal confederacy and incorporated the Mahajanapadas of Anga and Kashi.

Thus, while eastern India under the leadership of Magadha made a successful transition to statehood; the frontier tribes of the north-west were exposed to the Persian invasion. Consequently, certain areas of the Sindhu and Gandhara regions became a part of the Achaemenian Empire. The Persian hold continued up to 330 BC until the Macedonian invader Alexander destroyed it. During the Persian domination, some tribal settlements became states, whose rulers were allowed to rule independently without declaring allegiance to the Persian overlords. The short rule of the Greeks produced enduring results neither in the economic nor in the political sphere except that it opened up the gates of communication between Greece and India and laid the foundation for an intimate intercourse between the west and India. The only tangible result of Alexander's invasion was the extermination of tribal settlements of north-western India. Ultimately, the states of north-western India also came under the imperial rule of Magadha.

Non-Vedic Religions: Jainism and Buddhism

Besides the political developments of significance explained above, another far-reaching development was the momentous religious upheaval. This religious upheaval shook the foundations of the Vedic orthodoxy and gave rise to many heterodox religious movements. Though there arose eighty-two heterodox religious schools in the Gangetic valley, only Buddhism and Jainism stood the test of time and grew into well-organized popular religions, along with the *Sanatana Dharma*. Out of the 82 religious sects, Ajivika and Lokayata deserve notice. They preached materialistic doctrines and ethics. These heterodox sects arose primarily because the Vedic rituals and practices had become unduly elaborate and expensive. Further, the newly emerging socio-politico milieu made the other social groups acquire considerable economic power. The Kshatriyas, the merchants, the landed aristocrats, the Gahapatis and the Kutumbins began to raise their voice against the birth-based social status and they too began to aspire for a better social status. Thus, the negative attitude towards the existing Varna-based social order, either theoretical or practised, and the alternative basis of social order propagated by the Buddha and Mahavira attracted these new social groups to favour Buddhism and Jainism against sacrifice and Varna-based social order of the Brahmanical tradition. The newly emerging peasant communities who appear to have become dominant did not approve the killing of cattle in the sacrifice, as cattle wealth was very essential to supplement agricultural operations. The non-killing or *Ahimsa* preached by the heterodox sects appears to have made these social groups opt for the heterodox sects. Besides these factors, the patronage extended to trade and commerce in particular by Buddhism and Jainism made the merchants, rich and poor agriculturists and artisans to favour Buddhism and Jainism. The code of conduct prescribed for lay people by these new religions appeared to be more practical than performing protracted rites through the Brahmin priest. These causes led to the new socio-economic and political milieu that arose in the 6th century BC in the Gangetic valley.

India witnessed the birth of two outstanding teachers and thinkers, who moulded not only the way of life of the natives of Bharatavarsha but also of the entire humanity largely. They were Gautama, the Buddha, 'the enlightened', 'the awakened', 'the light of Asia' and 'the light of the World', the founder of Buddhism, and Nighantanata Putta or Mahavira, the 24th Thirthankara, well known as '*Jaina*', who popularized Jainism. Both, by their teachings and life made India a worthy nation among the comity of nations. Their teachings were as relevant at that time as they are today. The Buddha through his preachings provided a new dimension, the urge for social equality. Both the teachers also believed in the concept of constant travelling and preaching the principles. While the Buddha advocated a middle path, Mahavira advocated strict and extreme asceticism. Today, both Buddhism and Jainism are two living faiths for millions of devotees, like any other religion. Some think of Buddhism and Jainism as 'the two angry daughters of Hinduism' as there are certain similarities between those heterodox sects and the Brahmanical religion. If Hinduism is a way of life, these two religions also advocate a way of life. Both these religious doctrines are codified into texts to be scrupulously followed by their devotees and practitioners. There is also a view that Buddhism was a social movement that took the urban side in the contemporary rural-urban philosophical ideological struggle. For V.K. Thakur, Buddhism was definitely a religion seemingly fighting for the privileges of the powerful emerging urban groups hitherto denied any social recognition and prestige in a society dominated by the orthodox Brahmanical values. It is interesting to note that though both were contemporaries, neither the Buddhist literary tradition nor the Jaina literary texts record the meeting of their great teachers. There are again several new perceptions about the origin and growth of the heterodox religions. Some scholars today question the premise of heterodox sects rising as a reaction against Vedic traditions. The Vedic tradition during the birth of Buddhism and Jainism was still in state of flux and was yet to develop a strong ethic for or against a given religious percept. Such fullness on the Vedic tradition's behalf was reached only much later in history. Internal evidence gleaned from the Buddhist and Jaina texts of the early historic period do not seem to have any apathy towards the Vedic traditions. It may be said that heterodoxy, even according to the Vedic texts, was a very ancient system that ran parallel to the growth orthodoxy, as assigned to some sections of the Vedic liturgy like the Brahmanas.

The Buddhist Principles

As the origin and ancestry of the Buddha are well known to all, no reference is made to that aspect. The Buddha delivered his first sermon, called *Dharma Chakra Pravarthana* or turning of the wheel of law, at Sarnath.

The fundamental teachings of the Buddha are contained in the Four Noble Truths and the Eightfold Path (*Astangamarga*). The four noble truths are: (1) The world is full of suffering (*Sarvam Dukham*). (2) All sufferings have a cause, and '*Tanha*' or desire, ignorance and attachment are the cause of suffering (*Dukha Samuday*). (3) The suffering can be avoided by destroying the cause (*Dukha Nirodha*) and (4) Suffering can be ended by knowing and practising the right path (*Dukha Nirodha Gamini Pratipala*) and that right path is the eightfold path (*Astangamarga*). The Buddha's eightfold path consists of: (1) Knowing the right view, i.e., the world is full of sorrow because of desire and by ending desire, life can be liberated. (2) Right aims, i.e., not to love the pleasures of life but to love humanity and to strive for the increase of happiness in others. (3) Right speech, i.e., speaking truth alone. (4) Right action, i.e., doing action without selfish motive. (5) Right livelihood, i.e., man should obtain his livelihood by right means only. (6) Right effort, i.e., one should have control over his thoughts and should destroy desire and attachment. (7) Right-mindedness, i.e., knowing the impermanence of the body, and (8) Right concentration, i.e., observance of meditation that will unravel the truth. Buddha named the practice of these principles as *Majjhimamarg* or the middle path.

The Buddha laid great emphasis on the law of *Karma*. He taught that the present is determined by the actions of man in the past birth and the condition of a man in this life depends upon his earlier actions The Buddha's teachings made it clear that we are born repeatedly to reap the fruits of Karma. He propagated that if an individual does not commit sins he/she is not born again. The law of Karma is thus an essential element of his teachings. The Buddha preached that the ultimate goal in man's life is Nirvana or freedom from rebirth. Nirvana is possible only when we rid ourselves of desires and thereby end suffering. Therefore, for the Buddha, the annihilation of desire is the core issue. Normal, simple and virtuous life in this world can lead to salvation, and not sacrifices and prayers.

The Buddha neither rejected nor accepted the existence of God because he was more concerned about, the actions of the individual in this world as well as in his previous birth. Nor did he talk about the existence of soul as well. He gave more importance to the concept of love, which can be expressed by non-killing or non-injury or Ahimsa. He also denounced the two extremes – severe ascetism and excessive indulgence. He emphasized that there was no need for intermediaries between the individual and Nirvana or birthlessness. The Buddha rejected the animal offering as sacrifices. The preachings of the Buddha had been codified and brought out as collections or as Canon much later. These are the Buddhist canons, which are divided into three *Pitakas.* They are: (1) *Sutta Pitaka* (2) *Vinava Pitaka,* and (3) the *Abhidamma Pitaka*. The *Sutta*

Pitaka contains five '*Nikayas*' or religious discourses. The fifth Nikaya consists of Jataka tales or stories about the previous births of the Buddha. The *Vinaya Pitaka* contains the rules of monastic discipline. The *Abhidamma Pitaka* contains the philosophical ideas of the Buddha. Buddhism became popular among different sections of the society even during the lifetime of the Buddha as well as after the demise. Buddhism received state patronage at the hands of Ashoka and Kanishka. Consequently, it spread to Central Asia, West Asia and Sri Lanka, China and Japan.

Buddhism became popular because: (1) its emphasis was on a moral code of conduct that offered easily practicable and acceptable solutions to the problems faced by mankind, (2) the propagation of the ideal of social equality, (3) recognition accorded to merchants, artisans, courtesans and petty traders in the social hierarchy, (4) technique of teaching of the principles in common people's language, (5) royal recognition and patronage, and (6) the idea of a democratically constructed Sangha, that was open to all above the age of 15, except criminals, lepers and people suffering from infectious diseases. In the beginning women were not admitted into Sangha but later due to the persuasion of his step-mother Mahaprajapati Gautami and disciple Ananda, the, Buddha permitted women to be admitted into the Sangha. After admission into the Sangha, all the monks have to shave their heads and wear saffron robes and lead an austere life preaching and practising the Buddhist principles of love, compassion and equality. They have to live by the alms collected from lay devotees. Except in rainy season, during the rest of the year, they should be moving from place to place meditating and preaching the Buddhist doctrines. The members of Sangha should strictly follow the code of conduct prescribed; violation resulted in severe punishment.

Tradition records that after the death of the Buddha, the first Buddhist council was held in 483 BC in the Saptaparni cave near Rajagriha, which was presided over by Mahakassapa. Here, the two Pittakas – the Sutta and the Vinaya – were given shape. While Ananda led the group of Buddhist scholars who prepared the Sutta Pitaka, Upali led the group who prepared the text of Vinaya Pitaka. Later a schism took place among the Buddhists, and in order to bring about a rapprochement, the second council was held at Vaishali in 383 BC. The council failed to achieve its objective and the Buddhists were divided into Sthaviravadins and Mahasanghikas. The Sthaviravadins upheld the orthodox Vinaya Pitaka while the Mahasanghikas favoured new rules. During the reign of Ashoka, the third Buddhist council was held at Pataliputra, wherein Mogaliputta Tissa presided over it. This council prepared the third Pitaka, i.e., Abhidamma Pitaka. This council attempted to set right the house of the Buddhists in order. During the reign of Kanishka, the fourth Buddhist council was held at Kashmir. This council prepared three commentaries or *Vibhasas* of the three Pitakas. After this council, the Mahayana Buddhism developed. While the Hinayanists did not see the Buddha as God, the Mahayanists created the images of the Buddha and began to worship them. Thus by the 1st century AD, the Buddhists were divided into two different sects, Hinayana and Mahayana.

The Jaina Principles

The well-known personal antecedents of Mahavira need no recount. The Jaina literary tradition strongly advocates that the 24 Thirthankaras were responsible for the origin and development of Jainism, the other prominent heterodox religion. Of these, the historicity of the first twenty-two is very doubtful and it is said that with a view to claiming more antiquity for Jainism, these Thirthankaras might have been projected as the founders of Jainism. The twenty-third Thirtankara, Parsvanatha and the 24th Thirthankara Mahavira are historical figures and even the contemporary Buddhist literary tradition refers them.

Interestingly, the 23rd and the 24th Thirthankaras belong to the ruling Kshatriya community, both of them abdicated their thrones, and both became enlightened after severe penance. We notice resemblances in the pattern of enlightenment attained by the Buddha and Parsvanatha and Mahavira. This illustrates the urge of the ruling elite to compete with the ritually powerful Brahmins to claim the spiritual leadership of the community. Parsvanatha propagated the eternity of matter, the necessity to speak truth, the need for non-violence and non-possession of goods and Mahavira added celibacy or *Brahmacharya* to the already existing body of principles. He advocated that the Jiva (soul) and Ajiva (matter) are the two basic elements of the universal. Like the Buddha, he too opined that the soul of man is in a state of bondage created by desire, accumulated through previous births. He assured that with continued efforts, one can free oneself from bondage and this is final liberation or *Moksha* of the soul. As a result, it becomes a 'pure soul'. His three principles are known as *Ratnatraya* or *Triratnas*. The Triratnas are Right belief, Right knowledge and Right action. Extreme penance and severe ascetism were advocated by him to attain *Kaivalya* or the highest spiritual state like the Budha. He too had no faith in the supreme creator or God. He thought that the world functioned according to an eternal law of development and decay. He also advocated that all objects had a soul of their own and experienced pain or the impact of injury. He too rejected the sacred authority of the Vedas and objected to the supremacy of the Brahmans. He prescribed a code of conduct for both the householder and the monks. They have to follow the five vows – non-injury, non-stealing, non-adultery, non-possession and speaking only truth. Mahavira ordained that the *Grihasta* should feed the guests every day. Mahavira laid so much importance on the concept of non-violence, that lay Jains are prohibited from taking to the cultivation as in that process insects, small plants and animals that inhabit the cultivated land are destroyed forever.

Tradition records that all the doctrines taught by Mahavira were codified into 14 leaves known as '*Purras*'. The first Jaina council was held at Pataliputra and Sthulabhadra divided the Jaina cannon into 12 Angas. The Jains were divided into Swetambaras and Digambaras. In the second council held at Valabhi, new additions were made to what in the form of *Upagrayas* or minor sections to the existing Purras. The eleven disciples of Mahavira are known as Gandharas and one disciple Arya Sudhamma survived Mahavira and became the Thera or chief preceptor of the Jaina order. Both these heterodox religions survived along with the Brahmanic religion and in course of time we notice the impact of the Brahmanical doctrines on Buddhism and Jainism and vice versa. Another feature deserving notice is the fact that all religions were divided into different sects, based on regional or leadership consideration. It may be due to the vastness of the area as well as the diversity we notice in ecological and geographical matters. We can notice this tendency today in respect of political parties, as well as in art and literature.

The doctrines preached by these heterodox religions profoundly influenced the contemporary social thought and action. As such, the idea of social equality became one of the ideals to be achieved. Opening of doors of membership to all irrespective of birth made these religions more acceptable to all those who were denied access to equal social status by the hierarchical and graded social structure of *Sanatana Dharma*. Still social equality has proved to be elusive, in spite of the sincere efforts of progressive minded thinkers and preachers. It is accepted as a theoretical ideal, but traditions as well as the stakes of the privileged groups are so strong that we have yet to accept and approve social equality as practical reality. Acceptance of women as members of the Sangha is said to have increased the stature of woman. No doubt, due to the growth of these heterodox faiths, trade and commerce developed because of the recognition given to these professions as respectable, by these faiths. As such, we notice many Stupas, Chaithyas and Viharas on the trade routes patronized by trading and mercantile communities. As the preaching was carried on in mother tongues of the regions, Prakrit, Pali and Arthamagadhi gained strong foothold as languages of communication and of literature. Both these heterodox faiths had some similarities like emphasis on humanitarian values, ethical code of conduct, Karma doctrine and the principle of Ahimsa, and both of them opposed Vedic orthodoxy, Brahmanical supremacy, animal sacrifices and the concept of God. Yet, there are certain dissimilarities between them. Undoubtedly, they brought about a change in the attitude of the people and some began to challenge the established authority of the Brahmanical religion. The nature and tenacity of challenge was not uniform as it was vigorous at certain times and places and weak at certain other times and areas. As already explained, no religion was able to displace the other but all survived side by side with shifting impact from time to time.

A noteworthy feature of the religious scenario of early India is the coexistence of different religions leaving the people to choose their faith and the eschewing of suppression of other faiths as a general principle. A large literary tradition recorded in Brahmanical, Buddhist and Jaina texts refers to the socio-economic milieu of this age. Of this literate tradition, Grihyasutras, Srautasutras and Dharmasutras provide instruction in the performance of day-to-day rites and rituals. Dharma Sutras and Dharma Sastras explain the duties and privileges of the Varnas in the social order. Brahmans are accorded six professions, out of which teaching of Vedic knowledge and conducting religious rituals are important. This literary tradition specifically proclaims that only those who engage in pure professions and lead a life prescribed for them only are to be considered. Brahmins and those who violate the prescribed code are to be treated as Sudras. The Kshatriyas and Vaisyas are also advised to follow strictly the way of life prescribed to them. The Sudras are accorded four occupations: service, production of wealth, art and crafts. However, in real practice, more castes are known to have existed than the Varnasrama evidence. Perhaps, the *Varnasankara* theory was introduced in Dharmic literature to explain that the social order did not run as per the prescriptions of the Dharmasastras and to provide legality and legitimacy to the newly born Jatis as per the needs and demands of the changing socio-economic milieu. Simply accepting the normative tradition of literature does not appear to be true of the existing social system. Empirical evidence proves this fact. The contemporary Buddhist literary tradition depicts a different picture of society. This was the period when literate tradition began in India with the acquisition of the knowledge of writing and inventing a script known as Brahmi. This new acquisition made it possible to record the changes and transmit them to posterity through script. While the Brahmanical literature gives secondary rank to Kshatriyas in the social order, the heterodox literary, tradition places them in the first rank. This makes the historian cautious while making a generalization of the social order as the two traditions provide information from their divergent points of view. Likewise, the Brahmanical and the non-Brahmanical literatures also provide information from their point of view about the place of Sudras in the social order and how the higher Varnas oppressed them. Besides Sudras, we also come across dispossessed groups such as Pukkasas, Nishadas and Vennus, whose condition was very wretched. We have references to a group called Chandalas, who were considered impure because of their profession. Concepts like purity, impurity, pollution and distance began to take shape during this period. Though we come across the term Gahapati or Kutumbin representing the landed gentry who acted as Grihastas or householders, we also come across a group of *Parivrajakas* or *Sramanas*, who voluntarily renounced worldly pleasures and led a simple wandering life. The position of women deteriorated, as they became a non-entity in the social system. Thus, this was a period when the principle of social stratification can be seen in embryonic form, which made the social system experience the tremors of new winds blowing in the direction of equality.

Literary and archaeological sources provide sufficient evidence regarding the economy of this period. It saw the process of surplus production of agricultural goods, which was supplemented by domestication and rearing of cattle. Thus, this was a period of transition from subsistence economy to market economy. The introduction of coinage gave fillip to market economy. The exchange of commodities through coinage naturally led to greater mobility, acculturation and growth of trade and commerce, which facilitated the growth of complex economy. We find the growth of villages and towns. Pali texts refer to three types of settlements: (1) a typical settlement where we come across different Varnas and professional groups living in peace side by side, (2) a typical craft village or suburban village linked with a town, and (3) a border village, where hunting was still practised for survival and sustenance. Thus, the factors of surplus production, craft specialization, trade, markets of exchange, use of metallic currency, emergence of a large territorial unit with more power that is political and the beginning bureaucratic apparatus led to a new social formation where traders and craftsmen through their guilds began to claim dominance, along with the priestly and the warrior groups. In this process of historical change, we notice a struggle for identity among social groups as well as efforts by the lawgivers and the state apparatus to control the impact of this struggle on society, economy and polity. A significant event of political importance of this age along with the rise of Magadha is the invasion of Alexander on the north-west region inhabited by independence-loving hill tribes.

Alexander's Invasion and its Effects

Alexander, the son of Philip of Macedonia, is considered one of the great conquerors of the ancient world. He ascended the throne at the age of twenty in 335 BC. Alexander, who was fired by an ambition to become the world conqueror, gathered a large army and started his conquests in 334 BC. After consolidating his position by conquering neighbouring powers, he became busy in waging war with Persia between 334 and 330 BC and conquered Asia Minor, Syria and Egypt. In his wars with Persia, a decisive battle was fought at Arbela in 331 BC. Alexander captured and destroyed Persipolis, the capital of Persia and built a new city called Alexandria. By 328 BC, Alexander took the title of "Great King of Persia".

Alexander then turned his attention towards India and divided his army into two parts. Alexander himself led a part of the army while the other part was sent to India under the command of Hephaeston and Perdikkas, Alexander's army was opposed by the tribal chief Hasti or Aster, whose capital was Pushkalavati and after a bitter struggle Alexander won a victory. Later Alexander had to face the Asvayanas who fought very bravely before he defeated them. After a long seige, Alexander decided to cross the river Indus after consolidating his position in the conquered territories. It is said that he constructed a sixteen-mile bridge at Ohind and here the envoy of Ambhi, the ruler of Taxila, met Alexander. From Ohind Alexander proceeded to Taxila, where the ruler Ambhi and the ruler of the Abhisara tribe became subordinates to him. Purushottama or Porus, the ruler of the territory of Jhelum opposed Alexander in the battle of Hydaspes. In this battle, Purushottama was defeated by a stratagem, but in the end Alexander, recognizing the bravery and valour of Purushottama returned the territory to him. Purushottama appears to have accepted the overlordship of Alexander. Commemorating his victory, Alexander built the cities of Boukephala and Nikala near the Jhelum river.

Alexander then crossed the Chenab and defeated the tribes living between the Chenab and the Ravi. The army of Alexander revolted when asked to cross the Beas and as Alexander failed to convince them, he ordered retreat of the army in 326 BC, after constructing twelve huge altars on the river Beas. On the way back, Alexander had to face the opposition of many hill tribes and he died at the age of 33 in 323 BC in Babylon near Baghdad. His sudden death was followed by confusion and partition of the Greek empire in 321 BC and his power on the Indian soil was shattered to pieces.

A debate is going on among historians regarding the impact of the invasion of Alexander. There is a view that Alexander's invasion of India is a landmark in the history of India. There are also arguments that the significance of the event was much exaggerated, or that it was underestimated.

Interestingly, not even a single Indian literary text, Hindu, Buddhist or Jainas, of the contemporary times or of later date makes the faintest allusion to Alexander or his invasion. What could be the reason for this silence? Could it be that he could not come to the mainland of India, i.e., the Gangetic Valley and that he succeeded only over small, petty chieftains and hill tribes? It is a fact that he invaded the border area of India, but failed to establish a sound political power structure that could transit Greek ideas into India. His stay in India was only for 19 months, which was spent in fighting or planing to fight. Though there was no significant direct impact of his conquest, indirectly it opened up contacts between east and west culturally, and promoted trade contacts by opening up a communication network. We cannot accept the view of Hernesse that all the later developments of India depended indirectly upon the institutions of Alexander. Even V.A. Smith admits that India was not totally Hellenised but followed a policy of "splendid isolation". We may agree with the view of R.K. Mukherjee that the invasion of Alexander indirectly promoted the awareness and need for political unification under a large kingdom. We also can agree with R.C. Majumdar that it was only a raid leaving no permanent marks. Culturally, the Gandhara art is a good example of the impact of the Greek artistic tradition on Indian art. The Greek influence on Indian astronomy is remarkable, and the Greek influence on Indian coins is to be remembered. In conclusion, it can be said that though India was not Hellenised because of Alexander's invasion or raid, the Greek impact on Indian culture of later times is of considerable importance.

7

The Age of the Mauryas

Primary State Formation

Before a detailed analysis of the Mauryan polity is undertaken, it is imperative to recollect the process of state formation in the pre-Mauryan times, as we notice a continuity of political ideas with modifications necessitated by changing economic and social milieu of the times. For four decades, the focus of historical reconstruction has been revolving around the domain, function and role of the state. R.G. Gettell is of the view that the general form of the state that the 'Oriental world' created was a theocratic, despotic monarchy, with conquest or religion as sanction for authority. Subsequently, Gettell, on the authority of B.K. Sarkar, modified his view by conceding that the Hindu states were different from the other 'Oriental' political systems. Until the post-independent historiographical studies, it was the religious outlook that dominated the perception of many a scholar. Spengler called religion the prime symbol of Indian culture. Toynbee declared that the spirit of the Indian civilization was also religion based. From Sri Aurobindo to G.C. Pande, all are of the view that religion formed the foundation of Indian culture. A. Kumara Swamy, J. Gonda, J.C. Heasterman and I.W. Mabbett also emphasized the sacred character of the early Indian concept of state. It is so because the Brahmanas asserted that the notion of kingship originated from consecration rites. Further, Kumarilabhatta defined *Rajadharma* as something desirable producing a supra-sensible state of bliss. K.V. Rangaswamy Ayyangar maintains that all laws according to Smritis are fundamentally religious in nature. In recent times, the writings of A. Southall and Burton Stein once again reinforce the religious character of kingship of early India by looking at the performance of ritual obligation by the ruler as an important trait of the kingship. G.W. Spencer, H. Kulke, and S.K. Panda expressed the view that the ruling dynasties either by patronizing religious establishments or by integrating with and participating in the ritual system, validated their newly acquired power or buttressed their waning authority and thus used religion to legitimize their rule. No doubt, religion occupied a major place in the politico-legal life in early India, yet it cannot be accepted that religion alone can express the process and sanction of authority.

B.D. Chattopadhayaya and K.M. Srimali argue that though religion served as a legitimizing factor, "legitimization is a complex process and the instruments through which political authority seeks validation are varied".

There is a view among political thinkers and historians that there existed one type of state over the entire country. The domain, function and role of the state retained a uniformly fixed character over the long time spread from the Vedic period to the assumption of political power by the British. However, contradicting the above view, Sibesh Bhattacharya, argued that the nature of the state often experienced basic changes in its organizational set-up and pattern of authority. He suggested three typologies of transition of political authority: (1) pre-state, (2) centralized state, and (3) feudal state system in early India. He rightly and aptly cautions that these divisions are not watertight compartments, there is every possibility of overlap of traits as all history is a process and transition.

It is generally agreed upon that state formation and the growth of agriculture are interlinked. It is to be noted that the term 'state formation' has not been used in a uniform sense or context. It has been used to describe (a) the evolution of state from pre-state society, (b) extension of state system into areas that had not experienced state system before, (c) reintegration of a broken down state under a new ruling house, or creation of a state by piecing together parts of various previously existing ones. Here we are concerned only with the aspects 'a' and 'b' of the above explanation. We are now aware that there was a gradual transition from a lineage based society to a state system. Early state system originated in verdant river plains, perhaps with the need for control over the hydraulic system, which made Wittofogel propose the theory of Oriental Despotism. Irfan Habib criticized this theory of Wittofogel. The early state system originated in certain nuclear areas, which are very suitable for the development of agriculture and the resultant economic, social, and political processes and thus lineage societies flowered into states. Yet, it is to be noted that this process of state formation was not linear movement from lineage to state because while some graduated to state society through a new mode of production, i.e., agriculture, some appear to have persisted with their old ways of hunting and gathering. Consequently, we notice throughout our history a continuous tension between the settled communities based on agriculture that opted for state system and the groups of hunting-gathering communities who lived on the fringes. The *Rakshasas* could be none but the hunting-gathering peoples who waged a losing battle to preserve themselves against the settled agrarian communities. If we critically examine the growth of state system, we notice that a nuclear area, rich in agriculture gave rise to a state for the sake of protection, providing impetus for territorial expansion. The Santiparva of the Mahabharata and the Buddhist texts clearly state, "once there was no ruling authority, no king, no coercion and no coercer, people took care of each other out of a sense of neighbourliness". Nevertheless, the emergence of state system in the settled agrarian communities living on riverine plains was necessitated by the constant threat of disturbance by the forest dwelling communities, as well as a need to protect people from *arachaka* or a state of complete lawlessness and depravity. It is this constant fear of insecurity that drove them to accept the concept of kingship embodied in the king. As such, the king's primary function was *rakshana* or protection and *palana* or nourishing his *Praja* or people. The ancient Indian lawmakers like Manu and Narada, and Baudhayana Dharmasutra, Apastambha Dharmasutra and Gautama Dharmasutra echo this sentiment and as such, the king was endowed with the power to punish those who violate his orders. Hence, the Santiparva of Mahabharata clearly states that all Dharmas are merged in Rajadharma, that is at the head of all dharmas. Had there been no *Dandaneeti*, the Vanaparva declares, that this world would have disintegrated into pieces. We notice a gradual increase in the power and functions of the ruler. In Rigvedic age, we come across the term chieftain of Gana (Ganapati and Ganarajya), who protected the 'gana' from external enemies and saved the cows and buffaloes, and by the time we come to the post-Vedic age, the chieftain became a king and by the 6th century BC became very powerful. Post-Vedic literature popularized the concept of sovereign monarch and started attribution of some form of divinity to the institution of kingship.

From then onwards, the concept of the state revolved around the institution of kingship and included the concept of territory as can be gathered from the relevant literature. No doubt, the state provided a sort of cohesiveness to the territory within the borders but that cohesiveness remained superficial as it was confined to the administrative aspect alone. As such, the cohesiveness brought about by the state did not permeate spontaneously to the social and cultural levels, because the sense of belonging and loyalty were essentially local in character. The sense of identity was so deep-rooted that we come across the statement of Pasenadi as follows: "The master is a Kshatriya, I too am a Kshatriya. The master is Koshalan and I too am a Koshalan". Kuru culture is emphasized in the *Kurudhamma Jataka*. Patanjali records linguistic local peculiarities. Thus, caste identity, territorial identity, linguistic identity and identity of practices are to be taken into consideration while discussing the domain of the state. Sibesh Bhattacharya opines that the moment a state grew beyond local, it faces a bundle of heterogeneous cultures, which had to be forged into a cohesive polity. It is to be noted that the growth of the state implies both territorial expansion, and absorption of new people with their cultural traits. It also signifies a progressive growth and a greater degree of specialization and diversification of occupations. We gather from the writings of Rhys Davids, Mrs Rhys Davids, Fick, S.C. Bhattacharya and R.S. Sharma that the period beginning with the later Vedic age witnessed not only the process of state formation that resulted in the growth of the Magadhan empire but also witnessed a process of proliferation of crafts, guilds and Varna-jatis. Thus, a state had to accommodate a diversity of communities, traditions and cultures. The vitality and the strength of the state depend on its ability to harmonize both the contradictory pulls of homogenization and heterogenization. With this background of the state formation, let us try to understand the nature, domain and functions of the Mauryan state.

Political History

The emergence of Magadha, one of the sixteen Mahajanapadas, as a dominant kingdom between the 6th century BC and the 4th century BC heralded the beginning of a new era in the evolution of society, economy, polity and culture of the subcontinent of India. As history is a process and transition, we notice a transition: from pre-state society to state system, rural to urban, sacrificial ritual to individual meditation, from oral tradition to script and writing to record permanently, contributions in the realms of philosophy, science and literature, and minting of coinage with standard weight in metal, backed by legal and political sanction as exchange value of commodities which led to the growth of trade and commerce. These multiple factors are the cause and the effect of changes that shaped the material and intellectual milieu of Indian society.

Of the sixteen Mahajanapadas, only Magadha could play a seminal role at that time because of certain advantages: Geographically, Magadha had in its vicinity large tracts of alluvial soil suitable for producing agricultural surplus. The earliest capital Rajagriha was located in a strategic position in a comparatively isolated region, close to the availability of iron ore. The later capital of Magadha was located at Pataliputra, which was situated at the confluence of several rivers like Ganga, Gandak and Son, which makes it a waterfort or *Jaladurga*. This enabled the Magadha rulers to command effectively the *Uttarapatha* that is to the north of the river Ganga along the foothills of the Himalayas. The river Ganga helped them to stay connected with other regions and to develop transport on the river. These natural advantages made Magadha a dominant power. Further, recent studies have brought to light Magadha's access to iron ore, which enabled it to manufacture weapons for offensive and defensive use as well as implements necessary for agricultural operations. The alluvial soils of the Gangetic plain and adequate rainfall were very conducive for the expansion of agriculture.

This enabled Magadha to generate sustainable surplus to meet the growing needs of the state system in the form of taxes. Growth of towns and the use of metal currency encouraged large-scale trade and commerce. The taxes collected by the state machinery enabled the Magadhan rulers maintain a strong army. Their use of elephants gave them an added advantage over their enemies. Further, the racial admixture created an unorthodox social base that fostered solidarity among the inhabitants. All these factors encouraged Magadha to launch expeditions for territorial expansion. Magadha became a dominant kingdom under the Saisunagas and the Nanda political power structure became, what Romila Thapar calls "a Metropolitan state" under Mauryan rule.

A critical study of the available primary literary sources of the Buddhists – Tripitakas and the Jatakas, *Divya Vadana, Mahavamsa, Dipa Vamsa* and the Jaina texts *Acaranga Sutra* and *Sutra Kritanaa*. Classical writings in Greek and Latin, Megasthene's *Indica* that came to us through the quotations of Strabo, Deodorus and Arrian, Herodatus's account, Kautilya's *Arthasastra,* numismatic, and epigraphic evidences, and excavations help us in reconstructing the process of transition that took place during the pre-Mauryan and the Mauryan age.

Bimbisara, Ajatasatru and Udayin laid the foundation for the Magadhan supremacy. The Saisunagas and the Nandas continued the policy of acquiring new territories. It was during the rule of the Nandas that the Macedonian ruler Alexander invaded North-Western India in 326 BC. As already, mentioned, Alexander's invasion of India did not lead to any permanent political set-up but it initiated cultural contacts between India and Greece. Evidences show that the Nandas developed contacts with the South and the Deccan, and the Nanda political power structure ended by BC 321. Traditional accounts record that Chandragupta Maurya overthrew the oppressive rule of the Nandas in alliance with Kautilya or Chanakya. In spite of the dynastic fluctuations, Magadha continued to be a centre of political power by its location and natural advantages well into the medieval period.

The founding of the Mauryan empire by Chandragupta Maurya ushered a new era in the history of India. Not much reliable authentic data about the antecedents of Chandragupta is available. *Mudrarakshasa,* a play of the 6th century AD, records that he rose to political power with the help, blessings and cooperation of Kautilya the celebrated author of Arthasastra. The early years of Chandragupta's reign appear to be obscure. The Maurya was considered to be 'a low caste' or of 'tribal origin' by most of the historians. Classical sources also describe them as of low caste. The Puranas also describe them as Sudras but Buddhist literature mentions that Chandragupta was a member of the Moriya clan of Pippalivana, who are distantly related to the tribe of the Sakyas who are Kshatriyas. There is also a view that the Mauryas were Vaisyas as Chandra had 'Gupta' at the end of his name and Asoka married the daughter of a merchant of Vidisa. It may be concluded that the caste affiliations of the Mauryas remain obscure. The rise of Chandragupta Maurya to the throne proves beyond doubt that in spite of the dictates of the Varnasrama model the society and Dharma of the times accepted anyone who showed potential as a ruler. It may also be explained that the impact of heterodox sects on Magadha was so powerful that they could ignore the Varnasrama model. Whatever may be the reason, the accession and acceptance of Chandragupta, as a ruler appears to be revolutionary, though it is an isolated instance and not a general rule.

All the available sources record that Chandragupta overthrew the last of the Nanda kings and ascended the Magadha throne in or around 321 BC. Yet, there is no definite evidence regarding the year in which Chandragupta routed the Greeks and defeated the Nandas. Now, there is a general agreement that these two events must have taken place by 321 BC. Another important victory attributed to Chandragupta was the victory over Seleucus by 303 BC. This victory signifies that the territorial foundations of the Mauryas were well established within the Gangetic plains. Based on the later evidences, there is also a view that he conquered western India and Deccan too. The Jaina tradition proudly claims that he became a votary of Jainism and abdicated the throne and went south with a Jaina saint Bhadrabahu. Chandragupta spent the rest of his life at Sravana Belagola in Karnataka and ended his life performing Sallekhana, a Jaina way of attaining Nirvana.

His son Bindusara succeeded Chandragupta. He is said to have ascended the Mauryan throne in 297 BC. Neither Indian nor classical sources furnish any useful historical information about him. Classical sources call him *Amitraghata*. He had contacts with the Selucid king of Syria, Antiochous I. The Buddhist work of Taranatha, a very late source of the 16th century AD, recounts his war-like activities. Some scholars consider the thundering of the Mauryan chariots over the length and breadth of the territory depicted by early Tamil poets as reference to Bindusara's conquests. There is also a view that it was Bindusara, who firmly established Mauryan rule in the Deccan and the Mysore plateau as Asoka is said to have conquered Kalinga and then given up conquests. Though Binduasara had the title of Amitraghata, we are not sure of the foes killed by him and why he killed them. Bindusara appears to have been a follower of the Ajivika sect. The Buddhist texts are certain that he died around 273–272 BC, as there is a gap of three or four years before the crowning of Asoka; it is surmised that a succession war might have taken place among the sons of Bindusara aspiring for the throne.

Asoka's reign of more than three decades is the first fairly well documented period of the early history of India. Asoka left behind a series of major and minor rock edicts along with pillar edicts which enable us to know fairly well about his reign and deeds. Except the epigraphs at Maski and Sannati, none of the edicts refers to his name as Asoka. Epigraphs describe him as *Devanampiya* or beloved of the gods and *Piyadaso*. Till 1837, when James Princep desciphered these epigraphs and identified Devanampiya with Asoka Maurya with the corroborative evidence of other sources, Asoka was not a well-known historical figure of the early history of India. A stupa was discovered at Kanaganahalli, a tiny hamlet on the left bank of the river Bhima, 3 kms south of Sannati. The importance of this discovery is that an anthropomorphic representation of Emperor Asoka with his queen, with a legal in Brahmi reading 'Raya Asokasa' making a donation. It is quite interesting to come across an anthropomorphic representation at a far-off place from his core area and that too in a peripheral area. It makes one question: What could be the reason for this representation at Kanaganahalli with his queen? Perhaps, it could be to impress the people of this area about his attention for them that he and his queen made a donation. If that could be so, what could be the special reason? We have not yet found such a representation anywhere else. Perhaps, one of the beneficiaries of Asoka's deeds of charity out of gratitude or admiration might have been responsible for the anthropomorphic representation of Asoka at Kanaganahalli. Asoka attained eternal fame as 'Asoka the great' in the history of mankind because he happened to be the first ruler to give up 'Digvijaya' concept and start 'Dharma Vijaya' and to usher in a rule based on of Dharma. Because of this unique policy, the independent Republic of India selected Asoka's lion pillar as the emblem of the state.

Asoka started his political apprenticeship as the Governor of Taxila during his father's reign. He is credited to have successfully curbed the rebellions in the state. For sometime, he also was the Governor of Ujjain. The exact date and the precise circumstances in which he succeeded his father cannot be authentically proved. Nevertheless, the Buddhist sources are sure that Asoka ruthlessly eliminated his many brothers and declared himself the ruler in 269–270 BC. We may agree with Eggermont that this story was invented by the Buddhists to prove their point that prior to his transformation as 'Pious Asoka' he was wicked-minded and power-hungry. However, we may not subscribe to the Buddhist viewpoint, Asoka not being a Yuvaraja or heir apparent is certain and the war of succession appears to be a fact. Only Asoka's success in the war of succession made him the Mauryan ruler.

We have evidence to believe that Asoka's predecessors Chandragupta Maurya and Binduasara had intruded into the South and the Deccan and perhaps conquered parts of Kalinga, but still it had to be brought under their effective control. Asoka's first priority was the conquest of Kalinga as it controlled routes to South India both by land and by sea and as such, it was strategically important to have a firm sway over it. Around 260 BC, Asoka directed armies against Kalinga. The 13th Rock edict, Asoka vividly describes the conquest of Kalinga. Curiously, this epigraph is silent about the name of the defeated ruler but refers to the territorial entity of Kalinga. The edicts are categorical that a hundred and fifty thousand people were deported, a hundred thousand were killed and many times that number perished. The edict further records remorse expressed by Asoka over this loss of human lives and his urge for spiritual conquest or Dharma Vijaya. Based on this statement it was believed that he became a devout Buddhist immediately after the war. However, this is unlikely, as the Bhabru epigraph clearly states that it was only after two and a half years' gap after the war, that he became a staunch supporter of Buddhism under the influence of Upagupta, Buddhist monk. Asoka undertook a 256-day long *Dharmayatra* or holy pilgrimage to all the Buddhist holy places in northern India. Eggermont opines that after returning, Asoka celebrated a great festival of the Buddhist Sangha and began his extensive mission of propagating Buddhist doctrines, and convened the third Buddhist council at Pataliputra in 250 BC. However, curiously, none of his epigraphs refers to this event, or to the 'Enlightened One'. Perhaps, Asoka realized that in the larger interests of his empire, he should observe a clear-cut distinction between his personal faith and the polity, and should be unbiassed as the emperor as his subjects professed different religious faiths and beliefs.

Asoka does not appear to be a simple visionary or an idealist but quite practical and pragmatic in his approach. In order to propagate what he believed to be good for his populace and to translate those thoughts into action, in 257 BC, he ordered for large edicts to be cut in the frontier regions of his empire. The idea behind this order was that his message should reach the masses. The script employed by him was Brahmi and the language followed was the regional variations of Prakrit, known to all the common men. His target audiences were not the highly qualified literate groups but ordinary common folk. This displays his genuine concern for the moral well-being of the people. So far, eight versions of these edicts have been noticed. In all these edicts Asoka ordered all the citizens of his empire to put into practice non-violence, by not killing animals for food. He also prohibited illicit and immoral activities of people. He stressed the need for right conduct on their part and deputed messengers to spread this principle among his citizens. He himself put into practice this principle by being amicable with his neighbouring regions of the Cholas, Pandyas, Satyaputras, Keralaputras and Sri Lanka in the South and with King Antiyoka of Syria and his neighbours in the West. In addition to these measures, he instructed his officers to tour regularly to see that the people followed the rules of right conduct. This shows that Asoka was not simply a preacher but he also thought about the measures to implement his preaching. Asoka must have understood and realized that to bring about the required attitudinal change in the perception is not an easy task and needs constant observation and supervision by himself as well as by his officers. There is every reason to believe that right from the beginning, Asoka seems to have faced resistance to his ideas and orders. This can be inferred from the indirect evidence available to us from the inscription issued in the 13th year after his coronation. The epigraph reads as follows: "Virtuous deeds are difficult to accomplish. He who tries to accomplish them faces a hard task". Asoka appointed *Dharmamahamatras* in that year, to teach the principles of right conduct and to supervise the people. These new officers were ordered to travel widely and to report to him directly the outcome of their efforts. In the same year, he despatched *Dutas* or ambassadors to the distant countries in the west to propagate his Dhamma or philosophy as is known from the 13th rock edict. The epigraph records "where reigns the Greek King named Antiyoka and beyond the realm of that Antiyoga in the lands of the four Kings Tulamaya, Antekina, Maka, and Alikyashudata". These rulers are identified as Antiochus II Theos of Syria, the grandson of Seleucus Nicator; Ptolemy II of Philadelphus of Egypt; Antigonus Gonatices of Macedonia; Magas of Cyrene and Alexander of Epirus. Asoka, thus once again started contacts and communications deliberately to promote understanding based on mutual respect with the kingdoms beyond the subcontinent. Curiously, while the east was comparatively less explored, contacts with the west were carried on and we notice exchange of envoys. This resulted in the growth of mutual contacts and interests between the Hellenistic kingdoms and India.

The location of various rock edicts, and pillar edicts through which Asoka propagated his philosophy of Dhamma gives us a fair idea of the extent of the Magadhan territory under Asoka. There are 14 major rock edicts, seven pillar edicts and some minor rock epigraphs. The major rock edicts are located at Shabazgarhi and Manshera near Peshawar, Kalsi near Dehradun, Sopara in Thana district, Girnar near Junagarh in Kathiawar, Dhauli near Bhubaneswar and Jaugada in Ganjam district of Orissa. The minor rock edicts appear at Siddhapura, Jatinga Rameswara and Brahmagiri in Karnataka. Other, minor, rock edicts are also found at Rupanath near Jabalpur in Madhya Pradesh, Sahasram in Bihar, Bairat near Jaipur in Rajasthan and Maski in Karnataka. The pillar inscriptions of Asoka are found originally at Topra near Ambala and Meerut, which are now located at Delhi, Kausambi in Uttar Pradesh, Lauriya Araraj, Lauriya Nandangarh and Rampurva in Bihar, Sanchi near Bhopal, Saranth near Benaras, and Rumindei in Nepal. The edicts were placed deliberately after careful consideration on important trade routes linking trade and road traffic. Recent studies of the Mauryan period establish that the motivation of penetration of their rule appears to be a desire to have direct access to raw materials particularly of the Peninsula. The Magadhan Empire reached the greatest heights of territorial expansion under Asoka. Asoka's reign witnessed the expansion of empire and at the same time cessation of war as a means to expand the empire. Asoka's policy of non-violence as a state policy was never tried either prior to Asoka or by later rulers anywhere in India at any given time. Asoka made conscious efforts to unite under one umbrella the divergent populace, as one united entity, in the longer and larger interests of the security and stability of the Mauryan kingdom..As long as he lived and ruled, the empire remained intact but 50 years after his death, the Mauryan kingdom went into oblivion.

The rule of the first three Mauryas, viz., Chandragupta, Bindusara and Asoka, i.e., the first ninety years of the dynasty, was very impressive. The Mauryan rule is notable for drawing together the largely diverse elements of India under one umbrella. The Mauryans were the first to give expression to a vision of a politically unified India that influenced all political power structures in subsequent centuries. Only a few rulers could succeed in achieving the Mauryan ideal.

The available literary texts do not provide us definite information about the successors of Asoka. A sort of confusion can be noticed about what happened after Asoka. We come across various names like Kunala, Dasaratha, Samprati, Salisuka, Devavarman, Satadhanvan and Brihadradha and all of them are identified as the sons of Asoka. At this juncture with the available sources it very difficult to determine the precise dates or period of their rule. Most probably, the fragmentation of the empire into two parts, western and eastern, while frequent succession of rulers has hastened the process of disintegration of this first empire. It is suggested that Kunala ruled the western part and Samprati, who had to face the opposition of the Bactrian Greeks in the northwest, and Satavahanas in the northern Deccan. The eastern part of the empire was ruled by Dasaratha, Samprati, Salisuka, Devavarman, Satadhanvan and Brihadratha successively. His commander-in-chief, Pushyamitra Sunga, the founder of Sunga rule, killed the last of the Mauryas, Brihadratha.

Many causes are offered as an explanation for the disintegration of Mauryan rule. They are: (a) weak successors and division of empire, (b) failure to have a firm grip over administrative apparatus, (c) corrupt and oppressive bureaucracy, (d) failure of the spy system, (e) Asoka's policy of Dhamma and non-violence, (f) financial constraint, and (g) the rise of local polities in the north and south. We may conclude that directly or indirectly all the above causes contributed to the disintegration of the Mauryan polity. The Mauryans are credited with the establishment of the first centralized monarchical state apparatus supported by an established and efficient bureaucratic set-up. Kautilya's *Arthasastra*, Megasthenes' *Indica* and the Asokan edicts furnish an idea of the Mauryan administrative system.

Asoka's Policy of Dhamma

Asoka Maurya occupies a unique place among the rulers of India as well as of the world. He occupies a unique place in the history of the world not because of his conquests and the vast empire ruled by him but because of the policy of Dhamma or Dharma enunciated and implemented by him. Nevertheless, Asoka's policy of Dhamma has become a topic of debate among historians because different scholars interpreted the contents and nature of Dhamma of Asoka from different perspectives. For many years, historians have interpreted Asoka's Dhamma as a synonym for Buddhism and believed that he made Buddhism the state religion. However, this view has been questioned by modern historians who are of the opinion that Asoka's Dhamma is not merely piety, moral life and righteousness based on religious beliefs but an attitude of responsibility of a ruler in a pluralistic state. These modern scholars are of the opinion that the ultimate aim of Asoka's Dhamma is to create a harmonious atmosphere in the state where all people irrespective of their religious and cultural diversities, lived in peace and harmony as true friends recognizing their social responsibility with humanistic spirit in their day-to-day activities.

Our sources of knowledge about Asoka's Dhamma are his edicts and administrative measures. Asoka's major rock edicts, minor rock edicts and pillar edicts that were placed at different places in India contain his views about his Dhamma. By placing them at different localities, Asoka wanted them to be read by all people and translated into action by everyone. These epigraphs of years of his rule, clearly reveal an evolution of his policy of Dhamma. A critical study of the epigraphs and their contents show that Asoka made a distinction between personal faith and state policy. Asoka consciously made this distinction because he realized the necessity of such a policy for the stability and security of his kingdom to reduce the tensions created by the rise of new socio-economic formation during the Mauryan age.

Though there is no evidence, direct or otherwise, of the prevalence of tensions undermining the solidarity of the social fabric, politico-economic structure, and religious harmony, Asoka might have anticipated and realized that if no earnest conscious effort was made to arrest the undercurrent of incipient tensions, the stability of the Mauryan empire would be in danger and it made him choose a mechanism of Dhamma.

Romila Thapar's observation that Asoka's Dhamma was an attitude of social responsibility aimed at building of an attitude of mind in which the social responsibility, the behaviour of one person towards another, was considered to be of great relevance appears to be very near to the truth. Further, the Dhamma of Asoka was a plea for the recognition of the dignity of man, and for a humanistic spirit in the activities of society. Asoka found it necessary and useful to conceive a Dhamma on those lines because by family tradition, the Mauryans favoured heterodox sects that believed in the dignity of man. Tension in the shape of the status of the mercantile community, the power wielded by the urban guilds, the strain of a highly centralized political system and sheer size of the empire influenced Asoka to proclaim and practise such a Dhamma as would build bridges among all segments of society. The Dhamma of Asoka has traits like toleration, non-violence and welfare measures. Asoka defined tolerance as "consideration towards slaves and servants, obedience to mother and father, generosity towards friends, acquaintances and relatives as towards priests and monks. Its basis is the control of one's speech, so not to extol one's own sect or disparage that of another on unsuitable grounds. Therefore concord is to be commended so that men may hear one another's principle". Asoka's banning of gatherings at festivities indicates that he has perhaps, a lingering fear that such meetings may lead to declaration of open rebellion or may be the starting point of opposition to his policies. (Such attitude among kings is observed even during the medieval period when the Delhi Sultanate was ruling. Allaudin Khilji forbade his governors and subjects to gather on festive occasions.) Realizing this existing situation and understanding the vicissitudes of human behaviour, Asoka stressed on toleration and non-violence. For Asoka, non-violence implied both a renunciation of war and conquest by violence and a restraint on the killing of animals. Besides these two aspects of tolerance and non-violence, Asoka tried to put into practice what he considered to be the welfare measures of utmost importance for the good of both men and animals, like planting of trees on both sides of the roads, building of rest-houses, digging of wells, etc. In order to implement his concept of Dharma, he appointed Dharmamahamatras. However, in course of time, these appear to have become a type of priestly class interfering in the day-to-day activities of the people. The people naturally disliked their actions. It is to be admitted that though Asoka's Dhamma was theoretically a sound proposition in principle, yet because of its loftiness, the ordinary people could not appreciate it. They could not understand the ideals as an instrument to establish equity and a sign of his real concern for the well-being of his subjects a socially relevant responsibility. Yet, Asoka's concept of Dhamma deserves all praise because he was the first known ruler who realized the need and necessity of the principle of Dhamma as a binding force between men belonging to divergent creeds, cultures and faiths to live in peace. His vision and effort to establish a friction-free society makes him shine bright in the galaxy of kings. Asoka deserves our appreciation and praise for evolving a new philosophy suitable to govern a pluralist society.

Polity

The Mauryan administrative apparatus included in its range various levels of administration. They are: (i) the core area, i.e., Magadha, (ii) regional centres, (iii) peripheral areas, (iv) cities, and (v) villages. The Mauryan administration took care of sustaining the king's authority and maintaining order and a wide range of activities relating to justice, army, revenue, espionage and promotion of handicrafts to better the livelihood of the people. All the levels of administrative apparatus from the centre to the village in succession had their own administrative set-up. But all the levels of administration were under the control of the central authority. Though the Mauryan state was characterized by a centralized monarchical system, *Arthasastra* indicates that there existed certain tribal republics such as the Kambojas, Lichchavis, Vajjis and Panchalas were allowed to enjoy their privileges as long as they did not disrupt the Mauryan Empire.

The central administration of the Mauryas can be studied under the following headings: (i) the king, (ii) the council of ministers, (iii) city administration, (iv) army, (v) espionage network, (vi) law and justice, and (vii) public welfare.

In the Mauryan administrative structure, the king was the supreme head and all basic policy matters were to be decided by the king alone. Kautilya in his *Arthasastra* holds the view that the king is the primary limb of the state and as such should carry out a wide range of activities pertaining to material and spiritual welfare besides protecting the people from internal and external aggression. *Arthasastra* also mentions that if even on any issue, the *Sastras* diverge from the king's law; the king's law should prevail. However, *Arthasastra* thus gives supreme power and authority to the king; it also holds the opinion that a monarch functioning through an organized and efficient bureaucracy is the ideal of the government. Just as a single wheel cannot move, so also the king should employ 'mantrins' or should have a council of ministers (*Mantriparishad*). The *Saptangas* or seven limbs of the state according to Arthasastra are the king, the *Amatya*, *Janapada*, *Durga, Kosa, Danda* and *Mitras*. Romila Thapar points out – "the constituents of the Saptanga theory are noticeably absent in the earlier society, though the elements of Raja, Janapada and Rastra are referred to in earlier periods and the notion of concentration of power in the office of the Raja and notion of a defined territory are vague". These concepts took concrete shape by 3rd century BC. *Arthasastra* categorically states that it is the king who appoints and removes the ministers, defends the people and maintains the Kosa, works for the development and welfare of the people, punishes the evil doers and stands as an example by his conduct. Further, *Arthasastra* states that the king should be virtuous born in *Uchchakula* or higher status decided by birth, should have a sharp intellect for grasping the affairs of the state, and should be a truthful upholder of Dharma. Kautilya also states that the king should be active, ready to discharge his duties and should not hesitate to act wherever necessary. The king should not live in an ivory tower leading a luxurious life but should be accessible to officials both high and low and to people whenever they want to see him. The accounts of Megasthenes and the edicts of Asoka prove that the king followed the injuction of Kautilya in letter and spirit.

By the time of Asoka, we notice that though the king is the supreme head of the state, concentrating all powers in him he developed a paternal attitude towards his subjects. This is known from Asoka's Dhauli epigraph, which states, "All men are my children; on behalf of my own children, I desire that they may be provided by me with complete welfare and happiness in this world and in the other world, even so is my desire on behalf of all men". At the same time, he is aware of his absolute power, he instructs his officers at Tosali as follows, "Whatever I approve of that I desire either to achieve by taking action or to obtain by effective means, and these are my instructions to you". Thus, though Asoka made the welfare of his subjects the primary objective of his administrative philosophy, he appears to be an absolute monarch in terms of policy. By assuming the title of Devanampriya that is, beloved of the gods, Asoka, according to Romilá Thapar attempted to establish a connection between monarchy and divinity at a personal level and did away with intermediaries like the clergy or priests. Further, the ministers in the council or Mantriparishad were only his subordinate advisers in the true sense.

The Mauryan rulers had a Mantriparishad or council of ministers. *Arthasastra* and the Asokan inscriptions confirmed this. Girnar epigraph of Asoka records the function of the council. Whatever may be the functions of the council or of ministers, they appear to have been merely carrying out the orders issued by the king. We do not know the number of ministers and Kautilya is of the opinion that a large council is beneficial to the king. Though Kautilya suggests that the majority opinion of the council is to be implemented, he states that the verdict of the king is final. *Arthasastra* lays down certain qualifications for the selection of the ministers and one such qualification is that such person should be the purest of all or *Sarvopadasudhama*. Besides the council of ministers, there appears to have been an inner group of ministers called *Mantris*.

The *Arthasastra* refers to 18 departments or *Tirthas* of the central government and their duties in one chapter. *Arthasastra* refers to the superintendents of gold and goldsmiths, forest produce, commerce, armoury, weights and measures, tools, weaving, industry, agriculture, liquor dens, prostitutes, cows, etc.

The Mauryas maintained a standing army. While Pliny gives the strength of the army as 9,000 elephants, 3,000 cavalry and 6,000 infantry; Plutarch says that the Mauryan army consisted of 6,000 elephants, 8,000 horses, 2,000 foot-soldiers and 8,000 war chariots. We are not sure of the strength of the army but can say that they maintained a sufficiently large army. The army was divided into infantry, cavalry, elephants, chariots, transport; and navy of the fleet Kautilya refers only to *Chaturangabala* as the main components of the army. A commander was appointed over every branch. Kautilya refers to a medical corps attached to the army. There appears to be a hierarchy of military officers like *Senapati*, *Nayaka*, *Mukhyas* and *Adhyakshas* and the salary of the officer varied according to his rank. There was an officer called *Ayudhagaradhyaksha*, who looked into the production and maintenance of armaments. Likewise, every department of army has an Adhyaksha. *Arthasastra* describes in detail the plans of war, fortifications and policy of recruitment. The Mauryas had an efficiently organized spy system. Spies acted as the eyes and ears of the king, by supervising the officials and non-officials.

The Mauryan rulers established an efficient legal system to maintain the social order, the smooth and orderly functioning of administrative apparatus and for the uninterrupted collection of revenue. This is evident from *Arthasastra*, which is full of codes to punish the guilty. The offences mentioned in *Arthasastra* are varied like the violation of marriage law, divorce, murder, adulteration and wrong weights. There appears to have existed a hierarchy of judicial officers from the village level to the highest level. The practice refers to two types of courts *Dharmasthaniya,* i.e., courts which had jurisdiction over personal disputes and *Kantakasodhana* that has jurisdiction over cases involving the state and the individual. These courts followed prescribed regulations and gave an opportunity to produce the witnesses. They followed the *Dharmavyavahara*, i.e., existing legal code, *Charitra* or precedents, and *Rajasasana* or the law of the king. As the king was the upholder of Dharma, he had the supreme judicial power. Though Magasthanese wrote that the crime rate was not low in Mauryan India, *Arthasastra* gives a different picture and proves that there was no rule of law as the punishments varied from one Varna to another as prescribed by the Dharmasastras. We however do not know whether this was merely theoretical or also practised.

During the Mauryan period, the state derived revenue from various sources. According to Kautilya, the state received revenue from road and traffic (*Vanikpatra*), pastures (*Vraja*), plantations (*Setu*), forests (*Vana*), mines (*Khana*), rural areas (*Astra*), and cities (*Durgas*). An official called *Sannidhata* looked after the state treasury or Kosa. *Arthasastra* hints that twenty-one taxes were collected from the people of Durga, tax from Sita lands or new lands, land revenue or Bhaga from cultivators, taxes on orchards and ferry charges. The Mauryas collected taxes on road and waterways from the merchants and taxes on imports and exports also. There were a number of departments with officers to collect the revenues. This income was in turn spent on army, administration, salaries, king and public works. The king had the right to reduce or enhance the land tax. For we know that Asoka had reduced the state's share in agricultural produce to one-eight in the case of Lumbini, the birthplace of the Buddha.

Arthasastra and the accounts of Megasthanese reveal that adequate money was spent on public works that benefited the majority of people. Of such public works, the irrigation system was one. Megasthanese refers to a category of officials who supervised the irrigation facilities like dams, ponds, and canals. People were instructed to follow certain rules and regulations and those who violated them were punished by the state. An inscription of 2nd century AD of the time of Rudradaman, mentions the construction of *Tataka* (lake) *Sudarsana* during Chandragupta's time. Besides irrigational facilities, the state provided medical facilities to both men and women. The state appears to have taken care of the citizens during famines and floods. *Arthasastra* laid down that it is the duty of the state to take care of orphans and destitute women. Another important work was the laying of and repairing of roads and maintenance of inns. Asoka might have implemented all these activities on a large scale.

City administration is the last aspect of the central administration as it refers to the administration of the capital, Palibothra or Pataliputra known from the account of Megasthanese, and it is different from the account of the *Arthasastra.* Megasthanese states that the city council was divided into six sub-councils, or committees and each committee had five members.

The first committee was entrusted with the responsibility of industry and crafts. This committee inspected such centres and fixed wages for the artisans and labourers. The second committee took care of foreigners. Its function was to arrange for their food, stay, comfort and security. The third committee recorded births and deaths. The fourth committee took care of trade and commerce, and inspected weights and measures and controlled markets. The fifth committee was constituted to take care of the manufactured goods. Strict provision was made for their sale. Strict watch was also maintained to discriminate the first and second hand manufactured goods. The sixth committee collected the sales tax at the rate of 1/10 on goods sold.

The *Arthasastra* does not mention such committees though it gives a well-defined plan of city administration. It describes the head of the urban administration as *Nagarika*, who was assisted by Gopa and Sthanika. There appears to be a host of officials appointed by the state like *Bhandanagaradyaksha, Lokadyaksha* and *Sarvaraitha*. Thus, the Mauryas developed an efficient and well-organized city administration during this period that was elaborate and well planned. From these above accounts gathered from *Arthasastra* and Megasthanese, we are aware that the king was the supreme authority in the Mauryan state and that the core area was characterized by a highly centralized administrative system. But the vast area of the Mauryan empire could not be controlled effectively by a king, however supreme his authority. Hence, a mechanism to rule the distant areas had to be devised. In order to exercise effective control over distant regions, provincial and local administrative machinery was introduced. Provinces were entrusted to the rule of princes or Kumaras, as the representatives of the king. For example, we know that Asoka acted as the provincial ruler of Ujjaini and Taxila during the time of Bindusara before he became the king. Mahamatyas, Mahamatras, and a council of ministers assisted the Kumaras in Asoka's time. Asokan edicts refer to Tosali in the east, Ujjaini in the west, Suvarnagiri in the South and Taxila in the north as provincial capitals. Besides those provinces under the Kumaras, there were certain provinces that were ruled by minor rulers belonging to other royal families. For example, the 2nd century AD inscription of Rudradaman records that Tushaspa, a Yavana, was appointed the governor of Junagadh area in the time of Asoka. Further, the said record mentions Pushyagupta, a Vaisya, as the governor of the same area during Chandragupta Maurya. Perhaps, the council of ministers was appointed by the king to act as a check over Kumara and we may presume that this council of ministers must have direct access to the king. The provincial governor or the king appointed the senior officers like Mahamatras, Amatyas and Mahamatyas who are also a category of high officials and when they misused or abused their powers, the people revolted against them. This is known from the reigns of Bindusara and Asoka.

We come to know that the provinces were divided into districts that were under the control of Pradesihta, Rajuka and Yukta. Perhaps, Pradesihta was the overall incharge of the district, who appears to have had the functions of survey and assessment of land, tours and inspections, revenue collection and maintenance of law and order. As and when occasion demanded, the king maintained direct relations with these officials. For example, Asoka giving independent authority to the Rajuka to carry out his instructions in relation to public welfare is known from the fourth pillar edict. The Yukta appears to have assisted the Pradeshita and Rajuka as well. None of the officers was given total authority and checks and balances controlled them.

The Asokan edicts do not throw much light on village administration but *Arthasastra* refers to it. *Gramika*, an officer was appointed from among the local people, who ruled with the assistance and cooperation of the villagers. We notice that two officers *Gopa* and *Sthanika* were acting as intermediaries between the district and village level administration. There appears to be the practice of demarcating village boundaries, maintaining of records of lands used for various purposes, recording income and expenditure of people and noting down taxes, revenues and fines collected from the villagers. The villages appear to be enjoying certain amount of autonomy in the sphere of their administration. One of the interesting features of the Mauryan rule was the payment of salaries and services were paid in cash. This practice was not continued in later times.

The Mauryan rulers maintained cordial and friendly relations with their neighbouring kingdoms because of necessity of trade and of geographical proximity and diplomatic requirements. Thus, we find a shift from conquest and subjugation to friendly moral conquest in their relations with their neighbours.

Recent researchers raised a doubt about the centralization of power in the Mauryan Empire. Though contemporary historians think that the Mauryan Empire under Asoka was Unitarian and centralist, G.M. Bogard Levin says, "the degree of centralization and bureaucratization of the administrative system should not be overestimated. The Mauryan empire in fact was the first unified Indian state, and it consisted of numerous characteristics inherited from the former political structure and of tribal traditions. The Mauryan emperors tried to exercise effective control on all aspects of life and on all institutions. They instituted special monitoring systems and a secret police. The central administration made direct efforts to impose its authority on many provincial institutions. Nevertheless, it is not possible to speak of the strict control of the state, in that it concerns the heart of the empire. In the provinces, particularly in the far-flung ones, there were strong local institutions, and separatist tendencies could be seen in them". Gerrard Fussman, raising new questions concludes "one can thus assume that, contrary to general opinion, the Mauryan Empire functioned ... with a central absolute power, personal that is, dependent, on personal activity of the sovereign, relying on the army and on efficient officers, with a regional administration organized in a non-systematic fashion exercising royal authority, with more liberty further away from the royal power and putting into practice the king's orders only when they fitted in with local reality, with large provinces directly administered by royal agents, with traditional local powers (tribes, cities, feudal kingdoms), which, in many areas (taxes and rents, codes of Justice, customs, languages, culture and religious practices) continued to function as autonomous bodies under the more or less strict supervision of imperial officials ... what one sees under the Mauryas is a central power trying to bring under its sole authority preconstituted entities to which it leaves a greater or lesser degree of autonomy according to the place and circumstances. But, in the 3rd century BC history and geography precluded the constitution of a Unitarian state, which is not a reality even in the 20th century".

Material Milieu

Excavations conducted by archaeologists along with indigenous and classical Greek texts also throw valuable light on the material milieu of this epoch of Indian history. We are aware that during the second half of the first millennium BC, iron was used extensively to manufacture agricultural implements like socketed axes, sickles and possibly ploughshares. These iron agricultural implements made possible the clearance of thick forests of the eastern Gangetic plains and brought large tracts of land under efficient agricultural operations. We may postulate a hypothesis that the availability of surplus produce naturally brought about a transformation in the material milieu of the society. A natural corollary to this could be the emergence of new social groups with new occupations. Naturally, this growth of surplus produce and rise of new occupations led to the growth of towns and cities, which acted as market centres. Thus, besides flourishing agriculture, we find trade and commerce that necessarily led to urbanization. Arrian records that it is not possible to count the number of towns and cities, as they were so many. Further, Megasthanese's account of the city administration also reveals that cities were well organized with an efficient administrative apparatus to control the concentration of population in these cities. However, excavations have not so far brought to light substantial number of cities and surprisingly the remains of Mauryan architecture are not found in abundance. Excavations in Uttar Pradesh and Bihar reveal that burnt bricks were used on a large scale in the construction of buildings. Besides burnt bricks, they also used wood extensively for construction. Megasthanese also speaks of wooden structures at Pataliputra. Another feature to be noticed is the construction of ring wells on a large scale that supplied water to individual households. The availability of iron ore and the discovery of furnaces indicate that people were used to the manufacture of iron tools. *Arthasastra* makes it obligatory on the part of the state to have a monopoly of certain kinds of mining, as iron was essential to make military equipment as well as agricultural tools, necessary for expansion of the empire and to sustain economy and society. So far, we have learnt how knowledge of using iron transformed the economic and social set-up. Here, we have to find out the role of the state in the changed material milieu. By the time of Mauryas, the agrarian society took deep roots and it was in the process of expansion. This would not have been possible without the availability of labour on a large scale for production of food grains and other commodities in plenty. We know that a single household cannot undertake paddy cultivation. Therefore, the state encouraged the Sudras to establish new village settlements and to participate in large-scale agricultural operations and these new village settlement lands became Sita lands. The king and his officials exercised direct control over these lands. Thus, during the Mauryan period, the use and control of raw material like iron ore and successful inducements of large number of Sudras to agricultural operations made it possible for agrarian expansion to take place. Consequently, a new class known as *Gahapatis* and *Gramabhojakas*, landowning gentry, who appeared to have used hired labourers for agricultural operations emerged. During the Mauryan period, as we now know, two different types of agriculturists; a category who were working in the Sitas or crown lands, and another owned personal land. Magasthanese amply attests the fact that the Mauryan state laid much attention to providing irrigation facilities on large scale as the *Arthasastra* refers to an irrigation cess, amounting to a fifth or a fourth, or a third of the produce. Probably, the state provided irrigational facilities where rainfall was scant. In Saurastra, at a place called Girnar, a tank known as Sudarsanatataka was dug by Pushyagupta, one of the governors of Chandragupta. Land tax (*Bhaga*) was the major source of income for the Mauryan state. *Samharta* was the designation of the highest officer who assessed the land revenue that was collected in both cash and kind. Sannidhata was the custodian of the treasury. Certain villages that were newly developed and those that provided soldiers to the army appear to be exempted from the payment of taxes. Either one-fourth or one-sixth of the produce was collected as tax from the cultivator according to classical Greek writers as well as *Arthasastra.* We have an edict of Asoka that states that Asoka exempted the village of Lumbini from the payment of *Bali* or tribute and reduced the land tax to 1/8. Sharecroppers, who were provided with seeds, oxen and received arable land for cultivation, paid half of the produce as share of their land tax. Besides land tax, other taxes like *Pindakara*, *Hiranya* and *Bali* were taxes collected from the cultivators. *Arthasastra* deals with the aspect of land revenue in detail, as it was the main source of the state income. *Arthasastra* recommends that the taxes on land should depend on the fertility of the soil. The Mauryas must have given utmost importance to land revenue collection without which the government machinery and army cannot be maintained effectively.

Along with the flourishing agricultural operations on a large scale, two other developments, expansion of trade and commerce, and establishment of new market centres, and the growth of towns are also responsible for the stable economy of the Mauryas. While it is the growth of agrarian economy that provided a solid economic base to the Mauryan Empire in the Gangetic valley, the expansion of the commercial economy made it possible to extend the resource base to the other parts of the country. The Mauryan rulers gave importance to the growth of trade and commerce by maintaining peace and tranquillity in the kingdom. Further, the friendly relations maintained by Bindusara and Asoka with the neighbouring rulers gave fillip to foreign trade as well. Thus, both internal and external trade flourished due to the policy followed by the Mauryan state. Owing to the favourable atmosphere in the state policy, trade was carried on in different ways. We notice the emergence and functioning of artisan guilds during this period and the well-known artisan guilds are those of various kinds of metallurgists, carpenters, potters, leather workers, painters and textile workers. In the Gangetic valley making of the northern black polished ware (NBPW) had become a specialized craft because outside Ganga valley, the NBPW pottery was found in small quantities. Artisans used to live in a particular area of the town. As in the case of artisans, the merchants also had their guilds and some merchants had close contact with artisan guilds. Consequently the production and distribution of articles became easy, smooth and profitable. The state maintained strict supervision and control over the trading and commercial activity of the guilds of merchants and artisans. *Indica* and *Arthasastra* refer to a category of officers known as superintendents of commerce or *Panyadhyaksha*, *Samasthadhyaksha*, *Pantiyadhyaksha*, *Navadhyaksha* and *Sulkadhyaksha*; these officers controlled and supervised the mercantile activity of the merchant groups and artisan groups. The state also produced different types of goods that yielded high revenue, which were called *Rajapanya*. The process of urbanization, which started in the pre-Mauryan age, progressed in the Mauryan age. Officers of the government, artisans and merchants lived in the towns supported by the flourishing agriculture in rural areas. The towns were well-administered as seen from the description of the city administration by Megasthanese. Growth of urbanism promoted cash transactions and consequently led to the growth of coined money in the shape of punch-marked coins made of silver.

The above survey of the economy of the age clearly reveals that the Mauryan state maintained strict control and supervision over agriculture, trade and industry. Such a policy was necessary to control over the resources and taxes of the state. The Mauryas had effective state control over the areas that were economically useful for the soundness of the state. The conquests undertaken by the Mauryas appear to have been motivated by economic need rather than political necessity. For example, while the conquest of Kalinga brought fertile tracts suitable for agricultural operations into their possession, the conquest of Karnataka provided them with the monopoly over gold and other precious metals. Further, the Mauryan rulers made it their policy to bring more land under agriculture by converting the tribals into peasants.

The Mauryan state policy in the fields of agriculture, trade and industry became evident in different parts of India that came under its impact. It means, urban centres like towns and cities grew where different social groups lived using coins, script and sophisticated objects. Thus, we find change in the material culture in social organization and in ideas. According to some historians, the rise of local states in the post-Mauryan age was necessary for these developments within the Magadhan Empire.

Cultural Milieu

In the sphere of art and architecture including sculpture, thc Mauryan age is a landmark. As art reflects the culture of the age, in which it was produced, so also the Mauryan art and architecture is a representative specimen of the age. We notice new trends in the artistic activity of this age as the new social groups that arose from flourishing agriculture, trade and industry, patronized the artistic activity substantially. The most remarkable feature of the Mauryan age was the beginning of use of stone as a medium of creativity. Chunnar in the Bundelkhand area was mined extensively for the production of pillars on which edicts were inscribed. No worthy information is available about music and dance of the Mauryan age though *Arthasastra* makes certain references to dance and music. No specimen of the Mauryan painting has survived. Consequently, the only knowledge of architecture and sculpture derived from available vestiges helps us to understand and estimate the value and importance of the Mauryan art and architecture.

The architecture of the Mauryans can be studied under three heads: (a) palace remains which include forts, (b) columns, and (c) cave architecture. Classical writers Megasthanese and Strabo refer to the palace of the Mauryas. Their account is proved by the remains of the city brought to light by the excavations of Spooner and Waddel, who excavated the city wall and the huge wooden buildings at Kumarahara. Interestingly, Spooner brought to light an entire pillar in a perfect state of preservation. We come across a pillared hall supported by a wooden base, where the pillars were set in regular rows. The pillar brought to light by Spooner, resembles the Asokan pillar in style and ornamentation. Its surface is very smooth and highly polished. The entire Mauryan palace complex appears to have been built under the direct supervision and control of the rulers of the Mauryan age.

Undoubtedly, the best representative specimens of the Mauryan art are the columns. These columns are not only well proportioned but also tall, and imposing. These columns have slightly tapering monolithic shafts. They look complete and independent. The columns found at Meerut, Allahabad, Lauriya Araraj, Lauriya Nandangarh, Delhi, Topra, Sankisa, Sanchi and Saranath have the edicts of Asoka inscribed on them. At Rampurva while the column with lion capital has an edict, the column with bull capital does not have an inscription on it. Further, the column at Basarat Bakhira with single lion capital and the column at Kosam do not contain edicts. Rumindei and Nigalisagar columns contain dedicatory epigraphs. These columns are crowned by animals and birds, like lions, standing bull, Garuda, and horse. These animals and birds exhibit highly developed sculputral skill. What these animals and birds stand for is a debatable question. Some are of the opinion that the four animals, elephant, horse, bull and lion represent the four-cardinal points. These animals represent both Buddhist and Brahmanical motifs and the elephant is sacred to both the Buddhist and Brahmanical religions. The wheel, which is important for the Buddhist tradition is carved on the top of the column of Sarnath. The most interesting feature of these columns is that they have no base at all. It is remarkable because contemporaneous Acheminian counterparts have bull-shaped bases, plain rectangular block and plain circular moulding. While the Persians used bull as a base, the Mauryas used it as the capital of their columns. Interestingly, the Mouryan bull appears to have been derived from the lotus motif; the inverted lotus motif was a well-known design of those times.

Tradition records that many Stupas and Chaityas were built by Asoka but none of these remains exists in the original form today, except the Chaitya halls in the Barabara caves which bear the epigraphs of Asoka and Dasaratha. Of the Mauryan times, of the Barabar, the Nagarjuni caves, and the Sudama cave appears to be the earliest examples of Mauryan cave architecture. There is an epigraph of Asoka dated in his 12th year which dedicated the Sudama cave to the Ajivika sect. The Karnachauper cave contains an epigraph of Asoka dated in the 9th year of his rule. It is a plain rectangular hall with a round roof. The walls and roof of this cave are brightly polished. The Nagarjuni hill caves of the time of Dasaratha have an epigraph wherein Asoka is said to have dedicated this cave to the Ajivika sect. These three caves are known as Vahiyaka, Vadhika and Gopika.

We do not have large number of freestanding sculptures of the Mauryan age. We have evidences of animal sculptures crowning the Mauryan pillars. The elephant sculpture of Dhauli in Orissa is a good example of their sculptural skill. This shows that animals like elephant, horse, bull and lion were common during this age. These animal sculptures look like real ones endowed with life. Though terracotta figurines of animals and humans found at Taxila and other places have been assigned to the Mauryan period, art critics like Stella Kramrisch and Garden are of the opinion that they cannot be accurately dated. The Patna Museum has small terracotta figurines, terracotta plaques and terracotta seals recovered from the sites of interior Bihar. However, their artistic merit is negligible. Stella Kramarisch and other art critics are of definite opinion that the Mauryan art was not of high standard and was only an uninspiring interlude in the history of Indian art.

Religion

Though heterodox religions such as Buddhism, Jainism and the Ajivika sects were patronized by the Mauryas, the adherents of Sanatanadharma constituted a large segment during this period. The worship of the Vedic gods was in vogue. Patanjali's reference to the exhibition and sale of the images of Siva and Skanda makes us think that the practice of making images began to take shape during this period. The practice of performing sacrifices was also still in vogue. The hold of heterodox doctrines on certain sections of the people of Oudh, Bihar and Orissa was more than it was in other areas. Certain groups of people also practised

Vaishnavism or Bhagavatism, which promoted the Vasudeva cult. They also knew worship of the non-Indian deities like the Babylonian and Iranian deities. The above information on the state of religion clearly indicates that both Brahmanical and heterodox religions flourished and existed side by side.

Literature

Coming to the literary output of the age, tradition attributes to Kautilya the *Arthasastra,* to Bhadrabahu the *Kalpasutra* and the Buddhist to *Kathavathu* of the Mauryan period; but R.C. Majumdar, K.K. Datha and Roychoudary observe that it is difficult to assign any available Indian work definitely to the Mauryan age.

The term 'empire' is generally attributed to the Mauryan polity. This term is familiarized to us by the European historiographers basing their arguments on the knowledge of the Roman Empire. The observation of Romila Thapar, "the Mauryan state was an empire to the extent that it did control a large territory with culturally differentiated people and its nucleus, the state of Magadha, was enriched by the flow of revenue and resources from other regions" is very valid. However, the idea of unified unitary state never really took root in the Indian subcontinent because no state succeeded in its efforts to create new resource bases and because of their failure to restructure to any considerable extent, the economy of the core and peripheral areas. The same tendency is clearly visible in contemporary India also. Thus, the above discussion of the Mauryan age attempts to prove that it was an important formative period in the evolution of Indian culture and history. As already indicated, in the post-Mauryan age we notice the emergence of multiple power centres reflecting the aspirations of the local rulers, due to the failure of the state to create a strong unitary power structure. We now are aware that there was a gradual movement from a lineage-based society to state system in mid-first millennium BC as, Santiparva of Mahabharata and the Buddhist texts clearly indicate. In due course, as the idea of territorial sovereignty developed and gained prominence, royal authority was consolidated and strengthened by a military aristocracy and priesthood. While the process of transition from tribal settlements to smaller kingdoms took place in the pre-Mauryan period that from smaller kingdoms where the Mauryas completed a larger 'Metropolitan state'.

8

The Post-Mauryan Period

Sungas, Sathavahanas and Kushans

In the post-Mauryan period, Greek and Roman literary references and indigenous numismatics and epigraphical evidences indicate the rise of localism and the emergence of multiple power structures of small and large categories fighting for dominance. The period from 200 BC to AD 300 is called as the post-Mauryan period, is also characterized by some historians as the 'Dark Age' since during this period, power was shared by indigenous powers as well as foreigners like the Indo-Greeks, the Sakas, the Pallavas and the Kushans. Despite the absence of the concept of imperial unity as driving and integrating factor in the political sphere, in the socio-economic and cultural spheres it was a momentous period marked by the rise of trade networks, influx of foreigners and new ideas influencing philosophical trends, the rise of new sects based on devotionalism in all religions and the growth of cultural symbols like Chaitya, Stupa, Vihara and the temple along with new artistic and sculptural trends as reflected in Gandhara and Amaravati schools. In the social sphere too, this was not a period of rigid dogmatism, a sort of Catholicism appears to pervade. Accommodation, adjustment and acceptance rather than vigorous opposition to changes marked this phase in the socio-cultural milieu. This phase was marked more by the spirit of accommodation, adjustment and acceptance rather than vigorous opposition exchanges in the socio-cultural milieu, this can be seen by the inclusion of Varnasankara theory in the Dharmasastric literature to accommodate new sub-castes and Jatis into the Varnasasramadharma.

The final dismemberment of the Mauryan political structure took place in 187 BC. In Magadha, the Sungas, who ruled for a century and were followed by the Kanvas, succeeded the Mauryas. The Sunga lineage and the Kanva lineage are considered Brahmin dynasties and their founders were Pushyamitra Sunga and Vasudeva Kanvayana respectively. The Sunga dynasty consisted of nearly 10 kings. They are Pushyamitra Sunga, Agnimitra and the last ruler of the Sungas was Devabhuti who was killed by his minister Vasudeva Kanva. In the Kanva line Vasudeva, Bhumitra, Narayana and Susarman are the known rulers. Puranas state that Susarman was killed by *Andhrabhritya* Simuka or Chimuka, the founder of the Satavahana dynasty. After the decline of the Kanva power, there arose independent principalities at Ayodhya, Kausambi, Mathura and Ahichchatra, in Bareli, district of present-day Uttar Pradesh. The tribal states of the Arjunayanas, lying to the south-east of Mathura, the Audambaras, the Kunindas, the Trigartas, the Yaudheyas and the Agasiyas also declared their independence.

Around 200 BC, a number of invaders from central Asia and further west, began to enter India through the north-west and the first among such invaders were the Bactrian Greeks or the Yavanas. Demetrius, the Bactrian ruler wrested considerable territory in the north-west and occupied it with the title of 'King of the Indians'. Two Greek dynasties belonging to Eucratides and Ethedemos ruled northwestern India simultaneously. Menander (153 BC to 130 BC) who happens to be the most famous of the Indo-Greek rulers is credited with victory over Ayodhya and Patliputra. Menander is known as Milinda and appears to have been converted to Buddhism by Nagasena. The Indo-Greeks were the first to issue gold coins. They introduced the *Satrapal* system into India. They are responsible for introducing features of Greek art into the north-west frontier of India, which developed into Gandhara art. The Sanskrit term '*Horasastra*' for astrology is said to be derived from the Greek term horoscope. The Indo-Greek power in north-western India lasted for a short period and was followed by the Scythians or the Sakas. By the middle of the 1st century BC, the Saka power extended as far interior as Mathura. The first known Saka king was Maues or Moga, who is placed around 80 BC. The Sakas were divided into five branches and had their seats of power in Afghanistan, Mathura, Taksila, Malwa and Kathiawar. The Sakas of western India ruled for a longer time until the 4th century AD. They bore the title of *Kshatrapa*. Rudradaman I, who ruled between 139 and AD 150 was the most famous Saka ruler of western India He is well known for the repair of the Sudarsana Lake built by Chandragupta Maurya. Interestingly, Rudradaman's Junagadh inscription was the first chaste Sanskrit epigraph. Towards the end of the 1st century BC, Pahlavas or Indo-Parthians became the masters of north-western India. Gondophernes was the best-known Pahlava ruler and tradition avers that St. Thomas visited his court. Gondophernes is said to have ruled in the first half of the first century AD. The Kushanas, of Yuchchi tribe broke this Indo-Parthian power.

The Kushans

We come to know from a Chinese source that in the 1st century AD the Yuchchi chief Kujala Kadphises united the five Yuchchi tribes, crossed the Hindukush Mountains and occupied Kabul and Kashmir, driving away the Greeks. Kujala Kadphasies is regarded as the founder of the Dushanbe political power in India. After Kujala Kadphasies, his son Vima Kadphasies succeeded to the throne and is credited with the minting of gold coins, a momentous innovation. After Vima, Kanishka became the ruler. The relationship between Kanishka and his two predecessors cannot be established with certainty.

Kanishka is considered as the greatest of the Kushans and though a foreigner by birth, he made India his home by choice and made everlasting contribution to Indian culture. The date of his accession is a debatable issue and AD 78, the starting of Saka era has been accepted as the most probable date of his accession. The Kushan power reached its zenith and became a mighty force in these days. His sovereignty in India extended as far south as Kanchi and as far East as Benaras. He ruled extensive territories in central Asia. While Purushapura or Peshawar was his capital, Mathura was the second-most important city of the Kushan Empire.

Kanishka embraced Buddhism and for his service to the cause of Buddhism, he was justly considered, the second Asoka. Kanishka convened the fourth Buddhist council at Kundalavana in Kashmir under the presidentship of Vasumitra. In that council, they discussed the matters relating to Buddhist doctrines and theology. We come to know from Taranatha, the Tibetan historian that this council settled the dispute among 18 Buddhist orthodox schools. During this period, the old Hinayana form of Buddhism was replaced by Mahayanism, in which devotion and worship of the Buddha became important and Bodhisatva was created as an intermediary between the Buddha and the devotee. In this period, Sanskrit replaced Pali as the language in which literary texts are written. Kanishka encouraged missionary activities by sending Buddhist missions to Central Asia and China. He is credited with the construction of a multistoreyed tower containing the relic of the Buddha at Peshawar. This was attested by the Chinese traveller Hiuen Tsang of the seventh century AD and Alberuni, the Arab traveller and historian of the 11th century AD. Limited archaeological excavations have proved the existence of a Stupa, a Vihara, a reliquary by the discovery of figurative stone sculptures. Kanishka was also a great patron of art and letters. His period witnessed the growth of religious and secular literature of a high standard. Asvaghosha, the author of *Buddhacharita* and *Sutralankara*, Vasumitra, the author of *Mahavibhasasastra*, a commentary on the Tripitakas, Charaka, the author of *Charakasamhita* a book of authority on medicine, were patronized by him. Kanishka was a builder of great repute and his works are discovered at Mathura, Peshavar, Kanishkapura and Taxila. Mathura became a great centre of artistic activity. Kanishka combines in himself the qualities of a great conqueror, empire-builder and a great patron of art and letters, and ruled over a vast empire in Central Asia and India. His death was followed by the disintegration of Kushans political power structure. The Kushans became vassals by the middle of the 3rd century AD.

The Satavahanas

While the Kushans and the Sakas were ruling in northern and western India respectively, in the first century BC, there arose the kingdom of the Satavahan as north-western Deccan. Paithan or Pratishtana in Maharashtra has been accepted as the earliest capital of the Satavahanas. A debate is going on regarding their original home, chronology, caste and religious affiliations of the Satavahanas. It is now generally accepted that the Satavahanas are *Andhrajatiyulu*.

There are two views, one suggesting that they moved westward along the river Godavari and after the fall of the Mauryas founded the kingdom, the other view is that they originally belonged to western Deccan and slowly extended their sway over the east coast, which was called Andhra. D.N. Jha argues that as the earliest inscriptions of the Satavahanas found in western Deccan indicate that they moved from western Deccan to eastern Deccan in later times.

The sources for the reconstruction of the Satavahana history are the Puranas, *Brihatkatha* of Gunadhya, *Gatha Saptasati* composed by Hala, coins and 19 epigraphs from western Deccan and 7 epigraphs found in eastern Deccan. There is also a debate regarding the duration and number of rulers of the Satavahana dynasty. While some Puranas mention 19 rulers, some other Puranas mention 30 rulers. Regarding the duration of the rule also, there is discrepancy in the Puranas. As Andhras are mentioned in the edicts of Asoka, it is presumed that they were subordinates or officers in the court of the Mauryas. The founder of this dynasty is said to be Simuka, who destroyed the Kanva power.

The important rulers of the Satavahana dynasty are Kanha or Krishna, Satakarni I, Satakarni II, Hala, Gautamiputra Sri Satakarni, Pulamayi II, Vasisthiputra Sri Satakarni, Sivasri Pulamayi and Pulamayi IV. There was a long-drawn battle between the Satavahanas and the Sakas of the Kshaharata clan. As the coins and epigraphs of the Saka chief Nahapana were found around Nasik, it can be established without doubt, that the Sakas became dominant towards the close of the 1st century AD or the beginning of the 2nd century AD. Gautamiputra Satakarni, the 23rd ruler of the dynasty, revived the fortunes of the Satavahana political power. Gautamiputra Sri Satakarni was the greatest ruler of this dynasty. He is said to have ruled from AD 70 to AD 95. He has been described as the destroyer of the Sakas, Yavanas and Pahlavas. He is said to have exterminated the Kshatrapa Nahapana and recovered Aparanta, Anupa, Saurashtra, Kulura, Akara and Avanti from Nahapana. Gautamiputra had the title of *Tri Samudratoyapithavahana* which means the area encircled by the seas on three sides had been captured by him. His success against Nahapana appears to be short-lived, as the territories recovered by him were lost again to the Kardamakas. This view was based on the evidence of a study of the "Geography" of Ptolemy and of the Junagadh rock epigraph of Rudadaman, which states that he conquered the territory of Nahapana from the hands of Goutamiputra Sri Satakarni. A matrimonial alliance was concluded between Rudradaman and the son of Gautamiputra Sri Satakarni, Vasistiputra. In spite of the matrimonial alliance, the hostile relations between the Satavahanas and the Sakas continued.

After the death of Rudradaman, the Satavahanas regained their lost position by the end of the 2nd century AD. The Sathavahana power extended over Kathiawar in the west coast and Krishna delta and northern Tamil Nadu in the south-east. However, this extensive sway of the Satavahanas was short-lived. Slowly the Satavahana power was weakened in the next century as the local governors and the subordinate rulers declared independence. The Abhiras and the Traikutakas rose to power in western Deccan. In northern

Deccan, Vakatakas became a prominent power. In the northern Peninsula, the Kalachuri-Chedi dynasty asserted independence by founding an era in AD 248, 249. Numerous small kingdoms arose in the Ganga plain. Some of these rulers are identified as belonging to the Maghas, the Bodhis and the Nagas and the Mitras. Further south in the peninsula, political power passed into the hands of the Salankayanas, Brihatpalayanas and Ikshvakus in the 3rd and 4th centuries. Salankayanas and Brihatpalayanas ruled in the West Godavari and in the Masulipatnam region. The Ikshvakus can be located further south in the Krishna valley and are regarded as an indigenous tribe who assumed the lineage of the solar race or Suryavamsa after coming to power. Nagarjunakonda or Vijayapuri, a magnificent city was built by them. While the Ikshvaku rulers performed Vedic sacrifices, the womenfolk donated to the Buddhist Sangha. From a bird's eye view of the post Mauryan political history from 1st century BC to the 3rd century AD, we get a confusing picture of a group of contending tribes, kings and valiant invaders. However, for the Kushans and the Satavahanas, the rest were very small kingdoms.

The Hatigumpha epigraph records that in the east about the end of the 1st century BC, Kalinga or the present day Cuttack, Ganjam and Puri districts of Orissa state became powerful under the rule of Kharavela of Kalinga. He claimed to have conquered a number of rulers and assumed the title of *Kalingadhipati* or *Kalingachakravarti*. In ancient times, South India meant the region south of the river Krishna that was divided into three tribal territories: Chola on the Kaveri delta and the adjoining area, Pandya to the south of it and Chera extending along the west coast. In the 1st century BC, the Cholas became prominent under Karikalachola by defeating the Chera and the Pandyan rulers in the battle of Venni near Tanjore. Like Chola Karikala, the Pandya Chief Nedunjaliyan has been credited with the destruction of the Cholas and the Cheras in the battle of Talaiyalangam. Of the Cheras, none attained the fame either of Karikala Chola or of Nedunjaliyan.

There existed a number of small state powers with a known tribal background like the Naga feudatories of the Kushans in different parts of central and Northern India whose coins have been found in abundance. From the Gupta epigraphs, it is known that these were the Nagas of Vidisa, Kantipura, Mathura and Padmavati and these rulers appear to have been defeated by the Guptas. Coins of the local rulers ending with the surnames Mitra and Dutta have been found in the Mathura region. The above mentioned local rulers 'Mitras' and 'Duttas' are the vassals of the Kushans. They flourished in the second century AD. Coins of the Kushan feudatories, with names of local rulers ending in Mitra, Pala and Gupta, have been found in Ahichchatra. Coins from Ayodhya region contain names of vassals ending in Devadatta, Mitra, Varman and Sena. The Magha feudatories of the Kushans ruled in the Kausambi region and attained some degree of prominence. The Abhiras, the feudatories of the Sakas declared independence in north-western Deccan and they remained an independent power even in the 4th century AD. The Bodhis, another feudatory family of the Sakas, founded a principality in the north-west Deccan in the 3rd century AD.

Polity

In the sphere of polity, neither the Kushans nor the Satavahanas could maintain a centralized institution of monarchy assisted by bureaucracy like that of the Mauryas. Owing to the rise of localism or aspirations of local powers, both the Kushans and the Satavahanas realized the need to choose a new mechanism to keep the local powers in check by entering into feudatory relationships. These feudatories paid tribute to the sovereign power and rendered military service at needed times. Consequently, we may suggest that from now on exercise of direct administrative control over a large part of the country, as the Mauryas did in the earlier period, disappeared and was restricted to the core area, alone. The institution of monarchy became deep-rooted and, we notice the secondary state formation in Orissa and the eastern Deccan under Kharavela of Kalinga and the Satavahanas. In this period, the rise of centrifugal forces was curbed through the concept of divine rule associated with the king and the kingship. A Satavahana record compares Gautamiputra Satakarni to several gods in prowess. The Kushan rulers also tried to deify themselves by assuming the title of *Devaputra* or sons of God and created necessary temples to house the statues of the dead kings or *Devakula*. The indigenous texts of dharmasastras and legal commentaries stress the concept of divine origin of kings to make the people obey the ruler as they do of gods. D.N. Jha is of the opinion that this concept of the divine origin of king or kingship did not enhance substantially the administrative hold of the kingly authority over the ruler's territory, the reason being the weakening of the central authority of the ruler by the practice of donating lands with immunities of fiscal and administrative nature to the religious bodies of Buddhists and Brahmanas. Donation of land to priests had 'religious sanction' as is known from the sacred literature. Yet, the earliest epigraphical reference – to land grant in India comes from the 1st century BC which is the Satavahana epigraphs for Brahmins for performing Vedic sacrifices. In the beginning, such donees were exempted from paying taxes but in due course, the number of exemptions increased. A Satavahana record of the 2nd century AD of Gautamiputra warns the royal officials not to interfere with the administration of the donated field or village. This made historians like R.S. Sharma, D.N. Jha and others conclude that the villages gifted to religious bodies became semi-independent administrative pockets, which reduced royal control over the countryside. Though land grants were made to attain religious merit, the idea behind donating land was to expand the area of agricultural operations through individual efforts, as the government apparatus in the post-Mauryan age was not as effective as the Mauryan times. The Satavahanas initiated and encouraged land grants to individuals, as their administrative system was not assisted by an efficient bureaucracy that could not control human activities, like clearing of forests and founding of new settlements under state control. Therefore, the state depended on individual efforts for agricultural expansion. Buddhist works of contemporarious times refers to individual farmers in large numbers engaged in cultivation. *Manudharmasastra* also states that a field belonged to him who first cleared the timber, and a deer to him who first wounded it. We may suggest that the lawgiver Manu and Buddhist writers speak of the relevance of the principle only to encourage cultivation of virgin land by private individuals without state effort.

Economy

The post-Mauryan economy was based on the growth of agriculture, internal and long distance trade and on crafts and arts. The most important development of the period was the flourishing trade between India and the Western world. Improved internal communication system under the Mauryas was responsible for the growth of trade and commerce in the post-Mauryan phase. Land routes to South India developed during this period along the river valleys and the coasts and routes through mountain passes that helped trade and commerce. A landmark in the growth of external trade and commerce was the discovery of the monsoon winds by the Greek sailor Hippolus in around AD 46–47. This made possible, navigation across the Arabian Sea, by reducing the distance between Indian and west Asian ports. The invasions of the Indo-Greeks, Kushans and the Sakas increased and deepened contacts between India and western and central Asia. Central Asia acted as a link between China and India as Indian merchants acted as intermediaries in the silk trade of China. While the merchants of north-western India mostly traded with western and central Asia and China, the merchants of western and southern India concentrated on South Arabia, the Red Sea and Alexandria, which handled the bulk of the Roman trade.

The emergence of the Roman Empire was beneficial to the Indian trading community. *The Periplus of the Erythrean Sea,* written by an anonymous Greek navigator, records that Indians exported pepper, pearls, ivory, silk, diamonds, saffron, precious stones, tortoise shell and spikenard and imported topaz, thin cloth, linen, antimony, crude glass, copper, tin, lead, wine and wheat. The discovery of red glazed arretine ware at excavations of Arikemedu near Pondicherry (now Puducherry) makes us believe that the Romans not only exported this item but also had a settlement in that locality. So far, 68 hoards of gold and silver coins have been unearthed in India and interestingly nearly 57 hoards have been found south of the Vindhyas. Indians received as their share of profit nearly 50 million Sesterces (Roman currency) per year and this made Pliny remark that Rome was at disadvantage due to the favourable balance of payments towards India.

The phenomenal increase of long distance trade led to the vogue of money-economy during this period. While the imported coins were used as bullion, the indigenously minted coins were used for day-to-day transactions. Very few gold coins were minted by the Indo-Greeks, which the Kushans minted in considerable numbers. As gold and silver coins could not serve as medium of exchange, the Satavahanas issued coins of lead or potin. Copper coins were also issued by the Naga rulers and by several other indigenous local state powers. This clearly indicates that money economy had penetrated deep into the economic life and activities of the common people. As a corollary to the prevalence of cash economy and commerce, there arose a number of towns to which *Periplus* makes direct reference. Another interesting consequence of the growth of trade and commerce was the growth of towns, increasing affluence of certain sections, and cash economy that led to the proliferation of arts and crafts. Mahavastu, a Buddhist work of the 2nd century AD, which records that more than 36 kinds of workers lived in the town Rajgir, attests this. Further, *Milindapanho* another literary work related to the Buddhist discourse also refers to 75 occupations, 60 of which were connected with various kinds of crafts. Along with proliferation of crafts and arts, we also notice increasing specialization of skills of manufacturing items. While *Milindapanho* refers to specialized skill of artisans of metals such as gold, silver, lead, tin, copper, brass, iron and precious stones, *Periplus* refers to export of iron and steel to Egypt. In the sphere of textile manufacturing also, the superior skill of the Indians is known from *Milindapanho* and the works of Patanjali.

Increase in production and the consequent surplus required an efficient way of distribution to obtain sufficient reward for the people's hard labour. Both the artisans and the merchants involved in production and distribution of the goods developed collective bargaining strength by forming guilds and corporations respectively. It is very interesting to note that there existed more than two dozens of guilds of artisans. The Satavahana epigraphs refer to the guilds or Srenis of oil pressers, hydraulic machine operators, potters, weavers, corn dealers, bamboo workers and braziers. Besides these, many more might have existed. The Srenis also acted as banks that paid interest on money deposited in with them in these guilds and we come to know that Ushavadatta made two permanent endowments to Kalika Nigama or Sreni and one endowment made provision for new robes and the other for providing minor food necessities. This indicates the permanent financial soundness of the guilds. The existence of the guilds of traders (Sreni) in Kushan Mathura is known from a record, which refers to a perpetual endowment (*Akshayanivi*) in Purana currency made in two guilds enjoining to make payments out of the interest accrued on the deposit.

The Basarh seal of the Gupta times refers to Sreshti-Sarthavaha-Kulika-Nigama, which has been translated as guilds of merchants, of itinerant traders and of artisans. Epigraphs of this period refer to *Vanik* or merchant, *Sarthavaha* or itinerant or mobile trader and *Sresti*. Epigraphs attest to the existence of many guilds in the Mathura region and the western Deccan and in particular the town of Govardhana, which happens to be an important centre of guild of artisans. Some of the artisans and traders with the help of their guilds have become wealthy and emerged, as a dominant social group, having a say in the administrative structure of the period. Issue of coins by certain guilds indicates how powerful they had become during this period. Generally, a sovereign power only has the right to issue coins. Issue of coins by the merchant guilds of Taxila, Kausambi, Taripuri, Mahishmati or modern Mandhata, Vidisha, Eran and Varanasi indicates that they exercised considerable influence. Yet we have no clinching evidence to prove their actual participation in the administration. Every guild had its own insignia, banner and seal, which gave it individual identity. Every guild had its *Samayadharma* that had the strength of a law of the king. The guild provided social status to its members whereby also enabling them to earn reasonably good returns for their hard work. Every artisan had to follow the rules of work and quality for which price of the finished product and the guild laws were determined by the state.

The position of the Sudras who were artisans was economically better off and the economic distinction between the Vaisya and the Sudra appears to have been reduced considerably. The other Sudras earned their livelihood as hired labour and the *Manudharmasastra* and Patanjali imposed severe humiliating restrictions on the Sudras. This could be to safeguard the interests of the Brahmans against the Sudra opposition. The cultivators and the mercantile group were divided into a number of Grihas or homesteads or Kutumbins or Kulas or families. The head of a Griha was called a Gahapati or Kutumbin. The *Dasabrahmana Jataka* refers to Brahmanas working as tax collectors, hunters, traders, armed escorts, servants, wagon drivers and even menials of the kings. A chapter of the Mahabharata divides the Brahmanas into grades; those that are equivalent to the gods, the Kshatriyas, Vaisyas and Sudras based on their traits. B.N. Mukherjee states that the attempt to equate the Brahman with Kshatriya probably indicates that the former often took upon the jobs traditionally associated with the other castes. The *Kusa Jataka* refers to a prince or Kshatriya working successively as a potter, basket-maker, reed-worker garland-maker and cook. This makes B.N. Mukherjee observe that the Kshatriya could engage in activities not traditionally associated with his caste. In this period, it is not the birth in a caste that decided his role, but the profession in which he engaged himself. A number of Satavahana epigraphs refer to the issuer's professions, but not their caste. During this period, the Varna or the caste system was not as rigid as it is supposed to be. Though the rulers proclaim that they upheld the order of the Varnasrama dharma, in reality, the Varna model was theoretical and not actually practised. A view prevails that the traditional Varna model was threatened by the influx of foreigners. Since there is also a demographic evidence, it may be suggested that the number of foreigners was not such as to disturb the Varna model. Among the foreigners, compared to the Greeks, the Sakas and the Pahlavas, the number of Kushans appear to be more. By embracing Buddhism, the foreigners tried to find a foothold in India and as such, we notice the Indo-Greek kings, Agathocles and Menander displayed Buddhist symbols on their coins. A foreigner, Irila, built two cisterns for the monks at Junnar. We are very well aware of the patronage of Kanishka to Buddhism and how it became an international religion in his reign. As already noticed, the concept of Varna samkara or contamination of varnas was introduced to explain and justify the emergence of new castes in the Varna order because of Anuloma and Pratiloma marriages. The society of those days appears be less rigid and more catholic in temperament. It is only because of this spirit; a large number of foreigners settled in India and embraced the religions of their choice. We are aware that Rudradaman was a follower of Brahmanism and Heliodorous, an ambassador to Bhagabadra of Vidisa was a follower of Vishnu. D.R. Bhandarkar observes that in the cave inscriptions, Yavanas are frequently mentioned as making gifts in connection with Chaityas or monastic residences. At Karle, we have two names of Yavanas, Sihadhaya or Singhadyaja and Dharma. At Junar, we find mention of three Yavanas called Isila, Chitya or Chitra and Chandra. At Nasik, the name of only one Yavana is found, Indragnidatta, son of Dharmadeva. They all turned into Buddhist laymen and all of them except one had assumed Indian names.

Religion

In the post-Mauryan phase, people followed Vedic *Sanantanadharma*, Buddhism and Jainism. The rulers, in spite of their personal affiliation to a particular religion or deity never appear to have made that particular religion the state religion. It is misleading to speak of either 'Hindu India' or 'Muslim India' though it is true that religion played a very crucial role in the life pattern. Nevertheless, no religion dominated the socio-cultural milieu sufficient to ascribe the name of Hindu or Muslim to the entire society. The rulers generally do not refer to their caste or Varna in this period. Except the Sungas and the Kanvas, the Varna of other power structures cannot be mentioned definitely. It is not easy to identify the Varna of the Satavahanas, though they are thought to be Brahmans. The performance of sacrifice by some rulers made them to be considered as champions of Vedic ritualism and later Vedic devotionalism.

The Nanaghat epigraph of Naganika records that Satakarni I performed two Asvamedha sacrifices and one Rajasuya besides Agniyadhaya, Anarambhaniya, Gavamayana, Angirasatiratra, Aptoryama, Angirasamayana, Gangatiratha, Trayodasaratra, Dasarati, etc. Along with Yajna or sacrifice as the main component of Vedic ritualism, Bhagavatism or devotion to Vasudeva Krishna cult also was popular in this period. Further, only in this phase did the epics Mahabharata and Ramayana, attain the status of sacred literature. In due course of time, Bhagavatism transformed itself as Vishnavism. The Nasik epigraph of Pulomavi I, clearly states that Gautamiputra upheld the Puranic theism and coins and *Gathasaptasati* corroborate the epigraphic evidence of change from Vedic ritualism based on Yagna to Vedic theism based on devotion to personal gods Siva, Vishnu, Rama, Pasupati, Ganesh, Vasudeva, Samkarshana, Indra, Hari and Trivikrama. The worship of the Trinity – Brahma, Vishnu and Maheswara also developed in the Vedic theology. Vedic theism assimilated worship of popular cults of animals, trees and village deities.

Along with Vedic ritualism and Vedic theism, Vasudeva cult or Bhagavatism and Buddhism also flourished during this period. The Buddhist caves and epigraphs at Pitalkhora, Nasik, Bhaja, Bedsa, Kondone and Kuda and the Buddhist stupas at Bhattiprolu, Amaravati, Goli, Ghantasala, Gummididurru, Sanchi, Barhat, Nagarjunakonda, Karle, and many more places in the subcontinent show how Buddhism became popular. There was also emergence of different sects among the followers of Buddhism. The Bhadrayaniyas of Nasik and Kanheri, the Mahasanghikas of Karle, the Dhammottariyas of Sopara, Cheitikiya, Pubbasila, Aparasilia, Utayipabhati and Mahavinayasura are some of the well-known sects of Buddhism. The followers of Hinayana or the lesser vehicle claimed that their doctrine was the pure and original teaching of the Buddha and it became very popular in Ceylon (Sri Lanka), Burma (Myanmar) and the countries of South-East Asia. The followers of Mahayana or the greater vehicle became dominant in India, Central Asia, Tibet, China and Japan. One of the outstanding exponents of the doctrine of Mahayanism was Nagarjuna who is said to have converted into Buddhism from Brahmanism.

The most important tenet of Mahayanism was the doctrine of Bodhisatva, considered the logical development of the earlier Buddhist ideas. While Hinayana Buddhism stood for individual salvation, Mahayanism had for its goal the salvation of all beings. This concept of Bodhisattva was conceived as a series of previous incarnations of the Buddha and it tells that spiritual merit can be accumulated through births and it can be transferred to another person. Bodhisattva of Mahayanism was also a being of compassion and suffering who redeemed humanity through his own suffering. The Mahayanists elevated the Buddha from a religious teacher to a saviour god and introduced the image worship of the Buddha with elaborate rituals, formulae and charms. The earliest practice of worshipping the symbols of the Buddha continued along with image worship. During this period, the Buddha thus became a personal god and devotion to the Buddha became characteristic of the Mahayana Buddhism. Thus, we notice a transition from early Buddhism to the Mahayana Buddhism.

Like the Vedic Dharma or Sanatana Dharma and Buddhism, Jainism too underwent transformation. It split into *Digambaras* and *Swetambaras* by the 1st century AD. Digambaras claim to be pure and original Jainas and Swetambaras claim to be liberal. Jainism slowly moved from Magadha to Madhura and from there to Ujjain and finally reached Saurashtra on the west coast as well as Kalinga in the east and became prominent under Kharavela of Kalinga. We can postulate that Jains also developed image worship, as Kharavela in his Hathigumpha epigraph refers to the removal of an image of Jaina to Pataliputra from Kalinga and its recovery by him. Many well-carved Jaina images and votive tablets with Jaina figures are discovered at Madhura, which substantiates the view of the development of image worship by the Jains, like the Buddhists and the devotees of Sanatanadharma.

An offshoot of this new development of Bhakti cult or devotion to a personal deity in all the existing religions led to the growth of new cultural symbols – Stupa, Chaitya and Vihara of the Buddhists, Jaina Basadis and temples of the Sanathanadharma or Puranic theism.

Cultural symbols as reflected in the contemporary architecture can be broadly divided into (a) secular symbols or structures and (b) religious structures. The evidence on secular structures is scanty as it appears to have been built of wood, a perishable material. Literary texts like *Milindapanho* describes a city with ramparts, moats and gate homes, well laid out streets, markets, tanks, lakes and places of worship and also houses of several storeys. The dwellings of the rural people appear to be of perishable material.

Much significant evidence has not come from excavations regarding the earliest temple specimens. The temple at Jhandial (Taxila), the Sankarshana temple at Nagari (Rajasthan) the temple at Besanagar (Madhya Pradesh) and an apsidal temple at Nagarjunakonda (Andhra Pradesh) happen to be the earliest known examples of temples of this particular period. Fahien, a Chinese traveller of the Gupta times records the existence of a tower of 13 storeys with an iron column with imposing umbrellas of the time of Kanishka.

The practice of preserving the remains of holy persons below the earth has been in vogue for a long time. Buddhists adopted and followed this practice and the structure built over such a site was known as a 'stupa'. Buddhist tradition records that the sacred remains of the Buddha's body were divided into many parts and placed under various Stupas. The places where Stupas are built are known as the Buddhist sacred places and this led to a specific type of architecture for the construction of the stupas. In general, the Stupas have the shape of a bowl turned upside down. The top portion that is a little bit flat is known as *harmika* or the abode of the gods. In this *harmika* only, the urns containing the sacred relics are kept in a gold or silver casket. We also notice a wooden pole or Yasti in the middle and the bottom of the rod that was fixed on the top of the stupa. We also notice on the top of this pole three small umbrella type discs symbolic of respect, veneration and magnanimity.

Most prominent stupas venerated by the Buddhists are located at Bodhgaya (Bihar), Sanchi (Madhya Pradesh), Barhut, Amaravati and Nagarjunakonda in Andhra Pradesh and in Taxila. Besides Stupas, the Buddhists and the Jains built Chaityas and Viharas as places of worship. A 'chiatya' is a shrine cell where a votive stupa is placed in the centre. Viharas are places where the monks resided. These chaityas and viharas are generally of rock-cut architecture, and we notice them at Bhaja, Karle, Kondane, Nasik, Chitaldo, Ajanta and Kanheri of the western region and at Udayagiri in the eastern region. Every chaitya has the following features: a long rectangular hall ending in a semicircle at the rear end that is internally divided into a nave and apse and two-side aisles and the aisles are separated from the nave by two rows of pillars. These pillars cover the votive stupa placed in the centre of the apsidal part of the nave. The hall has a barrel-vaulted ceiling. The doorway is generally placed facing the votive stupa. The facade had horseshoe shaped windows called the chaitya windows.

The vihara has the following features: a square or oblong hall in the centre and preceded by a pillared verandah. A number of small square cells and halls are provided with raised benches for the use of monks. Bhaja, Bedsa, Ajanta, Pitalkora, Nasik and Karle are the earliest viharas of western India. Udayagiri and Khandagiri are Jaina viharas built by Kharavela. The double storeyed

Ranigumpha cave on the Udayagiri hills is the largest of all these. A knowledge of the sculptural art is necessary as sculpture forms an essential part of a total sacred complex like stupa or chaitya. We notice an interesting phenomenon of blend of regional or local styles such as Gandhara and Mathura styles of the north and Amaravati School of art in the Krishna-Godavari Valley in Andhra Pradesh. While the earlier Mauryan Art was palace-based, the later art had a wider social base. Relief sculptures and images of the Buddha reflect the skill of the artists of this age as seen in the stupa railings, gateways and plinths and on the facades and walls of the viharas and the chaityas. Compared to the Buddhist sculptures, Brahmanical sculptures of this period are fewer. It is not easy to point out who influenced whom in the making of the images. There is a view that the different Brahmanical gods and goddesses were conceived following the Buddhists and the Jains. Interestingly, the Yakshas and the Yakshinis occupy an important place among the sculptures of this period. Worship of icons is to be noticed from the Sunga period among the Jains and became popular by the 1st century AD. The Mahayana sect of the Buddhists advocated and propagated image worship. We come across seated and standing images of the Buddha in the style of the schools of Mathura and Gandhara.

Gandhara Art

The Kushan age has become famous for flourishing Gandhara art. Gandhara was situated in the north-western part of the Indian subcontinent on the banks of river Indus. Right from the time of the Buddha, the region has played an important role in the promotion and propagation of Buddhism in the whole of Central Asia. It is difficult to determine the geographical boundaries of Gandhara as they have always been shifting. Takshasila, also called Taxila, the capital of Gandhara was famous for higher education as well as woollen clothes. Gandhara was connected by trade routes to almost all important cities of Northern India. The art and architecture of Gandhara continued to develop until the 7th century AD. After independence, it became a part of Pakistan. Ancient Gandhara included the valley of Peshawar, Swat, Buner and Bajjora, and was ruled by the Achaenamids of Iran, the Greeks, the Mauryas, the Sakas, the Pahlavas and the Kushans in succession; consequently, it developed a cosmopolitan culture and Hellenism or Hellenistic art influence on its art. Gandhara art is primarily Buddhist art. V.A. Smith is of the view that the Gandhara style is Greeco-Roman, based on the art of Asia Minor and the Roman Empire. Nihar Ranjan Ray states that the Gandhara art was active from about the middle of the 1st century BC to about the 5th century AD. Gandhara art is considered to be influenced by the Hellenstic art because of the depiction of transparent garments draped in the Greeco-Roman fashion and the very curly hair of the Buddhist idols. B.N. Puri opines that in the Gandhara art foreign elements are conspicuous, though Indian iconography dominates. Stella Kramerish also argues that Gandhara art may be considered as an eastward expansion of the Hellenistic civilization and as westward expansion of Indian culture in western garb. We may conclude that the Gandhara art is certainly Indian in subject and content, though Hellinestic in form and execution. There is a debate regarding the influence of the Gandhara art. Paul Masson Oursel is of the view that this art exercised a twofold influence. We can notice the influence of Gandhara art in Central Asia, China and Japan, Indo-China and Indian subcontinent. Mathura art is said to be influenced by the Gandhara art.

The Mathura School of Art

The Mathura School of Art belongs to the age of the Kushanas. R.C. Sharma argues that this school of art has six styles and finds Gandhara art's influence on Mathura sculptural art only at the end of the reign of Kanishka. In this Mathura School, the images of the Buddha, the Bodhisattva and Jaina Thirthankaras became the prominent elements. The specimens of the Mathura School are found at Mathura, Saranath, Sanchi and Kosam. The beginning of the Mathura art style can be traced to the 2nd century BC and by the 1st century AD, Mathura had become a major centre of art and was in great demand at far-off places too. The sculptural pieces were carved out of a local variety of black and red sandstone. The characteristics of the idol of the Buddha are: (a) Buddha sitting under a Bodhi tree with right hand in Abhaya posture, (b) Dharma Chakra and Triratna chiselled in palms and at the bottom of the feet, and (c) except for one lock, the entire head is shaven. Mathura was a sacred centre of Buddhists, the Jains as well as the followers of the Brahmanical faith. Some images of the Brahmanical faith have been found at Mathura. The earliest representations of Siva, Lakshmi, Surya and Sankarshana or Balarama are found here. During the Kushan age, the images of Kartikeya, Vishnu, Sarasvati, Kubera and the Nagas were chiselled on stone. Mother Goddess worship was prevalent during this period. A number of Yaksha and Yakshini images have been discovered at Mathura. Very interestingly, we come across the images of Kanishka, Vima and Chastana from Mat, very near to Mathura. This practice appears to have been copied from Central Asia along with the Central Asian mode of dress.

The Amaravati School of Art

The Amaravati School inspired by Buddhist ideas, developed in the lower valleys of the Krishna of the Eastern Deccan, was patronized by the Satavahanas, the Ikshvakus, and the nobles, officials and merchants of their time. Art was inspired by the Buddhist themes. The main centres of this art were Nagarjunakonda, Amaravati, Goli, Ghantasala and Jaggayyapeta. This school of art reached its heights during 150 BC and AD 150. The stupa railings, plinths and other parts show sculptural themes. The stupas of Amaravathi are the largest and most interesting. The dome of the stupa was 20 feet high with four rectangular offsets. A railing 192 feet in diameter and 600 feet in circumference surrounded it. Sir John Marshall observes that there is greater originality, freedom of treatment and spontaneous exuberance in the art of Amaravati. The reliefs of Amaravati indeed appear to be as truly Indian in style as those of Barhut and Ellora. They seem to follow as a natural sequence of the Mauryan art, when that art was finding expression in forms that are more conventional. They have certain motifs and types that filtered from the north-west, but these elements have been completely absorbed and assimilated without materially influencing the indigenous character of the sculptures. This art depicts the Buddha as a divine being receiving worship. In Gandhara, the Buddha is portrayed as a Guru or preceptor. At Mathura, he assumes the garb of a local Yogin while Amaravati transforms him into a preaching monk or a public orator. We may conclude with a remark that the Amaravati School: "struck a quite novel and unique chord in the symphony of Indian plastic art. The Amaravati School exerted significant influence on the later south Indian sculpture. It also influenced in the skill of the sculptors of Ceylon and south east Asian countries". The Amaravati art served as a link between the earlier and the later art traditions. Nihar Ranjan Ray aptly observes, "Never so far was the delicate and voluptuous beauty of the human frame so richly and luxuriously conceived and were never technical skill and efficiency more adequate for realisation of the conception".

9

The Sangam Age

Literature, Society and Culture

In the evolution of Indian history and culture, the role of South India is no less significant. While the historiography of the British and the European scholars was based on Euro-centric perception, the historiography of Indian scholars was based on the perspective of the Gangetic basin in analysing the factors in the evolution of culture and history of India. In the past five decades, new archaeological material has come to light and a critical examination of literary forces has proved that *Tamilham* or Deep South has contributed significantly from times immemorial. Maurya Asoka's edicts and Hathigumpha epigraph of Kharavela also refer to the earliest chiefdoms of Chola, Chera and Pandya and their transition from chiefdom to kingdom finds reflection in the Sangam literature.

The beginnings of the historical phase in Tamilham or Deep South can be traced to the Sangam age. K.K. Pillai aptly states, "The Sangam is a unique institution of the early Tamils. It has lent its name to a number of classical works with the result that Sangam literature and Sangam age have acquired certain specific connotations, though in respect of details, doubts still continue to persist". The word *Sangam* is the Tamil form of the Sanskrit word Sangha and in this particular context, the Tamil Sangam is understood as an academy of poets and bards patronized by the Pandyan rulers with its headquarters at Madurai. It is very difficult to precisely date this Sangam age. The period between 300 BC and AD 300 is generally called the Sangam age. Likewise, it is also very difficult to fix the chronology of the works of the Sangam age. N. Subramanyam is of the opinion that the Sangam literature is attributable to pre-Pallavan age. Tamilham as described by its literature, is the region between the hills of Venkatam and Kanyakumari. This region is a combination of diverse eco-zones of hills surrounded by forests, undulating terrain, wetlands, long sea coast, pastures and arid zones. This region was under the political control of the three principal powers, the Cheras, the Cholas and the Pandyas. These were only chiefdoms and not kingdoms. The most important political centres in this region were Karur and the well-known ancient port of Muciris (Cragnore) under the Cheras, Uraiyur and Puhar on the Coramandal coast under the Cholas, and Madurai and Saliyur, a port under the Pandyas. The Sangam literature or heroic poetry refers to the concept of '*Aithinai*' or five eco-zones and these five eco-zones are: (a) *Kurunji* or hilly backwoods, (b) *Palai* or arid zone, (c) *Mullai* or pastoral tracts, (d) *Maruttam* or wetland, and (e) *Neital* the sea coast. The occupations and lifestyle the people of these eco-zones is varied. Hunting and gathering was the occupation of Kurunji inhabitants. The people living in Palai depended on plundering and cattle-lifting. Shifting cultivation and animal husbandry were the occupation of the people of the Mullai zone. The people of Marutam pursued plough agriculture, and fishing and salt-making were the occupations of the people of Neital eco-zones. We also notice bartering of goods produced by one eco-zone people with other eco-zone inhabitants. Gradually, these small social groups living in different eco-zones became integrated through interaction and interdependence. Where there was better productivity, they developed social divisions of labour and in other areas of lesser productivity, people led a simple life as clans. Though all the people of different eco-zones shared a common culture, the society comprised unevenly developed components. In the sphere of political structures also, we come across simple chiefdoms of clans and complex chiefdoms of ruling houses. A full-fledged state system was yet to take shape here as compared to Andhra and Maharashtra region where we notice the emergence of state system under the Satavahanas.

In Tamilham, there existed several chiefdoms big and small. The chiefs of these were addressed as the great son *Perumakan* or *Komakan* or younger son. There existed three types of chiefdoms – *Kizar* or little chiefs, *Velir* or bigger chiefs and *Vedar* or the biggest chief. The Chera, the Chola and the Pandya were the three principal ruling houses and were called as *Muvendar* or three Candar. The relations between the chiefs and the people was based on kinship. In order to augment their resources, the chiefs resorted to plunder and cattle-raids. The booty was redistributed among the warriors, bards and mendicants besides their own relatives. In this society, gift giving or *Kodai* also was very much in vogue. Sangam literature praises the generosity of the chieftains.

Livelihood of the people in Tamilham depended on hunting and gathering forest produce, cattle rearing, plough agriculture, fishing and salt-making and wayside robbery. By the time of Iron Age, we notice a spread of settlements from the upland areas to the fertile river valleys and the rise of agricultural economy. That agriculture was carried on with the help of the iron plough is known from literature and epigraphs. Interestingly, a dealer in ploughshare figures as a donor in one of the inscriptions. Irrigation facilities were looked after by the people of the region as well as by chieftains and kings. At Kaveripattinam in Tamilham, remains of an ancient reservoir has been discovered. The cultivators of the land known as *Uzhavar* or ploughmen, and *Vellar*, or cultivators of the soil grew paddy, sugarcane and pulses. We also come across a category of *Atiyor*, who may be slaves and *Vinaivalar* or wages workers as can be gathered from literature. Sangam literature mentions that people of this age had great knowledge of seasons, which was essential for successful cultivation to feed diverse population of different groups of specialist artisans like blacksmiths, carpenters, bards, priests and monks.

We come to know from Sangam literature that the chiefs received two types of contributions – *Irai* or regular contribution and *Tirai* or tribute. The chiefs gathered the village resources such as cattle at one place and redistributed them as gifts to the priests and warriors by way of remuneration for their services. Tamilham society of this period was essentially tribal, characterized by kinship organizations, totem worship and such tribal cults and practices. While tribal customs prevailed in all the eco-zones, in the Maruttam or the agricultural region, society appears to have become complex by the gradual break-up of old kinship ties and the introduction of the Varna concept. Social stratification based on 'high' and low' groups took shape in course of time. Besides agriculture, there were other professions such as blacksmiths, carpenters and weavers. Most of the people followed old tribal rituals of religious worship and cult practices, and the society was not priest-dominated. Trade and commerce was possible because of surplus production of goods; we come across traders – *Umanan* or salt merchant, *Kogla vanikan* or corn merchant, *Aruvai vanikan* or textile merchant and *Pon vanikan* or gold merchant. *Tolkappiyam*, the earliest Tamil grammar text indicates that Varna system entered into Tamilham as the above-mentioned traders were given the status of Vaisyas and the chieftains of the Maruttam region started claiming descent from Suryavamsa or Chandravamsa. Thus, in the agrarian zones, we notice amalgamation of old tribal practice and Brahmanical ideas.

The economy of Tamilham depended on trade and commerce besides agricultural production. There existed three levels of trade: (1) local, (2) overland, and (3) overseas. In the local trade sphere, barter was the most common mode of transaction to obtain perishable commodities of daily use; paddy and salt were the only two items that had an exchange rate. Long distance overland trade and long distance sea trade resulted in the growth of urban centres as well as seaports. There was a flourishing trade between Rome and Tamilham. Tamilham also had commercial contacts with Sri Lanka and South-East Asia. Roman as well as Sri Lankan trade settlements are in evidence. Growth of trade and commerce led to the use of coins as medium of commerce in this period. The coins may be divided into local and Roman coins. Sangam literature refers to locally available coins of *Kasu, Kanam, Pon* and *Venpon* but coins with these names have not been found so far. Roman coins generally of gold and silver and rarely, copper coins were in circulation. In Tamilham of this period, ruling chieftains and kings derived considerable income from trade and commerce from toll or *Ulka* collected by agents from the traders. Revenue was collected in cash and kind as well. Artisans paid a tax known as *Karukara*. Coming to weights and measures, in Tamilham, land was measured as *Ma* and *Veil*. Large measure called *Ambanam*, and small measures such as *Nali, Ulakan* and *Alakka* were prevalent.

Sangam literature and other literary texts refer to rural exchange centres, internal market, towns and port towns. Inland towns like Uraiyur located near modern Tiruchirapalli, Kanchi or Kanchipuram and Madurai developed into rudimentary market centres. Besides, there were port towns like Puhar or Kaveripattinam, Arikamedu, Colobil, Musiri and Tyndis. Bacare and Neleyamda were centres of maritime trade. It is also said that Musiris was a busy centre with a port crowded with large warehouses and markets. These port towns did not have close links with rural or local exchange centres, as they catered to the needs of the nobility and the ruling group. The vitality of these depended on the success of foreign trade and when overseas trade declined, these centres too declined and disappeared as port towns or *Pattinams*.

By 1st century BC, Tamil appears to have become a literary language. The earliest cave epigraphs prove this point beyond doubt. Label inscriptions found at Arittappatti, Ḳarumgalakkuti and Kongarpuliyamkulam had both Tamil and Prakrit/Pali/Sanskrit words. Besides these label inscriptions, the Tamil heroic poems of Sangam literature constitute the important evidence for the old Tamil literary tradition. The literary tradition states that there existed originally three Sangams of which only the last one has survived. Sangam literature is characterized by specific poetic themes. Broadly, this literature is grouped into *Ettuttogai* or the eight collections of poems and *Pattupattu* or the Ten Idylls. *Narrinai, Kurandogai, Aingurunuru, Padirruppattu* are some of the anthologies grouped under *Ettuttogai, Mullaippattu, Madurikku*; and *Karunjipputtu*, belong to the anthologies in *Pattupattu*. The entire collection includes 2,279 poems composed by 473 poets. The length of the poems varies from three lines to 80 lines. Interestingly, there were some women poets also. The anthologies are divided based on the theme or the subject: *Akam* or love and *Puram* or glorification of plunder or raid. Apart from these heroic anthologies, Sangam literature includes *Tolkappiyam*, a treatise on Tamil grammar and *Patinenkizkanakkse*, a collection of eighteen didactic texts. The most outstanding example of this category being *Tirukkural* of Tiruvalluvar. K.A. Nilakanta Sastri writes that doubtless what has survived is only a part of the much vaster literature of these remote times. Some scholars consider the twin epics *Silappadikaram* and *Manimekhalai* as contemporaneous with heroic poems but they appear to be later compositions. The literary piece *Pattinappalai* provides a detailed account of the activity of customs officials in Puhar. The literature advocated moderation in taxation. The *Kalavali* poems offer much interesting information on military matters. The twin arts of music and dance were highly developed. There are many references to variety of musical instruments, including drums. Karikala is famous as the master of the seven notes of music. Poems also furnish valuable hints on popular beliefs and customs. In this period, we notice the influence of northern ideas entering into the sphere of religion and ethics. People worshipped Murugan or Subrahmanyam, Siva, Balarama, Vishnu, Krishna, Arthanariswara and Anantasayi. *Manimekhalai* refers to a temple of Saraswati.

Thus, by the end of the Sangam period the joyous faith in good living found in the literature gives way to a pessimistic outlook indicating a change in the general outlook on life and K.A. Nilakanta Sastri aptly describes "a long historical night ensues after the close of the Sangam age". Until 6th century AD, or the rise of the Pallavas, Tamilham was under the rule of Kalabaras or Kalappalar. We can conclude with the statement of K.A. Nilakanta Sastri that the literature of the Sangam age gives an unusually complex and true picture of the life of the people of Tamilham in the beginning of the historical period.

10

The Gupta Age

The Revival of Empire

The period from 200 BC to AD 300, has been aptly characterized as the age of "the disintegration of the concept of empire". In this period, we notice the rise of many state structures in different parts of India that failed in their attempt to evolve into large kingdoms. Once again, the idea of an empire became a reality with the emergence of the Guptas in 4th century AD. In this background of small state structures in important parts of India, the Guptas of uncertain origin rose to prominence, whose core region appears to be eastern Uttar Pradesh.

A conscious effort is made by historians to portray this Gupta age as the age of 'Imperial Guptas' and 'the Classical Age'. These scholars, in the words of B.D. Chattopadhyaya, were of the opinion, "that an empire is perceived as a political structure assiduously built by the military exploits of several charismatic royal personalities; it was simultaneously an outcome of the liberation of Northern India from long standing foreign rule and political unification achieved by successfully suppressing centrifugal elements". With this perspective, R.C. Majumdar observed, "the Gupta Empire, at full maturity, once more brings unity, peace and prosperity over nearly the whole of Northern India". Echoing the same sentimental perspective U.N. Ghoshal also observed, "The greater part of the country undoubtedly enjoyed high prosperity". K.K. Dasgupta and R.C. Majumdar also observed, "The imperial Guptas with whom the volume opens, ably countered the centrifugal forces in Northern India and the kingdom, established by Chandragupta I was shortly converted by his son, Samudragupta into an empire. The Gupta Empire, reared by a succession of competent rulers, gave North India not only political stability and imperial peace but also set an exemplary standard in all departments of life and culture. Indeed, the advent of the Guptas on the political stage ushered an epoch which has rightly been called the Golden Age or the classical period of Indian history". This perception of an imperial, golden and classical age of the Guptas is created, sustained and perpetuated by a group of scholars as they witnessed in the rise of the Guptas an attempt to unite the different pockets of power in northern India. As described by B. Lahiri, "those controlled by the last rulers of the 'foreign' Kusanas; the Gana Sangha, Janapadas, unevenly distributed between Punjab and Uttar Pradesh, Himalayas to Haryana and Rajasthan, and petty rulers of what have been called 'indigenous states'."

Source material available to reconstruct the history of the Gupta age is scarce. However, what is available may be classified as: (1) literary, (2) archaeological, and (3) Chinese travellers' accounts.

Literary Sources

Of all the literary sources, the Puranas occupy an important place. The major Puranas, Vayu, Vishnu, Matsya, Brahmanda and Bhagavata Puranas are very helpful to the students of history. These Puranas were compiled and brought out in written form during this age. Based on the Puranic evidence it is believed that the founder of the Gupta lineage ruled over Prayaga, Saketa and Magadha. Kalidasa, the famous Sanskrit dramatist and poet is considered to belong to this period but V. Ramachandra Dikshitar thinks that Kalidas' works do not help us as a source material of the Gupta age. Further, Kamandaka's *Nitisara*, Pravarasena's *Setubandha Kavya*, *Kaumudimahotsava* a drama, whose authorship is debatable, Visakhadatta's *Devichandraguptam* and *Mudrarakshasa* and Bana's *Harshacharita* are the other valuable literary sources to reconstruct the history of the Guptas.

Archaeological Sources

Epigraphs, coins, seals, monuments and paintings constitute the archaeological source material. A critical examination of Gupta coins helps us not only to deduce the extent of the empire, the artistic excellence and religious beliefs but also the economic soundness of the Gupta period. Gold, silver and copper coins of the Guptas are found in abundance. Generally, the gold coins of the Guptas have the figure of the king on the obverse and a goddess on the reverse with associated symbols like figures of altars, Garuda a dwarf or Tulasi plant. Gold coins of Chandragupta I, Samudragupta, Chandragupta II, Kumaragupta and Skandagupta have become known. We have also gold coins of Purugupta, Kumaragupta II and Narasimhagupta Baladitya. There are silver coins of Chandragupta II, Kumaragupta I and Skandagupta. We have copper coins issued by Chandragupta II and Kumaragupta I. The coins contained legends that indicated their reverence for goddesses, and their epitaphs. The coins of Chandragupta I and his queen Kumaradevi exhibit the importance they attached to the matrimonial alliance with the Lichchavis as a means of gaining political authority while the superior gold coins of Samudragupta reflect the economic of the period prosperity. The inferior gold coins of the later Guptas reflect the deteriorating economic conditions of their period. The coins with Asvamedha symbol reflect their claim to sovereignty. We may conclude by observing that the gold, silver and copper coins of the Guptas bear testimony to the metal working skill and artisanship of the artisans of that period besides their economic condition.

Epigraphs

Nearly 42 epigraphs of the Gupta times covering a period from AD 360 to AD 466, besides a number of non-Gupta epigraphs and later inscriptions enable us to reconstruct the history and times of the Gupta period. Of the 42 epigraphs, 19 are official, while the remaining 23 are private records issued by private individuals. Among these epigraphs, 27 are carved on stone and the rest are copper or Tamra Sasanas. The Prasasthis of Samudragupta and two Prasasthis of Skandagupta are very useful in reconstructing the Gupta history. We have also a Prasasthi of Chandragupta II engraved on an iron pillar at Mehrauli in Delhi and the rest of the fourteen copper plates. Generally, the Prasasthis and the copper plates provide us with the geneology of the recipient and the donor. The private records show the donation of land or utensils to a religious establishment and these private records sometimes mentioned the name and occasionally the achievements of the ruling king. Of the Gupta epigraphs, the most valuable is the Allahabad pillar edict of Samudragupta, written by Harisena, the Mahadandanayaka of Samudragupta. It is a very long Prasasthi as it records the exploits of Samudragupta. Unfortunately, it is undated. It was written in a verse form in classical Sanskrit. Interestingly, 33 lines of this epigraph form a single lengthy sentence. Likewise, the Eran stone epigraph of Samudragupta also provides a glimpse of his achievements. The hero of the Mehrauli iron pillar, Chandra, has been identified with Chandragupta II and this epigraph deals with his achievements. Chandragupta II's conquests of western India are recorded in the Udayagiri cave inscription. So also, the Gadhwal stone epigraph, the Bilsad stone pillar epigraph and Mankuar stone-image inscription refer to the achievements of Kumaragupta. The Bhitari pillar epigraph near Benaras contains details of the fight between the Guptas and the Pushyamitras and the Hunas of the time of Skandagupta, the crown prince of Kumaragupta. The Junagadh rock epigraphs and the Kahum pillar edict are attributed to the time of Skandagupta. Likewise, non-Gupta epigraphs also refer to events that happened during the Gupta regime. An inscription of Kakutsthavarman of the Kadamba dynasty refers to his marriage with the daughters of the Gupta dynasty. A contemporary inscription of Varman dynasty reveals that they ruled the greater part of Malwa. The inscription does not acknowledge the hegemony of the Guptas. These also provide a clue to the time when the Guptas occupied that territory. About the disintegration and decline of the Gupta Empire, the epigraphs of Toramana and Mihirakula provide valuable information. The importance of these epigraphs lies in the fact that they enable us to corroborate the information given in the epigraphs of the Guptas. The later dated epigraph of the Rastrakutas, the Saranath epigraph of Pakaditya and the Nalanda record of Yasodharman also indirectly refer to the Guptas and their times.

Monuments

Besides epigraphs, the monuments of the Gupta period – temples, monasteries and Chaityas – also throw valuable light on the religious and artistic excellence of the Gupta age. There were three different schools of art and architecture

(i) Mathura, (ii) Benaras, and (iii) Nalanda, during this period. The cave paintings of Ajanta and Ellora of the Gupta times reflect the artistic tastes and excellence, social life, festivities and Jatras of that time. Likewise, numerous seals found at Vaishali and its neighbourhood provides very valuable information on the provincial and local government of the Guptas.

Chinese Travellers' Accounts

The information obtained about the Guptas from the literary and archaeological sources can be corroborated from the accounts of the Chinese Buddhist pilgrim Fahien; and a later dated account of Itsing who visited the region of the Guptas and recorded his impressions. Fahien spent nine years in India, six of them in the Gupta court, interestingly; he spent three years at Pataliputra itself and visited the other places like Kanauj, Ayodhya, Sravasti, Kapilavastu, Vaishali and Kusinagara. His account *Fo-Kuo-Kie* or 'The Record of Buddhist Kingdoms' gives very interesting information regarding different aspects of the Gupta age. Fahien is oddly silent about the name of the Gupta king. His account alone cannot be accepted as a truthful picture of the Gupta times; we have to carefully corroborate the information with other sources. Itsing visited India during the closing years of 7th century AD. He refers to the construction of a place of worship for the Chinese pilgrims at Mrigasikhavana by Sri Gupta. A fair amount of knowledge about the times of the Guptas can be gathered from these sources so that the history of this period can be reconstructed with some sources.

Political History of the Guptas

The beginnings of the Gupta dynasty are shrouded in mystery. As very little is known about their ancestors, various speculations are made regarding their original home and ancestors. The rise of the Guptas as political masters and their acceptance as an imperial power strongly suggests that the Sastric dictum that only the people of Kshatriya Varna are eligible to be the rulers was not a binding condition. Further, the epigraphs of the Sunga and the Satavahana dynasties refer to the name Gupta, in particular reference to Sivagupta that led some to postulate they are as ancient as the Satavahanas.

However, it is certainly conceded that the Guptas are not of royal origin. This becomes clear from Chandragupta I's attaching importance to his marriage alliance with the Lichchavi princess Kumaradevi and the first two rulers not recording any details except their titles. If they were of royal origin, the first two rulers would have claimed royal ancestry and Chandragupta I need not have attached much of significance to his matrimonial alliance with the Lichchavis, who were a well-known tribal royal family by that time. Hence, it is clear that the Guptas are of uncertain origin and rose to prominence taking advantage of the prevailing political uncertainty with the decline of Kushan power in northern India. Different theories have been offered about the original home of the Guptas. Some scholars placed their original home in North Bengal, while some placed it in Magadha in Bihar and U.P. Nevertheless, many historians now tentatively accept that their original home lay in Eastern Uttar Pradesh.

The advocates of this theory point out that they come to this conclusion based on the following: (a) the Puranas, in particular the Vayu Purana refered to alludes to eastern Uttar Pradesh as early Gupta territory, (b) a number of coin hordes are found in this region, and (c) the earliest epigraph of the Guptas recording the achievements of Samudragupta, the Allahabad pillar epigraph also comes from this region. Further, it is said that of the fifteen inscriptions that refer to the first one hundred and fifty years of the Gupta rule, eight come from Uttar Pradesh, two from Magadha and five, which belong to a later period come from Bengal. The Gaya inscription, indirectly clinches the issue by stating the intimate relations of the Guptas with Eastern Uttar Pradesh. All the above evidence conclusively proves that the Prayaga region of eastern Uttar Pradesh was the core area of the early Guptas. Though the literary and archaeological sources clearly reveal that the Guptas started their independent rule in the second decade of 4th century AD, it may be surmised that they were vassals of the later Kushans in north-western India in the closing decades of the 3rd century AD.

Epigraphs inform us that Srigupta was the first king of the Gupta dynasty followed by Ghatotkacha Gupta. Prabhavati Gupta's two records from Poona and Rithpur refer to Ghatotkacha Gupta as the first king and the recently discovered Rewa epigraphs refer to him as the founder of the Gupta family. Perhaps, compared to Srigupta, Ghatotkacha made some notable conquests that have yet to come to light that led him to be considered as the founder by the Rewa record. He appears to have assumed the title of 'Maharaja' which however does not imply that he was ruling independently.

Ghatotkacha's son and successor, Chandragupta I ascended the throne of the Guptas in AD 319–320 and commenced the Gupta era. In 1887, J.F. Fleet propounded the theory that Chandragupta was the founder of the Gupta dynasty and started 'the Gupta era'. He assumed the title of 'Maharajadhiraja', which clearly indicates that he started the independent rule of the Guptas. Beyond his marriage with Kumaradevi, the princess of the Lichchavi clan, nothing much is known about his rule. His successors record this matrimonial alliance with pride, and this makes us believe that this matrimonial alliance undoubtedly helped him in consolidating his kingdom. This can be further proved by the fact that Samudragupta, the successor of Chandragupta I, proudly declares himself as Lichchavi Dauhitra, the son of the daughter of the Lichchavis. Chandragupta I issued a coin with the figures of himself and Kumaradevi on the obverse with their names and on the reverse, a goddess seated on a lion along with the legend Lichchavanyah. The specific issue of a gold coin by Chandragupta I proclaiming his marriage with Kumaradevi, and the legend *Lichchavanyah* definitely indicates that this marriage had political significance. The Guptas in general and Chandragupta I in particular were benefited by this marriage. This marriage brought both respectability and legitimacy to the Guptas as rulers because they contracted a matrimonial alliance with one of the age-old and well-established ruling dynasties of northern India. We may safely presume that by this marriage, the incipient Gupta state power and the Lichchavi state power merged, leading to the emergence a strong power in eastern Uttar Pradesh and Magadha. There are no definite evidences to determine the boundaries of the kingdom of Chandragupta I. But, it is believed that his kingdom covered parts of Bihar, Uttar Pradesh and Bengal. Chandragupta is also credited with initiating the Gupta era, immediately after his accession to the throne in AD 319–320. The spatial extent of the use of this term 'Gupta era' by the non-Gupta rulers is an indication of the power wielded by the Guptas. Likewise, the non-mention of this era in later dated epigraphs would point out to the decay and decline of the Gupta power. The solid foundations laid by Chandragupta I appear to have made the middle Ganga Valley and the region around Pataliputra, a political centre of importance. The Gupta political power and polity were firmly rooted in the central sector of the Ganga Valley. Chandragupta successfully placed the Guptas in firm control of the middle Ganga Valley to both the north and south of the river. Samudragupta, the son of Chandragupta I and Kumaradevi, succeeded his father, and ruled for a period of five decades from AD 325 to AD 375 or from AD 330 to AD 380. Samudragupta had been acclaimed as the greatest of the Gupta lineage as well as one of the illustrious sovereigns of early Indian history. He has been praised as the real founder of the Gupta Empire. Allahabad Prasasti epigraph, inscribed on the original Asoka edict, by Harisena, the minister for war of Samudragupta vividly describes in detail the achievements of Samudragupta as a warrior as also his other qualities as a person and administrator. The Allahabad Prasasti specifically mentions that Smudragupta was specially chosen by Chandragupta I to succeed him among many aspirants for the throne. From this, we may infer that Chandragupta I had more than one son and he had chosen Samudragupta to succeed him. It is suggested that Samudragupta did succeed peacefully without opposition from his other brothers who aspired for the throne. It is believed that one of the disgruntled brothers, Kacha declared himself as ruler of the Gupta Empire, and ruled for some time as coins bearing the name of Kacha are found. Based on the evidence of the coins of Kacha, it is suggested that a civil war had taken place, though there is no direct or indirect evidence either way this. Samudragupta must have driven Kacha away and occupied the Gupta throne. This theory gained currency as the gold coins of Kacha are similar to those of Samudragupta but interestingly, the Gupta epigraphs are silent about Kacha.

After successfully establishing himself on the throne, Samudragupta appears to have started his invasions against the powerful contemporary rulers to expand and consolidate the Gupta hegemony. From the undated Allahabad Prasasthi, we come to know of his policy of conquests. Believed by some was the minister for war under Samudragupta. What the epigraph narrates is a faithful record in the order of the happenings. However, R. Sathianath Iyer opines that the order of events given in the inscription is not representing the chronological order. Further, the said inscription is silent about the Aswamedha sacrifice; so this inscription must have been composed immediately after his victorious campaigns and there must be a considerable gap between the issue of the said epigraph and performance of the Aswamedha sacrifice.

First, let us take Samudragupta's campaign in Aryavarta. The question of the number of campaigns he supposedly led has been questioned by scholars. Some historians hold that Samudragupta uprooted his opponents of Aryavarta in one campaign but some others, relying on the authenticity of the record argue that he campaigned twice against the rulers of Aryavarta. We are not sure whether they were undertaken successively or whether there was any gap between these two campaigns. By his successful campaigns in Aryavartha, Samudragupta became the master of the whole of Gangetic Valley and of Eran in the central part of India. Samudragupta employed the diplomatic technique of encircling the valley with a ring of tributary states, which are Atavika or forest tribes, to make this core territory secure and safe, and adopted a mild policy towards these states. The tribal frontier states of Malawas, the Arjunayanas, the Yaudheyas and the Madrakas, accepted the sovereignty of Samudragupta. Further, the Abhiras, the Ararjunas, the Sanakanikas, the Kakas and the Kharaparihas; tribes that ruled in the north and east of Bhilsa also acknowledged his sovereignty.

Now let us consider campaigns in Dakshinapatha. There is a controversy regarding the number of his invasions against Dakshinapatha and about the route followed by Samudragupta. The Allahabad Prasasti clearly states that he defeated all the kings of Dakshinapata. There is a view that he invaded the South twice, but the Allahabad Prasasti gives no hint to that effect. It clearly gives a list of twelve names of the rulers along with the names of the kingdoms. The kings and kingdoms defeated by Samudragupta are Mahendra of Kosala, Vyaghraraja of Mahakantara, Mantaraja of Korala, Mahendra of Pistapura, Swamidatta of Kottura, Damana of Erandapalli, Vishnugopa of Kanchi, Nilaraja of Avamukta, Hastivarman of Vengi, Ugrasena of Pallakka, Kubera of Devarastra and Dhananjaya of Kusashtalapura: The Allahabad Prasasti clearly mentions that with regard to the kings of Dakshinapatha, Samudragupta followed a policy of Grahana or capture of the enemy, Moksha or liberation and Anugraha or reinstating him. This policy of "grahana-moksha-anugraha" reveals the diplomatic skill and foresight of Samudragupta, as he knew that in those days when there was no proper and speedy communication network it would be very difficult to have a constant control on these distant areas, and decided to be satisfied with their acknowledging his overloadship rather than bringing them under his direct control. R.K. Mukherjee rightly observes, "This policy may be taken to be the only policy that a conqueror could pursue in distant South where he was only anxious that his position as the paramount sovereign of India should be recognised". Samudragupta's not trying to annex these southern kingdoms clearly reveals his farsighted wisdom and realistic approach.

There are historians who believe that the list of kingdoms and kings given in the Allahabad Prasasti is the route of the southern campaign of Samudragupta. Very recently, P.V.P. Sastri came out with a theory that Samudragupta's expedition to South India was merely prompted more by a desire to establish Sanatana Dharma in the south, than to gain any wealth or political advantage. Whatever the reason, the southern expedition of Samudragupta was a reality and established him as a victorious warrior.

The Allahabad pillar Prasasti also states that independent or semi-independent principalities also acknowledged his supremacy. But, it is very difficult to identify these except Simhala or Ceylon (now Sri Lanka). The epigraph refers to a term "Daivaputra Shahi-Shahanushahi-Saka-Murundas". Out of this compound term, we are very well aware that Daivaputra-Shahi-Shahanushahi are the titles of the Kushan rulers who were divided into three small principalities by that time. But, we are not sure of the names of the principalities of the Kushan rulers who are supposed to have accepted the suzerainty of Samudragupta.

A critical examination of the conquests of Samudragupta and the policy adopted by him towards his enemies reveals him as a political realist who had the geopolitical interests of the Gupta kingdom at heart. While he followed a policy of Unmulya or annihilation towards the rulers of Aryavarta, he followed a policy of "Grahana, Anugraha and Moksha" towards the southern rulers. His decision to annihilate his enemies in Aryavarta was motivated by his ambition to make himself the unquestioned master of the core area. As already indicated, his southern conquests were undertaken to prove his prowess as a warrior and a general striking awe in the minds of the contemporary rulers. His decision to create a ring of dependencies around the core area of his territory and maintaining friendly relations with distant frontier tribes and rulers was a masterstroke of diplomacy. The view of some of the scholars that Samudragupta had in his mind an international system of goodwill and peace, through violence, aggression and war appears to be far-fetched. Further, the opinion of R.K. Mukherjee that he earned fame as one who vanquished kings whom he reinstated in their kingdoms in a new order of peaceful partnership does not appear to be an overstatement. Samudragupta was not a bloodthirsty general but only a pragmatic imperialist. His pragmatic imperialism made him follow a policy of peaceful partnership with distant southern kingdoms, frontier tribes and frontier kings but not with enemies in the neighbourhood of his core area.

Samudragupta should be credited with raising the fortunes of the Gupta kingdom and establishing himself as a ruler of the entire Aryavarta and laying solid foundations for the military prowess of the Guptas. He is undoubtedly a good warrior and a capable general, equally interested in the fine arts of music and literature. None of his poetry is available, but he had the title of Kaviraja. That Samudragupta was also a patron of Sanatana Dharma could be deduced from his revival of Asvamedha sacrifice. It is also true that he is a typical representative of the ideology of the age that king is the image of God on earth. However, a patron of Sanathana Dharma, he was not obsessed with that ideology. This is proved by placing his son under the tutorship of Vasubandhu, a great Buddhist scholar. His coins bear testimony to the fact that he was of robust build. In one of his recently found coins, we come across the title of Srivikramah indicating his great prowess as victor and suggesting that he was as great as the legendary Vikramaditya.

Some scholars hold the opinion that the Gupta era starts not from the year of the accession of Chandragupta I, but from the accession of Samudragupta, because the copper plate grants of Samudragupta from Nalanda and Gaya are dated in the fifth and ninth years of the Gupta era. However, the most accepted view is that it was Chandragupta I who started the Gupta era and not Samudragupta. We can say that it was Chandragupta I who started the independent rule of the Guptas and it was Samudragupta who made the Gupta independence a reality by making the Guptas the real masters of northern India. Though family details of Samudragupta are not available in any source, the availability of some coins bearing the name Ramagupta and references to a fratricidal war between Chandragupta and Ramagupta in works like *Natyadarpana, Kavyamimamsa, Harshacharita* and *Devi Chandraguptam,* have prompted scholars to postulate a hypothesis that Ramagupta, his elder son, succeeded Samudragupta. On the basis of the available epigraphic and literary evidence, it is suggested that immediately after the death of Samudragupta, Gupta state was attacked by Sakas and that the Guptas had to face political humiliation and agree to handover Dhruvadevi, who is known from the Gupta epigraphs as the wife Chandragupta II, as demanded by the Sakas. But literary evidence indicates that Dhruvadevi was the wife of Ramagupta, who was supposed to have succeeded Samudragupta. The story in the literary evidence is as follows: Chandragupta, the brother, of the king disgusted at the meek surrender of his brother, went in the disguise of Dhruvadevi to the Saka king and killed him. His elder brother did not like this action of Chandragupta and hence Chandragupta killed his brother and married Dhruvadevi. Scholars of the stature of H.C. Raychaudhari rejected the above literary and numismatic evidence as untrustworthy and belonging to a later date. For some scholars, Chandragupta II, was chosen by Samudragupta as a worthy successor to him. At this juncture, we can only say that Chandragupta became heir to the Gupta throne at a time when their political fortunes and state power were at stake due to the rise of their enemies and this is supported by the fact that Chandragupta II had to wage wars again to re-establish the Gupta hegemony. Chandragupta II like his grandfather Chandragupta I entered into matrimonial alliances with Nagas by marrying Kuberanaga and their offspring Prabhavati Gupta was given in marriage to Rudrasena II of the Vakataka family. Chandragupta's policy of matrimonial alliances must have strengthened his position as the Nagas and the Vakatakas were powerful ruling lineages in North India and the Deccan and by making them his allies, he could wage war against the Sakas of Gujarat and Kathiawar.

The details of the conquests and campaigns of Chandragupta II are not known as any record like the Allahabad pillar, Prasasti of Samudragupta has become known. However, the Udayagiri hill epigraph of Virasena, his minister for peace and war, the epigraph of Sanakanika Maharaja near Bhilsa and the Sanchi epigraph of Amrakardeva, a military commander, testify to his camping at Malwa with his retinue to attack the Saka territories. In this conquest, Chandragupta defeated and killed the last Saka king Rudrasimha III. His total success against the Sakas is proved by the absence of Saka coins minted after this period, and the positive evidence of Chandragupta minting Saka type of silver coins and the legend of Sakari Vikramaditya, i.e., Vikramaditya who was an enemy of the Sakas. The victory against the Saka and the annexation of Gujarat-Kathiawar region was a very significant event, as he not only ousted foreign rule but also obtained access to the Arabian Sea and important ports and trading centres on the western coast. By this conquest, Chandragupta II improved the resource base of the Gupta kingdom, as he secured an advantage in the field of internal and external trade with the western world.

Chandragupta is also said to have extended his empire in the east by his conquest of Vanga or eastern Bengal. The Mehrauli pillar inscription, of one Chandra who is identified as Chandragupta II, proves this. There is a controversy regarding the identification of Chandra of the Mehrauli epigraph. Various scholars have identified this Chandra of Mehrauli with Chandragupta Maurya, Chandragupta I and Chandragupta II. However, the most persuasive identification is with Chandragupta II. We are already aware that his father Samudragupta had conquered Vanga or eastern Bengal and made it a tributary state, so the reason for his invasion appears to be a rebellion at Vanga or the desire of Chandragupta II to bring eastern Bengal under his direct rule. Whatever the reason, that Vanga was brought under the direct control of the Guptas is proved by the rule of the Guptas in the early years of the 6th century AD.

Chandragupta is also believed to have crossed the Sindh region and defeated Vahika, which is identified with Bactria, based on the exploits mentioned in the Mehrauli iron pillar inscription. The Kushan type of coins bearing Chandra's name further proves this fact. It is now established, based on available epigraphic, numismatic and literary evidence that Chandragupta II extended the frontiers of the Gupta Empire to western, north-western and eastern India.

Chandragupta is compared to the illustrious legendary ruler Vikramaditya of Ujjain and to the hero of Raghuvamsa of Kalidasa. Undoubtedly, Chandragupta II occupies a place of eminence among the Gupta rulers and among the great rulers produced in early historic period. Chandragupta II is unquestionably a worthy son, who was a conqueror of reputation and a patron of letters. It is also said that Chandragupta II patronized the Navaratnas, one of whom is the great poet and dramatist Kalidasa. Another important event of this era is the visit of Fahien, the Chinese Buddhist pilgrim, who stayed in his court for a period of nearly six years. Curiously, Fahein is silent about the name of the ruler who patronized him, though he gives a vivid account of the social and administrative aspects of his patron's reign. Chandragupta II ruled from 380 to AD 415–416.

Kumaragupta, the son of Chandragupta II, succeeded his father and ruled for forty years from AD 415 to AD 455. Nothing eventful occurred in his reign to be remembered by posterity, except keeping intact the vast empire bequeathed by his father. The cracks began to appear in the solid foundations of the state power of the Guptas in the form of the attack of Pushyamitras, a barbaric hoard from Mekala in the Narmada valley along with the foreigners, the Hunas. The Bilsad epigraph portrays his reign as one of ever-extending victory and says that he performed Asvamedha sacrifice and issued coins commemorating that event. However, we are not certain of his victories. He also proudly styles himself as Mahendraditya. He is said to have founded the Nalanda University and patronized Kalidasa. It is also learnt from one of the epigraphs that a group of silk weavers migrated to his territory and prospered there. His son Skandagupta is said to have played a crucial role in quelling the attacks of the Pushyamitras and the Hunas. The important epigraphs that refer to Kumaragupta are the Bilsad inscription, the Damodarpur copper plate inscriptions of AD 433 and AD 477, a stone inscription from Mandasor and the Karamdand epigraphs dated AD 436. While the Karamdand epigraph mentions that his fame spread to the four oceans, a stone inscription from Mandasor mentions Kumaragupta as reigning over the whole earth. The Damodarpur inscription refers to his title Maharajadhiraja. He appears to have maintained cordial relations with the Vakatakas with whom he had matrimonial relations.

Skandagupta succeeded his father Kumaragupta and ruled for a period of twelve years from AD 455 to AD 467. He was perhaps the last powerful Gupta emperor. His reign witnessed the attacks of the Hunas and AD 467 appears to be the last known date of his reign. Romila Thapar correctly observes, "Skandagupta battled valiantly, but he faced domestic problem as well, such as the breaking away of his feudatories, and there are indications of an economic crisis which would explain the debasing of the coinage". It is to be noted that in comparison to the gold coins of the earlier rulers, the gold coins minted by Skandagupta are fewer in number. It is also an established fact that though his gold coins are heavier in weight, the gold content in them is less than that of the earlier coins. In spite of the economic crisis faced by the kingdom and constant attacks of the Hunas, his Junagadh epigraph informs us that he undertook public works during his reign. We have come to know from the said epigraph, that when the Sudarsana Lake was damaged due to heavy rains, his governor Purnadatta got it repaired. Some scholars hold the view that the Gupta territory was partitioned between him and his half-brother Purugupta. Skandagupta assumed the title of Vikramaditya and 'Kramaditya'. After his death, the central authority of the Guptas appears to have declined fast. The succession of the various kings that followed him is uncertain. A number of administrative seals have been discovered with the names of the same kings, but following a varied order of succession, which points to a confused end to the dynasty. Epigraphs record that after Skandagupta, Budhagupta, Vainyagupta, Bhanugupta, Narasimhagupta, Baladitya, Kumaragupta II and Vishnugupta succeeded as rulers. Though we come across so many names, it is not very clear in what order these kings ruled the Gupta territories. Though epigraphs inform us that the Guptas ruled until AD 550, gradual disintegration of the empire started from the end of Skandagupta's rule. It is believed that the Guptas lost Kathiawar and portions of Malwa by AD 477. The repeated Huna invasions under Toramana and Mihirakula from AD 500 further weakened their rule. This gave scope for the subordinate kings of the Valabhi to rise in revolt and the rise of Yasodharman of Malwa and finally the Maukharis eclipsed the main Gupta line, which lingered on in eastern India for some more time.

Causes for the Disintegration of the Gupta State Power

The Guptas began to rule independently from AD 319–320. Though they ruled until AD 550, the effective period of their rule is not more than a hundred and fifty years, i.e., till the end of Skandagupta. After that, they figure oftly as rulers only in name, but without any effective power structure to back them. Generally, the reasons for the disintegration of any power structure are explained, as a combination of external factors with internal weaknesses.

1. It is generally agreed upon by almost all historians that the Huna invasions were the main or at least one of the principal causes for the decline of the Gupta power. It is no exaggeration to state that the Huna attacks dealt a severe blow to the Gupta authority particularly in northern and western regions. Further, the internal attacks of the Pushyamitras, who are identified with the Patumitras and Durmitras of the Puranas, also caused notable destabilization to the state power of the Guptas.
2. Another cause for the disintegration was the succession of weak rulers after Skandagupta.
3. Yet another factor behind the disintegration of the Gupta state power was the administrative weakness. Guptas made no efforts to impose an effective control over their regions. Their control was effective as long as powerful rulers occupied the Gupta throne and exercised their authority effectively. However, crisis of succession or weak monarchs led local chiefs to declare independence. This naturally resulted in constant military preparedness that led to the crippling of the financial resources of the Gupta Empire. Though Skandagupta thwarted the early attacks of the Hunas, the struggle disrupted the international trade of north-western India and eroded one of the most important financial bases of the Guptas.
4. By the end of the 5th century AD and beginning of the 6th century AD, taking advantage of the chaotic condition of the Gupta Empire, many regional powers asserted themselves by declaring independence. Further, for some historians, another cause for the disintegration of the Gupta Empire was the beginning of feudalization of the polity, economy and society. They argue that this process of fuedalization with the issue of land grants first to religious and later to secular beneficiaries, resulted in loss of revenue and diminished administrative control over the kingdom. Further, the growing importance of Samantas weakened the central authority.
5. Another cause for the decline and disintegration of the Guptas is said to be their tilt towards the asceticism of Buddhism during the reign of Kumaragupta and Buddhagupta. It is suggested that the founding of Nalanda University by Kumaragupta and of Buddhist learning and the patronage extended by Buddhagupta are index of their tilt towards

Buddhism that advocates non-violence. It is true that they patronized Buddhist educational institutions but this does not mean that they renounced violence even for protection of their territories from external and internal disorders, nor is there any conclusive evidence to prove that they disowned their royal duties and spent their lives as ascetics, embracing Buddhist philosophy.

All the above causes were either directly or indirectly responsible for the decay and disintegration of the Gupta power structure.

Polity

The main sources for understanding the polity of the Guptas are literary and archaeological. Among the literary sources, mention must be made of Kamandaka's *Neetisara* and *Manusmriti,* or *Manu Dharmasastra,* the codified Vedic and Puranic literature along with the contemporary literary pieces and foreign accounts. Among archaeological sources, mention must be made of royal Prasastis like the Allahabad or Prayaga Prasasti of Samudra Gupta and many other epigraphs, and the coins and clay seals issued by the Gupta rulers, in particular the Aswamedha type of coins with titles of the kings on them. The above-mentioned sources give an idea of the nature and dynamics of the Gupta polity. Generally, the rule of the Guptas in northern India is characterized as imperial government. However, this is not very correct, as centralized control of the Gupta polity does not appear to be a fact. N.N. Bhattacharya observes, "The Allahabad Pillar inscription refers to Samudragupta quite in accordance with Manu's concept of Kingship as a God dwelling on earth and that the Gupta kings, like their predecessors, the Kushanas and the Mauryas, tried to put this idea into practice, but it was possible only on a limited scale, in areas which lay within a manageable distance from the capital. The rest of the empire and the occupied territories were put in charge of the local rulers, mostly by erstwhile masters of the land, acting almost independently as feudatories or vassals who paid only a token submission to the imperial authority".

Central Administration and the King

The king was the central figure in the administration. They assumed titles like Maharajadhiraja, Samrat, Ekadhiraja, Chakravarthi, Paramabhattaraka, Paramadaivata and Parameswara. The Allahabad Prasasti of Samudragupta eulogizes the king as "equal to the Gods; Dhanada (Kubera), Varuna (Rain God), Indra and Antaka (Yama), who had no antagonist of equal power in the world". In Bhitari pillar inscription, Skandagupta is glorified as a person who "subdued the earth and became merciful to the conquered people, but he became neither proud nor arrogant though his glory was increasing day by day". Kumaragupta is said to have followed the true path of religion. From the above statements we come to know that the kings in spite of being called gods living on earth, had to follow a righteous path by putting into practice the following duties: (1) to decide the policy of the state during war or peace, (2) to lead the army in times of war, (3) to protect the subjects against foreign invasion and internal disturbances, (4) to support religious and pious people, (5) to venerate learned people, (6) to act as supreme judge and decide cases on the basis of religious precepts and existing customs, (7) to appoint central and provincial officers, and (8) to nominate or appoint a successor to the king as recorded in the Allahabad Prasasti and the Apratihata type coins of Kumaragupta. One more feature is the continuation of an office by various kings in their regions once they accepted the sovereignty of the Guptas and non-interference of the emperor in the administration of such regions.

A council of ministers and other officials who were appointed by him assisted the king. Though the Gupta epigraphs refer to ministers, they do not clearly mention the functions and the hierarchy of the ministers. The king used to take counsel of his ministers and issue written orders to officials on all important matters. The exact strength of the Mantrimandali or Mantriparishad is not known. Besides the Mantries or ministers, the Gupta epigraphs refer to Mahabaladhikrita or Commander-in-Chief, Mahadandanayaka or the Chief Executive General and Mahapratihara or the Chief of the palace guards. For the first time in the Gupta epigraphs, reference to a high imperial officer Sandhivigrahika or Minister for peace and war looking after external affairs is made. Officials like Kumaramatyas and Ayuktakas acted as a link between the centre and provincial administration. Perhaps, the Guptas appointed their princes as agents of central administration and such were called 'Kumaramatyas'. The suggested criterion for ministers and high officials was that only individuals with character, wisdom, and dedication to service of state were selected. However, there is evidence to prove that in many instances these offices were hereditary in nature. It is suggested that there existed besides Mantri Mandali, a war council or a Sabha with certain powers. The exact nature and scope of the war council or Sabha are not known. The royal household appears to have used the services of a number of officers such as Mahapratihara or the chief usher of the palace, Vinayasura, who conducted visitors to the king, and Khadyatapallika or superintendent of the royal kitchen. The Guptas do not appear to have divided the jobs into civil and military, because sometimes Kumaramatyas also acted as Mahadandanayakas.

Provincial Administration

The Gupta Empire was divided for the sake of administrative convenience into Tira Bhukti, etc. Pundravardhana Bhukti is identified as North Bengal and Tira Bhukti is identified as North Bihar. The king directly appointed the Uparika, who was the ruler of a Bhukti. Some scholars hold the view that viceroys, who were invariably princes, ruled the provinces or Bhuktis. It is also suggested that these Kumaramatyas acted as a link between the centre and the provinces. The 'bhuktis' or 'desas' and 'rashtras' were further divided into districts, called Vishayas. Vishayapatis ruled these Vishayas in some cases and Ayukthakas in other cases. Gupta epigraphs from Bengal suggest the head of desas, rashtras and bhuktis. The epigraphs refer to Rundravardhana Bhukti and of the district or Adhikarana are associated with a number of representatives of the major community of the locality, like the Nagara Sresti head of the city merchants, Sardhavaha caravan leader, Pradhama Kulika head of the artisan community, and Pradhama Kayastha head of the Kayasthas. There were officers known as Pustapalas whose duty was to manage and maintain records. It is also suggested that there existed units of group of villages between the Vishaya and the lowest unit, Grama. Sometimes a group of villages was called Pithaka or Samtaka. We do not know whether there was a separate body administering the cities but somehow a view prevails that a body comprising Nagarasresti, Sardhavaha, Pradhama Kulika, Pradhama Kayastha and Pustapala administered the city. We are not certain whether the city had a separate set-up or was a part of the Vishaya. The village was the lowest unit of the administrative structure. The headman of the village was known as Gramapati or Gramadyaksha. It appears that the Gramavriddhas or village elders decided disputes in the villages. There are references to Asthakuladhikarana, Gramikas, Kutumbins and Mahattaras though it is not certain whether these terms, refer to designations or units of administration. N.N. Bhattacharya is of the opinion that the mahattaras are the village elders. He suggests that a property owner's area is known as Bhoga. The Deo-Baranak epigraph of the later Guptas refers to the following administrative divisions: Bhukti, Mandala, Vishaya, Grama and Agrahara. Thus, we find different units of administration under the Guptas about which much cannot be said at this juncture. During the time of the Guptas, a number of vassals or feudatories exercised independent control in their domains while recognizing the sovereignty of the Guptas. At least three categories of feudatories may be identified: (i) feudatory lines existing before the rise of the suzerain power but reduced to vassalage; (ii) feudatory lines established by junior branches of the imperial dynasty; and (iii) feudatories through imperial creation. During the Gupta period, the first category of feudatories were very common. The fact that Gupta control on feudatories was not strong can be substantiated by the following instances. The Vallabhi princes issued coins mentioning the names of the Gupta kings but with their own symbol of trident instead of the peacock symbol of the Guptas, likewise the Parivrajaka Maharaja land grants refer to the Gupta era without recording the names of the Gupta rulers. There are instances that reveal that the Gupta polity was not centralized, but layered. The Gupta polity became layered because of the strategy adopted by the rulers. How and why the Gupta polity became layered will be discussed at a later stage.

Military

The invasions and conquests of the Guptas, the appearance of the designation of Sandhivigrhika for the first time as also of the official title of Mahabaladhikrita mentioned in the epigraphs presupposes that the Guptas maintained a standing army. But, there is no evidence as to the strength of this army The reference to officers like Pilupati or the head of elephants, Asvapati or the head of horses and

Narapati or the head of foot-soldiers, establishes that the army consisted of these divisions and it may be suggested that they were under the control of Mahabaladhikrita. We also come across a reference to another officer by name Ranabhandagarika, identified as the officer-in-charge of stores, who maintained and supervised the offensive and defensive armament of the army. In times of war, the king himself personally led the armies. They used battle-axes, bows and arrows, spear spikes, swords, lances and javelins in the battlefield. It is not known whether the army was structured in gradation form or not. It is believed that the army was paid in cash but it is doubtful, as the resource base of the Guptas does not appear to be very large, sound enough to meet the demand of a large standing army.

Revenue

The Gupta state was based on land revenue and other taxes collected from traders and others. An officer, Gopaswamin worked as Akshapatabaladhikrita in the time of Samudragupta. The duty of this officer appears to be to maintain detailed account registers, and keep a close watch over the financial transactions. An officer by designation Pustapala is identified as record keeper of all the transactions. As land revenue was the major source of income, they maintained a regular department for the proper survey and measurements of lands as well as proper collection of the land tax. From Kalidasa's works and Kamandaka's *Neetisara* that the state collected one-sixth of the produce as the land tax. Besides this tax, the state levied a tax called Uparikara on cloth and oil at different points of sale. The state collected Sulka for permitting the traders to carry on their trade and in case of defaulters; the state collected a fine eight times of the original Sulka. The king as a right enforced Vishti or forced labour, Bali and other contributions. The income from the royal lands was treated as the personal income of the king. Besides these, the king controlled treasure troves, jewels and valuable articles accidentally found while digging the earth and on mines and manufacture of salt. A view prevails that the state did not get substantial income from trade and commerce as long-distance trade declined, leading to an urban decay during this period.

Another important aspect that deserves our consideration and bears on the economy and polity was the issue of land grants to Brahmins and secular beneficiaries for their services to the state. This practice of making land grants with the right to collect one-third or one-half of the produce from the cultivator with immunities from what led to reduced state control over them and loss of the income to the state. Slowly the king lost control and right over large tracts of land. This practice created a class of landed intermediaries who became a dominant economic group, and the officers and vassals became stronger in course of time and began to threaten the stability and security of the empire. The vassals developed audacity and proclaimed themselves Nripa, Narapati and Kshitipa as can be seen in Raghuvamsa and epigraphs of the period.

One of the consequences of this feature was the slow and gradual fragmentation of political power between the centre and peripheral areas ruled by the vassals, and the rise of a political hierarchy of Samanta, Mahasamanta, Mandalesvara and Mahamandaleswara and eventually to the feudalization of state power. This made B.D. Chattopadhyaya observe, "Corrosion of centralisation acquired a faster pace in the Gupta period" and R.S. Sharma to call the Gupta phase "Proto-feudal Polity". A.L. Basham's observation "they (the Guptas) failed to establish an adequate administrative setup" appears to be right. Though the Gupta phase is designated as imperial, a critical examination of the polity of the Guptas makes it clear that the Guptas followed a policy of status quo and short-term gains instead of a vision of a pan-Indian empire, though they had the resources and ability to achieve that objective. Raghavendra Vajpai comments that by their short-sighted policy they paved the way for the pan-Indian manifestation of feudalism in the so-called 'golden age of early Indian history'.

Economy

Agriculture was the main occupation of the people and the state received the maximum income from the agricultural operations. There existed many social groups engaged in different crafts, commerce and trade. However, trade and commerce appear to be limited to internal consumption alone during this period. Consequently, we find increasing ruralization of economy and the practice of making land grants to religious and secular beneficiaries for their services. Though a large number of gold, silver and copper coins of the Guptas were available, there is no clear evidence that salaries were paid in cash. It is suggested that the changes in the pattern of economic production brought about changes in relations between social groups also.

The Gupta epigraphs refer to various types of land, depending on use and utility. Land under cultivation is generally known as Kshetra and lands not under cultivation or kept fallow are called Khila or Aprahata. A study of the epigraphs further reveals that more and more Khila land became Kshetra in course of time. The Guptas classified land according to soil, fertility and the use to which it was put. Land was measured but the method of measurement differed from place to place. While in some areas, the land was measured as Nivartanas, in Bengal it was known as Kulyavapa and Dronavapa. The Gupta cultivators knew and grew crops like barley, wheat, paddy, all varieties of pulses, grains, vegetables, and cash crops like sugarcane and cotton. As agriculture was the main occupation of the majority of people and the major source of income to the state, the state took care of promoting irrigation facilities. For example, when Sudarsan lake was severely damaged during the time of Skandagupta, Parnadatta, the Governor of Saurashtra and Chakrapalita, ensured that water drawn from wells was supplied through channels. Probably, the type of mechanism known as Araghatta was also in vogue. But, mostly, rainwater collected in the ponds was used for irrigation. Overall, compared to the Mauryan period, government intervention in provision of irrigation facilities appears to be minimal in the Gupta age. By the time of the Guptas, the land or Kshetra appears to have become a commodity that could be sold and purchased. There is sufficient evidence to prove that land was purchased by individuals from the government and granted in turn to Brahmins, Buddhists, or Jainas and to secular beneficiaries like small rulers. With the growth of ruling families of small localities, the land that was granted to them also increased. Therefore, a new class of landowners who did not cultivate land came into existence. Further, society began to recognize and praise those who gifted land as noble and pious persons, indicating change in the attitude of society. This new class of landowners was ascribed to a superior Varna. Probably, the Gramikas, Kutumbins and Mahattaras often mentioned in epigraphs are of this category. Compared to the new class of landed gentry, the condition of the ordinary cultivators known by names such as Krishivala, Karshaka or Kinass appears to be lowly; through they did not occupy a low position as postulated by some historians. There were both male and female slaves. The Kamasutra of Vatsyayana described graphically how their masters put the female slaves to a lot of hardship. With the growth of non-cultivating owners of land, the burden of taxation fell largely on the shoulders of the actual tillers of the soil. The number of taxes imposed and collected grew in number. Added to these, the imposition of Vishti or forced or unpaid labour made the condition of marginal tillers of the soil very depressing.

Crafts

Production of domestic and luxury items was very much in vogue during this period. The artisans made items like earthen pots, baskets, metal tools and furniture for daily use along with luxury items of jewellery made of gold, silver and precious stones, ivory objects, fine cotton cloth and silks. While some were manufactured locally, some were available imported through trade. Though literature graphically describes various items, these are not found in the archaeological excavations. Contemporary Sanskrit texts like *Amarakosa* and *Brihatsamhita* mention different categories of artisans manufacturing different items. Archaeological reports of excavations at Taxila, Ahichchatra, Mathura, Rayaghar, Kausambi and Pataliputra in the Gangetic valley record a variety of objects like earthenware, terracotta objects, beads made of different stones, objects of glass and items made of metals. The Gupta period also witnessed considerable increase of trade. This can be deduced from a number of metal coins issued by them in gold, silver and copper that must have been used for commercial exchange. Based on the representation given to the Nagarasresti and the Sarthavaha in the administration of the city scholars suggest that merchants ranked in society. Both artisans and merchants had their organizations to carry on their activities, and to take care of the interests of their members. These organizations are called 'srenis' or guilds. In this age, the status and position of artisans was not uniform, because Dharmasastras that were codified during this period assigned different ranks to different groups of artisans; they were given a status lower than three castes of the varna model and each craftsman group formed into a Jati or caste. The guilds maintained their own armies for their safety and issued their own seals to protect their merchandise. Interestingly, numerous seals belonging to a joint guild of bankers, traders and transport merchants having branches in different parts of northern India are found at Vaisali, the modern Basarh.

Textile and metal industries appear to have flourished in this age. Though there was a great demand for textiles in domestic market, there was decline in silk cloth industry due to the absence of long distance trade outside India. This made members of silk weaving guild of western India give up the manufacture of silk and take to other occupations. One of these is iron making, the best example of which is the Mehrauli pillar. This pillar of Chandra is regarded as a marvel of metallurgical skill. The iron pillar is 7 metres tall and weighs over 6,000 kgs. Its specialty is that it has not rusted or corroded, though kept in an open space through all these centuries. A.L. Basham writes that the metallurgical skill of ancient India is further attested by the fact that this pillar, though it has weathered the torrential rains for over 1,500 monsoons, shows no signs of rusting. This is not because the Indians had discovered some form of stainless steel alloy, for the column is of iron almost chemically pure. Several suggestions have been put forward to account for the remarkable durability of the iron pillar but no fully satisfactory explanation has been given. The theory, confidently proposed in the scientific journal (J.C. Hudson, *Nature,* 12. IX, 53, p. 499) that the dry atmosphere of Delhi is sufficient causer is quite inadequate since Delhi is very humid during the rainy season, when ordinary iron quickly rusts. Since the process of oxidization demands a catalyst, it may be the great purity of the metal that has preserved the iron pillar so long, as another memorial to India's technical skill. Iron of superior quality was manufactured and exported. Besides iron industry, the manufacture of gold and silver ornaments also reached a high peak. Cutting and polishing of precious stones, ivory crafts, sculpture, pottery and pearl industries also flourished, increasing aridity and a deadline in the quality of life of the people. Fahien might have found the conditions in Gupta India better than what he had seen elsewhere. Fahien, the Chinese Buddhist who spent years in the Gupta court pays glowing tribute to the economic prosperity of the Gupta age. "(Magadha) has the largest cities and towns. Its people are rich and thriving and emulate one another in practising charity of heart and duty to one's neighbour. The elders and gentry of this country have instituted in their capital free hospitals and hither came all poor and helpless patients, orphans, widows and cripples. They are all well taken care of, a doctor attended on them, and food and medicines supplied according to their needs. They are all more comfortable and when they are cured they go away". This statement of Fahien appears to be an exaggeration to some historians. M.K. Dhavalikar suggests that historical archaeology proves that the number of historical sites relating to the Gupta and the post-Gupta periods declined to more than half, i.e., from 353 sites to 118 and this indicates that occupation of the sites of the Gupta period betrays deterioration in the quality of life.

Society

The general perception prevalent among scholars is that Indian society remained static throughout the ages without any perceptible changes in the nature and functions of social order. However, this is not very correct as change and continuity cannot be seen in the practices of the society. Though, the Chaturvarna system is considered the basis of the Gupta society, we notice deviations and departure in actual observance of Smriti law. During the Gupta age the relationship between caste and occupation was observed; there was no rigid rule of following the occupations prescribed by the Chaturvarna system. By this time, the Dharmasastras accepted intermarriage or Varnasankara, and many foreign families of Scythian origin of the pre-Gupta period were accorded the semi-Kshatriya or Vratyakshatriya status and tribals who were absorbed into the Sanatana Dharma society were given fictitious origins. The Dharmasastras also sanction Apaddharma or conduct to be followed during emergencies. As a result, we find Brahmans and Kshatriyas adopting occupations not allowed by the Dharmasastras. Another feature is that the Sudras and Vaisyas tried to imitate the upper castes. Society was in a flux, accommodating the interests of the new social groups, though Brahmins continued to wield considerable influence because of their skill and proficiency in learning. The practice of issuing land grants to Brahmins itself was a deviation from the Dharmasastra injunction, which practice made them become in course of time landholders of significance, though tilling was the occupation of the Sudras. It is to be noted that only the highly learned among the Brahmins could become landholders; it may be recognition of their scholarship, and the term Dwija began to be used increasingly. Brahmin offenders and criminals were not let off altogether and were often expelled from the state. A.L. Basham writes, "Even in the Gupta Period, however, the regulations were by no means rigid. Hypergamous inter-marriage was recognised and the rule of craft exclusiveness was often ignored, or circumvented by the convenient escape clauses of Apadharma, and in the earlier law books, the Brahmin was permitted to accept food from any Aryan".

The Gupta period witnessed a rise in the status of the Sudras because the Dharmasastras made a distinction between the slaves and the Sudras, or they themselves belonged to Dharanagotra, a gotra of the agricultural community. Romila Thapar attributes this feature to the failure on the part of the Guptas to introduce a centralized administrative structure in turn reduced the pressure on the Sudras. However, that the position of outcastes remained as before is testified by the statements of Fahien. Though there was acculturation process throughout the course of Indian history, some of the aboriginal tribes remained outside the pale Sanatana Dharma. Not only did slavery continue during this period, but also more rules were framed regarding slavery. It was declared by Dharmasastras that a Brahmin could never be a slave and purchase and sale of a Brahmin woman was declared void. It is further stated, that if a Brahman woman marries a slave, she would become a slave but a slave woman giving birth to a child to her master is made a free woman.

Though Dharmasastras prescribe marriages between the same castes, inter-Varna marriages were accepted as a norm. The joint family system was in vogue and property was divided between the father and the sons equally. The position of woman continued to be one of subordination to man. Limited educational facilities were provided to upper caste women and their right to property was recognized, and marriage of young girls was in vogue. Arranged marriage by the parents was the norm but Gandharva type of marriages were known. The position of widows was highly deplorable, as they had to lead a strict life of celibacy. Brihaspati, as an alternative to widowhood, recommended the custom of Sati. This practice was commended as well as criticized during the Gupta period. An Eran inscription of 6th century AD contains a reference to Sati. Marriage of widows, though disfavoured, was not completely forbidden. Even if a widow remarried, she did not enjoy social status. According to Dharma Sastras, the function of a woman was only to be an ideal wife and ideal mother. Interestingly, the Dharmasastras accord the status of Sudra to a woman.

Another aspect of social life that deserves mention is the difference between the urban rich and rural poor social life. The city dweller or Nagarika led a life of luxury and affluence. Vatsayana's Kamasutra and other literary texts give a graphic description of the affluent class of Nagarikas. The poor of the city as well as of the village lived at subsistence level. A normal feature of city life was the presence of the courtesans. As a social group, they enjoyed considerable esteem and freedom. Some of them are well known for their accomplishment and beauty. The institution of Devadasi, or girls dedicated to God is known from records. Some women took to prostitution as livelihood. Thus, there is considerable disparity in the standard of living of Nagarika and of the rural poor villages. While the royalty lived in magnificent buildings and the affluent in cities in comparative luxury, the poor lived in bamboo houses. Amarakosa gives a list of different kinds of ornaments worn by royalty and the rich. While the affluent used silver and gold, the poor had to be satisfied with iron, copper and pottery utensils. Terracotta figures available show us the ornaments and dresses of the Gupta times worn by the rich and the affluent. It appears that they gave due importance to cleanliness. Fahien's statement that killing animals, drinking wine, eating onions and garlic were unknown throughout Madhyadesa appears to be incorrect as wine drinking among the rich class was an established fact. The ordinary and rich alike had faith in omens, portents and the like.

Literature and Fine Arts

Sanskrit as the language of the elite, and Prakrit as the language of common man were in vogue during the Gupta period. It is believed that Sanskrit language entered its classical phase in this age, considered the golden age of Sanskrit literature. Royal patronage on a large scale was responsible for the wonderful Sanskrit dramas and Kavyas produced in this age. The greatest Sanskrit poets and dramatists, Kalidasa, is said to have adorned the court of Chandragupta II, as one of the Navaratnas. His classical epics Raghuvamsa and Kumara Sambhava, dramas like the Sakuntalam and Malavikgnimitram and lyrics like Meghasandesa and Ritusamhara are testimony to his literary excellence, as a dramatist and poet. Sudraka's *Mrichchakatika* or the little clay cart, Visakhadatta's *Mudrarakshasa* and *Devichandraguptam*. Bharavi's *Kirataarjuniyam*, Subhandu's *Vasavadatta* and Vishnusarma's *Panchatantra* are the other great literary products of this age. Dandin's *Kavyadarsa* and *Dasakumaracharitra* are also of the same age. Dharmasastras supposed to be written by Narada and Brihaspati belong to this period. All the eighteen Puranas and Upapuranas were codified during this period. Philosophical works like Sabara's, *Bhasya* or the *Mimamsa* of Jaimini, Isvarakrishna's *Sankhya Karika* and Patanjali's *Vyasa Bhasthya*, *Nyaya Bhasya* of Vatsyanyana, *Yoga Bashya* of Vyasa are said to be products of this age. In the field of science, it was really a remarkable age where we find Aryabhata's *Aryabhatia*, Varahamihira's *Brihatsamhita*, *Panchasidhantika*, and Vagbhatta's *Astangasangraha*. There is also the classic on erotics, *Kamasutra* written by Vatsyayana. Thus, this age produced works of immortal value in all branches of learning in Sanskrit.

While Sanskrit was patronized by royalty, the commoners promoted and patronized Prakrit literature. Jains and the Buddhists did yeomen service to Prakrit and Pali languages. While the elitist class spoke Sanskrit, the Sudras and women spoke Prakrit in the Sanskrit dramas. The Buddhist writers Buddhghosa, Asanga, Vasubandhu and Dignaga are the great writers on Mahayana Buddhism. Budhaghosa's *Visudhamagga*, Asanga's *Yogacharabhumisastra* and *Mahayana Samparigraha*, Vasubandhu's *Abhidhammakosa* and Dignaga's *Pramanasamuchchaya* are the most renowned works in the Sanskrit. It is believed that Dignaga also wrote a Sanskrit drama Kundamala. The Jaina scholars, Umasvati and Siddhasena also wrote on philosophy. The Allahabad pillar Prasasti and Mehrauli pillar inscription are two examples of the Sanskrit inscriptions of that age.

Art

Some historians are of the opinion that political unification, the newly emerged national spirit and economic prosperity led to a creative cultural movement under the Guptas. Consequently, it is said that art which was imitative until then became creative and artists abandoned copying of foreign forms. We are all aware that Hellenistic style and Mahayana Buddhism influenced the post-Mauryan and pre-Gupta art. However, in this age, art and architecture were influenced by Puranic dharma. It is said by many scholars that this age reflected unprecedented artistic activity all over India. Art critics acclaim that various forms of art attained maturity, balance and naturalness of expression that is still to be surpassed. R.D. Banerji observes, "Gupta art is really a renaissance due to the transformation of the ideals of the people. This was based on an assimilation of what was old and an elimination of what was exotic and foreign and finally a systematic production of something new and essentially Indian". Let us take a specific view of each of the braches of art.

Architecture

In the history of architectural evolution of India, the Gupta age represents a definite dividing line, and the beginning of a new era. This Gupta age laid the foundations of a typical style of Indian architecture. Romila Thapar observes, "This was the age which saw attempts at building small stone temples to the Hindu deities, temples which within half a millennium were to become the dominant focuses of society in many parts of the subcontinent. Together with the temples came the carving of images and popular legends in stone". A.L. Basham also rightly observes, "There are no remains of free standing Hindu temples erected before the Gupta period, because by this time they must long have been built in perishable wood, clay and brick. From the Gupta period, however, several examples survive, chiefly in Western India all showing the same general pattern. Pillars were usually ornate, with heavy bell shaped capitals surmounted by animal motifs, and the entrances were often carved with mythological scenes and figures. All the Gupta temples were small, and most had flat roofs. Their masonry was held together without mortar, and was far larger and thicker than was necessary for the comparatively small buildings. Evidently the builders had not yet fully mastered their technique, and were still thinking in terms of cave". The finest Gupta temple, at Deogarh near Jhansi, probably of the 5th century AD, marks a great advance. "Here iron dowels were used to hold the masonry together, and a small tower arose above the sanctum. The portal veranda was continued all around the building, making a covered walk". Art critics divide the Gupta temples into three groups. The first group of temples of Sanchi, Tigwa and Eran are flat-roofed square temples in this group; we first come across the Garbhagriha, a cubical cellar with a single entrance and a Mandapa or porch. The Vishnu temple at Tigwa is the most typical example of this type. The pillars of this temple consist of "a massive abacus surrounded by a device of lions, a capital resembling a vase (Kalasa) or inverted lotus; a short shaft of many sides and a plain square or pedestal". Purnakalasa or the vessal indicative of plenty is an important feature of the Gupta capital. At this stage or in the first group, we find a link with the pre-Guptan art features. For example, it is suggested, that the design of the pillar looks like the Garudadhwaja of Besnagar and the lions, like those of the Asokan capital. The new feature of Tigwa temple is the shape and ornamentions as well as the picture of Yamuna seated on tortoise on one side and Gariga seated on a crocodile on the other side distinguish from the pre-Gupta pictures. This became a prominent feature of the doors of the temples of the later Gupta age. The second group is represented by flat-roofed square sanctum-cellar inside a similar roofed cloister around the sanctum preceded by a porch, which are open and pillared with the projection of a flight of steps. The Parvati temple at Nachana Kothura and Siva temple at Bhumara are the best examples of the second group of temples. The Bhumara temple is well known for its ornamental sculptures, decorated gateways, fine arabesque medallions, Kirthimukhas, Ganas and ceiling decorated with carving of foliage and creepers. Its Sikhara or tower distinguishes the third group over the Garbhagudi, the sanctum sanctorum. Though the Sikharas are not available now, it is suggested that they represent a straight-edged pyramidical form. The most noted temples of the third group are Dasavatara temple at Deograph built of stone and the Bhitargan temple of brick. It is further said that there is also a rectangular temple with apsilate backs and barrel-vaulted roof above, examples of which temples are Durga temple and Kapotesvara temple at Aihole, another such is circular temple with, shallow projection at the four cardinal points, examples of which can be seen in the Maniyar Math. Romila Thapar explained the reason for the style of the temple as follows: "The free standing temple became necessary with the growth of image worship, since the image had to be appropriately housed and a cave was not adequate for this purpose. Gradually the image came to be surrounded by a host of attendant deities and figures, leading eventually to the rich sculptural ornamentation associated with later styles. Manuals of the construction of stone temple were written giving minute details of construction and these were faithfully followed."

The Guptas continued the excavation of rock-cut caves but introduced extensive ornamentation of the facade, and improved the design of the pillars in the interior. The most important of such caves are found at Ajanta, Ellora and Bagh. Most of these rock caves exhibit the Buddhist faith and rarely do we come across Brahmanical and Jaina images in these. In the Gupta period, stupas and monasteries were also built. Of the stupas of this period, the stupa at Mirpur Khan in Sindh, Dhamekh Stupa at Saranadh, and the Buddhist Stupa at Ratnagiri deserve mention. Excavations conducted at Sarnath and Nalanda have brought to light a number of Buddhist monasteries of the Gupta times. Interestingly, many of the Chaityas and Vihara caves of Ajanta were of the Gupta times but it is doubtful whether they enjoyed direct Gupta patronage. Of the 28 caves at Ajanta, 23 belong to the Gupta times. Of these 23, only two are Chaityas and the rest are Viharas. Caves No. 12, 17, and 19 that are very ornate and considered the best specimens of this period. There are 11 Viharas at Aurangabad. It appears that the Jaina art of this period is very meagre. Besides temples, Gupta art can be known from the Mehrauli iron pillar and Buddha Gupta's monolithic pillar at Eran. A lion abacus surmounts the shaft of the Eran pillar and it supports the images of God Vishnu. The Eran pillar is 13 metres in height, whereas Mehrauli iron pillar is 7 metres in height. Contemporary Gupta epigraphs and later evidence of Hieuen Tsang testified to the fact that many structures were built in this period, but curiously, we have not many survivals of this legacy. As an answer to this phenomenon, it is suggested that the Islamic invaders might have destroyed many structures. Romila Thapar observes, "unfortunately, not much has survived of the architectural achievements of the Guptas. It is often said that the iconoclasm of the Muslims five centuries later destroyed the temples of Northern India and this accounts for the lack of the Gupta remains. But it is probably nearer to the truth to say that the Gupta temples were unimpressive shrines which were either absorbed in domestic architecture or else were built over in later centuries". Whatever may be the reason for their absence now, the fact remains that they paved the way for the two distinct temple styles: the 'Nagara' and the 'Dravida', which dominated northern and southern Indian architecture of later times. One more feature to be observed is the survival of the remains of Buddhist structures even today.

Sculpture

The artists of the Gupta age left behind for posterity excellent sculptural representations. Human figurines sculpted by the artists of this period are notable for their poise, flowing rhythm and grace. Elegance of form was achieved through the use of transparent dresses and restrained use of ornamentation. Images of several Hindu gods and goddesses as well as images of the Buddha and Bodhisattva reflect natural grace, perception and spiritual aura. Art critics estimate that the Bhuvardha at the Udayagiri cave, Seshasayee Vishnu, Gajendra, Varadanda and Nara Narayana at Deogarh are the best specimens of Gupta age sculpture. Further, the Siva Parvati reliefs from Kosam and Ramayana panels of the Dasavatara temple at Deogarh are good instances of Gupta sculptural art. Likewise, the most outstanding specimens of Buddhist sculptural art are the seated Buddha at Saranath and the standing Buddha at Mathura in sand stone. Besides the stone sculptures, the artists made bronze and copper images of the Buddha. Of them, the most impressive are the ones found at Sultanganj, Nalanda and Sarnath. Besides the images installed and worshipped in Garbhagriha, the preparation of Utsavavigrahas played important role in festivals and rituals begun in the Gupta era. All these developments in architecture and sculpture took place because, in the words of Romila Thapar, "Hinduism had by this time evolved from the beliefs of the Vedic period into a human and sophisticated religion. Perhaps the most fundamental changes were the two features that arose partially out of the heterodox challenge to early Hinduism. The first of these was the tendency towards monotheism, which was stressed by the increasing worship of either of the two deities Vishnu and Siva. Then came the change in favour of personal devotion rather than sacrifice. Thus Hinduism revitalised itself and was able slowly to supplant the heterodox religions". This was strengthened by the codification of the Puranas and the emergence of Mahabharata and Ramayana. This change in the nature and functioning of Hinduism and Buddhism led to the making of images and a house to place them and a place to worship them, which ultimately led to the building of permanent stone structures.

Terracottas

Terracotta tablets, plaques and seals portraying the Buddhist pantheon, Ramayana panels, and design of flora and fauna have been discovered in Harvan in Kashmir, Kosam, Ahichchatra, Bikaner, Pawaya, Patna and several places in Maharashtra. We have every reason to believe that terracotta beads were used by ordinary people as ornaments. The Buddhist religious places were covered with a facade of terracotta plaques depicting stories about the Buddha and his times.

Coins

Gupta coins are known for their exquisite artistic taste. Though the early Gupta coins reflect the impact of Kushans and the Greeks in their manufacture, the later Gupta coins reflect the creative and artistic perfection of the Gupta artisans and their skill in metal workmanship. Gupta artisans made gold and silver coins with smooth and even wedges. The figures of Hindu deities like Kartikeya or Skanda, Vishnu and Lakshmi are portrayed perfectly on the coins. They also portrayed other motifs such as chakra, the bow and the arrow, the Asvamedha horse, peacock, Garuda and spear very skilfully and perfectly. The dress and every part of the human body are also clearly visible on the coins.

Painting

The wonderful frescoes at Bagh and Ajanta caves clearly reveal that the art of painting reached a high point during the Gupta period. The world-renowned Ajanta paintings are acclaimed by art critics throughout the world as being balanced in composition, and superb in execution. Gupta painters successfully depicted different Rasas like Karuna or compassion, and beauty in their paintings like the "Dark Princess", and "Bodhisattva Padmapani". The paintings also reveal the dress and ornaments, the flora and fauna and the customs and traditions of that period. Art historians like Stella Kramrisch and Ananda Coomaraswamy acclaim the paintings of this period as masterpieces.

Religion and Philosophy

The Gupta age was one of resurgence of modified Vedic Dharma. It incorporated Bhagavatism and the worship of the Puranic gods. It was in this age that the important aspects of Hinduism like the image worship, building of temples to worship the images, growth of the Bhakti cult in the form of worship of individual gods like Siva and Vishnu along with Sakti became predominant. The Gupta artists popularized Ekamukha and Chaturmukha Siva Lingas. Though most of the Gupta rulers were personally great devotees of Vishnu and proclaimed themselves Paramabhagavatas, they appear to be more pragmatic than dogmatic in their outlook. They never proclaimed Hinduism or in particular, Vaishnavism as their state religion but gave equal respect to other religions like Buddhism and Jainism. Their individual faith did not influence their royal patronage; they extended patronage equally to all religions though they were responsible for the codification of the Puranas, popularizing the Mahabharata and the Ramayana as sacred texts, putting Hindu deities like Vishnu, Siva, Lakshmi and Skanda on their coins and performed the revived Aswamedha sacrifice. Religions of Buddhism and Jainism also attracted the attention of royalty as well as commoners. The Buddhist Stupa at Saranath was rebuilt and the Buddhist scholar Vasubandhu was patronized during this period. Mahayana Buddhism was not considered hostile to Hinduism during this period as they found certain common features in both of them. Along with Buddhism, Jainism flourished in western India, south India and the Deccan.

The second Jaina council met at Valabhi in the early 6th century and it was here the Jaina canon was settled as it is today. Jainism also took roots in the Malabar region. Syrian Christian church was established in Malabar. Mediterranean writers speak of a Syrian church in the land of Male, where pepper grows. The port of Caliana or Kalyana near Bombay is said to have had a Bishop appointed there. An important feature of the intellectual life of the Gupta times was the lively philosophical debates, among the scholars of different religious faiths. Consequent to the debates six systems of Hindu philosophy emerged to influence the intellectual thought and philosophy. The six systems were: (1) Nyaya or analysis, (2) Vaiseshika or particular characteristics, (3) Sankhya or enumeration, (4) Yoga or application, (5) Mimamsa or inquiry, and (6) Vedanta or end of the Veda. Nyaya was based on logic and it was used against the Buddhist philosophers to disprove their theories. Vaiseshika was a type of atomistic philosophy that advocates that there are separate universes of matter and soul. Sankhya is theistic in nature and tries to explain the cause of creation based on 25 principles. Yoga is a method employed to control body and mind to attain ultimate knowledge. Mimamsa believes in the ultimate validity of the Vedas. Vedanta advocates that the end of life is the union of the individual and the absolute soul after physical death.

Buddhist philosophy was based on four schools of thought: (1) Vaibhashika, (2) Sautrantika, (3) Madhyamika, and (4) Yogachara. The first two belong to the Hinayana school and the other two to the Mahayana school. Jaina philosophy laid emphasis on the logical side during this period. The Jaina philosophers Akalanka, Pujyapada and others developed the doctrines of Svadvada and Nayavada. About the same time, the Hindu thinkers evolved a cyclic theory of time. The cycle was called Kalpa and it was equivalent to 4,320 million years. Romila Thapar observes, "there is a curious similarity between these ideas and the idea of Millennium, as it was current in Europe and elsewhere".

In the field of science and technology also, the Gupta age stands out. During this period careful categorization, of divergent philosophical schools was carried out. Many scientific works that have stood the test of time were produced. Scientific knowledge of that age included medical, metallurgical, arithmetical and astronomical branches. Medical knowledge travelled to west and created interest among west Asian physicians. Copper plate charters, bronze images, the famous Mehrauli iron pillar and the beautifully executed metal coins in gold, silver and copper exhibit the metallurgical skill of the Gupta age. The concept of zero and the use of place notation of numerals are the gifts of Indian mathematics. The famous astronomer Aryabhatta calculated the length of the solar year as 365 days and calculated T as 31,416. He advocated that the earth was a sphere rotating on its own axis revolving around the sun. He also explained that the shadow of the earth falling on the moon caused eclipses. Many scholars are of the opinion that by the time of the Guptas, the mathematical knowledge of the Indians was far superior to that of their contemporaries in other nations. They developed a clear concept of the abstract number distinct from numerical quantity. Indians devised a simple algebra that enabled one to do complicated calculation compared to the Greeks. It is to the credit of the Indians that they devised nine digits and a zero with a place of notation for the tens and the hundreds. The decimal system was the legacy of the Indians and the Arabs who learnt it from the Indians passed it on to Europe and called it Hindisat or Indian art. *Aryabhatiaya,* the work of Aryabhatta belonged to AD 499. Another great astronomer mathematician of this time was Bhaskara, who wrote Siddhanta Siromani, in four parts: (1) *Lilavati* (2) *Bijaganita* (3) *Grahaganita* and (4) *Goladyaya. Lilavati* deals with geometry and arithmetic. *Karnakutuhala* a manual of astronomical calculation, which is used even today, is his work. Varahamihira's, *Brihatsamhita* is another great work in astrology of this period. The metallurgical skill of the Gupta artisans has been mentioned in the earlier part of this chapter. There is a view that Varahamihira's *Panchasiddhantika* reflects a close knowledge of Greek astronomy. Interestingly, religion and commerce in the early history of India were responsible for spreading Indian culture and way of life beyond the shores of India. Among the religions of India, Buddhism took initiative to introduce Indian culture into various parts of Asia, where it was patronized by the ruling elite and the rich merchants. The evidence at the site of Bamiyan conclusively proves that Afghanistan had cultured contacts with India. Buddhism, which travelled to China, was made a state religion in AD 379, when the Guptas were ruling India. Gupta age saw the revival of Vedic Dharma in a modified form of Hinduism of today. This phenomenon made the Chinese Buddhist pilgrims Fahien, Hiuen Tsang and Itsing to come to India between AD 400 to 700 due to which we find both countries developing trade and cultural contacts. Further, the demands of trade made Indians develop trading contracts with South-East Asia. Indians preferred South-East Asia because it was rich in gold, spices and scented resins and wood. Slowly and gradually, trade led to the growth of colonies. Consequently, Indian influence penetrated peacefully into the regions of Thailand, Cambodia and Java. Chinese annals mention Funan (the Mekong Delta) as the first sphere of activity of Indians. There were small settlements in the Malay Peninsula, which was closely connected with the east maritime trading centres of India. Ships sailed to Burma, Martaban and Indonesia from Amaravati and Tamralipti. Both the south coast and west coast had trade with Tennassrim, Troy and the straits of Malacca and Java. However, initially it was Buddhism that went beyond India and influenced China and central Asia, in later days, Hinduism influenced the South-East Asian countries. In the countries where the Brahmanical religion travelled, we find the strong impact of those elements in all spheres of activity.

A popular perception prevails that the Gupta age was classical or a golden age. However, some historians question this description of the Gupta age and a heated debate is going on the subject. There is also a view that as history is a process, there cannot be either dark ages or golden ages. Leaving the debate to scholars, we may agree that in the cultural sphere the Gupta age is remarkable yet, not so in the economic and social spheres.

Part II
Medieval India

11

The Post-Gupta Period in Northern India

The post-Gupta era is a period that witnessed the beginnings of the regional identities that took deep roots in course of time. This formative period requires a detailed study, since many institutions and problems of present-day India owe their origin to this period. With the disintegration of the Gupta political power centre, the northern half of the subcontinent splintered into 'warring kingdoms' and each tried to become a sovereign power. The basis of this sovereignty was distinct regionalism and localism that achieved a clear picture and structure in later centuries. The political heirs to the Gupta political power attempted to recreate an empire but, with the exception of the Pratihara kingdom, the attempts of others remained only a distant dream. The ability to establish large kingdoms and empires appears to have shifted to the region beyond the Vindhyas, i.e., the powers of the Deccan and the Tamil country. These powers of the Deccan and the south, the Chalukyas, the Rashtrakutas, the Pallavas and the Cholas showed the greatest vitality in the evolution of the classical Indian civilization.

The decline of the Gupta kingdom in the 6th century AD slowly and gradually led to the growth of many small kingdoms. In this process, certain regions witnessed the emergence of new kingdoms; and in other regions, the erstwhile Gupta vassals freed themselves from the sovereignty of the Guptas, founding independent kingdoms. Of the new political powers that emerged, the important ones are kings like Yasodharman, and powers such as the Maukharis, the Hunas and the later Magadhan Guptas. Along with these new powers, the Pushyabhutis, the Gaudas, the Varmans and the Maitrakas also became important powers to be reckoned with at that time. The political scenario of this period is to be understood against this background of the emergence of regional identities represented by the new political powers. The first to be studied is Yasodharman.

Yasodharman

Bandhuvarman, a feudatory of Kumaragupta I, ruled Mandasor, in Malwa. This Bandhuvarman of Aulikara family appeared to have ruled until the beginning of the 6th century as can be seen from the two stone pillars of Mandasor, one of which is dated to AD 532 refers to the achievements of Yasodharman. The epigraph glorifies him as a conqueror of the areas that were not even conquered by the Guptas. Except the name of Mihirakula, no other name is mentioned in the epigraph. It is suggested that Yasodharman must have ruled from AD 528 to 543, by which year his power appears to have disappeared. The Maukharis were an old royal family. Patanjali is known to have referred to them. There is also a view that the Maukharis were the descendants of Asvapati. The Barabar and Nagarjuni epigraphs refer to three Maukhari rulers, who ruled Gaya before they ruled from Kanauj as independent rulers. These three rulers of the said above epigraphs could be Yagnavarman, Sardulavarman and Anantavarman. As they had only the title of Samanta, it is believed that they accepted the suzerainty of the Guptas. One Asirgarh copper seal refers to Harivarman, Isanavarman and Sarvavarman as the rulers of Kanauj. While Isanavarman had the title of Maharajadhiraja, the rest had the title of Maharaja. It is presumed that Isanavarman set up an independent kingdom. The later Guptas appear to have had good relations with the early Maukharis but Isanavarman's declaration of independence must have strained their relations as the Apshal inscription of Kumaragupta of the later Gupta family of Magadha mentions a victory over Isanavarman. There existed hostile relations between the later Guptas and the Maukharis. This can be proved by the fact that Sarvavarman, the second son of Isanavarman is said to have defeated Damodara Gupta of the later Gupta dynasty. The last one in Maukhari line is Grihavarman. He married Rajyasri, the sister of Harshavardhana. Deva Gupta, the king of Malwa defeated and killed Grihavarman and thus the line of Maukharis ended. The Maukhari rulers appear to have ruled over modern Uttar Pradesh and parts of Magadha. However, the wars between the Maukharis and later Guptas resulted in the shifting of boundaries between them.

The Maukharis patronized Brahmanical religion and defended their territories against the invasions of the Hunas like the Guptas. One of the epigraphs of Kumaragupta proudly states that he defeated the elephant forces of the Maukhris, which defeated the Hunas. By their success against the Hunas, the Maukharis must have paved the way for Prabhakara Vardhana of the Pushyabhuti dynasty to easily override the Hunas.

Later Guptas or Magadhan Guptas

A.L. Basham observes, "By the middle of the sixth century a line of rulers with the same surname, but not connected in their official geneology with the imperial line, ruled in Bihar and parts of Uttarapradesh". The Aphsad epigraph of Aditya Sena gives the following names as belonging to the Gupta line of Magadha. They are: (1) Krishna Gupta, (2) Harsha Gupta, (3) Jivita Gupta, (4) Kumaragupta, (5) Damodara Gupta, (6) Mahasena Gupta, (7) Madhava Gupta, and (8) Aditya Sena. These rulers are said to have ruled between the 6th and 7th centuries AD. Their rule appeared to have been confined to Magadha and some times to Malwa also. Most of the time, they had hostile relations with their western neighbours namely the Maukharies of the upper and middle Gangetic valley. Finally, the Gaudas of Bengal, who in turn were overthrown by Yasodharman of Kanauj, overthrew the later Guptas.

Besides these powers, the Maitrakas of Valabhi ruled the Kathiawar region in western India. The Maitrakas were also originally the subordinates of the Guptas but they asserted themselves after the decline of the Gupta political power. The Gurjaras ruled in Rajaputana and Gujarat. Harishchandra was the founder of this line and his three successors ruled until AD 640. Gauda, the region of north and north-west of Bengal was under Sasanka, which, as an independent kingdom became prominent in Orissa. However, both these kingdoms faced setbacks because of the rise of Sasanka of Gauda and Harshavardhana of Kanauj.

The Pushyabhutis of Thaneswar and Kanauj

Of all the dynasties and personalities that left an indelible imprint on the post-Gupta era, the most important is the dynasty of Pushyabhutis of Thaneswar and Kanauj, and of them Harshavardhana of the Pushyabhuti line. There are both literary and archaeological sources to reconstruct the history, achievements and place of the Pushyabhutis of Thaneswar and Kanauj in general and in particular that of Harshavardhana. *Harshacharita* of Banabhatta, *Si-yu-ki* or travels of Hiuen Tsang, the Chinese traveller and some inscriptions and coins are important for these sources. Banabhatta, the court poet of Harshavardhana and an ardent admirer of Harsha, glorified and extolled him. Bana mixed up history and romance and hence *Harshacharita* is an unreliable history of Harsha. It contains eight chapters. Regarding the historical value of Bana's *Harshacharita,* one should not accept in toto what was written, but at the same time, it cannot be ruled out as totally without historical value. In spite of its historical inaccuracies, and admiration for Harsha, it has historical value. "The court, the camp, the quiet villages and the still more quiet monasteries and retreats, whether of the Brahmanas or the Buddhists, are all painted with singular power and his (Bana's) narrative illustrates and supplements the Chinese traveller's found at every turn" is the observation of Cowell and Thomas. *Si-yu-ki* of Hiuen Tsang is also an equally important literary text to know about of Harshavardhana. Hiuen Tsang visited many parts of India between AD 629 and AD 644 and recorded what he saw and heard. In spite of certain drawbacks, *Si-yu-ki* of Hiuen Tsang is a veritable fund of information about Harshavardhana.

The available epigraphs of Harsha and of his contemporaries do not throw much light on the reign and achievements. Harsha's Banskhera and Madhuban copper plate epigraphs contain his sentiments towards Buddhism. The Banskhera epigraph is very important as it contains the fascimile of his signature and proves beyond doubt that he is a good calligraphist. The Badami Chalukyan epigraph records the defeat of Harsha at the hands of Pulakesin II but Harsha's epigraphs are silent about the event. Likewise, the epigraphs of the Gurjaras of Broach also throw light on their role in the conflict between Harsha and the ruler of Valabhi. The available seals also throw much light. For example, the Nalanda seal gives information on the history of Kanauj after the death of Grihavarman. It informs us that Grihavarman was a *Paramabhattaraka*. The silver coins of Harsha dated in the year of Harsha also throw some light and appear to be imitations of the Gupta 'peacock-type coins'. The legends on the coins describe him as a world conqueror and conqueror of heaven. Banabhatta, the author of *Harshacharita* informs us that Pushyabhuti was the founder of this dynasty. Curiously, the inscriptions of Harsha do not refer to Pushyabhuti. Even the Banskhera and Madhuban plates and royal seals of Harsha mention five earlier rulers of whom three assumed the title of Maharaja and the fourth one Prabhakaravardhana is described as a *Maharajadhiraja*. It can be inferred that Prabhakaravardhana declared his independence and started independent rule and cultivated friendship with the Maukharis by offering the hand of his daughter Rajyasri to Grihavarman. As Banabhatta described Prabhakaravardhana as a lion to the 'Huna deer', it can be presumed that the Hunas from the western side attacked Thaneswar sometime about AD 604. Bana informs us that Rajyavardhana, the eldest son of Prabhakaravardhana was despatched to meet the Hunas but suddenly had to come back as his father was seriously ill. The sudden death of Prabhakaravardhana was a great setback to the newly declared independence of the Pushyabhutis. Taking advantage of this new development, the Malwa king Deva Gupta killed Grihavarman and imprisoned Rajyasri. Further, the later Gupta king, Deva Gupta entered into an alliance with Gauda Sasanka and threatened Thaneswar the capital of the Pushyabhutis. Rajyavardhana rose to the occasion and gave a fitting reply by defeating the Malwas but was killed treacherously by Gauda Sasanka. In these unfavourable circumstances, Harsha reluctantly ascended the throne. However, the death of his brother; and the imprisonment of his sister and her attempt to commit suicide brought about a sudden change in the mental make-up of Harshavardhana who gave fitting reply to his rival and enemies. In AD 606, Harsha ascended the throne of Thaneswar and started his conquests by sending his armies against Gauda Sasanka who treacherously killed his brother and helped Deva Gupta, the Malwa king to kill Grihavarman, Harsha's brother-in-law. Before starting his march, he entered into a political friendship with Bhaskaravarman, the ruler of Pragiyotisha or Assam, as he was opposed to Gauda Sasanka. It was a master stroke of diplomacy and indicates the far-sightedness of Harsha. There is no positive evidence to know whether Harsha attacked Sasanka directly or not. However, one positive effect is the release of Rajyasri from imprisonment. The result was the merger of Thaneswar and Kanauj, and Harsha started ruling from Kanauj. Hiuen Tsang refers to Harsha as the ruler of Kanauj. Both Bana and Hiuen Tsang mention that Harsha took a vow to defeat his other enemies.

Conquests

Harsha appears to have fought with the Valabhis, though there is no positive evidence except the indirect reference to his fight against the Valabhi ruler. From the evidence of Hiuen Tsang and an inscription of Dhruvasena II dated in

AD 640–41, we learn that political fortunes shifted between Harsha and the ruler of Valabhi – "who this ruler of Valabhi is a big question". Banabhatta writes that Harsha won a victory over Sind. However, Hiuen Tsang contradicts that statement of Banabhatta by writing that Sind was a powerful and independent territory when he visited it. This made some to suggest that Harsha's wars against Sind did not bear fruit. Though Harsha took a vow to free the earth from the hands of Sasanka of Gouda as per the statement of Bana, there is no positive evidence to prove that he defeated Sasanka. It is known from Hiuen Tsang that about the beginning of AD 643, Harsha finished the subjection of Kongonda and Orissa and was halting at Kajangala or Rajamahal on the bank of the Ganga. Harsha maintained friendly relations with Bhaskara Varma the king of Kamarupa. The war between Harsha and Pulakesin II of Badami Chalukyan dynasty is another event of significance in the reign of Hashavardana. The cause for the friction and resultant war between the two appears to be their interest in the overlordship of the Lata, the Malwas and the Gurjaras. While Harsha was actively engaged in consolidating his unquestionable hold over the entire Uttarprapatha, Pulakesin's desire to extend his sphere of activity to northern India could be the reason for the hostility and the war. While Banabhatta was totally silent about this war and its result, Rayikirti the court poet of Pulakesin II and the author of the Aihole epigraph implies by pun that Harsha, "whose lotus feet were arranged with the rays of the jewels of the diamonds of hosts of feudatories prosperous with unmeasured might, through Pulakesin II had his *harsha* (mirth) melted away by fear, having become loathsome with the rows of his lordly elephants fallen in battle". While the epigraphs of Harsha are silent, even the Aihole Prasasti does not positively indicate that Pulakesin II achieved victory over Harsha except that the happiness of Harsha melted away in fear. However, a reading of the sense in-between lines suggests that Harsha was not successful. The successors of Pulakesin II are certain that Harsha was defeated and hence gave lot of importance to this event, and mentioned that Pulakesin II acquired the title of 'Parameswara' after defeating Harsha. Interestingly, we have unconfirmed evidence to know where the battle took place. Based on the available Chinese evidence, V.A. Smith places the war in the year AD 620. As Hyderabad inscription of Pulakesin II mentions the title of Parameswara, R.K. Mukhreji assigns the date AD 612. There is also another view that the conflict took place in AD 630. Some scholars hold the view that Harsha defeated the Pallava ruler Mahendravarman and some other southern rulers too. However, there is no definite conclusive evidence to give it credence. As the Harsha era was in vogue in Orissa state, we may state that Orissa was conquered by Harsha. There is also a controversy regarding the extent of Harsha's empire. Though some modern biographers of Harsha believe that he ruled over the whole of Uttarapatha, Bihar, Bengal, and Orissa and areas of Kashmir, the Punjab, Sind, Rajaputana, and Kamarupa did not become a part of his empire because Hiuen Tsang mentions them as independent kingdoms. While there is a view, that the ruler of Valabhi was a feudatory of Harsha and hence his kingdom included Malwa, Gujarat, Kutch and Kathiawar. However, Hiuen Tsang categorically states that these territories were independent. Hence, we can conclude that, Rajasthan, Uttar Pradesh, Bihar and Orissa were under his direct rule and the peripheral areas of Kashmir, Sind, Valabhi and Kamarupa acknowledged his suzerainty. Harsha era was in vogue in Nepal, some scholars argue that Nepal was also part of the kingdom of Harsha. Harsha also maintained friendly relations with China. While Harsha sent an envoy to China in AD 641, China sent three envoys and by the time the third envoy reached India, Harsha was no more.

Harshavardhana adopted the administrative structure and mechanism of the Guptas with minor modifications. Hiuen Tsang tells in his work, "He was just in his administration and punctilious in the discharge of his duties. He forgot sleep and food in devotion to good work. The king's day was divided into three periods, of which one was given to activities of the government, and the remaining two were devoted to religious works. He was indefatigable and the day was too short for him". We can say that Harsha did not totally depend on his officers, and vassals, but took personal interest in matters of administration. Hiuen Tsang graphically describes this, in his words, "if there was any irregularity in the manners of the people of the cities, he went amongst them to punish evil doers and reward the good people". Further, he stated, "the King made visits of inspection throughout his dominions not residing long at any place but having temporary building erected for his residence at each place thus it can be said that Harsha took personal interest and moved from place to place". Though it is said that his was a centralized monarchical system, there is a view that his administration had become relatively decentralized and feudal. Bana's *Harshacharita* and epigraphs refer to state functionaries of civil and military nature like *Mahasandhivigrahaka*, *Devikrita*, *Mahabaladhikrita*, *Baladevikrita*, *Senapati*, *Catabhata*, the *Dutas*, *Rajasthaniya*, *Kumaramatya*, *Uparika*, *Vishayapati*, *Mahathalavara*, *Bhogapati*, *Mahapratihara*, *Pariyata*, *Dutaka* and *Karamikas* that made historians suggest the existence of a well-organized civil and military bureaucracy to assist and help Harsha. For administrative convenience, Harsha's kingdom was divided into Bhukthis or provinces, Vishayas or districts, Pathakars or taluks and finally Gramas or Villages. Hiuen Tsang is all praise for the administration of Harsha. We understand from his observation, that the state did not interfere in the day-to-day life of the people as he says, "Society was not choked by a grinding bureaucracy or overburdened by system of heavy taxation". The State collected the following taxes as referred to in the epigraphs – traditional one-sixth of the produce from the tiller, *Tulyamanya* or tax based on weight and measure of commodities, *Bhagabhoga*, *Kanashiranyadi* or share of the enjoyment. Hiuen Tsang states, "Of the royal land, there is fourfold division. One part is set apart for the expenses of the government and state worship, one for endowment of great public Services, one to reward high intellectual eminence, and one for acquiring religious merit by gifts to various sections". Officials and ministers were not paid in cash but land was apportioned to them by the state for their maintenance. Crimes were rare because punishments were severe and brutal. Overall, according to Hiuen Tsang, crimes were at a minimum. Though Harsha is said to have ruled benignly, he appears to have maintained a large standing army besides the army supplied by the Samantas or feudatories. The army consisted of infantry, cavalry, elephants and chariots. The strength of the army and its division appear to be exaggerated.

While what has been described above is the traditional scholar's perspective on the nature and structure of the administration of Harsha, recent researchers offer a different perspective on the same. However, in its dimensions his vast kingdom appears very much as that of the Gupta Empire; for a critical observer however, the internal structure appears to be quite different from that of the Gupta Empire. It is suggested that the core area of his kingdom, the *doab* between Kanauj and Prayaga and east Varanasi was under his control. Based on the cancellation of a land grant to a Brahmin because of the spurious nature of the grant situated nearly 250 miles away from Kanauj, it is suggested that he also exercised central control like the Mauryas and the Guptas. However, in other respects, the administrative mechanism looks more decentralized. Harsha's authority over the other parts of his kingdom and the peripheral areas was not very effective. For example, Purnavarman of the Maukhari dynasty as a representative of Harsha ruled Magadha. Though Purnavarman ruled on behalf of Harsha, he enjoyed a certain amount of autonomy. Likewise, Bengal appears to have been divided between Harsha and Bhaskaravarma, his ally and the ruler of Kamarupa, after Sasanka's death and there is no direct proof to state that Harsha ruled over Bengal. Compared to Harsha, the Guptas exercised effective power in appointing governors and district officers in Magadha and Bengal. Based on the Madhuban epigraph of AD 632, it is suggested that there was a different type of control in the core area that reflects a 'definite' change in the organization of administration. The inscription refers to 'great neighbours' (*Mahasamantas*), great kings (*Maharaja*), guardians of the royal gateway *(Daushadhika)*, Judges (*Pramahara*), Viceregents (*Rajasthaniya*), ministers belonging to the royal family (*Kumaramatyas*) Governors of provinces (*Uparikas*) district officers (*Vishayapatis*) regular and irregular troops (*Bhata, Chata*) ordinary people and servants (*Janapada*) as the ones who guaranteed the validity of the grant. This inscription makes us think that political power was fragmented between the various executives mentioned above. Further, as the epigraph begins with a Mahasamanta but not a Kumaramatya, it makes us postulate a hypothesis that the institution of Samanta appears to have taken deep roots. Originally Samantha is understood as a neighbour but by the 6th century, Samanta had come to mean a subject but reinstated prince of a realm. While these Samantas played an important role in the border areas under the Guptas, in the time of Harsha the Samantas had begun to exercise more authority in the core area also. Thus, according to latest researches, it is suggested that 'Samantization' became the practice of the time of Harsha and was called the Indian variety of feudalism. This process appears to have been accelerated by the two factors. The ruralization of economy and decline of long-distance trade which led to urban decay and paucity of coins which forced the king to pay salaries through land assignments with definite rights, also because of the growth of a feeling that the prestige of the king depended on Samanta Chakra or circle of tributory princes. In course of time, Samantization slowly eroded the power-base of the ruler in the core area of his kingdom, as this assignment of prebends reduced and limited the area directly controlled by the central administration.

Harsha's Religion

Bana writes that Harsha was a worshipper of *Nilalohita* or Siva in the beginning. This corroborated by the Banskhera epigraph, which calls him Paramamaheswara and the Madhuban record which also, says that he was a devotee of Maheswara. However, Hiuen Tsang is of the view that he became a Mahayana Buddhist at the beginning of his reign with the title of *Siladitya*. Hiuen Tsang records that Harsha erected thousands of stupas and built monasteries and generously furnished Chaityas, and that he convened an assemblage of Buddhist monks every year and looked after them for 21 days. Harsha honoured the true Buddhist scholars in this assembly. Hiuen Tsang records that at a special function at Kanauj he was honoured with rich presents in the presence of 20 rulers, 1,000 scholars from Nalanda, 3,000 Buddhist monks of Hinayana and Mahayana sects and 3,000 Brahmanas and Jains, and was taken in procession on an elephant. We also come to know that a special tower was built where a Buddhist statue of gold of considerable height was installed. It appears that religious discussions took place for 23 days. Hiuen Tsang records that Brahmans who did not like his patronage of Buddhism planned to kill Harsha but that the attempt failed and Harsha punished the ringleaders. This does not mean that he neglected other religions and patronized Buddhism exclusively. Taking into consideration the fact that his kingdom consisted of different religions, he realized that as a ruler he should respect all religions.

Harsha not only prohibited meat eating but also did away with execution of culprits guilty of serious offences. He also provided rest houses for all travellers. He established royal kitchens where every day 1,000 Buddhist monks and Brahmans were fed by the state. Harsha followed the practice of convening quinquennial convocation "Maha Moksha Parishad" every five years. Hiuen Tsang is said to have attended the sixth convocation at Prayaga, where the Buddha, the Sun God and Siva were worshipped.

Harsha's Contribution to Culture

Harsha was not only an able administrator, and a conqueror of Uttarapatha but also a literary genius of considerable merit. He authored three dramas in Sanskrit: *Ratnavali*, *Priyadarsika* and *Nagananda*. Some expressed doubt about the authorship of these three dramas. Harsha himself composed the Banshkera and Madhuban copper plate epigraphs. Two Sanskrit *stotras* and a grammatical work are attributed to him. Harsha was not only a poet and a dramatist of considerable repute but he also patronized poets. Bana adorned his court along with Mayurasena. Bana wrote *Kadambari* besides *Harshacharita*. Some attribute *Parvati Parinaya* and *Chandisataka* to him. Mayura is credited with the writing of *Suryasataka* and *Astaka*. Besides Bana and Mayura, Harsha is also said to have patronized Diwakara who is identified with the Jaina writer who was also the author of *Bhakkamara Stotra*. Some others identify him with Siddhasena Diwakara, the author of *Kalyanamandira Stotra*. It is not clear whether Bhartrihari, the famous poet, philosopher and grammarian, had any connection with Harsha. It is said that Harsha had set apart one-fourth of his revenue for honouring eminent scholars. He was a great patron of the Nalanda University. A story in circulation states that he showered favours on one Jaya, a native of Saurashtra. Hiuen Tsang wrote that Harsha built a magnificent monastery and a temple at Nalanda.

Estimate of Harsha

Harshavardhana is considered the last great Hindu king and is often compared to Asoka, Samudragupta and Akbar. But this comparison does not appear to be right to some historians as Harsha had not made Buddhism a living religion like Asoka, nor can we compare him to Samudragupta because he was not a great soldier, nor to Akbar because Harsha was not a nationalist like Akbar. Yet, commitment to the welfare of the people makes him one of the greatest kings of early India.

The Vakatakas

Next in importance to the Pushyabhuti lineage, the Vakatakas deserve our attention. In early India, the chronology and genealogy of dynasties cannot be established with absolute certainty, as the source material is inadequate to postulate a definite chronology. The Vakataka dynasty is one among them. Therefore, the details available about them are mostly conjectural. In the absence of ascertainable details, we have to depend on conjectures.

The Vakatakas, who were probably the feudatories of the Satavahanas, became the most important political power in the Deccan and Central India, after the disappearance of their overlords for a period of three centuries from 3rd century to the 6th century AD. Their original home is not yet very satisfactorily established and their origin is shrouded in mystery. Some scholars hold the view that they were Brahmins and their original home was Malwa. Others are of the view that they came from South India or the Eastern Deccan. However, as most of their inscriptions have been found in Madhya Pradesh, R.C. Majumdar concludes that their original home could be today's Madhya Pradesh. Though the Vakatakas at one stage of their existence, ruled over dominions extending from former Bundelkhand in the north to Hyderabad in the south, the core area of their rule appears to be confined to modern Madhya Pradesh. Until recently, the period of their rule was very controversial but the Poona copper plate of Prabhavathi Gupta clinched the issue by proving that the

Vakatakas were the contemporaries of the Guptas. However, it is interesting to note that they do not figure in the list of vanquished rulers subdued by Samudragupta. Though on a smaller scale, the Vakatakas too made significant contributions to Indian culture by adding substantially to the famous gallery of cave temples and paintings at Ajanta. The founder of the Vakataka dynasty was Vindhyasakti. He is said to have ruled from Purika, in the last quarter of 3rd century AD. He is credited to have extended his political power by occupying Malwa. He is also said to have performed a number of Vedic sacrifices and thus revived Brahmanical rituals, which were in abeyance during the rule of the later Satavahanas. Vindhayasakti's son and successor Pravarasena I, who is said to have ruled from AD 280 to 340, is considered the founder of the real power and greatness of the Vakatakas. As he assumed the title of *Samrat* and as he happened to be the only ruler who assumed that title, it is believed that he must have enlarged his kingdom in all directions. His son Gautamiputra married the daughter of Bhanaga of the Bharashiva dynasty. By this marriage alliance, he appears to have improved the political stature of the Vakataka dynasty.

Thus, by military exploits and matrimonial alliances, Pravarasena, extended his kingdom from Bundelkhand in the north to Hyderabad in the south and to commemorate his victories, he performed an Asvamedha sacrifice and one Vajapeya sacrifice. Pravarasena had four sons who were ruling independently in separate provinces. The Puranas mention that on the death of Pravarasena, his four sons divided the empire and declared their independence. It appears that Gautamiputra died during the lifetime of his father and hence, his son Rudrasena I succeeded his grandfather Pravarsena to the throne and ruled from Nandivardhana, near modern Nagpur. Sarvasena, another son of Pravarasena, started ruling independently from Vastugulma, which is identified as modern Bassien in Vidarbha as his captital. We do not have any knowledge of the other two sons of Pravarasena. Thus, by AD 340, the Vakatakas were divided into two lines, one ruling from Nandivardhana and the other ruling from Vastugulma. In spite of these happening in the Vakataka kingdom, the contemporary Gupta rulers never attacked the Vakatakas. It could be because the Guptas thought that the Vakatakas would be useful to them in defeating the Western Kashtrapas. Rudrasena is said to have ruled from AD 340 to 365 but as no inscription of this is available, nothing can be said about the events that took place during his reign. He is known to have been a worshipper of Lord Mahabhairava, another name of Siva. Rudrasena was followed by his son Prithvısena I, who ruled from AD 365 to 390. He appears to have spent his time in consolidating his kingdom and the chief feature of his reign appears to be a political alliance between Chandragupta II and himself. Together they defeated the Saka Satraps of Malwa and Kathiawar. It was during his reign that the Guptas and the Vakatakas entered into a matrimonial alliance. Prithvisena's son Rudrasena II, the crown prince was married to Prabhavati Gupta, the daughter of Chandragupta II. Prithivisena also was a Saiva like his father. Rudrasena II ruled only for a period of five years from AD 390–395. As he died prematurely leaving behind two minor sons Diwakarasena and Damodarasena, his wife Prabhavatigupta ruled as the regent until AD 410. Unfortunately, Diwakarasena also died prematurely so that Damodarasena became the ruler. Damodarasena ruled for a period of 35 years and assumed the title of Pravarasena II. A dozen copper-plate grants of his were discovered in different parts of Vidarbha. He is credited with the founding of a new capital at Pravarapura, which is identified as Paonar in the present-day Wardha district. He was also a poet in Prakrit and was the author of *Setubandhakavya* that won appreciation from contemporary poets and scholars. He entered into a matrimonial alliance with the contemporary Kadamba ruler as his son Narendrasena was married to a princess of Kuntala, Ajihata Bhattarika, the daughter of Kakutsavarman of the Kadamba dynasty. Narendrasena ruled for a decade from 455–465 AD. He had to face the invasion of Nala Bhavadottavarman both in the beginning and at the end of his reign. In-between, he made some conquests and yet he had to face the stiff opposition from Nalas. His son Prithvisena II succeeded Narendrasena. He is credited with having retrieved the fallen fortunes of the Vakatakas. He had to face thrice the invasion of Harisena of Vastugulma branch and the invasion of Bhavadottavarman of the Nala dynasty. He also appears to have fought with the Traikutaka king, Dahrasena of southern Gujarat. He is the known last ruler of Nandivardhana branch of the Vakataka dynasty. We may conclude that after his death, during the time of his successors, Harisena of the Vastugulma branch conquered them and united that kingdom with his own kingdom.

The founder of the Vastugulma line of the Vakatakas was Sarvasena, the son of Pravarasena I. It is believed that his successor Vindhyasena or Vindhyasakti ruled over the southern part of Vidarbha, the northern part of Hyderabad state and some other adjoining territories. He is said to have defeated a Kadamba ruler of Kuntala. He ruled for four decades. His son and successor Pravarasena II appears to have ruled for a period of fifteen years. Devasena, who was a pleasure-seeking ruler, followed him but luckily a very capable minister, Hasthibhoja, served him. His successor Harisena II was the ablest and the greatest ruler of this line, who ruled from AD 480 to 515. He united the two Vakataka kingdoms and extended his territories by conquering Kuntala, Avanti, Kalinga, Konkan and Andhra. Dandin, a poet of 6th century AD described Harisena as "powerful, truthful and bountiful, glorious, lofty, and a penetrating critic of ethical and economic compendia". His kingdom extended from Malwa in the north to south Maharashtra in the south and from the Bay of Bengal in the east to the Arabian Sea in the west. With the death of Harisena II, the glory of the Vakatakas ended and the Nalas, the Kadambas, the Kalachuris and Yasodharman of Malwa occupied their territory. Walter M. Spink observes that what Harisena did was to stave off the seam of decay he presided over the final thrust of the Classical Age by his patronage of the Ajanta cave paintings. As the Western Chalukyas of Badami never claimed to have defeated the Vakatakas, the Vakataka power must have disappeared by the middle of the 6th century AD. The Vakatakas played an effective role in the political game of the Deccan for more than two and a half centuries, and made significant contributions to the growth of culture. The silence over Samudragupta's exploits against the Vakatakas in the Allahabad pillar Prasasti and the matrimonial alliance contracted by Chandragupta II made some scholars postulate a theory that the Vakatakas were also powerful contemporaries of the Guptas. It is also suggested that their rule and achievements were overshadowed by the Guptas' glory and grandeur. Further, the revival of Brahmanical religion is also attributed to them as they performed many Asvamedhas and other religious ceremonies and made substantial land grants to Brahmans. At the same time, it is also said that they were liberal in outlook and patronized Buddhism and literature, and kings like Pravarasena II and Sarvasena were themselves poets of great repute in Prakrit. Pravarasena II is the celebrated author of *Setubandhakavya* and Sarvasena was the author of *Harivijaya*, another work of considerable merit in Prakrit. A style by name *Vaidharbhariti* was developed in Sanskrit during their rule, which was praised by the poets, Kalidasa, Banabhatta and Dandin. They are also credited with having built a few temples in Tigwa and Nachanakuthara. They do not however, show their individual style but indicate continuation of Indo-Persepolitan style. They made a remarkable contribution in the field of painting and Ajanta cave numbers XVI, XVII and XIX are the best examples of Vakataka excellence in the field of painting and in particular the painting *Mahabhinishkramana*. Not only the Vakataka rulers, but their ministers or governors Hastibhoja and Varahadeva too extended their benevolent patronage to the Ajanta cave painters. Thus, the Vakatakas leave behind them as patrons of art and letters, a stamp of their own.

Minor Dynasties

The epigraphs of the feudatories of the Guptas from the time of Puru Gupta and Budha Gupta bear testimony to the fact that they began to assert themselves particularly in Bengal and Malwa. Of such families was one Maitrakas of the Kathiawar peninsula. The founder of this lineage Bhatarka was a general of the Guptas. While he and his successor Dharasena called themselves *Senapatis*, the successor of Dharasena, Dronasimha assumed the title of *Maharaja* by AD 502 as his inscription testified. Though Dhruvasena accepted the suzerainty of the Guptas, his successors Maharaja Dharapatta and Maharaja Gahasena declared total independence between AD 545 and 570.

Inscriptions testify to the fact that the Parivrajaka dynasty of the Bundelkhand region, the dynasty of King Jayanga of Vichakalpa, the Pandu dynasty of Banda and Baghelkhand, the dynasty of Maharaja Lakshmana of the Allahabad and Rewa region, the dynasty of Maharaja Subandu of Mahishmati were also feudatories of the Guptas when Narasimhagupta was in power. Yajnavarman, Sudhula Varman and Anantavarman, who belonged to the Maukhari lineage, appear to be feudatories of the Guptas in Bihar and Uttar Pradesh. Another branch of Maukharis that includes the rulers Harivarman, Adityavarman and Isanavarman, belonging to another line, bore the titles of

Maharaja. The successors of Isanavarman bore the title of *Maharajadhiraja*, which indicates that they became independent of Gupta rule by AD 554, the first known date of Isanavarman. We come across a family of the Guptas ruling in the Magadha region declaring independence by AD 570–576.

In the 6th century AD, when the Guptas became decadent, one Harichandra of the Gurjara tribe established independent authority in Jodhpur and his sons increased their influence in Rajasthan. Another branch of the Gurjara tribe ruled Broach or Barukachcha region.

Gauda and Vanga, two independent kingdoms arose in Bengal. While the Gauda comprised northern and western Bengal, the Vanga comprised southern and eastern Bengal. We come to know from some copper plates the existence of three kings of Vanga region: Gopachandra, Dharmaditya and Samacaradeva. These three kings must have ruled between AD 525 and 575. The Kalinga area was divided among a number of small powers and of these, the eastern Gangas were prominent. Sarabhapuriyas controlled South Kosala until the Panduvamsis who had their seats of power in South Kosala and Mahakosala replaced them.

In the far south, the period from the 4th century to the 6th century, the Kalabhras, a people of uncertain origin occupied the region. Not much is known about the far south during the period. It is only at the end of the 6th century, that the Pandyas, freeing themselves from the Kalabhras, began to assert themselves. In the Karnataka region, the important political powers were the western Gangas of Talkadu and the Kadambas. The Kadambas became the vassals of the Pallavas of Kanchi of the line of Simhavishnu. Pulakesin I of the Western Chalukya lineage of Badami was a subordinate of the Kadambas. The Badami Chalukyas became prominent in the 7th and 8th centuries. Around 6th century AD, the king of Kamarupa, Narayana Varman repudiated the Guptas and declared independence.

While the Guptas were having their sway in northern India, the region comprising Deccan and South India and also parts of Central India and the Kalinga region was outside the purview of the Gupta Empire. We have read in the preceding pages how the Vakatakas ruled in the Deccan. A tribe of Bhojas ruled the Goa region. One Mirad copper plate epigraph refers to a Bhoja chief named Devaraja, who had his administrative centre at Chandrapura, modern Chander in Goa. The Traikutaka tribe ruled Aparanta or northern Konkan region. We come to know from numismatic and epigraphic evidence that Traikutaka chiefs Indradatta, Dharamasena and Vyaghrasena ruled over the western coastal area from Surat to Kanheri. By the middle of the 6th century AD, Gurjaras and Kalachuris overthrew the Traikutakas. Southern Maharahstra was ruled by one Mananka of Rashtrakuta dynasty from Manapura, modern Mann in the Satara district. We know about his grandson Avidheya and his successor Devaraja from the Pandurangapalli inscription. The Chalukyas overthrew this dynasty eventually. We also come across a number of small kingdoms ruled by petty rulers in different parts of India. The Nalas, who claimed descent from the epic hero Nala, ended the Vakataka rule of ancient Vidarbha or modern Berar in central Deccan. Epigraphs make us think that they occupied Koraput and Bastar areas on the borders of present-day Madhya Pradesh and Orissa. However, the fortunes of the Nalas received a blow either from the Panduvamsis of Kosala or from the rising power of the Chalukyas of the Deccan. The Bhojas occupied the Amaravati region in Maharashtra, the erstwhile Vakataka region, and their kingdom was called *Bhojakatakarajya*. Besides the Nalas and the Bhojas, there existed the kingdom of the Traikutakas, who ruled the region from Kanheri to Surats along the western coast. The Kalachuris who held a firm command, over the whole of Malwa started a new era by name the Traikutaka – Kalachuri era in AD 248, which replaces the Gupta era in coastal Gujarat. It indicates the growing power of the Traikutakas. The Traikutakas in association with Abhiras waged a war against the Kadambas of coastal Karnataka.

The valleys and the deltas of the Godavari and Krishna constitute the most significant territory in the eastern Deccan. While the present Guntur region was occupied by the Ananda *gotras* for a short while, the Salankayanas had their sway over the Vengi region. From 6th to 7th century, Vishnukundins dominated the western Deccan.

An examination of the political scenario of the post-Gupta era until the rise of the Rajput kingdoms and the invasions of Muslims presents a bewildering picture of regional, supra-local and local powers fighting for ascendency. However, recent researches, of the last three decades, stress that his period was extremely crucial from the perception of local and regional states based on the assertion of local and regional aspirations. R.S. Sharma rightly observes: "we can count sixty-nine states spread all over the country. Out of these, forty-eight could be attributed to Maharashtra, eastern Madhya Pradesh, Andhra Pradesh, Orissa and Bengal. A good part of the zone was a forested plateau lying largely in the Vindhyan region". B.D. Chattopadhyaya points out that the number mentioned is not definitive and this process was not applicable to this period alone. We also notice this feature in later times.

Despite the emergence of regional, supra-local and local power structures throughout the subcontinent, the traditional historiography perceives the political structure of every state as being built by the military exploits of charismatic royal personalities and political unification achieved by suppressing centrifugal elements through centralized monarchical power structure assisted by a council of ministers and a bureaucratic set-up. Recent scholarship suggests that the power or authority was not centralized in a monarch of a state structure with a stable territorial base, but there arose a hierarchy of authority, fragmented and multilayered, due to the changes in the material base which made the social groups claim their space in the political structure. The developments that took place in the politico-economic cultural sphere are perceived from the models and blanket concepts of medievalism, feudalism, segmentary and integrative social formations based on empirical validation. In all the above concepts, common element is the fragmentation of authority and power between different layers of the state structure. This resulted in decentralized administration and political hierarchy. While the protagonists of feudalism stress the issue of land grants, the advocates of segmentary state emphasize the aspect a of ritual sovereignty, and the advocates of integrative approach stress that political process is to be seen as part of the whole of contemporary economic, social and religious development. Nihar Ranjan Ray, the advocate of medievalism, highlighted the political order represented by Samantas and Mahasamantas, the reduced control of the central power over the Janapadas and the tenuous bonds with political parties.

Whatever may be the name given to the model, our central concern is to understand the process of historical change by in-depth analysis of linkages between polity, economy, society and culture. During this period, the salient feature of economy was ruralization and localization along with the emergence of hierarchized layers of landed intermediaries. Because of ruralization of economy and localism, villages appear to have become self-sufficient units and produced what was needed for their consumption; this might have led to the lack of surplus produce needed for markets. Lack of marketable goods, necessarily led to the decline of trade and commerce. Therefore, the urban centres of this age were not market centres but pilgrimage centres and political centres of minor rulers and officials. However, we should not be misled to think that trade was totally absent or had totally declined. Trade was controlled and administered by the rulers. Medhatithi refers to royal monopoly on elephants, saffron, fine cloth and wool, horses, precious stones and pearls and all these were exclusively meant for the use of royalty and nobility. There is a view that a sizeable portion of the meagre trade that existed was in the nature of exchange of gifts. It is said that Bhaskaravarman, the ruler of Assam sent twenty-six articles to Harsha as presents. H.S. Bhatia and Tan Chung state that between the 7th and the 10th centuries, India had sent 44 missions to China with gifts. During this period, trade appears to have been restricted to luxury goods. We also notice the decline of urban settlements and paucity of metal currency and frequent migrations of artisans as well as Brahmans. There is a view that during this period the peasantry experienced forced immobilization and a lot of hardship due to the enforcement of *visti* or forced labour. There is also a view that the economic and social status of the artisans and producing groups was at its lowest ebb. Vivekanand Jha and Suvira Jaiswal point that this period was the most crucial phase in terms of the ascendancy of ritual impurity as an institutional form, leading to untouchability. In this period, the social groups of the *Charmakara* or leather workers, *Rajaka*, the washermen, bamboo workers and basket makers and blacksmiths became *Antyajas*. Coming to the status of Brahmins, David Shulman observes: "However much the Brahmin may vaunt his purity and independence, his historical reality is one constant compromise above all through the acceptance of royal gifts. The vast number of land grants to the Brahmins throughout the south, right up to the beginning of the modern period, attest to the strength of this pattern and to the royal need for Brahmin legitimization which underlies it". During this phase only, as Chattopadhyaya states, the tribals – the Abhiras, the Gurjaras, the Bhils and the Medas in Rajasthan, had become peasants in the process of acculturization. Lahiri also proved that the same process took place in the Brahmaputra valley. About this process and its impact, R.S. Sharma observes, "... in order to assimilate numerous aboriginal tribes and foreign elements Manu made a far greater use of the fiction of Varnasankara (intermixture of Varnas) than was done by his predecessors. In the majority of instances, the mixed castes were lumped with the Sudras in respect to their hereditary duties. They pursued their old occupation and were possibly taught new methods of agriculture which gradually turned them into tax paying peasants". Robert Deliege states, "The process of transformation of tribal groups into castes is the passage from equality to hierarchy". The society of the post-Gupta era, though based on Varna model, does not appear to be static and rigid; but rather elastic. Women enjoyed security and status. Women rulers like Didda and Sugandha; learned women like Ubhayabharathi, wife of Mandana Misra and poet of Kanauj indicate that women also played an important role in society. Bana testified to the existence of the practice of Sati. Widow's hair was not tonsured in those days. Anuloma marriages were in vogue.

In this period, large Buddhist Viharas were built in eastern and northern India and were endowed with land and villages. The production of metal sculpture was popular in eastern India, Kashmir, Gujarat, Deccan and Tamil Nadu. Hieun Tsang recorded a colossal 80 feet-high bronze image of the Buddha at Nalanda. The Vajrayana Buddhist pantheon had become very popular during this period. The art and architecture of this period had become regional in outlook. We also notice the growth of regional languages during this period. As stated in the beginning, the post-Gupta age was a formative period in the evolution of Indian society and culture.

12

The Post-Gupta Period in the Deccan and the Peninsula

Chronologically, the period from the 6th century to the 14th century is called the early medieval period. This was a formative period in the history of Deccan and peninsular India. During this phase, two groups of states: (i) The kingdoms of the Deccan plateau, and (ii) Tamilham in the south emerged as very important and dominant players in the political and cultural domains. The Chalukyas of Badami or Vatapi, the Rashtrakutas of Manyakheta and the Chalukyas of Kalyani were the important ruling families in the Deccan. The Pallavas of Kanchi, the Pandyas of Madurai and the Cholas of Tanjhavur are the important players of the Tamilham. While traditional historians viewed the continuous struggle between these ruling families as a dynastic struggle for political hegemony, the latest researches made some historians view this conflict from the geopolitical perspective. The reason for the continued conflict between the western Deccan kingdoms and the kingdoms of Tamilham is the desire to control the Vengi region and Raichur *doab*, where the deltas happen to be prime agricultural lands and the east coast is a well-known trade network. These kingdoms appear to be more interested in improving their resource base to sustain themselves as imperial powers. Lack of vast fertile plains in the peninsula resulted in the establishment of smaller regional kingdoms. As such, we notice the regional loyalties taking deep-rooted shape in the form of language, script, art, architecture, sculpture and music and yet having a common syncretic thread as a unifying factor. It was a period where we notice the transmission of northern Indian values and beliefs and faiths in the Peninsula that led to an interface between the assertion of local culture and that of the expanding Sanskritic culture based on Puranic Dharma. We also notice an expansion of agricultural operations by bringing more and more of forest lands under irrigation by the mechanism of issuing land grants to religious and secular benificiaries, growth of trade and commerce, formation of guilds of merchants and artisans, temple-centred devotionalism as ideology and the emergence of a new social economic formation and state society. In this background, a study of the ruling families of western Deccan for an understanding of the historical process is necessary.

The Chalukyas of Badami or Vatapi

The Chalukyas of Badami or Vatapi, who came into prominence in the 6th century, played a crucial role in the politics of Deccan and South India in particular, and played a significant role in the history of India as well. The Chalukyas of Vatapi were great patrons of art and architecture. They are originally the tributary princes under the Kadambas of Banavasi who ruled the Kanara coast from about the 4th century AD. In the 6th century AD, the Chalukyan King Pulakesin I established his capital at Vatapi and declared his independence by performing the Aswamedha as a mark of his independence. The Chalukyas are said to have started from Badami or Vatapi and adjacent Aihole, moved northwards and annexed the territories around Nasik and the upper Godavari, which were previously ruled by the Vakatakas. The Chalukyas of Badami ruled until AD 757 but the Samangad epigraph dated in AD 754 proves that by that time, Dantidurga, the founder of the Rashtrakuta dynasty occupied the northern provinces of the Chalukyas of Badami. The origin of the Chalukyas of Badami is debatable. Different scholars have put different theories forward. Primarily, there are two theories: (i) foreign, and (ii) indigenous. Those who designate them as foreigners depend on the similarity between the terms Chalukyas and Seleucid. Because of that similarity, they identify them as Seleucid. Contrary to the above view, Bilhana in his famous Kavya *Vikramarnkadevacharita* presents a mythical story that the Chalukyas originated from moon and associates them with Ayodhya. Bilhana suggests that the first Chalukya was created from the hollow of the hand of Brahma (*Chalki*) and the word Chalukya is derived from the word *Chulika*. However, this theory is not accepted on the ground that Chalukya is not a Sanskrit word. There are other theories, which identify them as Solankis of Gujarat and others as indigenous Kannadigas who claimed Kshatriya status, and still others identify them as Sulikas or Sulkis of Orissa. Their Vamsika Prasasti resembles those of Kadambas and Gangas. From the similarities of Vamsika Prasasti, it can be argued that the Chalukyas considered themselves as the full-fledged successors of the Kadambas, not only in the political sphere but in the matter of patronizing the Vedic religion also.

Pulakesin I, the son of Ranaranga, is regarded as the founder of the dynasty of the Chalukyas of Vatapi or Badami. From the Vatapi Chalukyan records, we come to know that Pulakesin I was acknowledged by posterity as the defacto inaugurator of the Chalukya dynasty as a ruling house of the Deccan and to be conferred with title of *Maharaja* performed an Aswamedha sacrifice and the title *Vallabha* was regarded as an integral part of his name. He had also the second name *Ranavikrama* as known from Godachi, Mahakuta, Satara and Timmapuram epigraphs. He also happens to be the first to use the dynastic attribute of *Satyasraya*. His only dated Badami rock cliff-epigraph dated AD 543–44 refers to him as *Chalukya Vallabheswara*. He appears to have styled himself as Maharaja and is known as *Dharmamaharaja* like the Vakataka rulers. His performance of horse sacrifice was not only recorded by him but also referred to in the later dated epigraphs. His founding of the city of Vatapi was commemorated even in later times by the Chalukyas of Kalyani. He is also credited with having constructed the hill fortress of Vatapi. Besides being a military adventurer, full time warrior, founder of a dynasty and the citadel, and performer of religious sacrifices, Pulakesi was also a scholar as known from Nerur plates of Mangalesa. He had two sons, Kirtivarman and Mangalesa. Besides constructing the fortification at Vatapi as a strategist, he also initiated as a devotee and as a connoisseur of art, the construction of temples, in and around Vatapi. He appears to have built the Mahakuteswara temple with a small pavilion and installed the deity of Makutesvara Matha. Besides this temple, he also built another ancient temple known by an uncommon name Banantigudi. Makuteswara temple was said to be the earliest free-standing temple of the Vatapi Chalukyas. Thus a kingdom was born at the time of Pulakesin I. Pulakesin I was succeeded by his son Kirtivarman I, who is referred to as the annexer of the kingdoms of Nalas, the Konkana Mauryas and the Kadambas. By the conquests, Kirtivarman appears to have made himself not only the master of the whole of northern Karnataka by eliminating the Kadambas, but also spread his hegemony westwards and eastwards, by defeating the Konkana Mauryas who were ruling a petty kingdom in Goa region and the Nalas who were holding sway over Bellary-Kurnool region. Mangalesa in his Mahakuta pillar inscription lists fourteen kingdoms defeated by Kirtivarman, of which Vanga, Kalinga, Anga, Vattura, Magadha and Madraka are located in the north, while the remaining eight; Kerala, Ganga, Mushaka, Pandya, Dramila, Choliya, Senka and Vaijayaniti were to its south. However, there is no direct evidence that the temple at Aihole called Chikkigudi is attributed to Kirtivarman. Three sons were born to him at advanced age and he died in AD 591–592. The Badami Vaishnava cave temple is attributed to Mangalesa, Kiritivarman's brother. As the three sons of Kirtivarman were very young, Mangalesa, the uncle of the three infants, acted as the regent, with a promise that he would vacate as and when Pulakesin II, the eldest son of Kirtivarman was old enough to rule. There are two dates regarding the accession of Mangalesa, sometime in AD 597–598 or AD 591–592. Not much is known of the martial exploits of Mangalesa, who appears to have made grants to the existing structural temple of Mukuteswara and also Ravalaphadi or Ravanaphadi cave, where the image of Nataraja is said to be represented flanked by *Saptamatrikas*. K.V. Ramesh goes to the extent of saying that Ravalaphadi cave was conceived by Mangalesa as a royal portrait gallery and accordingly, he even had himself portrayed in the deified form of Nataraja and gave it a dynastic touch by enflanking the *Saptamatrika* images. Mangalesa did not yield to the wishes of the grown up Pulakesin II and he was forcibly ousted and killed in the battle of AD 609–610. The Aihole epigraphs and the undated Modlimb plates of Pulakesin II say that he had earned his kingdom by his own might. After his victory over his uncle, he assumed the title of *Satyasraya prithvivallabhamaharajadhiaja-paramaheswara-bhattaraka*.

The Aihole epigraph of Pulakesin II, written by Ravikirti, gives the details of the military expeditions undertaken by him after he assumed sovereign power. K.V Ramesh observes, "from a study of Ravikirti's Aihole inscription, it is indeed possible to deduce that the victories of his master therein narrated in their topographical sequence, though no tangible clue can be found as to the chronological succession of those events. All that we can say, with a certain amount of conviction, is that the Aihloe inscription implies that Pulakesin II's conquests were carried out at four different levels; two of them in the early years of his reign and the other two, a decade and a half later, each one of them contributing to a steady and successive improvement in his stature as one of the leading emperors of the subcontinent."

Taking advantage of the civil war, the Gangas of Talakkad, the Kadambas of Banavasi, the Alupas of Aluvakheda and the Mauryas of Konkan appear to have withdrawn their allegiance. Pulakesin marched his armies against them and successfully brought them into his fold. He then appears to have turned northwards and defeated the rulers of Malwa, Lata and Gurjara. Perhaps, the newly earned hegemony of Pulakesin incensed Harsha and resulted in a battle between the two. Bana's *Harsha Charita* is silent about this war. However, Hiuen Tsang mentions the war between the two indirectly. Ravikirti had two verses in his Aihole epigraph. "The powerful Harsha, whose feet were even worshipped by an army of extremely prosperous feudatories, lost his mirth because of his defeat at his hands and was disgusted at the sight of rows of his lordly elephants fallen in the battle. Having returned from that war, while he (i.e., Pulakesin II) was ruling over the earth, with the help of his huge army, the Vindhyan neighbourhood, which was already lustrous with myriad Sandanks of the Reva, i.e., Narmada, became by the addition of his own greatness, even more lustrous, being avoided by the mountainous elephants which, in their size competed with the Vindhyan mountains." Pulakesin II appears to have led a peaceful life for 15 years, before he undertook his other campaigns.

The undated Timmapuram plates and Kopparam plates reveal that Pulakesin II with the assistance of Vishnuvardhana subdued Pistapura, a land fortress and Kunala, a lake fortress. As a reward, Pulakesin appointed Kubja Vishnuvardhana his official Viceroy (Pruthviyuvaraja) in the conquered Andhra territories and allowed him to rule independently. Pulakesin appears to have started his eastern and southern expeditions in AD 631 or AD 634 and won a victory over Pallava Narasimhavarman. It is said that the latter wracked his vengeance by defeating the Chalukyas totally and conquering Vatapi. The Pallava ruler claims to have put an end to the life of Pulakesin II. Nevertheless, there is a controversy regarding the Pallava ruler who was attacked by Pulakesin II and about the result. While K.V. Ramesh is of the view that the Pallava ruler defeated by Pulekesin II was Narasimhavarman I, others are of the opinion that he could be Mahendravarman. It cannot be said definitely, how many wars took place between the Chalukyas of Badami and the Pallavas of Kanchi during the time of Pulakesin II. It is certain that the Pallavas had the upper hand in the end and consequent to the success of Pallava Narasimhavarman, the Chalukyan territory had become a victim of anarchy and confusion, while Pallava Narasimhavarman assumed the title of Vatapikonda and the Pallava epigraphs boast of his victory over *Vallabha*. It appears that many subordinates raised banners of revolt and there arose a civil war for succession among the children of Pulakesin II.

Vikramaditya I, the worthy son of a worthy father, who assumed the titles of *Vallabha*, *Prithwivallabha*, *Maheswara*, *Paramamaheswara*, *Maharajadhiraja*, *Satyasraya*, and *Ranarasika* and *Rajanadha* waged a battle of vendetta against the Pallavas to revive the lost glory and prestige of the Chalukyas claims that he reclaimed his families' fortunes as well as the title *Parameswara* after defeating the enemies in all directions. Epigraphs testify that he won success over three Pallava rulers, Narasimhavarman, Mahendravarman II and Parameswara Varman I. We also learn from the undated Hyderabad epigraph that the city of Kanchi was taken by force by Vikramaditya I from Parameswara Varman. Vinayaditya, the son and successor of Vikramaditya also actively helped his father in all his conquests as attested by the Alampur Prasasti. Pulakesin II had four sons – Adityavaman, Chandraditya, Vikramaditya I, and Dharasraya Jayasimha Varman. Vikramaditya ruled from AD 654 to 681. His son, Vinayaditya appears to have inherited a fairly peaceful and prosperous empire from his father Vikramaditya I, and ruled from AD 681 to 697.

His son Vijayadatya who ruled a fairly peaceful and prosperous empire from AD 696 to 753 succeeded Vinayaditya. His rule was the longest of the Badami Chalukyas, and also the most prosperous and peaceful. His reign has been characterised as 'the era of Benevolence'. We can agree with K.V. Ramesh that the expression *Samastabhuvanasraya*, which became one of the distinctive and opening epithets of the Kalyani Chalukyas was for the first time brought into use by Vijayaditya. He is said to have won a victory over the Pallavas. It is also said that he captured Kanchi and forced its ruler Parameswaravarman to pay a huge war indemnity as tribute. Vijayaditya died a natural death in AD 733. Vikramaditya II, son and successor of Vijayaditya ruled from AD 733 to 744. During the first part of his reign, the Arabs, after establishing their power in Sindh attempted to push into the Deccan, though their attempts were foiled by Avani Janasraya Pulakesin, the, son of Jayasimha, and the brother of Vikramaditya II. Another feudatory, Dantivarman of the Rashtrakuta line also helped him. He revived the Pallava Chalukya rivalry. It is suggested that two expeditions were despatched against the Pallava ruler Nandi Varman Pallava Malla or Nandi Potavarman. In the first expedition led by Vikramaditya, Nandivarman Pallava Malla was defeated and Kanchi was occupied by Vikramadhitya. A Kannada inscription at Kailasanadha temple records that he returned back huge blocks of gold, which belonged to the temple. The expedition led by his son Kirtivarman at the end of his reign was marked by success. Kirtivarman II, the son and successor of Vikramaditya II, was the last of the Badami Chalukyan rulers. His reign witnessed the 'total eclipse' of the political power, glory and prestige of the Badami Chalukyas due to the rise of their feudatories, the Rashtrakutas. Dantidurga, the founder of the independent Rashtrakuta line defeated Kirtivarman II and assumed sovereign power. Kirtivarman II attempted regaining of the lost glory, but failed. The continuous struggle with the Pallavas appears to be one of the reasons for the disintegration and decline of the Badami Chalukyan power.

Administration

The Badami Chalukyas adopted a monarchical form of government. The hereditary principle was followed generally and when it was violated occasionally, it led to a war of succession. In case a minor ascended the throne, a regent looked after the administration. Generally, the eldest son was nominated *Yuvaraja*. Sons of the king were trained with necessary skills in the art of warfare and peace. The rulers generally assumed high-sounding titles like *Paramabhattaraka, Maharajadhiraja* and *Parameswara.* Theoretically, the king wielded unlimited power, though in practice he was controlled by political needs of the Samantas who wielded considerable power – the power structure was hierarchical. The king was assisted by a Mantrimandali and a set of high officials. Mahasandhivigrahika is very often mentioned in the records. We come across the three important military officers: (i) *Baladhikrita*, (ii) *Dandanayaka,* and (iii) *Mahaprachanda Dandanayaka* in the epigraphs. The Amatyas looked after revenue matters. The kingdom consisted of two parts: one ruled by the king directly and the other ruled by Samantas. The position of the Samantas also varied. The king exercised control over the Samantas through his representative stationed in the feudatory kingdom.

For administrative convenience, the kingdom was divided into *Rastras, Vishaya, Bhukti*, and *Grama.* The head of Vishaya was called *Vishayapati*, the head of Bhukti was called *Bhogapati* and the Gramabhogikas or *Gamundas* were incharge of the villages. The towns were under the control of Narapatis or *Nagarapatis.* The principal source of revenue for the state was land revenue. The rulers collected money through direct and indirect taxes resulting in high incidence of taxation on the common man. Land tax was collected in kind.

The Chalukyas of Badami were well known as patrons of art, architecture, education and literature. The rulers gave *Agraharas* as gifts to learned Brahmins. Besides Agraharas, we come across *Ghatikas* or Vedic colleges. The Aihole epigraph prepared by Ravikirti is a testimony to the scholarship attained by him. Both Sanskrit and Kannada received impetus. Vijayanka or Vijaya Bhattarika, identified as the wife of Chandraditya, son of Pulakesin II is also a recognized Sanskrit scholar of those times. Pujyapada wrote a treatise on medicine entitled *Kalyanakaraka* in Sanskrit. Two eminent scholars of reputation, Syamakundacharya and Srivardhadeva also flourished during the reign of the Chalukyas of Badami. Srivardhadeva also known as Tumburacharya wrote a commentary on Tattvardha Mahasastra with the title of *Cudamani.* Qualitatively, the Badami Chalukyas made remarkable contributions to art and architecture. In Karnataka proper and in the neighbouring areas, nearly a hundred monuments are attributed to the Chalukyan patronage. The beautifully carved caves, free-standing temples and sculptures of this period undoubtedly constitute a landmark in the art history of India. The majority of structures were built for Hindu deities, while a few are also built for the Jain and the Buddhist worshippers. While Badami, Aihole and Pattadakal constitute the major centres of artistic excellence, minor centres like Lakkundi cave temples, one each for the Buddhists, the Jainas and the Hindus, are found at Aihole. Similar rock-cut caves are also found at Badami. Groups of four pillared rock art halls of the same type are found at Badami, of which three are Hindu caves and one Jain. Each cave comprised a pillared verandah, a columned hall and a small square cellar cut deep into the rock. Of the three Hindu caves, one is a Vaishnava cave belonging to AD 578. The cave contains fine reliefs of Vishnu seated, and of Anantapadmanabha and Narasimha. Both of them are located in the verandah. These reliefs exhibit a high degree of technical perfection. Aihole and Badami temples reflect the first stage of the Chalukyan architectural style. Aihole is a town of temples and appears to be a sacred centre. It contains many structures, out of which four deserve special recognition: (i) Ladh Khan, (ii) Durga, (iii) Hucimalligudi and in the Jaina temple of Megati. Ladh Khan is a 15 metre square low flat-roofed building with a small square cell and porch set on the roof. The art critic Percy Brown thinks that it was a moot hall converted into a temple. In the construction of Durga temple also, we notice an effort to adapt the Buddhist Chaitya to a Brahmanical temple. In this temple, we find a Sikhara curvilinear in shape after the northern style, rising above the sanctorum. Hucimalligudi is a construction that appears to be similar to that of the temple of Durga. The Jaina temple of Meguti, though unfinished, exhibits some development in the direction of erection of structural temples. Of the temples at Badami, the Melagatti Sivalaya, though small is finely proportioned and magnificently constructed.

The Pattadakal temples embody an important stage in the history of the Chalukyan architecture. Pattadakal has ten temples. Out of them, four were built in northern style, while the rest are in the southern style. The Papanasa temple attributed to AD 680 was built in the northern style. One view is that an attempt was made here to combine both northern and southern styles without success. The most notable example of the southern style is the Virupaksha temple built by a queen of Vikramaditya II, Loksanmahadevi of the Haihaya royal family. Though it was vastly improved in design and execution, it appears to be an imitation of Kailasanatha temple of Kanchi and to have been built by the artisans brought from Kanchi. The Sangameswara temple was also built in the same style but on an open mandapa. Percy Brown, an eminent art historian observes, "There is a bold beauty in the appearance of the Virupaksha Temple as a whole which is best seen in the exterior. It is a comprehensive scheme as it consists not only of the central structure, but of a detached Nandi Pavilion in front, and it is contained within a walled enclosure entered by an appropriate gateway". K.A.N. Sastri remarks that the heaviness of the stonework is relieved by an increase in the amount and quality of the sculpture. Percy Brown further observes that the Virupaksha temple is one of those rare buildings of the past in which the spirit of the men who conceived it and wrought it with their hands still lingers. The Badami Chalukyas professed faith in Brahmanical Hinduism by performing Vedic sacrifices and rituals, though they respected other heterodox faiths. Pulakesin I proudly proclaims himself as the performer of Aswamedha sacrifice. Besides Vedic Dharma, Puranic Dharma also appears to have become the dominant religious ideology, which promoted the construction of temples to Vishnu, Siva and other gods. We notice from the writings of Hiuen Tsang, that Buddhism was on the decline in western India while Jainism was still popular.

There is a view that the Badami Chalukyan period of nearly two centuries is marked by frequent invasions and plunder. It is because the resources of the state were limited and long-distance trade and commerce was in decaying condition and the Chalukyan land was rocky and infertile. Hence, the Chalukyas took the offensive by attacking the neighbouring rulers as well as the Pallavas in the south and Harshavardhana in the north. Contrary to the above view, L.N. Swamy, argues that the rise of the Chalukyas as a political power in the Deccan gave rise to manifold cultural expansions of Karnataka both in the subcontinent and foreign countries especially in South-East Asia, Persia and China. Based on the depiction of ship and sun symbol on coins found at Elephanta, Swamy holds that during the reign of Chalukyas of Badami maritime trade was flourishing. Relying on evidence of Hiuen Tsang, K.A. Nilakanta Sastri and Yazdani are of the view that Pulakesi II maintained a powerful navy. Swamy suggests that Badami Chalukyas had trade relations with Persia, Greece, Ceylon, Cambodia, Malayan Peninsula, Siam, Burma and China. At that time, the ports of western India, Puri, Revatidvipa, Kalyana, Mangalore, and Chaul carried on trade with the countries mentioned above. India exported rare wood, silk, and precious and semi-precious stones during this period and imported silk from China, sandalwood from Malaya, ivory and emeralds from Africa and horses from Persia. The Badami Chalukyas also maintained diplomatic relations with Persia and China and the Chalukyas received tributes from the kings of Persia, Simhala and Cambodia. The Arab historian, Tabariz confirms that the Persian king Khusru II sent an embassy to the court of Pulakesin II. A painting in cave 1 at Ajanta also proves this fact. Further, Khusru II, the ruler of Persia states that "Two Years ago, Pulakesi, King of India sent to us in the thirty sixth year of our reign, ambassadors carrying letters imparting to us news and presents, for you and our other sons".

Eastern Chalukyas or the Chalukyas of Vengi

Eastern or Vengi Chalukyas a collateral branch of the Vatapi lineage, played an important role in the history of Andhradesa for more than four centuries. There is a belief that they were the ancestors of the feudatories of the later Satavahanas and the Ikshvakus of Vijayapuri. Further, there is also a view that the homeland of the Chalukyas, *Chalukyavishaya* consists of the northern parts of Rayalaseema and the south-western portion of Telangana. The Chalukyas claim themselves to be the descendants of Hariti and belonging to Manavasyagotra like the *Andhrabhrityas* and the Kadambas of the Puranic lore. During the tenure of the later Chalukyas, a new chapter began in the history of the Telugus. Nannaya Bhattaraka, the Court poet of Rajaraja Narendra started the translation of Sanskrit Mahabharata into Telugu and earned fame and name as 'Adikavi' or the 'first poet', although Telugu was used in epigraphs since the time of Kubja Vishnuvardhana, the founder of this dynasty and we come across thousands of lithic epigraphs in Telugu inscribed on temple pillars of Andhradesa.

The founder of the Eastern or Vengi Chalukya power structure was Kubja Vishnuvardhana, the brother of Pulakesin II of Vatapi Chalukyan lineage. Pulakesin II after conquering coastal Andhradesa, appointed Kubja Vishnuvardhana as his viceroy in AD 624. We come to know from Kopparam epigraph dated in AD 631, that Pulakesin II permitted Kubja Vishnuvardhana to rule independently. The Vengi Chalukyas ruled coastal Andhra as independent sovereigns for more that four and a half centuries from AD 631 to 1070.

The Eastern Chalukyas had to fight with contemporary Pallavas of Kanchi as well as with the Rashtrakutas of Manyakheta, who replaced the Vatapi Chalukyas. Consequent to the continuous warfare with their neighbours, the Chalukyas of Kalyani or later Western Chalukayas, the Vengi Chalukyas entered into matrimonial alliances with the Cholas of Tanjore to succeed in safeguarding their interests in Vengi territory. As a result the Chalukyas of Vengi became pawns in the Chola-Chalukya struggle for supremacy over Vengi area. History and culture of the Eastern Chalukyan period could be constructed with the help of nearly a hundred copper plates and a number of lithic records found in different parts of Andhradesa. The Eastern Chalukyan rulers were also patrons of art and letters and they showed religious tolerance by patronizing Brahmanical as well as Jaina faiths.

Kubja Vishnuvardhana, founder of the Eastern Chalukyan line ruled from AD 624 to 641. He had the title of *Vishamasiddhi* and he had his capital at Pishtapura or modern Pithapuram. He appears to have undertaken conquests and extended his kingdom. He was followed by his son Jayasimha I, who ruled from AD 641 to 673. Jayasimha I was a worshipper of Vishnu. His Vipparla epigraph happens to be one of the earliest Telugu records and it helps us to know the evolution of Telugu language. Jayasimha I was followed by his brother Indrabhattaraka, who ruled for a very short period. Indrabhattaraka was followed by Vishnuvardhana II, who ruled for nine years from AD 673–682. He was followed by Mangi Yuvaraja Vijayaditya, who ruled for a period of 25 years from AD 692 to 706. Jayasimha II ruled from AD 706 to 719 after which started the internecine war between cousins for the throne. In AD 755, Vijayaditya II ascended the Chalukya throne and ruled till AD 772 and appears to have been defeated by Rashtrakuta heir-apparent Govinda III in AD 769. Vijayaditya II was followed by Vishnuvardhana IV, who ruled from AD 772 to 808. He too was defeated by Rashtrakuta Dhruva and offered his daughter Seelamahadevi to Dhruva in marriage. The wars between the Rashtrakutas and the Eastern Chalukyas continued for a long time.

Gunaga Vijayaditya III, the eldest son of Kali Vishnuvardhana and the most famous of the Eastern Chalukyas of Vengi ruled from AD 849 to 892. He had the title Gunakenallata (The lover of excellence or virtue). The historian N. Venkataramanayya suggests that there were three definite stages in the history of his reign: (a) a short period of victory and expansion, (b) a disastrous defeat and prolonged subjection to foreign rule, and (c) a period of brilliant military victories leading to the assumption of imperial authority over the whole of the Deccan. He won victories over Boya Kotams with the help of his Brahmin general Panduranga. He acquired the Pali banner the symbol of the insignia of Rashtrakuta, imperial title of *Vallabha* and proclaimed himself the Lord Paramount of the entire Dakshinapatha. Krishna II of the Rashtrakuta dynasty accepted the sovereignty of the Eastern Chalukyas. His Satuluru copper plate grant records his victories over the Pallavas and the Pandyas. Undoubtedly, Vijayaditya III or Gunaga Vijayaditya was the greatest conqueror and ruler of the Eastern Chalukyan line. During his reign, Eastern Chalukyas rule extended from Mahendragiri in the north to the Pulicat in the south. After him the Chalukyan power began to decline due to wars of succession among the brothers and their children. The son of Vikramaditya IV, Chalukya Bhima II ascended the Chalukya throne in AD 934 and ruled for 12 years. He is credited with the victory over the Rashtrakutas. *Vishnuvardhana, Raja Bhima* or *Brihath Bhima* and *Rajamartanda* were the titles assumed by him. Chalukya Bhima had two sons Danarnava and Ammaraja through different wives. Ammaraja drove away Danarnava and occupied the Chalukyan throne and once again there was conflict between Danarnava and Ammaraja and by AD 970, Danarnava occupied the Chalukya throne. Danarnava ruled for 3 years and was followed by his son Saktivarma. Jatachoda Bhima of Pedakallu defeated and killed Danarnava. The death of Danarnava led to Telugu-Chola interregnum period from AD 973 to 1000. Danaranava's sons Saktivarma and Vimaladitya fled to Chola territory and sought the help of Rajarajachola. Saktivarma regained the Eastern Chalukyan throne in AD 1001–2. In this war, Jatachoda Bhima and his General Ekavira lost their lives. This led to a new struggle between the Cholas and the Kalyani Chalukyas for the hegemony of the Vengi territory. Saktivarma ruled from AD 1002 to 1011 and was followed by his brother Vimaladitya, who ruled from AD 1011 to 1018.

Vimaladitya had two wives, Kundava, a Chola princess and Medamba, a Telugu-Chola princess. Kundava gave birth to Rajaraja Narendra and Medamba gave birth to Vijayaditya VII. Once again we witness a fratricidal war for the throne in which the Cholas supported Rajaraja Narendra and the Kalyani Chalukyas supported Vijayaditya VII. Political fortunes shifted from time to time and Rajaraja Narendra died in AD 1061. Rajaraja Narendra's reign was full of difficulties because of constant threat from his half-brother, Vijayaditya who in cooperation with the Chalukyas of Kalyani gave him trouble. Before his death in AD 1061 he lost his throne and regained it by fighting with the Chalukyas of Kalyani and ultimately he became an ally of the Chalukyas of Kalyani. Rajaraja was followed by Saktivarma II the son of Vijayaditya VII who ruled for a very short time. Vijayaditya VII, the brother of Rajaraja Narendra ruled Vengi in AD 1078 and Vengi then passed on into the hands of the sons of Kulottunga Chola, the son of Rajaraja Narendra.

Polity

Epigraphical and literary sources do not provide adequate evidences to construct the state of government and society. Yet a sketchy picture can be formed. There is a view that the Eastern Chalukyas also followed the hereditary monarchical form of government, wherein the king was the head of the civil, military and judicial branches. In recent times, A. Aruna in her book *State Formation in the Eastern Deccan (7th Century AD–13th Century AD)*, 2000 opines that polity in Eastern Chalukyan period is an integrative rather than centralized or decentralized state. The king was not an absolute autocrat and was assisted by a council of ministers in the business of general administration. They divided their territory into administrative divisions like *Rastra*, *Vishaya* and *Kottams* for administrative convenience. *Rastras* were kept under the control of the collateral branches of the ruling house such as Chalukyas of Elamanchili, Mudigonda, Pithapuram and Srikurmam. As the provincial rulers had internal freedom in the process of administration, it is likely that the administration was feudalized and decentralized. This was the main feature of their polity. *Grameyaka* or the *Rastrakutamohattara,* i.e., the chief cultivator of the village was entrusted with the village administration. Besides *Gremeyaka* there existed a government nominee or representative directly looking after the village administration.

It is generally believed that the social structure was based on Varnasrama model though it seems to be less rigid. We also notice the practice of people taking to new professions leaving aside the assigned professions by dharmasastric tradition. Social tensions were not visibly present during this period.

Puranic dharma was prevalent along with Jaina faith. Jaina monks were very active in the Chalukyan territory. Ammaraju II of the Eastern Chalukyan family extended considerable patronage to Jaina monks. Most of the Eastern Chalukyan rulers were Saivities calling themselves *Paramamahehsvaras*. Whatever their personal faith, the Chalukyan rulers showed religious toleration as a policy.

Classical Telugu literature owes its origin to the Eastern Chalukyan patronage. Rajaraja Narendra patronized Nannayya Bhattaraka, who started the translation of Sanskrit "Mahabhrata" into Telugu and completed *Adiparva*, *Sabha Parva* and a part of *Aaranya Parva*. Arudra observes, "Though he has introduced many Tatsamas and Sanakritic features, Nannayya wrote in the live language of his day". Nanne Choda of the Telugu Chola family was his contemporary. He wrote "Kumarasambhavam". He called himself as Kaviraja Sikhamani. Puvuluri Mallanna was another contemporary of Nannayya. He translated a Sanskrit treatise on mathematics entitled *Sarasangrahaganita*, written by Mahaviracharyulu. Interestingly, Mallanna was a Saivite and Mahaviracharyulu was as a Jaina. This mathematical work of Mahaviracharyulu contains a chapter on mensuration, measurement of shadows, proper and mixed fractions and the theory of numbers.

The Eastern Chalukyas took interest in the construction of temples. All the temples were dedicated to Siva. Chalukya Bhima I was responsible for the construction of Bhimeswara temple at Samarlakota and at Draksharama. Vijayaditya II is said to have constructed 108 temples. Yuddhamalla I built a temple to Kartikeya at Bezawada. Gunaga Vijayaditya constructed the Rajarajeswara, Golingesvara and Chandrasekhara temples at Biccavolu in the East Godavari District. The well-known Mahasena temple at Chebrolu was constructed by them. Rajaraja Narendra erected three memorial structures at Kalidindi in the West Godavari District. The Eastern Chalukyan style of architecture is prominently visible at Draksharama and Biceavolu. The Golingeswara temple at Biccavolu contains some richly carved out sculptures of deities like Arthanarisvara, Siva, Vishnu, Agni, Chamundi and Surya. During this period the Buddha was worshipped as Vishnu and as such Buddhism lost its separate identity. The Jatara of Mahasena at Chebrolu was a famous spectacle of this period. The Jatara used to start at Chebrolu in the Guntur district and reach Vijayawada and from there it returned to Chebrolu. The Eastern Chalukyan rule provided an identity to the coastal Andhras.

The Rashtrakutas of Manyakheta or Malkhead

The Rashtrakutas of Manyakheta or Malkhead rose to prominence in Western Deccan after the decline of the Badami or Vatapi Chalukyas. The Rastrakutas played in important role in the history of Deccan and South India for a period of nearly two centuries from AD 753 to 973. Romila Thapar aptly observes that the geographical position of the Rastrakutas led to their involvement in wars and alliances with both the northern and more frequently, the southern neighbours. The Rashtrakuta's effective interference in the politics of Kanauj made them masters of Kanauj for a brief period in the early tenth century. This imbued them with confidence and made them feel a great, strong power.

The origin of the Rashtrakutas is shrouded in mystery, in spite of a number of theories professing to identify the origin of this ruling lineage. The term Rashtrakuta does not signify any particular community, caste or a Jati. Later-dated epigraphs of the Rastrakutas claim descent from Satyaki, a close associate of Krishna of the epic tradition. Some historians identify the Rashtrakutas with the Reddy community of Andhradesa. Other historians consider them as a branch of the Kshatriyas who figure in the records of Asoka. Several Chalukyan epigraphs of Eastern Deccan refer to the term *Rashtrakutapramukhanam* who are identified as agriculturists of the Andhradesa.

R.C. Majumdar, K.K. Datta and H.C. Raychaudhari are of the view that it is not improbable that the Rashtrakutas were originally Dravidian agriculturists who obtained hereditary governorships of the provinces under the Chalukyas. It is suggested that, as the Sanskrit literature and epigraphs refer to the administration of a territory of Rastra or province as Rastrika or Rastriya and Ratthi in Prakrit, some of the officials in charge of the administration of the Rashtras might have declared independence and assumed royal titles and became rulers. We come to know from Undikavatika copper plate of Rashtrakuta Abhimanyu that there existed a Rashtrakuta kingdom in southern Maharashtra with Manapura or Manyapura as its capital. We also come to know that prior to the establishment of the Chalukyan power in Badami area, there existed a Rashtrakuta power and with the establishment of Chalukyan power, the Rashtrakuta power disappeared. We do not have any evidence to establish the relationship between the Rashtrakutas of Manyakheta and the earlier Rashtrakuta families of southern Maharashtra or Vidarbha or Badami. Rashtrakutas proclaimed themselves as 'rulers of Lattaluru' and it is identified with Latur presently situated in Osmanabad district of Marathwada.

The first ruler of Rastrakuta family appears to be Nannaraja, who ruled between AD 630–650. We have references to Dantivarma, Indrabhattarakaraja, Govindaraja, Karkkaraja and they are said to have ruled in between AD 650 and 735. The founder of the independent Rastrakuta power was Dantigdurga, who was an official of high rank under the Chalukyas of Badami till AD 742 and after the death of Badami Chalukya Vijayaditya II in 747, Dantidurga appears to have declared independence and ruled till AD 755. Dantidurga was followed by his paternal uncle Krishna I, who ruled between AD 756 and 772. Krishna I consolidated and extended the Rashtrakuta power. He became famous as the patron who caused the carving of the Kailasa cave temple at Ellora.

The death of Krishna I resulted in a civil war between his sons Govinda and Dhruva. In this civil war Dhruva won victory in AD 780 and ruled till AD 793. Dhruva is said to have defeated the Gangas, Pallavas and Vengi Chalukyas and he led his armies against northern Indian rulers, and occupied Kanauj and defeated Dharmapala. He also acquired Ganga Yamuna Torana and Palidhwaja. By these conquests Dhruva made Rashrakutas, a very strong and formidable power. He nominated his son Govinda III as ruler in AD 793. He ruled with the titles of 'Rajadhiraja' and 'Rajaparamesvara', 'Sri Vallabha', 'Janavallabha', 'Tribhuvanamalla' and 'Kirtinarayana'. Govinda III had to face the opposition of his eldest brother Stambha who took advantage of disturbances in the Rashtrakuta territory. Dharmapala reconquered Kanauj. But Govinda III successfully curbed his brother and regained the lost ground and by AD 795. He re-established the Rashtrakuta power. He once again led his armies north and gained victory over Dharmapala before AD 810. He also defeated Eastern Chalukya Vijayaditya II and occupied Kanchi by AD 802. The whole of South India acknowledged his sovereignty and even the ruler of Ceylon sought his friendship by offering presents. Undoubtedly, Govinda III is an eminent conqueror and statesman of repute among the Rashtrakutas. By his conquests over Pala and Pratihara rulers in the north, he established the greatness of the Rashtrakuta power. The political influence of the Rashtrakutas extended from the plains of the Ganges in the north to Kanyakumari in the south.

After Govinda III, his son Sarvudu with the name of Amoghavarsha ascended the throne in AD 814. But as he was a mere boy of thirteen, Karkka was appointed as regent. Amoghavarsha had the titles of Nrpatunga and Viranarayana. We come to know from the Sirur epigraph of Amoghavarsha that he defeated the rulers of Anga, Vanga, Magadha, Malava and Vengi. Amoghavarsha built the city of Manyakheta and changed his capital to that city in AD 860. He was also a patron of art and letters. He himself authored "Kavirajamarga" in Kannada. Jainasena, the author of "Adipurana" and Sakatayana, the author of "Ganitasara Sangraha" belong to his times. He professed Jainism yet showed religious tolerance. Amoghavarsha was not a blood-thirsty conqueror but was a peace loving ruler.

Amoghavarsha died in AD 878 and was followed by Krishna II. He married the daughter of the Chedi ruler Kokalla. He gave his daughter in marriage to Adityachola, the Chola ruler of Thanjavoor. He fought with Prathihara Bhoja and Eastern Chalukya Bhima I. Krishna II died in AD 914 and was followed by Indra III.

After Krishna II, his grandson, Indra III ascended the throne in AD 914 and ruled till AD 922. He was also a conqueror of repute and led his armies against Gurjara Prathihara Mahipala and defeated him. After his sudden death, his son Amoghavarsha II became ruler but he too was killed by his brother Govinda IV. As Govinda IV proved to be very wicked, he was replaced by Amoghavarsha III in AD 939. After Amoghavarsha III, his son Krishna III ruled from AD 940 to 968.

Krishna III continued hostilities with the Cholas. Sometime in AD 943, he attacked the Cholas and secured control of Tondaimandalam. In AD 949, Krishna III defeated the Cholas in the battle of Takkolam and proceeded to Rameshwaram to erect a pillar of victory and he built the temples of Krishnesvara and Gandamartandaditya at Rameshwararam. He also led an expedition to northern India in AD 963, but not much is known about the consequences of this expedition. He appears to have succeeded in placing his nominee on the Vengi throne. Though he cannot be compared to Dhruva, Govinda III or Indra III he too occupies an important place in the line of the Rashtrakutas as the lord of the large part of the Deccan and parts of South India. Thus, the Rashtrakuta power ruled over a vast territory in its heyday extended from South Gujarat, Malwa and Baghel Khand in the north to Thanjavoor in the south. The contemporaneous Arab writers rank them as one of the four great sovereigns of the world, alongwith the emperors of China, the Caliphs of Baghdad and the emperor of Constantinople.

Krishna III was followed by his younger brother Khottiga in AD 967. During his reign, Paramara Siyaka invaded the Rashtrakuta territory and devastated Manyakheta and this led to the death of Khottiga. Khottiga was succeeded by Karkka II. Tailapa II of the Chalukyas of Kalyani defeated and drove away Karkka II and became the overlord of the Deccan.

Polity

The Rashtrakutas also followed monarchical form of government, wherein the king was the head of the state and exercised control over judiciary, executive and legislative functions. The Yuvaraja was assigned a key role. The king was usually assisted by a council of ministers. The Rashtrakutas do not appear to have had any organized bureaucracy. For administrative convenience, they divided their territory into administrative units – *Rastras* and *Vishayas*, *Bhuktis* and Villages.

The Rashtrakutas promoted agricultural operations and trade and commerce. The Rashtrakutas appointed Arabs as officers and governors in their territory and made use of their services to enrich their economy. In order to continue commercial relations with West Asia, the Rastrakutas utilized the services of the Arabs appointing them in the Sanjan area, which are very essential and useful for commercial relations with Western Asia. Epigraphic reference is available about an Arab Muslim who called himself Maduramati, who has became a governor granting land to a wealthy Brahman 'matha'. The same epigraph further affirms that the said governor controlled many of the harbour officers on behalf of the Rashtrakutas. This makes us suggest that there was long distance sea trade during the time of the Rashtrakutas.

The worship of Siva and Vishnu was popular in the Rashtrakuta territory. Epigraphs refer to various gods and they performed *Hiranyagarbhadana* and *Tuladana*. They too constructed temples to promote Bhakti based worship of Saiva and Vaishnava deities. Besides Puranic dharma, there prevailed the faith of Jainism. The Rastrakuta rulers Amoghavarsha I, Indra III, Krishna II and Indra IV patronized Jainism.

The Rashtrakutas made significant contribution to Indian art. The rock-cut temples at Ellora and Elephanta belong to this period. The culmination of rock-cut architecture reached its highest stage in the monolithic temple of Kailasa, which was carved out of the live rock. This monolithic temple was excavated during the reign of Rashtrakuta Krishna I. K.A.N. Sastri, observes "in its general plan, it bears a certain resemblance to the Virupaksha temple at Pattadakal, though it is more than twice its size. The Kailasa temple has four parts – the main body, entrance gateway, a Nandi shrine in between, and cloisters around the court yard. The temple's main body, measures roughly 150 by 100 feet with projections at intervals throughout the entire height of its structure." Percy Brown, the eminent art historian describes this temple as follows: "Standing high on this plinth is the temple proper, approached by flights of steps leading to a pillared porch in its Western side and it is here that its designers rose to the greatest' heights. There is no pronounced departure from the conventional combination of the Mandapa and the Vimana, but the manner in which various architectural elements, all definite and sharply outlined, such as cornices, pilasters, niches and porticos, have been assembled in an orderly and artistic manner to form a unified whole, which is masterly. Then rises the stately tower in three tiers, with its prominently projecting gable-front, and surmounted by a shapely cupola, reaching up to a total height of 95 feet while the interior consists of a pillared hall, from which a vestibule leads to the cells. This hall is a well proportioned compartment measuring 72 by 62 feet having sixteen square pieces in groups of four in each quarter, an arrangement which produces cruciform central aisle with an effect of great dignity". The sculptured panels of Dasavatara, Bhairava, and Ravana shaking the mount Kailasa, dancing Siva and Vishnu and Lakshmi listening to music are superb. We may agree with Percy Brown that the "Kailasa temple is an illustration of one of those occasions when mens' mind, hearts and heads work in unison towards the consummation of a supreme ideal. It was under such conditions of religious and cultural stability that this grand monolithic representation of Siva's paradise was produced".

We may agree with the view of A.S. Altekar that the period of Rastrakuta ascendancy in the Deccan from about AD 753 to 975 constitutes perhaps the most brilliant chapter in its history. No other ruling dynasty in the Deccan played such a dominant part in the history of India till the rise of the Marathas as an imperial power in the eighteenth century.

The Chalukyas of Kalyani

The later Western Chalukyas or Chalukyas of Kalyani or Kalyana played a dominant role for two centuries from AD 973 to 1200 in the politics of the Deccan and South India. M.K.L.N. Sastry states that the Chalukyas of Kalyani followed the imperial traditions of the Vatapi Chalukyas and the Rashtrakutas of Manyakheta and their period of more than two hundred years was a period of cultural efflorescence of Karnataka. Innumerable lithic records and some copper plates and literary texts like *Vikramankadevacharita*, *Manasollasa* and *Vikramankabhyudaya* of Bhulokamalla Somevara, *Mitakshara* of Vignaneswara, Merutunga's *Prabandhachintamani* and Ranna's *Gadayuddha* and *Ajitapurana* are very helpful to a student of history in reconstructing the historical and cultural edifice of the times of Kalyani Chalukyas. The Chalukyas of Kalyani claim to be the close kith and kin of the Vatapi Chalukyas. But the origin of this family is debatable. After a close study of the available evidences, B.R. Gopal held the view that the Chalukayas were an indigenous Kannada family belonging to the occupation of agriculture and military background, who settled in and around and the Badami region. B.R. Gopal further thinks the word Chalukya is an archaic Kannada term.

The founder of the Chalukyas of Kalyani line Tailapa II, who was a feudatory of Rashtrakuta Krishna III, declared independence and started his reign from AD 973. He ruled for a period of 24 years from AD 973 to 997 and is credited with victories over Chedi, Orissa, Nepal and Kuntala. He is also said to have killed Munja, the Paramara ruler of Malwa. Taila was succeeded by his son

Satyasraya, who claims to have won a victory over a Chola invader. Satyasraya was followed in succession by Vikramaditya V, Jayasimha I and Jagadekamalla. Jagadekamalla claims to have defeated Paramara Bhoja, the ruler of Malwa and the ruler of Chedi and Rajendra of the Chola line.

Jagadekamalla was followed by Somesvara I who ruled from AD 1042 to 1068 with the titles of *Ahavamalla* and *Trailokyamalla*. Bilhana in his *Vikramankadevacharita* states that Somesvara I built the city of Kalyana and made it his capital. V. Venkataraya Sastry is of the view that Kalyana appears to have been in existence even during the reign of Jayasimha II and was one of his Nelavidus or Skandhavaras. As Sankaracharya in his *Soundrayalahari* mentions the city of Kalyana as great Devipitha, it can be safely surmised that Somesvara I made Kalyana a well guarded city and shifted his capital to Kalyana in the longer and larger interest of the safety from the invaders. Jayasimha Jagadekamalla's records refer to Etagiri, Kolhapur, Poltalakera or Patancheruvu, Kolippakai as Nelavidus or Skandhavaras or capitals and further a record dated AD 1044 refers to Pottalakere as the capital of Somesvara I. B.R. Gopal is of the view that it was only after AD 1044 that the capital was shifted to Kalyani, now in the Bidar district of the Karnataka region 48 miles north-east from Malkhed, the capital of the Rashtrakutas. Somesvara I carried on the struggle with the contemporary Chola power. While the Chalukyas claim victory over the Cholas, the Cholas stoutly deny it. Chola epigraphs claim that Somesvara I was defeated at Koppam in AD 1055 and again at Kudalasangamam in AD 1061. It appears that Dharavarsha, the Nagavamsi ruler of Chakrakuta accepted his supremacy and the territories of Kosala and Kalinga were occupied by him. After Somesvara I, his son Somesvara II became the ruler with the title of *Bhuvanaikamalla* and ruled till AD 1076. From Bilhana, we come to know that Somesvara I wanted to make his second son Vikramaditya his successor and after the refusal of the offer by Vikramaditya, Somesvara II was made the ruler. It appears that the relations between the brothers strained as Somesvara II took to evil ways. A civil war broke out and in the end, Vikramaditya won and became the ruler.

Vikramaditya VI had the title of *Tribhuvanamalla* even before he assumed the sovereignty. Vikramaditya bore the title of *Tribhuvanamalla* from AD 1071 and ruled from AD 1076 to 1126. Vikramaditya started a new era of Chalukya Vikrama era and continued wars against the Cholas. K.A.N. Sastri argues that both Vikramaditya VI and his Chola contemporary realised their parity in might and the futility of continuing hostilities and they suspended their raids into each other's territories. This is only partially correct as Vikramaditya continued his designs against Vengi and in the meanwhile he had to take measures to suppress the rebellious ambitions of Ballala I and Bittiga Vishnu Vardhana of the Hoyasalas, his subordinates. After a protrated battle with Hoyasalas, Vikramaditya succeeded in mastering the Hoyasalas and made them submissive to him. Along with subjugating the Hoysalas Vikramaditya renewed hostilities against Vengi and by AD 1118 or 1119, Anatapala Dandanayaka the famous general of Vikramaditya gained control over Vengi. For all practical purposes, the Chola power disappeared from the other parts of Andhra too. Vikramaditya appointed his younger brother Jayasimha as Yuvaraja who however revolted against his brother in AD 1083. Bilhana and Vignaneswara were patronized by him. Vikramaditya VI was followed by his son, Somesvara III, who ruled from AD 1126 to 1135. He assumed the titles of *Bhulokamalla* and *Sarvajna Chakravarti*. He also started a new era by name Bhulokamalla era. He appears to be a peace-loving ruler. Somesvara III was the author of *Manasollasa* and *Vikramankabhyudaya* in Kannada. He was succeeded by Jagadekamalla II who ruled from AD 1135 to 1151. Jagadekamalla II was followed by his son Tailapa III, who ruled from AD 1151 to 1163.

As Tailapa III was a very weak and incompetent ruler the Kalachuri chieftain Bijjala, slowly and gradually usurped power by AD 1157 and Tailapa III died while fighting with the Kakatiyas. Somesvara IV, the son of Talipa III ascended the Chalukya throne but he failed to safeguard the Chalukyan power and was defeated in AD 1190 by the Hoysala Balala II and thus ended the Western Chalukyan power of Kalyani. The death of Vikramaditya VI saw the beginning of the decline of Chalukyan power. Their subordinates the Kakatiyas of Warangal, the Yadavas of Devagiri, the Hoyasalas of Dwarasamudra and the Kalachuris began to take advantage of the weakness of the rulers and began to make preparation to declare their independence. The Chalukyas of Kalyani disappeared from the arena of political power by AD 1190 during the reign of Somesvara IV.

Polity

The Chalukyas of Kalyani also followed the hereditary monarchical form of government, wherein the king was the head of the state with effective power. They bore the titles of *Samastabhuvanasraya* and *Vijayaditya*. Their insignia was a boar signifying the *Varahavatara* of Lord Vishnu that protected the earth. Interestingly the Chalukyan queens and other family members actively participated in the administrative process. Queen Lakshmidevi, wife of Vikramaditya VI claimed in an epigraph to be ruling from Kalyana. We have some more evidence of Lachchala Mahadevi, wife of Somesvara I and Ketaladevi another queen of Somesvara I participating in administration. *Manasollasa* prescribes the qualities of the ministers and mostly ministers' posts were hereditary. *Manasollasa* suggested the number of ministers to be 7 or 8. There is a view that the Western Chalukyan polity had elements of feudalism because of the existence of graded powerful political intermediaries like *Samanta*, *Mahasamata*, *Mahasamantadhipati* and *Mahamandalesvara* along with *Senapathi*, *Dandaanayaka*, *Mahadandanayaka* and *Meghaprachandadandanayaka* of the military service. For administrative convenience the territory was divided as *Rashtra*, *Vishaya*, *Nadu*, *Kampana* and *Thana*. There is no clear-cut demarcation between *Rashtra* and *Vishaya* and *Nadu* except that *Vishaya* and *Nadu* are considered as smaller units than *Rashtra*. All the copper plate charters reconciling important transactions are addressed to all

Rastrapatis, *Vishayapatis*, *Gramakutakas*, *Ayuktakas*, *Niyuktakas*, *Adhikarikas*, *Mohattaras* and others. The above indicates the channels of communication between the ruler and the ruled to be collective.

It is believed that during the rule of the Chalukyas of Kalyani, social life was based on traditional *Varnasarama* model. Though caste was universal and hereditary, the connection between caste and occupation was not rigid. The woman of higher strata of society played an important role in social and administrative matters; S.L. Shantakumari writes that the epigraphical records pertaining to this period reveal the names of a number of women not only belonging to royal families but also those of others lower in rank who distinguished themselves in almost all walks of life like administration, religion, social and cultural aspects of life of the period. Akkamahadevi, a Chalukya princess also led the armies in battle.

The Chalukyas of Kalyani patronized fine arts. An epigraph dated in AD 1045 refers to the construction of a *Natakasala* or theatre in the premises of a Jaina temple. We have epigraphic references to a flutist, songsters, florists, drummers and dancers, being given grants for their maintenance. On the basis of epigraphical evidences, K.A.N. Sastri holds the view that next to the court, the temple was the great promoter of fine arts. Architecture, sculpture in stone and metal, and painting were promoted by the temples. An inscription dated AD 1085 from Nagai refers to a great sculptor Nagoja, who is called *Kandarana Vidyadhirajam*, the master of the art of engraving and we have references to other sculptures and engravings. We have evidence of an epigraph from Shirur which states that *Kankana* or bracelet, *Katisutra* or waistband, *Nupura* or anklet and three sets of necklaces with suitable pendents were offered to the temple of Vishnu. We have reference to a merchant Sovisetti who supplied precious stones to the emperor and to General Barmadeva.

Trade and commence and agriculture were the backbones of the economy of the Chalukyan state. Majority of the people were engaged in agriculture as an occupation. The rulers encouraged agricultural operations by providing irrigational facilities like excavation of tanks, construction of irrigation canals which increased the fertility of the soil. A number of epigraphs testify to the above mentioned activities. Epigraphs refer to the classifications of cultivated land as wet land, dry land and garden land, and tax collected from agriculturalists was not uniform and it varied from area to area. An inscription from Kolhipaikkai records that the lands were classified as *Uttama*, *Madhayama* and *Adhama* and even the villages were classified as above on the basis of fertility and yield. There existed private ownership of land along with joint ownership in villages. What epigraphs prove of this period is that economic disparities among different sections of the populace are noticeable. Traders were organized into a number of autonomous guilds, with their own traditions and insignia and *Prasasti*. The most celebrated of such merchant guilds was the 500 Swamis of Ayyavolepura; who claim to be the protectors of *Vira Bananjadharama,* i.e., the law of the noble merchants. G.S. Dikshit is of the view that the period of the

Chalukyas of Kalyana was the heyday of the guilds like the reign of their enemies the Cholas. The most important guild of Ayyavola, Ainurrvar, Virabalanja or Valanjiyar or Nanadesi had its origin in Aihole in Bijapur district. This guild was very active in the regions of Tamil Nadu, coastal Andhra, Rayalseema, Telengana and Kerala; it had its activities overseas such as Burma, Malaya and Sumatra. The growth of trade and commerce led to the growth of market towns in all the above mentioned regions.

What we notice during this period in the religious domain is a general atmosphere of spiritual conciliation in which many creeds lived together on a basis of mutual tolerance. Saivism and Vaishnavism were the major branches of Pauranic Dharma of the present-day Hinduism. Sakti was also worshipped as Kollapura Mahalakshmi and Kartikeya was also worshipped and the main centre of Kartikeya worship was Kudidatani in Bellary district. Next in order, Jainism was also very popular and commanded a larger following. Basavesvara's Virasaivism was also very popular. Saivism appears to have become the dominant faith of the country and Srisailam was visited by the royalty. We come to know from epigraphs that Attinabbe, the daughter-in-law of Dhalla and wife of Nagadeva was a Jaina celebrity. She is also known as *Danachintamani* and appears to have constructed a big Jaina *basadi* at Lokinagundi. Buddhism too flourished at Belagave and Dambal.

Kannada and Sanskrit languages flourished during this period. Santinatha, the author of *Sukumarachaitra*, Nagavarmacharya, the author of *Chandrachudamanijattaka* are well-known scholars. Ranna rose to the position of *Kavichakravarty* or poet laureate in the court of Tailapa II and wrote *Ajitapurana* in AD 993. Ranna described his work as *Kavyaratna* and *Puranatilaka*. Durgasimha, the author of *Panchatantra* belonged to the time of Jayasimha II Jagadekmalla. One Sridharacharya, a Jaina Brahmin of the time of Ahavamalla Somesvara claims to have written the first Kannada work on Jyotisha or astrology by name *Jatakatilaka* in AD 1049. Nagachandra or Abhinava Pampa wrote *Mallinathapurana* and *Ramachandracaritapurana* or *Pampa Ramayana*. Nayasena completed his *Dharmamrita* in AD 1182. Besides the above Jaina scholars, a number of Virasaiva scholars also promoted Kannada languages and literature. There were more than 100 writers, many women among them with Mahadeviyakka as a leader, among the Virasaiva teachers and writers. The Vairasaiva works are known as *Vachanas*. Besides *Vachanas*, distinctive Kannada metres like *Shatpadi*, *Tripadi* and *Vagadas* have also come into use.

Coming to Sanskrit literature, most well known are Bilhana's *Vikramankadevacharia* historical Kavya on the life of Vikramaditya VI and *Manasollasa* of Somesvara III, the Kalyani Chhalukyan ruler and *Mitkshara* of Vignanesvara. Chalukya Jagadekamalla, who ruled between AD 1138–1150, is credited with the writing of musical treatise *Sangitachudamani* in Sanskrit.

K.A.N. Sastri observes that the art of Chalukyas of Kalyani found its fulfilment in the architecture and sculpture of Hoysala temples in Mysore. Art historians point out that the Kalyani Chalukyan temples had their principal entrances at the sides, and the decoration of their exterior was singularly graceful and lavish. The art critics further observe that the Kalyani Chalukyan *Vimanas* were a compromise between the plain stopped storeys of the early Chalukyan style and the closely moulded tiers of the Hoysala temples. The doorways of the temples were elaborately carved. Temples of Ittagi are a perfect example of their artistic and sculptural glory. The Chalukyas of Kalyani earned a place of permanence in the evolution of Indian culture by their contribution of arts, agriculture, sculpture, painting and languages of Kannada and Sanskrit and by their liberal religious and realistic political policies.

Religious Developments

A survey of the religious phenomenon in the Indian context from the perspective of space and time reveals that it was never static but constantly underwent modifications by assimilating and absorbing new features of practices and worship. *Sanatanadharma*, the forerunner of the later day Hinduism, advocated *Jnana*, *Vairagya*, *Bhakti* and *Karma* paths to reach God, while *Jnana* and *Vairagya* paths were followed by superior intellectual groups, the *Karma* and *Bhakti* paths are followed by common folk. It is a well-known fact of history that Vedic Yagnas, worship of primitive deities with offering of blood, meat and toddy, the domestic rituals and worship of icon in temples, heterodox beliefs like Jainism and Buddhism flourished side by side, sometimes competing for space and sometimes adjusting, accommodating and absorbing other rituals into its fold. We have already noted that initiation of puranic dharma in the Gupta and post-Gupta era along with devotionalism of an individual God – Siva and Vishnu and Sakthi worship revived the age-old *Bhakti Marga* as a popular way to attain God and to achieve liberation. It is to be noted that the Bhakti movement evolved in the South due to the efforts of saints, was different from the early Bhagavata cult of northern India. There is no unanimity among scholars regarding the nature of the Bhakti cult. K.A.N. Sastri observes that this movement was strongly theistic in its character and definitely aimed at putting down Jainism and Buddhism. R. Champakalakshmi points out that the religious changes of the 7th to 9th centuries are hence viewed as a revival of orthodox forms, though not strictly a revival of Vedic religion per se. The Bhakti movement has often been characterized as a popular movement of dissent or protest against the social hierarchy of the Brahmanical order. Kesavan Veluthat and M.G.S. Narayanan suggest that the Bhakti movement represented an ideology which sought to reflect and legitimize the emerging socio-political order which developed as an unpremeditated by-product of the new Brahmanical agrarian settlements centred on temples, partly as a means of fulfilling their missions and partly as an antithesis. Whatever may have been the objective and nature of the Bhakti movement, an ardent personalized devotion to Siva and Vishnu become deep-rooted in the psyche of the common people.

The Saiva saints are known as Nayanars and the Vishnava saints are known as Alvars. We have references to 63 Nayanars and 12 Alvars. Soul-stirring songs were composed in Tamil in praise of Siva and Vishnu and sung in temples. The most important of the Nayanars were Tirunavakkarasu, a Vellala, Jnanasambandar, a Brahmin and Sundaramurthi, another Brahman. Nambi Anadr collected the hymns of the above three in a canonical work called *Thevaram*. Another Saint Nayanar Manikkavasagar was also very popular. We also come across a female Nayanar from Karaikkal, Nandanar, a pariah, whose hymns attracted the attention of many devotees. The well-known Vaishnav Alvars were Nammalvar, Timmankaialvar and well-respected and revered woman-poet Andal. The Vaishanav saints' compositions are collected in a canonical work called *Nalayirajaprabandham*. Although there were some Brahmins, among the saints, most of them were of the lower castes, belonging to the community of cultivators and artisans.

The sacred texts of the *Divyaprabhandam* reveal that Vaishnavism had its major centres in the northern and southernmost parts of Tamil Nadu and a few in the Kaveri region. Contrary to the Vaishnava impact the Saiva centres had their greatest concentration in the Chola region, i.e., Kaveri valley, in around the Pallava and Pandya capitals Kanchipuram and Madurai and their centres appear to be more than the Vishnava centres. By the time of the Cholas, Saiva centres proliferated beyond the Kaveri region. Saivism could acquire a more popular and stronger base through the incorporation of mother-goddess worship, along with tribal and popular forms of worship. The inclusion of Murugan, a tribal deity into the Saiva pantheon was also a clever move which made Saivism very popular. While Saivism gained ground among agricultural and artisanal groups belonging to lower social order, Vaishnavism was popular among the dominant peasant groups and ruling elite.

The rise and popularity of the Bhakti movements led to the construction of temples in a large scale as centres of activity in different parts of the subcontinent in general, and particularly in the peninsula. Temple construction activity was undertaken by royalty as well as the subordinate chiefs of the king. It is no wonder that at this time the temple became an institutional base for socio-religious and political order. It is well illustrated by the Thanjavur and Gangaikonda Cholapuram temples. By associating variety of people from various walks of life as active participants in the construction of the temple, the kings opened up channels of social communication and economic activity. Further, the establishment of educational institutions like *Ghatikas*, hospitals and *Mathas* was undertaken with the purpose of showing the concern of the religious and political elite in the interests of the common people. In a way Bhakti movement indirectly helped the growth of the power of royalty.

Another significant aspect of religious development to be noted is that of revival of *Sanatanadharma* or the Brahmanical religion. Kumarila Bhatta and Sankaracharya, by their effort revived the Brahmanical tradition. Both Kumarila Bhatta and Sankara were known as *Smarthas* or traditionalists who championed and revived the ancient Brahmanical religion. Kumarila Bhatta participated in religious discussions with the Buddhists and defeated many

Buddhist scholars. Kumarila enunciated the philosophy of ritualism or Mimamsa. Sankaracharya was born at Kaladi on the banks of the Alwaye river in North Travancore in the family of Nambudri Brahmins. Govindayogi was his guru. He is believed to be born in AD 788. He lost his father very early and became an ascetic at a very early age. Sankara toured the whole of India propagating his Advaita philosophy and established four Mathas in different corners; Sringeri, Dwaraka, Badrinath and Puri and thereby tried to propagate his new philosophy of rigorously consistent monoism. Ramanujacharya the greatest of the Vaishnava acharyas was born at Sriperumbudur near Madras in the first quarter of the eleventh century. He became the head of Srirangam matha after the demise of Yamunacharya. He propagated *Visistaadvaita* philosophy which reconciled devotion to personal God with the philosophy of the Vedanta. He affirmed that the soul, though of the same substance as God and emitted from him rather than created; can obtain bliss not in absorption but its existence near him. He is said to have weaned the Hoysala king Vishnuvardhana from Jainism and established a well organized Matha at Melkote. Ramanuja went ahead of all the religious reformers by throwing open the temples to the outcastes one day in a year. Ramanujacharya died in AD 1137 and he is worshipped as an *Avatara* even today. In due course of time schism developed among the devotees of Ramanuja who were divided as *Vadagalai* (northern branch) and *Tengalai* (southern). Another great acharya of the 13th century was Madhvacharya the advocate of *Dvaita* or dualism. He was born shortly before AD 1200 in a Brahmin family at Kalyanapura in Udipi Taluk of South Kannada district. He too became a 'sanyasi' at a young age and toured India. He built a temple for Lord Krishna at Udipi and lived and preached his philosophy. He authored 37 books and of them, the most important are commentary on *Brahmasutras* and on *Bhagavadgita* and a book called *Anuvyakyana*. His central teaching was an acceptance of the world's realities and of the distinction between *Jeevatma* and *Brahman*. The *Jivatman, Brahman* and the world were eternal realities and all the three had independent existence. He advocated that salvation could be attained through the grace of Vishnu and *Brahman* could be realized in himself and this was nothing but bliss. Basava is famous as the founder of Virasaivism or the Lingayat cult. It is known as Aradhya Saivism in the Andhradesa. There are differences between Virasaivism or Lingayat religion and Aradhyasaivism of Andhradesa. Basava rejected the authority of the Vedas and injunctions and the prohibitions of the Brahmins and founded a new priesthood called the *Jangamas*. He ridiculed pilgrimages and sacrifices and preached equality of men and women. Basava laid more emphasis on social problems than on theology. He stood for the abolition of caste distinctions and encouragement of manual labour based on professions and simple living along with a singleness of purpose. In North India this period saw the emergence of Islam as a major component of the cultural evolution of India. In Malabar region of Kerala, Christianity was making a similar impact.

13

The Pallavas of Kanchi

Society, Polity, Economy and Culture

The significance of the Pallava period is that it is the culmination of what had been a gradual process of assimilating the Aryan culture and the emergence of the Tamil personality. During this period, the political relations among powers of the Deccan and further south were based on the geo-political interests, which led to conflict between the Pallavas of Kanchipuram, the Chalukyas of Badami and the Pandyas of Madurai. By the beginning of the 7th century AD, the Pallavas with Kanchipuram as their capital emerged as an important power after replacing the Kalabhras. A serious debate is going on about the origin and homeland of the Pallavas. Primarily there are two theories, (i) foreign, and (ii) indigenous, about their origin. Lewis Rice based on the resemblance of the words Pallavas and Pahlavas concludes that the Pallavas were the descendants of the Pahlavas, a branch of the Persians and argues that the word Pallava is a Sanskritized form of 'Pahlavas'. On the other hand, N. Srinivasa Ayyangar maintains that the Pallavas were of Naga origin based on a reference to Naga-Chola alliance in *Manimekhalai*, which appears to be more realistic given the fact that Nagas in the reference can be adduced to the Andhras and the early Pallavas ruled the region of the lower Krishna valley. K.P. Jaiswal who regards Pallavas as a branch of the Vakatakas further strengthens this theory. R. Sathianatha Iyer relying on the Asokan epigraphs and on the prevalence of the regional names like Pulinada, Puliyaraw in Tondaimandalam, considers them as Pulindas. On the basis of the fact that the early Pallava epigraphs are found in Andhra region, K.A.N. Sastri, R. Gopalan and C. Meenakshi consider them as chieftains under the Satavahanas who became independent after the decline of the Satavahanas. Contrasting the above identification, R. Raghava Iyangar and S. Krishnaswamy Iyangar are of the opinion that they are Tamils, basing their arguments on the information furnished by the epic *Manimekhalai Tondaiyar* is the name given to the Pallavas by Thirmangai Alwar. Romila Thapar thinks that the traditions woven around the story of a young prince falling in love with a Naga princess and the story of binding the child with a creeper or twig, points a foreign origin of the Pallavas. For the last fifty years and more, the origin of the Pallavas has remained a mystery to be unlocked.

Though the Pallavas became an important political power in the beginning of the 7th century, theirs is an old power. The Pallavas, who ruled prior to the beginning of the 7th century, are known in history as early Pallavas. The early Pallavas issued two types of epigraphs: (i) in Prakrit, and (ii) in Sanskrit. There is a view that the Pallavas were the feudatories of the Satavahanas and started ruling independently after the fall of the Satavahanas. As all the inscriptions of the early Pallavas were discovered in the districts of Guntur and Nellore, it is believed that the Telugu country south of the Krishna river formed the bulk of the Pallava kingdom until the last quarter of the 6th century AD. We come to know from Sanskrit epigraphs of the Pallavas that they ruled from AD 350 to 550. The following are the rulers of this line known through their genealogical lists: Simhavarma I, Skandavarma I, Skandavarma II, Kumaravishnu II, Buddavarman, Kumaravishnu III, Skandavarman III and Vishnuvarman II. We learn from one of the epigraphs that Buddavarman has been described a 'submarine fire' to the ocean of the Chola army. From this, it can be inferred that there was hostility between the early Pallavas and the early Cholas and after subduing the Kalabhras the Pallavas became the rulers of Kanchi and established a secondary lineage. Simhavishnu, who ruled from AD 555 to 590, is considered the founder of the line of the Greater Pallavas. Simhavishnu, the founder of the Great Pallava line assumed the title of *Avanisimha* or lion of the earth. He was not only a great general who conquered Cholamandalam, the kings of Ceylon and the three Tamil states and brought peace and order by subduing the Kalabhras but also a patron of Bharavi, the author of *Kiratarjuniya.* The Adivaraha temple at Mahabalipuram provides the relief of Simhavishnu, his two queens and his son Mahendravarman. Mahendravarman I, son and successor of Simhavishnu, ascended the Pallava throne and ruled from AD 590 to 630. He assumed many titles like *Chitrumalla*, *Gunabhara, Vichitrachitta, Mattavilasa, Sankimajati, Chitrakarapuli* and *Avanibhajana*, each one reflecting his versatile accomplishments. It was Mahendravarman, who was responsible for the growing political strength of the Pallavas, and made the dynasty the arbiters and patrons of Tamil culture. He was a contemporary of Harsha of Thaneswar, and Pulakesin II of Badami. The most important political aspect to be noted is the beginning of the long-drawn rivalry for political supremacy between the Pallavas and the Chalukyas of Badami. Pulakesin II's Aihole epigraph bears testimony to the fact of the success of Chalukyas against Mahendravarman. The epigraph proudly proclaims that Pulakesin II "caused the splendours of the lord of the Pallavas to be obscured by the dust of his army and to vanish behind the walls of Kanchipura".

Originally a Jaina by faith, he appears to have been converted to Saivism by Appar, who himself was a convert to Saivism from Jaina faith. In spite of his defeat at the hands of Pulakesin II, Mahendravarman earned eternal fame by his scholarship, interest in music and by his patronage of art and architecture. Mahendravarman was a renowned builder of rock-cut temples in Trichinapally, Chengalpat, North Arcot and South Arcot districts. He also built temples in honour of Vishnu, Isvara and Brahma. The Mandagapatti epigraph informs us "This brickless, timberless, metalless and mortarless temple which is a mansion for Brahma, Isvara and Vishnu, was caused to be erected by the King *Vichitrachitta*". He also excavated a rock-cut temple in honour of Vishnu, on the banks of the Mahendravadi near Arkonam in the North Arcot district, which is known as Mahendra Vishnugraham. The rock-cut temples at Vellam, Dalavanur, Mahendrawadi and Mamandur are the best examples of rock-cut architecture. His reign is famous for popularization of rock-cut architecture and his title *Vichitrachitta* or the man with new or curious ideas is indicative of his personality. Mahendravarman's abiding and deep interest and love for fine arts is unparalleled. His title *Chitrakarapuli* is also very significant because the paintings on the ceiling of a rock-cut temple at Sittanvasal in the Pudukkottai region are attributed to him. His proficiency in music can be known from his Kudimiyamalai inscription that contains a musical tabular note. We may surmise from this that he has taken the title of *Sankimajati*. He composed two works in Sanskrit, *Mattavilasa Prahasana* and *Bhogavadajjuka*. His construction of a town Mahendramangalam or Mahendravadi and the tank at Mamandur known as *Chitramegatatakam* prove his interest in irrigation and promotion of secular engineering skills.

Mehendravarman I was succeeded by his son Narasimhavarman I, who ruled from AD 630 to 668. Narasimhavarman I followed his father's example and raised the glory and prestige of the Pallavas by his conquests and artistic achievements. He is popularly known as *Mamalla*. His reign of 39 years is full of significant events. Narasimhavarman decided to reconquer the territories lost by his father to the Chalukyas of Badami. He with the help of a King of Ceylon succeeded in defeating Pulakesin II in AD 642. He not only defeated him but also occupied Vatapi and as a mark of that assumed the title of *Vatapikonda* (the conqueror of Vatapi). He also undertook a successful naval campaign against the ruler of Ceylon. Besides these political victories, he made himself eternally remembered by introducing the Mamalla style of architecture. Mamallapuram bears eloquent testimony to his style of architecture. Paramesawra Varman mentions his victory over the Chalukyas in his Kurram plates. Another event of great significance was the visit of Hiuen Tsang who provides a graphic description of the fertility of the soil, learning habits of the people, and the condition of Buddhism and Jainism in the Pallava kingdom. Narasimhavarman was succeeded by his son Mahendravarman II, who ruled only for a period of two years from AD 668 to 670. His reign witnessed the invasion of the Chalukyas under Virkramaditya I, son of Pulakesin, who defeated him. Mahendravarman II was succeeded by his son Paramesvara Varman I. From the Udayendram plates, we come to know that he won a victory over the Chalukyas at Peruvalanallur. Paramesvara Varman was a known devotee of Siva and he built many temples for Siva and granted Parameswara Mangalam village to the Siva temple built by him at that village. Paramesvara Varman was succeeded by his son Narasimha Varman II, who ruled for 28 years from about AD 700–728.

He assumed the titles of *Rajasimha* (lion among kings), *Agamapriya* (lover of scriptures) and *Sankarabhakta* (devotee of Siva). True to his title of *Sankarabhakta*, he built the Kailasanatha temple or Rajasimhesvaram at Kanchi, the Siva temple at Penamalai and a famous shore temple at Mamallapuram. We know from the inscription available at the Kailasanatha temple that he had a queen by name Rangapataka and the crown prince Mahendravarman III. He patronized the famous poet Dandin. He sent an embassy to China. Interestingly the Chinese annals provide information regarding his efforts to counter act the efforts of the Arabs. Paramesvara Varman II, one of the sons of Narasimha Varman succeeded him and ruled for a short period of three years from about AD 728 to 731. Once again, he had to face the invasion of the Chalukyas of Vatapi led by Vikramaditya, who was helped by a Ganga prince Nandivarman Pallava Malla, the next great Pallava ruler who ruled from AD 731 to 796. It is said that the Pallava kingdom was plunged into crisis after the death of Paramesvara Varman II. In that period of crisis, the officials of the court chose a twelve-year-old boy Nandivarman as the ruler. He had to fight against the contemporaneous Chalukya, Rashtrakuta and the Pandya kings. Vikramaditya II of the Chalukyas of Vatapi appears to have gained a short-term victory over him. Rajasimha I, the Pandya king at Pennagadem, also defeated him. In these difficult days, the Pallavas entered into matrimonial alliance with Dantidurga of the Rashrakutas. Because of the marriage Dantivaman was born, who became the successor of Nandivarman Pailavamalla. The construction of Vaikunta Perumal temple at Kanchi and patronage of Tirumangai Alwar suggest that he must be a Vaishnavite. He is also said to have built a temple at Kanchi known as Paramesvara Visnagaram and a Kesavaperumal temple at Karam. Dantivarman, the son and successor of Nandivarman Pallava Malla ruled from AD 796–847. He had to face the invasion of Govinda III of the Rashtrakuta line. The decline of the Pallava power set in during his reign. The disintegration of the Pallava political power structure accelerated during the reign of Nandivarman III, who ruled from AD 847–849. He had the title of *Avanivaranam* and was defeated by the Pandyas at Kumbakonam. After his death, his three sons began to quarrel over succession and it gave scope for the Cholas and the Pandyas to participate in the civil war. In this civil war, Nrupatunga, one of the sons of Nandivarman III died and Aditya Chola and Kamavarman defeated Aparajita, another son. The last became a feudatory of the Cholas. The Pallava power ended.

Polity

Theoretically, the king was the sole source of authority. The Pallavas maintained that as they were the descendants of Brahma, the kingship was of divine origin and was hereditary. We find the election of a king when there was no direct heir to the throne, as happened in the case of Nandivarman Pallava Malla. Generally, kings assumed high-sounding titles like *Maharajadhiraja*, *Dharmamaharajadhiraja* and more unusual *Agnistoma-Vajapeya-Aswamedhayaji*. All these titles indicate the impact of the Aryan culture and the process of assimilation that took place during that period. As we are aware, the performance of Vedic sacrifice does not have any special significance as in the days of later Vedic age; but during this period these performances appear to have had special political connotation as they served to legitimize the right to rule independently of the Pallava overlords. Owing to the change in religious milieu, we find a change in the ideal of kingship and performance of the Vedic sacrifices by kings disappear. A number of ministers who appear to have gained more powers during the later Pallava rule assisted the king. These ministers also bore semi-royal titles and at times, they were appointed from among the subordinate allies or feudatories. These kings followed the practice of appointing a Yuvaraja or crown prince and generally, he played an active role in the administration or in wars as we come to know from the epigraphs of the period. Besides the ministers and the Yuvaraja, we come across a number of officials of various ranks who performed many duties on behalf of the king.

For administrative convenience, the kingdom was divided into a hierarchy of administrative units. The provincial administration was entrusted to a hierarchy of offices. In the Pallava kingdom, the *Nadu* the equivalent of the modern district emerged as the main unit of administration. Below the *Nadu*, we have villages. In the villages, the basic assembly was entrusted with matters relating to the village, like endowments, irrigational activities, cultivable land, punishments of crime, census records and all other necessary activities, The Sabha that was a formal institution worked very closely with the *Ur*, an informal gathering of the entire inhabitants of the village. The village headman acted as both the leader of the village and mediator with the government and was the link between the village assembly and the royal administration. As the king was regarded as the owner of the land, he had the right to make revenue grants to his officers, religious establishments, or get the land cultivated by small farmers and big property owners. The predominant practice of this time was entrusting collection of land revenue right to big landlords. There existed both crown lands and private lands. Crown lands were rented out to tenants at will. Grants of lands were given to officers in lieu of salaries. We do not come across the practice of supplying troops or giving revenue to the state as was in the regular feudal structure. As such, there is a controversy regarding the nature of relationship between the sovereign and minor rulers and chieftains or important royal dignitaries. There is one view that it was the ritual status of the anointed king that made minor chieftains or royal dignitaries obey him. Some others consider the minor rulers as feudatories but as we do not find feudal relation between the two, this view is discarded. It is suggested that it would be better to designate them as subordinate allies instead of feudatories or ascribing ritual status to powerful rulers. A striking feature of the Pallava polity was the importance attached to innumerable local groups based on caste, craft, profession or religious faith. We come across associations of artisans; association of merchants, of ascetics, of temple priests each with its own samayadharma or code of conduct. In Pallava polity, we notice three important territorial assemblies: *Ur*, Sabha and Nagaram. Generally, the *Ur* was a non-Brahmanical assembly while the *Nagara* was an assembly of mercantile groups. All these local assemblies or bodies used to meet regularly every year while the day-to-day tasks were taken care of by a small executive body. Every group had its autonomy in accordance with its own constitution based on custom and usage and solved the problems of members at the local level itself. In matters of common interest affecting the lives of more than one group, decisions were arrived at after mutual consultations. By giving powers or accepting the decisions of the local autonomous corporate groups to resolve their problems at local level, the burden of the government was lessened largely and this strategy adopted by the Pallavas minimized the opposition of the people towards the government. Though the Pallava rulers did not involve themselves at the local level, they seem to have strengthened their base by creating more and more *Brahmadeya* or *Agrahara* or *Devadana* villages. Interestingly, these Brahmana settlements were created throughout the core area of the kingdom, which depended on rice cultivation for its prosperity, and sustainability. In due course, the *Sabha* or *Mahasabha* of the Brahmin settlements evolved into a system of governance through committees. This is known as *Variyam* or committee system, which became a hallmark of self-government in the Brahman settlements. The Sabha through its *Variyam* system supervised the maintenance of roads and tanks, management of charitable donations, regulation of irrigational rights and temple affairs. Consequently, the *Brahmadeya* and *Agrahara* villages became predominant during the Pallava period.

The people knew rice, coconut, palm plantations, palmyra and areca palm, orchards of mangoes and plantains. Many of the villages depended on tank irrigation and this land was known as *Eripatti* or tank. Besides tanks, they knew well-irrigation. Fitting of sluices regulated water flow through canals.

Two types of taxes were collected: (i) land revenue at the rate of one-sixth to one-tenth of produce value from each cultivator was collected and paid to the state and (ii) a tax, collected and utilized for local needs. They also collected taxes on draught cattle toddy tappers, marriage parties and professions. The amount of tax levied on these was not known. Romila Thapar thinks that as there were no large areas under cultivation, the land revenue income of the Pallavas was small. There is a view that during this period the state did not receive substantial amount of income from trade and commerce. Much of the royal revenue was spent on maintaining the army. The Pallavas appear to have depended on the standing army rather than on troops supplied by the subordinate allies. The army consisted of infantry and cavalry alone. Chariots and elephants were almost absent. The Pallavas appear to have classified their officers as civil and military. They also developed navy and built dockyards at Mahabalipuram and Nagapattanam and developed maritime trade with South-East Asia, in particular with Kamboja, Cambodia, Champa (Annam), and Srivijaya, the southern Malay Peninsula and Sumatra seems to have flourished in the period.

Society

The social structure of the Pallava period witnessed the growing impact of the Aryan culture. Because of this impact, a pre-eminent position was assigned to the Brahmins both in status and in grant of lands. Further, Aryanization was evident in the sphere of education. During the Pallava period, the Brahmins superseded the Jains and the Buddhists in formulating policies. Though the Jaina and the Buddhist centres of education continued to exist, they lost the royal patronage. Ghatikas, the educational institutions catering to the needs of resurgent Sanantana Dharma were pervading. Every temple in general had a Ghatika attached to it. Though in the beginning, any twice-born was admitted into these Ghatikas, gradually they became the centres of Brahmanical students. The Ghatikas in due course became important centres of political activity supporting the cause of monarchy as a political institution. In those days, the University of Kanchi was the most well-known educational institution comparable to the Nalanda University. However, by the 8th century, the Matha, a combination of a rest house, a feeding centre and a seminary began to play a crucial role in the spread of education of a particular sect. Sanskrit continued to be the court language and the language of literature, Bharavi's *Kiratarjuniya* and Dandin's *Dasakumaracharita,* two outstanding standard Sanskrit works were produced in the South. On the other hand, the prominent Bhakti saints of this period popularized Tamil through their hymns and songs composed and sung in praise of the popular deities, Siva and Vishnu. Tamil devotionalism that became very popular in the 6th and 7th centuries can be known from the Tamil songs and works of the Nayanar and the Alwar saints. Of the Saivite saints, the most popular was Appar, who converted king Mahendravarman to Saivism from Jaina faith. Another feature to be noticed is that the majority of these saints came from lower castes of artisans and cultivators. The Bhakti movement led to the popularization of musical instruments like the flute, and the dance form of Bharatanatyam at temples. During the Pallava period, we notice some prosperous temples maintaining a group of dancers. The devotionalism in turn led to the construction of temples on a large scale, which reflected the Pallava style of art and architecture.

Percy Brown, the famous art historian and critic, points out: "of all the great powers that together made the history of Southern India, none had a more marked effect on the architecture of their reign than the earliest of all, that of the Pallavas, whose productions provided the foundation of the Dravidian style". K.A.N. Sastri aptly observes that the Pallavas bridged the transition from rock architecture to structural stone temples. The temple architecture of the Pallavas is divided into rock-cut and structural. The rock-cut temples are further divided into excavated pillared halls and monolithic shrines known as Rathas. Romila Thapar states, "Pallava temples were usually free standing buildings, but the tradition set by the Buddhists for cave temples still continued". The Brahmans and the Buddhists vied with each other in cutting shrines and temples into the Deccan hills, where, by this time, worship at these shrines may have been open to any one, the rivalry between the two religions not being particularly felt by ordinary people. The most impressive of these cave temples are the Buddhist shrines at Ajanta and the Buddhist and Hindu temples at Ellora. Even the Jains joined in and excavated a few temples at the latter site.

Mahendravarman I started the building of the rock-cut temples in South India. He built Mahabalipuram or Mamallapuram, an immortal centre of artistic excellence by making it 'the birth place of South Indian architecture and sculpture'. The excavated shrines initiated by Mahendravarman are simple pillared halls cut into the back or sides of walls. An interesting feature of the cave temples built by Mahendravarman I is the presence of inscriptions giving details about them. For example, the cave temple at Madagapattu in South Arcot district refers to his construction of a temple dedicated to Vishnu, Siva and Brahma without using brick, mortar, timber or metal. He built a five-celled cave temple with an elaborate plan at Pallavaram near Madras. Four more cave temples were built at Mamamundur in North Arcot district. He also built another temple for Siva at Siyamangalam, known as Avanibhanjana Pallaveswaram. The upper rock-cut temple at Tiruchiraplli is considered by far the best of his cave temples. Here in this temple, we notice the first representation of Gangadhara. Here we have direct evidence about his conversion to Saivism in the shape of an inscription treating Jainism as an alien faith. A portrait of an individual worshipping Siva in this temple is identified as that of Mahendravarman himself. He cut rock temples for Siva and for Vishnu. We find two Vishnu temples built by him in the North Arcot at Mahendravadi and Sivagaram known as Mahendra Vishnugriha and Ranganadha temple respectively. The Ekambareswara temple at Kanchi has a pillar mentioning his titles. As a Jain, prior to his conversion to Saivism, he built a cave temple at Sittanvassal. It is said that a few sculptures found in the Gunadharmeswara temple belonged to his times. His subordinate Kandesina constructed a cave temple at Vallam, near Tirukkalakkunram. Post-Mahendravarman art and architectural pieces are found at Mamallapuram. They are divided as: (i) cut-in cave temples popularly known as Mandapas, (2) rock-cut monolithic temples popularly called *Rathas*, (3) structural temples, and (4) bas-relief sculptures found in the open air on rocks. Of the first category of cave temples, only some are nearly complete and they are of modest proportion. The plan of these cave temples is not the same. At some places, the sanctums are cut at the backwall. In others, we find them projected into the hall from the rear wall. We also notice a pillared pavilion in front beside the sanctums, and sanctums cut in the outer wall of the rock face. Thus, we find no uniform pattern. The main factor seems to have been the convenience of the architect. While most of the caves are plain without sculptures, the Mahishasuramardini cave, the Adivaraha cave, the Varaha and the Trimurti caves have sculptures. Differing from the other cave temples, the Panchapandava cave was the biggest cave with sanctum in the centre with provision for a circumbulatory path around. In the other category, the most famous are the *Panchapandavarathas* or seven Pagodas, of Dharmaraja,

Bhima, Arjuna, Draupadi and Sahadeva. These are not uniform in shape. While Draupadi Ratha is a simple hut-shaped temple, the Arjuna Ratha is two storeyed, the Bhima Ratha is a rectangular Vimana and Dharmaraja Ratha is three storeyed. Their plans are also different. The Sahadeva Ratha is an apsidal temple with a portico in front. The other three Rathas are of Ganesha, Pillari and Valaiyam Kuttai. There is a controversy regarding the ruler who built these at Mamallapuram. Some are of the view that they were built during the reigns beginning with that of Narasimhavarman and ending with Narasimhavarman Rajasimha. Some others ascribe them to Rajasimha based on the epigraphical evidence that appears to be more rational. The Pallava age saw a transition from rock-cut architecture to free-standing temples. Rajasimha was responsible for this transition. He is credited with the construction of three structural temples at Mamallapuram. The most significant of them is the shore temple, which happens to be the earliest free-standing temples in South India. Rajasimha also built such structural temples at Panamalai and at Kanchi. Kailasanatha temple built at Kanchi has all the features of the Pallava style, a Pyramidal Viman and a detached pillared hall or Mandapa in front. In later centuries, Arthamandapa joined the Mandapa and the other structures. His successors also continued the temple building activity. Temples were built at Oragadam, Tiruttani and Gudimallam. Mulakeswara and Matangeswara temples were built at Kanchi. While the pillars of the Mamalla style are slender and supported by squatting lions, rampant lions support the pillars of Rajasimha style, which are also slender. K.A.N. Sastri observes that to the Pallavas, however, belongs the credit of having kept up and developed the tradition of Amaravati, and transmitted it to lands beyond the seas where in course of time there arose vast monuments that threw even the splendid achievements of the mother country into the shade. The Pallava rock-cut caves and structural temples are filled with sculptures. The sculptures in the rock-cut cave temples display well-rounded limbs, an elongated face, a double chin, snubnose and thick lips. During the post-Mahendravarman times, both religious and secular paintings are found in abundance. Sculptural depictions that received the acclaim of art critics were found at Mamallapuram. They are depictions of Lord Krishna lifting Mount Govardhana, Arjuna's penance and the killing of Mahishasura. Various forms of Siva such as Lingodbhava mounts and Tripurantaka are depicted in sculptural panels. The favourite theme of the sculptors appears to be different forms of Siva. The tiny Gopura makes its earliest appearance here. The Pallava age witnessed a lot of development in the field of painting also. The rich heritage of the Pallava paintings can be seen in the Jain cave temple at Sittanvassal, the Kailasanath temple at Kanchi and the Talagiriswara temple at Panamalai. In these paintings, dark colours predominate and the painters appear to have used dry surface that was given a thin coat of lime. In the words of Romila Thapar "to cover the walls of deep cut caves with murals was an achievement of no mean order, considering the difficulty of inadequate lighting and poor working conditions in these caves and structural temples". In those days, the colours were made from minerals and plants and their uniqueness is that they retain some of their original brilliance. The paintings were both religious and secular. It is already stated how music was patronized by them. In conclusion, it can be said that during the Pallava period the penetration of the Aryan culture of North India into the South led to the assimilation of some of the patterns, ideas and institutions and rejection or modification of certain other aspects. Tamil devotional culture was one of the results of this interaction. The Pallavas consciously laid foundation for a synthesis of the broad based Indian culture and made their place in the history of India secure.

14

The Cholas of Tanjore

Society, Polity, Economy and Culture

The Cholas were an ancient political power, mentioned in the Asokan epigraphs and the Sangam literature. Karikalachola was the earliest well-known ruler of the earliest Chola line. Urayur was their capital. Once again, the Cholas rose to the imperial position during the period AD 850 to 1200. Chola Aditya I, son of Vijayalaya crushed the political power of Aparajita, the Pallava king, in the last quarter of the 9th century and laid foundations for the rule of the Cholas of Vijayalaya line. The history of this period was dominated by the rivalry of the Cholas with the Rashtrakutas of Manyakheta and later with the Chalukyas of Kalyani.

Vijayalaya, who ruled between AD 846 and 871 was the founder of the imperial Chola line, well known in the history of India as conquerors of repute, efficient administrators and patrons of art and architecture. Originally, a feudatory of the Pallavas, Vijayalaya took the city of Tanjavur from the Mutharaiyar of Pudukkottai and made Tanjavur his headquarters. This initial success strengthened the power of the Cholas. Taking advantage of the civil war between the Pallava heirs Nriptunga and Aparajita, Chola Aditya joined hands with Aparajita. Both Aparijata and Aditya won a decisive victory over Pallava Nriptunga at Sripurambiyam near Kumbakonam in AD 885. Later Aparajita rewarded Aditya by granting additional territory. However, a dissatisfied Aditya waged war against Aparajita, killed him in AD 903, and annexed the whole of Tondaimandalam. Later, Aditya annexed the Kongu country and thereby made the Pandyas accept his sovereignty. The crown prince Parantaka in all these conquests helped Aditya. Parantaka's rule followed that of Aditya from AD 907 to 955 for a period of 48 years. His reign was marked by success and prosperity except towards the end of his career. His death was followed that of by anarchy and confusion that was ended by Rajaraja I, who ascended the Chola throne in AD 985 and ushered in the imperial phase of the Chola rule of the Vijayalaya line. Rajaraja I successfully united the entire Tamil country into a single powerful state by his successful conquests. He first attempted to weaken the confederacy of the rulers of Pandya, Kerala and Simhala. First, he crushed the power of the Pandyas and then brought Kerala under his control, He also despatched a naval force against Simhala and occupied the northern half of the island, destroying Anuradhapura and making Polonnaruwa the capital of the Chola province in Simhala.

Rajaraja extended the frontiers of his kingdom by conquering certain areas of Karnataka and knocking at the gates of Tailapa II the Chalukyan ruler of Kalyani. Further, Rajaraja made the eastern Chalukyan kingdom of Vengi, a Chola protectorate by offering the hand of his daughter Kundavai to Vimaladitya and installed Saktivarman, (Vimaladitya's brother) as the ruler of Vengi. After successfully extending his control over Vengi, Rajaraja turned his attention towards Satyasraya, the western Chalukya ruler. Rajaraja claims that Satyasraya prayed for peace and the Chola army returned with immense booty, which was used for the construction of the magnificent Rajarajeswara or Brihadiswara temple at Tanjavur. Rajaraja is said to have conquered Maldives towards the end of his reign. He also maintained friendly relations with Srivijaya, the maritime kingdom of Sumatra. In AD 1041, after a long and successful reign, Rajaraja passed away and was succeeded by his son Rajendra, a worthy successor and son to Rajaraja. He made his son Rajadhiraja the *Yuvaraja* in AD 1018. He completed the conquest of Ceylon; yet he had to face constant trouble from them as the Ceylonese were not reconciled to his conquest. It is suggested that the motive behind invasion and conquest of Ceylon was his desire to rob them and use the booty for the local betterment of the Chola state. He constituted a separate viceroyalty for the Pandya and Kerala territories with the headquarters at Madura. Rajendra claims to have supported Rajaraja to Vengi throne, and proceeded to Kalinga to teach a lesson to the eastern Ganga ruler who opposed Rajaraja at Vengi, from then he proceeded to the Ganges valley. After his successful invasion, he assumed the title of *Gangaikonda* and built a new capital named 'Gangaikonda Cholapuram' and the tank of this new capital was filled with the water of Ganga, which is called 'liquid pillar of victory'. Rajendra also despatched a large naval fleet against Srivijaya in AD 1025. The reason for this invasion appears to be the desire to control the route to China for diplomatic and commercial purposes. Rajendra occupied Srivijaya and Kadaram or Kedah on the west coast of Malaya. He is also credited with the suppression of rebellions in the Pandyan and the Kerala territories, also led an expedition to Ceylon in AD 1041, and ruthlessly put down the rebellion. After a successful reign of three decades and after making the Chola power supreme, he died in AD 1044. Rajadhiraja, who ascended the Chola throne after his father, continued Rajendra's aggressive policy of expansion. He fought with the Chalukyas of Kalyani and defeated them in a battle at Pundur on the Krishna, gained Yadgir and sacked the new Chalukyan capital Kalyani. He performed Virabhisheka and assumed the title of Vijayarajendra. As a mark of his victory at Kalyani, he took away with him the image of the Dwarapalaka that can be seen even today at the museum in Thanjavur. The Cholas continued their wars with the western Chalukyas of Kalyani and the eastern Chalukyas of Vengi.

With Kulottunga Chola's accession in AD 1070, a new era commenced in the history of the Chola empire. Kulottunga Chola was more of a statesman than an expansionist, but continued the policy of fighting for the control of Vengi region and Tungabhadra *doab* against the Chalukyas of Kalyani. He reinstated the local rulers and wisely concluded a peace with Ceylon by giving his daughter in marriage to the Simhalese prince Viraperumal. In AD 1077, a Chola embassy of merchants was despatched to China. Epigraphic evidence reveals the existence of a Tamil merchant guild at Srivijaya. Kulottnga's sons ruled over Vengi as viceroys. When the eastern Ganga ruler failed to pay tribute, he despatched an army under Karunakara Tondaiman against Kalinga. Jayagonda's celebrated war poem in Tamil *Kalingattupparani* records vividly the Kalinga invasion. Except for the loss of Ceylon, the rest of the territory remained intact under his rule. He maintained diplomatic relations with Kanauj of northern India and the rulers of Burma and Kamboja in Indo-China. However, towards the close of his reign, he had to forgo certain territories due to the revolts in Karnataka and Vengi. Consequently, Chola territory was confined to Tamil Nadu including Malabar region. Kulottunga Chola ruled until AD 1120, though his son Vikrama Chola is said to have started his rule from AD 1118. Vikrama Chola's rule was marked by peace. He is credited with renovating the temple of Nataraja at Chidambaram and with the improvement of Ranganatha temple of Srirangam. After Vikramachola, his son Kulottunga II ruled from AD 1135 to 1150. He carried on the construction of the Chidambaram temple. His son Rajaraja II ruled from AD 1150 to 1173. The Chola political fortunes began to decline and powerful feudatories emerged as rulers of different parts of their territory. Kulottunga III, the last great ruler of the dynasty, followed him. He again revived the glory of the Cholas by defeating Vira Pandya of the Pandyas of Madurai. He defeated the Cheras and Hoysala Ballala II and had *Vijayabhishekha* performed at Karuvar in AD 1193. He had to wage a war against the Pandyas as Kulasekhara Pandya, the successor of Vira Pandya revolted. The Chola Kulottunga III sacked Madurai and demolished the coronation hall of the Pandyas in AD 1205. This led to further wars between the Cholas and the Pandyas. Once again, a war arose between Kulottunga III and his son Rajaraja III, and Sundara Pandya. In this war, Sundara Pandya drove away the Cholas. The Cholas appealed to Hoysala Ballala II. It is said that realizing the impending danger, Sundara Pandya discretely restored to Cholas their throne and assumed the title of 'Sonadu-valangiyaruliya', i.e., who was pleased toi give away the Chola kingdom. Rajaraja Chola III ruled from AD 1216 to 1256 and appears to have been defeated by Sundara Pandya and Pallava Kopperajanga. Narasimha II of Hoysala helped Rajaraja Chola to regain his throne in AD 1231 and the friendship between the Cholas and Hoysalas continued for some time. Yet, Jatavarma Sundara Pandya defeated Chola Rajendra, the successor of Rajaraja III, Rajendra III was the last of the Vijayalaya line and his latest regnal year is 33, corresponding to AD 1279. At this time the Chola empire suffered an eclipse and became a part of the Pandyan empire.

Administration

Generally, the Chola kingdom was characterized as a centralized bureaucratic state where the sovereigns lived in magnificent palaces. They were assisted by a graded bureaucracy. In recent years vigorous research by scholars with a thorough examination of the available epigraphs and structural constructions suggests a new perspective to the study of the Chola state and society. Burton Stein, an American historian suggested that the Chola state was a segmentary state, but some critics point out that this segmentary state concept was untenable as the insistence on dual sovereignty, i.e., political and ritual was not a reality. Another perspective suggested was that of the model of the feudal state by historians like R.S. Sharma, D.N. Jha and Champaka Lakshmi. Spencer, another American historian argues that the viability and stability of the Chola state depended upon the plunder of the contemporary neighbouring states in the guise of constant invasions. B.D. Chattopadhyaya suggests that the model of the integrative state is applicable to the Chola state. Romila Thapar is very critical of the above theories and argues that the relationship between the relatively autonomous, local, agrarian, commercial, and religious organizations and the hierarchical political authority needs further critical investigation before we arrive at a theoretical model. The Chola state carefully surveyed and classified all land suitable for irrigation into taxable and non-taxable lands, as land revenue was the major source of income. We come to know that the village was assessed as a whole and revenue was payable either in cash or in kind. Granting of lands to the beneficiaries for the services rendered to the king was very common. It is suggested that in the Chola period the Brahmins and the Vellalas were the two landowning groups, who were classified as the wealthy and less wealthy. We come across tenants and cultivators also. Brahmadeyas or the Agraharas existed in large numbers in the Chola state. The local bodies and the state provided irrigation facilities. A feature which needs to be noticed is the emergence of individual ownership of land from the village controlled land in the later part of the Chola rule. In the Indian context, peasant uprisings are few but we come across sporadic instances of agrarian discontentment. For administrative convenience, the Chola Empire was divided into *Valanadu* or *Mandalam*, *Nadu* and *Kurram* in descending order. Large townships formed a separate Kurram called as *Tanniyuror, Tankurram*; *Mandalam* or *Valanadu* was the largest administrative unit, which can be compared to a province. K.A.N. Sastri observes that 'the most striking feature of the Chola period was the unusual vigour and efficiency that characterized the functioning of the autonomous rural institutions. Romila Thapar suggests that the village assemblies were crucial to Chola administration. The earliest references to village Sabha in the Tamil land are found in the epigraphs of the close of the 8th century AD from the Pandya and the Pallava territories. K.A.N. Sastri maintains that the origin and early history of these assemblies is at present very obscure, although their general prevalence over the whole of southern India is widely proved by innumerable inscriptions. Two Uttrameruru epigraphs of Parantaka give us valuable information regarding the functioning of village assemblies. The two epigraphs record resolutions passed by the local Mahasabha on the constitution of Variyam or executive committees. We come to know that each village was divided into 30 wards. Each ward had to nominate selected persons possessing certain qualifications like: (a) ownership of more than one-fourth *veli* of land, (b) residence in own house on one's own site, (c) aged between 35 and 70, (d) knowledge of Vedic mantras and of being a Brahmana. The records further state that as an alternative, one who had one-fourth *veli* of land and knowledge of one Veda and a Bhashya can be nominated. The epigraph also specifies those to be excluded from the process of nomination. They are: (a) individuals who were on the committee for the past three years, (b) those who being members of the committee failed to submit accounts, and (c) those who committed incest or great sins and those who had stolen the property of others. From among such nominees who met prescribed norms, one had to be chosen for each *Kudumba* or ward through the process of *Kuduvolai* or pot ticket. Of the 30 who were elected by this process, 12 were appointed to the annual committee – 12 to the garden committee and six to the tank committee. Besides these committees, there also existed a standing committee and a gold committee. The number of committees and membership also varied from village to village. The members of the committees were known as *Variyapperumakkal*. Generally, regular royal courts, besides the village panchayats, administered justice. The courts followed the practice of depending on evidence. The Chola rulers spent a good amount of money on public utility services. They looked after the maintenance of roads, bridges and ferries. They undertook irrigation facilities such as construction of the dams, artificial reservoirs, tanks, and wells. The Cholas maintained a huge standing army and navy. Chola epigraphs refer to seventeen regiments of army, consisting of infantry, cavalry and elephants. The kings actively lead the army assembly, met in a temple and sometimes, it met on the bank of a tank or under the shade of a tree. These assemblies managed all the activities of the entire village. They were not only the sole proprietors of the village lands but also collected total amount of the tax revenue due to the state. They were empowered to act as a court of justice. Thus, the village assemblies were entrusted with the general welfare of the local activities of the village. The ordinary peasant villages met at an assembly called the 'ur' and in the Brahmadeya villages, the assembly met at the Sabha. It appears that royal officials were present at the meeting. Their role was restricted to being present in the battlefield, and Rajaditya and Rajadhi Raja I died the on battlefields of Takkolam and Koppam. The Chola rulers were ruthless in war and caused misery to the people who were in no way connected with the war. They possessed a strong navy which enabled them to control the Coromandel and the Malabar coasts. This navy also helped them to conquer other countries like Ceylon, Maldives, Sumatra and the Malayan Peninsula.

Society

During the Chola period, society was in a flux, and was organized based on Varnasrama model. K.A.N. Sastri observes that the general atmosphere was one of social harmony and contentment with the existing order. Differences and disputes were there but were seldom acrimonious. Epigraphs state that towards the close of the reign of Kulottunga I, the 'bhattars' of a village consulted the codes and laid down the professions to be followed by the Anuloma caste of Rathakaras. Another epigraph testifies that the Chola ruler granted the privileges of the blowing of two conches, the beating of drums and so on, at domestic occurances, good or bad; the use of sandals when people went out of their homes and the plastering of the walls of their residences with lime plaster. We also notice proliferation of subcastes like Kaikkala, Chatti, Cheek, Kammalar, and Rathakara besides the regular four Varnas. Another feature to be noted is the further division of the subcaste into *Valangai* and *Idangai* or the right hand and left hand castes. This division appears to be based on the social position of the subcastes in the society.

The Chola kings were Saivites and constructed a number of Siva temples. The Vaishnava faith was also prevalent during this period. Because of the growth of temple-based Bhakti movement, the temple became the centre of all activities in each village. K.A.N. Sastri observes that the temple became a landlord, an employer, a consumer of goods and services, a hospital, and a theatre, in short, a nucleus, which gathered round itself all that was the best in the art of civilized existence and regulated the people with the humanness born of the spirit of Dharma. The medieval Indian temple had few parallels in human society. In the literary sphere too, the Chola period constitutes, the most creative epoch of South Indian history. Tamil literature made rapid strides during this period. Owing to the growth of devotion based temple worship of icons of Siva and Vishnu, the saints propagated their faith in the vernacular language of Tamil. Of this category, the most important one was that of Sekkiliar's *Periapuranam* or *Tiru Hondapurana*. This work is venerated as the sixth Veda. The other important devotional literary works are *Tiruvalaiyadala Puranam* of Nandi and *Ramanuja-Nurrandai* of Amundanor. Among secular literary works, the most important are *Sivakasindamani* of Tirukkadevar, Kamba's *Ramayana* and Jayagondar's *Kalingattupparani*. Vikramachola Kulottuga II and Rajaraja II patronized Ottakuttan as a court poet. Ottakuttan wrote an *Ula* on each of his patrons. He also appears to have written Parani recording of Vikrama Chola's Kalinga War and *Pillaittamil* on Kulottuga II. Coming to grammar, *Virasoliyam* of Budhamitra and *Nannul* by Pavanandi are very important works. Sanskrit literature was also encouraged by the Chola rulers. Vaishnava religious works were composed in Sanskrit. We may conclude with the statement of K.A.N. Sastri that the age of the imperial Cholas was the golden age of the Tamil culture. It was naturally marked by the widespread practice and patronage of literature. The Prabandha form became dominant and the systematic treatment of Saiva 'siddhanta' in philosophical treatises began. A quantum of Vaishnava devotional literature and commentaries on the canon also came into existence. Interestingly, Jaina and Buddhist authors also flourished in this period. The picture of religious practices, beliefs and life in the Chola period is quite complex. There appears to have been a perpetual stirring and mixing of various creeds, each influencing the other and being influenced in turn. K.A.N. Sastry aptly remarks that because of this long process of assimilation the Buddhist Vihara, the Jaina Palli, and the Hindu temple presented many similarities in their worship, organization and festivities in the midst of equally striking differences; and the ideals of asceticism and renunciation made a common appeal to all religions alike. It is a fact that there existed religious differences, but they did not tend to social discord. We can say that the religious environment did not create animosity between followers of different faiths.

Art and Architecture

The Cholas, who ruled for centuries in the early medieval period, inherited and continued the traditions of the Pallavas and Pandyas in the promotion of art and architecture. They built many stone temples throughout their kingdom. The early Chola stone structural temples are not very large and the district of Pudukkottai has a number of temples and among them, the Vijayalaya Cholesvara temple at Narttamalai claims our attention. This temple is said to have been built by Vijayalaya, the first Chola ruler; undoubtedly, it is a fine example of the early Chola style. Temple building activity appears to have received great impetus during the reign of Rajaraja I and his famous son Rajendra.

Rajaraja I built many temples in the early years of his rule and one of such unique structures was the Tiruvalisvaraswami temple at Brahmadesam in the Tirunevelli district. Its wealth of sculpture is unique. The Uttara Kailasa shrine at Tiruvadi in Tanjore district, the Vaidyanatha temple at Tirunelavadi in Trichinopoly district, the twin temples of Siva and Vishnu at Dadapuram in South Arcot district, and Sivadevala 2 at Polonnaruva in Ceylon are the other notable examples of Rajaraja's encouragement of temple construction The maturity of Chola temple architecture finds expression in the two magnificent temples of Tanjore and Gangaikonda Cholapuram. The superbly executed Siva or Brihadisvara temple that took six years or more for completion is a fitting memorial to the material advancement of the time of Rajaraja. It is the largest and the tallest of all temples of India. The Vimana, the Arthamandapa, the Mahamandapa and the large Nandi pavilion in front are all aligned in the centre of a spacious walled enclosure, 500 ft by 250 ft, with a Gopura gateway on the east. The main feature of the whole scheme is the great Vimana reaching a height of nearly 200 feet over the Garbhagriha in the west and dominating everything in its vicinity. A massive dome consisting of a single block of stone, 25 ft high and weighing 80 tons covers this temple. The temple structure is covered from the base to the top with sculptures and decorative mouldings. Percy Brown, the famous art historian praises the Tanjore Vimana as a touchstone of Indian architecture as a whole. K.A.N. Sastri aptly observes "the Tanjore temple as a whole is the finest monument of a splendid period of South Indian history and the most exquisite specimen of Tamil architecture at its best. The temple is remarkably alike for its stupendous proportions and for the simplicity of its design". He further observes that the temple's great dignity is due to the simplicity of its parts, the square vertical base, the tall tapering body, and overall the graceful domical finial. Rajendra, the worthy son of Rajaraja I built the temple of Gangaikondacholapuram. Today this temple stands in lonely wilderness but for mud huts and a nearby small village. It was built in the style of Rajarajeswara or the Brihadeswara temple at Tanjore. This temple is larger in plan, but is not as tall as the Tanjore temple. Its Vimana is 100 ft square at the base and 186 feet high. This temple is a large rectangle 340 feet long and 110 feet wide. The temple occupies the middle of the immense walled enclosure. The existence of a substantial bastion at the south-east angle and a smaller one in the west made scholars suggest that it was designed for defence purposes. The temple's main entrance is located in the east, next to it is located the Mahamandapa. It is a low building 175 ft by 95 ft with over 150 pillars of ordinary design. There are similarities as well as dissimilarities between the two temples built by Rajaraja and Rajendra. The scheme of decoration and sculpture is more ornate in this temple compared to Tanjavur temple. Of the Chola temples of the later times, the temple of Airavatesvara at Darasaram of Tanjore district and the Kampaharesvara temple at Tribhuvanam near Kumbakonam built by Rajaraja II and Kulottunga III deserve special mention. The architecture and sculpture of both these temples have many features in common with their predecessors. In the Darasuram temple, one of the Mandapas is designed in the shape of a chariot drawn by elephants.

Art historians and critics point out that the influence of Chola art can be noticed in the conception and execution of the temples of Indo-China and Far East. Ananda K. Coomara Swamy found a parallel of Chola architectural and sculptural designs in a temple of old Zayton or modern Chun Chow, opposite to Farmosa. The Chola phase is also well known for masterpieces of sculptures and bronzes. Bronze images of Siva, Brahma, the Saptamatrikas, Vishnu and his consorts Lakshmi and Bhudevi, Rama and Sita with their attendants, Sambandar, a Saiva Saint and the infant Krishna dancing on the serpent Kaliya are famous examples of their artistic skill. Coming to sculpture, it is said that the Chola sculpture shows classic grace, grandeur and perfect taste. Portraits, icons and decorative sculpture are the main items of sculpture. Among the Chola bronzes, the image of Nataraja occupies a unique place. The Nataraja of the Nagesvara temple is one of the largest and finest images known. Grousset describes the divine dancer, Nataraja as follows, "whether he be surrounded or not by the flaming aureole of the *Tiruvasi (Prabhamandala)* the circle of the world which he both fills and oversteps – the king of dance is all rhythm and exaltation. The Tambourine that he sounds with one of his right hands draws all creatures into this rhythmic motion and they dance in his company. The conventionalised locks of flying hair and the blown scarfs tell of the speed of his universal movement, which crystalizes matter and reduces it to powder in turn. One of his left hands holds the fire that animates and devours the worlds in this cosmic whirl. One of the God's feet is crushing a titan, for 'this dance is danced upon the bodies of the dead'. Yet one of the right hands is making the gesture of reassurance or Abhayamudra, so true it is that, seen from the cosmic points of view and, indeed, on more than one of our bronzes, the king of dance wears a broad smile. He smiles at death and at life, at pain and at joy alike, or rather, if we may be allowed so to express it, his smile is both death and life, both joy and pain. Here art is the faithful interpreter of the philosophical concept".

The Cholas continued the tradition of Pallavas and the Pandyas in painting too. Of the Chola paintings, the most important are to be found in the Pradakshina passage round the sanctum of the Tanjore temple built by Rajaraja and Rajendra. Invariably the theme of the painting is religious. In art, religion and letters, foreign trade and maritime activity, the Chola period reaches heights of excellence never reached either in the past or in the succeeding periods.

India's Cultural Contacts with South-East Asia

India or Indians never lived in splendid isolation but since times immemorial Indians had cultural and trade contacts with the outside world. By the beginning of the first millennium, the civilization and culture of India began to penetrate slowly across the Bay of Bengal into both inland and mainland South-East Asia. By the 5th century AD, the Indian religions Sanatana Dharma, Buddhism, and cultural traditions took deep roots in the regions of Burma, Thailand, Indo-China, Malaysia and Indonesia. The impact of the eastward spread of these regions was not sudden but took place in waves. The cultures of modern South-East Asia offer evidence of a long period of contact with India. We can notice the influence of classical language of India on South-East Asian languages and scripts. Likewise, the theory of kingship, traditional dance and puppetry, and place names, customs and traditions exhibit Indian influence.

Romila Thapar suggests that religion found an ally in commerce to carry the Indian way of life outside India. In this process, Buddhism acted as a catalyst introducing Indian culture to different parts of Asia. The demands of trade with eastern Mediterranean made Indian entrepreneurs enter South-East Asia, as it was the land of spices and semi-precious stones. Invariably, trade leads to closer interaction between the settlers and the original inhabitants. Through contact and interaction, Indian cultural influence slowly and gradually penetrated into the local pattern of life particularly in present-day Thailand, Cambodia and Java. Chinese annals testify to Indian activities in Funan or the Mekong delta as the first sphere of influence. Indians also established small settlements in the Malay Peninsula as it was connected with maritime centres on the east coast of India. Evidence is available of ships sailing from Tamralipti and Armaravati to Myanmar or Burma, Martabam and Indonesia. Ships sailed from the ports of South India to Tennaserim, Trang, the straits of Malacca and Java; the western parts of India also participated in the promotion of trade and commerce. In this context, Romila Thapar is of the view that the nature of the Indian connection varied according to the region from where it came and kind of relations it had with the host country. The available epigraphic and literary evidences prove that from the first century onwards, systematic colonization of these areas was undertaken. Ptolemy's reference to Yavanadvipa proves that such influence existed in the first century AD itself. We know the existence of Indian communities in Funan or Cambodia. Further, we have a reference to a Brahmin, Kaundinya as a founder of a dynasty in southern Thailand. The kingdom established by Kaundinya appears to have flourished for a few centuries and evidences of epigraphy and literature testify that by the beginning of the 5th century AD, Indian influence in South-East Asia was firmly established.

By 6th century AD, the Sailendra Empire rose in the Malayan peninsula, where we notice the caste system, the Brahmanical faith and its rituals and Sanskrit language within a century of its rule. It reached its glory in the 7th century within a span of three centuries; the Sailendra Empire began to fight with the mighty Cholas. Here we notice a sort of mingling of Brahmanical and Buddhist faiths and the famous and the magnificent Buddhist monuments of Borobudur were built. The Sailendra empire included the islands of Sumatra, Java and Borneo. By the 9th century, Java became independent. Kamboja, a former vassal state of Funan gained importance as it is said to have ruled for 900 years. Of this kingdom and its rulers, Jayavarman I and II, Yasovarman and Suryavarman II are considered the most important. This kingdom of Kamboja is said to have included modern Cambodia, Laos, Vietnam, Thailand and parts of Burma and the Malayan Peninsula. The kings were the followers of Saivism, and Sanskrit became the language of the country. The famous temple of Angkorvat built by King Suryavarman II and the ruins of Angkorthom stand as testimony to the greatness of Kamboja. Angkorthom was the capital of Kambhoja, which was built in the form of a perfect square. The kingdom of Kamboja appears to have declined after Jayavarman II, but it continued to exist as a small principality till the end of the 13th century.

Champa or modern Thailand was another famous kingdom, which included the southern portion of Indochina or South Vietnam, Cambodia, some parts of Thailand, Laos and North Vietnam. It too was established in the 1st century AD with Indrapura as its capital. It is said that more than 19 dynasties belonging to Indian origin ruled over the region for more than 11 centuries. Most of the rulers appear to be worshippers of Siva but some of them also worshipped Vishnu. The Champa kingdom disappeared after a prolonged struggle with the kingdom of Annam.

Coming to the erstwhile Ceylon, the connection between India and Ceylon is as old as our epic, the *Ramayana*. The regular colonization of Ceylon begins with the conquest of this island by Vijaya, the founder of the Simhalese dynasty. It is a well-known fact that Asoka Maurya sent Mahindra and his sister Sanghamitta to Ceylon to spread Buddhism. Slowly and gradually, Buddhism became a religion of significance and popularity in Ceylon. History testifies to intimate contacts between these two countries. Burma or *Suvarnabhumi* also had contacts with India since times immemorial. There is evidence to prove that relationship between the two is as old as the Buddha himself. Ashoka is credited with sending of Sonna and Uttara, missionaries of Buddhism to Burma who successfully converted Burma into a land of Buddhists. Hindu settlements were set up in Arakan, Srikshetra, Thalin and Peger; Indian influence is very visible in Burma too. Thus, what we see in 'Greater India' or 'further India' is the spread of Indian pattern of life into these territories and a blending and mixing of local pattern with the Indian pattern. It is quite an exaggeration to state that these territories were more Indianized by the adventurous efforts of traders than by religious missionaries of Buddhism and Brahmanical faith of Sanatanadharma.

15

The Age of Rajputs

Society, Economy and Culture

In the perspective of traditional historians, the period from the post-Gupta era to the establishment of the Delhi Sultanate, is a dark period. Absence of unified large empires and division of India into smaller territorial states based on lineages is the reason to depict this period as a dark age in contrast to the so-called golden age of the Guptas. For some historians, this assumption implies political chaos in the absence of large empires. In the 20th century, as the focus of the historians shifted to the study of regions it is now agreed that this period was seminal to significant historical changes in form and space.

We can observe that from the early decades of the 7th century AD upto the establishment of the Delhi Sultanate, history of India appears to have been dominated by certain individuals motivated by a desire for expansion, who waged war with their neighbours. After the death of such individuals once again India slipped into political fragmentation. By the end of Harsha's reign, northern India became a prey to political disorder and natural famines which caused misery to the people. Later Guptas resumed the Gupta rule in Magadha and were displaced by Yasovarman of Kanauj in the middle of the 9th century. Bengal or Vanga or Gauda came under the rule of the Palas and later the Senas. Gopala, who was elected king by the people, was the founder of the Pala dynasty. Gopala, Dharmapala and Devapala were rulers of significance and Indra Dumnapala was the last of the Pala dynasty. Senas succeeded to the throne of Bengal towards the end of the 12th century. Vijayasena and Vallalasena were important rulers and it was Vallalasena who reorganized caste system and introduced *Kulinism* among the Brahmins. Lakshmana Sena of this line partronized Jayadeva, the author of *Gita Govinda*. While the Palas were patrons of Buddhism, Senas patronized Vaishnavism of the Purnanic Dharma. Assam or Kamarupa was for sometime ruled by the Palas of Bengal and the Ahoms invaded Assam in AD 1228 and occupied it till the time of AD 1825. Nothing is heard of Kanauj, until Yasovarman, a Maukhari king became its ruler. The political fortunes of Kanauj, the cultural capital of northern India shifted frequently until AD 1294, when it fell into the hands of Mahammad of Ghor.

Western India, particularly Gujarat and Malwa, was ruled by the Gurjara Pratiharas. The Gurjara Pratiharas resisted the Arab incursions and at a later date Gujarat was occupied by the Rashtrakutas.

In the post-10th century of Central and Western India, we notice the rise of numerous political powers, who claimed to be Rajputs and feudatories of the Gurjara Pratiharas. It is also to be noted that the political developments in North, Western and Central India were greatly influenced by the developments in the contemporary West and Central Asia. We are well aware that the entry of Arabs in the 7th and the 8th centuries as traders and later as invaders made significant impact on India and specifically on the Gurjara Pratiharas. Palas and Rashtrakutas had to meet the Arab challenge in economic and political spheres. Punjab and Multan went under the control of Mohammad of Ghazni, who plundered and took away wealth to consolidate his position in Central Asia. We will be reading in detail about the invasions of Ghazni and Ghori and their impact which led to the establishment of the Delhi Sultanate in AD 1206 in the next chapter.

Rajputs: Origin

The issue of the origin of Rajput lineage is highly complex and controversial. Some historians are of the view that the Rajputs descended from Central Asian migrants perhaps, Hunas or possibly Gurjaras. But this view appears to be shaky. There is also a view that they were the Kshatriyas of the lunar race of Somavamshi and also the Kshatriyas of the solar race. Rajasthan's bards and chroniclers consider them as fire-born or Agnikula Kshatriyas. The legends in currency refer to four fire-born clans – Paramara or Pawar, Pratihara or Parihar, Chahamana or Chouhan, and Chalukya or Solanki. The legends state that four heroes emanated from the sacrificial fire pit of Sage Vasishta on Mount Abu. These are considered to be the ancestors of the chief Rajput clans and this is mentioned in Chand Bardai's *Prithivirajraso*. The birth of Rajput heroes from the sacrificial fire pit implies that they were purified by Agni or fire and if it is so, what could be the reason? It is very difficult to answer this in one sentence and we can agree with Romila Thapar that the discussions of Rajput identity are related to process of historical change characteristic of this period, particularly the widespread phenomenon of families from varied backgrounds rising to royal authority. They also claim a Brahama Kshatriya status. Bardic tradition holds that there were 36 Rajput founding clans and interestingly the list varies from source to source.

Early Rajput activities were dominated by the four clans claiming Agnikula origin. The new Pratiharas ruled in southern Rajasthan. The Chahamanas or Chauhans originally were based at Sakambhari, near Delhi but developed separate lines at Nado, Ranathambhor, Jalor and Sanchor in Rajasthan. Chalukya or Solanki power was concentrated at Gujarat and Kathiawar. The Paramaras established their rule in Malwa with their capital at Dhar near Indore.

Others, claiming to be Rajputs started their career as local kings in various parts of western and central India. Of such, the Chandelas of Khajuraho,

Guhillars of Mewar, the Tomaras of Delhi, the Kalachuris of Tripura and the Chedis are important powers to be reckoned with and during the nearly five centuries of their rule they exercised control over a vast region in western Rajasthan and Gujarat.

The Pratiharas or the Gurjara Pratiharas

Of the four fire-born clans, the most important were the Gurjara Pratiharas. Aihole epigraph of AD 634 first refers to them and Hieun Tsang also refers to them as *Kuchelo*. It is agreed upon that they ruled from the 8th century to the beginning of the 11th century. Their capital appears to be Bhimamal. The founder of the line of the Pratiharas was Nagabhatta I. Nearly 12 rulers are known of this dynasty and out of them Vatsaraja, who ruled between AD 775 –800, Nagabhatta II who ruled between AD 800–833, are important rulers and with the rise of the Chalukyan kingdom of Anhilvara in AD 961, the Gurjara Pratiharas lost their political and historical significance.

The Ghadwalas or Gharwars came into prominence in the later half of the 10th century and were in power till AD 1194. Govindachandra, who ruled between AD 1104 and 1155, was the greatest of this line. The Chahamanas or the Chauhans are known to have ruled from AD 700 from Sakambari. In this lineage come Vigraharaj IV and Prithviraja, the Rai of Pithora of legend and song and who opposed and died in war with Muhammad Ghor at the battle of Tarain in AD 1192 was the most important. The Chalukyas or Solankis ruled from Anhilpura from AD 974 to the beginning of the 13th century. They patronized Jainism. Mularaja was the founder of this line. The Solankis fought with contemporary Chauhans and the Paramaras of Dhara. The Paramara kingdom was established by Upendra or Krishnaraja early in the 10th century. The glory of the Paramaras comes to an end with the end of Paramara Bhoja and his successors continued as local rulers till the beginning of the 13th century. Another Rajput kingdom of importance was the Chandelas of Bundelkhand or Jajakabhukti. Dhanga was one of the most powerful kings of this line, who ruled between AD 954 and AD 1002. He was a great temple builder and even today the temples of Khajuraho are world famous. The last worthy king of this line was Paramardideva who was defeated by both Prithviraj Chauhan in AD 1182 and again by Qutubudin Aibak in AD 1203. The Chandela authority comes to a close and it lingered as a titular kingdom till AD 1310, when it was annexed to the Delhi Sultanate. They had dynastic and political relations with their southern neighbours, the Kalachuris of Chedi. The Chedi kingdom comprised two parts – northern part of ancient Dahala and southern Kosala. Tripuri or Tewar in Jabalpur was the capital of Dahala and Ratnapura or Bilaspur was the capital of Dakshina Kosala. There was enmity between the Chandelas and the Kalchuris and on account of mutual warfare; the Kalachuris of Chedi became weak and later disappeared. Thus, all the Rajput clans, in spite of their great individual valour and freedom loving temperaments failed to stop the invaders because of their mutual jealousies and desire to expand their political power base at the cost of other powers.

Socio-economic Conditions: Rajput Contribution to the Culture of India

During the post-Harsha period and the establishment of the Delhi Sultanate extremely wide ranging source material comprising epigraphic and literary is available to reconstruct the society of the period in general and that of the Rajputs in particular. Among the literary works, Kalhana's *Rajatarangini*, *Prabandhachintamani* of Merutunga, Soudhala's *Udayasundarikatha* and *Adipurana* of Jinasena, the 'Dohas' of Siddhas and many more are useful for reconstructing the social matrix of India.

Though it is generally agreed that this society was based on Varnasrama model, the social relations underwent changes due to the changing material base and the emergence of new social groups, vying for space in hierarchical order. We have to take cognizance of the fact that no Varna seemed to have remained homogenous but underwent fragmentation on account of territorial affiliation, purity of 'Gotras' and pursuance of specific crafts, professions and vocations. We have references to Brahmans as Senapatis and horse-dealers and betel-nut sellers. For example, Prithviraj Chauhan's Senapati Skanda was a Brahmin. In Gujarat and Rajasthan, the Brahmins were identified in terms of their Mula or original place of habitation and divided into Madha, Udichya, Nagara, etc., while intermediary Varnas of the Kshatriyas and the Vaisyas were absent in Bengal and in South India. The ranks of Kshatriyas multiplied during this period in North India. Many literary works and bardic recitations provide varying lists of 36 clans of Rajputs in North India and it is agreed upon that they arose out of different strata of population of tribals, foreign invaders, Kshatriyas and Brahmans. It appears that some among the captured respectable men were enrolled as the Shekhawat and the Wadhela tribes of Rajputs, while the lower categories were constituted to the castes of Kolis, Khantas and Mers. The political annals of the Rajput dynasties such as the Chahamanas of Rajasthan and the Paramaras of Southern Rajasthan, Gujarat and Malwa offer examples of the clan-based distribution of political authority. The bardic chronicles of Marwar testify to the fact that Dharaṇivaraha of the Paramara dynasty of Abu first made himself the master of the Navakot Marwar which he afterwards divided between his nine brothers. We have besides the Paramaras of Malwa, the Paramaras of Abu, Bhinmal, Jalor and Vagoda. We have Chahamanas of Bhroach as well that of Pratapgarh. Further Chahamanas of Shakambhari were divided into Chahamanas of Nadol, Jalor, Satyapura and Abu. Likewise, the Chapas ruled over small areas like Bhillamala, Vadhiyar in Kathiawad and Anhilapataka in Gujarat. Thus, the new clans and subdivision of earlier clans were drawn into the Rajput political network in a variety of ways. We also notice the process of caste proliferation among the Vaishyas and the Sudras. The Vaishyas were also identified with regional variations and they are called Shrimals, Palliwals, Nagars and Disawats among others. We also witness the crystallization of the professions of artisans into castes.

Economy

During this period more and more land was brought under cultivation and relations in society revolved around land grants. It also means the use of advanced agricultural techniques of plough cultivation and irrigation. Institutional management of agricultural process sometime, led to social tensions in rural set-up. However, regional variations and ecological factors are to be taken into consideration before we assess the impact of expansion of agriculture. Land grant system began in western Indian regions of Gujarat and Rajasthan between the 5th and the 7th centuries AD. In Rajasthan water-lifting devices such as *Araghatta* and big ploughs were in use. As Rajasthan and Gujarat were having less rainfall, the agriculturists must have depended on age-old practice of depending on wells. Trade and commerce also flourished. *Nagarams* or markets in those days were located on trade routes at points of exchange. In Rajasthan, where the exchange centres were located on the basis of agrarian production, the rural settlements clustered. These also acted as centres of traffic of varying origins. We also witness a certain measure of hierarchy among merchant families of the 11th and the 12th centuries. The important merchant families based on the origin of place are Osawal (Osia) Shrimalis (Bhinmal), Palliwalas and Khandelwalas. These merchant families integrated the resource bases or rural production centres, the main routes for the flow or resources or urban centres and centres of exchange; or *Nagarams*. Rajasthan provided the necessary commercial links between Gujarat, Central India and the valley of Ganges. The traders maintained links through towns like Pali between the coast and towns like Dwaraka and Brigukachcha or Broach with central and north India. Bayana in Rajasthan was such a crucial market junction.

Culture

The Rajput rulers patronized arts and literature. Paramara rulers Munja and Bhoja are well-known scholars of great repute. The following are the works of Bhoja – *Ayurvedasarvasva*, *Rajamriganka*, *Vyavaharasamuchchaya*, *Sabdanusasana* and *Yuktikalpataru*. Bhoja patronized literary giants such as Padmagupta, Dhanika, Halayudha, Dhananjaya and Amitragati. Rajasekhara, the author of the drama of *Karpuramanjari* in Prakrit was patronized by Mahendrapala of Kanauj. Jayadeva, the author of *Gita Govinda* was patronized by King Lakshmana Sena of Bengal. Kalhana, the author of *Rajtarangini*, Somadevasuri, the author of *Kathasaritsagara*, Chand Bardai, the author *Prithiviraj Raso* and *Brihatkathamanjari*, belonged to this period. Vernacular literature also made a beginning in this period. Hemachanda Suri, a great Jain poet deserves to be remembered for his services.

The Rajputs were also great builders. Art historians divide their period into two halves, the first part from AD 600–900 and the second part from AD 900–1200. We notice more of ornamentation in the second period. Their important specimens of secular art are the fortresses located at Chittorgarh, Ranathanbhor and Kumbalgarh in Rajasthan along with Mandu, Gwalior,

Chandai and Asirgarh in Madhya Pradesh. The palaces in Rajasthan are also beautiful examples of art and architecture they fostered. The Rajputs also constructed a number of temples. The Khajuraho group of temples numbering 80, built by the Chandella rulers stand in good testimony to the artistic excellence of the Rajput artists and craftsmen, where each temple exhibits individual architectural character. These temples are famous for elegant proportions, graceful contours and rich surface treatment. The Sikharas of these temples are most refined and elegant. We have both Brahmanical and Jaina temples. The Jaina complex at Mount Abu is very remarkable for its marble halls, a central dome of 11 concentric rings and richly carved vaulted ceiling and pillars. They also built Siva temples at Nemavar and Udaipur. It is said that Rudramala temple is one of the largest and most decorated religious monuments in India.

The Rajputs by their individual courage, valour and spirit of liberty played the role of defenders of Indian culture from the inroads of ruthless invaders like Ghajni and Ghori, leading to the postponement for the establishment of Muslim power in India. But, the Rajputs failed in preventing the establishment of the Delhi Sultanate by their narrow and clannish outlook, lack of foresight and failure to realize the impending danger knocking at their gates and importance of burying mutual jealousies for a common good.

16

The Invasions of the Arabs

Ghaznavids and Ghories

In the early medieval age India was on the threshold of phenomenal changes in the domains of polity, economy, society and culture. The impact of these changes is visible even today influencing the growth of India as one nation. The regional lineage-based territorial kingdoms that arose in different parts of India promoted regionalism based on script and language. The cultural traits, art and architecture, and the temple-centred devotional movement under Alvars and Nayanars, in peninsular India of Tamil Nadu were creating a new social ethos in the stratified Indian social organization. At that juncture a new power born on the Arabian soil professing a different faith, Islam entered India as a political power in the 8th century AD. Arabia was the birthplace of Islam. Prophet Muhammad of Arabia was the founder of Islam. He was born in AD 570 at Mecca in Arabia and passed away in AD 632. S. Abid Hussain is of the view that Islam, the new message of hope and faith, which the Prophet of Arabia delivered to the world was not a new religion. The original source of the teachings of Islam is the Quaran. It states, "there is no God but Allah and Muhammad is the Prophet of Allah".

While regionalism was taking deep roots on the Indian soil, many significant events were taking place in Europe and Asia in the post-Harsha era, which directly and indirectly influenced the course of our history. In AD 711 the ruler of Sindh, Raja Dahir was attacked by Mahammed Bin Kasim and Sindh was occupied by the Arabs for a short time. Thus, with the Arab conquest of Sindh began the impact of Islamic forces on India and its culture. Just as Buddhism enabled India to develop links with East Asia, the encounter with Islam forged new links with West Asia. A protracted debate and dialogue is going on about the impact of Islam on India. While some emphasize that this encounter enriched the Indian culture, some others vehemently condemn this encounter as having destroyed the original creative spirit of the Indians, and characterize this period a Dark Age. The truth lies between these two extremes.

The rise of Islam acted as an instrument in forging unity among the warring tribes of Arabs into a powerful political entity and started a new movement of expansion. It is erroneously believed that Islam entered India in the 8th century whereas the Arabs had been carrying on trade and commerce with the Malabar Coast for a long time prior to the conquest of Sindh. In 636 AD Osam Sakifi, the governor of Bahrain sent a fleet to India but the policy of armed intervention was abandoned with the advice of Khalifa. By AD 711 the Arabs captured Gibralter and started their conquest of Spain. By AD 712, Bukhara in Central Asia succumbed to the Islamic conquerors and by that time Sindh was already in Arab control.

The invasion of Sindh took place on the pretext of a very insignificant event. The king of Sri Lanka dispatched a group of Muslim orphans in a ship to the Governor of Iraq. On the way, sea pirates captured the ship. The ruler of Iraq demanded that the Raja of Sindh, punish the pirates. When the king refused to yield to the demand, Muhammad Bin Kasim, the son-in-law of the Governor of Iraq came with army and conquered southern Sindh. This invasion and conquest of Sindh was supported by the Khalifa. The new Khalifa ordered the execution of Kasim but this did not put an end to the conquest. In AD 725 the Arabs again invaded and occupied Kathiawar and Gujarat as far as southern Rajasthan. The Arab's thirst for further conquests was put to an end by the valiant efforts of the Chalukyas and Rashtrakutas in western India, while the Gurjara Pratiharas stopped their conquests in northern India. Masudi, a Muslim traveller who visited India in AD 915 testifies to the efforts of the Gujara Pratiharas by keeping a large army to stall the invasions of the Arabs. Sulaiman, another Muslim traveller also mentions the Rashtrakutas as one among the four mightiest rulers of the world. Till AD 861, Sindh along with Punjab was under the direct control of the Khalifa but in that year the rulers declared their independence and lived in peace with the Hindus. A large number of Arab traders settled outside the Muslim occupied territories on the coastal region from Sindh to Gujarat and Kathiawar. As a result of this harmony, contacts developed between the Hindus and the Arabs.

The Arab occupation of Sindh did not last long and the first chapter of Muslim occupation of Sindh comes to an end with the death of Muhammad Bin Kasim. Politically this was not a great event and yet it left an impact on the Arab culture. Satish Chandra aptly observes, "Unfortunately, we have only limited knowledge of India's economic and cultural relations with the Arab world during the period and of India's scientific contributions to it". The Arab conquest of Sindh in the 8th century did not lead to the establishment of close cultural relations between Arabs and the rest of India. Between AD 757 and 774, during the reign of Khalifa Mansur, some Hindu scholars visited Baghdad and brought with them Brahmagupta's *Brahmasiddhanta* and *Khandakdhayaka* which Al-Fazani translated into Arabic. During the time of Harun many Sanskrit books were translated into Arabic and this process continued as long as the Abbasids held control over Baghdad. We are fairly certain that Indian mathematics and works on astronomy were translated into Arabic and definitely Aryabhata's *Suryasiddhanta* is one of such translated works into Arabic. Indian traders and merchants continued to explore the markets of Iraq and Iran while Indian physicians and master craftsmen were welcomed by the Khalifa at Baghdad. It is no exaggeration to suggest that *Panchatantra* was translated into Arabic and formed the basis of Aesop's fables in the West. Further, Masudi, a Muslim traveller who visited India in the 10th century observes that the Hindu king of Cambay was interested in religious discourses and exchanged ideas with Muslims and other peoples who visited him. On the whole, the relations were neither very hostile nor very cordial between the Arabs and the Indians. By their secularization of Hindu religious knowledge, the Arabs laid foundation of Western experimental science, which has often appropriated the credit of discoveries which actually belong to the Buddhist and Hindu India.

The Ghaznavid Turks

After the Arab penetration into Sindh, it was the Turks who once again made inroads into India in the 11th century. After the decline of the Abbasid power, Samanid dynasty ruled from AD 874–999. Later Ghaznavids came to power in AD 962 and ruled till AD 1186. Alaptagin, a Turkish slave of the Samanid king Abdul Malik founded the Ghaznavid dynasty. He occupied Ghazni in Afghanistan and made it his capital. Alaptagin ruled till AD 969. He was followed by his son-in-law Sabaktagin who was the ruler of Ghazni in AD 997. Jaipal, the ruler of Lahore in the Punjab was defeated at Lamghan by Sabaktagin. Sabaktagin was followed by his son Ismail, who was overthrown by Muhammad, his brother in AD 998, who became famous in history as Muhammad of Ghazni, the capital of a state corresponding to what is now called Afghanistan together with a part of Iran.

Availability of the finest horses and iron useful for the manufacture of arms-making, made the Turks strong and adventurous and the growing Ghazni spirit in West Asia enticed the newly converted Turks to attack India. In AD 999 Mahammad ascended the throne of Ghazni and took a vow to organize every year a raid into India. After the successful initial raids, in 1001 he marched against the Shahis and reached Waihind or Peshawar and defeated Jayapala. Again in 1006, Muhammad conquered the upper Indus region, which gave him access to the Punjab. In 1009, Muhammad defeated Anandapala and occupied the fort of Bhimnagar or Nagarkot and accepted Anandapala as his feudatory. Once again in AD 1015 Muhammad plundered Lahore but his attempt to conquer Kashmir in the same year ended in failure, due to inclement weather. This happens to be the first defeat of Muhammad's armies in India. By now, the way was open for the Turkish advance into the Gangetic plains. By the end of 1015, Muhammad defeated a local Rajput ruler at Baran or Bulendashar but at Mathura he had to face the stiff opposition of Kalachuri Kokala II. But Mohammad was successful in this raid which was considered to be the most spectacular and profitable one in the Gangetic valley. Again in AD 1019 and 1021, he undertook two raids into the Gangetic valley and in 1025 he attacked Somanath, the famous holy town and shrine and after destroying and plundering it, he returned to Ghazni. This successful expedition demonstrated their capacity of swift movement over unknown and hostile territory and a spirit of daring enterprise rare even among the Turkish nomadic tribes of the times. Thus, ended the 17 raids of Mohammad Ghazni who captured places as far apart as Saurashtra of Gujarat and Kanauaj, the capital of the Gurjara Pratiharas. Looting of holy places in Thaneswar, Mathura and the loss of 50,000 people defending Somanath temple and destruction of the Shiva Linga with his own hands made the Hindus hate him as a fanatic Muslim. It is difficult to explain the motive for these wanton destructions, when he never wanted to establish his empire in India. Even if we agree that he looted the wealth of India to enrich his power base in central Asia, the question that defies explanation is his wanton destruction of temples. Mohammad was greatly honoured by the Khalifa for his successful feats in India.

None can dispute the military capabilities of Muhammad Ghazni. Undoubtedly, he was a bold and brave warrior and a born leader of men who single-handedly carved out one of the biggest empires in west and central Asia as described by Satish Chandra. He beautified his capital Ghazni with magnificent buildings with the wealth of plunder of the Indian territories. He patronized Firadausi, the author of *Shahnama* and Alberuni, the author of *Hindu ul kitab*. We may conclude with the statement of Satish Chandra "thus, despite his political and military achievements Muhammad is remembered in India as a ruthless plunderer and even did not earn a good name among his contemporaries outside India". By the end of the tenth century the Muslims had only touched the periphery of Indian culture but were far away from its centre. The real and meaningful contact between the Hindu and Muslim cultures did not begin with the occupation of the Punjab and Multan in the 11th century. It had to wait till the beginning of the Delhi Sultanate. The Ghazani rule lasted for a hundred and fifty years over Peshawar and a large part of western Punjab.

After Muhammad's death, India experienced temporary peace for more than a century before Muhammad Ghori descended upon the plains of India from Afghanistan. There was a gap of nearly a century and half before Ghori invaded India again and this was a period of great flux in northen India. Unfortunately, Indians did not learn any useful political lesson from Ghazni's raids and they failed to develop foresight necessary to meet the new challenge. Instead, they indulged in constant internecine warfare between the various Rajput principalities, which ultimately weakened all the Rajput states. In spite of the weakening of the power of Ghazni, the successors of Muhammad continued their raids into the Doab as far as Benaras and yet the Rajputs never realized the need for sustained united effort to drive away the Muslims invaders. It is Muhammad Ghori, who once again initiated raids into the Indian soil to expand his territory into India at the end of the 12th century.

Ghorian Raids

Towards the middle of the 12th century, another group of Turkish tribesmen, who were partly Buddhist and partly Pagan, rose to prominence and of such the

Ghurid kingdom based at Ghor in north-west Afghanistan was the most important. The Ghurids were the vassals of Ghazni and taking advantage of the weakness of Ghaznis, Ghurid Sultan Allauddin destroyed their power. As the Ghurids had to face the enmity of the Khwarizmi kingdom, who were also contenders for central Asia, the Ghurid, decided to move towards India.

In AD 1163, Ghiyasuddin Muhammad became the ruler of Ghor and appointed his brother Shihabuddin or Muizzudin Muhammad as the governor of Ghazni in AD 1173–74. This Shihabuddin is well known in history of India as Muhammad Ghori and he laid the foundations of the Muslim rule in India. With a view to bring back the Muslim provinces of India under his control, in AD 1175 he took Multan and next he occupied the fortress of Uch. His raid against Anihilwara in 1177, failed but gradually he overcame all his Muslim rivals in India. In 1182, he conquered Sindh and Punjab. In the first battle of Tarain that took place in 1191, he attacked and captured the fortress of Tabarhinda which was strategically important for the defence of Delhi. In this battle, Prithviraj Chauhan defeated Muhammad Ghor. Prithviraj, however, appears to have underestimated his enemy and within one year Muhammad Ghori once again attacked Prithviraj at the same battle ground of Tarain in AD 1192.

The second battle of Tarain of 1192, is well known as one of the turning points in Indian history. There is a difference of opinion between Minhaj Siraj, a contemporary chronicler and Ferishta, a later dated chronicler regarding the strength of the army of both. Muhammad Ghor overthrew Prithviraj Chauhan and his allies and killed Prithviraj. Muhammad conquered Ajmer and the Hindu states of that kingdom. After massacring the inhabitants and selling the remaining as slaves, Muhammad advanced to Delhi. In AD 1193, Qutubuddin Aibak, his general captured it, and it remained the capital throughout, till the British shifted the capital to Calcutta. In AD 1194 Muhammad defeated Jayachandra at Benaras and Kanauj. After the death of his brother Ghiyasuddin, Muhammad became the ruler of a vast empire in West Asia as well as India. Muhammad appointed Qutubuddin Aibak as his viceroy in Delhi and it was he who extended the influence of Muhammad over many Rajput states of Gwalior, Ajmer and Anhilwara, the capital of Gujarat. Muhammad Bhaktiyar Khilji, a general of Muhammad Ghori brought eastern India under the sway of Muhammad Ghori. Bhaktiyar Khilji captured Bihar, destroyed the University of Nalanda, in AD 1202, and defeated Lakshmana Sena of Bengal. It is said that Bhaktiyar Khilji ruled autonomously but not as a subordinate. By 1206, the year of the death of Muhammad Ghori, the Turks extended their sway up to Laknauti in Bengal, Ajmer and Ranathambhor in Rajasthan, upto the boundaries of Ujjain in the south, and Multan and Uch in Sindh. In 1206, after Muhammad Ghori's death, Aibak declared independence and laid the foundation of Delhi Sultanate.

Impact of Ghazni and Ghori's Raids or Invasions

Two distinct patterns of relations developed, and were at work between the Hindus and the Muslims on account of the invasions of Ghazni and Ghori.

One was the lure for plunder among the successors of Ghazni in the Gangetic valley and Rajputana. On the other hand, many Rajput rulers stoutly opposed the invading armies and won individual victories against the Ghaznavid armies. As the Ghaznavid armies were not very strong, the success of Rajputs made them complacent, which proved too expensive. At another level, the Muslim traders and merchants were welcomed, as they augmented the resources of the state. Consequently, colonies of Muslim traders sprang up in market centres and towns. Along with Muslim traders, there were Muslim religious preachers called the Sufis. The Sufis preached the gospel of love, faith and belief in one God. Though their preachings were primarily directed towards the Muslim population, they indirectly influenced the thought process of the Hindus also. Thus, a process of interaction developed between Islam and Hindu religions and society and also between the dogmatism of Muslims and liberal views of the Sufis. Lahore became a centre of Arabic and Persian languages and literature. Hindu soldiers and generals, took part in the service of the Muslims. In spite of the positive tendencies as mentioned, negative predispositions of aversion, hatred and suspicion developed due to the destructive attitude of the invaders. The important cause was the failure of the Rajputs against the superior war-like tribes of West Asia and also the better cavalry used by the invaders supported by their superior arms. These successful invasions left a deep impact on the course, direction and developments of Indian society in all spheres.

17

The Rise and Fall of the Delhi Sultanate

Socio-economic and Cultural Study

After the death of Muhammad of Ghor, Aibak declared independence and established the Delhi Sultanate in AD 1206. The Delhi Sultanate lasted for a period of 320 years from AD 1206 to 1526. This period of three hundred twenty years was shared by the Mamluks or slaves, Khiljis, Tughlaks, Sayyads and Lodis. Of the Mamluk dynasty, the most important rulers are Iltutmish and Balban, while Alauddin Khilji was the most important; of the Tughlak line the most important are Muhammad bin Tughlak and Ferozshah Tughlak and of the Lodis the important one is Ibrahim Lodi. Timur invaded India and destroyed Delhi during this period towards the end of 15th century.

The Delhi Sultanate in its existence of more than three centuries gave birth to political, social and economic institutions which differed from the earlier ones. Yet these institutions represent a unique combination of the Turkish and the earlier Indian institutions. The contact between the Turks and the Indians led to two major processes of military conflict and commercial activity along with cultural transactions. There were mutual hostility on account of cultural differences and conflicting political interests and partial assimilation and acculturation as a result of realization that they have to coexist as neighbours because the invading Turks made India their new home. There is also a debate about the causes for the success of the Turks. While the contemporary chronicles view their success as the 'Will of God', the British historians hold the view that the invading armies consisted of war-like tribes with better horses and better arms and the Indians were pacifists by nature and were not given to war. This view is disproved by the fact that the Indians were not lacking in bravery and martial spirit. Some Indian historians attribute the success of Turks to the peculiar social structure created by Islam. There are many causes for the defeat of the Indians, chief of them the superior military technology and fighting skills of the Turks. They were also helped by 'lack of unity of command' among the army of the Indians. The use of iron stirrups and horse shoes reinforced the striking power and stamina of the Arab cavalry. The horse-shoes provided greater mobility to the horses and the stirrups gave the soldiers a distinct advantage. We may conclude that the Turks were successful primarily due to their military technology and that the armies of the Indian rulers lacked unity of command as they were under the control of regional local lords or feudatories of doubtful loyalties, their greatest weakness.

The Turkish occupation of India brought about far reaching changes in the polity, society and economy of India. Though changes introduced by them were far reaching, the basic structure remained the same with some necessary modifications. First, let us take up polity or political process of the Delhi Sultanate. Before we go into details of the structure and nature of the polity, it is essential to have an idea of the Islamic theory of society. After the death of Prophet Mohammad, the institution of the Caliphate came into existence and gradually took shape. Khalifa was considered the head of the Muslim community or Umma or Ummat. In Islamic world view, the Khalifa combined in himself the duty of the guardian of religion and the upholder of the political order. In the early Islamic world, there was no provision for a head of the State like Sultan, as Khalifa was vested with that authority. In theory the Khalifa was the head of the Islamic community but in reality with the decline of the stature of Khalifa in due course of time the emergence of Sultan as independent powerful sovereign over a certain geographical area became a fact. But as the institution of Khalifa survived though only in a theoretical and formal sense, it became necessary to obtain legitimization of political authority of the Sultan by granting of titles, allowing the name of the Caliph inscribed on coins and reading of Khutba in Friday prayer. By this the Sultan obtained legitimacy for his authority and developed a link with the Islamic world. Further, the Delhi Sultans in theory recognized the supremacy of the Islamic law or Shariath but in reality they did not hesitate to deviate from Shariath. Political expediency prevailed over dogmatic approach in the conduct of the Sultans. Satish Chandra aptly remarks that the Turks evolved a number of new institutions and concepts which led to a centralization of power so far unknown in India.

The institution of monarchy has no place in Shariath and it was not an Islamic institution. The original concept of government in Islam was that of the Imam who was chosen by the faithful, who led a simple and austere life and combined in himself both political and spiritual authority. The disintegration of the Abbasid Caliphate was responsible for the emergence of the institution of Sultan. In course of time, the Sultan became all powerful. As he became the source of honour and patronage, he claimed divine attributes. Like the Hindus, the Islamic thinkers also made the office of the Sultan divine. Barauni writes that the heart of a monarch was a mirror of God and it reflected the wishes of God so that the actions of the King Sultan could not be questioned. Balban was the first of the Delhi Sultans, who assumed the title of *Zill Allah* or Shadow of God and introduced the ceremonies of *Sijda* and *Pabos* (prostration on the ground, bending down to touch one's feet). The Shariath allows these practices only for Allah but no one else. The Delhi Sultans though appear to be exercising unlimited power cannot be considered absolute despotic rulers.

Was the state governed by the Sultans of Delhi and Mughal emperors theocratic, purely based on Shariath? This aspect has attracted the attention of the modern scholars of history. The Islamic law stipulates that the entire world is divided into *Dar-ul-harb* or abode of war and *Dar-ul-Islam* or abode of Islam. Idolaters have no place in an Islamic country and they are to be killed or enslaved. But this canonical law could not be implemented in India as the non-Muslim population was in majority and it is impossible to enslave or convert all idolaters in India. Yet, there is a strong belief that the medieval state under the Muslim rule was definitely a theocracy, as it had the essential elements; the sovereignty of God and Government by the direction of God through Ulemas or the priestly group in accordance with divine law. The Sultans of Delhi considered themselves as deputies or assistants of Calipha who was God's vice-regent. Though the Delhi Sultans recognized the supremacy of the Islamic Laws, they had to supplement them by framing non-religious regulations (*Zawabti*) too. It indicates that for all practical purposes, the medieval state and sultan cared more for the stability and security of the young state rather than blind implementation of Shariath. We can say that the needs of the emergent state influenced the policies and practices not always consistent with the Islamic laws. To prove this point, we have the example of Sultan Iltutmish, when Shafai Muslim divines enjoined him to enforce the Islamic law strictly, i.e., giving the Hindus the option of Islam or death, his Wazir, Junaidi replied the Muslims are now like salt in a dish of food. We have also the evidences of Alauddin Khilji and Muhammad bin Tughlak who did not accept the authority of the Ulemas. Jalaluddin Khilji, the founder of the Khilji dynasty, being a pious Muslim considered as unrealistic the policy of forcible conversion of the Hindus or their humiliation as demanded by some theologians and also defended the policy of allowing Hindus to worship idols, preach their beliefs and observe practices which were considered the hallmark of infidelity according to the Quran. He also put forward the concept of a new type of state, one which was based fundamentally on the goodwill and support of the people of all communities and one which was basically benevolent and looked after the welfare of its subjects. Alauddin Khilji's statement, "I do not know what is lawful or unlawful according to Shariath, whatever I consider necessary for the state or for its welfare, I decree" also is an example to indicate that Shariath is not implemented in toto.

These instances prove that, in practice the Turkish state was not theocratic but evolved according to its special needs of the state which were paramount. Yet there are instances when the ruler gave importance to observance of Shariath strictly as in the reign of Ferozshah Tughlak. One of the despicable instances of bigotry on the part of Ferozshah Tughlak was public burning of a Brahmin on the ground that he openly performed idol worship at his house in which both Hindus and Muslims participated and that he had converted a Muslim woman. Ferozshah even collected *Zizia* from Brahmins, who were exempted till then. He was so dogmatic that he imposed this also against

Muslims who adhered to Sufism. While Muhammad bin Tughlak took measures to create a composite ruling class consisting of Muslims and Hindus. Ferozshah reversed the same by giving importance to orthodox elements of Islam. Later, Lodis once again revived the practice of composite administrative machinery, which was taken to its logical end by Akbar.

The Sultanate of Delhi had to face a number of political and administrative obstacles which created a crisis and then a decline. The Sultans did not find it smooth sailing to conquer, expand and consolidate their power. The Sultans had to face opposition from the indigenous Hindu rulers, conflict between the nobility and the Sultan and threat from Mongols besides the rise of regional kingdoms. In course of time, the Sultanate had to decline because as long as the Sultan could contain opposition, suppress rebellion and keep his flock together the kingdom survived, but when weak rulers ascended the throne, then came decline of the Sultanate. This is apparent since the success of monarchical system depends on the king's personality and individual qualities of leadership and ability to grasp the needs and requirements of the moment.

While in the earlier ages, the law of primogeniture was accepted, no clear and well-defined law of succession prevailed in the age of the Sultanate. Though the hereditary principle was accepted, no strict adherence to that principle was observed. Consequently, in a way, law of jungle or Darwinism prevailed, where anyone with the sharpest sword and the strongest desire could claim the throne by offering bribes or by treachery. As and when a ruler died, intrigues and strife became very common which shook the foundations of royalty. The nobles or *Umra* played a crucial role in the constructive and destructive activities of the Sultanate. The nobles always tried to manipulate the situation to obtain economic and political gains. This led to uncertainty and a sort of anarchical situation as there were divisions supporting and opposing the claimant to the throne.

Further, the rise of regional states under the Bahmanis in AD 1347 and the rise of the kingdoms like Jaunapur, Malwa and Gujarat respectively under Khwaja Jahan in 1394, Dilawar Khan in 1401 and Zabar Khan in 1407, weakened the Sultanate as the Sultans lost the fertile regions of Bengal, Malwa, Jaunapur and Gujarat and their revenue to the State. By the first decade of the 16th century the effective control of the Sultanate became nominal and the Sultanate came on the verge of collapse in the hands of a determined aggressor with minimum effort. The assaults of the Mongols at regular intervals further sapped the vitality of the Sultanate, but it appears that the Mongol forays did not affect the Sultan's political and economical fortunes.

Central Administration

The Sultan took the help of a number of ministers in performing his task as a ruler. We have no definite idea about the number of ministers employed by the Sultan and there was no council of ministers. The ministers were appointed by the Sultan and they remained in office as long as they enjoyed the confidence of the Sultan. We come across four ministers designated; the *Wazir, Ariz-i-mamlik, Diwan-i-Insha* and *Diwan-i-Risalat.* We also come across officers known as *Wakil-i-dar, Amir Hazib, Barid-i-Khas* and many more minor officials to execute the orders issued by their superiors.

Provincial Administration

We have only limited knowledge about the provincial and local administration. The provincial and local administration was only nominal. It is because the Sultans of Delhi were less successful in consolidating an empire comprising a large part of India. Though they had the military strength required to do so, they were not successful in establishing an administrative set-up which could penetrate deep into the countryside and strengthen their control. The Sultan had to be invariably dependent on the alien nobility through the bondage of Islam as in the past too the ruling elite of different parts of India depended on their *Samantas* or feudal lords. None of Sultans, except Alauddin, could succeed in penetrating into the rural sector by introducing a direct revenue assessment with a view to subdue the Hindu middlemen, but he could gain partial success only in the core area of his region. Even if Alauddin attempted this in provinces, it could have boomeranged as the provincial lords did not like to be cowed down. The Sultan's scheme of satisfying those who helped them in conquest, by granting feudal fiefs or *Iqtas*, though beneficial to the Sultanate in the initial stages, in the long run the exclusivity of alien nobles impeded the administrative reach deep into the rural areas. Further, the aloofness of the ruling elite was as an obstacle in integration of the political system. Besides their aloofness, their emphasis on conversions to some extent and the excesses committed by some Sultans was mainly responsible for the Sultanate's failure to extend their effective control into the deep interior of the subcontinent. In a way the Sultanate accelerated the process of political unification and can be considered as the precursor of a nation state, which has been our cherished ideal. In theory, the Delhi Sultanate appears to be a unitary state but in actuality it was a confederation of semi-independent territorial units ruled by military chiefs or governors. The administrative organization of the Sultanate was a composite structure. The age-old local institutions such as village and caste councils continued. Further, on these the Sultans superimposed certain measures like the system of taxation and law of succession which are not in conformity with the law of the faith. While their monarchy was fashioned on the Persian tradition, their army was organized on Turko-Mongol system.

Local Administration

The Sultans divided their kingdom into provinces but the hold of the Sultan appears to be nominal as every governor behaved as an autonomous one. The provinces were again divided into *Shiqs* and *Paraganas* which were placed under the *Shiqdars* and *Amils*. In that period *Paragana* was the smallest unit of administration. The provinces were called Iqtas. The number of Iqtas varied and there was no uniformity in the administration of the Iqtas. The head of the *Iqta* was called *Naib, Sultan, Nazim, Mukti* or *Wali*. During the period of Alauddin Khilji, Iqtas were divided into two categories as those under the Delhi Sultanate from the beginning and which were subsequently brought under the control of Alauddin Khilji. Besides the Iqtas, there also existed tribute paying states of South India who acknowledged the sovereign power of the Sultan. Each Iqta had besides Mukti, number of officers of central government. A *Wazir*, an *Ariz* and a *Quaji* in each Iqta were also placed as representatives of the central government. The smallest unit of administration was the village which was administered by local hereditary officers and the Panchayat of the village. The *Chaudari*, the *Patuari*, the *Khur*, the *Chaukidar* and the *Muqdam* were the hereditary officers of the village who helped the government in the collection of revenue but they lost these privileges during the reign of Alauddin Khilji.

The Panchayat of the village looked after education, sanitation, etc., and acted as a judicial body also. There is a controversy regarding Sultans' attitude towards their Hindu and Muslim subjects. One view holds that the Delhi Sultans pursued a policy of discrimination among the Hindu peasants; the Muslim peasants paid less revenue. The Hindu traders paid double trade tax and the Muslim traders paid less tax. Even among the Muslims, the Indian Muslims and converted Muslims were treated lowly and only foreign Muslims enjoyed higher status and the Hindus were treated as second rate citizens, experiencing hardships. What was narrated above was the view of the traditional historians who believed that the Muslim rule was based on the Islamic law but a section of the modern historians argued that the Sultan's policies are not determined by religious considerations but by economic interests. This view is questioned on the ground that the medieval period was period of faith and the faith of the rulers motivated them to be bigoted in their approach. As a general rule all the Sultans can be considered as bigots and it is true that some are really bigoted compared to the rest and on the basis of that we cannot say that the Muslim rule was full of conversion from Hinduism to Islam.

The occupation and the establishment of the Delhi Sultanate initiated changes in the economic structure as well as the general political structure of India. Though they were aware of and conversant with well defined concepts and practices of tax collection, the structure, distribution system and minting of coinage, in the beginning they superimposed their ideas on the existing system and slowly and gradually introduced modifications up to the end of the 15th century. The slave labour played a crucial role in providing the accustomed luxurious life to the nobility, depending on their taste and habits. Muhammad Habib holds that the economic changes that occurred during this period created an organization considerably superior to that which existed prior to their occupation. Habib further states that the changes in economic sphere were so drastic that they deserve the designation of urban and rural revolutions;

D.D. Kosambi argues that the Islamic raiders intensified already existing elements of feudalism in the subcontinent. The Sultans after bringing new areas under their occupation divided the new areas among the commanders who were allowed to plunder and extract tribute from the defeated and subjugated rural lords. The commanders paid salaries to the members of army in cash.

Land revenue was the major source for the resource base of the state. The Sultans introduced a mechanism for simultaneous collection and distribution of revenue. In this period the *Iqta* system combined the twin functions of revenue collection and distribution. It did not endanger the unity of the political structure. The *Mukti* is authorized to collect land tax and other taxes due to the state and had to maintain troops; and to provide them to the state at the time of need. It is a transferable job. The territory from which the Sultan collected tax directly and deposited in his own treasury is called *Khalisa*, only core area of the Sultan, i.e., the territory around Delhi and parts of Doab remained in *Khalisa*. The area under *Khalisa* shifted from time to time depending on the success of the Sultan in expanding his territorial gains. While Alauddin paid cash to his soldiers, Iltutmish, Balban and the Tughlaks assigned land or villages to soldiers in lieu of salaries. Such assignments were called *Wajh* and its holders as *Wajhadars*. These were permanent and hereditary appointments. Balban, by appointing *Khwaja* or accountant, started streamlining the tax collected by *Iqta* holder. Alauddin Khilji also brought Iqta under the preview of the central finance department or *Diwan-i-Wijarat.* The central intervention reached its climax during the time of Muhammad bin Tughlak. By the time we come to Lodis, the administrative changes and revenue assignments were combined together, instead of *Iqtas*, we now come across terms like *Paraganas* or *Sarkars*. By the time of Sikandar Lodi, we notice sub-infeudation in these areas. The Sultans also made land grants to *Darghas*, mosques, Madarsas and they are called *Milk*, *Idrar* and *Inam*. The land tax in Islamic tradition was called *Kharaj* but till the time of Alauddin Khilji no serious attempt appears to have been made to streamline the assessment and realization of *Kharaj*. Alauddin aimed at increasing the revenue collection by enhancing the demand and also introduced direct collection to cut down the outflow due to intermediaries. The system of tax collection introduced by Alauddin continued till the time of Ghiyasuddin Tughlak who modified and expected the *Khots* and *Muqqaddams* from paying tax on their cultivation and cattle. Muhammad bin Tughlak extended this system of Alauddin Khilji to Gujarat, Malwa, Deccan, South India and Bengal. He introduced new imposts and collected taxes very rigorously. He was the first Sultan to contemplate formulation of an agricultural policy. He introduced the practice of providing agricultural loans called *Sondhar* for increasing the area under cultivation and to dig wells for irrigation purposes. It is estimated that Muhammad bin Tughlak spent a huge amount as *Sondhar*, but only a small amount of it reached the peasantry. He created a new ministry designated *Diwan-i-amir-i-Kohi* to promote agriculture. The two main functions of this ministry were to extend area under cultivation and reclaim the land that was out of cultivation, and efforts were also made to improve the cropping pattern.

Muhammad bin Tughlak's time saw sugarcane being replaced by grapes and dates; wheat was given up for sugarcane. Though in theory all these plans were good, in practice they did not yield the necessary result and his successor Ferozshah replaced all these measures. Alauddin Khilji also introduced measures to regulate the prices of all the essential commodities in the market. He not only fixed the prices of the commodities but ensured supervision over the market prices and saw that they were under control. The followers of Alauddin gave up these measures. The establishment of the Delhi Sultanate was marked by a considerable growth of monetization of economy as evidenced by the currency system or coins in circulation. There was no pure silver coinage prior to the establishment of the Delhi Sultanate. Iltutmish introduced gold and silver *Tanka* and a copper *Jital* that was specially at 1/48th of a *Tanka* in North India and 1/50th in the Deccan after the conquest of Devagiri and a ratio of 1:10 between gold and silver was established by him. The silver currency remained dominant till the reign of Alauddin but later silver coinage slowly disappeared. Muhammad bin Tughlak introduced a coin of copper and brass alloy and reckoned it at the value of silver Tanka. For the first time, this coin had an engraving in Persian. Introduction of token currency by Muhammad bin Tughlak ended in a thorough failure. Slavery and slave trade flourished throughout the Delhi Sultanate period.

As land and man relationship was very favourable, and agricultural land was in abundance, double cropping was prevalent around Delhi. They raised food crops like wheat, barley, paddy, millets, Jowar, and pulses and cash crops like sugarcane cotton, oil seeds and sesame linseed, etc. The Sultans encouraged digging canals to promote agriculture. Ghiyasuddin was the first to dig canals while Ferozshah also dug two canals from the river Yamuna and it was considered the largest canal network in India till the 19th century. Cultivation was based on individual peasant farming, but the peasant economy was not at all egalitarian and the divide was immense. We notice the occurrence of intermediaries between the peasant and the state in the *Khot* and the *Muqqaddams* and they were designated Zamindars and Chowdharies under Ferozshah Tughlak, which continued under the Mughals also.

There is a view that on the eve of Ghorian conquest of India, the urban economy was in decline. The towns were fewer and smaller in extent in the centuries prior to the founding of Delhi Sultanate. D.D. Kosambi remarks that the capital was a camp on the move and the urban ruling elite was on the whole along with the army while lower levels of the community were totally ruralized. R.S. Sharma is also of the same view. On the other hand, we have the evidence of the contemporary citings of administrative centres, Delhi, Multan, Anihilwara (Patna) Cambay, Kara Lakhnauti and Daultabad or Devagiri. Most of the 13th century towns are headquarters of *Iqta* like Hansi, Kara and Anihilwara. The need for new luxuries of life made the ruling elite depend on numerous artisans and craftsmen skilled in their areas of specialization, who migrated from other countries. Urban craftsmen, who provided these new goods with the help of new technological devices, came to India. The arrival of spinning wheel or *Charkha* increased the production of yarn manifold. This very important mechanical device is referred to in Isami's *Futuha-s-Salatin* datable to AD 1350. Lymn White Jr. points out that spinning wheel was unknown in ancient India and this must have led to large-scale manufacture and production of cloth during the Sultanate. The weaving of silk cloth, a luxury item began in the middle of the Sultanate period. Carpet weaving on the vertical loom also appeared during this period. Most notably, paper manufacturing craft was also established and the earliest surviving piece of paper datable to 13th century comes from Gujarat. The building industry underwent a considerable technological transformation. The important new techniques were the use of cementing lime and vaulted roofing, with exclusive use of the true arch and dome. Consequently, we also came across large brick and rubble structures.

The Sultanate coinage reflects pre-eminently the growth of commerce, internal and external. The demand for cavalry horses in the Sultanate made them import these from as far as Ukraine and Russian steppes. During the period, the export exceeded imports and there was a large flow of bullion. Irfan Habib remarks that what the Sultans thus brought about was not a social revolution in any modern sense but the creation of a new system of agrarian exploitation, with a parasitical urban growth based upon it. It united political power with economic power more fully than ever before, vesting the control over the bulk of the surplus in the hands of a ruling class whose composition was determined not by inheritance but formally by the will of the sovereign, and whose individual members remained permanently unattached to any particular parcels of land. Irfan Habib also sees the traits of feudalism in the denial of rights to the peasants and oriental despotism due to the excessive centralization of power.

Sources of Revenue

The chief source of income of the state was land reyenue known as *Kharaj* and originally it signified all taxes including *Jiziyah* raised from the non-Muslims, who were called *Kharajguzars*. The land tax was raised from the earlier one-sixth or less at least one-third and one-half of the gross produce by Alauddin Khilji, *Jiziyah*, a sort of capitation tax levied upon every adult Hindu made with independent means of maintenance, *Zakat*, a tax raised from well-to-do Muslims for ihe sake of helping the needy Muslims, *Khams* or *Ghaninah*, the booty taken in war, transit and octroi duties, mines, forests, treasure troves and heirless property were also the sources of revenue to the state.

Military

The main prop of the Delhi Sultanate was military force and as such both the Delhi Sultanate and the Mughals gave top priority to the military force. Under Alauddin Khilji, the military objectives decided his policy and action. Though the Delhi Sultanate was not a military state primarily, separate status was given to military department both at the centre and in the provinces. The main branch of the army was the cavalry and the Sultan maintained constant vigilance on the frontiers because of the threat and incursions of the Mongols. To safeguard frontiers, a series of garrison posts and fortresses were either repaired or newly constructed at strategic places. The elephant corps was an important branch of the army and was meant to pull heavy loads. The Sultanate also took care to organize judiciary and police and the final court of appeal and judgment was the Sultan. There is an officer called *Mohatasibs* to inspect the civil and religious behaviour of the Muslims, while the policing of cities and towns was entrusted to *Kotwals* and that of the rural areas to the *Faujdar*.

Society

Society during the Sultanate period was in flux. On the religious level, people were broadly divided as Hindus and Muslims. Even the two major religious sects were further divided into separate groups. Stratification appears in both the communities. Among the Muslims, there were divisions of (a) nobility, (b) the chiefs or the emergent Zamindars and besides the ruling class there prevailed judicial and junior administrative cadre and the Ulema and slaves. The nobles were divided into three categories, the Khans, the Maliks and the Amirs. We do not have any definite idea of the number of nobles in office at any time. Most of the nobles are Turkish and Persian Muslims. But during the Khilji and Tughlak rule, Indian Muslims began to ascend the social ladder due to their personal efficiency. However, preferential treatment of the foreign Muslims continued and even when a noble lost his power and position, the tradition of former dignity and social honour passed on to his descendants. Along the clergy, the nobles called *Ashraf* or the respected sections enjoyed privileged position on the social set-up and this naturally heightened the social stratification among Muslims. When Muhammad bin Tughlak appointed people of low status with efficiency to high posts, there was social resentment. Nobles led a luxurious life because of their position and emoluments. Very little information is available about the education and the cultural outlook and values of Turkish or Persian nobles. Gradually, warrior nobles metamorphasized into patrons of culture.

Political relationship between the Turkish rulers and the Hindu Rajput chiefs or Rais was also common in those days in spite of the relationship; the position of the chiefs was one of considerable uncertainty because of the see-saw battle between the two political powers. By the beginning of the 14th century, references to Zamindars who were hereditary intermediaries are noticed. The term was first used by Amir Khusru and later on it was applied to Khots and Muqqaddams and Chowdharies. There is little idea of the lifestyle of the privileged rural sections but they too appear to have lived affluently. The nobles were helped by religious and judicial functionaries (*Qazis* and *Muftis*). We have reference to *Mehtasib* who supervised the behavioural pattern of Muslims in following *Shariath* besides checking weights and measures. All these are paid posts and their numbers increased when the population of Muslims grew in size. We have little idea of the social base of this large and amorphous group of people. Reference to a number of clerks and petty officials is noticeable. Slave population was in considerable numbers and played a crucial role in politics and society.

There was no remarkable change in the structure of society of the Hindus. The Smriti literature prescribes strict rules for the maintenance of stratified Varna structure, but reality appears to be different. In the position of women, there was little change. During this period, the Purdah system became widespread. Muslim society remained divided into ethnic and racial group with deep economic disparities. The Turks, Iranians, Afghans and Indian Muslims rarely had marital contacts. In fact, these groups developed a sort of caste exclusiveness similar to that of the Hindus. Hindu converts to Islam who formed lower economic and social groups were looked down upon. For administrative purposes and conveniences, we find a mingling of the Hindus and the Muslims. The local machinery of administration was untouched by the influence of the Muslims and it remained almost entirely in the hands of the Hindus. Occasions for mutual intercourse were many. To say that the communities kept strictly aloof from each other is thus not true. No doubt, to a certain extent conflicts of interest as well as differences in social and cultural ideas, practices and beliefs did create tensions and slowed down the process of mutual understanding and cultural assimilation. We may agree with Satish Chandra that both processes of conflict and rapprochement continued side by side, with setbacks under some rulers and in some regions, and faster development under some other rulers.

Culture

During the Sultanate period, there arose many socio-religious movements in North and East India and Maharashtra. Emphasis on Bhakti or devotional surrender to a personal god for attaining salvation and the striving for religious equality were the two common features of the earlier Bhakti movement of South India and the present Bhakti movement of North India, East India and Maharashtra. There is a view that this Bhakti movement was a continuation of the earlier Bhakti movement. Critical examinations of the two movements reveal that there were differences between the two and also differences in the North Indian Bhakti movement. In the present context, we notice the popular monotheistic and Vaishanava Bhakti movement. It is also accepted that to a certain extent Islam also influenced the rise of the two movements of popular monotheistic and Vaishanava Bhakti. Scholars are of the opinion that the political factor of the decline of Rajput-Brahman alliance, and the socio-economic factor of rising aspiration of the common people against oppression are the most important reasons for the rise of the Bhakti movement.

Monotheistic movement of North India was led by religious teachers like Kabir, Gurunanak, Dhanna and Pipa. We notice certain common characteristic features in this movement: (a) Most of the monotheists belonged to the low castes, (b) all the monotheists are influenced to a great extent by the Vaishanava concept of Bhakti, the Nathpanthi movement and Sufism of Islam, (c) communion with God is possible through following *Nirguna* Bhakti, repetition of divine name, a spiritual guru, community singing of devotional songs or Keerthana and companionship of saints or Satsang, (d) opposition of caste systems and idolatry, (e) use of vernacular language, (f) being a *Grihasta* and not an ascetic, and (g) organization of exclusive *Panths*.

Ramananda was the most famous saint scholar of the Vaishnavabhakti and he belonged to the Vaishanava school of Ramanuja of South India. Yet, he differed in certain aspects:

1. He looked upon Ram but not Vishnu as the object of Bhakti.
2. He preached his Bhakti in common man's language.
3. He stressed that caste should be left out and ate food along with low caste people.

Vallabhacharya was another prominent Vaishanava Bhakti preacher. He is a Telugu Brahmin. He was the founder of *Pushtimarga* or way of grace. He preached Krishna Bhakti. Another Saint scholar of Vaishnavabhakti, Surdas was his follower.

Bengal had a Vaishanava Bhakti movement of its own and it differs from both the South Indian and North Indian Bhakti movement. The Bengali Vaishnavabhakti is said to be influenced by the tradition of *Bhagavata Purana* and Sahajiya Buddhist and *Nathpanthi* tradition. *Gita Govinda* of Jayadeva also played a crucial role in shaping the Vaishnavabhakti of Bengal. Chaitanya was the most prominent Vaishanava Saint and his influence was so pervading that he is regarded as an incarnation. Through disregard for caste, creed and sex, he gave a popular base to Vaishanava Bhakti. His favourite disciple Haridas was originally a Muslim, who exercised great influence on the Bengali mind and culture.

The Bhakti movement also drew its inspiration from Bhagavata Purana to a certain extent and also from Saiva Nathapanthis, who were very popular among the lower strata of Maharashtrian society. Jnaneswar (AD 1275–1296) was the pioneer of Bhakti movement in Maharashtra and authored a commentary on Bhagavad-Gita by name *Jnanesweri*. This is not only the earliest literary work of Marathi but also served as the foundation of *Bhakti Marga* in Maharashtra. He advocated that there was no room for caste distinctions in following Bhakti Marga to attain the Moksha. Namdeva was another famous Bhakti Saint of Maharashtra and he is considered to be as one of the leaders of the *Varkari* stream of the Vaishanava devotional tradition. Eknath and Tukaram, also from Maharashtra propagated Bhakti Marga during the 16th and 17th centuries.

In other regions of India, Bhakti movement flourished and Saiva Bhakti was popular in Kashmir in the 14th century while the Vallabha sect prevailed in Gujarat. In Karnataka, Virasaivism preached by Basava became popular in the 12th and 13th Centuries. In Assam, Sankaradeva, a non-Brahmin by birth, preached absolute devotion to Vishnu or his incarnation Krishna. He preached Bhakti Marga to devotees through the medium of dance-drama and music in people's language. He also started the institution of *Satras*, where people belonging to all castes met for religious and social purposes. His sect is called Mahapurushiya sect. It is to be agreed upon that the Bhakti movement of the

Sultanate period was influenced by the Bhakti tradition of Bhagavata Purana and this Purana is regarded as the unifying bond between various Vaishanava Bhakti movements. We have to remember that Kabir and Nanak did not subscribe to the Bhagavata Purana tradition of Bhakti and they rejected the Brahmanical and scriptural authority totally.

Nathpanthi preachers known as Siddhas who belonged to the lower castes – Doma, Chamara, washermen, oil-pressers, fishermen, woodcutters, cobbler, etc., became popular by 13th and 14th centuries. They allowed anyone irrespective of caste to be initiated into Nathpanthi sect. These Nathpanthis are non-conformists and opposed to the Brahmanical tradition. There is a strong view that the Bhakti movement of the Sultanate period was the outcome of Islamic influence and in particular Sufism, both before and after the 12th century. It cannot be denied that Islam did influence the Bhakti movement and in particular the popular monotheistic movement. Likewise the Sufi concepts of Pir and mystic union with the god coincide with the non-conformist saint's concepts of Guru and devotional surrender to god. An interaction direct or indirect between Islam and the Bhakti movement is inevitable because of their existing side by side for many decades and of common features like the worship of one god, who can be Rama, Vishnu, Siva or Allah.

In the domain of culture, another feature is the growth of Sufism or *Tassawwif*, which has the aim of establishing direct communion between God and man through personal experience of Islamic mysticism. Sufism was based on the spirit of Quaranic piety. The Sufis, besides following Shariath also wanted to develop direct communion with God. Sufis, (1) stressed the importance and need to follow the Sufi path or *Tariqa* to reach divine reality or *Haquiqat*, (2) advocated that one has to pass through different stages *Muqqameet* and changing psychological states of mind to experience God, (3) stressed that a spiritual preceptor only can guide one to reach God, (4) believed that a disciple progresses through the stages of self-mortification and chanting of God's name to attain *Zikr* or concentration and contemplation. The Sufis also believe in music recital or *Sama* as a mechanism to induce mystical state of ecstasy in a disciple. The Sufis are divided into various orders or *Silsila* in the name of a particular Sufi saint. Each Sufi order has a hospice or centre (*Khanquah*) where the Pir or spiritual Guru imparted spiritual training to a disciple and these hospices were maintained by endowments and charity.

Sufism developed from the 7th to the 13th centuries and had its beginnings in India from the 11th century. Al Huzwari, the author of *Kashf-ul-Mahjub*, a Persian treatise of Sufism, was the earliest to settle in India and he is said to have lived around AD 1088. But Sufism became popular during the Sultanate period. During this period, we notice the prevalence of six orders: (1) the Suhrawardi Silsila, (2) the Chisti Silsila, (3) Firdausi, (4) the Qadiri, (5) the Shattari, and (6) the Qalandari Silsila. Of the above orders, the Chisti Silsila was popular. The founder of Suhrawardi Silsila was Sheik Baharddin Zakariya, who lived during the period AD 1182 to 1262. The founder of the Chisti Silsila was Khwaja

Moinuddin Chisti, who came to India with Muhammad Ghori and settled in Ajmer about AD 1206. Even today his tomb at Ajmer is a great pilgrimage centre. Sufis played a crucial role in the social life of the period. We notice a sort of distrust between the Ulemas and the Sufis because of differences in practices. There was a cultural synthesis in the art, music and literature of this period.

Art and Architecture

It is generally accepted that a culture of the period is truly manifested in art and architecture as they are the visual expressions of the mind and spirit of the society in time and space. The period of Delhi Sultanate heralded a new expression in art. During that period, what is now called Indo-Islamic art took shape. Painting, calligraphy and book illumination also flourished in this period.

The structural remains of the palaces, mosques and temples that are wholly or partially in well-preserved condition reveal the style and techniques employed by the builders. They used lime mortar as the basic cementing material. The artisans started using the true arches and vaults and domes instead of lintel and beam. Percy Brown records that in the buildings of the Khilji period a new method of stone masonry was practised. Gypsum was commonly used to plaster buildings. The decorative element of Sultanate architecture was based on calligraphy, geometry and foliation. As calligraphy formed an important element of decoration, the Quaranic sayings were inscribed on buildings in an angular, sober and monumental script, known as *Kufi*. These are written on stone, stucco and painting. Geometric shapes are used in bewildering variety of combination on buildings. They used circles to develop a square, a triangle or a polygon of the foliations, the most common feature appears to be a stem-and-leaves combination.

Indo-Islamic architecture begins in the year in AD 1198 with the completion of Jama Masjid or Quwatul Islam which was built after destroying a number of Hindu and Jain temples. As this mosque was constructed by Indian artisans, we find Indian influence in this mosque, but from the construction of Qutub Minar onwards we notice fully Islamic tradition in detail of decoration and construction techniques. The most celebrated and the most magnificent building of the Delhi Sultanate period was Qutub Minar. Its height is 71.4 metres or 238 feet. Originally its height was only four-storied but Ferozshah Tughlak added the fifth storey. The basic beauty lies in the skilful manner in which balconies have been projected yet linked with the tower by a device called Stalectic honey-combing. The best example for the early form of Islamic architecture was the mausoleum of Balban built in AD 1286–87. We notice a marked change in this respect during the time of Khiljis and the characteristic feature of this age is the use of pointed horse-shoe shape of true porch and the emergence of the true dome with recessed arches under the squinch and also the use of new building materials of red sand stone. The other features of this period are decorative marble relief and the appearance of lotus bud foliage on the under side of the arch and the use of profuse geometric and calligraphic motifs. By the time of Tughlaks, a new style of architecture characterized by the use of stone rubble as the principal building material and plastering of walls in most cases, use of four centred arch, a pointed dome and construction of tombs on octagonal plan. In the final phase Delhi and its surrounding areas emerged as a sprawling grave yard. Stagnation set in the art and architecture of the Sultanate from the 15th century and Delhi Sultanate was replaced by the Mughals in AD 1526.

Besides royal palaces, tombs and mosques, we have evidence of the existence of a number of public buildings, Sarais, bridges, irrigation tanks, wells, dams, Katcheris, prison houses, Kotwali, Dak Chowki, Hammam and Katra or market places. Compared to architecture, painting in this period is less known. We have literary evidence for murals in this period as analysed by Simon Degby. As already explained calligraphy was the most revered art of this period and it was used for decorative purposes in buildings and mosques. The earliest copy of Quran is datable to AD 1399 of Gwalior. Music does not appear to have received any patronage. Amir Khusru of the time of Alauddin Khilji made significant contribution to music. He is said to have introduced for the first time the Qawwali mode of singing into the country side, Khayal form of singing by abandoning the traditional Dhrupad, and a new musical instrument called sitar by combining the old Indian Vina and the Iranian Tanpura.

The regional states of Bengal, Jaunpur, Gujarat, Malwa, and the Deccan kingdoms of Gulbarga, and Vijayanagara too patronized art and architecture. Interestingly, both painting and art and architecture developed at the same place in all the regions. Satish Chandra aptly remarks "thus, we not only see an outburst of architectural activity but a coming together of the Muslim and Hindu traditions and forms of architecture in the various regional kingdoms which arose during the 15th century, attempts were made to combine the style of architecture which had developed at Delhi with regional architectural traditions".

Language and Literature

It is generally assumed that due to the change of political power into the hands of the Muslims, Sanskrit would be neglected but what happened was different. Sanskrit remained a link language of entire India and Sanskrit literature flourished in this period. It is a fact that Persian had become the court or official language and yet there was no decline in the quality of literary output in Sanskrit. Kavyas, philosophical treatises, grammar, drama, stories, books on science on astronomy, medicine and digests of law books and commentaries on Vedas were produced in large numbers during this period.

Arabic, the language of Prophet Muhammad and of Islamic theology and religion was in limited prominence as it was used by a band of Islamic scholars and philosophers. Many Arabic scholars sought asylum in India in the reign of Iltutmish, when Bukhara was sacked by Chengiz Khan. Mujuddin Ferozabadi prepared a great Arabic dictionary *Qams* under the patronage of Ferozshah Tughlak with the help of Sanskrit scholars. Arabic was promoted and patronized by provincial rulers also.

We also notice great interaction between the languages of Sanskrit and Persian. In the middle of the 14th century Zia Nakshabid was the first scholar to translate Sanskrit stories into Persian. Zian-ul-abedin, the well-known Kashmiri ruler of the 15th century got *Mahabharata* and *Rajatarangani* translated into Persian. The languages of Hindi, Urdu, Punjabi, Bengali, Assamese, Marathi, Gujarati, Tamil, Telugu, Kannada, and Malayalam, also received impetus during this age from the regional kingdoms. The growing Bhakti or devotionalism also contributed to the growth of literature in these regional languages. The period of Delhi Sultanate was a formative period of significance in the history of India, which moulded the spirit of Indian culture and civilisation. We may concluded this chapter by agreeing with Satish Chandra that the Sultanate period far from being a dark age as postulated by some, saw the breaking of the rigid, narrow economic and social mould which had dominated the country between the 8th through 12th centuries and created an atmosphere for a limited development.

During the rule of the Ghaznavids in Punjab a new language, Persian was introduced. The earliest known Persian poet was Masud Sad Salman. Among the Persian poets, Amir Khusru stands as a colossus. The rule of the Khiljis was a very significant period in the growth and promotion of Persian literature. Amir Khusru's original name was Abdul Hasan. He was a prolific and versatile writer and it is said that he composed half a million verses and 99 works on different themes. His poetry consists of genres of lyric, ode, epic and elegy. Amir Khusru created a new style of Persian which later on came to be known as *Sabaq-i-Hindi* or the Indian style. *Mutla-ul-Anwas*, *Shirin Khasran*, *Laila Majnu*, *Alyina-i-Sikindari* and *Hasli Bhishit* are regarded as the literary masterpieces. These are dedicated to Alauddin Khilji. He also composed *Diwans* and also wrote *Masnavis* or narratives of the Delhi Sultanate.

Amir Khusru was born in India of an immigrant Turk. He loved India very dearly. He proudly says "I have praised India for two reasons; Firstly, because India is the land of my birth and our country. Love of the country is an important obligation. Hindustan is like heaven. Its climate is better than that of Khurasan. It is green and full of flowers all the year round. The Brahmins here are as learned as Aristotle and there are many scholars in various fields". Khusru composed verses in Hindavi or Hindi and paved the way for the future development of the Urdu language. Sheik Nizamudin Hasan was a well-known poet in Persian and was a friend and contemporary of Amir Khusru. Bahmani rulers patronized Persian poets. Historical works like *Tabaqat-i-nasiri* of Minhaj Siraj, *Futuha-s-Salatin* of Isami and *Tarikh-i-Firozshi* of Sham Siraj Afif were produced during this period. Sultan Ferozshah Tughlak was also the author of *Futuhat-i-Firuzshah*. It is an important historical work of significance. One the greatest historians of this period was Ziauddin Barauni, whose work *Tarikh-i-Firozshi* is also a good example of history. He also wrote a book on political theory called *Fatwa-i-Jahandani*.

A number of religious and philosophical works were written in Persian during this period. The Sufi preachers wrote their discourses in Persian and of them *Fawaid-u-Fuid* written by Amir Hasan Sifzi deals with the conversations or discourses of Sheik Nizamudin Auliya, the famous Chisti Sufi saint and scholars Mir Khwurdis. *Siyaram-ul-Aulia* is the well-known biographical dictionary of the Sufi saints.

Causes For the Fall of Delhi Sultanate

In the historical process of any country the rise and fall of dynasties of kingdoms is a natural phenomenon. Internal and external factors facilitate the atmosphere for the rise and fall of kingdoms. Cumulative effect of both internal and external factors was responsible for this phenomenon.

The disintegration of the Delhi Sultanate was not sudden but it began by the end of the reign of Ferozshah Tughlak in AD 1388 and it was completed by the invasion of Timur who caused destruction of the city of Delhi between the years of AD 1398–99. Timur's invasion resulted in the spread of death and destruction in Delhi and its neighbourhood and also carried away a number of artisans to beautify Samarqand. Definitely, this invasion paralysed the Delhi Sultanate beyond recovery, though it lingered for more than a century. Some attribute the disintegration to the actions of Muhammad bin Tughlak and the bigotry of Ferozshah Tughlak. But it is to be remembered that no individual Sultan can be held responsible for the downfall. It is the deep-rooted regionalism and a number of political chiefs of regions who were waiting for an opportunity to rise and declare independence as and when they found weaknesses in the central government. The Sultans tried to stop this trend by creating a band of slaves, loyal to them and also loyal people among the nobility. But the individual selfishness was also responsible for the failure of these checks. Religion could hardly unite people and it could not prevent rebellion from kith and kin. The problem of succession also hastened the disintegration of the Delhi Sultanate. All these factors were responsible for the failure of the Sultanate.

18

The Impact of Islam on Indian Culture

Bhakti and Sufi Movements

Culture is a complex and a very sensitive phenomenon. Each culture claims to be unique and uninfluenced by any other culture. However, such rigid view of culture cannot be truthful and realistic when specified geographical area is shared by people of different cultures and there is more than a likelihood of ideas, beliefs and practices mixing with one another. Satish Chandra rightly observes that the 13th century with the coming of the Turks into India and the establishment of the Delhi Sultanate was a period of both turmoil and development. The first phase was one of death and destruction on a large scale with many sacred, beautiful symbols of culture – temples being destroyed and palaces and cities being ravaged. This rather was a continuous process throughout the period of expansion and consolidation of the Delhi Sultanate along with the process of development and peaceful co-existence as well.

Contact between the two cultures started much earlier to the coming of Islam to India but the interaction quickened after Islam arrived. It is true that some bigoted Ulemas such as Nasiruddin Mubarak Ghaznavi of the regime of Iltutmish advocated a policy of inveterate hostility towards the Brahmins of the Hindu community as some of the very orthodox Hindus resented the Muslim entry into India. In due course of time, in spite of the seemingly irreconcilable nature of Islam and Hinduism, with Islam advocating strict monotheism, rejecting the image worship and worship of innumerable gods through Bhakti and Karma paths. Yet we notice the development of a gradual process of mutual adjustment and accommodation along with conflict and rapprochment.

No doubt, with setbacks under some rulers in some regions and faster development under some other rulers, travellers and saints played a key role as agents of transmission of ideas of one cultural adherents to another group. By the time Delhi Sultanate was established, it is rightly suggested that the main features of early Islam underwent many changes. It is also said that outwardly the migrants of Islamic religion professed to be fervent followers and showed respect to the Islamic rites and prayers appear to have imbibed many non-Islamic ideas of the upper strata of the Persian society, retaining some elements of its original simplicity, tribal democracy and social justice. Some Hindus who were opposed to the caste oppression and hierarchical ordering of social structure appear to have preferred conversion to Islam while some were forced into conversion while there were others lured by pecuniary gains. As Tarachand states, it is hardly possible to exaggerate the extent of Muslim influence over Indian life in all departments. But nowhere else is it shown so vividly and as picturesquely as in customs, in intimate details of domestic life, in music, in the fashion of dress, in the ceremonies of marriage, and fairs, and in the courtly institutions and etiquette. It is to be admitted that though these cultures lived for ages side by side, there was no real fusion of cultures but the impact of each on the other cannot be underestimated.

Tarachand further observes the influence exercised by Muslim mystics and their religious thought, which inspired a number of reform movements among Hindus, which spread over the whole of the country and profusely affected the Hindu outlook. S. Abid Husain writes that one of the most powerful factors, which contributed to the reconciliation was the historic mediating role played by the Muslim Sufis and Hindus saints of the later Bhakti school.

The Sufi Movement

Sufism or *Tasawwuf* is the composite name for various mystical tendencies and movements of Islam. Its object was to establish direct communication between God and man through personal experience of inherent mysticism. It is also based on the spirit of Quranic purity. There is an evolution in the growth and development of Sufism up to the 10th century, where we notice a formative stage of growth of organized Sufi movement. This was also the period of emergence of Sufi poetry in Persian. Fariduddin Attar, who died in AD 1220 and Jalaluddin Rumi, who died in AD 1273 were its two great exponents. The early Sufi mystics stressed on the virtues of repentance, abstinence, renunciation, poverty and trust in God. The early Sufis were wanderers but in due course of time the Sufi groups have become orders and while in Arab regions there developed hostels called *Ribat* and in Iran there developed hospices or *Kanquash*, where the Sufi mystics stayed in the late 12th and 13th centuries. We notice the formation of Sufi orders or *Salsilas*. Al Hujwiri of the late 11th century was the earliest Sufi saint to settle in India. He was the author of *Kasf-ul-mahjub*, a famous treatise on Sufism in Persian. After the establishment of the Delhi Sultanate, many Sufi orders were established in different parts of India and Sufism became very influential by the 14th century. Some of the most important *Silsilas* during the period of the Sultanate are as follows:

1. The Suhrawardi Silsila which was founded in India by Shaik Bahauddin Zakaria (AD 1182–1262).
2. The Chisti Silsila introduced in India by Khwaja Moinuddin Chisti, who died in AD 1236. Even today he is venerated by Muslims and his tomb is located at Ajmer, which became a sacred pilgrimage.

   Besides the above two orders, there existed the orders of the Firdausi, the Qadiri, the Shatauri, Qalandari, etc.

A critical study of the tenets of Sufism indicates that it was acquainted with Hinduism and Hindu thought and had imbibed certain elements of Indian idealism and adopted many Yogic practices and also was influenced by Upanishadic idealism and Vedanta. The early Sufis were not only ascetics but also lived a life of voluntary poverty shunning all types of worldly pleasures. Khwaja Fariduddin, popularly known as Baba declared, "The main purpose of this path is the concentration of heart which can be achieved only by the abstination from prohibited means of livelihood and association with kings". Thus, most of the Sufis in India conceived and preached divine unity in terms of idealistic monoism while many Hindus found the Sufi ideas very similar to those of Vedantic philosophy. The lower strata of Hindu community appears to be greatly attracted by the ideas of social equality and fraternity of Islam. Thus the simplicity, toleration and liberation of the Sufis in India released syncretic forces and led to a sort of cultural synthesis.

The Bhakti Movement

Abid Hussian is of the view that another great force that created a general atmosphere of religious harmony between the Hindus and the Muslims was the Bhakti movement that swept northern India between the 14th through 17th century. Bhakti as a path of salvation was as old as the Vedas. The Bhakti stresses mystic realization of God within oneself and the ultimate union of the individual with God based on loving devotion on the part of the devotee and gods is a given popular concept in India. There are two aspects of Bhakti:

(i) The path of devotion based on service to God by the devotee or *Bhakta* throwing himself completely on the mercy of God or *Prapatti*.

(ii) The path of bond based on pure love based on equality rather than service and the ideal being participation in the life divine.

We notice the currency of these two aspects of Bhakti in early medieval period in South India and in the later medieval period in northen India. There is a controversy regarding the origin and relationship between the Bhakti movement of the Nayanars and Alvars of South India and the popular Bhakti movement of northern India. One view is that the new situation created by the coming of the Turks, the defeat of Rajput states, the wanton destruction of the temples and trampling of images, lowering of the image of Brahmins and the failure of the Rajput and the Brahman alliance to stem the tide of Turks led to the popular Bhakti movement in many parts of northern India. Max Weber, a well-known sociologist suggested that an apocalyptic movement such as Bhakti was often the ideology of a defeated ruling class with aspects of quietism and suffering being emphasized. Satish Chandra disagrees with the view of Max Weber as the Bhakti movement was a mass-based popular movement but not an ideology of a defeated ruling class with a vested interest. There is also another view that the movement grew in the north as a kind a defence mechanism to safeguard the Hindu social organization from the threat of Turkish onslaughts of and the challenge faced from the Islamic ideology, which was based on ideas of brotherhood and equality. However, even this view does not take into account the totality of the situation as both the Hindus and the Muslims realized the futility of the efforts to forcibly convert Hindus to Islam. Both Sultans and saints such as Nizamuddin Auliya, admitted that the Hindu faith was too strong to be affected either by threats of force or the concept of brotherhood and equality held out by Islam. Further, it is to be remembered that the concept of social equality as a bonding factor long disappeared in Indian Islam as the Turkish ruling group looked down upon Hindu converts from the low strata of society. It is suggested that the Sufi emphasis on monotheism, on the role of the *Pir* or Guru, on mystical union with the beloved happen to be elements of Hinduism that influenced saints and people to come together. Satish Chandra says, "Thus the Bhakti movement marks a phase of symbiosis where common elements were emphasized and this aspect is more important than the claim of mutual borrowings which is always a matter dispute".

K. Damodaran writes that the Bhakti movements in India have many points of resemblance to the Reformation movement led by Wycliff and Thomas More – it was not a purely religious movement, it expressed itself in the cultural field as a national renaissance; in its social content, it represented a revolt of great significance against domination and injustices of the caste system. It gave a new impetus to the growth of diverse nationalities in India, to the development of national languages and their literature. The doctrine that all men high and low were equal before God became the central idea, which pulled wide sections of the masses to fight caste tyranny. Thus, this great movement of the middle ages not only helped the development of a composite Indian culture embracing different linguistic and religious communities, but also paved the way for united struggle, against feudal oppression. J.T.F. Jordans observes: "During medieval times (13th through 17th century) Hinduism underwent a transformation as great as that of Christianity by the Reformation. The focus of religious activities moved from the great gods and the liturgies connected with polytheism to one god, and his avatars, especially Krishna and Rama. A new attitude to God, emotional, passionate Bhakti replaced the old approaches of sacrificial rites and monoistic meditation, just a new mysticism, practical yet ecstatic, replaced the former philosophical type. Forms of religious expression changed: love songs to the Lord were sung, and group singing created a new popular cultural form, the *Kirtan*. Finally, the Bhakti movement without destroying the Hindu social frame work fostered ideas of brotherhood and equality before the loving God and its saints drawn from all levels of society proclaimed that in Bhakti, caste had no meaning".

In conclusion, we can say that though there was no visible direct evidence of positive impact of Islam on Indian culture, interactions between common Hindus and Muslims, Sufi and Bhakti saints created an environment for the emergence of a Hindustanic culture, wherein we can witness the mutual borrowings from both cultures. As cultures are dynamic but not static when two people, two cultures meet, cultural interaction either positive or negative is inevitable and the same happened in India during the rule of Delhi Sultanate. The initial suspicion, dislike, animosity and hatred did not quite disappear but the slow and gradual realization that the Muslims and the Hindus have to live side by side occupying and sharing geographical space made them reconcile, adjust, accommodate and adapt themselves to the changing circumstances with their identities reflected in their cultural practices and symbols.

19

The Age of the Kakatiyas

Society, Economy, Polity and Culture

The Kakatiyas, a known indigenous Andhra power, presided over the destiny of Andhradesa from the 10th century AD to the first quarter of the 14th century AD. Even today the memory of the Kakatiya rule is green in the minds and hearts of the *Andhrajati* as the Kakatiyas shaped and moulded the identity of the Andhras by establishing a unified political and cultural hegemony over the entire Telugu-speaking region.

Like the rest of the political power structures, there is no unanimity among historians regarding the origin and caste of the Kakatiyas. The literary text *Prataparudrayasobhushana* of Vidyanatha records that this family of rulers was called Kakatiyas as they were known to have worshipped the goddess Kakati. The Kakatiyas are also known as worshippers of Svayambhudeva, i.e., Siva. The Bayyaram tank epigraph now definitely proves that Venna was the earliest member of the family and he ruled from a town called Kakati and as such his descendants are styled as Kakatiyas. The epigraphs of the Kakatiyas refer to them as the lords of Kakatipura. On the basis of these literary and epigraphical evidences, it can be suggested that Kakati was a Pura or town and the family name Kakatiya might have been based on the original connection of the family with that town. The epigraphs further state that the Kakatiyas were originally of some Ratta or Rashtrakuta family and hence *Chaturdhakulajas* or Sudras. The Kakatiyas claim that they belonged to the Durjaya family whose very remote ancestor Karikalachola founded Kakatipura.

The first known historical personage among the Kakatiyas was Gundaya Rashtrakuta. Gundaya is known from the Mangallu record of Danarnava. Gundaya, the commander of Rashtrakuta Krishna II died in the battlefield fighting with the Eastern Chalukyas. The Rastrakuta Krishna II rewarded Ereya, the son of Gundaya with the governorship of the Korivi region for the loyal service rendered by Gundaya and his family. During the 9th and 10th century, they were the subordinates of the Rashtrakutas. After the overthrow of the Rashtrakuta power by the Western Chalukyas of Kalyani, the Kakatiyas became their feudatories or *Mahamandalesvaras* under the Chalukyas of Kalyani. Kakatiya rulers Beta I, Prola I, Beta II and Prola II served the Western Chalukya rulers; Somesvara I, Vikramadity VI, Somesvara III and Jagadekamalla II. After the fall of the Western Chalukyan power during the reign of Tailapa III, the Kakatiya ruler Rudradeva declared independence in AD 1158. Thus the role of the Kakatiyas as sovereign power starts from Rudradeva.

Rudradeva, who ruled form AD 1158 to 1195, was the son and successor of Prola II. He was the founder of the Kakatiya lineage as he declared independence and started independent rule. The Hanumakonda epigraph dated AD 1162 gives graphic details of his conquests over his neighbours and how he extended his sway over coastal Andhra by subduing the Velanaticholas. We learn from Jalhana's *Suktimuktavali* and Hemadri's *Vratakhanda*, that Rudradeva faced defeat in the conflict with the Yadavas of Devagiri. He is credited with laying foundation stone for a new fort near Warangal, which became the capital of the Kakatiyas. As Rudradeva had no children, he was succeeded to the throne by his brother Mahadeva, who ruled from AD 1195 to AD 1198–99. Mahadeva was defeated by the Yadava Jaitugi and he lost his life in the battle and his son Ganapatideva was captured as prisoner by the Yadavas. Political instability and disorder gripped the Kakatiyas because of the captivity of Ganapati Deva and the death of Mahadeva. At that juncture, Recharla Rudra, the loyal commander-in-chief of the Kakatiyas saved the kingdom. Ultimately, Ganapatideva was released by the Yadavas from prison and was sent to the Kakatiya kingdom. It is argued that political pressures experienced by the Yadavas from other quarters were responsible for this release of Ganapatideva.

Ganapatideva ruled from AD 1199 to 1262. Though he faced defeat and failure initially, in the end his reign forms a brilliant epoch in the history of the Kakatiya rule. Ganapatideva expanded the Kakatiya territorial state by capturing coastal Andhra by defeating the Velanati chief, Prithviswera and later he led an expedition to Nellore and placed Manumasiddhi on the throne of Nellore. But Ganapatideva's efforts to bring Kalinga under his sway were not successful. Ganapatideva in his attempt to safeguard Manumasiddhi against the attack of Jatavarma Sundara Pandya was unsuccessful and Jatavarma Sundarapandya, after defeating Manumasiddhi and Ganapathideva, performed *Virabhishekha* at Nellore and Kanchi. Ganapatideva successfully united the entire Telugu-speaking people under his sway and shifted his capital from Hanumankonda to Warangal.

As Ganapatideva had no male issue, his daughter Rudramadevi ruled from AD 1262 to 1289. Ganapatideva had two daughters; Rudrama and Ganapamba. He selected his eldest daughter Rudrama to succeed him and made her his co-regent from AD 1260 to 1262 to enable her to gain experience in the art of rulership. The accession of Rudrama to the Kakatiya throne was a remarkable and memorable event of medieval South India as she was the first woman ruler of Andhra region. Rudramadevi proved to be a woman of substance and rose to the occasion and put the state in order, subduing all those who opposed her internally. She successfully repulsed the Yadava attack and drove the Yadavas up to Devagiri as is known from the Bidar epigraph. We come to know from the Chandupatla epigraph that Rudrama and her general Mallikarjuna died in the battlefield while opposing Kayasta Ambadeva, who defeated her. Rudrama was followed by daughter Mummadamba's son, Prataparudradeva, who ruled from AD 1289 to AD 1323. Prataparudra defeated Kayashta Ambadeva and his allies and the Yadavas who supported Ambadeva. By these victories, once again the prestige and glory of the Kakatiyas was revived. It was during his reign that the Delhi Sultans, first Allauddin Khilji and later Muhammad bin Tughlak turned their attention towards South India and began to invade the Kakatiya territories. Finally, the Kakatiya power came to an end in AD 1323, with the failure and defeat of Prataparudra by Muhammad bin Tuglak's armies. The Kakatiya rule came to an end with the defeat and death of Prataparudra.

Polity

The Kakatiya polity was based on monarchical system. The Kakatiya ruler was the pivot of the entire administrative structure, yet he was not an absolute autocrat. Generally, in the process of succession, they followed the law of primogeniture and as already referred, a woman coming to the throne was a remarkable exception. The power appears to be decentralized between the ruler and the subordinates who owed allegiance to the ruler. P.V. Prabrahma Sastry rightly observes, "The peculiar type of political relationship between the Kakatiya rulers and their subordinates during the reign of nearly two centuries makes us believe that they tried to introduce a new type of polity other than imperialism. The subordinates were allowed to have their freedom in all respects except military matters. The only concern for the king was to check their overgrowth in power". This made some scholars characterize Kakatiya polity as a feudal polity of personalized rule by a warrior elite and a socio-economic formation marked by oppression of the peasantry, economic stagnation and de-urbanization. But a critical examination proves that this image was inappropriate in the case of Kakatiya Andhradesa. Another alternative model of segmentary state suggested by Burton Stein does not appear to be applicable to the Kakatiya state. Cynthia Talbot maintains, "Stein himself excluded internal Andhra from the South Indian macro region characterized by the segmentary state and ritual sovereignty, calling Telengana, a shatter region on the borders of South India proper". Cynthia Talbot, after a thorough discussion of the suitability of the models – feudal, segmentary and integrative, declares the Kakatiya state as best understood as a fluctuating political network composed in large part of a multitude of personalities between lords and underlings. Some of the fibres in the fabric of Kakatiya polity united the rulers directly to their primary subordinates, others led from these subordinates to different tiers of associates in a densely ramified pattern. Connections extended horizontally, integrating localities spread over a wide territory, as well as vertically reaching down into villages and towns". Cynthia Talbot is of the view that the Kakatiya polity is closely approximating to Weber's patrimonial model of the state, i.e., personalized authority of a ruler through a class of dependent officials. R. Champakalakshmi is of the view that Cynthia Talbot has no specific model to offer for Andhra polity. Talbot views the Kakatiya polity as a regional variant of a pan-Indian complex, a dynamic and an expansionist world. There is also a view that Kakatiya polity is an integrative polity. The Kakatiya rulers were assisted by a council of ministers and a host of officers at the centre as well as the provincial and local level. They took care to see that the territorial segments were properly divided and ruled effectively by loyal officials. *Mandala, Nadu, Sthala, Seema* and *Bhumi* were the names of the territorial divisions.

The Kakatiya state was a military-state ready to face the threat of internal and external enemies. The military organization of the Kakatiyas was based on *Nayamkara* system. In this system the ruler assigned fiefs to the Nayaks in lieu of their salaries and the Nayaks were to maintain some army for the ruler's use. The number of soldiers, horses, and elephants that are to be maintained by the Nayak were fixed by the king as per the fiefs enjoyed by the Nayak. Apart from the army that was supplied by the Nayaks, the Kakatiyas also maintained a standing army under the control of the commanders, who were directly responsible to the ruler. In the military organization, forts played crucial role and the epigraphs refer to *Giridurgas*, like Anumakonda, Raichur, Gandikota and the *Vanadurgas*, like Kandur and Narayanavanam, the *Jaladurgas*, like Divi and Kolanu and the *Sthaladurgas*, like Warangal and Dharanikota. *Nitisara* of Prataparudra refers to the above mentioned four types of *Durgas*. The military organization enabled the Kakatiyas to be aggressive and rapidly expand as an Andhra power from the core region or nuclear zone of Telangana to the coastal districts and hence to Rayalaseema or South-West Andhra and to penetrate to the Tamil region also. Talbot gives importance to the strategy adopted by the Kakatiyas in patronizing warrior chiefs, and promoting martial ethos and assumption of martial epithets by the rulers. The relationships between Nayaks and rulers are marked by layers of lord-subordinate relationships loosely bound through personal loyalties of allegiance and service.

Society

Relying on the evidence furnished by the Dharmasastric literature, traditional historians perceive the society as based on the *Varnasramadharma* model and divided into fourfold Varnas; Brahman, Kshatriya, Vaisya and Sudra. We also notice the emergence of sub-castes and Brahmins being divided on the basis of sub-regions as Velanatis, Veginatis and Mulakanatis, besides Srotriyas and Niyogis. Interestingly, the community of Brahmins besides being scholars and teachers also acted as *Dandanayakas* or commanders and *Amatyas* or ministers. Rulership was not the monopoly of the Kshatriyas alone and the prominence of the Kshatriya community as rulers appears to have diminished to a large extent. Anyone could become a ruler, provided he had the necessary qualities and abilities. One of the prominent features of medieval Andhra was the emergence of Sudras as the new political elite and the other social groups accepted the superiority of the Sudras as rulers. Further, it is believed that kings made it their duty to uphold the Brahmanical Dharma and took measures to see that each caste followed the duties assigned to it. There is a strong belief that in medieval Andhra, the Brahmans occupied superior place in social order and the social order itself depended on their dictates. Cynthia Talbot rejects the image of a static village and a caste based organization during this period as Varna and Jati are less visible in the Kakatiya lithic records and hence she argues that the idealized paradigm of Varna and Jati are not relevant. Identities on the basis of local, familial and occupational associations are highlighted and very interestingly neither the ruling family nor the warrior elite claimed the superior Varna status, to prove their high ancestry. Instead, clan and lineage were taken as the greater signifiers of social status with considerable divergence of status within the larger clan-Varna affiliation. Such claim was made by the Brahmins in the epigraphs by referring to their Gotras or Sakhas and Varna status only in situations of contention about power and resources. Kakatiya lithic records hail the Sudras as the bravest of the four Varnas and also the best. Cynthia Talbot is of the view that the individual eminence, military service and administrative ranking were the main basis for identities, and claim to social importance. Mobility in turn indicates social typologies. Considerable social fluidity among all non-Brahmins and the existence of occupational groups like merchants makes it too complex a situation for applying any standard model for Kakatiya Andhra society.

Temple epigraphs testify to the practice of *Saani* being added to the women of the royal family and those attached to the temple. Women made donations referring themselves as somebody's wife or daughter. That women had right to *Stridhana* and other forms of property is evident as women comprise 11 per cent of all individual donors. Epigraphs also record donation of livestock, temple buildings and metal items used in ritual worship, along with irrigational facilities and cash. Interestingly, most of the temple women or *Gudisanis* were daughters of respectable men like *Nayakas* and *Settis* and temple women were not barred from marriage. Cynthia Talbot is of the view that the condition of women in Kakatiya age was by no means deplorable as was presumed by traditionalist observers basing their conclusions on legal and epic literature. It can be concluded that multiplicity of social foci existed in Kakatiya phase, wherein both kingship ties and territorial proximity created linkages among people based on factors like military service, a common sectarian membership or similar occupation. Social rigidity was less noticeable due to dynamism and fluidity witnessed in social relations. For example, the literary test *Palanativirulakatha* refers to the war and the friends Balachandra from diverse backgrounds: a Brahmin, a blacksmith, a goldsmith, a washerman, a potter, and a barber and all of them call themselves 'brothers' and dine together before going to battle. Merchants and artisan association appear to be the largest category of collective donors known from the epigraphs of the Kakatiyas. Social relationships appear to be based on common interest and occupations rather than Varna and Jati as social identities were not expressed in terms of Varna or Jati.

Economy

Kakatiya epigraphs bear testimony to the economic development witnessed by Andhradesa due to the cumulative effect of the steps taken by rulers and feudatories and officials from AD 1158 to 1324. Both agriculture and trade and commerce, particularly long distance trade acted as a catalyst in carrying the Kakatiya state and making it economically sound. Cynthia Talbot writes "During the Kakatiya era, inland Andhra economy underwent considerable growth due to the extension of agriculture into uncultivated territories, the boosting of agricultural productivity through the construction of irrigational facilities and an overall rise in trade and commerce in which the temple as an institution was ultimately intertwined".

Though the core area of the Kakatiyas was ecologically in dry zone with scanty rainfall, with soil not very fertile, the Kakatiyas paid much attention to agriculture, the main occupation of majority of its population. They employed tank irrigation as a necessary technique to provide water for cultivation. In order to encourage more people to undertake the digging of tanks, wells and canals, tank construction was made one of the *Saptasantanas* which confers merit. Kakatiya epigraphs refer to more than 38 tanks of considerable size which provided water through artificial channels to thousands of acres. Of all the tanks, the Ramappa and the Pakala lakes are of large size and require special mention. Ramappa Lake adjoins the well-known Ramappa temple at Palampet in Mulug taluk of Warangal district. Gopal Reddy and P.V.P. Sastry state that this lake had a colossal bund only one side that extends over 200 feet and rises up to 56 feet. The lake has a ring of hills on three sides. Kakati Ganapati Deva's *Senapati*, Recharla Rudra constructed this lake in AD 1213. Pakala lake in Narasampet taluk of Warangal district is larger than Ramappa lake, with a dam composed of laterite pebbles and earth that is one mile long from which 40 artificial channels have been extended. This lake was also constructed in the time of Ganapati Deva by a subordinate, Jagadala Mummadi, the son of a minister or *Mantri*. The multitude of historical traces confirms that a boom in the building of tanks occurred in inland Andhra while the Kakatiyas were ruling. The tank foundation inscriptions are distributed throughout Telengana, the southern coastal districts, and in Cuddapah of Rayalaseema. They are more concentrated in the districts of Khammam and Warangal. Along with tank construction, we also notice the construction of temples with a tank in the interior as well as addition of a tank to the existing temples. Cynthia Talbot observes the frequency of new temples is notably higher in the Telangana than in coastal Andhra. The temple construction also led to the growth of new settlements of people who brought uncultivated virgin land into cultivation. By these processes of tank construction and temple construction, the Kakatiyas achieved the twin objective of improving productivity by bringing new areas under cultivation and also the formation of Andhra as a regional society, noted by Talbot.

Cultivable land was classified as wet and dry land. Wet land is further divided as paddy growing land and garden land. Dry lands are those where crops like millet, sesame, indigo, mustard, castor, etc., were grown which needed less water. Forests and pastures were kept exclusively for gazing cattle. Land was surveyed and measured, where the ruler collected one-fourth to one-half of the produce as revenue. The revenue was collected either in cash or in kind. The Kakatiyas levied different taxes like tax on grazing, property tax, income tax, profession tax, marriage tax, tax on herds of sheep and tax on salt. Heavy taxation by the state appears to be the feature of Kakatiya polity.

In the Kakatiya Andhra, trade was carried on by well-organized *Srenis* or guilds. Both the merchants and artisans had their own guilds. Epigraphs refer to guild of weavers, agriculturists, oil pressers, mat makers, smiths, potters and jewelers. The guilds obtained a license to conduct business in a particular town or fair. Fairs or weekly markets were held regularly at specified places. The merchandise was transported by means of carts, oxen, horses, etc., and to a great extent by boats and barges through the rivers Govadari and Krishna.

Kakatiyas recognized the importance of long distance trade. One indication that they wanted to encourage maritime trade, comes from the famous Motupalli epigraph which runs as follows: "This inscribed guarantee has been granted by his majesty the king Ganapati Deva which assures and welcomes the traders from other areas going back and forth through selected area to all countries and towns. In the past, kings forcibly seized all the cargo such as gold, elephants, horses, jewels, etc., when sea-going vessels journeying from one region to another were caught in storms, wrecked and cast on shore. But we for the sake of our reputation and religious merit and out of pity for those who have incurred the grave risk of a sea voyage thinking that wealth is more valuable than life give up all but the customary tariff." Motupalli must have been the chief port of the Kakatiyas and this port was visited by the Venitian traveller, Marco Polo.

The Motupalli epigraph specifies the rates assessed on a variety of items, including scents such as sandal, camphor, rose-water, ivory, pearls, corals, a range of metals like copper, zinc and lead, silk, pepper, and areca nuts. This above list gives an idea of exports and imports from Motupalli port to other Indian regions along the coast as well to foreign territories. One Warangal epigraph issued by merchant groups, who traded in the main markets of Warangal, refers to the same commodities mentioned above. Another epigraph notes that a number of agricultural products offered for sale in Warangal market included rice, wheat, and other grains and assorted vegetables, coconuts, mangoes, tamarind and other fruits, sesame seeds, green lentils, mustard, honey, ghee, oil, turmeric and ginger. We have epigraphic reference to the activities of Pekkandru, a guild which was carrying on long distance trade. Besides, Motupalli, Krishnapattanam, Chinaganajam, Nellore, and Divi also played a very crucial role in fostering sea-borne trade. Thus, flourishing agriculture and surplus produce and long distance trade carried on by guilds like Pekkandru was the base for the sound economic position of Kakatiya Andhra.

Religion

The early Kakatiya rulers were adherents of Jainism of the Digambara sect. They are credited with the construction of Padmakshi temple at Hanumakonda. Though there are strong references to the worship of Buddhism, it had lost its impetus and Buddha has been identified with Vishnu and Buddhism was absorbed into Brahmanical religion. Saivism was the most predominant faith in Kakatiya Andhra; Beta II and Prola II of this lineage are known to be the adherents of the Kalamukha school of Saivism. During the reign of Ganapati Deva, the Pasupata sect of Saivism had become very popular and Visveswara Sivacharya became the Rajaguru of Ganapati Deva. The Malakapuram inscription of Rudramadevi helps us to know about the growth of Pasupata sect and Golaki Matha activities in Andhradesa. During this period another sect of Saivism, Aradhya Saivism also emerged and Mallikarjuna Pandita was a well-known pioneer of this sect. In the past three decades, western scholars like Herman Kulke and Burton Stein have stressed that religions patronage by royalty was a critical element of state formation. Further scholars like Spencer, Brackenbridge, and Appadurai also opine that by religious patronage, kings enhanced their royal authority. There is a view that Brahmanical rituals legitimized and conferred royal power on the kings of the Sudra community. Cynthia Talbot observes; "Contrary to what one might expect from the secondary literature, we have seen that the religious patronage of the Kakatiyas was quite limited. Altogether, the five independent Kakatiya rulers left behind only 26 inscriptions documenting their religious gifts spanning over a period of 150 years (Rudradevas – six grants; Mahadeva – one Ganapatideva independently – 14 and with Rudramadevi – one; Rudramadevi independently – 4 and Prataparudra – 4). Rudradeva, the first independent ruler constructed the Thousand-pillared temple at Hanumankonda and laid the foundation for a new capital at Warangal along with a temple to the tutelary deity of Svayambhudeva. Ganapati Deva also built temple at Motupalli because by that time this area had become a secondary core area of the Kakatiyas. It may be suggested that the Kakatiyas regarded divine legitimation and the support of the institutionalized religion as important assets to royal authority, and not necessarily the foundation for their sustenance as effective rulers. The model of Dharmic kingship does not apply to the Kakatiya rule as the Kakatiyas understood that political interests differed from religious interests.

Culture and Literature

Andhra under the Kakatiyas witnessed considerable literary activity. Sanskrit occupied the place of pride and was the language of the educated few. Many epigraphs of this period are written in Kavya-style of Sanskrit. The noted poets who were the authors of the epigraphs of this age are Nandi, Acchitendra Antantasuri and Iswarasuri. The greatest Sanskrit poets of this age were Vidyanadha and Jayapasenani. Vidyanatha wrote *Parataparudrayasobhushana*. Jayapasenani was the author of *Nrityaratnavali* and *Gitaratnavali*. Coming to

Telugu literature, the most important are Tikkanna Somayaji who wrote *Nirvachananottararamayam*, Mantri Bhaskara who wrote *Bhaskara Ramayana*, Gona Budda Reddi who wrote *Ranganatha Ramayanam*, Nanne Choda, the author of *Kumara Sambhavama,* Baddena the author of *Sumati Satakam* and Palkuriki Somanadha, the author of *Basavapuranam*, and *Panditaradhyacharita*. Of the above *Ranganadha Ramayanam*, occupies a unique place as a *Dvipadakavya*.

The Kakatiyas inherited the Chalukyan architecture but the distinctive feature of their architecture is the display of more indigenous art than that allowed by the texts. The architects used locally available granite and sandstone in the main structure of the *Vimana* and used bricks and lime in constructing superstructure. They used black granite for pillars, jambs, lintels, decorative motifs and icons. Their temple architecture reflects great sophistication and the 'Thousand-pillared temple' is a landmark in the evolution of the Kakatiyan architectural style. The great Rudresvara temple was built by Recharla Rudra, the commander in chief of Ganapati Deva; in the words of Y. Gopala Reddi it marks the climax of the Kakatiyan style. The Gomateswara temple at Manthani, the Erakesvara and the Namesvara temples at Pillalamarri and the temple at Naguladu are the masterpieces of the Kakatiyan style of architecture.

About the Kakatiya sculptures, we have very little evidence to study it. Their main decoration was *Kirtimukha* or *Krititorana*. Nandis are a special feature of the Kakatiya sculpture. The Nandi images at Palampet, Thousand-pillared temple, Sambhuni Gudi, Ghanapur, Kolanupalli are some of the best examples with profuse bell ornamentation. The sculptural presence of *Hamsa* or swan motifs, on the gateways and friezes is to be noticed for their grace and beauty. Of the decorative sculptures, the motifs of dancers and *Kolata* are worth recording. It is also suggested by scholars that, they represent the dance styles of Jayapasenani. The Narasimha temple at Parivela near Nalgonda consists of profusely carved lintels and jambs. The temples at Nandigonda contain richly furnished Mandapa pillars and ceilings.

The Kakatiyas also extended patronage to the art of painting. The traces of painting that are found on ceilings of the pillared halls of the temples at Ghanapur and Palampet bear testimony to the painting skill of that period. The defaced painting of the 'Churning of the Milk Ocean' found on the ceiling of the Sabha Mandepa of the Namevara temple at Pillalamarri is also a good example of their painting skill.

The Kakatiya rule in Andhra was a period of transition and ushered the beginning of an era in the 13th century. The Kakatiyas by their support of art and their integrative polity improved agriculture, commerce and trade in the interior and construction of temples in Telangana, Rayalaseema and coastal Andhra.

20

The Vijayanagara-Bahmani Kingdoms

In the history of India in general and South India in particular, the Vijayanagara kingdom is remembered even today for its extensive political control of a large territorial state, for its legacy of architectural wonder of Hampi and magnificent religious structures throughout South India. These kings are also remembered for their policy of promotion of agriculture, trade and commerce, and by their contribution to the greatest literary surge in Sanskrit, Kannada, Telugu and Tamil. They made themselves memorable by their policy of separating religious dogmatism from the sphere of politics. Foreign travellers' accounts of Abdul Razak, Nicolo Conti, Domingo Paes and other Portuguese traders paint a picture of affluence and wealth enjoyed by the kings, nobles and courtiers, while the common people led the life of subsistence due to excessive taxation.

The origin and early history of the Vijayanagara kingdom is shrouded in mystery. Historians are not unanimous regarding the original home or the founders of the kingdom. Though all historians agree on the role played by Harihara and Bukka, in the foundation of the kingdom and the role of Sage Vidyaranya in inspiring and helping them, there is a difference of opinion regarding their original place of birth and mother-tongue. Literary traditions and epigraphs testify that Vijayanagara kingdom was founded in AD 1336 by Harihara and Bukka, the two Sangama brothers. Robert Sewell, who brought to light this "Forgotten Empire", refers to seven 'traditions' regarding the origin of the foundations of this Vijayanagara kingdom. Rev. Fr. Heras, S. Krishnaswamy Ayyangar, B.A. Saletore, P.B. Desai, G.S. Gai and some other scholars support the theory of Kannada origin by associating the founders with Hoyasala Ballala III. Numerous traditions like *Kumararama Katha*, *Kampiliyuddha,* etc. in Kannada refer to the Kampili origin of the founders of Vijayanagara. Robert Sewell, N. Venkata Ramanayya, M. Somasekhara Sarma are of the view that the founders of the Vijayanagara kingdom were Andhras, in the service of Prataparudra of the Kakatiya dynasty. Whatever may be the original home of the founders of Vijayanagara kingdom, it is to be noted that in building their system of administration, the Vijayanagara rulers used the Tamil traditions of the Cholas, Kannada traditions of the Hoyasalas and the Telugu traditions of the Kakatiyas as they represented themselves as rulers of entire South India.

There is also a controversy regarding the role of Sage Vidyaranya in founding the city of Vijayanagara. As the city of Vijayanagara has an alternate name of Vidyanagara, it is believed that Sage Vidyaranya was responsible for the construction of the city also. Inscriptions contain certain evidence that Vijayanagara was founded and completed by the two brothers Harihara and Bukka. Treating the epigraphs that refer to Vidyaranya as spurious, Fleet, Rice, Fr. Heras, Narasimhachar and Gopinadha Rao question the role of Vidyaranya in founding the city as well as the kingdom.

A strong belief prevails that the primary objective of establishing the Vijayanagara kingdom was to stop the penetration of Islamic way of life and worship into South India as well as to preserve and conserve the age-old Dharmic culture of the *Sanatanadharma* from pollution. Vidyaranya's role is minimized by the advocates of this view, who also point out that the Vijayanagara rulers ruled as trustees of the kingdom on behalf of their tutelary deity Virupaksha. This view is rejected by others who argue that the decline of the Delhi Sultanate was the main reason for the emergence of Vijayanagara state in South India. There is no definite proof that Vijayanagara rulers were fanatical Hindu revivalists or champions of Hindu faith. A critical examination of their pragmatic religious policy and other policies and their relations with contemporary political power centres, indicate that political considerations and self-interests outweighed protecting Hindu Dharma against Islam. The recruitment of proficient archers belonging to Islamic faith, construction of a mosque and venerating Islamic religious text Quran and the title of *Yavanarajyasthapanacharya* by Krishnadevaraya are some examples to suggest that the Vijayanagara rulers were not influenced by religious consideration in framing their policy. Taking advantage of the decline of the Delhi Sultanate after the Tughlaks and the disintegration of the erstwhile power centres of the Yadavas, the Kakatiyas, the Hoyasalas, and the Pandyas, the resultant vacuum was filled by the Vijayanagara rulers.

The Vijayanagara and Bahmani kingdoms were contemporary power centres, one located in Karnataka and the other in the upper Deccan. While the Vijayanagara kingdom was established in AD 1336, the Bahmani kingdom was founded in AD 1347. Vijayanagara and Bahmani rulers opposed each other at regular intervals, until their energies and resources were dissipated in this constant struggle for control of fertile zones. Satish Chandra rightly observes that the interests of the Vijayanagara rulers and the Bahmani Sultans clashed in three separate and distinct areas in the Tungabhadra Doab, in the Krishna-Godavari delta and in the Marathwada country. The Tungabhadra Doab was the region between the rivers Krishna and Tungabhadra. On account of its wealth and economic resources, it had been the bone of contention between rival political powers for a long time. The struggle for mastery of the fertile Krishna-Godavari basin, which on account of numerous ports controlled the long distance sea trade of the region, was often linked with the struggle for the Tungabhadra Doab. The smaller powers of the time either allied with Vijayanagara or Bahmani rulers depending on their immediate interests. In the Marathwada region, the main contention was for the control of the Konkan and the area, which gave access to it. The Konkan is a narrow strip of land between the Western Ghats and the sea. Its principal port Goa, was thus of great importance to the southern states. Further, the military conflict between the Vijayanagara and the Bahmani kingdom was a constant feature throughout the existence of these two kingdoms. This constant friction based on rivalry made both these states ever ready for war. They are in fact viewed as military states given the fact that they belonged to two distinct religions. The struggle therefore was also given a religious colour, although it does not seem to be so as there are other factors that came into play. Yet, the religious dimension cannot, however, be ignored totally as it made the conflict more bitter, leading to wide spread devastation in the contested areas with significant loss and destruction. The rivalry started in AD 1356 and continued with political fluctuations till the end of Aravidu dynasty of the Vijayanagara kingdom. The battles between Vijayanagara and the Bahmanis are described in great detail by medieval writers favouring either the Bahmanis or the Vijayanagara rulers, where the victim was the truth and the villain was parochialism.

The Vijayanagara kingdom witnessed the rule of four dynasties: Sangama, Saluva, Tuluva and Aravidu. Sangama dynasty ruled for a period of 150 years from AD 1336 to 1486. The important rulers of this dynasty were Harihara and Bukka I, the founders of the Vijayanagara kingdom. Devaraya I who ruled from AD 1406 to 1422 was made memorable by constructing a dam across the Tungabhadra river to irrigate cultivable land lying waste and to relieve Vijayanagara of water shortage. Devaraya II, who ruled from AD 1422 to 1446, was the greatest of this dynasty. It is he who recruited 2,000 Muslims in the army and gave them Jagirs. During his reign two foreign travellers, Nicolo Conti, an Italian traveller and Abdul Razak, an envoy from Persia visited his court in AD 1420 and 1443 respectively. The last of the Sangamas, Virupaksha II was overthrown by Saluva Narasimha in AD 1486. Saluva dynasty ruled from AD 1486 to 1505. Viranarasimha of the Tuluva dynasty usurped the Vijayanagara throne in AD 1505.

During reign of the Tuluva dynasty, the prestige and glory of Vijayanagara reached its climax particularly under the rule of Krishnadevaraya. But disintegration also set in towards the end of the Tuluva dynasty. Krishnadevaraya is appropriately considered the greatest ruler of South India. The throne ascended by Krishnadevaraya was not a bed of roses but full of thorns and the Vijayanagara kingdom's prestige was in its lowest ebb. Krishnadevaraya had to establish once again the internal law and order and to deal with the enemies of Vijayanagara, the successor states of the Bahamani kingdom, Bijapur, Bidar, Golkonda, Ahmadnagar and Berar and the Gajapatis of Kalinga who usurped many Vijayanagara territories. He also had to face the growing power of the

Portuguese. Krishnadevaraya rose to the occasion as a warrior, general and statesman and in a series of battles lasting seven years. Krishnadevaraya successfully compelled Gajapatis to restore to Vijayanagara all the territories up to the river Krishna. After strengthening his position, Krishnadevaraya restarted the old struggle for the control of Tungabhadra Doab and made the necessary preparations to teach a lesson to Gajapatis and the successor states of the Bahmani. He completely defeated Bijapur by AD 1520 and destroyed Gulbarga and a truce was entered into. With this, Krishnadevaraya's wars with old enemies came to an end, and Vijayanagara emerged as the strongest military power in South India. Krishnadevaraya like the earlier Cholas committed the mistake of paying scant attention to the development of a naval force and forgot the threat of danger from the sea-power of the Portuguese.

Krishnadevaraya had no male issue for a long time and at last, his chief queen Tirumaladeva gave birth to a son called Tirumaladeva Maharaja. Krishnadevaraya, out of paternal love and affection, crowned the young prince and himself became the Prime Minister. Unfortunately, the Crown Prince passed away within eight months and his death was attributed to the poisoning by Timmanadadanayaka. In a fit of anger, Krishnadevaraya appears to have ordered for the execution of Timmana and his father Timmarasu to be blinded. This was a sad conclusion to a glorious reign.

The foreign travellers who visited his court testify to the prosperity, affluence and pomp of the kingdom under Krishnadevaraya. Paes, an Italian, who spent a number of years at his court remarks: "He is a great ruler and a man of much justice, but subject to sudden fits of rage". His paternal attitude towards his subjects and his concern for their welfare are proverbial. Paes describes Krishnadevaraya as a man of medium height, and of fair complexion and good figure; rather fat than thin; he had on his face signs of smallpox. He is the most feared and as perfect a king as could possibly be. Krishnadevaraya's reign has been recognized as the greatest because in the words of Burton Stein "it is obvious that the resources capable of being regularly appropriated by the (Vijayanagara) kings were those in the Tungabhadra heartland of the kingdom. This was not a small region, nor was its resources meagre. The Tuluva kings of the first half of the 16th century drew upon a large agricultural zone in the midst of whose dominantly dry cropped fields were small regions of high agriculture based on tank irrigation. In this region there were among the best cotton soils in the peninsula as well as some of the largest pasturages that supported the herding of both cattle and sheep. Thus, cotton and woolen goods were exported from the region as well as bullocks. Bullocks were used in large numbers because they pulled the guns that now appeared in all armies. This explains how Krishnadevaraya could maintain armies to win battles and undertake welfare measures for the people".

Krishnadevaraya was a warrior and a general of outstanding reputation. He was also a great builder. He built a new town named Nagulapuram near Vijayanagara in memory of his mother Nagulamba and dug an extensive tank for irrigation. He was a gifted scholar in Sanskrit and Telugu and had the broad mind to patronize the contemporary regional languages Tamil and Kannada by creating *Asthadiggajas*, or *Navaratnas* (?) and building *Bhuvanavijayam*. That his administration was efficient and effective is attested by Barbosa, Nunez and Paes who visited his court. Barbosa, writes that the king allows such freedom that every man could come and go, and lives according to his own creed, without suffering from annoyance, without enquiry whether he was Christian, Jew, Moor or Heathen. The greatest achievement of Krishnadevaraya's reign was his liberal mindset which enabled him to establish justice and equity among his kingdom. Krishnadevaraya was succeeded by his half-brother Atchyutadevaraya in AD 1529–30 and who, was followed by his son Venkata in AD 1540–41. In the same year the throne passed on to Sadasivaraya, nephew of Atchyutadevaraya. Sadasiva became a puppet of Ramaraya, the Prime Minister and bad days began for the kingdom.

Ramaraya of the Aravidu dynasty, the Prime Minister of Vijayanagara, was an able schemer determined to raise the sunken prestige of the Vijayanagara after the death of Krishnadevaraya. He followed the strategy of entering into alliance of a commercial nature with the Portuguese and made them stop the supply of horses to Bijapur Sultan and defeated the Sultan in a series of battles. With the cooperation of the temporary ally, the Bijapur Sultan, he inflicted a crushing defeat on Ahmadnagar and Golkonda. Ramaraya's policy yielded dividends in the shorter run and as planned by him, he could successfully establish a balance of power favourable to Vijayanagara. But in course of time, the Sultans realizing the real intentions of Ramaraya, decided to forget their personal interests and forged a common alliance cemented by matrimonial alliances, to take revenge against Vijayanagara. In this coalition except Berar, the rest have become active partners and met the Vijayanagara armies at Tallikota in AD 1565. It is also known as the battle of Bannihati. In the battle the Sultans won and the victorious armies damaged the city of Vijayanagara. The defeat was a vital blow to Vijayanagara kingdom, yet it continued to exit till the end of the 17th century. Ranga III of the Aravidu dynasty, was the last ruler of significance.

Polity

The Vijayanagara rulers built a vast territorial state apparatus by conquests and expansion, consolidation and integration of the different regions comprising different languages and cultures by an effective administrative system. Monarchical form of government was no doubt the order of the day. They followed a policy of benevolent and benign despotism and the king was never an autocrat. Krishnadevaraya, in his *Amuktamalyada*, a *Prabandha Kavya* describes vividly the 'do's and don'ts' of a ruler, who is interested in the welfare of his subjects. In a nutshell, the philosophy of a ruler should be that "with great care and according to power of the King should attend to the work of protecting (the good) and punishing (the wicked) without neglecting anything that you can see or hear".

The king is to be the fountainhead of all power. His authority is supreme in all matters pertaining to the interests of the state. The king should follow the injunctions of the Dharmasastras. The king should take the assistance of skilled personnel in matters of administration. The king should utilize the mineral wealth of the state for the economic uplift of the people inhabiting the kingdom. The king should not impose too many taxes and make the people miserable but should levy moderate taxes. He should employ force through a strong and efficient military and maintain peace and order in the state, driving away the external and the internal enemies of the state. He should exhibit paternal love and affection towards his subjects and be their loving protector. The king should be dependent on Brahmanical order as the strength and security of the kingdom depended on the successful maintenance of Brahmanical Dharma.

The king was assisted by a *Mantrimandali* or council of ministers. There was no clear-cut demarcation between civil and military assignments. The ministers were appointed from the Brahmin, Kshatriya and Vaisya communities. Rarely was the post of the minister hereditary. The Prime Minster occupied a very important position in the council of ministers. We have references to the officers like the Chief Treasurer, custodian of jewels and the Prefect of police. A dark feature to be noted is the rampant corruption prevailing in the administrative set-up at the higher levels in particular. For administrative convenience, the kingdom was divided into *Rajyas* or *Mandalams* or provinces below which were *Nadu* (district), *Sthala* (sub-district) and *Grama* or village. During this period, it is believed that the Chola tradition of village self-government was considerably weakened.

For effective administration the vast territory of the *Rajya* was divided as vassal states and provinces ruled directly by the king's direct representatives. While the vassal states were administered by the *Nayakas* or *Samantas*, the territories directly under the king were called *Rajyas, Mandalas* and sometimes *Chavadis*. The governors appear to have enjoyed greater amount of autonomy, leading to the disruption of the empire under its competent rulers.

The other provinces were ruled by the *Samatas* or *Nayakas* and this type of administration was known as *Nayankara* system. This is an important feature of the Vijayanagara provincial organization. The term *Nayankara* is an abbreviation of *Amaranayankara* composed of three words; Amara, Nayaka and Kara. Amara literally stands for a command of a thousand foot soldiers. Nayaka stands for the military-chief who held land for the king. Kara probably means an office. The term *Amaranayankara* may be taken to refer to a military chief who was granted land, yielding fixed revenue for the sovereign. This system of Nayankara is not a new phenomenon. It existed during the Kakatiya period under the same name and was called *Iqta* during the Delhi Sultanate period and *Munsabdari* system of the Mughals. All these need not necessarily be one and the same; there were minor differences. The Nayaka and the provincial governor's role appear to be different and neither of them enjoyed the same level of autonomy. The Nayakas had to maintain two agents, one military and the other civil representing his interests at the capital city. Nayaka appears to be military vassal who has to render military and financial assistance to the king. The office of Nayaka was not transferable from one person to another person. The Vijayanagara epigraphs and later Mackenzie manuscripts refer to the Nayakas as territorial magnets with political aspirations which at times differed from those of the rulers. Krishnaswamy views the Nayankara systems as feudal, but N. Venkata Ramanayya states that the Nayankara system cannot be feudal because it did not contain the elements of fealty, homage and sub-infeudation. D.C. Sircar also refutes the theory of feudalism and explains it as a kind of landlordism, a variant of feudalism in which land was allotted to the Amara Nayankara for military services rendered by them to the king. The importance and dependence on Nayakas can be understood from the fact that three-fourth of the area of land in Vijayanagara territory was alienated under the Nayaka system. The Nayankara system had both merits and demerits. As long as the king was powerful and strong, the Nayakas were under control but once the king became weak, the Nayakas behaved as independent rulers and destabilized the kingdom. The merits of this system were the formations of new settlements, extension of irrigation facilities bringing new areas under cultivation and measures to preserve and conserve age-old culture.

The Rajyas or Mandals are further sub-divided for administrative convenience and to ensure efficient and effective administration. The nomenclature of the subdivided divisions differed from locality to locality. They are known as *Kottams* or Ventures or districts, *Nadus* or *Seemas* or *Talukas* or present-day *Mandalams* and *Sthala* or a group of villages. The village was the basic unit, and each village is said to be a self-sufficient one in all aspects, which is debatable. There is an accepted view that during this period autonomous local institutions experienced a setback in Tamil, Karnataka and Andhra regions. The *Ayagar* system became widely prevalent in the macro-Vijayanagara region. The Ayagars were village servants or functionaries and consisted of group of families. These Ayagars were headman of the village (Reddi or Gaunda or Gauda or Maniyam), accountant (Karnam or Senabhova) and watchman or Talari or Talavari. These Ayagars were given land either tax free or as *Manya* and these were provisions for payment in kind for their services by the villagers. Other Ayagars like washermen, potter, blacksmith, carpenter, watchman and charmakara were also allotted land and paid in kind for their services. There is a view that these payments were provided for the first time to village servants holding a particular office.

Law and Justice

The king was the supreme authority in the matter of justice. His verdict was final and irrevocable. The subjects of the kingdom, in case of injustice could submit a petition either to the king or the prime minister – judgement was delivered as per the merits of the petition. Hindu law and tradition was the basis of law. Trial by jury was in practice. Criminal justice was very severe and harsh. The Nayakas and Gaundas were given authority to settle cases in their jurisdiction.

K.A. Nilakanta Sastri seems to be right in stating that the Vijayanagara state was a military confederacy of many chieftains cooperating among themselves under the leadership of the strongest among them. This view gains strength because of the importance given to the Amara Nayaka system by the Vijayanagara rulers as already referred to above. The Vijayanagara rulers maintained a large standing army besides the army supplied by the Amarnayakas. The army consisted of infantry, cavalry, elephantry and artillery. The rulers selected and recruited into army from all castes and creeds. While Devaraya I maintained 10,000 Muslim soldiers, Devaraya II appointed 2,000 Muslims to teach archery to the Hindus. Vijayanagara rulers strengthened cavalry by importing good breed of horses from Hormaz with the help of the Portuguese merchants.

The Vijayanagara rulers organized a military department called *Kandachara* under the control of the Dandanayaka and forts played crucial role in the military organization. Like our Republic Day festival, Maharnavami festival was used by Krishnadevaraya to exhibit the strength of his armed forces and rewards were presented to the winners in various competitions.

Nature of the State

There is a great deal of debate among historians about the nature of the Vijayanagara state. In the last three decades and more, debate on state-formation and its apparent nature has come to occupy a key position in discourses on Indian history. K.A. Nilakanta Sastri, a traditional historian, regards the Vijayanagara state as an example of a war state. Satish Chandra however argues, Vijayanagara was a war state only in the sense that all medieval states had to be constantly ready for war. There is also a view that the Vijayanagara state was a loose association of semi-autonomous military and territorial leaders and that it was not a centralized state like that of the Delhi Sultanate. In this connection, Satish Chandra distinguishes between Amaram and Iqta and holds that Amaram cannot be equated to the Turkish Iqta system. Further, Burton Stein regards the Vijayanagara state as a segmentary state and suggests that absolute political sovereignty rested with the centre and symbolic or ritual sovereignty rested with the Nayakas and the Brahmin commanders in the periphery. He also thinks that the relationship between the segments and the centre was pyramidally arranged and the distance between the segments and the centre decided the nature of relationship between the two. Disagreeing with the view of Burton Stein, R.S. Sharma, D.N. Jha and R. Champakalakshmi try to fix Vijayanagara state in the model of a feudal polity and society. These scholars stress that the practice of giving land grants to Brahmins was an important factor that led to the rise of feudal segments and these feudal lords in turn gave lands to their subordinates and thus paved way for sub-infeudation. The proponents of feudal model argue that the extent of the empire and the absence of adequate means of transport and communication made it necessary for the rulers to delegate power to these feudal segments and to depend on them.

Noboru Karashima and Y. Subbarayalu also noticed feudal elements in the Vijayanagara state to a certain extent. Cynthia Talbot also suggests that the pre-colonial state structures in South India cannot be fixed into any particular models of segmentary, feudal or integrative state. At our present state of knowledge, it is not easy to fix in a certain model, the pre-colonial medieval supra-regional powers like Vijayanagara. The debate is still going on regarding the nature of the state of Vijayanagara as well of medieval and late medieval state structures of south India and the accepted view so far is a monarchical system based on the loose association of supra-local leaders or Samantas and vassals.

Society

Society under the Vijayanagara kingdom was in a state of flux. The components of the society consisted of the native indigenous population and the foreigners like the Portuguese, the French, the Dutch and the British along with Muslims of Turkish origin. The indigenous population was divided into Varnas and Jatis and also we notice the proliferation of sub-castes based on new professions and occupations needed for the changing social and economic orders. Consequently, new ideas and values began to influence the society. Brahmins, the custodians of scholarship, living with religious rituals and practices had begun to perform secular functions as landlords, and Dandanayakas in charge of forts, commanders, managers of religious structures-temples and Mathas. Some Brahmins possessing land and political power became dominant but they were in a very small number.

Another factor to be reckoned with was the territorial segmentation of society. It means that the social groups were divided on the basis of natural sub-regions inhabited by them along with occupational patterns associated with them. These social groups practised exclusivity by preferring consanguineous marriages.

Another feature to be noticed under the Vijayanagara rule in the Tamil region was the dual division of lower castes into *Idangai* and *Vadangai* to the right-hand and left-hand castes. This division does not appear to be in vogue in Andhra and Karnataka. Those castes which were engaged in primary agricultural production were called right-hand castes and the mobile artisan communities engaged in non-agricultural pursuits were called left-hand castes. Owing to increase in the temple construction, extensive agricultural operations and growth of internal trade and commerce, the economic and social conditions of the artisans improved and they began to claim a sacred social and ritual status and thus we come across a social group of people calling themselves *Satsudras* among the Sudra community. Further, the social space accorded to a caste or Jati is determined by their participation in the worship of a particular deity in temple management and ritual. The entire caste spectrum appears to have been given due representation by the state. The same is the case with the Mathas; where both Brahmins and non-Brahmin social groups enjoyed social space. Yet in that social structure, the Brahmans, the right-and left-hand castes and

Satsudra social groups of Vellalas and among the artisans the weavers occupied a better position. The social structure thus was not static but reflected the spirit of the times. The influence and the impact of the Dharmasastric literature were overshadowed by pragmatic social and political consideration.

Abdul Razak testifies that the courtesans of the age had a place of honour in the social order. They not only participated in royal processions and festivals but also paid taxes to the state treasury. The practice of child marriages, payment of dowry, *Satisahagamana*, sacrifice of animals at the time of *Jataras* and human sacrifice were some of the defects to be noticed during this age. Mostly women were viewed as objects of luxury and not as equal participants in social system.

The economic soundness of the Vijayanagara kingdom depended on flourishing agriculture along with trade and commerce. Agriculture was the main occupation of the large sections of the people. The Vijayanagara rulers promoted agricultural operations on a large scale by constructing tanks and by providing canals to supply water continuously for irrigational purposes. They allotted to small farmers cultivable land lying waste and even provided loans at lower rate of interest. Further, they repaired old irrigational tanks and constructed dams and dykes. Rice was the main crop of the region. Besides, cereals like gram and pulses, spices like black pepper, coconut and betel nuts were produced in good quantities. Land revenue differed from region to region and depended on fertility of the soil. Generally, it is one-sixth of the produce but in some cases it went up to one-fourth also. The rise in land revenue was exempted in the case of Brahmins and temples as 1/20 to 1/30 respectively. The land revenue was paid in cash or in kind. Vijayanagara epigraphs refer to three categories of land tenure: *Amara*, *Bhandaravada* and *Manya*. The Bhandaravada villages are crown villages, and a part of this revenue was utilized for the maintenance of forts. Manya land villages were tax-free lands and Amara lands or villages, were allotted to Samantas or vassals who utilized the revenue to maintain the armies to be supplied to the king as and when needed.

Besides land tax the Vijayanagara rulers imposed taxes on shopkeepers, farm servants, shepherds, washermen, potters, shoemakers and musicians. Further, they collected tax on property owned by individuals, House tax, and taxes on grazing land were collected. Village officers were maintained by the state with the money collected from the villagers. The state also collected transit duties in the *Sthaladayam*, *Magadayam* and *Manuladayam* and also earned income through *Dasavanda* in the Tamil country and *Kattukadage* in Andhra and Karnataka for providing irrigation facilities in semi-arid zones, which were conducive for carrying out development projects. Land was held not only by the crown and individuals but by temples also. Some big temples become landowners and the state appointed officers to collect and to supervise proper spending of the money collected from Devadana villages. During this period, the temples became important centres of economic activity.

The travelogues of contemporary foreign travellers testify that local and long distance trade flourished under Vijayanagara regime. The state provided reasonably good roads and facilities for travellers between towns. For short distance transport, carts were in vogue. The travellers refer to riverine shipping especially the backwater system on the west coast. Pack animals were put to use in long distance transport. Armed guards protected the goods and merchandise for long distance traders. Local officials and nobility also gave sufficient encouragement to trade and commerce by organizing fairs at regular intervals. Merchants and traders formed into *Srenis* and head of the guild of traders was known as *Pattana Swami*. The literary works and the epigraphs of the 14th to the 16th centuries record that there existed 80 major trade centres. We also notice the growth of urban centres, of these some were religious and others were commercial and administrative centres. Markets were divided on the basis of commodities sold there. Markets existed separately for agricultural and non-agricultural products of the right-and left-hand castes. In temple towns, the items needed by pilgrims were sold. Traders and artisan communities of the medieval times were identified with certain towns. For example, the oil pressers or the Telikas claim to be the inhabitants of the town of Bezwada. The temple epigraphs and the foreign traveller's account refer to the economic prosperity and prestige of the merchants and traders in the towns.

Krishnadevaraya's *Amuktamalyada*, the accounts of Domingo Peas and Nunez provide a vivid description of horse-trade carried on at that time. The role of the Indian merchants in the long distance foreign trade was nominal. Barbosa testifies that the Indian overseas trade was completely controlled by the Muslim merchants. The rulers realizing the importance of long distance trade provided special facilities to the foreign traders by providing a bodyguard, a *Chetti* accountant and a broker for help in local dealings. Even the royal monopoly of pearl fisheries was given to Muslim merchants. In the beginning, the Arabs and later the Portuguese controlled horse-trade. Horses were brought from Arabia, Syria and Turkey to the ports on the west coast. Besides horses, ivory, pearls, spices, precious stones, coconuts, palm-sugar, and salt were also imported while white rice, sugar cane and iron were exported from Vijayanagara. Nunez states that the diamond mines of the Vijayanagara times were the richest in the world and were located on the banks of the river Krishna in Kurnool and Anantapur. The availability of diamonds in large numbers led to the promotion of diamond-cutting and polishing of diamonds, sapphires and rubies in Vijayanagara and Malabar. Honnavar Bhatkal, Nagapatnam and Pulicat were the important ports of the Vijayanagara times. Krishnadevaraya in *Amuktamalyada* states: "A king should improve the harbours of his country and encourage its commerce so that horses, elephants, precious gems, sandalwood, pearls and other articles are freely imported. He should arrange that the foreign sailors who land in his country on account of storms, illness and exhaustion are looked after in a manner suitable to their nationalities. Make the merchants of distant foreign countries who import elephants and good horses attached to you by providing them with daily audience, presents and allowing decent profits. Then those articles will never go to your enemies". The recent researches of

Sanjay Subramanyam on trade and the regional economy of South India offer valuable new evidence on the relationship of overseas, coastal and inland trade and changes in political fortunes. On account of growth of trade and commerce foreign Muslims and Indian Muslims or Mappallas dominated the south-west coast long distance trade and coastal and local trade respectively. Overseas trade was dominated by Arabs, Jews, Armenians and Christians of Portuguese origin. While Sarasvat Brahmins dominated as traders on the Karnataka coast, in the northern Coromandal Telugu speaking Balija Naidus, Berichettis and Komatis dominated. In this age trade was no longer the monopoly of the Vaishyas or Komatis. Sanjay Subrahmanyam postulates a hypothesis that this age saw the beginning of 'Portfolio capitalists'.

Religion

The Vijayanagara rulers followed a policy of providing social space to all religions and their adherents. In the larger and longer interests of stability and security of the empire, they made a clear-cut distinction between their personal faith and religious sentiments of their subjects. Duerate Barbosa states that Krishnadevaraya treated Saivites, Vaishnavites, Jainas, Christians, Jews and Moors with kindness compassion and love, though Krishnadevaraya's personal faith was Vaishnavism. Atchyutadevaraya was a follower of Vishnu but he gave donations to Saiva temples at Kanchi and Lepakshi. Ramaraya is said to have had the Quran placed before him when Muslim soldiers rendered obedience to him. Further, Ramaraya appears to have allowed the Muslims to kill cows in the city of Vijayanagara. Some epigraphs testify that there were sectarian rivalries, but were amicably settled. But there is a strong view that religion and religious groups played a crucial role in political, social and economic life of the kingdom. Maharnavami festival or the annual royal ceremony was celebrated for nine days and it ended as Dasarah festival on the 10th day. It is viewed as ritual kingship. Celebration of Dasarah by the ruler may also be taken as a gesture on the part of the ruler to identify himself with the collective interests of the population rather than ritual kingship. No doubt, there existed relationship between kings, sects and temples. Large number of temples came into existence during the Vijayanagara rule and it is said that the temple acted as an integrative factor and as a central place of multifarious activities. The Vijayanagara rulers built large number of temples by donations and took measures for their upkeep and regular maintenance.

Patronage of Literature

The Vijayanagara rulers exhibited keen interest in promoting Sanskrit and Telugu, Tamil and Kannada literature. T.V. Mahalingam aptly remarks: "The foundation of Vijayanagara empire coincided in point of time with the outburst of a momentous literary movement in South India. As language and literature are recognized as binding forces of oneness in a region, the rulers for their enlightened self-interest promoted and developed Sanskrit as well as regional languages spoken in their territory of rule. Vast literary output in Sanskrit was produced by eminent scholars like Vidyasankara, Vidyaranya, Sayana and his son Madhava Mantri. Sayana's *Vedantaprakasa*, a commentary on the Vedas was undoubtedly the greatest of work of the period. Iswara Dikshita wrote two commentaries on Ramayana during this period. Vedanta Desika, Srikantha Pandita and Jaya Thirtha wrote on Vaishanava, Saiva and Madhva sects respectively. Gangaamba and Tirumalamba wrote historical Kavyas *Madhuravijayam* and *Varadambikaparinayam* respectively.

Among the rulers Devaraya II is known to be the author of *Mahanataka Sudhanidhi* and Krishnadevaraya wrote *Amuktamalyada* besides *Madalasacharitra*, *Rasamanjari* and *Jambavati Kalyanam*. Celebrated books on music, erotics, medicine and grammar were written during this period. Of such works, Vidyarayana's *Sangitasara* on music, Sayana's *Ayurveda Sudhanidhi* and Lakshmana Pandita's *Vaidyarajya Vallabham*' are outstanding works.

The reign of Krishnadevaraya is a well-known *Prabandhayugam* of Telugu literature. Krishnadevaraya himself was scholar, musician and a poet and he loved to gather around him poets, philosophers and religious teachers whom he honoured and respected by offering gifts and lands. Krishnadevaraya patronized a group of eight poets or Asthadiggajas and conducted literary salons in famous Bhuvana Vijayam specially built for this purpose. The Asthadiggajas are: (1) Allasani Peddana, the author of *Manucharita*, (2) Timmana, the author of *Parijatapaharanam* (3) Dhurjati, the author of *Kalahastisvaramahatyam* (4) Ramaraja Bhushana or Bhattumurti, the author of *Vasucharitra*, (5) Pingali Surana, the author of *Raghavapandaviyam* and *Kalapurnodayam*, (6) Tenali Ramakrishna Kavi the author of *Pandurangamahatyam* and *Ghatikachalamahatyam*, and (7) *Ayyalaraju Ramabhadra, the author of Ramabhyudayam* and (8) *Madayagari Mallana.*

Kannada literature also flourished during this age. Literary texts in Kannada dealing with Jainism, Virasaivism and Brahmanism appeared in this age. Of the Jaina Kannada literature, mention has to be made of Mathura's *Dharmanathapurana*, Vritha Vilasa's *Dharmapariksha Sastrasara*, and Saiva's Jain version of Mahabharata also deserve to be mentioned. The Virasaiva scholars promoted Kannada prose. Chamarasa, the author of *Prabhuragalila* along with Bommarasa, Kallarasa, Tontada and Siddhesvara were well-known Kannada literary giants. Kumaravyasa and Timmana were well-known popular Brahmanical writers. Sripadaraya, Purandharadasa and Kanakadasa are well-known Kannada composers of musical Kirtanas.

In the history of Tamil literature, the period of 450 years from AD 1200 to 1650 is considered to be the last great period. It was a period of large output of philosophical works, commentaries, Puranas and Prabandhas. The numerous authors professed faith in both Vaishnavism and Saivism along with Jainism. K.A. Nilakanta Sastri states that though Vijayanagara rulers patronized Sanskrit and Telugu languages, there is no setback to the promotion and development of Tamil literature. Svarupananda Desika and his pupil Tattuvarayar at the end of the 14th and the beginning of the 15th century wrote the celebrated book on Advaita. Haridasa, the author of *Irusamaya Vilakkam*, an exposition on

Vaishnavism and Saivism was patronized by Krishnadevaraya as a court poet. Turasai Ambalavana Desikar of the 16th century, wrote many religious works like *Sittanta Sikhamani*, *Nittai Vilakkam* and *Sammargasittiyar* and *Puppilai-Atavanai*. We come across much stress on the religious and philosophical aspect in the Tamil literature. In lexicography, the most popular lexicon *Nigandu Chudamani* was composed by Mandala Purusha, who is doubtfully said to be of the time of Krishnadevaraya.

Architecture, Art and Painting

The Vijayanagara rulers left behind marvellous architectural edifices, both religious and secular, whose ruins make us to look at them with awe and wonder. It was a remarkable period in the sphere of art, sculpture and painting. Vijayanagara or the city of victory is the capital as well as the name of the kingdom and it can be safely identified as Hampi and its present surroundings.

Nearly 77 epigraphs of the Vijayanagara rulers have been found here. George Mitchell, architectural historian who had documented the city of Vijayanagara delineated three board zones: (1) the sacred centre, (2) the urban core, and (3) the royal centre. These three zones are separated from each other by an irrigation canal. In the sacred centre of the city, which is along the river side of the Tungabhadra, we notice the temple complexes dedicated to Virupaksha, Balakrishna, Tiruvengalanatha Vittala, Raghunatha and Pattabhirama. All these temples reflect the Vijayanagara temple style. Domingo Paes records, "the King has made Vijayanagara a very strong city, fortified it with walls and towers, and the gates at the entrance are very strong, these walls are not made like those of other cities, but are made of very strong masonry and inside very beautiful rows of buildings with flat roofs. There live many merchants, and it is filled with a high population because the King induces many honourable merchants to go there from his cities". Paes further reports that "before the Ramachandra temple there was a broad and beautiful street full of fine houses. And it is understood that the houses belong to Merchants, and there you find all sorts of rubies, and diamonds, and emeralds and pearls and clothes and every sort of thing there is on the earth that you may wish to buy. There you have every evening a fair where they sell many common horses, and also many citrons, and limes, and oranges and grapes, and every kind of garden stuff and wood, you have all this in the street (which) leads to the palace". In the royal centre, we witness a system of roads, many stone-paved, radiating outward for main open area in front of the Ramachandra temple and reaching all parts of the site south of the agricultural zone and a few of these extending northward to the Tungabhadra. Thirty or so palaces have been noted in various parts of the city and mostly in royal centre one of the most striking of all of Hampi structures is Maharnavami or Dassarahdibba. We also come across a two-storeyed pavilion, the 'Lotus Mahal' which is full of Hindu and Muslim elements. We also have an evidence of an elephant stable with eleven domes and a guard's quarter and a pavilion for royal bath. Thus, Vijayanagara was a royal city, a commercial centre and a place where kings spent most of their time conducting royal duties.

K.A. Nilakanta Sastri rightly observes: "under Vijayanagara, South Indian art attained a certain fullness and freedom of rich expression in keeping with the general consciousness of the great task of the empire, namely the preservation and development of all that remained of Hinduism against the onslaught of Islam. In this period, temple became very elaborate both in structure and organization; even the old temples were amplified by the addition of pillared halls, pavilions and other subordinate structures. The most characteristic addition to the temple is the Kalyana Mandapa, which is a very ornate pillared platform in the centre for the reception of the deity and his consort at the annual celebration of their marriage ceremony. Another feature to be noted is the 'Thousand Pillared Mandapa', a huge hall with many rows of pillars. The most striking feature of the Vijayanagara style was the varied and complicated treatment of the pillars, and all pillars had ornamental brackets as part of these capitals and below the bracket we come across an inverted lotus bud. Another feature of Vijayanagara style is the tall entrance or Gopura. The principal temples of Vittala and the Hazara Rama are the most important exhibits of Vijayanagara style. Vittala temple is by far the most ornate. These temples had three entrances with Gopuras and those on the east and south are considered to be the most important. The Hazara Rama temple is a modest but perfectly finished example of the Vijayanagara style. Besides the main temple, there is a shrine for the goddess, a Kalyana Mandapa and other subsidiary temples all enclosed in a courtyard by a wall of 24 feet height. Vellore, Kumbakonam, Kanchipuram, Tadipatri and Srirangam temples are also perfect examples of the Vijayanagara style. The Kalyana Mandapa of Vellore is considered to be the most beautiful structure with its tall tower or Gopura. Two Gopuras of the temple of Rameswara at Tadipatri are remarkable for their rich and exquisite carvings. Ferguson is of the view that these carvings are in better taste than anything else in this style. Percy Brown observes that Seshagirimandapa at Srirangam contains a colonnade of furiously fighting steeds each rearing up to a height of nearly nine feet, the whole executed in a technique ... not like stone but hardened steel". Madhura Nayakas also encouraged the Vijayanagara style of architecture in the later stage. The art of casting bronzes flourished under the rule of the Vijayanagara rulers. The subject of sculpture is made memorable by the life-size statues of Krishnadevaraya and his two wives located at Tirupati.

In the end, we can conclude with the statement of Burton Stein that the Vijayanagara epoch saw the transition of South Indian society from its medieval past to its modern future based on modernization and urbanism or economy backed by flourishing surplus agriculture and trade and commerce with modern weapons of warfare guns. It can be the study of the kings which indicates that Vijayanagara age is a synthesis of the age-old Indian tradition and values of life.

The Bahmanis

Polity, Society, Economy and Culture

An Afghan noble, Alauddin Hassan established the Bahmani kingdom in AD 1347. Prior to the foundation of the Bahmani kingdom, Hassan's ancestors rose to prominence in the service of Alauddin Khilji. A tradition in circulation, as recorded in *Ferishta* of later times informs that Hassan rose to importance in the service of a Brahmin, Gangu and was therefore known as Hassan Gangu. After founding the Bahmani kingdom, Alauddin Hassan claimed his descent from the Iranian heroes, Isfandar and Bahman and added Shah to his name. Consequently, the kingdom was called the Bahmani Kingdom.

The political fortunes of the Bahmani kingdom can be divided into two phases. The first phase was between AD 1347–1422 and the second phase was between AD 1422–1538. In the first phase, the centre of activity was Gulbarga and in the second, the centre of activity was shifted to Bidar because of its strategic location. The Bahmani kingdom was a contemporary of the Vijayanagara power, which was founded in AD 1336. Throughout their existence, both the Vijayanagara and the Bahmanis constantly fought for supremacy in three distinct areas, in the Tungabhadra Doab, in the Krishna Godavari delta and in the Marathwada country. The reasons for continued hostility were primarily the economic interest, but the religious dimension also influenced the hostility between the two powers to some extent. Alauddin Hassan Bahman Shah ruled from AD 1347 to 1358. He was followed by his son Muhammad I (1358–1375). He was followed by his son Alauddin Mujahid (1375–78). Mujahid was killed by his uncle Dawood I, who ruled for nearly a month and was followed by his brother Muhammad II (1378–1397). Muhammad II was succeeded by Tajuddin Firoz Shah, who ruled from AD 1397 to 1422. He was followed by Shihabuddin Ahmad or Muhammad Shah, who ruled for a period of 14 years from AD 1422 to 1436. He was followed by Alauddin Ahmad II or Alauddin II, who ruled from AD 1436–1458. He was succeeded by Alauddin Humayun who ruled form AD 1458 to 1461. He was followed by Muhammad III, who ruled from AD 1463–1482. The last noteworthy Bahmani ruler Shihabuddin Ahmad died in AD 1518. After him, his sons Ahmad Shah IV, Alauddin Shah, Kaliyuka and Kalimulla ruled till AD 1528. With the death of Kalimulla, the Bahmani kingdom disappeared. Throughout this period, the wars between the Bahmanis and the Vijayanagara rulers were taking place affecting the fortunes of these two kingdoms. There was hardly any decade that passed without a clash of arms between these two kingdoms. Though, contemporary chroniclers describe the wars as Jihads or holy wars, this perception does not appear to be quite true.

Of the twelve Bahmani Sultans, the most remarkable was Firuzshah Bahamani who ruled for a quarter of a century from AD 1397 to 1422. Firuz was a well-read scholar, a good calligraphist and a poet of eminence; he was also proficient in many languages. He had the vision of making Deccan a cultural centre of

India. He was liberal in outlook and inducted Hindus in large number into administrative cadres. He took all the necessary measures to improve the principal parts of his kingdom Chaul and Dabhol, where the foreign ships used to anchor. He was defeated by Devaraya-I. His successor Ahamad Shah shifted the capital from Gulbarga to Bidar.

In the early decades of the foundation of Bahmanis, there arose strife among nobles. The nobles were divided as old timers or newcomers or *Deccanis* and *Afaqis*. This division created havoc in the history of the Bahamani kingdom, between AD 1482–1518, the clash among nobles reached its climax, which led to the dismemberment of the Bahmani kingdom. In the history of the Bahmani kingdom, the period between AD 1463–1482 saw the rise of Muhammad Gawan as the Prime Minister of the kingdom. Nothing important is known about the early life of Muhammad Gawan. Gawan was an Iranian by birth and he was first noticed in AD 1456 and in 1461 he was made a member of the council of regency. In AD 1463 he was appointed as *Vakil-i-Sultanat* with the title of *Khawaja-i-Sehan* and *Malik-ul-Tajjar*. He dominated the affairs of the State for twenty years. Gawan tried his best to extend the frontiers of the Bahmanis and the expansion of the Bahmanis kingdom towards the east and west led to a resurgence of the conflict with Vijayanagara. Gawan appears to have annexed the Tungabhadra Doab and made a deep raid into the Vijayanagara territories reaching as far south as Kanchi. Gawan also introduced a number of internal reforms which benefited the Bahmani kingdom. He was a great patron of arts. He built a magnificent Madarsa in the capital city of Bidar and on his invitation some of the most famous scholars of Iran and Iraq visited the Madarsa. The Deccani nobles poisoned the ears of the Sultan and got him executed at the age of 70. The death of Gawan sounded the death knell of the Bahmani kingdom.

The Bahmani rulers followed the administrative structure of the Delhi Sultanate. The Sultan was the head of the state and supreme authority followed by *Wakil*, *Wazir*, *Bakshi* and *Qazi* and a host of officials like *Dabir* or Secretary, Mufti or interpreter of law, *Kotwal*, *Mehtasib* or censor of public morals and *Munhihans* or spies. The Bahmani kingdom was divided into 4 *Tarafs* or provinces. They maintained a strong army of soldiers, cavalry and elephants and they knew the use of gun powder in the battles.

Systematic measurement of land fixing boundaries of the villages and towns was undertaken by Muhammad Gawan. By this process, Gawan streamlined the revenue system and improved the revenue collection of the state. Further, by this process the income of the state was known in advance and corruption of the nobles was also minimized. From the statements of Nikitin, a Russian traveller who visited Deccan during AD 1469–1474, we come to know that trade and commerce too flourished in the Bahmani kingdom. Nikitin mentions that horses, cloth, salt, and pepper were the main items of merchandise and Mustafabad-Dabul as a centre of the commercial activity. Horses were imported form Arabia, Khurasan and Turkistan. Musk and fur were imported from China. Interestingly, trade and commerce was mostly in the hands of Hindu merchants, whereas in Vijayanagara kingdom, coastal trade and long distance trade was in the hands of foreign and indigenous Muslims.

Bahmani rulers were mostly Sunnis, but the Bahmani society was cosmopolitan in character. The Muslims, local and foreign, Hindus and the Portuguese were the components of the society. Consequent to multi-Jati composition of the society, we notice multiple languages Persian, Marathi, Dakhini or proto-Urdu, Kannada and Telugu being spoken by different social groups. Economically, the population of the Bahmani state appears to be divided as poor and the affluent nobles, according to Nikitin. He says that the nobles were carried on their silver beds, preceded by 20 gold caparisoned horses and followed by 300 men on horseback and 500 on foot along with 10 torch bearers. Nikitin also describes the luxurious lifestyle of Muhammad Gawan. He observes that every day, 500 men dined with Gawan and 100 armed personnel kept watch over his palace. Besides these two social classes, we also come across the community of merchants who were not as affluent as nobles and as poor as common people.

In the Bahmani kingdom, we notice the predominant influence of the Sufis of the Chisti, Qadiri and Shattari orders. Bidar has emerged as one of the most important centres of the Qadiri order. Sheikh Sirajuddin Junaidi was the first Sufi to receive the royal honour. The famous Chisti saint of Delhi, Syed Muhammad Gesu Daraz migrated to Gulbarga in AD 1402–03 and Sultan Firuz granted a number of villages for the maintenance of Khanquah of Gesu Daraz. With the influx of Afaqis, the Shia population of the Bahmani kingdom also increased. An interesting feature of the communal life is the mingling of Muslim and Hindu traditions and in particular, during the *Ursu* celebrations, the *Jangam*, a Lingayat in a Muslim cap blew the conch and offered flowers to the Muslim saint. Thus, the Bahmani culture was composite and tolerant.

In the art and architecture, the Bahmanis were influenced by the style of the Delhi Sultanate. The Bahmani rulers generously patronized art, science, learning and the court was the centre of poets, scholars and artists. Art critics and historians of architecture noticed the influence of the military architecture of Europe and civil architecture of Persia. The Persian architects' hand and skill is very visible in the Jamil Masjid of Gulbarga. The Chand Minar of Daultabad and the Madarsa at Bidar also reflect Persian craftsmanship. The capital cities of Gulbarga and Bidar were the centres of the civil architecture of the Bahmanis. The royal tombs of Gulbarga fall into two patterns: (1) single tombs, and (2) double tombs. Single tombs consist of simple square chambers, crowned with battlements and corner turrets and roofed by a single dome, the whole standing on a low square plinth while the double tombs are merely duplicate of the single ones. The Bahmani architecture has its own peculiarities like square arches of its cloisters.

In conclusion, it can be said that the Bahmani kingdom acted as a cultural bridge between the north and the south and had close contacts with some of the leading countries of West Asia, including Iran and Turkey. The culture which developed as a result had its own distinctive features which were continued by the successor states and also influenced the development of Mughal culture.

21

The Mughal Period

A Survey of Sources

In this volume, in the backdrop of chronological framework of AD 1526 to 1964 or under the label of periodization of late medieval to contemporary, we are going to witness the changes in the political, economic, social and cultural spheres which effected and evolved in the structural and institutional set-up of the Indian subcontinent. Nearly 450 years of this period make a period of transition which transformed the Indian society and culture from that of traditional, superstition-ridden and inward-looking society to the brave new world of democratic values based on equity and social justice and looking forward with hope and determination to usher in a new economic and social order. One notices in this period of study the theme of continuity and change as is seen in the earlier period of pre-colonial society and culture. In spite of the imposition of colonial and imperialistic hegemony and efforts to make us 'mimics' of western cultural traditions and scientific and technological innovations, the Indians retained their individuality in protecting their basic nature. We can notice this in our endeavour to 'become a nation' for more than a century. In this period only the new concepts of globalization, transnationalism and international capitalism took deep roots and strengthened to pose a threat to the survival of the nations as independent sovereign democracies. In order to understand and appreciate the historical change that took place in India, we have abundant source material. Broadly, this phase of 450 years can be divided as the period or the Mughals and their successor states up to 1757, the colonial and imperialist regime up to 1947 and post-independent India up to 1964. First, let us take up the source material pertaining to the Mughals and successor states up to 1757. During this period, even before the Mughals landed in India as conquerors, the first European nation – the Portuguese entered India as traders and during the Mughal rule, the other Europeans: the Dutch, the British and the French entered India as traders by obtaining the permission of the sovereign powers.

The Mughal Sources

Tuzuk-i-Babur or *Babarnama* written by Babur, the founder of the Mughal power as autobiography in his mother tongue, Chagtai Turki occupies the first place. It is a true reflection of his account of India and it gives information from Babur's birth to AD 1529. *Humayun Nama* written by Gulbadan Begum, the daughter of Babur and sister of Humayan records a brief account of Babur and a detailed account of Humayan. This was written at the instance of Akbar.

The *Tuhfa-i-Akbari Shahi* (*Tarikh-i-Shershahi*) of Abbas Khan Sarwani provides details of the life and works of Shershah. Abdul Qadir Badauni's *Muntakhab-ut-Tawarikh* is not dedicated to Akbar as Badauni was very critical of the 'innovations' of Akbar. It is written in three volumes. It deals in detail with various important matters mentioned in *Akbar Nama* of Abul Fazl. Abul Fazl's *Akbar Nama* consists of three volumes; the third volume is the *Aini Akbari*. While the first two volumes cover the period of Akbar up to the close of his 46th year, the third volume *'Ain-i Akbar'* gives an account of the various imperial departments and also of the revenue and administrative officials, revenue rates of measured land and revenue statistics of Subhas, Sarkars and Paraganas. Khwaja Nizamuddin Ahmad Harawi's *Tabaquat-i-Akbari* was completed in the year 1593–94 and it was composed in nine parts from the advent of Islam up to AD 1593–94. *Tuzuk-i-Jahangiri* was the autobiography of Jahangir. It is also called *Tarikh-i-Salim Shahi* and *Jahangirinama*. Muhammad Qasim Uindu Shah Astrabadi's *Tarikh-i-Firishtah,* deals with the history of the Sultans of the Deccan. *Padshanama* of Abdul Hamid Lahori is a biographical account of Shahjahan from his childhood to 1649. It is rated as the first-rate authority on the reign of Shahjahan. Besides this biography, Muhammad Amir Khan Qazyni and Muhammad Waris, a pupil of Lahori also wrote two biographies with the name *Padshahnama*. Of these two, the first one gives an account of the first 10 years and the other the last ten years' rule of Shahjahan. Inayat Khan, a high official of Shahjahan also wrote *Shajahannama* and another *Shahjahannama* was written by Muhamad Sadiq Khan. This covers the historical events from the death of Jahangir to the accession of Aurangzeb. Muhammad Saki Mustaid Khan was the author of Maasir-e-Alamgiri. This was written after the death of Aurangzeb with the help of state records. Mirza Muhammad Qazim was the author of *Alamgirnama*. This is a good detailed history of the first ten years of Aurangzeb's reign.

Muhammad Hashim Khafi Khan's *Muntakhab-ul-Lubab Muhammad Shahi* is a voluminous history from the Muslim conquest of India up to the Mughal emperor Muhammad Shah. Besides these histories written in Persian, administrative and accountancy manuals, statistical tables, Firmanas, Mishans or Parwanas, letters and dictionaries also serve useful purpose as primary source material. A number of books based on primary sources written in the last seventy-five years provide useful insights into the different reigns of the Mughal rulers. Further, the contemporaneous Portuguese, Dutch, English and French records and accounts provide useful information of the various aspects of Indian life. Memoirs, travelogues, letters of the Jesuit fathers, and factory records come under the above category. Antorio Monserette, a Jesuit in his commentary published in 1597 written in Portuguese, provides a graphic account of the court of Akbar. William Hawkins' work graphically describes Jahangir's court. Sir Thomas Roe's embassy (1615–1619) of Jahangir's time offers political and economic information. Similarly, the Dutch factor, Pelsaert's account, the travels of Peter Mundy, and Fray Sebastian Manrique, the travels of Francois Bernier and *Storia do Mogor* of Niccolo Manucci also throw very useful light on the contemporary Indian society. Regarding the company rule and its impact, the primary sources are factory records, despatches from Fort St. George, Fort William and transaction between different Presidencies of Bombay, Madras and Bengal, despatches between Indian presidencies and East India Company officials, etc. Newspapers, journals and memoirs of the British officials also are very useful. There is abundant source material to understand the response of the Indians towards the British policies in the shape of petitions submitted by the Indians. About the freedom movement in India too we have abundant source material in the state archives of all states and also books written by freedom fighters. Oral tradition is employed to elicit information from the participants in the freedom struggle from Quit India movement onwards. There is also abundant source material of secondary nature to understand the nature and course of the National movement. Speeches, government records, parliamentary debates, newspaper editorials and reports throw a flood of light on the events of the contemporary period till 1964. A historian, by using the source material judiciously and by analysing the authenticity of different sources, can arrive at proper understanding of the historical process without being subjective in choosing a fact. The objective of the historian or the history text book writer is not to sit on judgment of the past but to understand the process and relate it to the present and future.

Advent of Mughals

The advent of the Mughals or the Timurids in India in the early decades of the sixteenth century is a significant landmark in the evolution of Indian nation and its culture. In the initial years, the Mughals had to face stiff opposition from the Afghans, who were replaced by the Mughals, and the Rajputs. Shershah Suri, the founder of the Second Afghan Empire by his prowess as a general and by his administrative genius laid the future foundations for the edifice of the Mughal polity. A brilliant chapter began in the history of the Mughal rule from the middle of the sixteenth century with the accession of Akbar. By the first decade of the seventeenth century, the Mughals consolidated and expanded their sway over the whole of India and worked in the direction of establishing law and order along with the promotion of arts and letters. The sunset of the Mughal polity was completed by the sixth decade of the 18th century and the power lingered on nominally till the end of the first war of Indian independence in 1857, when the last of the Mughal lineage Bahadur Shah was hanged by the British, who became the sovereign power in India from that event of historical significance.

By the time Babur, the petty chieftain of Ferghana, lost his power and his strong desire to be the ruler of Samarqand became utterly futile and he started looking towards India as his new destination, as the power and prestige of the Lodis, the last of the dynasties of Delhi Sultanate was at its lowest ebb. Political disunity was the order of the day and there arose innumerable centres of political authority, quarrelling mutually among themselves to acquire legitimacy as sovereigns over a vast area. Iswari Prasad, aptly remarks that India was "a congeries of states at the opening of the 16th century and likely to be easy prey of an invader who had the strength and will to attempt her conquest". Percival Spear also remarks that by the time of Babur's invasion "Hindusthan was ruled by Afghan chiefs whose kingdoms were tumultuous confederacies of nobles rather than well organized states". Babur in his memoirs also refers to "five Musalman rulers and two Pagans". The five Muslim rulers were the Lodies, and the rulers of Gujarat, Malwa, Bahamani and Bengal and the two pagans were Rana Sanga of Mewar and the king of Vijayanagar. Besides these major powers, there existed innumerable Afghan chieftains around Agra. While the above was the political situation in India, in central Asia the power of the Timurids was on decline, the Uzbeks captured firm foothold in Transoxonia and the Safavis captured Iran. As a consequence, Babur the ruler of the small principality of Ferghana had to give up his long cherished desire of ruling over Samarqand by 1512 and turn his attention towards opening of gates of India by successive invasions from 1519 to 1526. Abul Fazl, the historian of the time of Akbar the grandson of Babur, pertinently notes that the meagre resources of Kabul and rich resources of India might have attracted Babur towards India. In 1526 Babur defeated Ibrahim Lodi in the battle of Panipat and founded the Mughal power in India. Iswari Prasad rightly observes, "The battle of Panipat placed the empire of Delhi in Babur's hands. The power of the Lodi dynasty was shattered to pieces and the sovereignty of Hindusthan passed to the Chagatai Turks". R.P. Tripathi also observes "the victory of Panipat laid the foundation of the great Mughal empire which in grandeur and power and culture was the greatest in the Muslim world". By this victory, Babur had not become secure, and he had to face the threat of the Rajputs, who were determined to restore their lost power. Babur fought against the Rajputs led by Rana Sanga at Kanwah in 1527 and succeeded in defeating them. R.P. Tripathi observes, "the consequences of this battle were indeed far reaching". After this victory, Babur defeated the Rajputs in the battle of Chanderi in 1528 and defeated the Afghans in the battle of Ghogra in 1529. In a series of three successive battles, Babur successfully achieved his objective of starting his reign in India. Babur lived for only a short time and breathed his last in 1530, leaving behind an unstable and insecure power structure as the Afghans and the Rajputs were still waiting for an opportunity to snatch the newly established power of the Mughals. Babur, the link between central Asia and India, between predatory hordes and imperial government of Asia, a fearless warrior and an able general, scholar and poet, occupies a unique place among the medieval rulers of India. We can conclude with the statements of V.A. Smith "Babur was a most brilliant Asiatic prince of his age and worthy of a high place among the sovereigns of India". Babur had four sons, Humayun, Kamran, Askari and, Hindal and in 1530, his son Humayun, 'the fortunate' ascended the throne. Humayun failed to prove himself a worthy son to a determined conqueror like Babur and his life and reign was one of wasted chances in teaching a strong lesson to his opponents, the Afghan and the Rajputs. Humayun was replaced by Shershah Suri, who ruled for only a period of five years from AD 1540–45 but earned an eternal place in the galaxy of able rulers by his administrative genius. Humayun's efforts to regain his lost power ended in dismal failure.

The Second Afghan Empire

Before we start the phase of consolidation and expansion of the Mughal power structure under the successors of Humayun, Akbar, Jahangir, Shahjahan and Aurangzeb, we have to study the rise of Afghans as a significant political entity in Indo-Muslim India in the 16th century. It is necessary to study this aspect as the Afghans were the main adversaries of the Mughals among the Muslim nationalities and the Mughals owed much to the legacy of the administrative genius and organizational capabilities of a unique Afghan, Shershah Suri or Shershah Sura and his successors for their rule of 15 years in the 16th century. The Afghans after sub-planting the Turks and the Persians became the most powerful and widely spread foreign Muslim group in northern India. Burton Stein's statement, "Alone of the Muslim ruling clans from 1200, the Afghan clan leaders persistently and successfully planted roots in the Indian communities to which their military offices took them, whether in the Gangetic plain or in distant Deccan" explains the rise of the Afghan power on the Indian soil. The head of the Afghan Lodi clan Bahlul Khan seized the throne of Delhi in 1451 and laid the foundation of the first Afghan kingdom in India. While Bahlul Khan provided the scope for the Afghan dominance, his son Sikandar continued his father's efforts very successfully till 1517. Though Sikandar proved it easy to control the inter-tribal conflicts among the Afghan nobles, his successor Ibrahim failed in the endeavour and it is a well-known established fact that one of his disaffected nobles, Daulat Khan Lodi, the governor of Punjab invited Babur to invade. But, Babur, by using matchlocksmen and field cannons against the Afghan cavalry won the war of Panipat. It is this technological advantage, which was responsible for the victory of Babur. Added to this technological disadvantage carving out petty kingdoms of Jaunpur, Meerut, Bayana, Dholpur, Gwalior, Rapri, Etawa, Kalpi and Sambhal, etc., by the Afghan chieftains weakened the Afghan power. Though there is a strong view that the enmity of the Rajputs was more formidable than that of the Afghans on religious differences, the reality does not appear to be so. Decline and disintegration of the Lodi power gave a way to Suras to fit into the shoes of the Lodis. The greatest of the Sura lineage, which lasted for a very short time in between Humayun and Akbar as a brilliant interlude has to be remembered with admiration and respect. Sher Shah's grandfather Ibrahim Sur and his father Hussain migrated from Afghanistan to India in search of new pastures. The father and son pair in the beginning joined the service of Bahlul Lodi in the Punjab. It is said that Farid, the later-day popular hero and sovereign Sher Shah, was born in Punjab in AD 1472. During the tenure of Sikandar Lodi, Hussain became the Jagirdar of Sasram, Khawanpur and Tanda. Farid learnt and practised the art of administration for full 21 years as the future ruler of his father's Jagir with the blessings of his benefactor Jamal Khan. But Farid had to face the stiff opposition of his stepmother as she was determined to ruin him. There was a civil war between brothers for the possession of the family Jagir and Farid had also to face the opposition of the Lohanis and other Afghan nobles. As there was no other solution to his problem, Farid joined the Mughal Service in 1527, and as a reward for his loyal service, Babur granted his Jagir to him. Not able to withstand the vanity of the Mughal ruler Babur, he gave up his service with the Mughals in 1528, and in due course he became a ruler of reckoning. Sher Shah proved to be a better match to Humayun, and made Humayun wander from place to place and in the meanwhile Sher Shah ruled from 1538 to 1545, when he finally died in the battle. In his brief reign, Sher Shah proved himself to be a military genius of the calibre of Babur and an extraordinary man of vision as an administrator like Akbar the Great. At the time of his death, the Sura political power extended from the Punjab to the eastern borders of the Ganges delta including the town of Chittagong and from the Narmada valley to Kashmir in the north. The extent of his political sway is equivalent to that of Akbar at the end of his reign and greater than the Lodis at their highest glory. Leaving behind two sons, Adil and Jalal, Sher Shah died in 1545 while in battle to capture Kalanjar fort. His son Jalal, by assuming the title of Islam Shah ruled from AD 1545 to 1553. He was succeeded by Muhammad Adil who ruled for four years from 1553–57. With the victory of Humayun in the second battle of Panipat the second Afghan empire came to an end.

Administration: Economic and Technological Developments

The second Afghan empire survived for less than two decades as a significant political entity. With Sher Shah's reputation as an efficient administrator and as an effective executioner of his philosophy, the second Afghan empire did leave permanent footprints. Undoubtedly, Sher Shah deserves comparison with the Mughal emperor Akbar the Great, and a debate is still going on regarding the place of each in the history of India. No doubt, Sher Shah is justified in being designated as the forerunner of Akbar, as Akbar followed the good and useful aspects of Sher Shah's policies. Even Sher Shah was not a real and true innovator, as he too borrowed from his predecessors what he thought to be good for his philosophy of administration. Any wise person will necessarily try to retain the universally applicable aspects of his predecessors and add or modify to the existing needs and demands of his times. This applies to all those enlightened rulers like Alauddin Khilji, Sher Shah and Akbar.

Sher Shah believed that the essence of royal protection consists in protecting the life and property of the subjects. They should use the principles of justice and equality in all their dealings with all classes of peoples, and instruct powerful officers so that they may try their best to prevent cruelty and oppression in their jurisdiction. His administrative structure appears to be autocratic as power was entirely concentrated in the hands of the single individual for executing orders and implementing through his subordinates or bureaucracy responsible to him. In practice the king was no autocrat but only an enlightened despot who took keen personal interest with alertness in the matters of administration and acted with vigour in discharging his duties. Sher Shah's state was neither a police state nor a welfare state but an apparently autocratic state with the welfare of the subjects as its motto. Sher Shah took the help and assistance of a group of ministers in discharging his duties. They were: (1) *Diwan-i-Inshah,* (2) *Diwan-i-Wizarat,* (3) *Diwan-i-Ariz,* and (4) *Diwan-i-Risallat.* Besides these four ministers, there also existed *Diwan-i-Qaza* and *Diwan-i-Barid*.

1. *Diwan-i-Wazarat* (or *Wizarat*): The Wazir was the head of Diwan-i-Wazarat. Total income and expenditure of the state was controlled by him. He also exercised general supervision over the rest of the ministers.
2. *Diwan-i-Ariz*: *Arizi-i-Mamlik* was the head of the department. It was he, who recruited, organized and disciplined the army. Payment of salaries was his duty. Sher Shah intervened actively in the affairs of the army, as his stability as a ruler and importance as a conqueror depended on the strength of the army.
3. *Diwan-i-Risalat* was the minister of foreign affairs. It was the responsibility of *Diwan-i-Risalat* to effectively supervise and control the ambassadors, envoys and foreign correspondence. Besides, he had to look after charity and endowments.
4. *Diwan-i-Insha* was the minister of information and correspondence. It was his duty to draft the royal proclamations, preserve and despatch them and he was also the custodian of government records. It was he who maintained correspondence with the provincial and local administrative set-up.

Diwan-i-Qaza was under the headship of the chief Qazi. He supervised the administrative structure of judiciary.

Diwan-i-Barid was government's intelligence department. It had a very vast effective network covering the whole of the territory acting as ears and eyes of the rulers. Besides the above known ministers, there also existed a minister controlling the royal household. He appears to have exercised great influence because of his nearness to the kith and kin of the king. For administrative convenience, Sher Shah divided his empire into different territorial segments – the Sarkar, the Paragana and the village. We are not very clear whether the sarkar or the province existed next to the imperial structure. Kanungo is of the view that the highest division during Sher Shah's time was the sarkar and not the province and he further goes on to state that the province was the creation of Akbar. Saran contradicts this view stating that the provinces existed in the past and it is not right to think that sarkar was the highest division of the state.

Sarkar in Persian language means government and authority. Burton Stein suggests that it was at the sarkar level that the Lodi Sultan's military and civil officers encountered and sought to dominate the countryside and town. Realizing the administrative and economic importance of this unit, Sher Shah appointed two officers: Shiqdar-i-Shiqdarin and Munsif-i-Musifon over each sarkar. While Shiqdar-i-Shiqdarin maintained law and order Munisf-i-Munsifon acted as the judge of civil cases and supervised over armies. Appointment of two officers with specific responsibilities and jurisdiction was only to avoid concentration of authority in one single individual and also to see that one acts as a check over the other.

Sarkars were further subdivided as paraganas. In each paragana a Shiqdar, an Amin, a Fotehdar, a Munsif, a Hindi writer and a Persian writer were appointed besides the Patwari, Chaudari and the Muqaddam who acted as the intermediaries between the government and the people. The duty of the Shiqdar was to maintain law and order, to collect the revenue and also decide the legal matters. The Amin was in charge of collection of the land revenue and he too tried civil and revenue cases. The Amin and the Shiqdar were of the same rank. The treasurer was Fotehdar and the entire amount collected was kept in his custody. He also maintained account of the income and expenditure of the paragana. Clerks or Karkuns were appointed to maintain duplicate accounts in Hindi and Persian. Shershah introduced the practice of transferring the Shiqdar and the Amin of the paraganas for every two years as a precaution to see that they do not become too familiar with the locality and people and indulge in rebellions.

Burton Stein writing on the role of sarkars and paraganas observes, "On the frontiers of the realm, Sarkars were joined together under the supervisory responsibility of an Afghan noble, who was a deputy of the sultan". Burton Stein further observes, "In this way, attempts were made to contain the two levels of political authority that is, on the one hand, provided the regime's principal income in tribute and was controlled by the Afghan nobles, and on the other hand, consisted of the core tracts of traditional political and economic integration – the paraganas – which were overseen by non-Afghans of various kinds. In paraganas, local dominance continued and it is estimated that there existed nearly a lakh paraganas with particular local tradition and authority. The administrative apparatus of the levels of sarkars and paraganas provided the foundation for Akbar's times also". Satish Chandra thinks that a number of sarkars were grouped into provinces, but authentic evidence is lacking to know about the pattern of the provincial administration in Shershah's time. The role of the governors varied depending on their individual capacities.

Revenue Administration

As land revenue was the main source of income to the State, Shershah introduced certain improvements in the method of collection and assessment of land revenue, keeping in mind the interests of the cultivators. Shershah had the belief that "the cultivators are blameless, they submit to those in power, and if I oppress them they will abandon their villages, and the country will be ruined and deserted, and it will be a long time before it again becomes prosperous". Shershah demanded the cultivator to pay one-third of the expected crop in kind as tax. For that purpose, the land was measured and recorded against the cultivator by name. He employed the yard of Sikandar Lodi, 32 digits long as the unit of measurement. By taking into consideration the fertility of the soil, an average was reached of the best, the middling and the worst land for every crop. Shershah's revenue officials prepared a per bigha schedule in kind. On the basis of this he asked the cultivator to pay the land revenue as per the crops sown in the area recorded against his name. The collection of land revenue was assigned to the village headman and for the labour involved in this work, he charged 5 per cent addition as his labour. The village headman also collected 5 per cent more to take care of visiting public servants. Shershah introduced the system of remitting land tax in case of damage of the crop by the army. Shershah introduced measures to bring more land under cultivation by these measures, i.e., by providing loans without interest, by encouraging to cultivate valuable crops, by asking the officials to be lenient at the time of assessment, and to be very strict at the time of collection by instructing the army not to destroy the crops of the cultivators on their march and by paying compensation to the cultivator, if crop was destroyed by the army.

In spite of the best intentions to be friendly with the cultivators, in reality in operation we notice certain defects in the land revenue system. As the land revenue was fixed at one-third of the gross produce, the cultivator cultivating the bad land was overtaxed compared to the cultivator of the best land. Besides this defect, the corruption among the officials created problems to the cultivators. While R.P. Tripathi was critical of the revenue administrative measures, Moreland observes that Shershah's land reforms "formed the starting point of the series of experiments in administration which marked the first half of Akbar's reign". Satish Chandra rightly observes, "Since there was plenty of land available for cultivation in those days, the desertion of the villages by the peasants in case of oppression was a real threat and it helped in putting a limit on the exploitation of peasants by the rulers".

Justice and Police

Shershah showed no discrimination in the policy of administering justice on any ground. Shershah believed, "justice is the most excellent of religious rites, and it is approved alike by the king of infidels and of the faithful". The courts were presided over by the Qazi and Mir Adil, who administered civil justice. Village panchayats and Zamindars also disposed petty civil cases in the villages and rural areas. Punishments appear to be severe, so that in future no one would dare to repeat the same mistake. Shershah's son, Islam Shah, took a big leap in the dispensation of justice by codifying the laws, so that they became standardized.

It appears that what the police did today was carried on by the army in the days of Shershah. We are already aware in the Sarkar and paragana that the

Shiqdar-i-Shiqdarin and the Shiqdar respectively were in charge of the police duty of maintaining law and order with the help of army. Shershah's innovation was the introduction of local responsibility and it worked for the advantage of the people. Shershah's police policy won the accolades of one and all. Abbas Khan Sarwani, a contemporary historian of the time of Shershah records that Shershah gave top priority for the maintenance of law and order and fear of Shershah made the Zamindars not to raise the banner of revolt against him or to molest the innocent travellers passing through their territories. Realizing that the prosperity of the state and society depends on the growth of commerce and trade and in turn it depends on proper communication system of linking of roads, Shershah took measures in that direction. First, he took measures to restore the old imperial road later called the Grand Trunk road, from the river Indus in the West to Sonargaon in Bengal. In order to have direct communication link with the Gujarat sea port, he built a road from Agra to Jodhpur and Chithod or Chithore and another road from Lahore to Multan. Shershah not only built roads but also took steps for the safe stay of travellers and merchants by constructing sarais at every 2 kms. Sarai or rest house was a fortified place where provision was made for the safe custody of merchandise and provision was also made for horses and grain for horses. Separate rest places were provided for the Hindus and the Muslims. Each sarai had a Shadna or custodian under whose watchful eyes many watchmen worked day and night taking due care of the travellers. It is estimated that there existed seventeen hundred sarais. It is no exaggeration to state that the roads and the sarais are called the arteries of the empire. In course of time each sarai developed into a market town or Quasbas to which peasants gathered to sell their goods. These sarais also served as Dak Chowki stages. By means of Dak Chowkis, Shershah used to gather information about the developments in the state. In order the give fillip to the growth of trade and commerce, Shershah took measures to abolish the vexatious duties collected at various points of entry and the state imposed only two duties, i.e., at the time of entry into the country and at the time of sale. Shershah removed by a stroke of pen all internal customs and thereby goods had become cheaper comparatively.

Shershah reorganized the currency system by abolishing the old mixed metal currency and introducing a new coin called *Dam*. The coins bore the name of the coin in the Devanagari script. He also introduced gold coins. Satish Chandra states that Shershah's attempt to introduce standard weights and measures all over the empire along with currency reforms helped in the growth of trade and commerce. He struck fine coins of gold, silver and copper of uniform standard and his silver Rupee was so carefully executed that it remained a model standard coin for centuries to come. The ratio of exchange between the Dam and the Rupee was fixed at 64 to 1. As all the states of medieval times were 'war ready' and readiness of war required a strong and efficient army with necessary arms and equipment, Shershah took measures to reorganize the army under the strict discipline of the ruler. Shershah gave up dependence on feudal levies or tribal levies whose loyalty is always doubtful and instead recruited soldiers directly into the army, after scrupulous verification of their character. He continued the practice of recruiting and maintaining of the descriptive role of every soldier and horses given to soldiers are branded with imperial sign to avoid substitution of inferior horses by certain unscrupulous elements. Shershah's army is estimated to consist of 1,50,000 cavalry and 25,000 infantry armed with matchlocks or bows, 5,000 elephants and a pack of artillery. Shershah also set up cantonments in different parts of the empire and a strong garrison in each of them.

Shershah followed a religious policy suited to the needs and demands of a plural state with multiple beliefs and faiths practised by different segments. Shershah is very conscious of his role in such a state and preferred to be liberal rather than dogmatic in his approach to religious and social spheres of life. Satish Chandra argues that he was not a bigot but did not initiate any new liberal policy. He continued the practice of collecting Jijiya from the Hindus and also continued the clanish mentality of the Afghans by drawing nobility from the Afghans alone. We may conclude by agreeing with Satish Chandra that the state under Shershah remained an Afghan institution based on race and tribe and Shershah was a statusquoist at the core rather than an innovator or a prochanger. Shershah was also a great builder of monuments of significance. His tomb constructed at Sasram is considered to be a masterpiece of architecture by art critics. Shershah also built a new city on the banks of the Yamuna near Delhi, and Puranaquila and the fine mosque within it are the two living legacies of old fort area built by Shershah. Shershah also patronized arts and letters. Sur buildings laid the ground work for the Mughal architectural splendour and glory. The architectural legacy of the Surs can be studied under two heads. The first phase belongs to Sasram in Bihar between 1530–1540. And the second phase is attributable to 1540–45 when Shershah wrested power from the Mughal Humayun. Art critics suggest that several architectural innovations were adopted which later matured in the Mughal times. The architectural phase of Sasram in Bihar is represented by a group of tombs, three of the ruling family and one of the architects, Aliwal Khan. These tombs reflect the ambition of Shershah that these monuments should be more glorious than those in Delhi. Among these the first one is that of Hasan Khan, the father of Shershah and it was conceived and executed in the conventional Lodi design. Shershah's tomb is of a beautiful pyramidical structure in five distinct stages and it was constructed of the finest chunar sandstone. It stands on a stepped square plinth on a terrace. The main building comprises an octagonal chamber surrounded by an arcade with domed canopies in each corner of the platform. This tomb, which is acclaimed as a masterpiece, reflects the capabilities of the Indian architects in achieving harmonious transition from square to octagon and to sphere. The second phase of the architectural splendour is reflected in the existing buildings of the old city of Delhi. Here in 1542, Shershah built Qilai Kuhna Masjid inside the Purana Qila citadel. The facade of the prayer hall is divided into five arched bays, the central one longer than the others and the facade is richly carved in black and white marble and red sand stone and the central arch is flanked by narrow, fluted pilasters. One notable feature of this building is the use of the four-centred Tudor arch of the Mughals.

In the first half of the 16th century, though we notice serious effort on the part of Shershah to improve the living standards of the people by reorganizing the administrative structure and system, the developments in the sphere of science and technology are not too significant as those of the later centuries of 17th and 18th. No breakthrough was made in scientific studies and at that time only the early Indian and Greeco-Arabic views on science were predominant. The age old-agricultural technology and textile technology continued. In the military sphere also, use of guns and canons developed. The guns were actually matchlocks. Ship-building was also known in those days. Glass technology had not taken deep roots on the Indian soil. Time reckoning devices were also in vogue. The time was ripe for a new threshold of vibrant economy and society into the impacts of Western scientific values in the next two centuries in the field of technology and science.

Shershah by his foresight, political wisdom, statesmanship and shrewd understanding of human nature carved out a second Afghan empire in India single-handedly and by anticipating Akbar, created an image that, if destiny had favoured Shershah, the great Mughals would not have found a place on the stage of history. Can there be a better tribute to him than the above one?

The Mughal Empire until 1707: Consolidation, Expansion and Diplomacy

Babur founded the Mughal empire in India in AD 1526 after his success in the first battle of Panipat. But after the sudden demise of Babur in 1530 and in between before the accession of Akbar in AD 1556, the Mughals had to struggle hard to retain their hold in India and in their effort they failed against the determined Afghans and the Rajputs. By the time Akbar ascended the throne in 1556 to claim his right, the Mughals were at their lowest ebb of prestige. It is their success in the second battle of Panipat in the year 1556 that provided secure space for the Mughals in India. Since 1556 to 1707, the Mughals, "the professional kings" strictly followed the dictum of the earlier Hindu and Muslim rulers of the past that "a monarch should ever be intent on conquest, otherwise his enemies rise in arms against him". The core philosophy of Akbar and his successors up to Aurangzeb was to expand the power of the Mughals over the entire subcontinent and to deepen their administrative control over the rural and urban subjects by a wise and liberal policy of integration. As John Fleet Richards observes, the dynamism of the Mughals was at its core military and the Mughal Empire was a war state. What J.F. Richards holds appears to be true. Yet the Mughals not only expanded their territorial extent by wars and conquests, they also devised administrative measures to consolidate themselves as rulers by winning the loyalty of their subjects. In the following pages, let us treat the twin policies of expansion and consolidation followed by Akbar, Jehangir, Shahjahan and Aurangzeb till 1707 along with diplomatic tactics adopted by them. Akbar's reign started shakily in 1556. Akbar's reign comes to a close by 1605. He had to regain his paternal kingdom after defeating the Sur successors of Shershah and their general, Hemu in the second battle of Panipat. During the regency of Bairam Khan, Ajmer, Malwa and Garhkatanga were added to the territory of the Mughals. Later on, Akbar brought the major part of Rajasthan under his control along with Gujarat (1584), Kabul (1585), Kashmir (1586–87), Sindh (1591), Bengal (1592) and Kandahar (1595) were annexed to the Mughal territory. Like his predecessor Sultans of Delhi, after establishing his sway over North India, Akbar turned his attention towards the Deccan and demanded them to accept his suzerainity. As the response was negative, Akbar despatched Abdul Rahim and prince Murad to attack Ahmadnagar in 1595. Chand Bibi, the regent offered stiff opposition and peace was concluded after acquiring Berar. By 1600, Akbar proceeded in person and occupied Burhanpur and sent his armies to annex Ahmadnagar. In 1601, the Mughals occupied the fort of Asirgarh and carved out three Subas of Ahmadnagar, Berar and Khandesh. Thus, within a period of five decades from 1556 to 1605, Akbar built a vast multi-regional empire by his repeated conquests and victories and provided a stable and secure administrative apparatus and structure catering to the needs and demands of his subjects. A.L. Srivastava rightly states, "Akbar invariably followed the policy of giving an organized administration to his conquered territories. As soon as a principality or a province was reduced to submission, he took steps to establish therein complete order and peace, and to appoint civil officers to carry out a revenue settlement which was based on the principles of measurement and classification of land. Religious toleration was extended to the newly conquered areas, social, religious as well as administrative reforms were introduced and the interests of the people were taken care of. Akbar, unlike his predecessors paved the way for the establishment of a common nationality in the land". By following a wise policy of liberal attitude towards all communities and by providing peace and order through his policy initiatives, he cemented the bond of relationship between people of different religions and cultures of India. It is no exaggeration to suggest that under his benign paternal outlook, not only the entire land mass stretching from the frontiers of Persia to Assam and Burma and from the Hindukush and the Himalayas to the Godavari river has grown into a coherent state ruled by one system of administration throughout India giving equal scope and place of honour to both the Hindus and the Muslims and for more than a century enjoyed cultural and artistic renaissance. Satish Chandra observes that along with political integration, importantly the cultural and emotional integration of the people within this vast empire had taken place at the same time. As a result of his reformistic zeal and liberal policy towards non-Muslims, the state became essentially secular, liberal and enlightened in social sphere and a harbinger of cultural integration.

Prince Salim, the eldest living son of Akbar ascended the Mughal throne with the title of Jehangir in 1605 against his own son prince Khusru, who was supported by a section of the nobility. Jehangir was not a great general and organizer like his father Akbar but continued his father's policies to the best of his ability having the long range interests of the Mughal Empire in his heart. Jehangir consolidated the administrative system, which was built by Akbar. He also maintained friendly alliance with the Rajputs and took measures to broaden the political base of the empire by seeking alliance with the powerful section of the Afghans and the Marathas. J.F. Richards is of the view that under Jehangir too, the Mughal Empire continued to be a war state attuned to aggressive conquests and territorial expansion. The important achievement of Jehangir was the settlement of the dispute with the Sisodia ruler of Mewar. Immediately after his accession in 1605, he took up the issue with all seriousness. By 1615, Jehangir completed the task begun by Akbar and further strengthened the alliance with the Rajputs. Jehangir conquered the fort of Kangra through the efforts of his son Prince Khurram and also conquered the district of Kistwar in 1620. Jahangir had to face the opposition of Malik Amber, the Peshwa of Ahmadnagar who defeated Abdul Rahim Khan-i-Khanan and recaptured Ahmadnagar in 1610. In spite of his best efforts, Jehangir could not reconquer Ahmadnagar till his death in 1627 and it was left to Shahjahan to totally capture Ahmadnagar after the death of Malik Amber. Along with Ahmadnagar, Kandahar could not be conquered by Jahangir during his reign. The dark patches of his reign are his failures to recapture Ahmadnagar, Kandahar and continuous unsuccessful wars with Ahoms for a number of years and execution of Guru Arjun Singh, which laid the seeds of religious discontentment of the Sikhs and his passion for Nurjahan, which made prince Khurram and Mahabat Khan rebel against him. The purple patch was his positive role in establishing relations with the neighbouring Asian powers Iran, the Uzbeks and the Ottoman Turks and opening of gates of India to foreigners by giving trade concessions and making the Mughal court a centre of cultural activity. We may conclude that his contribution for the expansion and consolidation of the empire was not very positive but at the same time not negative to the extent of causing harm to the prosperity and stability of the Mughal Empire. Prince Khurram, with the title of Shahjahan ascended the Mughal throne in 1628 after a bloody war of succession and ruled for three decades, i.e., up to 1658. By the time of his accession, Shahjahan was the master of vast territories with unmatched military power and massive wealth. Shahjahan proved himself to be a pastmaster in military campaigning, diplomatic negotiation, and political manoeuvring. Under his direction, the empire continued its expansion. J.F. Richards observes, even the previously remote refuge areas felt the imprint of the imperial power. Shahjahan's efforts on the north-western border and north-east ended in thorough failure. We come to know from the account of Abdul Hamid Lahori that by 1647, the Mughal domain stretched from Sind in the far north-west to Sylhet on the Brahmaputra, and from the newly conquered Balkh to the southern boundary of the Deccan provinces – 22 provinces contained 4,350 paraganas and the annual revenue of the empire was 8,800 million dams which was definitely higher than that of Jahangir. Shahjahan celebrated his success by constructing a new city of Shahjahanabad in Delhi and constructing the Taj Mahal and the Peacock throne. His regime witnessed a return to an earlier Islamic political culture deviating from the liberal policy, of his father and grandfather, his policy anticipating the future under his successor, Aurangzeb. Though the Mughal Empire appears to be invincible and wealthy on a scale unknown to the earlier Delhi Sultans, undoubtedly, the empire was moving towards its greatest political crisis. The greatest political crisis that seriously affected the fortunes of the empire was the polarization of liberal and conservative forces led by Dara Shukov and Aurangzeb and differences of opinion regarding major policy matters of the Deccan conquest and the Mughal's relations with Bijapur and Golkonda. By the time Shahjahan seriously fell ill, there started a bloody civil war between the brothers and finally Aurangzeb, the third son of Shahjahan ascended the Mughal throne as the champion of the conservative ideology of reviving the Islamic state in 1658 and ruled for more than a half century till 1707. Aurangzeb spent most of his time in the campaigns of Rajasthan and the Deccan. Aurangzeb's reign witnessed intense struggle with the Deccan and it is a fact of history that Aurangzeb spent the last twenty years in Deccan fighting against the Deccan kingdoms. These efforts yielded results and by 1687, the Deccan Shia states of Bijapur and Golkonda were annexed to the Mughal Empire. The major success of Aurangzeb in the north-east was annexation of Assam. This was followed by the capture of Chatgam in 1664 but by 1680, the Ahoms of Assam captured Kamarup and the Mughal control disappeared from Assam. Akbar initiated the policy of friendly relationship with the autonomous chieftains that spread over the whole of India with the objective of consolidating his empire and the same policy was continued by his successors. These chieftains had control over the core regions of the Subas of Delhi, Agra, Awadh, Aurangabad and the peripheral areas also. These chieftains belonged to the Rajput communities and also to all castes and communities including the Muslims. These chieftains possessed sufficiently extensive army and hundreds of acres of land yielding good amounts of revenue. Realizing the need to control them and to reduce his enemies, Akbar made 61 of them as Manasabs who were continued by his successors. Some were made Subedars, Diwans and Bakshis. They appear to pay tribute to the sovereign which was known as Peshkash. It was paid in either cash or kind. As a result of the Mughals' policy, both the chieftains and the Mughals became beneficiaries. While the Mughals obtained their support along with armies for new conquests and help in administering a large empire, the chieftains retained their territories with a right to administer them. By entering into matrimonial relations with certain chieftains also, the Mughals strengthened their hold over the territories as well as such chieftains. Thus, Akbar and his successors by following a wise policy of conciliation and conquest brought large areas in the east, west, north and south under the effective sway of the Mughal Empire. It was not the entire South, but only Deccan that came under the Mughals. As already explained, the conquest was followed by consolidation through measures of effective control of a unified administrative system. By the time of Aurangzeb, new areas of Golkonda and Bijapur of Decan and the north-east were added to the empire. The cracks in the edifice of the Mughal structure became visible in the lifetime of the last great Mughal, Aurangzeb himself.

Mughal Administration

The nature and structure and functioning of the Mughal administration can be comprehended by the study of the following sources: *Ain-i-Akbari* of Abul Fazl, *Dastur-ul-Amals* or official handbooks of the period of Shahjahan and Aurangzeb, *Iqbal-nama Jahangiri* by Muhamad Khan, *Padshahnamah* of Abdul Hamid Lahori, the *Tuzuki Jahangir,* and *Tabazat-i-Akbari* of Nizamuddin provide valuable and useful information. Besides the above books, the writings of foreigners – Sir Thomas Roe, Bernier, Hawkins, Manucci, Terry and the Factory records of the European trading companies also provide necessary information.

Political Ideas and Institutions

It is an established fact that every human settlement creates certain basic laws and code of conduct based on rules to sustain peace and order. Human experience recorded tells us that the laws and rules so framed from generation to generation undergo changes as needed by the societal needs and demands. The Mughal polity was no exception and was the result of a mixture or blend of Indian, Turkish, Persian and Mongol political ideas and institutions. The important political institution of the later medieval times was the monarchy represented by royalty or the sovereign. Jadunath Sarkar, who made a pioneering study of the Mughal administrative nature and structure comes to the conclusion that "the Mughal administration presented a combination of Indian and extra-Indian elements, or, more correctly it was the Persio-Arabic system in Indian setting". Though the Mughals imported principles of administration, and designation of officials, they modified the imported system as per the local needs and experiences and saw to it that it effectively worked at all levels. It is accepted by Irfan Habib and Athar Ali that the Mughal polity was highly centralized and absolute. It is suggested that this process is visible in the efficient working of the systems of land revenue, Mansabdari and Jagidari and uniform coinage. Contradicting the above view, Stephen P. Plake and J.F. Richards, while accepting the centralized tendencies point out that the Mughal state was 'patriomonial bureaucratic', i.e., everything revolves around the imperial household and the bureaucratic set-up. Strewsand discovers that the periphery was less centralized and Chetan Singh also echoes the same and argues that the local elements of the periphery could influence the policies at the centre. At this juncture, we can only say that theoretically, the Mughal administrative structure was highly centralized and bureaucratic but in practice it is a debatable issue as total centralization of the administrative structure appears to be doubtful.

Central Administration

Monarchy was the prevalent political institution with supreme authority vested in the head of the state. As such, the emperor was the head of the administrative structure. Both Babur and Humayun followed the Islamic theory of kingship but Akbar differed from them in his concept of royalty. Akbarnama states that a king "cannot be fit for the lofty office, if he does not inaugurate universal peace, and if he does not regard all classes of men and all sets of religions with a single eye for favour". We also notice divine element in the concept of royalty. While Babur adopted *Zil-ul-allah Filarz* or 'Shadow of God on earth', Akbar changed it as *Farri-i-Zidi* or 'The height of the God'; Akbar's concept of sovereignty makes him linked to God directly. Abul Fazl states that "royalty is a light emanating from God, a ray from the sun and the illuminator of the universe. The receptacle of all virtues". Abul Fazl further states: "No dignity is higher in the eyes of God than royalty. Royalty is a remedy for the spirit of rebellion". And thereby an emperor becomes "the origin of stability and possession." From the above statements of Abul Fazl and Akbar, we may conclude that king was appointed, guided and protected by God. Akbar differed from his father and grandfather's concept of Quaranic royalty and decided to be the ruler of all, and not of Muslims alone. Jahangir too was motivated like his father but his son Shahjahan and Aurangzeb were influenced by the Islamic theory of sovereignty. It is to be accepted that no Mughal emperor craved or cared for the recognition of Khalifa and this indicates that they exercised real sovereign power internally and externally too. Except Jahangir, the rest of the emperors took keen interest in the matters of administration and toiled for a number of hours to attend to the administrative work as the entire system was emperor-centric and the emperor was the highest authority in the state, who combined in himself the supreme executive, legislative and judicial authority. The emperor's prestige and glory was heightened by the Mughal court. The Mughal court was full of splendour and pomp with the emperor enjoying great respect from the courtiers. The emperor lived magnificently in the midst of his courtiers wearing gorgeous dress and valuable ornaments of gold and precious stones. The Mughals did not practise the law of primogeniture and as such wars of succession had become a common feature. Appointments, promotions, transfer and termination of officers was the prerogative of the emperor. We come across the designations *Wakil* and *Wazir, Diwani Khul*, *Mir Bakshi*, *Mir Saman*, *Sadir-us-Sudur*, *Qazi-ul-Quzzat*, *Miradi* and *Mahtasib* but we are not certain whether they are ministers or high officials. J.N. Sarkar states: "the Mughal emperor had no regular council of ministers". We may say that all the above designations indicate offices of highest officers but not ministers in the sense known to us now. The office of the Wazir was revived by the early Mughals. Both Babur and Humayun appointed Wazirs. In the regency of Bairam Khan, we notice the rise of Wakil-Wazir with unlimited powers but in 1564–65, the financial powers were given to the Diwani Khul, and the office of Wakil continued as the highest office in the Mughal bureaucratic set up. Diwani Khul was the head of the department of finance and revenue. His important duty was to supervise the imperial treasury and have an eye on all accounts. The revenue matters were divided under different sectors like Diwani Khalisa, Diwani Tan or payment of cash as salary, Diwani Jagir, etc. Each wing had a hierarchy of officers and clerks made responsible to his superiors in the order of hierarchy.

Mir Bakshi was in charge of the appointments of Mansabdars. Salary papers of the Mansabdars were endorsed and passed by him. He was also responsible for the branding of horses (dagh) and checked the rolls of soldiers. Mir Bakshi was directly responsible to the emperor. He controlled the provincial Bakshis and Waqai Navis. He was assisted by other Bakshis at the centre. Mir Saman or Khan Saman was the officer in charge of the royal Karkhanas and he had a number of subordinate officers working under him. The Sadir-us-Sudur was the head of the ecclesiastical duties like protecting the laws of Shariat and distribution of charities in cash or in kind. Before the time of Shahjahan, the post of Qazi-ul-Quzzat and Sadir-us-Sudur was combined and held by one individual but from the time of Aurangzeb the two posts were separated. The head of the judiciary was Quzi-ul-Quzzat and he appointed Quazi to the suba, sarkar, paragana and towns. Mir Adil executed the orders of the court. The Muhtasib acted as censor officer of the public morals and was also in charge of proper functioning of weights and measures and enforcing fair prices too. There also existed some other important officials: Mir Bahri or revenue secretary, Mir Barr or Superintendant of forests, Qur Bergi or lord Standard Bearer, Akht Bagi or superintendant of the Royal stud and Mir Arj or officer who presented petitions to the emperor.

Provincial Administration

It was Akbar the Great, who divided the empire into provinces or Subas in 1580. There existed twelve Subas. They were Kabul, Punjab, Multan, Delhi, Agra, Avadh, Allahabad, Bihar, Bengal, Malva, Ajmer and Gujarat. Later three more – Berar, Khandesh and Ahmadnagar were added after their conquest by Akbar. Jahangir separated Orissa from Bengal and created a separate province. During the rule of Shahjahan Kashmir, Sindh and Bidar provinces were carved out. Aurangzeb added the provinces of Bijapur and Golkonda. Each Suba was further subdivided into a number of sarkars and these were sub-divided into paraganas and Mahals. A cluster or number of paraganas was called Chakla unit by Shahjahan. The governor of Suba, the Subedar was directly appointed by the ruler. He was also called *Sahib-i-Subah* or Nain. In running the day-to-day administration, he was assisted by the Diwan, Bakshi, Faujdar, Kotwal, Qazi, Sadar, Amir, Bitkchi, Potdar or Khizamdar, Waqa-i-Navis, Kanungo and Patwari. The tenure of Subedar was for a period of 2 or 3 years and was liable for transfers. The most important duty of Subedar was to look after the welfare of the people and army. It was his duty to maintain law and order in the Suba. It is also the duty of Subedar to encourage agriculture, trade and commerce besides undertaking welfare activities like construction of Sarais, gardens, wells, water reservoirs, etc. He should be in the look out to improve the revenue of the state. The head of the revenue department was called Diwan and was appointed by the emperor. He is responsible to the centre. He is an independent officer. He maintained a *Razanama* or a daily register of the entries of amounts deposited in the royal treasury by revenue Collectors and Zamindars. He was assisted by a number of clerks. The Bakshi was a military officer of the Suba appointed with the recommendation of Mir Bakshi. He controlled the Mansabdars in the Suba and the soldiers. He also checked the horses used by the Mansabdars. The Faujadar was the commander of the troops of the Suba. He appears to have helped the Subedar and the Amir in their duties. Sadur was appointed by the central government to supervise Sayarghal or rent-free lands granted for charitable and religious purposes. The Amir was a revenue collector. He had to see that the Zamindars do not rebel. Bitkchi acted as a check on the Amir. Thus, the duties of every officer in the Suba were fixed and the centre maintained effective control over the Subas by a system of communication network of Darogha-l-dak, who were helped by runners or Mewras. The emperor appointed *Waqai Navis* and *Waqai Nugars* to report to the emperor directly. Thus, every effort was made by the Mughals to effectively control and have a check over the activities of the officials of the Subas.

Local Administration

The workings of administration at the level of Sarkar, Paragana and Manuja or village constitute the aspect of local administration. In Sarkar, the most important functionaries are the Faujdar and the Amalgujar. The duty of the Faujdar was to maintain law and order and thereby protect life and property of the people under his jurisdiction. He helped Amalgujar in revenue collection. Amir or Amalgujar was the revenue collector of the Sarkar. He maintained all the accounts of revenue and he is to send daily reports of income and expenditure to the Diwan. In those days army was kept at certain locations to maintain peace and order and such places are called Thanas. The incharge of the Thana is called Thanedar and he was generally placed under Faujadar. In each Paragana an executive head known as Shiqdar was appointed. He also assisted the Amir in revenue collection. A Quanungo was kept in charge of the records of the Paragana. He had to record the crops grown and the extent of land under cultivation was also to be recorded by him. The lowest unit of administration was the village and in each village was appointed a Muqaddam and a Patwari. The Mughals did not meddle with village administrative set-up introduced by Sher Shah. The Mughals took care to see that the administration of the cities and forts was carried on properly. A Kotwal was appointed by the centre in each city to maintain law and order. For every fort, they appointed a Qiladar and generally Mansabdars of high rank were appointed to forts located at strategic places. The Mughals also appointed officers in port towns known as Mutasaddi and he was empowered to collect taxes on merchandise and maintained a customs house. He was assisted by a subordinate Shah Bandar. Thus, the Mughals took keen interest in the administration of their territory by dividing it into administrative units and by keeping them under different offices and by strict vigilance and watch over their activities they made the officers responsible and responsive to the needs and demands of the time.

Land Revenue

Land revenue was the main source of income to the state, as agriculture was the main occupation of the majority of population of India since times immemorial. Coming to the Mughal period, the author of the land revenue system was Akbar. We notice evolution in the land revenue administration initiated and implemented by Akbar. In the beginning, Akbar followed the land revenue system of Sher Shah but as he found this system defective, he modified it. The Persian term for land revenue during the Mughal age was *Mai* and *Malwajib*. The process of land revenue collection had two stages: (a) assessment or *Tashkhis/Jama,* and (b) actual collection or Hasil. After the fixation of state demand in the process of assessment, the actual collection was undertaken separately for Kharif and Rabi seasons. The revenue officials issued a Patta or Qual or Qual Parar to the cultivator indicating the amount to be paid by him to the state. In return to the above mentioned demand notice or patta, the cultivator had to give Qabuliyat or acceptance of the obligation imposed by the state informing when and how he should pay it. During the Mughal period, the state commonly used the methods of: (a) Gallabakshi, (b) Kankut or Danabandi, and (c) Zabti. In certain areas Gallabakshi was also known as Bhaoli and Batai. Gallabakshi was nothing but crop sharing. *Ain-i-Akbari* mentions three types of crop sharing: (a) division of the crop at the threshing floor as per the agreement in the presence of both the parties, (b) division of the crop when the crop was not cut in the field by marking a division of the field, and (c) division of the crop by both the parties when the crop was cut and stacked in heaps. In practice, this system of sharing the crop proved to be too costly for the state when it was implemented by Aurangzeb. In the method of Kankut or Danabandi, grain yield or grain produced in a bigah was estimated. First, the land was measured by a rope or by pacing and later, on the basis of the productivity of the soil (good, medium and bad) the grain yield was estimated and then the revenue was fixed. Zabti or Dahsala was the most commonly used method for assessment of land revenue. In 1580, Akbar introduced this system. In this system, the average produce of different crops as well as the average prices prevailing over the last ten years was calculated. The state fixed one-third of the average produce as the share of the state and this was collected in cash. As the prices varied from region to region, the money to be paid was collected and decided on the basis of local prices. Thus, the main features of this system are: (a) measurement of land was essential, (b) fixed cash revenue rates known as Dastur-ul-Amal or Dastur for each crop, and (c) the entire amount was to be collected in cash. This system was introduced in Delhi, Allahabad, Awadh, Agra, Lahore and Multan. Besides Zabti or Dahsal, Nasqi method was also in vogue. It is said to be a rough calculation of the amount payable by the peasant on the basis of past payment. Revenue farming or Izara was another system in vogue. Though the Mughals disfavoured it, in some places it was in vogue, where land owners were not in a position to undertake cultivation. Jagirdars appear to come under this category. By the 18th century, Izara system had become a common form of revenue assessment and collection. On the basis of the continuity of cultivation, the lands were divided as Polaj, Parauti, Chachar and Banjar. The land cultivated every year was called Polaj and when the same land was uncultivated, it was called Parauti. The land that was uncultivated for 2 or 3 years continuously was called Chachar and if it is beyond 3 or 4 years it was called 'banjar'. Further, on the basis of productivity of the soil the land was known as good, middling and bad. Generally, one-third was the state demand, but it varied according to the productivity of the land and the method of assessment. The Mughals showed keen interest in the promotion of agricultural operations on a large scale and instructed officials to act like a parent to the peasants, to advance loans for seeds, implements, and animals in times of need and to encourage agriculturists to bring more land under cultivation. There is a view that rate of tax on land varied from region to region. Further, it is reported that revenue rates varied according to the class or caste of the revenue paying groups. For example, the Brahmins and Banias paid revenue in concessional rates in a certain paraganas of eastern Rajasthan. We come across a number of revenue officials like Karori, which post was created in 1574–75, amin, qanungo, chaudari, shiqdar, muqaddam and patwari, fotdar, bitkchi, diwan, faujdar, waqari navis and sawanih nigar.

The Mughals granted a large portion of the land of the empire to beneficiaries like the Jagirdars, and Muslim religious leaders. The Jagirs were temporary assignments. Jahangir introduced system of nullifying grants by the emperor himself personally. There existed Khalisa lands which were under the direct control of the imperial revenue department. The extent of Khalisa lands varied from region to region and time to time. While Jahangir decreased the extent of Khalisa lands, Shahjahan increased it. We notice the transfer of Khalisa lands to Jagir type and reverse also. *Ain-i-Akbari* provides a list of food and non-food crops produced in Rabi and Kharif and tobacco and maize were introduced into India during the 17th century. Sericulture and horticulture also made rapid strides during this period. The peasant group during this period was highly stratified. There was also considerable difference in the size of holdings, produce and resources of the peasants, Commercial crops were produced on large scale by the landed gentry. We also notice exploitation of the small peasants by rich peasants.

Mansabdari System

Akbar was the architect of the Mansabdari system, an institution of political and economic significance that played a critical role in the consolidation and disintegration of the Mughal Empire. We also notice an evolution in the beginning and the growth of this institution. The word Mansab means a place, a position, an honour and a rank, which happened to be an integral part of the elaborate Mughal bureaucracy. Percival Spear rightly points out that this Mansabdari system was elite within an elite. The Mansabdars were appointed to all civil and military posts except that of judiciary, and the positions like wazir, bakshi, faujdar and Subedar were held by the Mansabdars. The Mansabdar appears to be a central Asian institution. There is a view that this institution came to India with Babur. During Babur's time, instead of the term of Mansabdar, the term Wajahdar was used. There is a definite difference between these two terms of Mansabdari and Wajahdari system. Under the regime of Akbar, Mansabdari system became the basis of military and civil administration. It is also believed that Akbar followed the principles of Changiz Khan in fixing up the grades of Mansabdars. Abul Fazl states that Akbar provided 66 grades of Mansabdars ranging from commanders of 10 horsemen to 10,000 horsemen but he gives a list of 33 grades of Mansabdars. Thus, the term 'Mansab' decided the status of the holder in the graded official hierarchy, it also fixed the pay of the holder or the Mansabdar and it also made it obligatory to maintain a specified number of contingent with horses and necessary equipment. In the beginning and up to 1595–96, personal pay and the size of the contingent was represented by single rank of Jat but from 1595–96, both the Jat and sawar ranks began to decide the position and status of the Mansabdar. While Jat decided the Mansabdar's personal pay or Talabkhasa and his rank in the official hierarchy and sawar fixed the horses and horsemen to be maintained by the Mansabdar and the amount he received to maintain his contingent. Regarding the meaning and nature of sawar there is no unanimity of opinion. William Irvine, Abdul Aziz and Athar Ali offered different versions. Again in the year 1595–96, the Mansabdars were divided into three classes, first, second and the third. First class was in equal number to Jat and sawar, second class Jat and half or more than half of sawar and third class Jat and less than half of sawar. There was no fixing of the number of Mansabdars. While in 1595–96, Akbar maintained 1,803 Mansabdars, by the end of the reign of Aurangzeb, their number rose to 14,499. The emperor can raise the rank of the Mansabdar by increasing the number allotted to a Mansabdar. We also come to know that those who had 500 or less than 500 were called Mansabdars. Those who had more than 500 and below 2,500 were called Amirs and those above 2,500 were called *Amir-i-Umda* or *Amir-i-Azam* or *Amir-l-Aam* or *Amrahs*. Further, those Mansabdars, who were paid in cash, were called Naqdi and those paid through Jagirs were called Jagirdars. No mansabdar could hold on to the said Jagir for a long term and they were liable for transfer. The Mansab's post or honour or dignity was not hereditary and it lapsed after the death or dismissal of the Mansabdar and the property returned to the state after that. While the basic features of this system introduced by Akbar continued, new features were added during his successors' regimes. One such feature was the introduction of the use of conditional rank or Mashrut which means an increase of sawar rank for a short period. The reign of Jahangir saw an important innovation of the introduction of the Du-aspah She-aspah which means if a Mansabdar held a mansab of 4,000 Jat/4,000 sawar and he was eligible to 4,000 + 4,000 = 8,000 or both, the pay and obligation of the Mansabdar were doubled. Under Shahjahan, new regulations prescribing the size of the contingent under various sawar ranks were introduced. The increase of number of Mansabdars during the reign of Aurangzeb led to the Jagirdari and agrarian crisis which led to the collapse of the Mansabdari system. Though in theory, the Mansabdari position was open to all, in practice, the Mughals gave importance to heredity factor and as such Khanzads or house-born and Zamindars were given preference along with Turanis, Iranis, Afghans, Rajputs and Marathas and the Deccanis by Aurangzeb in particular for military reasons.

Jagirdari System

Assignment of a piece of land to an individual for the purpose of collection of revenue in lieu of cash salary is an age-old practice in India. In the Delhi Sultanate period such assignments were called Iqtas and the holders Iqtadars. The Mughal emperors also implemented this system and the areas assigned were called Jagirs and their holders, Jagirdars. It is to be remembered in this connection that it is not land that was assigned but the right to collect revenue or income from the piece of land. The framework of the Mughal Jagirdari system began during the reign of Akbar and in course of time it underwent modifications. Babur and Humayun continued the collection of revenue from the assigned territories through Wajahdars by fixing 'wajah'. In the time of Akbar, the territory was broadly divided as Khalisa and Jagir. The revenue of Khalisa territory was collected and deposited in the imperial treasury. Depending on the rank the Jagirdar was assigned the collection of revenue in lieu of salary in cash. The maximum area of the territory was assigned to Mansabdars on the basis of their rank. The estimated revenue from the territory was called 'jama ojamadari' as it was calculated in 'dam'. Dam is a small copper coin. Generally, the jama included land revenue, in-land transit duties, port customs and other taxes too. This is also known as 'sair jihat' and 'hasil' or the amount of revenue actually collected. There were various types of Jagirs or revenue assignments. They are: (1) Jagirs, which were given in lieu of pay known as Jagir Tankha, (2) Jagirs given to an individual on certain conditions called Mashrut Jagirs, (3) Jagirs with no involvement of obligations of service and were independent of rank known as Inam Jagirs, and (4) Jagirs, assigned to Zamindars in their home lands called Watan Jagirs. Of these varieties, Tankha Jagirs were transferable for every three or four years. Watan Jagirs were hereditary Jagirs and non-transferable. Yet, all these types of Jagirs were liable for conversion. Thus, the Jagirdars were allowed to collect only the stipulated amount fixed by the king. The Jagirdar collected the revenue through his own officials like Karkun, Amir and Fotedar. The imperial bureaucracy kept a vigilant watch over the Jagirdars. The Diwan of the Suba saw to it that the Jagirdars never harassed the peasants for excess payment. From the 20th year of the reign of Akbar, an Amir was posted in the Subha to see that the Jagirdars strictly implemented the royal orders. In times of difficulty, the Jagirdar took the help of faujdar for the collection of revenue. During the later period of Aurangzeb's reign, there arose a crisis in Jagirdari system and this in turn led to a crisis in the Mughal Empire. We also come across the term Zamindars besides Mansabdars and Jagirdars in the official Mughal records. In the Mughal period, the term was used in a very wide sense. It meant the petty land holders in the villages and descendants of old ruling families and the Rajputs and other autonomous chiefs who exercised administrative authority in their areas. They also maintained armed forces and forts depending on their status. The Zamindars were the local elite or rural aristocracy who exercised authority in their areas. We may conclude this chapter with the assertion that the Mansabdari and the Jagirdari were the two main institutions created by Akbar to consolidate and expand his empire which embraced both civil and military sectors of administration. Thus the Mansabdars, Jagirdars and Zamindars were a part of the Mughal nobility which acted as a prop of the Mughal administrative structure created by Akbar and nurtured by his successors. It is of great interest to note as observed by J.F. Richards, "the structure created by Akbar and his administration survived with surprisingly little change until the early years of the 18th century. Imposed and backed by the overwhelming Mughal power, this structure included beneath the tough defense of rural life and reshaped the economy, culture and society of Mughal India".

The General Conditions under Mughal Rule

In the past half century, there is a definite shift in the focus of the study of history. It is recognized that the history of a nation is not only the study of the dynamics of dynasties represented by individual rulers (i.e., the political aspect) but the study of social and economic aspects of different segments rural and urban, religious groups of the Hindus and the Muslims, customs and traditions, living standard and style of the agricultural and mercantile occupations, and artisans and craftsmen of different professions as a whole. Coming to Mughal India, R.C. Majumdar, H. Raychowdary and K.K. Datta are of the view, that the sources for studying it are indeed meagre, but valuable information can be gleaned from the account of contemporary European travellers and records of the European factories and incidental references available in contemporary historical works in Persian as well as vernacular literature of the period. In order to understand the social and economic aspects of Mughal India, Moreland was the first to arrive at a demographic calculation with the help of *Ain-i-Akbari* and concluded that the population of northern India was 30 to 40 million people at the end of the 16th century. He also concludes that the population of entire India was 100 million at the end of AD 1600. Kingsley Davis is of the view that the population of India was 125 million. Shireeen Moosvi estimates the population of India in the 17th century to be between 140 and 150 million. Ashok V. Desai also tried to estimate the population of India by 1,600 by using the method or concept of total and per capita land revenue but his efforts were questioned by Alan Heston and Shireen Moosvi. It is now agreed upon that the population at the end of Akbar's reign could be 100 million and the whole of India 145 million. Out of this population, Irfan Habib by using the method of pattern of consumption of agricultural produce comes to the conclusion that the urban population could be over 15 per cent of the total population and the rest of the population belongs to the rural setup. We come to know from Nizamuddin Ahmed's *Tabaquat-i-Akbari* that in Akbar's empire there existed 120 big towns and 32,000 townships. Contemporary European travellers also record the population of various big towns like Agra, Delhi, Lahore, Surat, Patna, Dacca and Masulipatnam, where the estimated population is given the maximum of 5,00,000 in Delhi and Agra, Lahore as 4,00,000, and 2,00,000 in the towns of Surat, Patna, Dacca and Masulipatnam. Another interesting aspect to be noted was that the rate of the growth of the population was 0.2 in the 17th and 18th centuries. The composition of the population was pluralistic but not homogenic. While the majority of the peoples were Hindus, considerable number were Muslims, who were divided as Sunnis and Shias, Sikhs, Jains, Buddhists and Christians also lived side by side. Each religious denomination had its cultural identity represented by its own social customs and traditions, having their own cultural symbols. The Hindus observed important festivals like Holi, Basant Panchami, Dushehra, Diwali, Shivaratri and Sankranti. The Muslims observed important festivals like Id-ul-Juha, Id-ul-Fitr, Shab-l-bharat, Muharram and Milad-un-nabi. In addition to the above, Navroj was also celebrated by the aristocratic group. The Buddhists, Jains and Christians celebrated their respective religious festivals. Hunting, animal fighting, pigeon honing, chess, mujra, and mushaira were pastimes. Sati, child-sacrifice, child marriage, *jauhar* and Purdah were common among the Hindus. Akbar attempted to ban sati. Both the Hindus and Muslims spent a lot of money on ornaments. Consumption of opium and liquor was common to both the communities. The Mughal emperors introduced new games like playing cards and modified some games. Religious festivals and fairs were conducted with gaity and pomp. We can trace the origin of many modern fairs to the Mughal period. Society of the Mughal period looked like a feudal organism with the sovereign at its apex followed by the nobility consisting of Mansabdars, Jagirdars and Zamindars, Ulemas followed by middle and lower classes. The most glaring aspect of the society was the wide gulf between the ruling group and the commoners and rural and urban, in standard of life and living pattern. The ruling group and the elite led a luxurious life living in huge palaces, enjoying the best of everything available, wearing jewels and, riding on horses. The urban pattern of life was different from the rural pattern. The rural masses led a very simple life living in mud houses with bare necessities for sustenance. Satish Chandra observes "although the life of the peasant was hard, he had enough to eat and to meet his simple requirements. In urban areas also, the largest social group consisting of artisans, servants and slaves, soldiers and petty shop keepers were poor".

Ulemas: As the majority of the population had strong belief and faith in religion in this period, the religious heads occupied a high place in social ladder. The Ulema or Muslim theologian naturally wanted the sovereign to follow Islamic code in the administrative measures and treat the non-Muslims as ordained by Shariat. During this age, as the Mughal sovereigns believed in autocracy, they never bothered to give importance to the position of Ulemas. The Mughal rulers' attitude towards religion varied according to the personal perception of the sovereigns. As such Ulemas did have high place in the minds of the ordinary folk but their role in state appears to be minimal.

Nobility: Satish Chandra is of the view that socially and economically, the Mughal nobility formed a privileged group of the ruling class. Though, theoretically the doors of nobility were open to anyone and everyone, in practice only persons of aristocratic birth, Indians or foreigners were given preference. The majority of the Mughal nobles were recruited from the homeland of the Mughals in the beginning and in due course, even the Afghans who were opposed to the Mughals were also recruited along with the Indian Muslims and the Hindus from the time of Akbar. The largest groups among the Hindus in the service of the Mughals were the Rajputs and even among the Rajputs Kachwahas were in predominant strength. The Rajputs who were recruited as nobles were either hereditary 'rajas' or belonged to the aristocrat families related to the rajas. This does not mean that, the entire nobility consisted of aristocratic families or rajas. It included the commoners in good number also. The nobility received considerable stability under Jehangir and Shahjahan. The Mansabdars, Jagirdars and Zamindars constitute the nobility or the ruling class. Thus, the nobility of the Mughal age was the creation of the sovereign and as such they were the main source of strength to the ruler. At the time of initiation into nobility, the newly recruited Khan has to take an oath of loyalty to the sovereign. In spite of their usefulness as loyal and obedient in the service of the ruler, there is a view that the prevalence of the hereditary privileges among the large section of the nobility hampered the growth of absolutism in the Mughal Empire. We also notice a number of examples where the nobles were dismissed, executed, punished, fired and banished. The Mughal state was beneficiary of the nobility to a certain extent but the rapid growth of the numbers of nobility in the 17th century, the resultant tensions among different groups and individual nobles led to a serious crisis of the functioning of the institution of nobility, which killed the vitality of the Mughal state. Satish Chandra is of the view, "The nobility of the Mughals, although it suffered from a number of internal weaknesses was on a broad view, a remarkable institution which wielded into a homogenous and harmonious whole. They were men belonging to different regions and tribes, speaking different languages and professing different religions and with different cultural traditions but the Mughals succeeded in inducing the nobles with a sense of common purpose and loyalty to the reigning dynasty and in imparting to them a distinctive cultural outlook, and in creating traditions of high efficiency and endeavour in administration. It was thus, a definite factor in securing for a century and half a remarkable degree of unity and good government in the country".

The Zamindars: The term Zamindars is derived from two Persian words; Zamin or land and *Dar* or holder. We come across Zamindars in every part of the region ruled by the Mughal sovereigns. They played a significant role in the agrarian structure as intermediaries of the Mughal age. Nurul Hassan divided them into three categories of primary, secondary and autonomous chiefs. The primary Zamindars are those who had proprietary rights over the land. The secondary Zamindars are those who held the intermediary rights and helped the state in collecting land revenue. The autonomous chiefs are those Zamindars who exercised autonomous rights in their territories and paid a fixed amount to the Mughal state. Thus, the Zamindars besides their principal fiscal claim also collected number of petty perquisites from the peasantry. The Zamindars also had their own militia to help them in proper collection of revenue and subjugation of the peasants. The Zamindars lived a luxurious life in forts. Abul Fazal in his *Ain-i-Akbari* records that the total strength of military force of the Zamindars was forty-four lakhs.

Peasantry: Peasantry constitutes the major chunk of the population. The peasantry was directly involved in the agricultural operations and as such it was the primary agricultural group in the society. The peasantry was not a homogenous entity as it consisted of different strata based on economic and social status. The tax collected from the peasantry constitutes the major source of income that sustained the state apparatus of the Mughals. We are already aware that the peasants had to part with a large part of the produce or the income of the produce as cash to the state as land tax. It is now agreed upon that the peasant had certain rights over the land he cultivated, except the right of free alienation of the land. The peasant was not disturbed as long as he paid the tax to the state exchequer through the intermediary appointed for that purpose. Big peasants with large resources acted as heads of villages (Maqaddam or Patel) and enjoyed a larger share in the produce of other peasants. Rich peasants are referred to as Khud kasht or self cultivated and the poor peasants as 'riza riaya' or small peasants. In each region these peasants both small and big were referred by different names. Below the category of the peasants, there existed innumerable number of menial workers or agricultural labourers and the contemporary literature described them as Chamars, Belaharas, Thoris and Dhanuks, etc. It can be justifiably suggested that this group was exploited by the peasants, Zamindars and the state. We come across various references to the migration of these labourers as well as small peasants to free themselves from exploitation.

Artisans: The Mughal age in India witnessed high level of craft production. Resultantly, we come across artisans engaged in non-agricultural production, particularly of textile, silk, wool, indigo sugar, and oil which come under the category of agro-based products; minerals, mining and metals, wood-based crafts and miscellaneous crafts like stone cutting, paper and pottery. There existed different forms of production from independent artisan level to the 'karkhanas' supported and run by the state. Further, the organization of production varied in different crafts and industries as per the needs and requirements of the craft. The artisans living in rural areas of villages produced articles of daily use for the residents of the villages. The most important artisans of the village were blacksmiths, carpenters, potters and shoemakers. They manufactured the basic tools like agricultural implements to satisfy the needs of the villagers for their sustenance. Further, the growth of long distance trade increased the number of artisans and their prosperity. Besides the villages craftsmen dependent on Jajmani system, there came into existence a number of independent craftsmen engaged in production for trade, either long distance or medium distance. We also notice a marked change from subsistence-oriented economy to money economy. Tapan Roy Choudari rightly observes, "By the 17th century, if not much earlier, exchange had made significant inroads into the subsistence-oriented system of manufacture by collectively maintained artisans. Payments in cash and kind for additional work, or entirely on a piece work basis, coexisted with the more widespread practice of allocating fixed shares of the rural produce or land to the artisan families". Another change to be noticed is the marked mobility of the rural artisan to urban markets with the increase in demand for their finished goods. Production for the market had become a common practice by the independent artisan and there emerged specialist craftsmen in all crafts. Interestingly a Dutch traveller, Pelesaert, who visited India in 1623, refers to a hundred specialized categories of artisans working in different crafts. A significant feature of these times was the localization of manufacture. In the area of textile manufacturing, we notice the highest level of specialization. Another feature of significance was the impact of merchant capital on profitable crafts like textile weaving. We come to know that one Kasi Veeranna, the biggest merchant who had under his control all the ports from Madras to Armagoan except Pulicat. The weaver settlements of this region were known as the "Veeranna villages". We do not have any reference to artisan guilds during this period like those of early and medieval periods. Besides independent artisans manufacturing goods for long and medium distance trade, 'karkhanas' maintained by the royalty and the nobility produced specialized goods for the consumption and use of the affluent social groups. These karkhanas enabled specialist artisans to cater to the requirements of the royal and the noble households. We notice that the process of production underwent a marked change in the Mughal age. Tapan Roy Choudari aptly remarks "The organization of manufacture in Mughal India did not remain unchanged. A lot was happening, but on a limited scale and the sum total of new developments did not amount to a break with the past. Continuity was the dominant characteristic. Yet the changes in organization were more basic than those in techniques".

Slaves: The institution of slavery was in vogue in the Mughal period as in that of the Delhi Sultanate. Bengal was known for slave markets. During this period, a feature to be noticed is the lack of opportunities for the slaves to improve their position and status. Though numerous domestic and personal slaves were employed by the royalty and the nobility, free employees appear to have outnumbered the slaves. As in the past, in this age too, the slaves served the emperor as harem guards. We do not have evidence for slaves in the service of military guards of any emperor during this age. Often slaves served as maid servants in the harem of the royalty as well as nobility. Domestic slavery appears to be limited to the Mughal royal household and nobility. Slave eunuches also played a crucial role in the affairs of royal kith and kin and nobles. These slaves acted as guards, servants and often as business agents for high-born women in the harem. There appears to have developed discrete sexual relationship between the master and women slaves and men slaves and women of harem.

Position of Women: In the Mughal age, the position of the women was not very different from that of the previous ages. Women had a second rate place. It is because the society was feudal and hierarchically arranged social order was in vogue. Though women are said to be the queens of the house, only the voice of the head of the family prevailed in many cases. In the Hindu community 'sati sahagamana' practice, child marriage and child sacrifices were very common. In Muslim community there existed the practice of polygamy and divorce by uttering Talaq thrice as per Shariat. Women of the stature of Nurjahan rarely existed. J.F Richards is of the view that the wives, concubines and female relatives of the master were ranked by seniority, blood ties and favour in a strictly prescribed hierarchy. The Muslim rulers and nobles maintained their harems with a number of wives and concubines and the prevailing view appears to treat women as object of pleasure. We may conclude by suggesting that the Mughal India was feudalistic and pluralistic in nature in the sphere of social relations.

Economic Conditions

The Mughal state took conscious interest in the promotion of agriculture, trade and commerce along with technological innovations as the prosperity of the state depended entirely on the taxes collected and deposited in treasury by bureaucracy. We have very meagre information of the economic conditions of India under Babur and Humayun, though Babur's Memoirs and *Humayun Nama* have references to the economic situation. We have ample evidence provided by *Ain-i-Akbari* and other documents of the period as well as of the European travellers' accounts to have a good knowledge of the economy of the Mughal state till the end of the great Mughals and the lesser Mughals. The view held by V.A. Smith and Moreland was that ordinary labourer was happier in those days than today. *Ain-i-Akbari* gives a list of the cost of food stuff like rice, wheat, barley, vegetables, sugar, and sheep and cow. The cost was cheap and the wages too were meagre but as their availability was much in vogue, people could purchase and be satisfied.

Agriculture

Agriculture was the main occupation of the vast majority of the population of India. Throughout the ages, agriculture was the main productive activity as the soil was fertile in most parts of India and people were known for their hard working nature and knowledge of agricultural operations. *Ain-i-Akbari* of AD 1595 and *Chahar Gulshan* of 1739–40 provide with figures of measured and unmeasured land under cultivation in all villages. Historians are of the view that the cultivated area doubled between the end of the 16th century and the beginning of the 20th century due to the factors of clearance of forests in Bihar, Awadh and parts of Bengal and by the spread of canal network in the Punjab and Sindh. As India was a vast country with different ecological set-up, fertility and nature of the soil also varied. So, the means and methods of cultivation varied from region to region. Generally, the plough was of wood and iron plough-share. The plough happens either to be of light weight or heavy weight depending on the nature of the soil. Generally, tillage was carried on by harnessing a pair of oxen to the plough. The peasant increased the fertility of the soil by using the droppings of the goat and the sheep. They knew the practice of rotation of crops. Sowing of the seeds was done by hand. The crop was cut by the use of a semicircular sickle. Agriculture in India was mostly dependent on monsoon. Besides rain water, the peasants depended on wells, lakes, tanks and reservoirs and canals for irrigation purposes. India produced a large variety of agricultural products. Rice and wheat were the two major food crops throughout the country. Barley was grown extensively in the central plains. Jowar and Bajra were also grown extensively. Maize was grown in Rajasthan and Maharashtra in large tracts. Pulses like gram, Jowar, moong, moth, urd and khesari were also in great use. Besides food crops, cash crops called in Persian records as Jimsi Kamil or Nimsi Ala or superior grade crops like sugar-cane, cotton, indigo and opium were also cultivated in large scale to supply to the markets. Cultivation of tobacco also began in India during the 16th century and it was introduced into India by the Portuguese. The cultivation of coffee was known from the 17th century. The beverage tea does not figure in the records of this period; oil was extracted from rapeseed, castor, and linseed which were grown extensively. The cultivation of other oil seeds was relatively less. Sericulture was undertaken in the provinces of Bengal, Assam, Kashmir and Western Coast. Horticulture was patronized by the rulers as well as nobles. Pineapple was brought to India by the Portuguese from Latin America. Papaya, cashewnuts, Leechi and Guava were known to them. Potato and tomato were introduced in the 17th century and thereafter. Cattle played a significant role in agricultural operations and production. The contemporary European travellers refer to a large number of cattle in Indian fields. Butter or ghee was consumed daily even by ordinary people as a part of the regular diet. Oxen were used for transporting goods as pack animals or for bullock carts. It is no exaggeration to suggest that there was abundance of agricultural products which enabled even the common people to fill their belly satisfactorily. Besides agricultural production, non-agricultural production of textiles, indigo, sugar, oil and various crafts received new heights. Abul Fazl provides a list of important centres of production of cotton textiles like Gujarat, Rajasthan, UP, Bengal, Bihar and Orissa, Masulipatnam and the Coromandal Coast. According to

Hameeda Naqui, forty-nine varieties of clothes were produced in five major production centres of the Mughal Empire. The European accounts mention more than one hundred varieties. Woodcraft and metal craft also received patronage from the royalty, nobility and the commoners. We can justifiably say that the salt produced in India at that time was sufficient to meet the needs of the domestic sector and saltpetre was exported on a large scale. More than substantial quantity of iron and steel was produced and the shipbuilding industry was highly developed. Royal Karkhanas produced luxury items needed by the royalty and the nobility. The Mughal age witnessed a change in the process of production of non-agricultural goods. In this age, thus, we notice abundance of commodity production in different regions of the country. As the volume of production was very much higher than the local demand and consumption, the surplus of production was turned to trade and commerce. The relative political stability and increased surplus production gave a fillip to trading activities. During this age, the volume of trade increased manifold. The entry of foreigners too increased both the inland and foreign trade.

Trade and Commerce

Inland trade is organized at local, regional and inter-regional levels. At the local level or village, much of the surplus was sold to banjaras or traditional grain merchants. Tavernier, a contemporary French traveller records that every village sold the surplus goods and to enable the merchants to carry on trade and each village had a Saraf or moneychanger. There existed periodic markets besides local markets. Banarsidas states that in the middle of the 17th century, Jaunpur had 52 paraganas, markets and wholesale markets or mandis each. We can postulate that there existed a network of small and big markets which were linked to bigger commercial centres in a region. Ahmedabad, Surat, Dhaka, Agra, Delhi, Lahore, Multan, Ajmer, Thatta, Burhanpur, Masulipatnam, Bijapur, Hyderabad, Calicut and Cochin were big trading centres of all commodities. There were special markets located at Delhi, Agra, Dhaka and Lahore for specific commodities. Owing to the growth of trade, a new class of sarfs and brokers emerged in these cities besides merchants. Burhanpur and Ahmedabad were famous for cotton 'mandis', Cambay was famous for gems, and Surat was famous for indigo market. Among the inter-regional centres, in the east Hugli, in the west Surat and Ahmedabad, in the north Agra and in the south coastal areas Masulipatnam and Malbar regions were very important markets. This inter-regional trade was carried out by coast to save time. The trade through eastern and western coasts was prominent. Piracy was rampant in the west coast. During the Mughal period too, India had a flourishing trade with a large number of foreign countries. The arrival of European traders increased foreign trade manifold. In those days, imports were very little and there were export of considerable Indian goods like textiles, indigo, spices and saltpetre. In the category of textiles, the main varieties of cotton fabrics were Baftas, Samanis, calico, Khairabadi and Dariabadi, Aruberty, and Qaimkhani and muslin were exported. Chintz or printed cotton textiles were the most favoured export. Carpets from Gujarat, Jaunpur and Bengal were also bought. Among exports, silk cloth from Gujarat and Bengal occupies a prominent place. Saltpetre was exported by the Dutch from the Coromondal coast in the 17th century. Later the English also joined in this export business of saltpetre. The export of indigo was started by the Portuguese in the last quarter of the 16th century and the Dutch and English joined the race in exporting indigo in the 17th century. The other items of export were opium, ginger, and turmeric. Among imports, silver was the main item followed by copper, lead and mercury. Silk and porcelain were imported from China. Quality wine, carpets and perfumes were imported from Persia. The state purchased horses of central Asia for military purposes. Musk was bought from Nepal and Bhutan. Boray was imported from Tibet and Nepal and in turn iron and food grains were supplied to these neighbouring hilly regions. This type of trade and commerce could take place because of the network of routes and a developed transport system.

The Mughal state created an elaborate network of trade routes linking all the commercial centres of the empire by the beginning of the 17th century. All the important routes had 'sarais' at short intervals to enable the travellers to take rest and then to proceed further. The important land trade routes were: (1) Agra-Delhi-Kabul; (2) Agra-Burhanpur-Surat; (3) Surat-Ahmedabad-Agra; and (4) Agra-Patna-Bengal. Quite interestingly, the river route from Bengal ran almost parallel to the land route. Coming to the routes to foreign trade, indigenous and foreign merchants used both the overland and overseas routes. Oxen played a major role in land transport. On high mountains, besides human labour, mules and hill ponies were used to carry heavy loads. Many rivers provided a network of river routes. Contemporary records testify to the fact of hundreds of boats plying between Agra and Bengal.

The Mughal state made it a policy to promote trading activities by removing hurdles of vexatious duties and taxes imposed on merchants. We come across a number of royal decrees abolishing taxes and customs on certain items. Almost all the European trading companies obtained royal orders for carrying merchandise without paying transit duties. While the state showed liberal attitude towards merchants who carried on trade, the officials at various levels looked for an opportunity to fleece the merchants. Sometimes, the nobles and officials also indulged in trading activity as it was not legally banned. As a result, we notice coercion of those in power over the other merchants. We come across a number of petitions and requests by foreign companies, merchants and individuals complaining against the high-handed attitude of the bureaucracy. In spite of the above hurdles, trade began to grow, attracting merchants from many countries. In consequence to the growth of trade and commerce, besides merchant community operating in different parts of India with different names there were specialized groups of brokers, 'sarafs' and moneylenders. During this period the system of bills of exchange and moneylending was highly developed. The interest rates were generally quite high. Rules and regulations for trading and commercial activities were made by well-organized merchant guilds. During the Mughal period, the Portuguese, the Dutch, the English and the French merchant companies established their trading centres and by the time the Mughal rule was at its end, the British East India Company emerged victorious and cultivated designs to establish a political power structure in India.

Technological Developments

The Mughal age did not witness any breathtaking discoveries in the fields of different branches of science. One of the renowned scientists of Akbar's time was Mir Fatullah Shirazi and he is credited with the invention of mechanical devices and the introduction of a true solar calendar (*Illahi*) exposed to the European learning; the impact of the European learning did not penetrate into the areas of Indian sciences. In the sphere of agricultural technology we do not notice any radical change with regard to the tools of agricultural operations like the plough, ploughshare and sickle, but as one significant development to be recorded is the introduction of some new crops, plants and fruits, which have been already referred to in this chapter in the section on agriculture. P.K. Gode is of the view that grafting became a common practice in India after AD 1550. As a result, new varieties of mango, Alfanso, Our Lady and Joani Perriera developed in India. Of all the Mughal emperors, Shahjahan appears to have built two canals – Nahr Faiz and Shah Nahr. During his period, in the sphere of textile technology, carpet weaving and production of silk and silk fabrics became popular. In 1770s, the Italian silk filatures were introduced into India. In the sphere of military technology, the fire arms – guns, canons, matchlocks, handguns and pistols were used commonly. In boat or ship manufacturing, Indians started the use of iron nails and clamps in the 16th century. In the beginning of the 16th century, Varthema records the use of iron nails in Indian ships at Calicut. The Mughal paintings and the works of art prove the use of iron nails. In ship building activity, iron anchors were begun to be used from the 17th century. From the second half of the 17th century, the use of chain pumps to draw the water from the ship became common. We notice the European or the British impact on metallurgy, glass technology and printing press. Time reckoning devices like sand-glass were in use. Babur Namah and Abul Fazl's works refer to such time-reckoning device. Two new discoveries of chemical sector – preparation of rose scent and the use of saltpetre for water cooling deserves to be credited to the Mughal period. Indian response to the exposure of European science does not appear to be uniformly the same and we appear to have gained less from the European exposure.

Policy of Religion

A unique feature of Indian society since ages is the prevalence of multiple religious faiths and rituals and the absence of a single religion dominating the behavioural pattern of the people of India as a whole. As a result of the multiplicity, we notice the emergence of a composite cultural ethos. By the time the Mughal power structure emerged in the 16th century, the religious scenario of India was reflected in the religious faiths, beliefs and practices, followed by the Hindus, Muslims, Christians, Buddhists and Jains. All these religious denominations have been living side by side being mutually influenced in varying degrees by one another. The most accepted principle was 'God is one'. No doubt, there were those who were intensely devoted to their particular faith and practices, there were those who disbelieved the existence of God, and there were those who were skeptical about the existence of God. Most of the people were those who peacefully lived and offered their personal prayers to their personal God of their choice and who viewed religion as purely belonging to personal domain rather than public domain of concern. Only the religious preachers who belonged to a minuscule minority exercise some influence in their denominations. By the time the Mughal rule started, the Indian society was in the state of fusion of different cultural strands of Hinduism and Islam through the concept of Bhakti ideology and Sufism advocated by Sufis. Suspicion and hatred towards the other faith was not very deep as reflected in the emergence of Hindusthani cultural ethos. In this backdrop of attempts of peaceful fusion, an attempt should be made to understand and appreciate the religious attitude or policy of the Mughals in general and in particular of Akbar, the so-called tolerant and liberal, and Aurangzeb, the so-called staunch believer of the Sunni faith of Islam, who was credited to have tried to convert India into a land of Islam from that of infidels. Before we take up the actual religious policy of Akbar and Aurangzeb, we have to remember that there was a perception that as the rulers were of Islamic faith, the state religion was Islam. On the basis of this perception, we know that medieval India is perceived as Islamic India and the time as Muslim period. A critical examination of the contemporary scenario disapproves this perception as an erroneous one and no ruler at any time equated personal faith with state religion and decided the state policy and administration under religious consideration. What each ruler did was only to extend his patronage to the extent that was not harmful to his tenure as a ruler and never to discriminate on religious consideration.

It should not be forgotten that during this period most of the people had a firm faith in their religion, and the rulers sometimes used religions for their personal and political ends and the religious preachers like Ulemas and Pithadhipats were held in high esteem. Yet, what is to be remembered is that religious consideration was not the only criteria that decided the policy of a ruler towards non-believers either Hindus or Muslims but the other factors like economic or political, made the rulers to adopt a different attitude towards the recalcitrant ones irrespective of the same religious denomination. What we have to ultimately remember is that religion of the ruler and the ruled was not the sole criteria in deciding the religious policy, but other factors influenced the religious policy or attitude of the ruler concerned, to a great extent.

Babur, the founder of the Mughal lineage in India and his son, Humayun were by faith Sunnis of Islam and most of their time was spent in wars in their attempts to consolidate their rule. Nothing is known about their religious attitude except that Babur married a Shia princess and Humayun also married a Shia princess and in distress Humayun sought asylum in the Rajput court. This clearly indicates them to be tolerant of other sects, if not of liberal disposition. Akbar ascended the Mughal throne in very precarious conditions in 1556 and ruled till 1605. The early bringing up and tutor Abdul Latif and his friends Faizi and Abul Fazl appear to have exercised great influence on the development of the personality of Akbar. Akbar is said to be a firm advocate of *sulh-l-kul* or peace for all. Akbar was a devout Muslim of Sunni sect. As he had a great desire of establishing an empire of long duration in India, he did not give much importance to the observation of the Islamic way of rule but throughout his life, he remained to be a seeker of truth in all religions which ultimately reflected in his spiritual quest and political segacity which made him to be considered as the first national monarch of India in its long history.

The measures taken by Akbar between 1560–65 – his matrimonial relations with Rajputs, abolition of the Pilgrims tax, abolition of *Jiziya* and non-imposition of force to convert Hindus into Islam, providing space for Hindus in bureaucratic set-up, establishment of translation department to reduce the distance between the Hindus and the Muslims and provision of liberty of worship made Akbar to be considered as one of a different mould. But the works like Gulzar-i-Abrar and Nafais-ul-Massir testify to his respect towards the Ulemas and their patronage by him. Now, the current opinion is that these measures motivated political concessions given to non-Muslims to win their support and it is also suggested that Akbar was influenced to take this decision by the lack of dependable Muslim support. After 1565, we notice a change in the attitude of Akbar towards his liberal outlook. We have a documentary proof of the reimposition of Jiziya tax in the year 1566, in the vicinity of Agra. There is another Fatahnama of Chittor, which states that he declared a war against the Rajputs as Jihad and took pride in destroying temples and in killing of the Kaffirs. Badauni states that in 1575, Akbar ordered the reimposition of Jiziya which did not work. What we notice during this period 1566–1579 was that most of the Rajput chieftains became collaborators of Akbar, in spite of the change in his religious outlook.

Another development that deserves our attention was the establishment of Ibadat Khana in 1575 at Fatehpur Sikri and this indicates an advanced step in the evolution of his religious policy. The original aim of the establishment of Ibadat Khana was to have free discussion on different aspects of Islamic theology. In the beginning, it was opened to Sunnis only but from 1578, the gates of Ibadat Khana were opened to Sufis, Shias, Brahmins, Jains, Christians, Jews and Parsis. This decision was taken by Akbar after the disillusionment with the quarrels of the Muslim theologians. The discussions made Akbar realize that the essence of faith was internal conviction based on reason. In 1579, Akbar proclaimed the 'Infallibility Decree' by which he became the Mujtahid and declared himself as Imam Adil. This declaration had given him the right to interpret legal aspects of Shariat and there is a view that Akbar became the king and the Pope by this declaration. This declaration of Mahzar was opposed by the orthodox Muslim community with a belief that he rejected Islam and its tenets. By this measure, Akbar successfully curbed the predominance of the orthodox elements of Islam. The next significant development in the religious views of Akbar was the promulgation of the *Din-i-Ilahi* or *Tauhid-i-Ilahi*. A lot of debate took place about the reasons why Akbar founded Din-i-Ilahi and what were the motives behind his decision. V.A. Smith, Iswari Prasad, S.R. Sharma and R.P. Tripathi and some of the learned scholars expressed different opinions about Akbar's decision to establish the Din-i-Ilahi. V.A. Smith is of the view that "it was the outcome of his ridiculous vanity, a monstrous growth of unrestrained autocracy". Iswari Prasad holds the view that "it was an eclectic pantheism containing the good points of all religions". S.R. Sharma is of the view that "it was the crowning expression of the idealism of Akbar". R.P. Tripathi observes "Shrewd as Akbar was, he must have felt that it was neither possible to melt all religions down into one, nor to launch a new religion which would have added one more to others. But he felt himself called upon to propagate his ideas among those who cared to listen to them. The sect had no scared book or scripture, no priestly hierarchy, no sacred place of worship and no rituals or ceremonies except that of initiation ... a member had to give a written promise of having ... accepted the four grades of entire devotion, viz., sacrifice of property, life, honour and religion ... [it] was not a religion and Akbar never intended to establish a church ... neither force nor money was employed to enlist disciples .... It was entirely a personal matter not between the emperor and the subjects, but between Akbar and those who chose to regard him as their peer guru". We may conclude that the *Din-i-Ilahi* or *Tauhid-i-Ilahi* had nothing to do with his religious or political policy except that he wanted to have a band of people around him who were willing to sacrifice their religion, honour, life and property for his sake and who were willing to be guided by him as their philosopher, friend and guide. Finally, it may be said that Akbar never showed discrimination on religious ground to any group but did not hesitate to suppress individuals who opposed his way.

Akbar's son and successor Jahangir on the whole made no deviation from the liberal policy of Akbar, Jahangir suspected the hand of Jains and Sikhs in the revolt of Prince Khussru and took action against Guru Arjun by ordering his execution and also drove the Jains from his kingdom. These actions were not the result of his religious persuasion but the result of intolerance of his son's revolt and suspicion. But by the time Shahjahan became the ruler, a change in the climate of tolerance and liberalism seemed to have set in. Shahjahan abolished Sifda or prostration before the emperor as it was a practice to be shown in the presence of almighty only. We come to know from Amal Sahib that 76 temples in the region of Benaras were demolished by the order of the emperor. But for this Shahjahan did not reverse the tolerant policy introduced by Akbar. The reign of Aurangzeb, the last of the great Mughals was considered to be the most intolerant and fanatical period of the Mughal age. In personal life, Aurangzeb was very simple, pious, and puritanical and led a very austere life. But his desire to convert India into Dar-ul-Islam and to treat non-Muslims according to the injunctions of Qaran and Shariat made scholars hold conflicting opinions. Jadunath Sarkar, S.R. Sharma and A.L. Srivastava condemn Aurangzeb for his religious bigotry and persecution. Shibhi Nomani, Zahiruddin Faruki and Ishtiaq Hussain Qureshi considered most of his actions political expedients. Satish Chandra and N. Aktar Ali tried to analyse his actions from the perspective of neutrality without subscribing to the perception of 'for and against policy' followed by other historians. All the actions or ordinances of Aurangzeb can be divided into minor inconsequential orders and major policy initiatives of the state. The forbidding of the Kalima being stamped on coins, abolition of the celebration of Nauroz, repairing of old mosques and appointment of Imans and Muezzins on regular basis, appointment of censors of morals or Muhtasib, stopping of Tuladana ceremony, banning of Holi and Diwali celebrations, and discontinuing the practice of 'zaroka darshan' after the 11th year of his reign and forbidding musicians from his court are the measures that made him to be regarded as intolerant and anti-Hindu. All these measures cannot be considered as anti-Hindu except forbidding the celebration of Holi and Diwali. The orders for the demolition of the newly constructed temples of Hindus in the Benaras region and not allowing the old temples to be repaired are definitely indicators of the anti-Hindu policy of Aurangzeb. As a consequence of this order, the temples of Viswanath at Benaras and the Keshav Rai temple of Mathura were put into disuse. Mathura was renamed as Islamabad. Another anti-Hindu measure was the imposition of Jiziya in 1679. While J.N. Sarkar considers this as anti-Hindu measure of bigotry, Satish Chandra points out that through this Aurangzeb desired to win the confidence of Muslims to save himself from the crisis of the Deccan problem. He also imposed economic restrictions on the Hindus in the case of purchases. Aurangzeb's personality appears to be enigmatic and the same Aurangzeb who ordered for the demolition of temples issued grants for the maintenance of temples and priests. Interestingly, Aurangzeb did not reduce the number of Hindu Mansabdars and retained many Hindus in high posts and two were appointed as governors. In the end, we can conclude that there was no constant and definite religious policy pursued by of the Mughlai state and it varied depending on the personal perceptions of the rulers.

Revivalist Movements and Composite Cultures

By the time the Mughal rule was established in India, the religious milieu of India was deeply influenced by the growth of Bhakti propagated by saints in different areas and by the Sufi Pirs in different parts of India. There was an earnest attempt for the fusion of two cultures resulting in a composite culture along with revivalism of the old Hindu faith to suit the needs of the time. Sikhism was founded by Guru Nanak in the 15th century. Guru Nanak preached the unity of God and laid emphasis on having a real and true guru and asked his followers to put into practice the principles of 'sach' or truth, 'halal' or lawful earnings, 'khair' or wishing well of others, 'niyat' or right intention and service of the lord. He denounced caste system and its inequality. He advocated universal brotherhood of men and equality of men and women. Sikhism gave importance to 'guru parampara' and we have 10 gurus who shaped Sikhism from that of peaceful sect to a militant one.

Dadu is another great saint inspired by the philosophy of Kabir. He lived in the second half of the 16th century and died in the first few years of the 17th century (1544–1603). His *Banifa* collection of hymns and poems regard Allah, Ram and Govind as his spiritual gurus. Dadu Panthis were the followers of Dadu. Dadu Panthis were also non-conformists and by the 18th century, after the decline of the Mughal rule, they became professional fighters. Gyaneshwara was the founder of the Maratha Vaishnavism and it was founded in the 13th century. Saints Tukaram, Namdev and Ramdass were famous in Maratha Vaishnavism in the 16th and 17th centuries. Tukaram and Ramdass, who exercised considerable influence on Shivaji in the 17th century are very much responsible for the growth of Maratha nationalism by preaching equality of all by denouncing caste system. This movement also led to the growth of Maratha vernacular literature as a literary language. Mahadeva Govinda Renade appropriately suggests that this movement led to the upliftment of the self-respect of the lower castes. Gaudiya Vaishnavism or Vaishnavism of Bengal also had a deep impact on the psyche of the Bengalees in particular, and on the social, religious and cultural life of the people of Assam, Bengal and Orissa. Chaitanya stands as a colossus among Gaudiya Vaishnava saints. By his preachings, desperate social classes belonging to subaltern groups joined this movement and enriched the consciousness of oneness.

By the 13th century, Sufis in India were divided into 14 orders or Silsilas. Of the 14 silsilas, the Chisti silsilah had become a predominant one. Shaik Abdul Qudders Gangoli, who died in 1537, was a great exponent of the unity in one being (Wahdat-ul-wizhad), which became very popular among the masses as well as the intelligent. Prince Dara Shukhoh was a great devotee of Miyan Mir, a Sufi saint of the Qadri order. After his death, Dara became the disciple of Mulla Shaik Badakhashi. During Akbar's reign, the influence of Chisti order rose to prominence. The Naqshbandi order was introduced into India by Khwaja Baqi Billah, who lived between 1563 and 1603. Shah Wallaullah, who lived between 1702 and 1762, was a noted scholar and a saint of the Naqsbandi order. He tried to reconcile the two doctrines of *Wahdat-ul-muj*ad and *Wahadat-ul-Shuhud* (apparentism). Khwaja Mir Dard, a famous Urdu poet, was another mystic of the Naqsbandi order and contemporary of Shah Wallullah. We also notice the Mahdavi movement that believed in the advent of a deliverer to save the mankind from the bondage of life of this world. Syed Mohammed of Jaunpur was the only Mahdair who did not crave for political power but was mainly interested in spiritualism and purifying Islam. In the background of anti-Islamic risings in India after the death cf Aurangzeb by the Sikhs, the Marathas and the Islamic revivalist movement was started by Shah Walliullah, who lived between 1703 and 1762. His religious and political thought influenced a group of religious reformers called Mujahiddins or holy warriors. They exercised good influence on the later developments of the Indian Muslim thought like development revivalism, the modernism of Sayyad Ahmad Khan and in the Aligarh movement, the nationalist theology of Deoband School and the neo-traditional *Ahihadith* or followers of Muhammad's traditions.

In the backdrop of the religious milieu of India as found expression in the individual policies of the Mughal rulers and the rise of the Bhakti School of devotion as represented by Sikhism, Maratha and Gaudiya, Vaishnavism and the growth of Sufi silsilas of Chisti, Qadri and Naskbandi and the revivalist movements, there arose a composite Hindustani culture which was yet to take deep roots on the basis of the concept of peaceful coexistence. In the contemporary times, when Europe was embroiled in crusades, the suppression of the liberal Islamic kingdom of Spain and the inquisition, India witnessed comparatively an era of inter-faith harmony and inter-religious comradery. The emergence of the Sufi Rishi culture in medieval Kashmir, testifies this. Ibrahim Khan a Pathan warrior of Uttar Pradesh becoming a lifelong devotee of Krishna and the author of famous *Premvatika* or the forest of love, Ibarhim Adil Shah of Bijapur commencing his work *Kitab-i-Nauras* with an invocation to goddess Saraswathi and Muhammad Quli Qutub Shah of Golkonda, Wali Deccani and many poets and writers of the Deccan also bear testimony to the above view. Dusan peak shows that in medieval Maharashtra a Muslim saint Chand Bodhale took the form of a Hindu god Dattatreya, and was the guru of Janardhan, himself the guru of Ekanath and concludes that in the sacred sphere of the divine game, Hindu can become Muslim or the other way round, which appears to be unbelievable to the ordinary souls and the believers of the present day.

A Study of Art, Architecture, Literature, Education and Fine Art (1526–1761)

The two centuries of the Mughal rule in India from AD 1526 to 1761 make an important watershed in the evolution of the Indian culture as they promoted and patronized literacy and arts. The Mughals were responsible for the creation of a rich legacy in the shape of literary masterpieces in Arabic, Persian and Urdu, wonderful specimens of architectural marvels in monuments, paintings and miniature paintings of astonishing colour combinations and vast gardens and lakes of their times exhibit their taste for the beauty of nature. All the above factors made the Mughal rule in India a memorable one, to be remembered for its creative intellectual activity. Satish Chandra is of the view that the Mughal age witnessed many-sided cultural activity leading to the emergence of a national culture. He further points out, that the Mughal period can be called a second classical age comparable to the Gupta age of the early period. In this culture we notice a synthesis of Turko-Iranian and Bharatiya cultures.

Literary Activity

The languages that received patronage of the Mughals were Arabic and Persian. Mostly, Arabic language was employed to compose philosophical treatises relating to religious and spiritual matters. Very few works of poetry in Arabic were also available. Persian was the official language of the court. Babur, the founder of the Mughal rule, was an accomplished poet in Turkish language and penned his memories in Turki. His *Baburnama* was translated into Persian by Abdul Rahim Khan-i-Khanan. Babur is also known to have written a didactic work *Mathnavi Mubin*. Babur and Humayun encouraged many Persian poets to come to India. A new Indian style of Persian literature known as Sabaq Hindi developed like the Indian English of the modern times. Notable among the poets were: Faizi, Urfi, Naziri, Talib Amali, Kalim, Ghani Kashmiri, Saib and Bedil developed the above said Sabaq Hindi style, which was patronized by the emperors from Akbar to Shahjahan. Some of the rulers and the princes were themselves poets in the Persian language. Akbar and Shahjahan patronized a number of poets in their courts. While Abdul Rahim Khan-i-Khanan, a great poet lived in the court of Akbar, the greatest poet of this age in Persian was Mirja Muhammed Ali Saib of Tabriz. He is credited to be a creator of a new style in Persian poetry. In the Deccan, Adil Shahi rulers of Bijapur patronized Persian poets and of them the best known were Malik Qummi and Mulla Zohuri. The Qutub Shahis of Golkonda also were well-known patrons of Persian scholarship and literature. *Burhan Qati* was a Persian dictionary compiled by Muhammad Hussain Tabrezi. During the Mughal rule, classical Indian texts were translated into Persian. During Akbar's period, *Singhasan Batisi, Ramayana* and *Rajatarangini* of Kalhana were translated. Besides Persian, Urdu, Punjabi, Phusthi, Sindhi, Beluchi and Kashmiri languages too flourished under regional powers' patronage. Even Sanskrit was patronized by the Mughals, in particular by Dara Shuhkoh and in the contemporary Vijayanagara court. After the debacle of Banihatti battle, the tradition of patronizing Sanskrit literature was continued by the Aravidu lineage of Vijayanagara, the Nayaks of Tanjore and the chiefs of Travancore and Cochin. Mahakavyas, Sreshta kavyas, Champukavyas, Natakas and historical 'kavyas' along with various genres of Sanskrit literature flourished under their patronage. Srinivasa Dikshita, author of 18 dramas and sixty kavyas; Govinda Dikshita, author of *Sahitya Sudha* and *Sangitasudhanidhi*; Appaya Dikshita, who is credited with the authorship of more than a hundred literary works; Nilakanta Dikshita, author of Mahakavya *Siva Leela* and the *Penance of Bhaghiratha;* and Chakrakavi, the author of *Janaki Parinaya* deserve to be remembered as the great Sanskrit poets of 16th through the 18th centuries. Women Sanskrit poets of this age that deserve special mention are Tirumalamba and Ramabhadramba, who wrote *Varadambikaparinaya* and *Raghunathabhyudaya* respectively. In tune with syncreticism of Hindu and Muslim cultures, while Pandith Jagannatha wrote *Jagadabh* in praise of Dara Shukoh and *Asatvilasa* in praise of Asaf Khan, Dara Shukoh himself wrote a *Prasasti* in honour of Nrisimhasaraswati of Benaras. Annambhatta wrote *Tarkasangraha* in 1625,

Vyasaraya wrote philosophical works *Bhadojjivana*, *Nyayamitra* and *Tatparyachandrika* and Vijeyandra authored *Upasamharavijaya* and *Madhavatantra makhabhushana*. As a result of the growth of vernacular literature, the output of Sanskrit literature appears to have reduced to a great extent. It is also because the Bhakti saints preached their devotional songs in their respective vernacular languages to bring home the truth and importance of Bhakti in one's own life. The most popular literary languages of northern India were Hindi, Urdu and Punjabi. Hindi language developed from the dialects of Brajbhasha, Awadhi, Rajasthani, Maithili, Bhojapuri, Malwi, etc. A mixed version of Hindi, Khadiboli became popular in the 15th and 16th centuries. Goswami Tulasi Das, the author of *Ramcharitamanas* was the most famous Hindi poet and he lived in 16th century. Tulasi Das inspired poets like Agra Das and Nabhagi Das who composed poetry on the lives of the Vaishnava saints. Urdu language developed as a dialect of the Muslims who inhabited Deccan and South India from the 14th century onwards and it was also called *Dakhani*. The major areas of Dakhani literature were Gujarat, Bijapur, Golkonda, Aurangabad and Bidar. The oldest writer of reputation of this language was the famous Sufi poet Sayyidi Banda Nawaz Geudoz Raz, the writer of *Meraj ul Ashiqi*. The Qutub Shahi rulers of Golkonda patronized Dakhani literature and among them Mahammad Quli Qutub Shah, remains unique. Ibrahim Adil Shah II, the Sultan of Bijapur was also a great patron of Dakhani literature. He himself was an author of a book on music. By 1750, Urdu language was well established in the Delhi region and declined with the conquest of Deccan by the Mughal ruler Aurangzeb.

The Punjabi language grew from Sauraseni Prakrit or Sauraseni Apabhramsa. Before Gurunanak, we have no written record of the existence of Punjabi literature. The earliest text in Punjabi was the *Adigrandh* written by Guru Arjun Dev in 1604. Besides the gurus of the Sikh 'parampara', the important Punjabi poets are Bhai Gurdas, the Hindi poet Aggara, Sultan Baha, Shah Hussain and Batha Shah. The other vernacular languages of significance are Gujarati, Marathi, Bengali, Assamese, Oriya, Tamil, Telugu, Malayalam and Kannada. In these vernacular languages, we notice a large output of kavyas by eminent poets. The major poets in Gujarati are Bhalana, Narasimha Mehta and Akho who lived in the 15th and 16th centuries. Among the Marathi poets, the great ones are Muktesvara, Tukaram, Ramdas and Varnana Pandita. In Bengali literature Chaitanya Chandramandas, Jayananda and Lochanadas deserved to be remembered. Muslim writers also enriched Bengali literature with their writings. Of such Muslim writers the first notable writer was Daulat Qazi. In Assamese, Sankardeva, Mathuradas and Gopala Chandra Durja are remembered even today. Till the 17th century, Oriya literature was under the influence of Sanskrit, and from the 17th century with *Haravali* of Rama Chandra Pattanayaka, the Oriya language developed a popular base. It was Upendra Bhanja, who ushered a new era in Oriya literature.

In Tamil literature, philosophical works, commentaries, Puranas and literary texts occupy a predominant place. Saiva sect and Vaishnava sect of Pouranika

Dharma dominate the literary texts. An exposition of Saivism and Vishnavism, *Irusamaya Vilakkam* was written by Haridas. In 1553 was written *Sivadarmottaram,* a Tamil work of significance by Marainanarbandar and he wrote *Saivasamayaneri* or the path of Siva. Kamalainanprakaras wrote a Purana on Tirumaluvadi and also another book on Saiva worship. Purana literature was enriched by Niramba Alagiya Desikar and his 'sishyas'. Desikar wrote *Setu Puranam* and the Puranas of *Tirupparangiri* and *Tiruvaiyaru*. In the 17th century, the important literary figure was Madai Tiruvengadanathar, an employee in the court of the Nayakas of Madura. He composed a long poem on Advaita Vedanta. Two important lexicons, *Niganduchudamoni* and *Kodaryram* were compiled in this period.

Telugu language was closely connected to Sanskrit, Tamil and Kannada languages. During this period, it was the Prabandha that dominated the Telugu literary scenario. Krishnadevaraya of Tuluva dynasty of Vijayanagara kingdom was the author of *Amuktamalyada* in Telugu. His court poet was Allasani Peddana. Krishnadevaraya patronized the Astadiggajas a group of eight great poets, that has been dealt with some detail in the preceding chapters. Interestingly, Quli Qutub Shah of the time of 1550–1583 also patronized Addanki Gangadhara kavi and Ponnaganti Telunguraya who dedicated their literary works *Tapatisamharanopakhyanam* and *Yayaticharitra* respectively to Quli Qutub Shah of Golkonda. In the 16th century, a book on horses was written by Manumanchi Bhatta with the title of *Hayalakshana*. After the disappearance of Vijayanagara Empire, their subordinates of Gandikota, Nellore, Siddhavatam, Gingee, Tanjore and Madurai patronized Telugu literature. Matli Ananta of Siddhavatam authored *Kakusthavijayam*. Pushapagiri Timmama translated *Niti Sataka* of Bhartruhari. The Tanjore Nayaka ruler Raghunatha Nayaka wrote a prose literary text *Valmiki Charitam*. Even during the 17th through the 18th century the contribution of the Jains to Kannada literature was really remarkable. In 1533, a prominent anthology of Kannada poets was prepared by Vadi Vidyananda of Geroppa with the little of *Kavyarasa*. Salva an important Jaina scholar wrote a number of works like *Bharata Ratnakaravarthi*, *Trilokarasa*, *Aparajita Sataka* and *Bharatesvaracharita* which deal with Jaina outlook on cosmology and philosophy. Adrisya's *Cennabasava Purana* and *Praudharayacarita* are the important literary pieces relating to the Lingayat sect. Of the Saiva literature, the most important examples are *Siddhesvarapurana* of Virakta Pantadeva and *Vivekachintamani* and *Sivayogapradipika* of Nijagunna Siva Yogi, *Bhava Chintaratna* and *Virasaivamrita* of Mallinarya Gubbi and *Sarvana Padagalu* of Servana Murthi. Vaishnava literature was also produced in this period. Purandaradasa popularized Vaishnavism through his compositions, which are very popular even today.

Malayalam which originated as dialect of Tamil in Odeyar region acquired separate independent status by the 14th century and Malayalam style of poetry began to develop from the 15th century. Rama Panikkar's, *Bharata Gatha*, *Savitri Mahatmyam*, *Brahmandapuranam* and *Bhagavatam* stand as unique examples. Cherusur Nambudiri of the 16th century is credited as the promoter and developer of modern Malayalam. *Krishnagatha* was his famous work and the other works of importance are Anju's *Tampuren Pattu* and *Eravikiittipilla Pattu*. It is believed that dance-drama literature known as *Attakatha* or Kathakali developed during the 16th century. One of the earliest Attakathas was Raman Attam. Malayalam literature was undoubtedly enriched by Attakathas or Kathakali literature. In this way Sanskrit, Persian, Urdu and different vernacular languages flourished in India during the 15th through the 17th centuries. Much information is not forthcoming about the structure and content of educational system under the Mughals. We do not come across the names of great institutions that promoted education of the majority of people. Education appears to be the prerogative of the rich and upper strata of society. The content of education was not uniform. Language teaching from childhood received good attention. Education was religion-oriented.

Art and Architecture

The Mughals left behind as legacy magnificent forts, palaces, gates, mosques, public utility buildings and baulis or water wells or tanks. Akbar was the first great Mughal who initiated the process of constructing on a large scale. Of all the forts of Akbar's time, the most famous example is the Agra fort. It was built in red sandstone and this fort had many magnificent structures. Fort building activity reached its peak with the construction of Red Fort by Shahjahan in Delhi. In 1572, Akbar began the construction of a palace-fort complex at Fatehpur Sikri or the city of victory, 36 km from Agra, atop a hill with an artificial lake. The most magnificent building or gateway at Fatehpur Sikri was Buland Darwaja or the lofty gate. It was built to celebrate the victory over Gujarat. In the reign of Jahangir, marble began to be used in the construction of buildings along with the wall decoration of floral design made of semi-precious stones. This method of decoration called 'pietra dura' became very common during the rule of Shahjahan and was used extensively in the Taj Mahal, which was called a jewel of the builders' art. Humayun's tomb at Delhi is considered to be the precursor of Taj. The double dome was an important feature of this building. The primary beauty of the Taj is the massive dome and the four slender minarets linking the platform to the main building. Mosque building also reached its zenith under Shahjahan, with the construction of Moti Masjid in Agra fort built with marble and Jama Masjid at Delhi built in red stone. While the pre-Mughal architecture was well known for its massiveness and simplicity, the Mughal architecture was known for its decoration and delicacy. In Mughal architecture we notice a fusion of Persian and Indian techniques.

The second half of the 16th century undoubtedly marks a watershed in the development of the art of painting and music in India and they reached their height of glory in the 17th century. Humayun's contribution to the evolution of painting is very significant. An important painting of the time of Humayun was the *Princes of the House of Timur*. It was done in the year 1550 on cloth, measuring approximately 1.15m square. Owing to the deep interest of Akbar, there emerged a distinctive school of painting of the Mughals. Akbar's reign has become famous with the illustration of the Hamza Nama through paintings. This project was started in 1562. In the project large numbers of artists were employed. The place where the painters worked was known as Tasveerkhana. S.P. Verma gives a list of 225 artists of the time of Akbar who worked in the Tasveerkhana. A careful scrutiny of the paintings reveals an evolution in the art of painting. In the beginning the impact of Persia is very visible but slowly it began to decline. The paintings contain the following features of symmetrical compositions – restricted movement of figures, fineness of the lines of drawing, flat depiction of architectural columns and profuse embellishment of buildings in the manner of jewels. By 1590, the painting under Akbar exhibited the following features of naturalism and rhythm and luxuriant depiction of foliage and brilliant blossoms. The Mughal painting reached its zenith during the reign of Jahangir who had an aptitude for painting. Jahangir claims that he had the capacity to discriminate the work of one from the other painter after looking into a painting drawn by more than one. Portrait painting and animal painting reached its climax under Jahangir. Of such painters, the name of Mansur stands very tall among the rest of the painters, Shahjahan too continued the traditions of painting and with the accession of Aurangzeb, patronage to painting began to decline and a number of painters left Aurangzeb's court and sought refuge in the regional head-quarters.

From the 17th century onwards, we notice the impact of European painting on Mughal painting. They borrowed some of the technique of the European painters. At the same time, a number of original European paintings were collected and preserved by Jahangir and Dara Shuhkov and several Mughal nobles. An important feature to be noticed in the Mughal paintings is their attempt to make them three dimensional. Though the European painting technique was adopted or borrowed, the Mughal painters did not prepare oil paintings and there was no work from this period that was executed in oil.

A distinct style of painting developed in the Deccan kingdoms of Ahmadnagar, Bijapur and Golconda in the 16th and 17th centuries, Rajasthani painting also deserves to be noted because by 1600 the art reached its consummation. Different Rajput kingdoms encouraged and patronized painting in the 17th and 18th centuries. The main centres of Rajasthani painting are: (a) Mewar School, (b) Bundi School and (c) Kishangarh School. The Rajasthani paintings contain pictures on hunting scenes, portraits and musical seasons. Nature was focused in their paintings because in their paintings we notice a variety of tree forms, dense foliage, singing birds and frolicking animals, rivers full of lotus blossoms and drops of rain falling from deep blue clouds. Fine arts of music and dance and drama were also patronized by regional kingdoms in the 16th through the 18th centuries. The development of music was due to the growth of bhakti. Swami Haridas of Brindavan promoted music in a big way. Tansen was patronized by Akbar and he is said to be the disciple of Haridas of Brindavan. Tansen is given credit for the introduction of the famous ragas *Mian Ki Malhar*, *Miyan ki Todi* and *Darbari*. Raja Man Singh of Gwalior is credited with the perfecting of *Dhrupad*, a variant style of the North Indian music. A later Mughal ruler Muhammed Shah provided great encouragement to music in North India by patronizing *Adranga* and *Sadaranga*, two great music composers of Khayal at his court. An interesting aspect was the incorporation of folk music into classical music of the court and to that category belong Thumri and Tappa. In the south too, music received patronage from the regional kingdoms like Tanjore. *Swaramelakalanithi*, a treatise on music was written by Ramamatya of Kondavidu in 1550. This book describes 20 Janak and 64 Janya ragas. Later in 1609, one Somanatha wrote *Ragavibodha* which incorporated some north Indian styles. *Çaturdandi Prakasika* the bedrock of the Carnatic music system was comp osed in 1650 at Tanjavur by Venkata Mukhi. Evidence for the promotion of dance and drama is lacking during this period. The following texts of *Abhinayachandrika* by Mahesvara Mahapatra, *Sangitha Damodara* by Raghunatha, *Tuljarayas*, *Natyavedangama* and Balavarman's *Balaramabharatam* and *Sangita Malika* of the court of Muhammed Shah deserve to be noted as they indicate the various styles of dance and drama in different parts of India. Thus in the domain of arts, the 16th and 17th centuries proved to be a period of experiments and fusion of north and south Indian concepts.

Decline and Disintegration of the Mughals

The Mughal rule in India established in 1526 by Babur gradually consolidated itself under the great Mughals: Akbar, Jahangir and Shahjahan and reached its pinnacle of glory as a vast empire in the first half of the reign of Aurangzeb, the last great Mughal. The twilight of the Mughal rule set in 1707 after the death of Aurangzeb and the decline and disintegration of the Mughal rule saw its logical end by AD 1761 and the empire lingered as a nominal power till 1857, the year in which the last of the Mughals, Bahadur Shah Zafar was deported to Rangoon in Burma and he was executed in 1862.

The causes for the decline and disintegration of the Mughal rule attracted the attention of a number of scholars, Indian and foreign. Many attempts were made to explain the process of decline and disintegration from different approaches and perspectives. The historiography of the decline and disintegration of the Mughal rule in India can be divided into two phases – pre-independent and post-independent approaches and perspectives. In the pre-independent era, the historians Jadunath Sarkar, Stanley Lanepoole, V.A. Smith, and W. Irvine followed the empire-centric approach and attributed the decline to a deterioration in the characters of rulers and their nobles. J.N. Sarkar, who had analysed the developments in the empire in the context of law and order, is of the view that Aurangzeb was mainly responsible for the decline and disintegration of the Mughal Empire and in particular by his religious fanaticism, Aurangzeb alienated the support of the Hindus to the empire. Further, it is argued that the Deccan policy was also responsible for the decline and V.A. Smith goes to the extent of saying that "The Deccan was the grave of his reputation as well as of his body". It is suggested that the despotic rule of Aurangzeb turned majority of the governors of the Subas hostile and ready to revolt waiting for an appropriate time. The death of Aurangzeb sounded the death knell of the empire by the revolts of provincial governors. Another cause offered was the weak successors of Aurangzeb. It is true that the later Mughals were mostly weak, imbecile and steeped in luxury and were partly responsible for the decline. Further, the deterioration in the valour and strength of the rulers coupled with the degeneration of the nobility and army hastened the process of disintegration. Added to the empire and emperor-centric perspective, the other causes that led to decline and disintegration of the Mughal rule were the alienness of the Mughals, widespread prevalence of corruption, the invasions of Ahmed Shah Abdali and Nadar Shah Abdali, financial bankruptcy and neglect of navy.

In the post-independent India, historians Satish Chandra, M. Athar Ali, S. Nurul Hassan and Irfan Habib, after analysing the political power structure of Mughal India offered crisis in the Jagirdari and agrarian spheres as mainly responsible for the decline and disintegration of the Mughal Empire. In this approach, the focus was shifted from personalities and policies of individual rulers to the study of the key institutions, Mansabdari and Jagirdari on which the Mughal super-structure was built. Irfan Habib is of the view that the mechanism of collection of revenue of the empire was inherently flawed and as a result of the peasant protests in different parts of India the political and social fabric of the empire was weakened. J.F. Richards, M.N. Pearson and P. Hardy undertook the re-examination of the crisis and differed in their conclusions from those of Satish Chandra, M. Athar Ali, S. Nurul Hassan and Irfan Habib. Pearson too suggests that the Jagirdari distress sounded the death knell of the Mughal system. Contradicting the empire-centric approach of the above learned scholars, Muzaffar Alam and Chetan Singh follow the region-centric approach to explain the decline of the Mughal Empire basing on the developments in the Mughal Subhas of Awadh and Punjab. Muzafar Alam holds the view that the Mughal Empire acted as a coordinating agency between the interests of the conflicting communities and the various indegenous socio-political systems at different levels. Muzafar Alam concludes that the Mughal decline in the 18th century was because of its failure to maintain checks and balances between the key institution holders, i.e., the Mansabdars, Jagirdars and the local indigenous elements. The decline and disintegration of the Mughal Empire appears to be very complex as many factors, empire-centric and region-centric were cumulatively responsible for bringing together the core and the periphery and for the emergence of regional identities in the successor states of Mughal India. In the end, we may conclude that the decline of the Mughal Empire was not the consequence of administrative maladjustment which led to the Jagirdari crisis which in its turn led to the emergence of regional powers as successor states of the Mughal-power in India. There is not one single common cause applicable to the whole of India but there are many factors which caused disequilibrium to the fragile political edifice of the Mughal polity and led to the revival of the regional identities as reflected in the emergence of regional powers.

22

The Marathas

The Rise, Growth and Decline

The rise of the Marathas as a strong political power under Chatrapati Shivaji, and their long-drawn rivalry with the Mughals in the 17th and the first half of the 18th centuries add a new dimension to the study of Indian history and culture. The Marathas were originally petty 'bhumiars' and soldiers in the service of the neighbouring Muslim kingdoms of Ahmadnagar and Bijapur, where they learnt the art of administration and had their first political training. The important sources for the study of the Marathas are: The literary source, Shivaji's biography or Bakhar written by Sabhasad in 1694 which was elaborated by Chitragupta. Sambhaji's *Adanapatra* or *Marathishahitil Rajaniti* of Ramachandra Pant Amatya written in 1716 is another important source. Jayarama Pande's *Radhamadhav Vilas Champu* written in Sanskrit is also a primary literary source on Shivaji. On Mughal-Maratha relations, the important source is Bhimasen's Persian work *Nushka-i-Dilkusha*. Kanhoji Jedhe and Jedhe Sakavali also provide much information on the activities of Shivaji, the founder of independent Maratha political power structure. Further, *Sivabharatam* written by Paramanand and *Sivaraj Rajyabhisheka Kalpataru* are also useful sources. The Persian-Sanskrit dictionary *Rajya Vyavaharakosam* prepared by Raghunath Hanumahte under the instructions of Shivaji also serves as a useful source. The writings of Kafi Khan and Bhimasen in Persian also throw good light on Shivaji. The records of the British East India Company, memoirs of Francois Martin, the travelogues of Bernier, Taverniar and Thevnot also furnish some useful information on Shivaji. Further, Peshwa 'daftars' or official records of the Peshwas, Persian records and Residency records also throw useful light on the activities of the Peshwas. The books of Grant Duff, Kirtane, Rajwade, V.S. Khare, P. Ranade, G.S. Sardesai and J.N. Sarkar constitute the secondary source-material to study and understand the Maratha history and culture.

Multiple factors like the physical features of the area of Maharashtra the land, the climate, the hilly areas, scanty rainfall, the impact of the preachings of the devotional saints Tukaram, Ramdas, Vaman Pandit and Eknath on the masses and the Maratha language and literature fostered a sense of oneness among the Marathas. Added to the above factors, the training they obtained in the Ahmadnagar and Bijapur courts made them to realize the need of a united stand to become a political power and the leadership of Shivaji enabled them to carve out a kingdom for themselves. J.N. Sarkar aptly remarks that nature developed in them "self-reliance, courage, perseverance, a stern simplicity, a rough straightforwardness, a sense of social equality and consequently pride in the dignity of man as man ... thus a remarkable community of language, creed and life was attained in the Maharashtra in the 17th century, even before political unity was conferred by Shivaji. Thus, in the end a tribe or a collection of tribes or castes was fused into a nation and by the end of the 18th century a Maratha people in the political and cultural sense of the term had been formed, though the caste distinctions still remained. Thus history has moulded society". The above are the generally accepted factors for the rise of Maratha nationalism. Yet, the rise of the Maratha nationalism received the deep attention of many a scholar, who perceived it differently. Grant Duff views the rise of the Maratha power as a result of the conflagration in the forests of Sahyadri along with the Mughal factor. M.G. Ranade holds the opinion that it was a national struggle of independence against foreign domination. J.N. Sarkar and G.S. Sardesai strongly believe the rise of the Marathas as a Hindu reaction against the fanatical religious policy of Aurangzeb. Andre Wink is of the view that it was because of the growing Mughal pressure on the Deccan Sultans. Satish Chandra is of the definite opinion that the socio-economic factors are responsible for the rise of the Maratha nation state. Satish Chandra postulates a view that Shivaji by curtailing the powers of the big landed intermediaries, i.e., Deshmukhs and by introducing necessary reforms created political space for petty landholders to have a say in the political management. Irfan Habib sees a connection between the rise of the Maratha power and the rebellious mood of the oppressed peasantry. The social content of the *Maratha Dharma* can be understood by the way Shivaji got prepared a Suryavamsa Kshyatriya lineage of his family with the willing support of Gangabhat, a Brahmin of Benaras. Along with Shivaji many of the people belonging to the agriculturalist profession might have succeeded in enhancing their social status. In this backdrop, the Bhakti movement spear-headed by Tukaram, Samarth Ramdas and Eknath gave scope for mobility in the Varna scale by individuals and groups which further crystalized into Maratha Dharma based on egalitarianism. M.G. Ranade and V.K. Rajwade formulated the idea that it was Maratha Dharma that led to the political independence of the Marathas based on aggressive Hinduism. The earliest reference to the term Maratha Dharma is found in the *Guru Charitra* of the 15th century in the context of an ethical policy of a great enlightened state. Samartha Ramdas, the spiritual guru of Shivaji who was very critical about the Turko-Afghan-Mughal rule gave impetus to Maratha nationalism. Shivaji made use of this saint-poet's statement to kindle popular ideological protest against the rule of the Mughals and the Deccani kingdoms of Bijapur and Golkonda. Tulja Bhavani, Vithobha and Mahadeva, the trinity of Maharashtra and the slogan *Hara Har Mahadeva* gave the needed religious sanction to Maratha Dharma. A big debating point is – can we identify Maratha Dharma with Hindu Swarajya. While some subscribe to the view that Hindu Swarajya and Maratha Dharma are identical, there are some who disagree with this view and regard that it was not primarily religion-oriented but opposed to the centralizing tendencies of the Mughals. We can agree with the view that taking advantage of the decline of Ahmadnagar kingdom, the Marathas wanted to carve out a bigger principality against the growing influence of the Mughals in the Deccan.

Formation of the Maratha State

Since the early 17th century, the Marathas emerged as new political elite by joining the service of Ahmadnagar, Bijapur and Golkonda courts in the Deccan. Some Marathas earned the titles of Raja, Naik and Rana and became petty chiefs of hill forts and Chander Rao Morey and Yaswanta Rao, Rao Naik Nimbalkar, Jujah Rao Ghatage, the Deshmukh of Mullore, were some of the important subordinates of the Deccan Sultans.

Maloji, the grandfather of Shivaji married the sister of Jagpal Rao Nail Nimbalkar the 'deshmukh' of Phultun. Maloji's son Shahji joined the count of Bijapur and was married to Jijiyabai. Shahji and Jijiyabai's youngest son was Shivaji. He was born at Shivaneri on April 10, 1627. As Shahji was busy till 1636 Shivaji was denied paternal attention. Shivaji was shifted to Poona under the guardianship of Dadaji Kondadev. In 1640–41 Shivaji married Saibai Nimbalkar and the administration of the Jagir of Poona was entrusted to Shivaji by Shahji Bhonsle under the guardianship of Dadaji Khonddev. With the death of Dadaji Khonddev in 1647, Shivaji became the independent agent of Shahji at Poona. Shivaji tactfully befriended the brave community of Maval chiefs who became loyal defenders to him. The Maval chieftains Jedhe Nayak of Kari and Bandal Nayak were the first to join hands with Shivaji. Shivaji developed a desire to recover as a legitimate heir of Shahji, the territories surrendered to Bijapur Sultan by the latter. But he could not execute his plans as his father Shahji was imprisoned by the Bijapur forces. Shivaji succeeded in 1649, on getting his father released from the prison. Shivaji occupied Purandar fort in 1648 and the fort of Javali in 1656, and also the fort of Rairi or Raigarh which became the capital of Shivaji's 'swarajya' in 1674.

The relations between the Marathas and the Mughals can be studied under four phases: (a) 1615 to 1664, (b) 1664 to 1667,(c) 1667 to 1680, and (d) 1680–1707. The Mughal rulers Jahangir and Shahjahan realized the importance of the Maratha chieftains of Deccan and started persuading them to defect to their side from that of the Deccan Sultans. Aurangzeb too tried to woo Shivaji to be his ally as early as 1657. Shivaji did not yield and continued with his raids and occupied Kalyan and Bhiwandi in 1657 and Mahuli in 1658 and the entire eastern half of the Kolaba district was occupied by Shivaji from the Siddis of Janjira. In order to cut short the efforts of Shivaji, the Adilshahi ruler of Bijapur dispatched Abdulah Bhatare Afzal Khan with a strong force against Shivaji in

1659. Shivaji got Afzal Khan killed by a stratagem and diplomacy and overpowered the Bijapur army by occupying Panhala and south Konkan but Shivaji lost Panhala after a short while in 1660. In order to reduce the growing power of Shivaji, the Mughal ruler Aurangzeb despatched Shaistha Khan as viceroy of Deccan in 1659. Shaistha Khan succeeded in occupying Chakan in 1660 and north Konkan in 1661 and there were hostilities between the Marathas and Aurangzeb in 1662–63. In 1663, Shivaji attacked Shaisth Khan at Poona and seriously wounded the Mughal viceroy of Deccan and sacked Surat in 1664. This gave a shock to Aurangzeb and Aurangzeb appointed Mirja Raja Jai Singh as the viceroy of Deccan. Raja Jai Singh raided the Maratha territory and occupied Purandhar in 1665 and persuaded Shivaji to enter into an alliance with the Mughals. Shivaji accepted the proposal of Jai Singh and the Treaty of Purandhar was concluded between the Mughal and Shivaji in 1665. Shivaji was made to visit Agra to meet Aurangzeb. At Agra, Shivaji got enraged when he was not treated with proper respect and expressed his dissatisfaction and he was imprisoned by the Mughal forces in Agra. In 1666, Shivaji escaped from Agra prison and Raja Jai Singh was replaced by prince Mauzzam in 1667 as the Mughal viceroy of Deccan.

Shivaji kept quiet for two years after his escape from Agra prison and again renewed his hostile attitude towards the Mughals as the Purandhar Treaty was not at all advantageous to him and he had to forgo 23 forts and territory worth 4 lakh huns to the Mughals without any compensation from Bijapur. He renewed hostilities by sacking Surat in 1670 for the second time and recovered a large number of forts, including Punandhar and made deep inroads into the Mughal territories of Berar and Khandesh. Simultaneously, he fought with Bijapur and secured Panhala and Satara by offering bribes and also raided Kanara country at leisure. The year 1674, was a memorable year in the life of Shivaji, as in that year the coronation of Shivaji with the appropriate title of Chatrapati took place at Raigarh. Definitely, the coronation was a declaration to the public that Shivaji was the foremost among the Marathas and an equivalent to the contemporary Sultans and the emperor. This was followed by his raids into Bijapur and Karnataka in 1676, in which Akkanna and Madanna of Golkonda offered him active support. The Qutub Shahi ruler of Golkonda entered into a friendly treaty with Shivaji but in due course the relations between them got strained as Shivaji did not agree to share the booty with Golkonda. This Karnataka expedition happened to be the last major expedition of Shivaji and Shivaji died in 1680, shortly after his successful return from the expedition of Karnataka. Shivaji, who was by birth a petty Bhumia or landlord belonging to the agricultural occupation, by virtue of his determination and foresight became a *Chatrapati* and *Haindava Dharmodharak* and carved out a considerably vast kingdom, which he bequeathed to his progeny. Shivaji's fame rests on his assertion of popular will as a representative of the popular Maratha Dharma against the Mughal penetration into Maharashtra. Shivaji was also an able administrator as well as a builder of independent kingdom by bringing together different elements.

Administration of Shivaji

The creator of the administrative structure and apparatus was none else than Shivaji, the founder of the Maratha state. The administrative structure of the Marathas is primarily based on the Deccan Sultans' administrative principles and some of the aspects of the contemporary Mughals. The Maratha polity was basically a centralized despotic but enlightened monarchy. The king was the pivot of the entire administrative process from the beginning to the end. "Raja Kalsya Karanam" or happiness and prosperity of their subjects were the motto of the Maratha rulers. However much interested and sincere, as it is not possible for a single individual to carryout the entire administrative process, the king was assisted by a council of ministers designated as Ashtapradhan or council of eight ministers. The ministers are: (1) *Peshwa* or Prime Minister, who was the head of civil and military matters, (2) *Majumdar* or auditor, who scrutinized the income and expenditure of the state, (3) *Waqenavis* or the person who was incharge of intelligence, costs and household affairs, (4) *Dabir* who was incharge of ceremonies and assisted the king in dealing with foreign powers, (5) *Shuru Navis* or Sachiv or who was incharge of all the official correspondence, (6) *Pandit Rao Danadhyakha* was incharge of eclesiastical affairs, (7) *Nyayadhish* or the Chief Justice and, (8) *Senapati* or the commander in Chief. Of the 8 members of the council of ministers except Panditrao and the Nyayadhisha, the rest were entrusted with military responsibility. During Shivaji's rule, all these posts were neither hereditary nor permanent. They were kept in their positions as long as they enjoyed the confidence of the king. They were liable for transfer. All these executive officers were paid in cash by the exchequer and no Jagir was given to any military or civil executive. But, by the time we come to Peshwas (1713–1761) this practice was given up and the posts became hereditary and permanent. Each of the Ashtapradhan was assisted by eight assistants, Diwan, Majumdar, Phadnis, Sabnis, Karkhanis, Chitnis, Jamadar and Potnis. Among the eight assistants, Chitnis or secretary appears to be next in rank to asthapradhans as he dealt with all diplomatic correspondences and drafted all royal letters. He also wrote letters to provincial and district officials. Fadnis was given the authority to respond to the letters of commanders of forts. By the time of Peshwas, the power and prestige of Phadnis grew and he become a prominent officer. The Potnis took care of the income and expenditure of the royal treasury. The Potedar acted as an assay officer.

Provincial Administration

The Marathas divided their kingdom hierarchically into 'mauzas', 'tarafs' and 'prants' for administrative efficiency and convenience. Mauza was the lowest unit of administrative structure. The head of the taraf or district was havaldar, Karkun or paripatyagar. The provinces were known as Subahs and their officers were called Subedars. Karkun or Mukhyadesadhikari or Sarsubedar supervised and controlled the work of the Subedars.

The stability and security of the kingdom depended on the efficiency of the military and their preparedness to meet the demands of the situation. In the history of the Marathas, forts played a crucial role and no single officer was entrusted with the sole responsibility of the fort. Instead, Shivaji appointed a havaldar, sabnis and a sarnobat for ordinary sized forts. For big forts, 5 to 10 tatsarnobats of equal status who were liable for transfers also were appointed. The keys of the fort were kept in the custody of the havaldar. The muster roll or attendance was taken care of by the sabnis. He was also in change of the revenue administration. The sarnobat was in charge of the garrison. Karkhanis used to take care of the grain stores and other material required. Shivaji applied a good system of checks and balances over his officials to keep them under control. No official was given absolute power in any sphere of activity. Shivaji had taken care that no caste group dominated in the bureaucratic set-up. It was clearly ordained that the havaldar and sarnobat had to be a Maratha, the sabnis a Brahmin and Karkhani, a Kayastha.

Shivaji maintained light cavalry and light infantry trained in guerilla and hilly warfare. Shivaji's most excellent troopers belonged to the Mavalis and Hetkaris. Shivaji's infantry structure was hierarchically arranged in a pyramidal shape from bottom to top. Naik-Havaldar-Jumladar-Hazari-Sarnobat. Same is the case with cavalry. His cavalry consisted of two classes – Bargirs and Silodars. Bargir troops were supplied with horses and arms by the state and silodars are those who brought their own horses and arms. The army of Shivaji was well served by an efficient intelligence department headed by Bahiraj Naik Jadhav. By the time of Peshwas, separate artillery department was created in the army. Discipline was given top priority by Shivaji and that became lax under the Peshwas. During the time of the Peshwas, the armies become a mobile town with all paraphernalia. Shivaji strengthened his military by a strong navy. His naval fleet consisted of Ihurabs or gunboats and galivats or row boats. Koli the sea faring tribe of Malabar manned his fleet. Shivaji established two squadrons of 200 vessels. There is a view that these figures are highly exaggerated as Robert Orme mentions just 57 fleets of Shivaji under the command of Admiral Daniya Sarang and Marnaik Bhandari. One more admiral of Shivaji's navy was Daulat Khan. The Marathas did not develop an organized judicial structure. At the village level; the village panchayat decided the legal issues. Criminal cases were decided by Patil. Hazir Majalis was the highest court for civil and criminal cases.

In the matters relating to land revenue system, Shivaji continued the regulations practised by Malik Amber in the Deccan states. Shivaji got the measurement of land under cultivation by using a Kathi or measuring rod. Twenty Kathis constituted a Bigha and 120 Bighas a Chavar. Shivaji entrusted the task of systematic assessment to Annaji Datto in 1678. Annaji Datto carried on assessment with the help of the Paragana and village officials. Shivaji collected one-third of the total value of the crop as land tax but later after abolishing other cesses, a consolidated share of 40 per cent was claimed by the state. A hierarchy of officials was there to look after the collection of land tax at various stages from the cultivators. Jadunath Sarkar holds the view that Shivaji did away with the intermediaries – Zamindars, Deshmukhs, Desais and Patils between the state and the cultivator. Contradicting the view of J.N. Sarkar, Satish Chandra holds the view that Shivaji curtailed the unlimited powers of these hereditary intermediaries and appointed his own men to collect the land tax, instructing them not to extract more than the due share of the state. Shivaji punished those officials who violated his orders. Peshwas introduced changes into the land tax collection system introduced by Shivaji. Shivaji attempted to take special measures to protect peasants from the oppressions of the revenue collector. Besides land tax, 'chauth' and 'sardeshmukhi' formed the major sources of income for the Marathas. Some criticized these measures as plunder and loot. Sardeshmukhi was an extraction of 10 per cent imposed upon the revenues of the entire Martha kingdom.

Shivaji claimed sardeshmukhi as his right as the supreme head of the Marathas. Further, he claimed chauth, i.e., percentage of the total revenue of the neighbouring chieftains whose territories did not form a part of swarajya. Shivaji was not an innovator and creator of new administrative ideas but modified the existing Daccani Sultan's administration and made it suitable for his swarajya. The only change introduce by him was more and more of centralization and he saw to it that there was no possibility of configuration of various groups to emerge as strong political elite. This system worked very effectively and efficiently as long as Shivaji survived and decline set in after his death. Shivaji was followed by his son Sambhaji who ruled from 1680 to 1689 and he was followed by his brother Rajaram, who ruled from 1689 to 1700. After the death of Rajaram, his wife Tarabai became regent on behalf of her son Shivaji II who ruled from 1700 to 1707. All these years the hostility with the Muguals continued and in spite of his best efforts, Aurangzeb failed to curb the spirit of the Marathas. Once again the Marathas became a prominent political force under the regime of the Peshwas during the years 1713 to 1761 during the reigns of Sahu 1707–1749 and Rama Raja in 1749–1777.

Part III

Modern and Post-Independent India

23

Colonial Advent

The Portuguese, the French and the English

India had contacts with Europe since time immemorial through land route, which affected both India and Europe culturally and materially. But the advent of European powers into India by discovering sea route to India had far-reaching consequences on the shape and course of Indian society and history from the middle of the 15th century. First to come to India as traders were the Portuguese, who were followed by the Dutch, the British and the French, who subsequently developed designs to be the political masters of India. Of all the European powers, the British succeeded in becoming the political masters of India. Indians continued their struggle against the European powers in the 18th and 19th centuries and only by the middle of the 20th century India could become independent after the partition of the subcontinent. Much water has flown under the bridge in these four hundred years in India, and India underwent transition from a feudal, conservative, exclusive social system to a capitalistic, progressive and inclusive social system during this period with self-assertion based on introspection and external stimuli of ideas of equality, liberty, fraternity and people's rule instead of rule of one man, i.e., from monarchy to democracy. What we notice in this transition process was the tendency of continuity and change in all the spheres effecting human activity on the Indian soil, in spite of the foreign domination of our country by the British from 1757 to 1947 and their efforts to bring about a total change in our basic attitudes and outlook. We can thus learn how India reacted to the western dominance and showed its resistance facing the challenge of its annihilation of cultural mosaic based on pluralistic cultural values inherited in its long history of more than five thousand years.

The factors of the emergence of nation states, renaissance and reformation, agricultural and industrial revolution, new economic doctrine of mercantilism, competition between nation states for breaking the mercantile monopoly of the merchants of Venice and Geneva over sea-borne trade, and a great advance in navigational technologies like compass gave strong impetus for geographical discoveries leading to the finding of new worlds and new sea routes. As a consequence of the above factors, a new route to the east via the Cape of Good Hope was discovered. This led to the European monopoly over the seas and the advent of Europeans into India in search of trade and commerce in spices, which were essential requirements of their food habits. Owing to the rivalry of European powers, India became the actual theatre of conflicts by the middle of the 18th century.

The Portuguese Power in India

India maintained long distance trade with South-East Asia and the west Asian countries but India never had direct contact of maritime trade with European nations bordering the Atlantic Ocean. Prince Henry, the Navigator (1398–1460), the ruler of Portugal took the lead among the European nations and promoted seafaring activity. During the regime of King John II, Bartholomew Diaz crossed the Cape of Good Hope. When King Emmanuel was ruling Portugal, Vasco de Gama started his expedition in 1497 and landed on the Indian soil (Calicut) in May 1498. Vasco de Gama's silent landing on the Indian soil ushered a new chapter of far-reaching consequences. He was cordially received by Zamorin of Calicut. Vasco de Gama came to India again in 1501 and returned to Portugal in 1503 and by that time they established trading centres at Calicut, Cochin and Cannanore and effectively suppressed the Arab resistence. De Almedia was appointed as the first viceroy in India in 1505 and he initiated the 'Blue Water' policy or the mastery of sea by strong naval power. In 1509, De Almedia was followed by Albuquerque as the second viceroy and he was in that power till 1515. Albuquerque laid the foundation of the Portuguese power in India by conquering Goa in 1510, and it became the headquarters of the Portuguese in India. In 1515, he conquered Ormuz, an island in the Persian Gulf. He also built a fort at Cochin with the approval of its ruler. The Portuguese obtained Diu and Bassein in 1534 and in 1538 they conquered Daman. Thus, the Portuguese power in India grew but their power and influence declined from the beginning of the 17th century. They failed in India due to various factors like their zeal to convert Indians to Christianity and the defeat of Portugal by Spain. But for the first time in the history of international trade, commercial treaties with Indian rulers were concluded, by the Portuguese alone. The present European contact revolutionalized the outlook of the Indians significantly with far-reaching impact on the future course of the Indian society. The production of cash crops, especially spices grew with an eye on international trade, and agricultural production had become enormously market-oriented.

The Dutch East India Company

By a charter of the Government of Holland, the Dutch East India Company was established in 1602. As the Dutch were very much interested in spice trade, they had their focus on the Far East and made India their trading depot. In 1606, they established their factories at Petapalli and Masulipatnam. Realizing that Indian textiles have a large market, they established factories at Pulicat in 1610,

Cambay in 1620, Surat and Agra in 1621, Hariharapur in 1633, Patna in 1638, Dacca in 1650, Udaiganj in 1651, Chinsura in 1653, Quasim Bazar, Barangore, Balasure and Nagapatnam in 1659–60. The Dutch withdrew from Golkonda by 1684. They also opened factories in Bengal, at Khankul in 1669 and at Malda in 1676 but both were closed down soon. The rising Dutch power was looked as a threat by the British and a truce was concluded between them in 1619 but it did not last long. By 1795, the British expelled the Dutch from India totally. In India, the factories of the Dutch were administered by a council consisting of the director, a senior factor, the incharge of the company's trade books, a law enforcement officer, the incharge of the warehouses, the incharge of the loading and unloading and six junior factors. Of the six, one acted as secretary to the council. Their headquarters was in Batavia. The Dutch received encouragement from the rulers of Golkonda, the Nayaks of Tanjore and Shahjahan, Aurangzeb and Jahandar Shah.

The English East India Company

'The English Association of the Merchant Adventurers' was established in 1599 with the objective of carrying on trade with the east. This company, which is popular as east India Company obtained a Royal Charter with trade monopoly in the east from Queen Elizabeth on 31 December, 1600. By 1608, the first factory at Surat was decided to be opened by the British. By 1619, they established factories at Agra, Ahmedabad and Broach. Even before these factories, one factory was established at Machilipatnam in 1611, one at Armagaon in 1625, and obtained Madras in 1639 and constructed Fort St. George. They acquired Bombay Island in 1668 and fortified it soon and it become the headquarters of the west in 1687. In the east, they established their factories in Orissa at Hariharapur and Balasore in 1633, in 1651 at Hughli and in 1698 they acquired the Zamindari of Sutnauti, Kalikata and Govindpur, where they built Fort William and in later days it grew into a big city known as Calcutta. The internal management of the East India Company was carried on by 'Court of Committee' for sometime and in 1709 the name was changed to 'Court of directors' which was based in London. The Company was empowered to make laws and judicial powers. In India, each factory was administered by a governor-in-council. There exists a close relationship between the company and the crown, and the crown and parliament controlled the East India Company through charters.

The French East India Company

The French were the last of the European powers to enter the eastern trade. The French East India Company was established in 1664. In 1668 the first French factory was established in Surat. The French established their second factory at Masulipatnam in 1669. The French obtained Pondicherry in 1673 and they built Chandranagore in 1690–92. There was rivalry between the French and the British and the Dutch for major share in the eastern trade.

Further the hostile relations between these powers in Europe also led to war in India. There was hostility between the French and the Dutch in India in 1690 and again in 1721. The French and the British companies clashed in India between 1742 and 1766. The French hopes of establishing their political powers came to an end in 18th century.

In the beginning the French had their headquarters at Surat but later they shifted it to Pondicherry. The supreme body of the French was known as "Superior Council of the Indies". It was headed by a Director General and he was placed in charge of the French affairs in India. The superior council consisted of a Governor and five members. The Governor's voice was final. One aspect to be noted is the mutual jealousies and quarrels between the French officials and the commanders in India, which ultimately affected the fortunes of the French in India. The French East India Company was a state controlled organization and from 1723, it was almost wholly controlled by the French government. The Directors now have become its representatives. The Directors have no powers for all practical purposes. After 1730 the French East India Company had became the national East India Company. After 1789, the French East India trade was thrown open to individuals. In a way it is the French who initiated the strategy of interfering in internal affairs of the Indian states to obtain political mileage and showed the way to the British. While the French failed in their strategy, it is the British who were successful. Besides the Portuguese, the Dutch, the British, and the French, the Danes entered India as traders in 1616 and obtained Trancquabar port from the Nayaks of Tanjore in 1620 and built a fort there. Though they started factories at Masulipatnam, port Novo, and Serampur, their success in trading business was short-lived as their sources were scanty. They sold their factories to the British and left India finally in 1845. Likewise, the Swedish East India did business for a short while and the activities of Flander's merchants were also limited to India alone for a short while. The discovery of the new sea route via the Cape of Good Hope, threw the eastern trade open to all European nations. Consequently, the Portuguese, the Dutch, the British and the French merchant companies opened their factories in Africa and Asia. These European companies exhibited interest in obtaining more and more concessions from the Indian rulers as each was very desirous of gaining a monopoly of eastern trade against the other powers. This desire for monopoly made them enter into conflicts with one another both on land and sea. By 1750, the fortune smiled at the British and the British emerged victorious and developed designs to establish their political supremacy in India. In the following sections we will be studying the strategies adopted by them to achieve their objective.

The Expansion and Consolidation of the British in India

The British East India Company slowly and gradually expanded its trading activities in India by getting permission from the then ruling powers, the Mughals and the local rulers. By the time the Mughal empire's decline started and it fragmented into successor states, the British East India Company developed designs of becoming a political power by the middle of the 18th century. The British East India Company in its desire to become a political power realized that it had to eliminate the other European companies from trading activity and so obtained permission to build forts and to improve its military strength. After making thorough preparations, the British East India Company acquired its foothold firmly in Bengal, Bihar, and Orissa by its victories in the battles of Plassey (1757) and Buxar (1765). Since then, the British East India Company adopted a threefold strategy of ideological, military and colonial administrative apparatus to expand and consolidate the British Indian Empire. In this process, we witness a transformation of trading connections into colonial relations of unequal nature. Now, let us understand how the British East India Company tried to justify its policy of acquiring political power through its ideological bases of mercantilism, orientalism, utilitarianism and evangelicalism.

The British were not just crude blood-thirsty annexationists or conquerors like the Arabs and the Turks. The British who came to India as traders, in course of time realized that in order to obtain the optimum profits from Indian trade, they have to secure political power, backed by force. What had never happened in the world's history so far happened in India and a trading company becomes sovereign political power. The British knew what they did was morally and ethically incorrect and to justify their action, they used ideological bases to brainwash the natives of India and the world that what they did in India was in the interest of the progress and development of India and it was their 'white man's burden' to 'civilize India' from a historical barbarian rule of the earlier centuries of Indian polity and culture. Romila Thapar rightly observes that the historical writings produced by the European scholars, beginning in the 18th century, were formulated in terms of the ideological attitudes then dominant in Europe. Further she states, "the European ideologies entailed a set of attitudes towards India which were for the most part highly critical as that of unchanging India, unhistorical, barbarian and uncivilized", in support of their design to conquer. In this backdrop let us take up the first aspect of expansion and consolidation of the British Indian empire, the ideological bases.

Mercantilism

By the beginning of the 16th century, we notice the decline of feudalism in Europe along with the emergence of new ideas which promoted the rise of nation state, urge for new geographical discoveries, seaborne long distance trade and colonization of new lands through migration and settlement of new colonies. Further, a new commercial outlook influenced by mercantalist ideas dominated Europe between the 17th and 18th centuries. Added to these the growth of science and technology in England made England an industrially developed country. In consequence, England had become a colonial power and a capitalist country. All these developments necessitated England to search for raw materials necessary for the manufacture of goods in England and new markets for their finished mechanized products. England wanted to achieve these objectives through colonialism in India, as merchants became an influential social class of England. Thus, by the 17th century the countries of Europe came under the impact of a set of economic ideas and practices called mercantilism. Mercantilism presupposes the volume of world trade as more or less fixed, precious metals silver and gold form the desirable national wealth, balance of trade should be the norm and for that purpose should impose high tariffs on imports. Colonization should be adopted and if necessary rival powers should be curbed by force of arms and finally colonial trade should be a monopoly of the mother country. The above-mentioned mercantilist ideas dominated the European nations between the 17th and 18th centuries and this system was criticized by Adam Smith, the author of *Wealth of Nations* published in 1776 and Maurice Dobb, the famous Marxist thinker as *The Mercantile System* was a system of state-regulated exploitation through trade which played a highly important role in the adolescent capitalist industry. It was essentially the economic policy of an age of primitive accumulation.

Orientalism

Orientalism is a concept that stresses the uniqueness of the culture and civilization of the Orient. Orientalists are also called Indologists. But Romila Thapar is of the view that the term 'Orientalist' was used in the wider sense of scholars interested in Asia and the term Indologists referred to those interested only in India. These orientalists started the first serious study of the past civilization and culture of India in particular in the late 18th century. Orientalists, who were conservative by nature pleaded for providing a framework of security without interference in the working of the religio-social institutions and cultural traditions. They argued that peace would promote the trade and it would be to Britain's advantage. This view of the orientalists was supported by the right wing Tories and they also opposed missionary activity of any sort in India. This serious study of the past of India became inevitable as the British East India company authorities decided that it was essential for officers of the British East India Company to be proficient about Indian culture and civilization to rule them properly. In order to encourage this type of study, the Asiatic Society was established in 1784 to undertake research into the past of Indian culture and civilization. William Jones, Wilkins, H.T. Colebrooke, W.H. Wilson and Max Muller who never visited India were the well-known orientalists. Owing to the efforts of the above orientalists, by the middle of the 19th century the interest in the past culture of India has become deep-rooted and spread to various parts of Europe. The most significant revelation of the orientalists was the relation between Sanskrit and certain European languages. Translations of the important Sanskrit classics were carried by orientalists of the Asiatic Society. As a consequence of the efforts of the orientalists, there was an infectious spread of the romantic fascination of India and her culture throughout Europe. Warren

Hastings, the Governor General of Bengal not only patronized Asiatic Society but desired to reconcile the British rule with the Indian institutions. In order to translate the vision of Hastings, Halhead prepared the 'Gentoo laws' with a view to ensure stability to the acquisitions of the British in India. To encourage further the study of the past of India, Wellesley established the Fort William College at Calcutta in 1800. The focus of the Fort William College was imparting scholarship in Indian languages to the students to enable them to become good administrators. The British consciously made every effort to educate every British officer to be aware of the customs and traditions of the locality of their posting. Besides languages, they also mastered the institutions like law and landed property as the British began to consolidate their conquests. The British followed the policy of learning about the Indian society to the extent that knowledge enabled the administrators to be conversant with laws and customs of Indians of various localities but never disturbing the Indian society by mediation or intervention.

Evangelicalism

Evangelicalism is a Protestant Christian movement of England of the 18th century. This movement in contrast to the Orthodox Church emphasized on personal experiences, individual reading of gospel rather than the traditions of the established church. While some Christian missionaries attempted to reform the 'degenerate Indian society' quietly, the evangelists were openly hostile to 'Indian barbarism' and desired to 'civilize India'. The influential members of the Evangalicalism were Wilberforce, the confidant of Pitt, Charles Grant, a chairman of the directors and his son who was a cabinet minister. They advocated to bring Christian West to the East and "India will reform herself as a flower to the Sun" Charles Grant propagated the policy of assimilation of India into the great civilizing mission of Britain. This attitude coincides with the liberalism advocated by Macaulay. The British East India Company too agreed upon this philosophy of civilizing India because they can acquire properties in India and they could have markets for their finished products in India due to the implementation of free trade policy. Charles Grant too supported this idea as civilizing process would lead to material prosperity. Thus, in the late 18th and the early 19th centuries the idea of 'improvement' became a part of the civilizing process. The then Governor General Cornwallis introduced permanent settlement in Bengal as a part of his vision of improvement as the magic touch of property would create capital and market in land. Munro was critical of the permanent settlement idea as it was an alien concept of English rule of law with its strict division of judiciary and executive. Murnro argued for the preservation of the stable heritage of village committees by introducing Ryotwari settlements. When Wiliam Bentink became the Governor General of India by the Charter Act of 1833, liberal minded Macaulay suggested that Indians should be civilized through the Western education system. There arose a debate between the orientalists who insisted that the old system of education be continued and the Anglicists who supported the move of Macaulay. Finally, the Western education system was introduced with the cooperation of the reformer, Raja Ramohan Roy.

The Utilitarians

The utilitarians too believed in the vision of civilizing and improving India like the evangelicalists and liberals. The utilitarians were radicals and humanists and had a strong faith in reason. The most important advocate of utilitarian philosophy was James Mill, the author of *History of India* published in 1817. Though, his book was studied by the employees of the British East India Company as a Bible, it caused immense harm to Indian society by laying the seeds of communalist approach to the study of Indian history and civilization. They advocated that introducing reforms into the problem of law and landed property they could attain the Benthamite principle of the 'greatest good of the greatest number'. They believed that law could be an instrument of change and through enactment of laws, Indian society could be transformed into a modern society from that of superstitious society. With the joining of James Mill in the East India Company's London office, a systematic attempt began to give a concrete shape to a vision of political reform in the philosophical premises of utilitarianism. Resultantly, a series of laws and penal codes were enacted to make India civilized and improved. The utilitarians opposed any form of representative government in India at that time as well as in near future. The utilitarian philosophy also influenced the views of Dalhousie in creating all-India departments with single heads. What we notice was the decline of the overall spirit of reform and the British administration was now dominated by the outlook of pragmatism and rationality. In the span of a hundred years (1757–1857) in this process of expansion and consolidation of the British power, the mission of the British was to civilize and improve India from a society of historical unchanging barbarian image by providing a unity of action in spite of differences in the perception of the orientalists, evangelicalists and the utilitarians led by Sir William Jones, Charles Grant and James Mill respectively. An objective analysis of the process reveals that these ideological bases and advocates of these ideologies were responsible in building the British empire in India.

Tools of Expansion: War and Diplomacy

Of all the European East India companies which came to India as traders in different periods of the 15th and 16th centuries, only the British and the French East India companies remained as dominant ones by the beginning of the 18th century. In the first decade of the 18th century, the fortunes of the then mighty Mughal empire began to decline and there emerged a number of successor states or regional powers or country powers in different parts of India. The two European trading companies after realizing the weakness of the then country powers decided to make sincere efforts to become a strong political power and to expand and consolidate their sway in India. It is the trade interest that made the two European companies chart out this process of territorial expansion. The European trading companies established their factories on the western, eastern and southern costal areas and in this process they extended their influence into the mainland territories of the Indian subcontinent. The expansion and consolidation of the British influence was achieved in a span of one hundred years, i.e., 1757 to 1857 by using the tools of war and diplomacy. Rabindra Nath Tagore, very aptly in a poetic way described this as "darkness settled on the face of the land then the weighing scales in the merchant's hand changed into the imperial sceptre".

The Carnatic Wars

The outbreak of the Austrian succession war in Europe in which the British and the French were in opposite camps and the outbreak of the succession war in Hyderabad, one of the country states, where the British and the French supported the claims of the rival claimants provided the first opportunity to the British and the French to put to test their relative military strengths and strategy of interfering in internal matters of regional powers. P.E. Roberts remarks aptly, "at the outbreak of the war the English and the French seemed about equally matched in strength and extent of possessions. It cannot be doubted that in financial power, in commercial wealth and in material resources the advantage lay considerably on the side of the English". In all the British and the French fought three wars, which are known as Carnatic wars between 1746–1763. The Carnatic wars ended in the resounding victory of the British, which ultimately resulted in the establishment of British hegemony in India. The first Carnatic war came to an end with the treaty of Aix-la-Chapelle concluded in 1748. The first Carnatic war did not effect any territorial changes. But it was a war of significance. We can agree with Dodwell that, "it demonstrated the overwhelming influence of sea power, it displayed the superiority of European methods of war over those followed by Indian armies, and it revealed the political delay that had eaten into the heart of the Indian state". The second Carnatic war took place between 1748–54 and concluded with the treaty of Pondicherry concluded by the French Governor Godeheu in 1755. As a result of this war, the influences of the British increased in Carnatic as well as in Hyderabad as Muhammed Ali and Salbat Jung, respectively were well disposed towards the British. Once again due to the outbreak of the seven years war in Europe, hostilities took the shape of third Carnatic war between the British and the French, in which the French wanted to revive their influence again but ultimately the fate of the French was sealed and they were made to give up their ambitious desire for political power. P.E. Roberts aptly remarks, "the fall of Pondicherry sounded the death knell of the French dominion in India". The French East India Company formally ended its career in 1769 and private traders continued to use the French factories. Many factors like the commercial superiority and better financial position of the British East India Company, the British employees' keen and sincere interest in promotion of trade, the realization of the British that success in trade was more important than territorial gains, marked superiority of the British Generals and finally the naval supremacy of the British and access to the resources of Bengal which was acquired in 1757, enabled the British East India Company to be a winner in the struggle and to carry on further annexations in other regions. We may agree with the view of V.A. Smith, "neither Alexander the great nor Napoleon could have won the empire of India by starting from Pondicherry as a base and contending with the power which held Bengal and command of the seas".

The Battles of Plassey and Buxar

While the Carnatic wars were going on between the British and the French in South India, Bengal was occupied by the British in the year 1757 by their victory in the battle of Plassey. Bengal became a hunting ground for all the European trading companies from the 17th century and by the 18th century Bengal provided 60 per cent of British imports from Asia. Thus, commercial viability of Bengal was the main cause of the British interest in this province. Siraj-ud-daula was the Nawab of Bengal in 1756. But, his accession was opposed by his cousin Shaukat Jung and his aunt Ghasiti Begum and the dominant group consisting of Jagat Seth, Unichand, Raj Ballesh and Mir Jafar. Further, the relations between the British and the Bengal Nawab were strained because of the activities of the British East India Company like the fortification around Calcutta without the permission of the Nawab, the misuse of the company's trade privileges by the officers of the East India Company for their private benefits and for granting shelter to Krishna Das son of Raja Ballesh, who fled with lot of money. Both Siraj and the British were suspicious of each other and in that situation the arrival of Robert Clive with a strong force deepened the suspicion of the Nawab of Bengal. Already there was a secret understanding between the foes of Nawab and the British. Nawab Siraj-ud-daula attacked the British factory at Kasimbazar, seized it and advanced towards Fort William and besieged it with an army of 50,000. This sudden attack surprised the British and the British were forced to surrender to the Nawab. The British recaptured Calcutta on 2 January, 1757 and attacked Siraj. This made Siraj enter into a peace treaty with the British on 9 February, 1757. By this treaty the British gained many advantages and yet not content they insisted for further concessions. The Nawab did not yield and evaded the issue. The British attacked the French possession of Chandranagore and captured it in 1757. The Nawab in turn gave protection to the French refugees. Realizing that war with Siraj was inevitable, the British conspired with the opponents of Siraj and made preparations to proceed to Plassey. The British despatched a letter to Siraj charging him of betraying them and violating the treaty of 9 February, 1757. On 23 June 1757, the actual battle of Plassey took place and as planned and agreed upon Mir Jafar and his army stood inactive and by the evening the success of the British became a reality. In this battle Siraj was captured and killed by the orders of Miraj, Mir Jafar's son. Thus, political power in Bengal passed into the hands of the British by their success in the battle of Plassey and the other European trading companies were eliminated from Bengal. This victory made the British in Bengal king makers and placed their protege Mir Jafar on the throne of Bengal and Mir Jafar was replaced by his son-in-law Mir Kasim. As Mir Kasim did not agree to be a loyal subordinate and satisfy the desires of the British, they planned to place Mir Jafar on the throne of Bengal again. A war broke out between the British and Mir Kasim in which Mir Kasim was driven away. Mir Kasim, Siraj-ud-daula and Shah Alam I joined together and fought with the British at Buxar in 1764. The British won victory in this battle and a treaty was concluded at Allahabad in 1765. By their victory in the battle of Buxar, the British became the political masters of Bengal, Bihar and Orissa. In a span of 8 years from 1757 to 1765, the political power in Bengal gradually and slowly was transferred from the hands of the Nawab of Bengal to a trading company, the British East India Company. We may conclude by stating that the economic and commercial interests of the company and its officials and the growth of factional politics in the courts of Nawab of Bengal and internal conflicts among different groups in the court acted as favourable factors for this political transformation of significance in the history of India. Thus by 1765, the British East India Company became a dominant political power in South India as well as in Bengal.

The Mysore Wars

Next, the British East India Company turned its attention to the annexation of Mysore which was under Haidar Ali and Tipu Sultan, who were opposed to the British East India Company and were ready to take the cooperation of the French in sustaining the kingdom of Mysore. Let us trace the backdrop that led to the actual wars between the Mysore state and the British East India Company. The 18th century India, in general witnessed complex power struggle between various groups of powers – native as well as European trading companies. It was a struggle to establish political hegemony between the colonial power and the Indian states and also among the Indian powers themselves; the Nizam, Mysore and the Marathas. While the main cause for struggle between colonial power and the Indian state was economic and commercial interest, and the struggle between native powers was for territorial expansion to augment their resources to sustain their power. In this backdrop, the rise of Mysore state under Haidar Ali and Tipu Sultan sent alarm signals of threat to the neighbouring kingdoms of the Marathas, the Nawab of Carnatic and the Nizam of Hyderabad as each kingdom was primarily interested in expansion and consolidation of their territorial boundaries. Each one was suspicious of the other power and there were syndicates of understanding and cooperation for immediate gain. This mutual suspicion and constant enmity among the country powers ultimately led to the effective intervention of the British and their success in establishing political hegemony.

The immediate cause for the British intervention was primarily the apprehension of the commercial loss in the spices trade of Malabar due to the control of Haidar Ali over Malabar and a possible threat to the control of Madras under the British. Further, the French alliance with Mysore hastened the British to follow and implement a more aggressive expanisonist policy in Mysore. Haidar Ali and Tipu Sultan fought four wars: (i) the first Anglo-Mysore war (1767–69), (ii) the second Anglo-Mysore war (1780–1784), (iii) the third Anglo-Mysore war in (1790–92) and (iv) the fourth Anglo-Mysore war (1799). In the first Anglo Mysore war, Haidar Ali successfully thwarted the designs of the Nizam, the Marathas and the British and was successful in his war against the British and their allies. The British became friends of Haidar Ali and when the Marathas invaded Mysore in 1771, he approached the British to respond but when they failed to respond, he lost his battle against the Marathas. Haidar Ali for diplomatic reasons kept quiet and in 1779, he joined hands with the Nizam and the Marathas against the British. There was a war between the British and Mysore, the Nizam and the Marathas. In the middle of the war Haidar Ali died in 1782 and his son Tipu Sultan continued the war and the peace treaty of Mangalore were concluded in 1784. The war ended indecisively. Again war broke out between Tipu Sultan and the British between 1790 and 1792 and in the end Tipu concluded the peace treaty of Srirangapatnam in March 1792.

Tipu had to surrender half of his kingdom which was shared by the English, the Marathas and the Nizam. The final showdown between Tipu and the British took place in 1799, wherein Tipu lost his life fighting heroically and Mysore was placed under the earlier Odayar family. Mysore became a dependency of the British by 1799. From the British perspective, the annexation of Mysore was a great event Majumdar, H.C. Raychaudhari and K.K. Dutta observe: "It secured for the company substantial territorial, economic, commercial and military advantages. It extended the company's dominion from sea to sea across the base of the peninsula encompassing the new kingdom of Mysore on all sides except in the north. When in 1800, the Nizam transferred his acquisitions from Mysore to the company, his kingdom was entirely encircled by the Pax Britannica".

The Maratha Wars

As in the case of Mysore, the primary cause for the British interest in the affairs of the Marathas and the desire to expand their sway into the Maratha territory was solely commercial, as the British developed lucrative cotton trade after 1784 to China from Gujarat through Bombay. Further, the growth of infantry and gunnery in Maharashtra created suspicion in the minds of the British that their objective of expansion of their territorial sway cannot be achieved unless the Marathas are reduced to submission. As in the case of the Nizam of Hyderabad and the Carnatic, the rivalry for succession among Narayana Rao, the younger brother of Peshwa Madhava Rao and Raghoba or Raghunath Rao, uncle of Peshwa Madhava Rao and the subsequent events between 1772 and 1775, necessitated the intervention of the British in the Maratha affairs. Consequently, there were three Anglo-Marartha wars: (i) Anglo-Maratha war 1775–1782, (ii) Maratha war 1803–1806, and (iii) Maratha war 1816–1817.

In the first Anglo-Maratha war, the British supported the claims of Raghoba who approached them but Nana Phadnavis opposed the move of Raghoba. Consequently, the first Anglo-Maratha war took place between 1775 and 1782, and the war came to an end by the treaty of Salbai of 1782. The British obtained Salsette and Madhava Rao Narayan, the posthumous son of Peshwa Madhavarao was confirmed as the rightful Peshwa. There was peace for two decades and taking advantage of the peaceful situation the British made Mysore their dependency. During this period there developed dissensions between Gaikwad of Baroda, Bhonsle of Nagpur, Holkar of Indore and Scindia of Gwalior and at this juncture Wellesley wanted the Marathas to enter into Subsidiary Alliance system. Understanding the real implications, the Marathas refused to oblige. At this juncture only, Nana Phadnavis died and taking advantage of this Jaswant Rao Holkar defeated Scindia along with the forces of Peshwa in 1800 and captured the city of Poona. This loss of Poona made the Peshwa once again to approach the British and thus started the second Aglo-Maratha war of 1803–1805. The Peshwa, Bajirao II entered into subsidiary alliance in 1802 and accepted the treaty of Bassein, which was opposed by Scindia and Bhonsle but they were defeated by the British. In 1804, Holkar made an effort to retrieve the lost prestige of the Marathas but he failed. Thus, ended the second Anglo Maratha war as Wellesley was called from India to England. Again in 1817–1819, Peshwa Baji Rao II made efforts to form a united coalition to drive the British, but his attempt also failed. Finally, the British succeeded in making the Marathas forgo their independence, and the dominions of Bhonsle and Holkar were annexed by the British. Thus by 1820, the British expanded their political sway over Carnatic, Nizam of Hyderabad, Mysore and the Marathas, and the British rule in India became a reality. In northern India, the decline of the Mughal power led to the emergence of country states of Awadh, Rohillas, Jats and Sikhs. We also witness conflict and cooperation among these powers and with the British in their pursuit of expansion and consolidation of their dominions. After the success in the battle of Buxar, the British East India Company forced a subsidiary alliance on Ayodhya or Awadh. Awadh become a buffer zone between the territories of the British and the regions of Western India. Despite the opposition of the British, the Nawab of Awadh maintained his hold effectively by restricting the trade by the company and other Europeans in Awadh territories between 1765 and 1775. As the defences of Awadh weakened between 1775 and 1801, the hold of the company over Awadh increased and the ruler of Awadh was isolated diplomatically and reduced financially. Lord Wellesley succeeded in forcing the Awadh Nawab to enter into a new treaty in 1801 by which he ceded Doab, Gorakhpur and Rohilkhand to the company. Further, by the third provision of this treaty the Nawab had to act with the advice in conformity to the council of the officers of the said Honourable Company. The British company slowly and gradually increased its hold over the mindset of the people of Awadh and made it a virtual dependent of the company and by 1856, Awadh was annexed to the British empire and the Resident took over the administration of Awadh as the Chief Commissioner. The British intervention in Rohilkhand is linked with the interests of Awadh. In the 18th century the Afghans who migrated to India in search of employment occupied and settled between Delhi and Agra in the west and Awadh and Allahabad in the east. The Rohillas became politically important under the leadership of Dadu and Ali Muhammad Khan. After the death of Ali Muhammad Khan, the possessions of the Rohillas were divided and there were skirmishes among the neighbouring states and by 1761 the Rohillas became independent. As the Rohillas were attacked by the Marathas, they entered into a treaty with the Nawab Wazir of Avadh in 1772. By this treaty, they agreed to pay 40 lakhs as the price for their help. In 1713, the Marathas attacked Rohilkhand but left after the approach of the British and Avadh troops. The Nawab Wazir demanded the Rohillas to pay the amount as per the treaty but they refused. The British troops in association with the troops of Avadh attacked Rohilkhand and Rohilkhand was annexed to Avadh. The occupation of Rohilkhand by Avadh with the help of the British was unjustifiable on any ground. It reflects the avariciousness of the Avadh ruler and the British.

The British East India Company while making efforts to weaken Awadh and capture it was planning to repeat the same story of annexation in Punjab also. By the time the British East India Company developed into a political power in India, the Sikhs became a power to be reckoned with by occupying all the territory extending from Saharanpur in the east to Attock in the west and from Jammu in the north to Kangra in the south. The Sikhs were divided into 12 *Misls* and generally they used to fight against each other. It was Ranjit Singh, the son of Sardar Mahasingh of Sukar Chakia clan, who ruled from 1792 to 1839, united the Sikhs into a unified state structure. Ranjit Singh with foresight maintained cordial relations with the British and never fought with them directly, in spite of the problems posed by them. Political instability that set in the Punjab after the death of Ranjit Singh in 1839 and quick succession of rulers in the Punjab and the high handedness of the military and Sikhs allies like Prime Minister Rajan Lai Singh, the Commander-in-Chief Misar Tej Singh and Dogra Raja Gulab Singh made the British intervention possible. The Sikhs fought two wars: (i) Sikh war 1845–1846 and (ii) Sikh war 1848–49. In the first Sikh war the British won and concluded the humiliating treaty of Lahore in 1846 and the British annexed the Jalandhar Doab and handed over Jammu & Kashmir to Raja Gulab Singh. A British resident was stationed at Lahore with extensive authority over all matters and expenses to be borne by the Lahore government. The revolt of Mulraj against the Lahore Durbar in 1848 led to the beginning of the second Sikh war in which the British defeated the Punjab and Punjab was annexed to the British empire in 1849. The British East India Company had chosen two tools of war and diplomacy to expand their political sway in India. In the preceding pages, we witnessed how the British expanded their territories by waging war with Bengal, Nizam, the Carnatic, Mysore, the Marathas, Avadh and the Punjab. Now, let us take up the aspect of diplomacy followed by the British. The two important policies of diplomatic nature are: (a) the subsidiary alliance of Wellesley, and (b) the Doctrine of Lapse of Dalhousie.

The Subsidiary Alliance of Wellesley

Besides the tool of war, the British East India Company, like a hungry wolf was anxiously waiting to use any means to expand its territorial holdings in India. Of such means Subsidiary Alliance is one. It is Welleseley, the Governor General of Bengal, who vigorously implemented this policy for the advantage of the company. Though, Wellesley is associated with Subsidiary Alliance, the author and originator was not Wellesley but Dupleix, the French Governor. Dupleix devised it and implemented it and later the same was followed by the British from Clive to Wellesley. Alfred Lyall notices four stages in the evolution of this system. In the first stage, the British East India Company supplied weapons and armies to the native ruler, as we notice the supply of arms and armies to the Nawab of Avadh against Rohillas during the tenure of Warren Hastings. In the second stage, the British with the help of the native ruler took the field. In the third stage, the British took money from the native ruler for the maintenance of the army separately for the defence of such state, e.g., Oudh in 1797. In the fourth stage, the British agreed to maintain a permanent and fixed subsidiary force within the territory of its ally in return for a payment of a sum or ceding certain territory permanently to the British. Further, Wellesley by this Subsidiary Alliance system made it mandatory for the ally to keep a British Resident in the court of the native ruler, not to employ any other European nationals in this service, not to maintain relations with any other native ruler without the prior approval of the British. The British agreed to protect the territory of such allies from foreign aggression and not to intervene in the internal affairs of such native ally who entered into this alliance. A critical review of this policy clearly reveals that this is advantageous to the British and disadvantageous to the native ruler. The policy was designed in such a way that it served the main interest of the British East India Company in expanding its hold in new territories of its allies without spending money from its coffers and to make these allies its dependencies.

The Doctrine of Lapse

Dalhousie, the last of the Governors General of the time of the Company was associated with this policy of the Doctrine of Lapse. By using this policy as a means, Dalhousie annexed the native states like Satara, Nagpur, Jhansi, Jaitpur and Sambhalpur. By denying the right of adoption to a Hindu native state as legitimate one, the British Governor General Dalhousie annexed the above native states to the British empire in India. His policy resulted in a political upheaval which threatened to destroy the solid foundations of the Company's rule in India in 1857, because his annexationist policy based on the Doctrine of Lapse has no legal, moral or expediency justification. The British East India Company expanded its control over a vast territory and also extended its influence beyond India in Sri Lanka in the south, Mauritius in the south-west,

Afghanistan in the north-west, Nepal in the north to Andamans and Nicobar, Burma, Malaya, and Philippines in the south-east. It can be said without any hesitation that it was mainly at the cost of India that England became the dominant power in the whole of South Asia and Asian lands on the Indian ocean by using the Indian sepoys like cannon fodder and draining the Indian treasury through unnecessary wars and diplomacy.

Colonial Administrative Apparatus and Ideological Influences

The British entered India as traders and their primary objective was to earn profits by carrying on trade in India. In order to earn maximum profits from Indian trade and commerce and to develop monopoly of trade and commerce they competed with other European powers. By the beginning of the middle of the 18th century, the British crippled the French interests in India and became a dominant trading power. The British also developed political interest to push in their monopoly of trade and commerce and initiated the process of expanding their political power in Bengal by the victory in the battle of Plassey and obtained the power of Diwani by the victory of Buxar through the treaty of Allahabad of 1765. From then on till 1857, the British East India Company through wars, diplomacy and administrative measures made it a policy to obtain more and more of economic benefits by fleecing the Indian farmer, artisan and small and medium traders. This process is called colonialism and India became a colony of the British. This colonialism bled the Indians and made India a de-industrialized power. In this span of seventy-five years from 1772 to 1857, the process and pattern of colonialism underwent different stages because the Charter Act of 1813 made by the British Parliament and Crown, abolished the monopoly of the British East India Company and opened the gates of trade and commerce to every British citizen. Further, by Charter Act of 1833, the Governor General of Bengal became the Governor General of India with control over the presidencies of Bombay and Madras and the British citizens were permitted to own. property in India and thereby we come across British landlords and planters of tea, coffee, indigo and cotton and also British capitalists investing surplus capital in Colonial India. Both these measures hastened the process of draining of the wealth of India by the colonialists with their colonial policies. Along with the colonialist measures, the British introduced ideology of mercantilism, orientalism, evangelicalism, utilitarianism and liberalism to justify their colonialist policies in India. In the name of 'improvement', 'progress' and 'whiteman's burden' the British administrators made it their avowed objective to introduce British laws and revenue measures into India. Added to the above ideological and philosophical tenets, the modernization process of Dalhousie also acted as the last straw on the camel's back, and the substance of colonialism remained the same throughout the period of seventy-five years. The colonial administrative apparatus from top to bottom was controlled by the Crown and Parliament through their Acts and Charter Acts. The British East India Company enjoyed a unique position at England as

King George III patronized it and its friends – fought with the help of the parliament. The British decided to control the company's Indian administration in the interest of Britain's influential elite group as a whole. The company was allowed to have monopoly "of the trade and Directors of the company" were given the control of Indian administration.

Before we take up in detail the administrative set-up of the colonial administrative apparatus, we have to bear in mind the fact that the pre-colonial India had well established administrative structure at different levels – centre, provincial and local, suited to the needs and demands of the time, relevant to the socio-economic formations. Another factor to be noted is that all the earlier invaders who established their power in India like the Indo-Greeks to Sakas, the Kushans and the Muslims added their principles of administration and modified the administrative structure and thus we notice the process of continuity and change in our administration in theory and practice. The major factor of difference to be noticed is, that the British East India Company replaced the old Indian administrative policies and introduced their system of law, justice, education, revenue and intellectual and social theories, in India. All these changes created a new value system. We also notice an evolution of the colonial administrative apparatus as per the reforms introduced by the earliest regulating Act of 1773 and ending with the Government of India Act of 1858.

The regulating Act of 1773 introduced provisions for the effective supervision of the executive of the company. It introduced changes in the constitution of the Court of directors of the company and the company affairs were put under the control of the government. The Governor of Bengal was made the Governor General of Bengal and a council with four members was constituted. The Governor General and council was given authority to supervise the presidencies of Bombay and Madras and the presidencies were brought under the control of Governor General in the council of Bengal. This Act provided for a Supreme Court of justice at Calcutta to take care of the justice of Europeans, employees and citizens of Calcutta. The Governor General in council was empowered to make laws for Bengal. The Pitt's India Act established a board of control with six members of whom two were to be cabinet ministers. This board was given power over the activities of the Court of directors. This Act provided three members to the Governor General in council and the Governor General was given a casting vote. The importance of the Pitt's India Act lies in the fact of laying the foundation for a centralized administration, a process which reached its climax towards the end of the 19th century and it tightened the control of parliament over the company. In 1786, the Presidencies were divided into districts and collectors were appointed. A revenue board was created with four members with the right to manage the treasury. The Charter Act of 1793 gave powers to the Governor General to override his council and also empowered him to exercise effective control over the Presidencies. Through this Act the British introduced the concept of a civil law enacted by a secular human agency, i.e., the government and applied universally in place of the personal rule of the past rulers. It is an important change to be noticed by everyone. The Charter Act of 1813 allowed the British subjects, access to Indian shore with their ships. By now the company's power spread over the whole of India except the Punjab, Nepal and the Sindh. To whatever political and economical philosophy the British subscribed, every Britisher was interested in the stability and security of the British territorial power in India. The most important development to be recorded is the deprival of the monopoly of trade and commerce of the British East India Company and throwing open the trade of India to all the British citizens. The East India Company was allowed to have monopoly of trade with China. Owing to the rapid growth of industrial revolution in Great Britain, the British followed laissez-faire philosophy in India which ultimately benefited the British industrialists and capitalists at the cost of the Indian farmers and artisans. There was a great demand in India for the abolition of the company rule and assumption of authority by the crown. In this backdrop the Charter Act of 1833 was passed which made the Governor General of Bengal, the Governor General of India. The president of the board of control became the minister of India and the board of control was given the power to supervise Indian affairs on behalf of the crown. Bombay, Madras and Bengal regions were placed under the direct rule of the Governor General in Council of India. Central government was given the power to exercise full control over revenue and expenditure of the British territories in India. The Governor General in Council was given legislative powers over the rest of the Indian presidencies which are applicable to everyone in India. By this Act, a new member by name law member was added to the executive council and the strength rose to four. Lord Macaulay, the new law member played a very crucial role in influencing the educational policy of the British. The number of members of the councils of the presidencies was reduced to two. Bombay and Madras were to keep their separate armies under the commander-in-chief and were kept under the control of the central government. The laws of India were codified by this Act through a law commission appointed by the Governor General. As a result of their effort, the Indian penal code and codes of civil and commercial law were enacted. The most significant aspect of this Act theoretically was abolishing discrimination towards Indians in appointments to the British East India Company, and it was more violated by non-implementation and it provided for Indians a sheet anchor towards agitations for equality of treatment to Indians. In the next two decades the political consciousness of Indians increased due to the introduction of Western education and realization among the Indians. Raja Ram Mohan Roy, the Bombay Association and the Madras Native Association submitted petitions to the parliamentary select committee demanding for the end of the reactionary rule of the company. By 1853 Charter Act, one more member was added to the executive council of Governor General to enact laws. The consent of the Governor General was mandatory for all legislative proposals. They added one more member from each province to the central legislative body. The Chief

Justice of the Supreme Court of Calcutta was also made the ex officio member of the legislative council. The legislative council's membership was limited – to 12 the Governor General, Commander-in-Chief, four members of Governor General's council and six legislative members. Thus, this Act separated the legislative body from the executive body and this legislative body became an Anglo-Indian House of Commons. The 1857 Great Revolt opened the eyes of the British and made it clear how the Indians hated the British rule for all their evil deeds and an attempt was made by the British to rectify their blunder by the Government of India Act of 1858. The Act replaced the British East India Company as ruler and transferred the powers to the crown along with the army. It abolished the Court of directors and the Board of Control. Their place was filled up by the secretary of state and the Indian council. They were given the powers to rule in the name of Her Majesty. But yet the ultimate power rested with the Parliament. India Council should consist of 15 members and it was to be an advisory body to the secretary of state. The Governor General is designated as Viceroy or Crown's representative and the Government of India's strings were in London.

The administrative structure that evolved in India from 1773 to 1858 was the result of the initiatives of many British administrators, thinkers and philosophers. As already indicated, the earliest influence on the thinking of British administrators and thinkers was their idea of improvement or progress. This process was initiated by Cornwallis by introducing the permanent land revenue settlements. Between 1830 and 1840, when Bentinck was the Governor General of India the initiatives of Benthamite reforms based on utilitarianism and Charles Grant's idea of evangelicalism and the British interests of monopoly of trade and maximum profits created the framework of administrative machinery and structure in India. Thus, the British administration in India was motivated by the maintenance of law and order and the perpetuation of the British regime. The British depended on three pillars, of civil service, the army and the police to achieve their objective. The term 'Civil Service' was first used in India by the company to distinguish military and ecclesiastical personnel from civil employees. In the beginning they were commercial-oriented but later on they became public servants. The civil service was graded from the beginning as apprentices, writers, factors, junior merchants and then finally senior merchants. High officers in India were selected from among the senior merchants. This system of grading continued till 1839. It is Cornwallis who increased the salaries of the civil servants and debarred them from taking bribes. It is Wellesley who introduced training for civil servants. For a long time, the civil servants were appointed through the process of patronage and in 1833, the selection through limited competition was introduced and by 1853 they selected civil servants through public competition and in 1858 the Civil Service Commission was started for the process of selection of civil servants. The chief officer in the district was the Collector and he was assisted by a Tahsildar, who was a native. The Collector had both magisterial and chief police functions. By these changes the Collector obtained total authority over the districts. In between the Collector and the Tahsildar, the post of Deputy Collector was created. It is Cornwallis who initiated the police system. Till then, the police functions were performed by the local Zamindars. The army was also disbanded along with stripping of the police functions of the Zamindars. The police force was organized into Thanas, headed by a Darogha, who was a native and these daroghas were kept under the supervision of the criminal judges. The post of district Superintendent of Police was created to head the police set-up in the district and sometime later the Collector controlled the police also. The judicial system was one of the main pillars of administrative structure and framework of the British in India. It is Lord Cornwallis, who started building up of the administrative machinery in India, It is he who separated the judicial functions from the revenue functions and laid foundation for the judicial system. Broadly the structure of the judicial system is divided as follows: in civil cases *Sadar Diwani Adalat* followed by provincial courts followed by district courts presided over by a district magistrate from civil service was introduced. A category of subordinate courts presided over by Indian judges called Munsiff and Amins was created. In criminal cases *Sadar Nizamat Adalat* in Calcutta and *Sadar Faujdari Adalat* in Madras and Bombay happened to be the highest, followed by the court of circuit presided over by civil servants followed by local courts presided over by Indian magistrates who are called principal Sadar Amins in Madras Presidency. First, all these courts in hierarchical order were experimented in Bengal. Both the *Sadar Diwani Adalt* and *Sadar Nizam Adalt* were located in Calcutta as the highest civil and criminal courts. The provincial courts of appeal both in civil and criminal cases, (circuit courts) were established in the towns of Calcutta, Dacca, Murshidabad and Patna. While the British occupied the superior position, the Indians occupied subordinate positions such as Munisiffs, Amins, the Quazis and the Pandits advising the judges in the Hindu and the Muhammadan laws. In subsequent years, the same was extended to other states and after some time a whole network of laws through the process of enactment of laws and codification of old laws was developed. By the time of Bentinck, the Indian penal code and Indian criminal procedure code were prepared. The entire judicial system was based on the notions of the 'rule of law' and 'equality before law' of the British. But in practice, the judicial system was not at all beneficial to the Indians as it became very costly and lengthy and Indians failed to comprehend the laws. To give an example of the lengthy process, the case in Madras Presidency may be quoted where a Zamindar went to a court of law in 1832 to settle inheritance and debt suits and the final judgment was delivered in 1896, i.e., after 64 years. In spite of the above demerits the judicial system created a consciousness of oneness. Thus, what we see in India as a result of the measures, administrative machinery was a network of laws applicable throughout the country and a vast administrative structure to implement the laws. In nature, the structure was modern and pan-Indian in its spread, while the administrative structure served the purpose of maintaining law and order in India from the British view point, it served as a ground to protest and challenge the authority of the British in India.

Economic Changes

In this chapter we are going to study the impact of the British East India Company's economic policies on the conditions of the peasants and artisans in particular and of the people of India in general. The British, who came to India as traders with the approval of the crown in AD 1600, acquired political power in Bengal, Bihar and Orissa by the middle of the 18th century and began to rule directly from 1772 onwards. Since then the British experimented with land revenue as the main source of income to the state. It was so because the main occupation of the majority of the people of India was agriculture and the experiments in land revenue were primarily motivated by the objective of multiplying the income of the state through land revenue and not to better the conditions of the peasants by providing better irrigational facilities and better seeds.

In 1772, Warren Hastings became the Governor of Bengal and he abolished the dual government and assumed direct responsibility of the Bengal province and initiated experiment of five-year settlement of land revenue by farming out cultivable lands to the highest bidders. Warren Hastings did not recognize the rights of Zamindars and did not depend on their services for tax collection. Realizing that the collectors of land tax have become corrupt, Warren Hastings replaced them with Indian Diwans in 1773. As the five-year land revenue settlement failed in operation, in 1777 Warren Hastings reverted to the annual settlement system and returned to open auction to the highest bidder. On the whole, the efforts of Warren Hastings did not yield the desired enhancement of land revenue and left behind a dark trail of misery and famine.

Cornwallis and Permanent Settlement of Bengal

Cornwallis, who followed Warren Hastings, as Governor General of Bengal was sent with specific instructions to improve the land revenue to be collected from Bengal. The British Parliament by an Act of 1784 directed the Court of directors to give up the practice of annual settlement of revenue to be collected and to fix up the collection of revenue of land on a permanent basis. Cornwallis appointed an inquiry committee under the headship of Sir John Shore and asked him to inquire about the usages, tenures and rents of land revenue collection in pre-colonial India. Sir John Shore submitted his report in 1789. On the basis of the report, Cornwallis introduced land revenue settlement for ten years with Zamindars in 1789 but the same was made permanent in 1793 by the proclamation of Cornwallis and it was known as Permanent Land Revenue settlement. The basic features of the settlement were as follows:

- The Zamindars were made hereditary owners of the land under their possession. They and their successors exercised total control over lands.
- The Zamindars could sell and purchase lands.
- The state had no direct contact with the peasants.
- The company's share in the revenue was fixed permanently with the Zamindars.

Thus the Permanent Land Revenue settlement involved three parties, the government, the Zamindar and the 'ryot' or the cultivator. As per this settlement, the role of the government and the Zamindar is fixed but the role of the ryot is not at all defined and the ryot is put at the mercy of the Zamindar and thus ryot is the worst effected due to this settlement.

Merits and Demerits of the Settlement

Scholars hold divergent opinions about this settlement. Marshman observed that it was a bold, brave and wise measure and the Fifth Report concludes: "The measure was a success and the government had taken every step in its power to remove the minor defects". R.C. Dutt also opines: "If the prosperity and happiness of a nation be the criterion of wisdom and success, Lord Cornwallis's permanent settlement of 1793 is the wisest and most successful measure which the British nation had adopted in India" and he adds, that it is "the one act of British nation within the century and a half of their rule in India which has most effectively safeguarded the economic welfare of the people". On the contrary, Holmes, James Mill, Thurston and Raja Rama Mohan Roy were very critical about this settlement. A critical analysis of the actual operation of this settlement in years to come proves that this settlement was not at all beneficial to any party – the government, Zamindar and the ryot. Charles Metcalfe is of the view that "Cornwallis instead of being the creator of the prosperity in India was the great destroyer of it. The cultivators who were reduced to the position of tenants suffered miserably at the hands of their landlords. The company therefore, did a grave injustice to the peasants". Bipan Chandra also writes that compared to the British landlord, Indian landlord paid as tax 10/11th of his income from the land. As such many landlords became defaulters of tax to the government and had to sell their lands to pay the tax. Thus, the permanent settlements proved harmful to all parties concerned and as such it was not introduced in other parts of India except northern circars in the south and in the districts of Benaras in the north. By 1811, the London authorities warned against the introduction of permanent settlement without a minute and detailed survey of the land.

Ryotwari Settlements

As a result of the criticism against the permanent settlement by Captain Read and Sir Thomas Munro, the select committee of the House of Commons suggested to the Crown and Parliament the necessity of not introducing permanent settlement anywhere in India and favoured Ryotwari system. The architect and prime advocate of Ryotwari system was Thomas Munro. Munro advocated that the prosperity of the large, number of people can be achieved by the introduction of the Ryotwani system further. He argued that this system was in vogue in pre-colonial India. The cultivator was made to pay a stipulated land tax to the government regularly keeping in view the area under cultivation and the prices of the agricultural produce. In this system, the ryot or cultivator becomes the landlord, labourer and the farmer. This system appeared to be more advantageous to both the government and the cultivator as it protected the interests of both the parties. Two important features of this system were the direct settlement between the ryot and the government and assessment for a short period. There would be no intermediary between the government and the ryot like Zamindar or Talukdar. Another significant feature was that the ryot obtained both hereditary and transferable rights of occupancy over the land tilled by him. Ryotwari settlement was introduced in Madras and Bombay presidencies and was in operation for three decades. In actual operation, it failed to make the cultivators prosperous and happy and the condition of the peasants worsened due to indebtedness to moneylenders. Most of the land passed into the hands of the moneyed class and a new social group of landless wage earners increased due to high land tax collected from the ryots. These after-effects of the Ryotwari system created considerable social tension and led to a major rural apprising in the Bombay Deccan in 1875. In practice the Ryotwari system too did not satisfy either the cultivator or the government.

The Mahalwari System

The failure of the permanent settlement of Cornwallis and the Ryotwari system of Munro made the British administrators think of an alternate settlement of land revenue to be implemented in the north-west provinces. Discussions on the need for new orientation on revenue policy made the British opt for the settlement proposed by an English official, Holt Mackenzie in 1819. Holt Mackenzie developed a theory that the Zamindars and Talukdars constitute the village community and land tax of that village is to be collected from the village community. Mackenzie's proposal was to gradually eliminate all the intermediate proprieters created by the British laws and to protect the rights of the actual cultivators, i.e., the village Zamindar and the Ryot in the village. It was introduced in the Gangetic valley, the north-west provinces, parts of central India and the Punjab. Under this Mahalwari system the revenue to be paid by the Ryot was fixed for a short period and the state's share was fixed as two-thirds of the gross produce. As it was too high, William Bentinck reduced the tax to the sixty-six per cent and afterwards to fifty per cent. As the tax was high and cultivators failed to pay the taxes, large areas of land began to pass into the hands of the moneylenders and merchants after 1833. The Mahalwari settlement brought impoverishment and widespread dispossession in the cultivating communities of North India between 1830 and 1840 and their resentment burst as 1857 revolt. Owing to the greed of the British administrators for more and more income from land tax, all the land revenue settlements experimented in India between 1772 and 1822 thoroughly failed and caused undue hardship and misery to the community of ryots or peasants.

Condition of Peasants: Rural Indebtedness and Recurrent Famines

One hundred years of colonial revenue policy of the British East India Company made the entire Indian peasantry impoverished and indebted to unscrupulous moneylenders and bankers. It is all because of the high incidence of land revenue fixed and imposed by the British, existence of many intermediaries between the cultivator and the state, subdivision and fragmentation of landholdings and pressure on agriculture due to the growth of population. Besides these factors, uncertain monsoons, poor means of irrigational facilities, and lack of modernization of agriculture also contributed to the impoverishment of the peasantry. Added to these factors, the most important feature was high demand for revenue and its constant increase year after year throughout the colonial period. The British collected as land revenue from Bengal in 1767 an amount of sixty lakh of rupees. By 1793, the amount rose to Rs 1,09,59,130. Besides high tax on the cultivator, many intermediaries exploiting the innocent and uneducated peasant by demanding tax at various levels made the cultivator approach the moneylender to pay the revenue due to the state. Consequently, the peasants were indebted and it led to rural indebtedness as rural industries based on rural handicrafts declined due to rapid industrialization of England and the drain of wealth from India to England. The early Indian nationalist thinkers Dadabai Naoroji, R.C. Dutt and Govind Mahadeva Ranade and many more, made minute studies of the drain of wealth and causes of rural indebtedness and finally came to the conclusion that it was all due to the British colonial interests destroying the Indian agriculture and rural industries. Bishwesvar Prasad aptly remarks that the prosperity of England beckoned poverty of India, for imperialism based on a colonial economy thrives on the exploitation of the dependent subjects. India had become the victim of colonialism and all the evils of imperialism had become evident before the power and position of the East India Company had been extinguished after the revolt of 1857. By 1911, the rural indebtedness was estimated as 300 crore and by 1937 it rose to 1,800 crore.

Further, besides man-made disasters, natural disasters like famines also affected the Indian peasants and made them impoverished. A number of major famines: 1759 (Sind), 1783 (UP, Kashmir, Rajasthan), 1800–1804 and 1837–38 (UP). Famines occurred in 1787, 1790–92, 1799–1804, 1812–13, 1819–20, 1824–25, 1833–34 in Maharashtra and Rajasthan, famines occurred in south Indian region in 1781–82, 1790–92, 1806–1807, 1833–34 in Maharashtra and Rajasthan. Of all the famines the most devastating was the 1770 famine of Bengal, where one crore people perished. The failure of the British colonial power to improve irrigation and the failure to tackle famines through a sustained policy also contributed to the impoverishment and indebtedness of rural India. We may conclude that the British colonial policy coupled with land revenue experiments made India an impoverished and debt-ridden country.

Nature of Colonial Economy

India became a colony of the British nation for nearly two centuries from 1757 to 1947. The British who came to India as traders developed political ambition and became political masters of Bengal, Bihar and Orissa by their victory in

1757 in the battle of Plassey. In the next hundred years by wars and diplomacy, they became the dominant political masters of the entire Indian subcontinent and introduced such policies which were beneficial to the economic interests of British nation. It is no exaggeration to state that the primary motive of British colonialism was economic exploitation of India. The final outcome of British colonialism was extreme poverty of the Indian population. India became a backward nation in all spheres of life. Thus, the British colonialism made India a poor and backward nation dependent on the mercy and charity of the British political masters. The view of Adam Smith as recorded in the *Wealth of Nations* that the government of an exclusive company of merchants is perhaps the worst of all governments for any country whatever, is true of India as pointed out by Ramesh Chandra Dutt, Ranade and Dadabhai Naoroji, the early nationalist critics of British colonialism. Bipan Chandra aptly points out that the early nationalist critiques by their efforts sowed the seeds of nationalism well and deep by a brilliant scientific analysis of the complex economic mechanism of modern colonialism and of the chief contradiction between the interests of the Indian people and the British rule.

Commercialization of Agriculture and Its Effects

Since time immemorial, agriculture was the main occupation of the people of India and surplus agricultural goods were sold in the markets in pre-colonial India, which promoted internal and external trade and commerce. We can say that commercialization of agriculture was not totally new to India but the form that it took under the British rule differed in many ways from that which existed in pre-colonial times. During the British colonial rule, what happened was production of agricultural goods which could be exported for the investment in Britain alone was encouraged in India only to feed the British industries or which could get maximum profits to the Britishers in the European or American markets. The sole objective of the commercialization of agriculture was to provide raw material and quality agricultural goods like cotton, indigo, tea and coffee, raw silk, jute, opium, pepper, and sugar.

The commercialization of agriculture of this period was beneficial only to the British planters, traders and manufacturers and a very minute section of Indian traders and moneylenders who worked as middlemen for the British capitalist group. The immediate effect of commercialization of agriculture was the reduction of area under cultivation of food crops. As a result in the words of Manilal Nanavati, former Deputy Governor of Reserve Bank of India, nearly 30 per cent of the population of India is estimated to be suffering from chronic malnutrition and undernutrition. The growth and export of commercial crops impoverished India instead of enriching Indians. Commercialization also added a fresh element of instability to rural markets as price fluctuations in global market had their impact on the fortunes of individual merchants and peasants. It is no exaggeration to state in the final analysis; the worst sufferers were the peasants who had been drawn by force and persuasion into the production of commercial crops. The commercialization of agriculture did not affect the social structure totally and widened the gulf between the rich and poor, and peasants have now become wage-earning agricultural labourers. It is true that the peasant were impoverished and he could survive because the European businessmen found it more advantageous to exploit the small peasants household than to take up large scale production with hired labour paying wages, as this commercialization of agriculture altered neither the methods nor the organization of production, and small farming based on family labour continued to be the predominant form in the rural localities of Indian subcontinent.

Decline of Cottage Industries

The economy of pre-colonial India was mainly based on agriculture and handicraft production or cottage industries. Livelihood of the rural masses passed off adequately because of the self-sufficiency of villages and village communities. In pre-colonial times more than 200 varieties of cotton and silk clothes were exported to foreign countries besides spices, ivory and other varieties of goods like indigo, saltpetre, and sea pearls. But the transfer of political authority to a trading company which was primarily interested in earning profits and investments in Britain and their colonial economic policies systematically ruined the trade in silk and cotton clothes and impoverished the weaving community. The process of industrialization that took place in Europe as a result of industrial revolution and invention of mechanical devices like spinning jenny in 1767, and water frame by Arkwright in 1769 destroyed the cottage industry of cotton and silk weaving in India. The import of finished silk made cloth available at cheaper rate and production and exports of raw cotton to Europe gave death blow to the cottage industries of India. Further, the tariff policy of the British government also destroyed the cottage industries of India. It is no exaggeration to suggest that the total destruction of Indian handicrafts and cottage industries contributed to the mass poverty in India.

Causes for Poverty in India

In pre-colonial India, in spite of uneven income levels of different segments of population, the demand in the home markets for consumer goods was fairly good among common people and the rich nobles provided market for high class luxury goods. Cotton textiles agro-based products like oil, tobacco, opium and ship building provided the necessary stimulus for the pre-colonial economy. In pre-colonial India, Indians were relatively better off compared to colonial India. The British colonial policies, in particular, the revenue policy of imposing high tax on agricultural sector, ruined the agrarian economy. The commercialization of agriculture, ruining of Indian handicrafts, import of finished mill-made cloth at cheaper rate, neglect of irrigation facilities till the second half of the 19th century and the greed of the British East India Company officials made India a poor country. The main cause for the poverty and impoverishment of Indian peasants and artisans was the colonial policy which resulted in 'Drain of Wealth' as proved by the early nationalists like Ramesh Chandra Dutt, Dadabai Naoroji, Ranade, G.V. Joshi and Malaviya.

Social Changes: Spread of Western Education

Pre-colonial India is well known for its system of indigenous education. There existed *Gurukulas* and *Patashalas* to promote education of the caste Hindus and *Madarasas* and *Maktabs* to promote the education of the Muslim community in India. This indigenous education gave more stress to scholarship of languages rather than science and technology and by the time the British came to India as traders, Persian was the court language and irrespective of religious faith, both Hindus and Muslims learnt Persian to obtain jobs under the rulers of pre-colonial India. Besides Madarsas and Patashalas, there too existed advanced centres of learning in languages along with ordinary schools teaching language proficiency based on oral tradition and memorization of the texts. The British who acquired territorial control and became political masters did not interfere in the educational field till 1813. After 1813, with the cooperation or a limited number of Indians, the British colonial rulers introduced the western system of education in India. There was a great debate among Indians and the British, known as 'Orientalists' and 'Anglicists' about the type of education needed by the Indians. For nearly more than half a century, the British followed a policy of neutrality or non-intervention in the matters of religion and culture of the indigenous people. But due to constant pressure from different sections – the Christian missionaries, the liberals, the utilitarians, and the Anglicists – the British yielded and agreed to take up the responsibility of promoting Western education. There is also a view that the educational policy was designed to legitimize the domination of the British colonial needs. No doubt, there also existed certain people among the British, who were genuinely interested in the promotion of oriental learning, like Warren Hastings who started Calcutta Madarasa in 1781, Jonathan Duncan who founded the Beneras Sanskrit College in 1791 and William James, who founded The Asiatic Society of Bengal in 1784. In this great debate, finally Anglicists, succeeded in introducing the western system of education in India. A general committee of public instruction was set up in 1823 to look after the development of education in India. Macaulay, the president of the General Committee of Public Instruction and Lord Bentinck overrode the orientalist view point and declared, "the great object of the British government in India is henceforth to be the promotion of European literature and science among natives of India and that all the funds appropriated for the purpose of education would be best employed on English education alone". Besides Macaulay and William Bentin, the efforts of Charles Grant and William Wilberforce deserve to be remembered in this aspect. William Bentinck announced in 1835 that English replaced Persian as the court language, books in English were made available at low prices and more funds were allotted to support the English education, and fund for the support of oriental learning was curtailed. Lord Auckland, who succeeded Bentnick as the Governor General also continued encouragement for the promotion of English learning by opening English colleges in Dacca, Patna, Benaras, Allahabad, Agra, Delhi and Barielly. In 1841, the General Committee of Public Instruction was abolished and in its place a council of education was established. Another landmark in the development of Western education was Wood's Despatch of 1854. The Despatch categorically states "the education that we desire to see extended in India is that which has for its object the diffusion of the improved arts, science, philosophy and literature of Europe, in short, of European knowledge". Charles Wood also recommended for the starting of universities at Calcutta, Bombay and Madras, for the establishment of a network of graded schools, high schools, middle schools and the elementary schools, promotion of vernacular schools and the establishment of teacher training institutions and the introduction of grant-in-aid system to non-government schools opened by charitable bodies and individuals. As per the recommendation of Wood, in 1857 three universities were established at Madras, Bombay and Calcutta. The Woods Despatch acted as a model for further development of education in India. Besides government support for Western learning in India, Christian missionaries and others took keen interest. The founding of Hindu College, which in later times was called Presidency College in Calcutta by David Hare and others helped the promotion of secular learning among the Hindus. Along with Western learning, woman's education also received wide patronage. The same pattern of promotion of education can be witnessed in Bombay and Madras presidencies too. We notice a slow and gradual promotion of Western learning in India which ultimately led to a new spirit of rationalism and a new critical outlook in the Indians which finally led to the emergence of a spirit of nationalism; championing of self-rule and self-reliance. It does not mean that Western learning was primarily responsible for the above narrated process, but it acted as a catalyst in fostering the awareness of the colonial economic exploitation. As the consequence of the spread of Western educational system, new notions of reason, justice and utilitarian concerns of welfare began to mould the minds of the educated Indians in search of an answer to the problems of poverty and impoverishment that plagued Indian society of the later 19th century. An interesting offshoot of the spread of Western education and transformation of British East India Company from that of trader-conqueror to that of rulers was the emergence of a middle class professional group to serve the interests of the British colonial and imperial interests.

Rise of Professional Classes and the Emerging Intelligentsia

The British colonial rule of India produced a new social group of bureaucrats and professionals like lawyers, teachers and doctors trained in Western medicine to heal the ailments and diseases. This social group is commonly known as 'Middle class" and 'Elite'. By 1870, India witnessed the rise and growth of middle-class consciousness which is reflected in the aspirations of native associations started in Madras, Bengal and Bombay presidencies. Sumit Sarkar remarks on the basis of evidence of J.R. Maclane, that by 1880, the total number of English-educated Indians rose to 50,000 and by 1907, the number of English-educated Indian rose to 5,05,000 and the circulation of English newspapers to 2,76,000. We can agree with Sumit Sarkar that English education gave its beneficiaries a unique capacity to establish contacts on a country-wide scale and opportunity to mould and mobilize public opinion either against or in favour of government policies. Further, Western education created awareness of world currents and ideologies which helped them to formulate conscious theories of nationalism. The ideology of the most of the English-educated elite was motivated by a desire of change rather than defending conservation or privileges of caste. The English-educated elite in many cases became the torch-bearers of modernity based on reason and social justice and made personal sacrifice to lead the Indian society on progressive lines of western outlook. Some of the English-educated elite emerged as intelligentsia and guided the destiny of Indian nation by their ideas and deeds. The intelligentsia of 19th century stood for reform and revival as in the case of Raja Ram Mohan Roy and Dayananda Saraswati and Bal Gangadhar Tilak. Some intellectuals impressed by the progressive ideas of the West, successfully convinced that the Indian society was in need of urgent social change and acted as catalysts in bringing out the desired change. But at the same time some intellectuals resisted total modernization based on secular values. Thus, middle-class elite played a critical role in-shaping and moulding the destiny of Mother India by their critical understanding of western outlook based on reason, social justice and equality.

Growth of the Press: English and Indian Languages

During the rule of the British East India Company, the Anglo-Indians and Europeans began to publish newspapers and journals. Hicky began to publish a weekly by name *The Bengal Gazette* in 1780 and did not hesitate to criticize the actions of the then Governor General Warren Hastings. Hicky is justifiably considered as the pioneer in the history of journalism in India. During the regimes of Cornwallis and Wellesley, the editor of *Indian World*, Duanna and Charles Maclean, the editor of *The Bengal Gazette* also attacked the policies and were deported to England. In 1818, J.S. Buckingham started the *Calcutta Journal* and also attacked the policies of the British officials and he too was deported to England. The British introduced the licensing system to publish papers. During 1860, *The Bengalee* and *The Amrita Bazar Patrika* were started in 'Bengalee language'. Lord Lytton wanted to control and regulate the vernacular press by his Vernacular Press Act of 1878. The press and literature played a very important role in moulding and shaping the national consciousness of the Indians. In particular, the role of the newspapers *The Indian Mirror*, *The Bombay Samachar*, and *The Hindu Patriot*, *The Amrita Bazar Patrika*, *The Hindu*, *The Kesari*, *The Bengalee*, *The Huriara*. *The Bengali Public Opinion*, *The Reis and Rayet*, *The Samprokash*, *The Sulabh Samachar*, *The Hitavadi*, *The Induprakash*, *The Swadeshimitran*, *The Advocate of Lucknow*, *The Herald of Bihar* are really noteworthy. By 1875, there was phenomenal growth of newspapers in India which rose to 475 in number. These newspapers created awareness among the masses of India about the need to be united and to act with one voice to achieve their goal of freedom from foreign yoke. Bipan Chandra observes that in the period from 1870 to 1918, powerful newspapers emerged under distinguished and fearless nationalists. The influence of the press extended far beyond its literate subscribers. Their influence was not limited to cities and large towns. Along with newspapers, library movement also kindled the spirit of nationalism and political participation on a large scale. One thing we have to remember is that newspapers in those days were started with the noble objective of public service by patriots par excellence. The newspapers were published with the sole objective of arousing political consciousness, to inculcate nationalism, to expose colonial rule and to preach disloyalty to the masses by opposing the unjust and harmful policies of the government. Along with the newspapers of English and vernacular languages, the literature produced by educated intellectuals belonging to different languages promoted patriotic consciousness among the masses of India. Of these writers, the most important are Raja Ram Mohan Roy, Ishwar Chandra Vidyasagar, Bankim Chandra, M.G. Ranade, and many more by their literary works fostered the spirit of patriotism and national consciousness among the masses.

Indian Renaissance

The success of the British in acquiring territorial possessions by displacing the old lineage-based political structures in different parts of India, the introduction of British law system, and revenue assessment through Permanent, Ryotwari and Mahalwari systems and cautious intervention in social system by objecting to infanticide, child marriages and sati sahagamana and ultimately the introduction of western system of education and ideas created a situation of re-examination of the pre-colonial values and ideas of the Indians in meeting the challenge posed by the west and its religious missionary zeal. There was a clash between the efficacy of the old ideals and values against the onslaught of new ideas of rationalism, human rights, social justice and equality based on rule of law. The cumulative effect of the clash of old and new ideas was Indian Renaissance of the 19th century. This Indian Renaissance resulted in the movement of revivalism, reform and rejection of existing cultural norms and values and welcoming of modernism based on secular values and outlook. The stimulus to the Indian Renaissance was both internal and external. Factors like general ideological interest, Western education and Theosophical Society gave impetus to the renaissance of the 19th century. Internally, the failure to meet the challenge of the West made the educated Indians introspect seriously the reasons for the failure of the Indians. Thus, both the internal and external stimuli led to Indian Renaissance of the 19th century. Literally, the term renaissance is composed of two Latin words *re* and *nasci* meaning 'again' and 'to be born'. Donald H. Bishop observes, "It involves a digging down the old and the temporarily submerged and bring it to the surface again". Bishop further observes "the Renaissance in India was a movement which confronted the threefold challenges of the past, the modern and the alien". The Indian Renaissance left the indelible threefold mark on the Indians. A section of the Indians denounced traditions of India and age-old caste system and became free inquirers after truth. Another section desired to retain the eternal essential truths of Sanatana Dharma and to do away with the corrupt practices that crept into it and wanted to build bridges between the Sanatana Dharma, Islam and Christianity. Another section wanted to revive and preserve the pure form of Sanatana Dharma. This Indian Renaissance first originated in Bengal and from there it spread to other parts of India and became finally an all-India phenomenon.

The basic tenets of Indian Renaissance are: (a) belief in equality of all, (b) faith in the belief of brotherhood, and (c) emphasis on the promotion of inherent capabilities and potentialities of all concerned. The objective of Indian Renaissance was not a limited perspective of social reform but the holistic perspective of total emancipation of Indians from all kinds of slavery and foreign yoke. It was such a comprehensive movement that included social, economic and political ideals of liberation from age-old cultural values of discrimination and differentiation based on birth, gender and power. Its impact can be seen in the socio-religious sphere, which is generally called social reform movements spearheaded by great intellectuals like Raja Ram Mohan Roy, Kesab Chandra Sen, Ishwara Chandra Vidyasagar, Devendranath Tagore, Dayanand Saraswati, Ramakrishna Paramahamsa, Vivekananda, Madam Blavatsky and Col. Alcott, Sir Sayyad Ahmed and Smt. Annie Besant and Jyotiba Phule, etc.

Socio-religious Movements and the Status of Women

In the history of pre-independent India, the 19th century was a period of transition and contestation in the socio-religious sphere as three streams: of reform, revival and rejection of ancient cultural values were woven around the socio-religious movement or social reform movement initiated by eminent intelligentsia of vision and foresight. This movement acted as a catalyst for the emergence of nationalism which ultimately drove away the British from India and made India an independent republic. This movement began in Bengal and spread to the other parts of India. It was a movement aimed at regenerating the sluggish spirit of India which was in a dazed condition due to the impact of the British rule. The pioneer of this movement of regeneration of India was Raja Ram Mohan Roy (1774–1833), the father of modern India who is acclaimed as the link between the fading past and dawning future, between the deep-rooted conservatism and radical reform, and between superstitious isolationism and progressive synthesis, in short, between reaction and progress. Ram Mohan Roy is also described as the arch which spanned the gulf between ancient caste and modern humanity, between superstition and science, between immovable custom and conservative progress, between a bewildering polytheism and a pure but vague theism. The intellectuals of the 19th century had a vision of the future India and in the words of M.G. Ranade the vision that inspired them was, "a change from constraint to freedom, from credulity to faith, from status to contract, from authority to reason, from unorganized to organized life, from bigotry to toleration, from blind fanaticism to a source of human dignity". In order to achieve this vision, all the intellectuals believed the spread of education, both western and Indian vernacular, to be the panacea for social transformation and national regeneration. It was not just a socio-religious movement but also a movement against economic exploitation and social discrimination of backward communities and women's emancipation from bondage and slavery. The movement which started as a minor stream in the first decade of the 19th century evolved into major water flow, engulfing the entire territorial borders of India.

Brahmo Samaj

In Eastern India, the socio-religious reform movement was spearheaded by Raja Ram Mohan Roy, a reputed linguist, and an erudite scholar born of affluent family. Ram Mohan started his career as an employee of the East India Company for 11 years from 1803 to 1814. In 1805, he published his first philosophical work, *Tulufat-ul-Muvaheddin*. In this book he examined and analysed the major religions in the light of reason and social content. Ram Mohan started his service activities from 1814 on settling at Calcutta after relinquishing his job in the East India Company. He started Atemiya Sabha in 1814 and carried on his struggle against idolatry and propagated monotheism by contributing articles in Bengali language to the newspapers. Ram Mohan was the first to use print media for the propagation of his views and philosophy to the public and for mobilization activity. The next step was the establishment of a new society, Brahma Sabha or Brahmo Samaj in 1828. Raja Ram Mohan advocated the principles, one 'Supreme Being' and the Brotherhood of Men and encouraged the followers of various religions to come together. He also refused to regard the Vedas as the last words of God and interpreted religion on the basis of reason and logic. Ram Mohan also criticized and denounced ritualism of Christianity. By incorporating the best principles of other religions he made Brahmo Samaj the advocate of humanism, monotheism and social regeneration. He preached monotheism and waged a crusade to better the condition of women by abolishing child marriages, by encouraging ascetic widowhood and putting a stop to sati, the inhuman practice of burning the wife along with the dead husband. He also condemned polygamy, early marriage and subjugation of women. He advocated that Western education and scientific knowledge had to be introduced in India. He supported the moves of Macaulay and William Bentinck in introducing English as medium of instruction. Ram Mohan took the socio-religious reform as a necessary step in the direction of nation building. He was a democrat to the core and an internationalist. Ram Mohan was not free from defects, but he stands as the first luminous star on the intellectual firmament of the 19th century. He breathed his last in 1835 at Bristol in England. The Brahmo Samaj's influence began to decline after Ram Mohan Roy's death but its influence was revived by Devendranath Tagore and Kesab Chandra Sen. In 1839, Devendranath Tagore founded the Tattva Bodhini Sabha to carry on further the ideology of Brahmo Samaj and in order to stop the rapid growth of Christianity in Bengal, he advocated the development of Vedantism. Devendranath Tagore emphasized more on the indigenous language and culture of India rather than on universalism of Ram Mohan Roy. In 1843, he established the *Tattva Bodhini Patrika* to propagate the new ideas of regenerated Brahmoism. It was another great intellectual of Bengal, Kesab Chandra Sen, who started a new organization known as Bharatiya Brahmo Samaj with the objective of bringing about a total social revolution. He dedicated his life to the cause of Indian social reform especially to the uplift of women. He published a pamphlet justifying the need for widow remarriage, submitted petitions to government, rendered valuable service for the cause of woman's education by opening 35 schools for girls, with his own money, encouraged intercaste marriages and advocated the renunciation of sacred thread. It is no exaggeration to suggest that by his effort only, the Widow Remarriage Act of 1856 was passed by the government. One more great intellectual of Bengal who contributed to the great renaissance of Bengal and emancipations of woman was Pandit Ishwara Chandra Vidyasagar. He was a great Sanskrit scholar and became the principal of the Sanskrit College in 1851. He opened the gates of Sanskrit College to non-Brahmin students. He introduced western thought as one of the subjects to be studied by the students of Sanskrit College. He was also the author of a Bengali premier which helped in the evolution of a distinct modern prose style in Bengal. He devoted his entire life for the emancipation of women particularly by promoting the cause of higher education among women and widow remarriage. Between 1855 and 1860, nearly 25 widow remarriages took place in Bengal under his leadership. He also fought against child marriage and polygamy. The Brahmo Samaj by its efforts created a pride among the Indians by reforming the evil-ridden Hinduism and by stressing humanism as an ideal, necessary for the welfare of mankind.

Arya Samaj

The social and religious reform movement through Arya Samaj in North India was led by Swami Dayanand Saraswati (1824–1883) who established the Arya Samaj in 1875. He, like the Brahmos, denounced idolatry, polytheism, Brahminical intervention in religious rituals and superstitious practices. He also advocated intercaste marriages and adult marriages. The Arya Samajists opposed caste rigidity and attacked vehemently the practice of untouchability. They pleaded for social equality and improvement in the condition of women. The major difference between Brahmo Samaj and Arya Samaj was claiming of the superiority of Hinduism compared to Islam and Christianity. Their slogan, 'go back to the Vedas' which Swami Dayanand considered infalliable gave the colour of revivalism along with reform. His teachings are noticable in his two famous works *Rigveda Bhashya Bhumika* and *Satyarthaprakasika*. He proudly proclaimed, "God is the primary cause of true knowledge and the Vedas were the only source of truth and in the matter of religion and in the domain of spirit the western mind has not reached either the depth or the heights commanded by the ancient sages". His teachings promoted natural identity based on Hinduism and provided confidence and self-esteem to the Hindus that theirs was in no way inferior to the Islamic and the western cultures. He was also the first intellectual to use the concept of Swadeshi and to think of Hindi as the national language of India. In a way he happens to be the pioneer of militant Hinduism which led to extreme nationalism, communal approach and division of India as the solution of the problems of India. Lala Lajpat Rai's remark on Arya Samaj is noteworthy. "Arya Samaj is a Hindu organization which engages in the work of reclaiming those who have left the Hindu society, and it converts every one who is prepared to accept its religious teachings. In this work it comes into direct conflict with the proselytising work of the Musalman Mullah, and the Christian missionary. But its greatest success lies in raising the social status of the classes among the Hindus and preventing the depressed from leaving Hinduism and joining other religious denominations".

Ramakrishna Mission

Towards the close of the 19th century, Ramakrishna Math was started (in 1887) by Vivekananda, the famous disciple of Ramakrishna Paramahansa. In 1896 the Math took the shape of Ramakrishna Mission. Narendranath Datta, popularly famous as Vivekananda was the last great thinker of Bengal of 19th century. His spiritual preceptor was Ramakrishna Paramahansa. Ramakrishna was a priest in the Kali Temple in Calcutta, who advised people to practice spiritualism of the Vedas and Upanishads and to lead a simple and pure life worshipping the God of their choice. His doctrine emphasized that service to mankind is service to God. Though Ramakrishna allowed idol worship, he gave importance to the spiritual aspects rather than to the ritual aspects. Vivekananda popularized the spirituality of Hinduism in the west by his lecture in the Parliament of World Religions at Chicago in 1893. His message became so popular that he founded a Vedanta Samaj in USA. Vivekananda had not blindly glorified the spiritual base of Hinduism but had the courage of conviction to admit the defects of Hinduism and to suggest ways and means to get rid of the defects. His greatness lies in the fact of imparting a social meaning to religion and asserting that wiping the tears in the eyes of a widow and quenching the hunger of the orphan by giving bread is better than worshipping an idol in a temple. He courageously pointed out: "him, I call a Mahatma whose heart bleeds for the poor, otherwise he is a Duratma. So long as millions live in hunger and ignorance, I hold every man a traitor who while educated at their expense, pays not the least heed to them". Ramakrishna Mission has been engaged in serving the poor, the needy, and the orphans, even now with the zeal and missionary belief of the founder. What Vivekananda did was to make social service a noble deed of serving God.

Socio-religious Reform Movements of Western India

The main objective of the movement in western India was removal or eradication of social discrimination prevalent against the various lower caste groups.

Thinkers like Vishnubawa Brahmachari, Jyotiba Phule, Ranade and many others played a crucial role in the development of this social awareness. The most important thinkers who initiated an intellectual revolt against the social discrimination were Bal Shastri Jambhakar (1812–1846), Dadoba Pandurang Tarkhadkar (1814–1882), and Bhaskar Pandurang Tarkhadkar (1816–1847), Gopal Hari Deshmukh popularly known as Lokhitwadi (1823–1882) and Vishnu Bhikaji Gokhale (1825–1873) popularly known as Vishnubawa Brahmachari. Of the above intellectuals, Jambhakar was the pioneer of the intellectual revolt with his writings and Dadoba gave to them an organizational shape by founding the Paramhansa Sabha in 1840. Bhaskar Pandurang was the first militant nationalist critic of the colonial rule of the British and by his eight long letters published in *Bombay Gazette* in 1841, exposed the colonial exploitation. By writing *Shatapatru* or 100 letters in the *Prabhakar*, a Marathi weekly between 1848 and 1856, *Lokhitavadi* broadened the scope of the intellectual revolt. *Lokhitavadi* also criticized casteism and emphasized the aspects of oneness of humanity. A Brahmin by birth he employed a Muslim cook and ate the food cooked by him. The Paramahansa Sabha is a secret society whose objective was the demolition of all caste distinctions. In the later half of the 19th century, the most notable intellectuals who spearheaded social reform movement were Pandit Vishnu Parasuram Shastri (1827–1876), Jyotiba Phule (1827–1890), R.G. Bhandarkar (1837–1925), Narayan Mahadev Paramanand (1838–1893) M.G. Ranade (1842–1901), Vishunasastri Chiplankar (1850–1882), K.T. Telang (1850–1893) Ganesh Vasudev Joshi (1851–1911), Narayan Ganesh Chandravarkar (1855–1923) and Gopal Ganesh Agarkar (1856–1895). Vishnu Parasuram Shastri Pandit advocated widow remarriages and also took active part in the women's emancipation movements. In 1865, he started Vidhava Vivaha Uttejaka Mandal and married a widow in 1875. He started the first school for untouchables in 1854 and in 1851 he with his wife started a girl's school at Poona. 'Maharshi' Bhandarkar performed the widow remarriage of his daughter in 1891 and advocated vigorously the Hindu Muslim unity Mahadev Govind Ranade reorganized Paramhansa Sabha in 1867 as Prarthana Samaj. It preached monotheism and denounced priestly domination and caste distinction. Chiplankar started *Nibandhamala* in 1874; a monthly Marathi magazine devoted to the cause of social reform. K.T. Telang was responsible for the introduction of compulsory primary education in Bombay. He was a brilliant academician who critically examined the economic policy of the British government. Chandravarkar also devoted his time for the propagation of Prarthana Samaj. Agarkar, another intellectual of commitment was an iconoclast of eminence and proved himself to be an uncompromising rationalist. Sumit Sarkar points out: "The anti-Brahmin toxin was first sounded in Maharashtra in the 1870s by Jyotiba Phule with his book, *Ghulamgiri* (1872) and his organization, the Satyasodhak Samaj (1873) which strongly pleaded for saving the lower castes from the hypocritical Brahmins and their opportunistic scriptures." Tamil Nadu was another area where we notice the anti-Brahmin movement being very strong. It is visible as a movement also in British administered Andhra. Satyasodhak Samaj launched direct attacks on the upper caste moneylenders and landlords and also challenged the ritual status of the Brahmins. Phule asserted that every individual irrespective of his birth in a caste and has his own individuality and identity. He wanted to uplift the people of the lower castes by encouraging them to be educated and started schools for girls and boys in 1848; and started a special school for untouchables in 1851. It is because of his constant efforts alone that the non-Brahmans secured special representation under Montague Chelmsford reforms. While the above were well-known reformers of Maharashtra, Naoroji Fudonzi, Dadabhai Naoroji and S.S. Bangalore are the well-known reformers of the city of Bombay. In 1851, they started a religious organization called the Rehnumai Maza Dayasan Sabha, which focused on the aspects of modernization of the Parsi religion and its social customs. This organization worked for the emancipation of women by spreading educational opportunities and by demanding uniform laws of inheritance and marriage for the Parsi community. In South India, the leader of the social reform movement, in the second half of the 19th century was Kandukuri Veeresalinagam Pantulu (1848–1919). Born in a poor family, and working as a teacher, he devoted his entire life and earnings for the emancipation of women by propagating widow remarriage and spread of education among women. His newspapers and books made him a father figure of social reform movements of the Andhra. In other parts of South India, we witness movements for social elevation of castes and opportunities for social mobility as is the case of Kongu Vellala Samsthan of the Gounder caste of Tamil Nadu, the Vokkaliga and Lingayat associations of Karnataka and the SNDP Yogam of the Iravas of Kerala.

The Theosophical Society and Other Social Reform Movements

The Theosophical Society also played a crucial role in moulding and shaping the socio-religious movement of the 19th century. It was founded by H.P. Blavatsky and Col. H.S. Olcott in 1875 in USA. Its headquarters were shifted to Adayar in Madras city in 1893. Its main exponent in India was Mrs Annie Besant. In her words, the mission of the Theosophical Society was the revival, strengthening and uplifting of ancient religions, Hinduism, Zoroastrianism and Buddhism. This brought with it a new sense of self-respect, a pride in the past, a belief in the future and as an inevitable result, a great wave of patriotic life, the beginning of the rebuilding of the nation. No doubt, it stood for revivalism but it sought for the abolition of child marriage, illiteracy and alcoholism. The other association that worked for revival of age-old culture was Deva Samaj formed by Satyanand Agnihotri in 1887, which was limited to the Punjab Sanatana Dharma. Rakshini Sabha of Bengal which was set up in 1883, the Madhava Siddhanta Unnayini Sabha set up in south in 1887 and Bharat Dharma Maha Mandal of Benaras with their urge for socio-religious reform movements among the Muslims and Sikhs was reflected in their efforts during the 19th century. In the regeneration of the Muslim society, two intellectuals, Sir Sayyad

Ahmed Khan and Maulvi Chirag Ali played an important role. Sir Sayyad Ahmed, a Western educated intellectual pleaded for the abolition of pardha, polygamy and child marriage and emphasized the need to impart Western education to the youth among Muslims. In 1875, he started the Muhammadan Anglo Oriental College at Aligarh for imparting Western education to the Muslims which was opposed by the orthodox Muslims, Sir Sayyad Ahmed considered Quran as the most authoritative and rational religious text for the Muslims. He also opposed religious bigotry and fanaticism. Maulvi Chirag Ali was another Muslim intellectual who made sustained effort to modernize the Muslim community by propagating monogamy and need to better the condition of Muslim women. Contrary to the above movements, Mirza Gulam Ahmed of Qadiun in Gurdaspur district started a movement to counter the missionary activities of Arya Samaj and Christianity and opposed western culture and education. The other important Muslim organizations that influenced the social and educational activities of the Muslims were Anjuman-i-Himayat-Islam established in 1885 at Lahore, Navakhat-ul-Ulema set up at Lucknow in 1894 and Khudai Khidmatgar started by Gafar Adbul Khan in North-Western frontier provinces.

The Sikhs of Punjab also made sincere efforts to purify the Sikh life and behaviour by creating the chief Khalsa Dewan along with local level assemblies, the Singh Sabhas. They also started schools and colleges for the promotion of education among the Sikhs.

Up to the present chapter we reviewed the movements for reform and revival of ancient Hindu, Muslim, Parsi and Sikh religions and culture. Now let us take up those who rejected in toto the ancient culture of India and preferred western culture. This movement was led by a group of young Bengali intellectuals known as the Young Bengal. The leader of this group was Henry Vivan Derozio (1809–1831), an Anglo-Indian teacher of Hindu College, who was a free thinker and a rationalist. His followers known as the Derozians denounced the old and 'decadent' customs and traditions and questioned the whole fabric of Hindu society and religion. Derozio was dismissed from the Hindu College in1831 for opposing the existing cultural values and he died shortly at a young age of 22. The Young Bengal movement could not attract the masses because of its radical ideas of rationalism. Their impact on contemporary Bengal in particular, and on India in general, cannot be minimized. They strengthened the movement of public enlightenment through mass media initiated by Ram Mohan Roy by spreading the ideas of freedom of press, trial by Jury, protection of cultivators from the oppression of the landlords and providing higher employment to Indians in civil administration. There is enough truth and justification in Surendranath Banerjee's statement that the Derozians were the pioneers of the modern civilization of Bengal. We may conclude the aspect of the socio-religious reform movement of the 19th century which identified the socio-cultural evils that plagued the Indian social order like the degraded position of women, child marriage, sati, polygamy, enforced widowhood, caste system, untouchability, idolatry, polytheism ritualism, priesthood and other superstitions and they were interwoven with new practices like upliftment of the position of women, abolition of infant marriages, monogamy, widow remarriage, elimination of caste distinctions that led to oppression and segregation, monotheism, humanism and brotherhood. In the words of Bipan Chandra, the nineteenth century witnessed a cultural ideological struggle against the backward elements of traditional culture on one hand, and the fast hegemonizing colonial culture and ideology on the other. Bipan Chandra further points that the cultural ideological struggle represented by the socio-religious movements was an integral part of the evolving national consciousness which aimed at the emergence of a new society with new values of equality, liberty, fraternity, social justice and democracy.

24

Resistance to Colonial Rule

Peasant and Tribal Movements

The British East India Company, a trading organization, slowly and gradually through wars and diplomacy transformed itself into a political power between 1757 and 1857. The British power made India a colony of the British and established colonial rule in India and introduced far-reaching changes into administrative, legal, social and religious spheres. Colonialism of the British and introduction of British values had shaken the Indian society. While this transformation was taking place, Indians did not keep quiet as passive spectators helplessly but the subaltern groups of peasants and tribals expressed their resentment through popular resistance, movements or civil disturbances mostly which were localized, sporadic, isolated and unorganized. These popular resistance movements reflect a certain kind of currents of political and social consciousness which influenced them to fight against the authority of the British to regain their identity and interests of theirs, prior to the British annexation of India.

Sumit Sarkar points out that in the past two decades intense research on civil disturbances makes it clear that Pax Britannica was largely a myth and we notice the revolts of the predominantly lower classes in social composition which are called subaltern groups and a study of this aspect is called 'Towards a History from Below'. Katherine Gough, an anthropologist, listed 77 per cent of peasant uprisings and classified them as 'restorative', 'religious', 'social banditary', and 'terrorist vengeance'. K. Suresh Singh observes, "the tribal insurrections were the most militant outbreaks and they revolted more often and far more violently than any other community including the peasants in India". Bipan Chandra records that the series of civil rebellions, which run like a thread through the first one hundred years of the British rule were led by impoverished Zamindars, landlords and poligars but the backbone of the rebellions, their mass base and striking power came from the rack rented peasants, ruined artisans, and demobilized soldiers. Bipan Chandra further observes that these sudden localized revolts often took place because of local grievances, although for periods they acquired a broad sweep, involving armed bands of a few hundreds to several thousands. We may agree with Bipan Chandra that the very foreign character of the British rule hurt the pride and made them rise in revolt to expel the foreigner from their lands. In Bengal and Bihar, we notice more than fifty major rebellions apart from hundreds of minor ones between 1756 and 1856.

In the series of uprisings of the period, the Sannyasi Rebellion of 1763–1800 needs to be mentioned as the first one. The East India Company's official records refer to this rebellion of northern Bengal. The targets of this group of sanyasis and fakirs were grain stocks of the rich and government officials. The rebellious sannyasis by adopting the guerilla techniques of fighting, also looted the local treasuries. They went to the extent of establishing an independent government in Bogra and Mymen Singh. One feature to be noted is the equal participation of Muslims and Hindus in it. Manjushah, Musashah, Bhawani Pathak and Debi Chaudhurani were some of the important leaders of this rebellion. Till 1800, the conflict between the British forces and the sannyasis and fakirs – became a common feature.

The Khasis, a primitive tribe, a resident of Jaintia and Garo hills in Assam also rebelled against the British authority. They came into contact in 1765 and since then hostilities continued between the Khasis and the British and it provided impetus to similar risings among the Singhas in 1890. The English Captain Neufvilie succeeded in suppressing the revolt. The revolts of the chief of Kapachor Akas, the Nagas and Kukus took place respectively in 1835, 1849 and 1826–1849. Mundas, a tribe of Chota Nagpur also revolted against the British in 1831. The primary reason for the revolt of the Mundas was the new policy of farming for outsiders and the revenue and judicial policies. It was suppressed by the British with the massive support of the British military force. The peasants of Rangapur and Dinajpur districts of Bengal rose in revolt in the year 1783 against the harsh and inhuman attitude of Debi Singh, the revenue contractor. It is because he and his agents created a reign of terror in these districts by beating and flogging the peasants. The peasants appealed to the government, seeking justice but the silence and apathy of the government made the peasants revolt under the leadership of Dinajnarain. They formed the government of their own and stopped payment of revenue and the government with great difficulty suppressed the revolt.

Between the period of 1818 and 1831, the Bhils of Khandesh ravaged the plains to show their anger against the occupation of their territory by the British in 1818. In spite of the use of force and conciliatory measures, the Bhils could not be suppressed. In 1830–31, the peasants of Nagar and other provinces rose in revolt under the leadership of Sardar Malla, the son of an ordinary ryot of Kremsi. They defied the authority of the ruler of Mysore and ultimately the British forces suppressed this rebellion and the territory of Mysore went into the hands of the British. In 1830–31, the Kols of Singabham, the tribals of Bihar opposed the British occupation of Singabham and rebelled against the British because their land was occupied by plains people, by which they were made to forgo their livelihood. The rebellion was active in the areas of Ranchi, Hazaribagh, Palamaw and Manbhum. Though they gained victory initially, ultimately they were defeated by the British militia. Between 1838 and 1851, the Foraizi sects founded by Haji Shariatullah of Faridpur rebelled against the oppression of the landlords and the British. The Fazis opposed the British legal system and maintained the village courts to settle their disputes. They opposed the British and the Zamindars for their excesses but they too were suppressed by the British and the Zamindars in the end and Dudi Miyan, the leader of the Fajai sect was imprisoned. Between 1836 and 1854, the Mappilla uprising of Kerala posed a great challenge to the British administration. These are the descendant of the Arabs and converted Muslims. Majority of them earned their living by working as daily agricultural labourers, petty traders and fishermen. They rebelled against the British for their brutal behaviour. The reasons for Mappilla rebellion are the transfer of Zamin to an independent owner, over-assessment, illegal taxes, forceful eviction from land and hostile attitude of the government. The religious leaders kindled unity among the Mappillas and they rose against the British government. Between 1836 and 1854, there were 22 uprisings against the government in Malabar and the participants were from the lower strata of society. It was a prolonged movement, wherein with great difficulty, the government subdued the Mappilla movement. The last of revolts before the 1857 great revolt was the Santhal rebellion of 1855–56. The Santhals inhabited the districts of Birbhum, Banlarua, Murshidabad, Palkur, Damka, Bhaglapur and Purnea. Their area is known as Daman-l-kosh or Santhal Paragana. As the plainsmen in collaboration with the local Zamindars began to settle in their area, it became inevitable to the Santhals to rebel for their motherland and livelihood. Interestingly, the Santhals, the tribals were supported by non-tribals belonging to the lower strata. Finally, in the end the superior arms and armaments of the British succeeded. A critical examination of the pre-1857 peasant and tribal uprisings reveal that they did not emerge in a 'full blown form'. It is because the consciousness of the insurgence and rebellion was limited in perspective and mostly it was shaped by their vision of the past and what they have forgone by the annexation of the British. We may say that the urge to recover their past provided them inspiration to struggle to regain that past from the newly established political power. Here the past refers to their identity as reflected in their livelihood and the land on which their forefathers have been living for ages. What this movement of peasants and tribal risings lacked is the awareness of the need for integrating consciousness of all those adversely effected by the British colonial policies. No doubt, all the peasants and tribal uprisings which we have studied in the preceding pages are localized and isolated, but they served as the forerunners for the great uprising of 1857 which reflected the deep frustration, agony and anger of all sections of the effected people which shook the fabric of the British regime to the core.

The Revolt of 1857: Causes, Nature and Results

The Revolt of 1857 which is called 'Sepoy Mutiny', 'Great Revolt' and the 'First War of Indian Independence' is the watershed in the history of pre-independent and early colonial India. It is so, as the one hundred years penetration of the British East India into different parts of India through wars and diplomacy and the introduction of alien revenue, judicial social intervention methods and language of English as the medium of instruction at the school and collegiate level destabilized the existing pre-British socio-cultural fabric. Added to this destabilization, the ruination of the Indian industries, handicrafts and agriculture led to rural indebtedness and the growth of daily wage earners and de-industrialization, and the rise of a capitalist class of moneylenders, rich landlords and Zamindars as collaborators of the British rule and hegemony created strong resentment against the British. Further the latest device of the Doctrine of Lapse implemented by Dalhousie dispossessed a group of native rulers and leaders and they joined hands with the rest of the population. Thus, by 1857 the situation was very stormy and ready for inflammation by any factor and the greased cartridge affair acted as the last straw on the camel's back. No single segment of population welcomed the rule of the British by 1857. The peasant and tribal revolts of which we have studied in the previous pages also clearly reveal how the British had to face the opposition of the peasants and the tribals. In the end, we may presume that the revolt of 1857 was the result of a culmination of popular dissatisfaction that had been simmering for a long time against the policies of the British in India – expansion, exploitation and economic drain and humiliation of the Indian spirit by advocating the white-man's civilizing mission – factors of multiple dimension of direct and indirect, long run and short run and of immediate nature led to the revolt of 1857. These multiple factors are: (1) political and administrative, (2) economic, (3) social and religious, and (4) military and the immediate affair of greased cartridges.

Political and Administrative Reasons

The expansionist and annexationist policies of the British power in India made all the Indian rulers, big and small, Hindu and Muslim look with suspicion and develop hatred towards the British power in India. Naturally, this type of reaction is justified as the Indians are the losers and the British gainers. Tara Chand observes, "Each region became, after annexation, a scene of resistance and revolt, in which land holders and peasants were involved and in which the disbanded soldiers of the landlords, the ministers of religion and the dismissed dependents participated", as a result of the British occupation by annexation. The native rulers were forced to disband their army who failed to obtain gainful employment elsewhere. Further, the open disrespect exhibited by the British towards the last of the Mughal ruler Bahadur Shah Zafar made the Muslims rise in revolt. The unjustified and unethical Doctrine of Lapse was the last straw on the camel's back which made the native rulers take up arms and start revolt. There is a view that resentment was brewing since 1832 which took a shape in 1857. It is difficult to accept the conspiracy theory of the native rulers against the British.

The Indians in general did not accept the administrative changes initiated and implemented, as most of them were alien in nature and replaced the age-old existing rules and regulations. Creation of a new administrative cadre, replacement of Persian by English and the colonial rule which created hardships to all sections of people and lack of personal touch between the ruler and the ruled led to a sort of distrust in the administrative set-up. This distrust hardened in due course as Indians were denied positions in all high civil and military jobs which were reserved for the Europeans and in particular to the British. Failure on the part of the British East India Company in honouring the provision of 1833 Charter Act that "no Indian shall by reason of his faith, place of birth, descent, complexion or any of them, be disabled from holding any place, office or employment under the East India Company", convinced the educated Indians of the arrogant racial hatred of the British towards the natives of India.

Economic Causes

Added to political and administrative distrust for the British East India Company, the economic policies of the British resulted in impoverishing all the segments of the Indian society except a handful of collaborators among the Indians. Owing to their colonial policies of economic exploitation, industry, trade commerce and agriculture languished and India became de-industrialized, impoverished and debt-ridden, while, William Bentinck himself admitted that by 1833–34 "The misery hardly finds a parallel in the history of commerce. The bones of cotton weavers are bleaching the plains of India". The parliamentary reports of 1840 also record that while the British cotton and silk goods imported into India paid a duty of *VA* per cent and woolen goods 2 per cent, Indian cotton goods exported to Britain paid 10 per cent, silk goods 20 per cent and the woolen goods 30 per cent. Further, the abolition of the monopoly of trade in 1813 of East India Company and the introduction of free trade by 1833 increased further the exploitation of the economy of India. The levels of exploitation of Indians were so high, that even the British felt so sad and disturbed that they wrote, "India is as much a manufacturing country as she is an agricultural one. She is a manufacturing country; her manufacturers of various descriptions have existed for ages, and have never been able to be competed by any nation wherever fair play has been given to them. To reduce her now to an agricultural country would be an injustice to India." While the above was the opinion of a Britisher, Mr Martin, another Britisher, Mr Cope made the following statement before the Parliamentary Committee in 1840: "I certainly pity the East Indian labourer, but at the same time I have a great feeling for my family than for the East Indian labourer's family. I think it is wrong to sacrifice the comforts of my family for the sake of the East Indian labourer because his condition happens to be worse than mine". As a result of the British economic exploitation all classes of people, peasants, landlords, traders, industrialists, labourers and middle class of India were badly affected and it is no exaggeration to state that unlimited poverty enveloped the entire society and made India an underdeveloped country.

Social and Religious Causes

Added to the already explained political and administrative distrust and hatred, the economic exploitation, the social and religious discrimination of superiority complex viewing the Indians as racially inferior and culturally backward and their belief that God had created the white men to civilize the Indians and intolerance of the idolatry of the Hindus by the Christian missionaries also created distrust between the natives and the British. The British were so arrogant and haughty, that a police regulation published by a magistrate at Agra categorically states "Every native, whatever his pretended rank may be, ought to be compelled, under heavy penalties, to salam all English gentlemen in the streets and if the native is on horse back or in a carriage, to dismount and stand in a respectful attitude until the European has passed him." Further, the missionary activities of charitable and philanthropic nature were looked with suspicion as the missionaries used to heckle the Hindus for worshipping many gods and goddesses, and their efforts to convert to Christianity many economically and socially backward community people and in their educational institutions they began to openly canvas about Christianity. All these made the Indians come to the conclusion that their religion was in danger and this suspicion aroused the religious and social sentiment of the Hindus against the British. Sir Syed Ahmed Khan admits that during the famines of 1837, many orphans became Christians. Further, the contents of the letter of Mr Edmund, a missionary also strengthened the apprehensions of the Hindus. The letter reads as follows: "As all India obeyed one government as in all parts of the country kept up constant communication with the other by means of the electric telegraph – and as the Railway system united the extremes of the Peninsula, it was necessary that there should be one religion also, and therefore that every one should embrace Christianity". Rev. Kennedy also observed, "Whatever misfortune may come on us, so long as our empire in India continues, so long let us not forget that our chief work of the propagation of Christianity in the land until Hindusthan from Cape Comorin to the Himalayas, embraces the religion of Christ and until it condemns the Hindu and Muslim religions, our effort must continue persistently. For this work, we must make all efforts we can and use all power and all the authority in our hands". The intervention of the British in social traditions by prohibiting the practice of Sati in 1829, passing laws relating to succession of property in 1832 and 1856, Widow Remarriage Act in 1856 and the Religious Disabilities Act of 1856 further strengthened the view of the conservatives that the Hindu religion and customs were being tampered by the British with the specific objective of Christianizing India. Sir Syed Ahmad Khan observes: "All persons, whether intelligent or ignorant, respectable or otherwise, believed that the government was really and sincerely desirous of interfering with the religion and customs of the people, converting them all, whether Hindus or Muhammadans to Christianity and forcing them to adopt the European manners and habits". In a way, partially the outburst of 1857 was a revolt of the old against the new, of Indian conservatism against the arrogant British hegemony and Christian indoctrination. The conservation of religion took the shape of rallying point in the revolt which was seen as a war of religion by the sepoys and the masses to some extent but religious grievances were not the total rallying points of the great revolt.

Military and Immediate Causes

Besides the above political and administrative, economic, social and religious grievances, another major cause was the unrest of the sepoys in the army of the British. We are aware that the action of Mangal Pandey, a sepoy of Barrackpore near Calcutta on 29 March, 1857 led to the mutiny of sepoys in the beginning which precipitated the revolt of the people. Mangal Pandey's action was not a spontaneous outburst against the British officer but it was a culmination of a simmering discontent brewing in the sepoys. Mangal Pandey was a representative of the totality of the sepoys' wrath against the British. The sepoys' revolts were not a new phenomena and go back to the first decade of the 19th century. There was a clash between the service conditions and religious practices of the upper caste sepoys due to the policies of the British. The army of Vellore mutinied against the British in 1806 opposing the replacement of turban by a leather cockade. In 1824, the sepoys of Barrakpore did not agree to proceed to Burma as their custom was against the crossing of the sea which results in the loss of the caste. In 1844, the Bengal army opposed the decision to go to Sind and wage war for the same reason mentioned above. Added to the above grievances, there was professional discontentment among the sepoys for the following reasons: (i) the British paid a paltry amount of Rs 7 per month to an infantry sepoy, (ii) the British paid Rs 27 for a cavalry sawar from which he had to meet the cost of maintaining uniform, food and upkeep of the horse, and (iii) the British publicly showed discrimination in treatment between the native sepoy and the British in the matters of promotion, pension and service provisions and fear of forgoing their jobs agitated the minds of the sepoys. Annexation of territories by the British also annoyed the sepoys. The general service establishment Act of 1856 of the time of Lord Canning was the immediate cause of discontentment as it stipulated that every sepoy must be ready to serve anywhere in India or abroad. Finally, the suspicion that the greased cartridge which was used in Enfield rifles was filled with the fat of cow and pig made the sepoys to openly rebel by killing a British officer. The event of March 29, 1857 of Barrackpore kindled the spirits of other sepoys and by the 11 May, 1857, almost half of the sepoys joined the great revolt. It can be conclusively said that the discontentment, suspicion, and hatred among all sections and displacement of earlier power structures led to the great revolt of 1857.

The mutiny of sepoys started at Barackpore on 29 March, 1857 spread to Meerut by May 1857, and to Delhi by 12 May, 1857. At Delhi, the sepoys selected Bahadur Shah Zafar as their leader and declared him as the emperor of India. Encouraged by the success at Delhi, the sepoys of Lucknow, Bareilly, Kanpur, Jhansi, Central India, Bundelkhand, etc., rebelled and by the middle of June 1857, the whole of Northern India was in revolt. South India was comparatively peaceful because of the lukewarm support to the cause of the sepoys. The Punjab and Hyderabad were absolutely peaceful. By July 1858, the revolt was totally crushed but for local risings in certain areas. In this revolt, human loss on both sides was considerable. The prominent leaders of 1857 revolt were:

(i) The Rani of Jhansi who sacrificed her life fighting in June 1858, (ii) Nanasaheb, the adopted son of the last Peshwa, Baji Rao II, who led the mutiny at Kanpur and escaped to Nepal in the beginning of 1859, (iii) Kunwar Singh of Avadh who had carved a base for himself in Azamgarh and Gazipur and breathed his last fighting in May 1858, (iv) Begum Hazarat Mahal who also escaped to Nepal, (v) Maulvi Ahmadullah who carried on the revolt around the borders of Avadh and Rohilkhand till his death in June 1858 and Tantia Tope, uprooted from his base on the Jamuna at Kalpi, reached Gwalior in June 1858, crossed the Narmada in October and was captured and put to death in 1859. All these leaders no doubt were affected by the policies of the British in the last hundred years and had genuine grievance against the British.

The factors like localizing of risings, loyalty of the native princes, lack of efficient generals, lack of commonly agreed national level leaders, lack of adequate arms, proven communication system of the British and control of sea by British were ultimately responsible for the failure of the revolt of 1857. Though the revolt failed, it shattered the myth of Pax Britannica and the invincibility of the British and created awareness in the Indians about the need for unified action in future to achieve their objective. It also made the British cautious in their approach to the Indian problem. Definitely the 1857 revolt was an eye-opener to the British as well as to the Indians.

Nature of the Revolt

There is no unanimity among scholars regarding the nature of the revolt of 1857 and a debate took place between 1950–1960 focusing attention on three perspectives: sepoy mutiny, national struggle or first war of independence or a manifestation of feudalist revival. All the British historians, in particular, Sir John Lawrance and Seelay are of the view that it was a sepoy mutiny as the sepoys refused to use the greased cartridges of the Enfield rifles and opposed the move. We notice an anxious conscious attempt on the part of the British to minimize the grievances of Indians and to restrict it only to a section of army's revolt. Further, the British tried to portray civil disturbances as the actions of selfish vested interests of the landholders and the princes. Their attempt was to prove that the colonial rule, if not welcomed, was not detested, as many Indian historians argue. L.E.R. Reese viewed it as a religious war against Christianity. J.R. Holmes expressed the opinion that it was a conflict between civilization and barbarism. Sir James Outram, W. Taylor and others are of the view that it was a conspiracy hatched by the Hindus and the Muslims against the British.

Contesting the British interpretation as that of sepoy mutiny only, the nationalist historians and in particular V.D. Savarkar in his banned book, *The Indian War of Independence of 1857*, published anonymously in 1912 argues that it was the first war of Indian independence inspired by the lofty ideal of self-rule by Indians through nationalist upsurge. Ashok Mehta in his book *The Great Rebellion* expressed the view that the revolt was national in character. Bishewswar Prasad observes "as the end of the alien rule was the essential object and the chief purpose and in this sense the revolt of 1857 may be termed a national war for freedom, though the sentiment of nationalism in the modern sense had not taken deep roots in the soil of India at that movement". Tara Chand described it as "War of Nation's Independence" in his book, *History of Freedom Movement in India*. Contradicting the above views of nationalist motivated perceptions, R.C. Majumdar concludes that it is difficult to avoid the conclusion that the so-called first national war of independence of 1857 is neither the first, nor national, nor a war of independence as it was not preplanned and was limited to certain pockets in North India. Surender Nath Sen is of the view that: "The mutiny became a revolt and assumed a political character when the mutineers of Meerut placed themselves under the king of Delhi and a section of the landed aristocracy and civil population declared, in his favour. What began as a fight for religion ended as a war of independence for there is not the slightest doubt that the rebels wanted to get rid of the alien government and restore the old order of which the king of Delhi was the rightful representative".

Since 1970, the historical perspective has shifted from the study of 'sepoy mutiny' or 'national revolt' to the examination of social roots of the revolt by understanding specific area studies. As a result of such studies, it is now established that the relationship between land revenue settlement and the revolt is very minimum. Further, it is now suggested that the roots of the revolt are traceable to the pockets of relative poverty due to ecological factors such as less fertile soil and severe revenue assessments imposed on arable land caused undue misery to the cultivator. It is believed that it is very difficult to make generalization of the 1857 event as the response of the people varied from one area to another and as such it is argued that the revolt of 1857 was not one movement but many. The nature of the 1857 event has become so emotive that it gave scope to multiple perspectives.

Results of the 1857 Revolt

The 1857 revolt though failed and crushed by the superior military force of the British was a significant event of far-reaching consequences in the history of British rule in India. It marks the end of an era of mercantile capitalism and early colonial rule and the beginning of direct imperial hegemony of the British crown. While in the first century, i.e., from 1757 to 1857, the British crown indirectly ruled India, in the second century, i.e., from 1858 to 1947, the British crown directly ruled India through the Viceroy appointed by the Monarch. The results of the 1857 revolt may be subdivided as: (i) constitutional changes, (ii) changes in the army, (iii) religious, judicial and diplomatic effects, and (iv) social effects.

Constitutional Changes

The most significant result of the mutiny was the transfer of power from a trading company to a sovereign power of Britain by the Government of India Act of 1858. This Act of 1858 completed the process initiated by the Charter Act of 1853. In the place of the President of the Board of Control, the Secretary of

State for India was appointed. The Secretary of State for India was assisted and helped by a 15-member body of India Council. Out of the fifteen, eight were appointed by the crown and the rest were to be appointed by the court of the directors. The designation of the Governor General of India was changed to Viceroy. In case of the rulers of the Indian states, the crown made categorical announcement that all the treaties and agreements entered into by the East India Company will be honoured and respected and made it clear that no renewal was necessary. The British crown gave up the policy of subordinate isolation and advocated a policy of subordinate union in respect of native states. The administrative apparatus in India was centralized effectively due to the improvement in communications. The British crown reinstated the Taluqdars of Oudh to their old positions. They gave up the idea of the ruthless expansionist policy of their territorial boundaries in and outside India.

Changes in the Army

Before the revolt of 1857, the army of the British in India was divided into two major divisions – king's forces and company's troops. As a result of the revolt the two forces were united and called king's forces and one-third of it should consist of the Europeans. The artillery section was exclusively kept under the British. As a consequence of more European soldiers in the army, the expenditure on the army doubled up. The Bengal Army was virtually abolished. They reduced the Brahmins from the army and recruited Gurkhas, Sikhs, Jats and Rajputs of the Punjab.

Religious, Judicial and Diplomatic Effects

Queen Victoria's proclamation of 1 November, 1858 guaranteed freedom of faith and equal treatment to all Indians. The Queen made it clear that there was to be no distinction between one individual and another on the pretext of race, religion, sex and creed. The British crown agreed to provide employment to the Indians in the bureaucratic structure of the times, which was denied previously. In the sphere of judiciary, the Sadar courts and Crown's Supreme Court were amalgamated into High Courts which were established in the presidency towns of Madras, Bombay and Calcutta. In the sphere of diplomatic ties between India and Britain, now there was a change and the British began to show greater interest in the internal development of India than in foreign affairs.

Social Effects

In the sphere of social relations, the gulf between the Europeans and the Indians not only widened but animosity and hatred between the two social groups became marked, and there was definite social estrangement between Indians and Europeans. Detestation, contempt, ferocity and vengeance became marked features of the British in India in the post-mutiny period. The Indians too did not lag behind in maintaining social distance. What we notice in this period was abandonment of social and educational welfare measures by the British purposefully and willingly. As if it is not sufficient, orthodoxy, religious superstitions, communal, caste and religious discrimination began to be practised by the Indians. The British who were quite aloof in the beginning realized their mistake and changed their policy with 1861 Indian Council Act.

A very disturbing feature of post-mutiny period in India was the growth of social distance between the Hindus and Muslims which ultimately led to communalization of social life and partition of India on communal lines. The post-mutiny period also witnessed setback to Muslim renaissance and efforts of modernity. At the end, we may conclude by agreeing with Tarachand: "imperialist Britain treated India as a satellite whose main function was to sweat and labour for the master, to subserve its economy and to enhance the glory and prestige of the empire".

25

The National Liberation Movement

Bipan Chandra characterizes the freedom struggle or the national movement or the national liberation movement as "undoubtedly one of the biggest mass movements modern society has ever seen. It was a movement which galvanized millions of people of all classes and ideologies into political action and brought to its knees a mighty colonial empire". Indian national movement is as relevant and significant as the modern revolutions which had the motto of altering the existing political and social structure and to establish a new politico-socio-economic system based on equality, social justice, rule of law and democratic outlook. The importance of the Indian national movement lies in the fact that it was the only available historical example where semi-democratic traditional and mostly illiterate social groups were motivated by an urge to free themselves from the colonial exploitation by writing and forging a common agenda forgetting their age-old social, economic and cultural moorings. Undoubtedly, the Indian national movement is the best example of mobilization of all segments of population having divergent political and ideological interests with a common goal of liberation or freedom from the foreign yoke. The objective of this national movement was not the single point of replacing the colonial rule of the British but a total transformation of the socio-politico-economic cultural mosaic of India with new values as engines of the driving force. The new values that inspired, influenced and provided the necessary moral strength and courage were democratic, civil libertarian and secular outlook based on a self-reliant, egalitarian social order and an independent foreign policy. As such the national movement of India had an ideology that is the most suitable for a multicultural, multi-linguistic and multi-layered pluralistic society of India. The fathers of this national movement are fully aware that 'India, was the nation in making' and hence they followed a strategy that could unite people based on the concept of 'unity in diversity'. Though, since time immemorial Indians living the different parts of India are aware of their 'geographical fundamental unity' as expressed in their daily prayer and cultural unity through pilgrimage centres and worship of rivers, mountains and nature, the most prevalent deep-rooted feeling was devotion to the head of the clan, the guru and the local ruler but not to the concept of a nation based on one religion, one culture, one language and territorial and geographical boundaries as we perceive nationalism today. As such it is to be admitted with a sense of hurt pride that the concept of nationalism was of a modern phenomena. It was perceived by different scholars in different ways. *Encyclopedia Britannica* describes nationalism "as a state of mind in which the supreme loyalty of the individual is to the nation state". Palmer and Perkins explain it as a desire "to exalt a state, and to add to its prestige drives men into carrying their flag, their culture, their language and their institutions into poor and backward regions of the world; and it compels the governments to justify, defend and champion the economic ventures of their nationals in foreign lands, especially weak ones". It is further observed that nationalism strives to unite the members into one nation, politically and territorially in a stage organization, when strong power exploits the weakness of the occupied political power rather than it becomes alive and opposes the imperialist tendencies. There is a view that the emergence of nationalism in India was the legacy of the British rule and prior to the rule of the British, India was never a nation. Percival Spear holds the view: "In looking for the roots of Indian nationalism we can begin with an emotion and a tradition. The emotion was dislike of the foreigner which in India for many ages had gone along with a tolerance of his presence. The tradition was that of Hinduism deeply rooted in the basis of what has been called the fundamental unity of India. But xenophobia and pride in tradition was not a sufficient foundation for a new movement to produce secular nationalism. It would require some sort of stimulus from outside." Spear locates the external stimuli in literature. Spear writes, "the ideas which were imbibed from the ruler's literature and attitudes were nationalism, civil liberties and constitutional self-government". Many British and the Indian scholars echoed his view. Ishwari Prasad observes: "the consciousness of the French that their troubles were due to the Bourbons led to the French Revolution, of the English that their troubles were due to the unrestrained prerogatives of the crown led to the civil war, and of the Indians that their troubles were due to the British rule led to the formation of the Indian National Congress in 1885, whose object was to secure India's liberation". A.R. Desai remarks, "Nationalism came into being during the British period as a result of the action and reaction of numerous subjective and objective forces and factors which developed within the Indian society under the conditions of the British rule and the impact of world forces". But this view is contested by the Indian historians who argue it would be wrong to assert that nationalism in India was solely the contribution of the British. S.L. Sikri rightly points, "Some of these factors sowed the seed; some nurtured into growth; some moulded its form; and some influenced its ideology and technique. Hence, the causes responsible for the origin, growth and rapid development of the Indian national movement were various and manifold". The origin and the growth of nationalism in India can be traced to the stimuli of internal and external factors.

Impact of the Western Culture and Discovery of the Past Pride of India

The foremost cause for the growth of Indian nationalism and national movement was India's contact with the nationalistic and political liberalism of the west through initiation into English language and literature. This initiation opened up their minds to the events of Italian and German unification in the last quarter of the 19th century and also provided common language to all the Indians to transact and express their views with one and the other. Further, orientalists like William Jones, James Princep, Max Muller and Ferguson and archaeologists like Alexander Cunningham enabled Indians to be aware of their pride in their past glories. This revelation of common heritage of a great culture and rich historical tradition imbued the natives of India with an idea of glorious common nationality. The revisiting of India's past, supplemented by the bond of a common religion, acted as a bond to bring them together and English served as lingua franca to strengthen the unity. In the view of R.C. Majumdar, "Nationalism was thus founded on the bedrock of common religion, culture and historical tradition. But this gave it a Hindu character which it has retained, consciously or unconsciously, ever since". This view of R.C. Majumdar is partially true to some extent but not the whole truth.

Socio-cultural Renaissance

Undoubtedly, the socio-cultural renaissance movement played an important role in emergence, nurturing, shaping and moulding of the nationalist spirit in India. They consciously promoted a sense of self-respect, unity and patriotism and made the Indians realize the need for internal introspection and to get rid of the social evils that divided the Indian society. This can be explained by quoting Vivekananda and Gandhi who observed that religion is of no avail when it cannot wipe the tears of a widow and we cannot feed a hungry man with preaching about God.

Colonialism and Discriminating Treatment

In the preceding pages, it is explained how the economic policies of the British East India Company ruined the economy of India by draining away the resources of India. Early nationalist leaders of India like Dadabhai Naoroji, the grand old man of India, Justice Mahadev Govind Ranade and Ramesh Chandra Dutt by their economic critique of the colonial policy educated the public of India as well as the British with their writings about the economic havoc caused by colonial policy. Bipan Chandra aptly remarks "of all the national movements in colonial countries, the Indian national movement was the most deeply and firmly rooted in an understanding of the nature and character of colonial economic domination and exploitation. Its early leaders known as Moderates were the first in the 19th century to develop an economic critique of colonialism. This critique was also, perhaps their most important contribution to the development of the national movement in India and the themes built around it were later popularized on a massive scale and formed the very pith and marrow of the nationalist agitation, through popular lectures, pamphlets, dramas, songs and prabhat pheris". Besides ruination of peasantry and artisan groups, de-industrialization, the wanton discrimination shown by the British towards the Indians for more than a century also seriously hurt the feelings of Indians and made them hate the white man and his government.

Improved Transport and Communication Facilities

The British indirectly promoted the growth of nationalism in India by providing an elaborate communication system network which enabled people of different parts to meet, discuss and exchange their grievances and chalk out plans and programmes of action. Thus, the network of communications and transport facilities helped in the growth of nationalism to a great extent.

Role of the Press

The role of the English and vernacular press in raising the level of consciousness of the Indians by explaining the misdeeds, and injustices perpetuated by the government is really commendable. Fearless reporting in newspapers of the misrule of the governmental agencies created national awakening which in turn led to the emergence of the spirit of nationalism. By 1875, there were no less than 478 newspapers in the country kindling the spirit of nationalism. The pen of Dinabandhu Hemachandra Banerjee, Navin Chandra Sen, Ravindranath Tagore and Bankim Chandra Chatterjee influenced innumerable people of India as freedom lovers. The influence and impact of Bankim was so great that his novel *Anadamath* and 'Vandemataram' song had become the Bible of Bengali patriotism.

Repressive Policy of Lord Lytton

In the history of colonial India the period from 1876 to 1884 had been aptly described "the seed time of Indian nationalism". The callous, indifferent and arrogant attitude of Lytton in organizing Delhi Darbar in 1877 very lavishly when many people perished due to the famine and his war against the Afghans, the notorious Vernacular Press Act and the Arms Act of 1878 accelerated the growth of nationalism in India. Even the British criticized the Vernacular Press Act as "a retrograde and ill-conceived measure injurious to the future progress of India" and Surendranath Banerjee observed that the Arms Act "Imposed upon us a badge of racial inferiority". Sprinkling salt on the injury, the Ilbert Bill controversy added fuel to the fire of Indian nationalism. This controversy convinced the Indians that unless they too resorted to agitational process, there was no salvation to the humiliation experienced by them.

Besides the above narrated episodes, the happenings outside India in America, France, Italy, Germany, China and Japan inspired the Indians to become united to free themselves from continuous humiliation of the white race. Thus, the emergence and the growth of the national movement in India was the cumulative effect of both internal and external factors. This nationalist spirit or urge lead to the formation of Indian National Congress in 1885, which spearheaded the liberation or freedom struggle in India from 1885 to 1947.

Indian National Congress

The Indian National Congress founded in 1885 was the institutionalized form of emergent Indian nationalism. It was the first organized expression of Indian nationalism on an all-India scale. The birth of the Indian National Congress was not a sudden event or a historical accident but the result of a gradual effort of a number of educated Indians of Bengal and other regions who were very much dissatisfied and disgusted by the exploitative nature of the alien British rule. In India, we notice a process of the beginning of political awakening since 1860, which took a major leap forward in 1870–1880 and finally led to the founding of the Indian National Congress in December 1885. R.C. Majumdar aptly observes, "The national conference held in Calcutta in 1883 forestalled it in all essential aspects". The forerunners of the Indian National Congress were many and among them the most important ones were: (a) the British Indian Association founded in Bengal in 1843, (b) British India Association founded in Bengal in 1851, (c) India League founded in 1875, (d) Indian Association in 1876, (e) Bombay Association founded in early fifties of the 19th century, (f) Poona Sarvajanik Sabha set up in 1886, and (g) National Conference in 1883. Besides these major regional organizations in India, some radicals in England founded the British India Society in 1837 to promote and create interest in the conditions of India. In the year 1843, the Bengal British India Society was founded by George Thompson with the goal of advancement of the public welfare by peaceful means while being completely loyal to the British crown. The British India Association actively campaigned for throwing open offices to all Indians, trial by jury, and establishment of provincial and central legislative councils with elected representatives. The Indian Association spearheaded by Surendranath Banerjee acted as a catalyst in creating awareness by undertaking mobilization activity against the injustices done to Indians in general and to Surendranath Banerjee in particular. Thus started an agitational strategy when age limit was reduced for Indians to appear for ICS and when a judge wanted an idol to be brought to the court. Surendranath Banerjee initiated all-India tour to propagate the idea of national self-respect and he may justifiably be called the first national leader of India. We can agree with Bipan Chandra that the foundation of the Congress was the natural outcome of the political awareness and work done by various bodies in the years between 1850 and 1885. In the process of the foundation of the Indian National Congress by 72 people in 1885 at Bombay, undoubtedly, A.O. Hume, a retired civil servant of India played a very crucial role along with other early nationalist leaders like Naoroji, Ranade, Banerjee and others. But a powerful and long-lasting myth, the myth of 'Safety Valve' has been in circulation, which states that the Indian National Congress was started by A.O. Hume and others under the official direction, guidance and advice of a no less a person than Lord Dufferin, the Viceroy, to provide a safe, mild, peaceful and constitutional outlet or 'safety valve' for the rising discontent among the masses, which was inevitably leading to a popular and violent revolution. Bipan Chandra after a detailed discussion about this myth and reality observes that the 'safety valve' theory is a myth but as 'time factor' was not ripe or suitable for the Indians to start an organization, the earliest nationalists Dadabhai Naoroji, Justice Mahadev Govind Ranade, Pherozeshah Mehta, G. Subrahmanya Iyer and Surendranath Banerjee cooperated with Hume because they did not like to arouse official hostility at such an early stage of their work. Gokhale aptly points out "No Indian could have started the Indian National Congress". If an Indian had come forward to start such a movement embracing all-India, the officials in India would not have allowed the movement to come into existence. If the founder of the Congress had not been a great Englishman and distinguished ex-official, such was the distrust of political agitation in those days that the authorities would have at once found some way or the other to suppress the movement. Bipan Chandra concludes this discussion on myth and reality as follows: "If Hume and other English liberals hoped to use the Congress as a safety-valve, the Congress leaders hoped to use Hume as a lightening conductor. And as later developments show, it was the congress leaders whose hopes were fulfilled". Percival Spear states, "at the start the Congress was a modest body, having only seventy delegates at its first session. But from the first it formed a focus for the new classes' political opinions. By 1900, it had spread all over India and was regarded by the forward looking members of the new class as the natural mouthpiece of their aspirations. Its support came mainly from the new professionals with a sprinkling of businessmen in Bombay and of landlords in Bengal". The first step in the direction of founding of Indian National Congress was initiated by Hume in March 1883 by appealing to the graduates of the Calcutta University to come together to form an association for the moral and political regeneration of the Indians. In his appeal he stressed "self-sacrifice and unselfishness as the only unfailing guides to freedom and happiness". In response to his appeal, Indian National Union was formed in 1884 under his leadership. Subsequently, it turned into Indian National Congress. The objectives of the Indian National Congress were proclaimed by its first president W. Chandra Banerjee as follows: (1) The promotion of personal intimacy and friendship among workers from various corners of India. (2) The eradication of all prejudices from the minds of every Indian towards the others and to foster sentiments of national unity among all the inhabitants of India. In the beginning, the Indian National Congress stood for piecemeal reforms by submitting petitions, resolutions and deputation to satisfy the demands of the Indians expressing their faith in the political liberalism of the British Raj. The Indian National Congress through resolution demanded for (i) the appointment of a commission to inquire into the working of the Indian government, (ii) the abolition of the India council of the Secretary of state for India, (iii) creation of legislative councils of the north-west provinces and Awadh and the Punjab, (iv) enhancement of the number of elected members in the central and provincial legislative councils with the right of interpolation and discussion of the budget and the creation of a standing committee in the house of commons to look into the demands of the people, (v) reduction of military expenditure and equitable division of expenditure between India and England, (vi) introduction of simultaneous Public Service Examinations in England and India and raising age of the candidates who wish to appear for ICS. Till 1905, the Indian National Congress, demanded only for piecemeal reforms through petitions and prayers. On the basis of the goal, strategy and technique adopted by the Indian National Congress, the national movement of India was divided as moderate phase (1885–1905), extremist phase (1905 to 1918) and the revolutionary phase and finally the Gandhian phase (1919 to 1947).

Era of Moderates or Moderate Nationalism

The first twenty years of Indian National Congress is generally perceived as that of a moderate phase. Sumit Sarkar is of the view that in spite of uniformities in the policy of the moderate phase, current research reveals that certain interesting variations existed over time and between regions. He further points out, "turning to the activities and organization of the Congress, three broad phases can be distinguished within the moderate era. From 1885 to 1893, the Congress was dominated by Hume. After his departure the affairs of the moderates were taken care of by W.C. Banerjee, Anandacharulu, Pherozeshah Mehta and Ranade and from 1899 it was Pherozeshah Mehta who controlled the reins of the moderates' phase of nationalism. It was so labelled due to its limited goal, techniques adopted and methods employed by them to spread the ideal of nationalist spirit. The main motto of these moderates appears to be politicization, political propaganda and education and formation and propagation of nationalist ideology. They carried out their mission by using the print media to arouse, train, mobilize and consolidate the public opinion. They have purposefully and knowingly chosen the methods of meeting, discussing, passing resolutions, submitting them to the government and pleading with the government to implement their needs but not demands. They adopted a conciliatory tone because their social base was restricted and India was still a nation in making, lacking the necessary cohesiveness of oneness to wage a direct battle with the mighty British power. They knew that the age-old traditional India of old values cannot be transformed into a nation, based on the new values of liberty, equality and democracy. Realizing their limitations, they constantly and conscientiously made it their goal to work hard with patience to develop the feeling of national unity by prompting and developing contacts and friendly relations among the people of the different parts of the country speaking different languages, professing different faiths. They have to overcome the stupendous task of inbuilt differences in various social groups – distanced by tendencies of cultural superiority and inferiority. It may be suggested that the time in which they started their ambitious goal of fostering national unity made them moderates. They placed before them the twin tasks of convincing the British government of their genuine need to improve the conditions of India and to educate the Indians about the need and necessity of oneness as a nation. The moderates expressed their faith in the fair play and justice of the British government and repeated again and again every year from the platform, perhaps with the objective of not making the British directly inimical to the Congress organization and its ideals. It was so because their social base was limited and they needed some more time to penetrate into the interiors of India with their ideology of unity. The statements of Dadabhai Naoroji, Surendranath Banerjee, Badruddin Tyabji and Rash Behari Ghosh clearly reveal their committed vision. For example, Tyabji observed, "Be moderate in your demands, just in your criticism, correct in your facts and logical in your conclusions". Rash Behari Ghose aptly cautioned, "You must have patience, you must learn to wait and everything will come to you in time".

Realizing the need to expand the social base of the Indian National Congress organization, the moderates demanded 'wider employment of Indians in higher offices in the public service and the establishment of representative institutions for the reduction of heavy land revenue payments, to provide cheap credit to the peasants through agricultural banks, to make available irrigational facilities on large scale, to improve the conditions of the plantation labourers, for the abolition of salt tax, for rapid introduction of modern industries, to give tariff protection to the industries of India. Finally, to stop the drain of wealth from India by encouraging indigenous crafts of artisans of India. These demands clearly indicate how they desired to improve their social base by highlighting the problems of the peasants, the labourers and the business community and of the artisans. Their patient educating methods slowly and gradually made the larger groups to understand the need for a common unity to improve their conditions. Thus, the moderates by their technique and strategy could obtain 'space' in public sphere to express the grievances of the Indians. There is a view that the Congress sessions that took place for three days in December were *tamashas* organized by highly educated affluent Indians who were Indians by birth but Britishers or Westerners by their choice of lifestyle, who spoke in English and travelled in luxury. This view is not totally correct. If we dispassionately examine critically what the moderates did and achieved, we have to agree that achievements were of considerable significance, when we take into consideration the attitude of the British Viceroys and officials. Lord Dufferin criticized the Congress organization as representing 'microscopic minority' of the people. Hamilton, Secretary of State accused the leaders as 'Seditious and double sided character', 'disloyal Baburs', 'Seditious Brahmins' and violent villains and 'a factory of sedition' and 'unclean thing'. Lord Elgin openly remarked, "India was conquered by the sword and by the sword it shall be held". In this backdrop of the hard British attitude, the moderates could influence in enacting the 1892 Indian Council Act. Bipan Chandra writes "the nationalist agitation forced the government to make some changes in legislative functioning by the Indian Council Act of 1892. The number of additional members of the Imperial and Provincial Legislative Councils was increased from the previous six to ten and from ten to sixteen. A few of these members could be elected indirectly through municipal committees, district boards etc., but the official majority remained. The members were given the right to discuss the annual budget but they could neither vote on it nor move a motion to amend it. They could also ask questions but were not allowed to put supplementary question or to discuss the answers. The 'reformed' Imperial Legislative Council met, during its tenure till 1909, on an average for only thirteen days in a year, and the number of unofficial Indian members present was only five out of twenty four". While the nationalists were totally dissatisfied with the provisions of the Act as they demanded a majority for non-official elected members with the right to vote on the budget and thus to control the public purse. It is neither correct nor true, to conclude that the efforts of the moderates failed totally and theirs was a futile exercise. Bipan Chandra writes, "the accomplishments of the national leaders of this period are many, provided success is not measured in terms of immediate gains. The moderates succeeded in creating a wide political awakening and arousing the middle and lower middle class Indians and the educated elite to feel that they were all one and their interests were one politically, economically and culturally. They also succeeded in popularizing the ideas of democracy and liberty. They also successfully exposed the true character of the British imperialism to the public of India as well as that of the world. Gopal Krishna Gokhale, an impeccable leader of the moderates had rightly pointed out: "The minds of the people have been familiarized with the idea of a united India working for salvation; a national public opinion has been created, close bonds of sympathy now knit together, the different provinces, castes and creeds hamper less and less the pursuit of common aims, and the dignity of a consciousness of national existence has spread over the whole land. Above all, there is a general perception now of the goal towards which we have to strive and a wide recognition of the arduous character of the struggle and the immerse sacrifices it requires". We can conclude by stating that the moderate leaders Dadabhai Naoroji, Pherozeshah Mehta, Gopal Krishna Gokhale, G.V. Subrahmanya Ayer and others by their cautious policy of mendicancy gave life to the organization of Congress and succeeded in spreading the message of the need for oneness among the different segments of India and by their demands widened the social base of the Indian national movement and built a strong foundation on which the extremists built up a sustained continuous movement, 'Swaraj' of India.

Extremism or Militant Nationalism and Revolutionary Terrorism

Extremism or militant nationalism became a predominant philosophy of Indian nationalism or Indian national movement from 1905 to 1917. Many factors contributed to the rise of extremism or militant nationalism. One such factor was the opposition of certain early nationalists in the strategy and technique adopted by the moderates' expression of faith in the fairness of the British, medicancy and appealing to the British government. The failure of the Indian Council Act of 1892 in satisfying the aspirations of the Indians is another important cause. Further, the callous attitude exhibited by the British towards the sufferings of the people due to the famine of 1897 was also one of the causes. The outbreak of the Bubonic plague in Bombay presidency and the means followed by the government created strong resentment in the minds of the people which led to the murder of Rand, the Plague Commissioner of Poona by the Chapekar brothers. Another factor was the exclusion of educated Indians from the public services also which led to the dissatisfaction for the moderate methods and the view of Lord Curzon, the Viceroy of India, "the highest ranks of civil employment must be a general rule, as held by Englishmen" made the blood of the Indians boil and think of resorting to violent means to redeem their honour. Lord Curzon's high-handed mission, commission and omissions – the Calcutta Corporation Act of 1899, and Calcutta University Act of 1904, along with the partition of Bengal in 1905 accelerated the extremist movement. Bal Gangadhar Tilak, the trail blazer of extremism rightly pointed "political rights will have to be fought for. The moderates think that these can be won by persuasion. We think that they can be only be obtained by strong pressure". The bases of extremists were Maharashtra, Punjab and Bengal. Tilak preached "protests are of no avail. Mere protests not backed by self-reliance will not help the people. Days of protests and prayers have gone". He further advised "prepare your forces, organize your power and then go to work so that they cannot refuse you what you demand".

The methods chosen by the extremists were boycott, Swadeshi and national education. Boycott implies refusal to use foreign goods and of government services, honours and titles and everything that is foreign. Bipan Chandra writes: "with the start of the Swadeshi movement at the turn of the century, the Indian national movement took a major leap forward. Women, students and a large section of the urban and rural population of Bengal and other parts of India became actively involved in politics for the first time". It indicates how the social base of the movement increased. He further states, "the next half a decade saw the emergence of almost all the major political trends of the Indian national movement. From conservative moderation to political extremism, from terrorism to incipient socialism, from petitioning and public speeches to passive resistance and boycott – all had their origins in the movement". The British realizing the sullen mood of the Indians and change in the attitude of the early nationalist leaders towards extremist measures resorted to the clever technique of 'divide and rule', and to woo the Muslims against the Congress demand of representative government. The idea of the partition of Bengal was in the air since 1903 in the pretext of better government and it was resented by the Congress organization through public meetings organized spontaneously in different parts of Bengal. The real intention of the partition of Bengal was the division of the people on religious or communal lines.

Lord Curzon wanted "to dethrone Calcutta" from its central position as Bengal was the centre of intrigue, by dividing Bengali-speaking population. Risely, the Home Secretary to Government of India pointed in 1904 in the month of December on 6th, "Bengal united is power. Bengal divided, will pull in several different ways". Even before the partition of Bengal materialized on October 15, 1905, the Swadeshi movement was announced on 7, August, 1905. The advocates of the Swadeshi movement undertook tours throughout India and roused the public opinion in favour of Swadeshi movement. The response was so favourable and positive; the sale of the British cloth fell by 5 to 15 times between September 1904 and September 1905. The message of Swadeshi and the boycott of foreign goods were carried on by Surendranath Banerjee, Anand Mohan Bose, Tilak, Lajpat Rai, Ajit Singh and Sayyad Haidar Raja to different parts of India. The Banaras session of Indian National Congress presided over by Gokhale endorsed the Swadeshi and boycott movements for Bengal. But Tilak, Bipan Chandra Pal, Lajpat Rai and Aurobindo Ghosh advocated for the spread of the movement throughout India along with the message of Swarajya as the objective. Tilak popularized the slogan 'Swaraj is my birth right and I will have it'. By 1906, the Indian National Congress declared 'self-government' or 'swaraj' like that of the United Kingdom or Colombo as its objective at the Calcutta session. In Bengal anti-partition movement and swadeshi and boycott movements became a mass movement and took the shape of non-cooperation and passive resistance through mass mobilization. Along with this movement, they made it their objective to promote 'self-reliance' or 'Atmasakti' and 'self-help' concept and 'national education policy' As a result, Bipan Chandra observes: "In sum, the Swadeshi movement with its multi-facetal programme and activity was able to draw for the first time a large section of society into active participation in modern nationalist politics and still larger sections into the ambit of modern political ideas. The social base of the national movement was now extended to include a certain jamindari section, the lower middle class in the cities and small towns and school and college students on a massive scale". Yet, the movement failed to draw the peasantry as well as the Muslims. The movement continued till 1908 and it became a burnt movement by mid-1908. The reasons for the gradual failure of the movement were the repressive measures of the government and the internal squabbles among the leaders that led to the well-known split of Surat of 1907. The Indian National Congress was divided as extremists and the Moderates openly and publicly professing different techniques and objectives. The movement lost its vitality and vigour but still the fire of rebellion was alive in the shape of individualized terrorist activity directed against the government through the method of sacrifice of life for the sake of motherland.

The British Viceroy Lord Minto adopted the strategy of pacifying Indians by promising the enactment of Morley-Minto Reforms of 1909 Act. The Act failed to come near to the aspirations of the people of India as the Moderates were a disillusioned lot. R.C. Majumdar observes, "For nine years after the

Surat fracas, the Moderates ruled over the Congress in splendid isolation with their ideals and programmes. But the country had lost faith in them, and the Congress had very little following. The Congress held its annual sessions as usual, but the spring had gone out of the year". In order to placate the Extremists, the British government annulled the partition of Bengal in 1911. The Indians realized that the British were using the same technique of 'divide and rule' to continue the split of Congress as Moderates and Extremists. In this backdrop, the First World War broke out in 1914 and it continued till 1919. In order to make the people actively cooperate in war effort, the British promised to introduce reforms by the 1919 Act, or Montague-Chelmsford reforms. This Act too did not come up to the expectations and aspirations of the Indians and the reforms were condemned as "inadequate, disappointing and unsatisfactory". Bipan Chandra points out "The outbreak of the First World War in 1914 gave a new lease of life to the nationalist movement which had been dormant since the heady days of the Swadeshi movement". It is so because after 1908 the intensity of the national movement as a whole declined and the same as expressed by Aurobindo in these words, "when I went to jail the whole country was alive with the cry of Bandemataram, alive with the hope of a nation, the hope of millions of men who had newly risen out of degradation. When I came out of jail I listened for that cry, but there was instead, a silence. A hush had fallen on the country". The later events reveal that the national movement was only dormant during this period and it picked up momentum from 1914 after Tilak became free. From the end of 1907, a new political trend of the path of individual heroism and revolutionary terrorism came to forefront in Bengal, which in course of time spread to different parts of India. The active participants of this revolutionary terrorism were the youth of Bengal. Bipan Chandra explained the origins of this phase as follows: "This was primarily because they could find no other way of expressing their patriotism. It is necessary at this point to reiterate the fact that, while the youth of Bengal might have been incensed at the British arrogance and repression, and the 'mendicancy' of the Congress moderates, they were also led to 'the politics of the bomb' by the extremists' failure to give a positive lead to the people'. In the backdrop of the repressive measures of the government and the failure of the moderate and the extremist tactics, the revolutionary youth decided to copy the methods of the Irish nationalists and Russian nihilists and populists". The revolutionary terrorists targeted to assassinate unpopular British officials and thereby kindle patriotic spirit and sustain the pace of the nationalist movement. In 1907, an unsuccessful attempt was made on the like of the Lieutenant Governor of Bengal. In April 1908, Prafulla Chaki and Khudiram Bose threw a bomb on the carriage which they believed to be occupied by Kingford, the unpopular judge of Muzaffarpur but the attempt misfired and it killed two English ladies. Prafulla Chaki shot himself dead with the feeling of guilt for killing two innocent women and the other accused Khadiram Bose was tried and hanged. Both of them had become popular heroes and earned a permanent place through folk songs composed in the praise of their selfless sacrifice. With these two episodes, the era of revolutionary terrorism had begun. Very soon secret societies of revolutionaries sprang up all over the country. Of such secret societies, the famous ones of long-standing credit were Anushilan Samity and Jugantar. Between 1908 and 1918, nearly 186 revolutionaries were killed or convicted for sedition. Two of the most, spectacular revolutionary terrorist activities of this period were the unsuccessful attempts under the leadership of Rash Behari Bose and Sachin Sanyal to assassinate the Viceroy, Lord Hardinge, who was wounded by the bomb thrown at him while he was riding an elephant in a state procession and the assassination of Curzon while in London by Madan Lal Dhingra. This type of revolutionary terrorist activities took place in important centres abroad. The most famous revolutionary terrorists acting abroad were Shyam Krishna Verma, V.D. Sarvarkar and Hardayal in London and Madame Cama and Ajit Singh in Europe. Sumit Sarkar writes: "Elite revolution did make substantial contributions to the national struggle. The British were often badly frightened, rare examples were set of death-defying heroism in the cause of complete independence and world wide contacts were sought in quests for shelter and arms, leading to important ideological consequences". Hemachandra Kanungo came back from Paris as an atheist with some interest in Marxism. It is no exaggeration to note that terrorist heroism evoked great admiration from very wide circles of educated Indians and sometimes from ordinary people. In spite of its selfless sacrifice, the elite revolutionary Hindu religious zeal acted as a check for others to join the movement and it postponed efforts to draw the masses into active political struggle. Yet, the importance and significance of this revolutionary terrorist phase cannot be minimized. One unique feature of Indian national movement was the simultaneous participation of Moderates, the extremists, the revolutionary terrorists side by side pursuing their definite paths making the people conscious the need of unity and creating a sense of apprehension in the minds of the British that time is nearing to leave India, from 1909 onwards till we achieved independence in 1947.

Constitutional Development up to 1919

A critical examination of the historical process in India under colonialism reveals an evolutionary transition in transfer of power from the British East India Company, a trading organization to the British crown and from the crown to the Indians in 1947. In this total process two stages can be noticeable. The first stage was from 1773 to 1857 and in this stage through the Charter Acts of 1793, 1813, 1833 and 1853 slowly and gradually power and authority was transferred from the Company to the Crown. This transfer of power was made legally valid by the Act of 1858. Throughout the 19th century, the progress towards constitutionalism was very tardy and Macaulay makes a significant statement that it was a period of walking in darkness as it had no plan and goal.

Indian Council Act of 1861

The Indian Council Act of 1861 was passed by the British Parliament in the backdrop of the proclamation of Queen Victoria and the Government of India

Act of 1858, which tried to apply soothing balm to the wounds of the Indians caused by ruthless suppression of the 1857 great revolt. The Queen's proclamation is undoubtedly a great landmark and in the words of Mukherje, it sealed the unity of Indian government and opened a new era. This memorable proclamation, justly called the 'Magna Carta' of India was published at every large town throughout the country and translated into vernacular languages".

Provisions of the Act

The new Act of 1861 abolished the 5th member of the Executive Council of the Viceroy.

- The Act introduced the portfolio allocation system.
- The Act added not less than 6 and not more than 12 by the method of nomination to the Executive Council of the Viceroy for purposes of legislation. Of these additional members, not less than half to be non-official members and thus for the first time inclusion of non-officials for legislative purposes was initiated.
- The Governors of Bombay and Madras too were given the powers of nominating the Advocate General and not less than four and not more than 8 members for legislative purposes. All the laws and amendments require the assent of the Governor General.
- The Governor General was given the power to create new provinces or divide or alter the limits of any presidency, province or territory.
- Though the Indian Councils Act of 1861 marked an important step in the constitutional history of India, it is considered retrograde in many respects by K.K. Datta. Yet, it is to be admitted that the act was in the right direction as for the first time non-official members were nominated to the Viceroy and Governor's executive councils. It is true that they are only ornamental figures with no right to deliberate on any issue. It is a halfway between the wishes of the people and response of the government.

Indian Council Act of 1892

Till 1892, the British government did not think that it was necessary to provide a further dose of reforms to the people of India. The Indian National Congress founded in 1885 vehemently and persistently demanded for the reform of the legislative councils, both at the central and provincial levels. The Congress demanded (a) establishment of councils in provinces in addition to those in Bengal, (b) expansion of the councils, (c) larger representation of elected members, and (d) grant of additional powers to the councils. Tara Chand opines "The resolutions reiterating the demand for responsible government and the speakers criticizing government measures especially condemning the imperialist forward policy and wars, were most unpalatable to the British rules. What seems to have irked them even more was the issue of pamphlets describing grievances. The British government in a bid to mollify the anti-governmental stand of the Congress, passed the 1892 Indian Council Act.

M. Venkata Rangayya rightly observes that this is the only Act which was directly influenced by the Congress.

Provisions of the Act

- The 1892 Indian Council Act enlarged the functions of the legislative councils. The members of the legislative council were authorized to discuss the annual financial statement under certain limits.
- The Act gave members of the council the right of addressing questions to the government on matters of public interest.
- The number of additional members to the council was increased. It was to be not less than 10 and not more than 16 in the case of the Supreme Council and not less than 8 and not more than 20 in the case of Madras and Bombay. The maximum number of Bengal Council was fixed at 20 and for NWF and Oudh 15. It also enumerated that 2/5 of the additional members were to be non-officials.
- Owing to the intense pressure from the Indian National Congress, the British government yielded to their demand and introduced election process under the rules but decided to nominate such elected members, so that the government will have a hold over such candidates.

The Indian Council Act of 1892 did not satisfy the aspirations of the people of India as "it was an attempt of compromise between the official view of the councils as pocket legislatures, and the educated Indian view of them as embryo parliaments". Gokhale observes, "The actual working of the Act manifested its hollowness". Pherozeshah Mehta aptly commented, the Bill as "a most superb steam engine in which the necessary material to generate steam was carefully excluded, substituting in its place coloured shams to look like it". W.C. Banerjee also comments, "the Act does not profess to give us much. We must go on with our agitation and not stop until we get what we all think and we all believe that which we have a right to get". Despite the drawbacks, "by sheer courage, debating skill, fearless criticism, deep knowledge and careful marshalling of data they kept up constant campaign against the government in the councils undermining its political and moral influence and generating a powerful anti-imperialist sentiment". Both Gopal Krishna Gokhale and Pherozeshah Mehta, the Moderate leaders became famous for being fearlessly independent and the bête noir of British officialdom in India: As a result of the efforts of the Moderate nationalist leaders, the Indian nationalist movement became vigorous and vibrant and the highhanded action of Curzon in partitioning Bengal led to the emergence of 'Swadeshi and Vandemataram' movements in Bengal in particular and also the growth of extremist tendencies coupled with individual terrorist activities and the split in the Congress at Surat in 1907. During this period only, the Indian Muslim League emerged as the champion of the interests of the Muslims. The period from 1907 to 1914, has been characterized as a phase of 'repression', 'conciliation' and 'divide and rule' by Sumit Sarkar. In the backdrop of storm and stress, Morley-Minto Reforms were introduced in 1909 as the Indian Council Act of 1909.

Indian Council Act of 1909

Provisions

- The Act of 1909 increased the size of the legislative councils as demanded by the nation. The additional members of the Governor General's council were increased up to a maximum of 60, those of Madras, Bengal, UP, Bombay, Bihar and Orissa to a maximum of 60 and those of the Punjab, Burma and Assam to 30.
- The Act provided for official majority in the imperial legislative council and non-official majority in the provincial legislative councils.
- The Act introduced separate or special electorates for due representation of the different communities, classes and interests. The rest of the seats were allotted to the municipalities and district boards which were called 'general electorates'.
- The functions of the legislative councils were increased. Members were given right to make discussion on the budget, and were allowed to put questions and supplementary questions for the purpose of elucidating any point. The members were provided with right to move resolution in the councils. Rules were made for the discussion of matters of general public interest in the legislative councils.
- The Act raised the number of the members of the executive councils in Bombay, Bengal and Madras to four. Even for a Lt. Governor provinces also, provision was made for the creation of the executive council.
- The university senates, landlords, district boards, municipalities and Chamber of Commerce of the provinces were to elect members. Muslims were provided with separate representation. The Act imposed disqualification. On political offenders the governments could remove these disqualifications, if it desired so.

The Morley-Minto Reforms became operative from 1912. This Act of 1909 too could not satisfy the growing aspirations of the majority of the nationalists, though Moderates like Gokhale appreciated this Act. Though Perceival Spear is of the view, "taken as a whole the act was a clear step towards representative and responsible Government", Sumit Sarkar holds the view, "The Indian Councils Act of 1909 proved to be the most short lived of all of Britains constitutional experiments in India, being totally revised within nine years by the Montague-Chelmsford Report of 1918. It quickly revealed itself to be a failure, both in rallying moderates and in keeping politically active Hindus and Muslim apart". Lord Montague aptly remarked that the Act remained inelastic and antediluvial and it neither contained the best of the old nor the best of the new. A.B. Keith is of the view, "The reforms of 1909 failed in their object if that was to check the propaganda for self-government". We conclude with the statement of Majumdar "the act was nothing but mere moon shine and 'it gave the people of India' shadow rather than the substance".

Montague-Chelmsford Reforms

Montague-Chelmsford Reforms or the Government of India Act of 1919 became operative in 1921. Before we take up the main provisions of the Act and criticism of its provisions, it is necessary to have an idea of the background in which the Montague-Chelmsford Reforms were introduced. The 1909 Act or the Morley-Minto Reforms could not satisfy the nationalist aspiration of having a responsible representative government of the Indians in India. The Muslims were in a restive mood and the decision of the British government to annul the partition of Bengal in 1911 annoyed the Muslims and the Hindus were not happy because they underwent suffering for a long period. The Indians settled in European countries were ill-treated. There was thus discontentment in all sections of the public of India against the British hegemony. In 1912, a serious attempt was made on the life of the Viceroy, Lord Hardinge by individual terrorist Rash Behari Bose, who fled to Japan and played an important role in organizing Indian National Army (INA) in Japan. In such an atmosphere of utter dissatisfaction and disillusionment the First World War broke out in 1914.

Sumit Sarkar aptly remarks, "The First World War (1914–18) brought about really crucial changes in the political life and socio-economic conditions of India". Taking advantage of the war, revolutionaries striving hard for immediate independence in particular the Ghadar Party became very active mobilizing like-minded individuals and groups in India and the British met the wartime threat by a formidable battery of repressive measures like the Defence of India Act of 1915. Many suspects were held without trial for years in Bengal and Punjab and special courts ordered extremely severe sentences. 'According to one estimate of the Ghadar trials, 46 executions and 64 life sentences were listed. Many Bengali terrorists, Punjabi Ghadarites and Radical Pan-Islamists were interned for years during the war and in some cases even afterwards., While the revolutionaries were waging continuous lone battle, the Indian National Congress at its Madras session passed a resolution in 1914, "expressing its profound devotion to the Throne and its unswerving allegiance to the British connection and its firm resolve to stand by the Empire at all hazards and at all costs". It is interesting to note Lord Pentland, Governor of Madras attended the session of the Congress. In this session only Surendranath Banerji moved a motion demanding: "In view of the profound and a vowed loyalty the people of India have manifested in the present crisis, this Congress appeals to the government to deepen and perpetuate it and make it an enduring and valuable asset of the Empire, by removing all invidious distinctions here and abroad between His Majesty's Indian and other subjects, by redeeming the pledges, Provincial Autonomy contained in the Dispatch of August 25th, 1911, and by taking such measures as may be necessary for the recognition of India as a component part of the Federal Empire, in the full and free enjoyment of the rights belonging to that status". While the war was going on, two important events of significance – the Home Rule league movement under the leadership of Tilak and Annie Besant started and the unity of the moderate and extremist elements at Lucknow in 1916 and another significant event was the Lucknow Pact in 1916 between the Congress and the Muslim League. In 1915 Bombay session, they passed a resolution insisting that time had arrived to introduce sustainable measure of reforms towards the introduction of self-government with provincial autonomy and financial independence. Realizing the determined mood for national self-government among the Indians, in order to placate the Indians, the British proclaimed their policy in August 1917. It reads as follows: "The policy of His Majesty's government, with which the Government of India are in complete accord, is that of increasing associations of Indians in every branch of administration and the gradual development of self-governing institutions with a view to the progressive realization of responsible government in India as an integral part of the British empire. They have decided that substantial steps in this direction should be taken as soon as possible". In November 1917, Lord Montague, the Secretary of State paid a visit to India to discuss the scheme with the Viceroy and the political parties. The Congress welcomed this move but finally when the report was submitted in 1918 July, it thoroughly dissatisfied the people of India. The Congress convened a special meeting at Bombay to discuss the report and passed a resolution urging the government that the principle of reforms contained in the Congress League scheme of "nothing less than self-government within the empire can satisfy the Indian people". At the same time, the national leaders taking cue of President Wilson's advocacy of self-government decided to make India a world issue. In such a background, where disenchantment and hope was all-rewarding, the Montague-Chelmsford Reforms were introduced in India and the Bill was passed in 1919 and it became operative from the year 1921.

Provisions

- The Government of India Act of 1919, made many changes in the administration of India. The most important change was that the Secretary of State for India is to be paid from the British revenues. Some functions of the Secretary of State for India were taken away from him and given to a High Commissioner for India who was to be appointed by the Government of India. The Governor General of India was made to carry out the orders of the Secretary of State.
- The Act of 1919 set up a bicameral legislature at the centre – the Central Legislative Assembly and the Council of State. The strength of the Council of State was fixed at 60. Out of 60; 33 were to be elected and 27 were to be nominated by the Governor General. The strength of the Legislative Assembly was fixed at 145. Out of 145; 103 were elected and the rest were nominated. Out of the 42 nominated, 25 were to be officials and the rest were to be non-officials. Out of the 103 elected members, 51 were elected from the general constituencies, 32 by communal constituencies (30 from Muslims and 2 from Sikhs) and 20 by special constituencies consisting of 7 landholders, 9 by Europeans and 4 by Indian commerce.

The life of the Central Legislative Assembly was fixed at 3 years and the Council of State was fixed at 5 years. The first speaker of the assembly was nominated by the government.

– The Franchise Committee had recommended a system of indirect elections to the Central Assembly and the right to vote was very much restricted.
– The Governor General was given power to summon, prorogue and dissolve the chambers. He was given the right to address the members of the two houses.
– The Central Legislature was given very wide powers and can make laws for all the Indian subjects. The crown can veto any law passed by the Central Legislature, if the crown doesn't like the law. Members were given the right to put supplementary question or move resolution, etc. Regarding the budgetary demands, certain items are classified as non-votable and without the approval or assent of the Governor General, they cannot be discussed in the Central Legislature.
– The Government of India Act of 1919 introduced a responsive but not a responsible government. It is to be noted that though the executive was independent of the legislature, the latter could influence its decisions.
– This new Act provided for two lists of subjects: the central list and the provincial list. The central subjects were defence, foreign and political relations, public debt, tariff and customs, posts & telegraphs, patents and copyrights, currency and coinage, communications, public works, commerce, etc. The provincial subjects were local self-government, public health, sanitation, irrigation, water supply, famine relief, agriculture, law and order, forests, etc. The size of the provincial legislature was considerably enlarged.
– An important and far-reaching provision of the Act was the introduction of diarchy in the provinces. Under this scheme, the subjects dealt by the provincial government were divided as transferred and reserved subjects. The transferred subjects were under the control of the governor and the ministers and the reserved subjects were put under the control of the governor and the executive. The system of diarchy worked in the provinces from 1921 to 1937, but many factors were against the satisfactory working of the system and many factors were responsible for the failure of diarchy in the provinces. It is pointed out that the very principle of diarchy was very faulty and the division of the subjects was also faulty. As the government did not encourage the principle of joint responsibility, the ministers never worked as a team.

In the view of Sir H. Butler, "In India it has almost become a term of abuse". Roberts, Appadorai, Palande, Punnaiah, Thompson and Garatt Coupland and Perceival Spear pointed out that diarchy in theory was good but in practice it failed. That the Montague-Chelmsford Reforms announced towards the end of 1919, with their ill-conceived diarchy satisfied few was the view of Bipan Chandra and others. Though liberal-imperialist scholars were ecstatic about the impact and nature of reforms for the Indians, in practice the reforms did not create ecstasy as of the imperialist scholars. Percival Spear makes an apt observation, "the present Indian government is the heir of Montague as well as of Gandhi."

Impact of the First World War

Sumit Sarkar aptly remarks, "the war and the immediate post-war years witnessed truly dramatic changes in Indian life, the three universally accepted crucial landmarks being constitutional reforms, the emergence of Gandhi as leader of a qualitatively new all India mass nationalism and important shifts in India's colonial economy". Bipan Chandra also writes, "The outbreak of the First World War in 1914 gave a new lease of life to the nationalist movement which had been dormant since the heady days of the Swadeshi movement". Bipan Chandra's remark: "Britain's difficulty was India's opportunity" was also very appropriate. From the perspective of Indian nationalism, this opportunity led to the rise of Ghadar movement and the Home Rule league movement. While the Ghadarites attempted a violent overthrow of British rule, the Home Rule leagues launched a nationwide agitation for Home Rule or Swaraj.

Sumit Sarkar argues, "Far more significant were the economic and social consequences of the First World War – drain of wealth, the decline of handicrafts, revenue pressures and impediments to indigenous capitalist growth. To state more categorically, the war affected Indian life through massive recruitments, heavy taxes and war loans, and a very sharp rise in prices. The First World War, no doubt effected different sections of the Indians people in varied and sometimes in opposite way and so sharpened tensions within Indian society, too".

The war led to a massive plunder of Indian human and material resources affecting the quality of life of the people. In theory, the recruitment to the army was voluntary but in practice it happened to be compulsory. It is proved that Michael O'Dwyer resorted to coercion in recruiting Indians to the army and in one year the percentage rose from 1: 150 to 1:4 in Gurjanawala district, which became militant during Rowlath Act disturbances.

There was 300 per cent increase in defence expenditure. As a result of this increase, there was sharp rise in war loans and taxes. Land revenue collection was so excessive; the ryots of Kheda resorted to Satyagraha in 1918 under the leadership of Gandhi. Not only the peasants, but other sections of people also experienced the burden of heavy taxation. Between 1913–1914 and 1920–1921, the share of customs in the total revenue went up from 8 to 14.8 per cent. Further, income tax collections also grew from 2 per cent of gross revenue to 11.75 in 1919–1920. The government demanded the submission of individual tax returns for the first time from 1917–1918 and in the same year supertax was imposed on industrial companies and undivided Hindu business families.

There was phenomenal increase in the prices of essential goods needed by the major chunk of public. Prices of coarse food-grains went up very fast compared to that of higher quality crops of rice or wheat. Sumit Sarkar points out that while the majority experienced fall in standard of living and misery, a small section of businessmen engaged in business of war goods obtained fabulous profits. Blessing in disguise was the certain shift in British Indian government policy towards Indian industrial development out of a combination of financial demands and a realization that a certain minimum of economic self-sufficiency was a strategic necessity.

The war and immediate post-war years mark the real beginning of the Indian trade union movement. The first of such unions was the Madras Labour Union of April 1918 and by November 1920, the number of such unions went up to 125. The first All-India Trade Union Congress met at Bombay in November 1925. The formation of trade unions led to the organization of strikes between 1918–1919 in different parts of India. Of such ones, the food riots in the Krishna-Godavari Delta region in May 1918, followed by three days of intensive riots in Madras city in September wherein both textile and railway workmen played an important role deserves to be noted.

Most far-reaching of all developments, the impact of the Bolshevik Revolution in November 1917 is very significant one. The Bolsheviks gave a new hope to the failing masses that they can overthrow the established government by unity of force and can usher a new set-up. Further, the 14 points announced by Woodrow Wilson, the President of USA gave a new lease of life and hope to the people of India, who were demanding a responsible government in India. Inspired by what is happening in other parts of the world, the new classes gave up the attitude of requesting for concessions and ushered in the attitude of demand of rights. As already mentioned in the preceding pages, realizing the tenacity of the nationalist's struggle for responsible government, the British announced their policy of gradual development of self-governing institutions in India. Finally, the war also provided an opportunity for the Muslims and the Hindus to come together, forgetting their fears and anticipated suspicions and forge unity by the Lucknow Pact of 1916. It was during this period only, the ghastly brutal episode of Jalianwalla Bagh happened, which left serious scars on the psyche of the Indians, making them more determined to secure self-rule soon by mass agitation.

Rise of Gandhi – Nature of Gandhian Movement

India's struggle for independence was actively shaped, influenced and nurtured by Mohandas Karamchand Gandhi, reverentially worshipped as Mahatma and respectfully adored as 'Father of the Nation' from 1920 to 1947 for a period of nearly three decades. During this momentous period of our history, Gandhi was undoubtedly the undisputed leader of millions of freedom loving Indians. He strode like an unrivalled colossus transforming the freedom movement to a broad-based mass movement by his policy of non-violence based non-cooperation and civil disobedience movement, and finally, his slogan 'Do or Die' inspired the Quit India movement. A critical examination of the strategy adopted by him reveals that it was 'Struggle-Truce-Struggle' as coined by Bipan Chandra. In between the phases of struggle-truce-struggle, Gandhi invented the constructive activity programme of eradication of untouchability, Hindu-Muslim unity, promotion of Khadi and village reconstruction to channelize the energies of the multitude of Indians by carrying on peaceful and continuous agitation of all-round mobilization of superstition ridden, illiterate, and ignorant masses about the need of self-help and self-reliance by precept and practice. Gandhi had justifiably become an icon of the 20th century to many Indians and non-Indian protagonists and time is not far off, when he is going to be another *avatar* of God.

Anil Seal, a Cambridge historian and an uncharitable critic of Gandhi observes, "Gandhi's own brand of social conservatism, which sought change through personal reformation rather than popular revolution, his project to uplift the Harijans while keeping them within the Hindu straight jacket, the very cause of their degradations, his desire to take India back to its traditional and rural roots, with support from many captains of industry, his commitment to harmony between the Hindus and the Muslims while stressing Hinduism as a distinctive force, and his hopes, through Satyagraha, of curbing the violence which lies just under the fragile crust of order in Indian society, all suggest that Gandhi's contribution has been as ambiguous as India's chequered past and its uncertain future". What Anil Seal perceives above about Gandhi is not the whole truth but only a partial biased perspective and there are many such who belittle his contribution. It is very difficult to understand and appreciate Gandhi, the 'charismatic saint', astute politician, social reformer, pure visionary and the greatest force for conservatism.

Gandhi was born at Porbandar, a small native state in Kathiawar in.1869. His father was the hereditary Diwan of that tiny state. He belonged to the Vaishya community which had close contacts with the Jains and. perhaps that could be the basis of his firm belief in *Ahimsa* or non-violence and Pacifism. His autobiography *The Story of My Experiments with Truth*, graphically, truthfully and vividly describes his life. Gandhi after becoming a bar-at-law went in search of new pastures to South Africa, where he developed as a mature lawyer-cum-political activist and put into practice his policy of passive resistance backed by non-violence. Sumit Sarkar aptly observes: "The South African experience (1893–1914) contributed in a number of different ways to the foundations of Gandhi's ideology and methods, as well as to his later achievements. In 1909 itself, Gandhi recorded his social ideals in *Hind Swaraj* wherein he categorically states that "the real enemy was not British political domination, but the whole of modern industrial civilization". Gandhi further advocated "Indian's salvation consists in unlearning what she had learnt during the past 50 years or so. The railways, telegraphs, hospitals, lawyers, doctors and such like, have all to go, and the so-called upper class have to learn to live consciously and deliberately the simple life of a peasant. By patriotism, I mean the welfare of the whole people". Sumit Sarkar points out, "The Gandhian Social Utopia as out lined in Hind Swaraj is undoubtedly unrealistic and indeed obscurantist if considered as a final remedy for the ills of India or of the world and it never had much appeal for sophisticated urban groups which by the 1930–1940 would turn increasingly to either capitalist or socialist solutions based on industrialization". Sumit Sarkar continues further by observing, "it did represent a response to the deeply alienating effects of 'modernization' particularly under colonial conditions the artisans ruined by factory industries, the peasants rural or small town intelligentsia. After his return to India, Gandhi concretized his message through programme of Khadi, village reconstruction and (somewhat later) Harijan welfare". Amartya Sen comments, "I personally believe Gandhiji was mistaken on many subjects including his opposition to modern technology, his opposition even to railways and his opposition to religious conversions. But to give credit where it is due, he was altogether visionary in understanding why what he called the Vivisection of the nation can be very detrimental to a harmonious society". Percival Spear observes that Gandhi by his philosophy of thought and action "envisaged a peasant society of self supporting workers, with simplicity as its ideal and purity as its hallmark, the state would be a lose federation of village republics. He rejected the mechanics of the west along with its glitter and preached the necessity of hand spinning and weaving while cheerfully receiving the contributions of Indian industrialists".

In January 1915, Gandhi returned to India and instead of plunging into action, he spent a year in understanding the situation in India by undertaking travelling and in the next year too he maintained distance from the ongoing Home Rule movement. During the course of 1917 and early 1918, he involved himself in three significant struggles in Champaran in Bihar, in Ahmedabad and in Kheda in Gujarat. In the words of Bipan Chandra "the common feature of these struggles was that they were related to specific local issues and that they were fought for the economic demands of the masses". Interestingly, these movements involved the impoverished peasants at Champaran and Kheda and industrial workers in Ahmedabad. Champaran, Ahmedabad and Kheda struggles made Gandhi find a place among the people of India as a determined and committed person to a cause which will better the conditions of the masses in India and to earn the goodwill and confidence of the younger workers. In such a mood of goodwill and successful experience at the age of 50, Gandhi called for a nationwide Satyagraha against the Rowlatt Act in March 1919. As the constitutional method failed, Gandhi initiated *Satyagraha*. A Satyagraha Sabha was formed and contacts were established with the people interested in participating in the agitation against Rowlatt Act. Gandhi proposed that the form of protest to be observed should be a nationwide hartal or strike followed by fasting and prayer. In addition to this form of protest, they decided to offer civil disobedience against specific laws. Though 6 April was fixed as the date on which Satyagraha was to be launched, due to some confusion, hartal was observed on 30 March at Delhi followed by street violence and disorder. Same pattern was also noticed in other parts too. The situation in Punjab, Gujarat and Bombay was very volatile. Gandhi was not allowed to visit Punjab and was detained at Bombay. Gandhi made it his mission to pacify the people. The Punjab Government by its action of arresting two local leaders precipitated the matter to the verge of violent protests. April 13, the Baisakhi day was the darkest day in the Punjab and on that day the British resorted to brutal shoot-out attack on an innocent gathering at Jallianwala Bagh, in which 179 died as per government account and many ware injured. This most inhuman and brutal act of General Dyer stunned the entire civilized Indians and anger and resentment knew no bounds and the entire nation was overwhelmed by the total atmosphere of violence and revengeful mood. Gandhi withdrew the movement on 18 April, as his philosophy of action was based on non-violence and he wanted to be a leader of the controlled mass action. Bipan Chandra et al. write, "This did not mean, however, that Gandhiji had lost faith either in his non-violent Satyagraha or in the capacity of the Indian people to adopt it as a method of struggle. A year later, he launched another nationwide struggle, on a scale bigger than that of the Rowlatt Satyagraha. The wrong inflicted on Punjab was one of the major reasons for launching it". Thus began the 'Indian Experiment' of Mahatma which lasted for more than two and a half decades in actively shaping and moulding the course of the national liberation struggle under the banner of Gandhian era.

The Non-cooperation Movement (1920–22)

The 'Indian Experiment' of 'The Non-cooperation Movement' of 1920–22 was undertaken by the Indian National Congress under the leadership and direction of Gandhi, when every segment of the Indian society was seething with discontentment and itching for action due to various reasons – Rowlatt Act, the Jallianwalla Bagh massacre, martial law in Punjab, the neglect of the Khilafat Committee aspirations, high prices of commodities, drought and epidemics.

The non-cooperation movement was launched formally on 1 August, 1920, the day on which Lokamanya Tilak breathed his last. The Congress gave a call to the people to: (a) surrender all titles and honorary offices and resign from nominated seats in local bodies, (b) refuse to attend government of semi-government functions, (c) withdraw slowly step by step children from schools and colleges, aided or controlled by the government (d) boycott of British courts by lawyers and litigants, (e) refusal for recruitment for military and other services in Mesopotamia, (f) boycott the elections to be held for councils as per the reforms of 1919, and (g) boycott of foreign goods. Besides the above-mentioned measures of non-cooperation with the government, it was decided to establish native educational institutions and native arbitration centres all over India and also to establish harmonious relations between the Hindus and the Muslims. In 1921–22, the movement continued with unabated zeal by the participation of masses. National institutions like Gujarat Vidyapith,

Bihar Vidyapith, Tilak Maharashtra Vidyapith, Kasi Vidyapith, the Bengal National University, and the Jamia Milia of Delhi were established. The Swadeshi concept became a household word. Khadi became a symbol of freedom. In order to finance the non-cooperation movement, Tilak Swaraj Fund was started to which money poured and within six months, nearly a crore of rupees was subscribed. When Prince of Wales visited India in 1921, a successful hartal was organized against his visit. On 5 February 1922, police station of Chaura, near Gorakhpur in UP was attacked by a mob of peasants. The mob burnt the police station and in that nearly 22 policemen died. This violent event disturbed the soul of Gandhi and he ordered for the immediate suspension of the programme.

Though many leaders were very unhappy with the decision of Gandhi, they accepted the decision in good faith. The non-cooperation movement definitely awakened tremendous national awareness for freedom and successfully erased the fear psychosis from the minds of the Indians and the movement thus inspired the people to be ready for further sacrifices and future struggles with confidence and hope. Discussing the impact and significance of the non-cooperation movement, Anil Seal concludes, "The non-cooperation movement of 1921–22 was in many respects a debacle". Bipan Chandra et al. are of the view "the battle was over, but the war would continue". Sumit Sarkar writes "An adequate understanding of the non-cooperation upsurge of 1921–22 requires an analysis at three levels – the phases of the all-India movement as sought to be determined by the Gandhian Congress leadership, the role of district social groups and classes, and most interesting and important of all perhaps, the regional and local variations". Sumit Sarkar further continues, "four phases may be distinguished in what may be termed the official movement. From January to March 1921, the central emphasis was on students and lawyers giving up practice. In the face of pressure from below, the Bombay AICC meeting of 28–30 July adopted a somewhat militant stance. Gandhi here gave a call for flooding the prisons with volunteers 'Our triumph consists in thousands being led to prisons like lambs in the slaughter house' and organization of volunteer bands was now given top priority. Despite the brakes, however, developments in the fourth phase between November 1921 and February 1922, very nearly brought the government to its knees and the entire movement was abruptly called off on 11 February, 1922". A.R. Desai is of the view, "with the section of workers and peasants participating in it, the national movement which was restricted to the upper and middle classes till 1917, got a mass basis for the first time". Griffith concludes, "Gandhi taught India new self-respect which could be content with nothing less than self-government. He inspired his countrymen with a tradition to suffer in the case of their country. Gandhi, who had himself learnt from Britain the meaning of justice and freedom, imparted these ideas to his fellow countrymen with such success that Indian nationality became a reality and Indian nationalism a unanimous expression of the feeling of the Indians". Gandhi in an article published in

Young India on February 23, 1922 declared, "it is high time that the British people were made to realize that the fight that was commenced in 1920 is a fight to the finish, whether it lasts one month or one year or many months or many years and whether the representatives of Britain re-enact all the indescribable orgies of the Mutiny days with redoubled force or whether they do not".

The abrupt suspension of non-cooperation movement led to a great divide among the Congress as pro-changers and no changers. The visit of Simon in 1927 was boycotted and was greeted with black flags. In 1929, the then Viceroy Lord Irvin declared that dominion status would be accorded to India in stages as its ultimate goal. As this proposal was not acceptable to the Congress, in its Lahore session of 1929, the Indian National Congress demanded Purnaswaraj or complete independence as its ultimate goal. As the British government adopted adamant attitude towards the aspirations of the people, the Indian National Congress under the direction of Gandhi started civil disobedience movement.

Civil Disobedience Movement (1930–34)

Gandhi addressed an ultimatum to Viceroy Lord Irwin on 31 January, asking him to remove the evils of the British rule and also informed of his decision to undertake Dandi Satyagraha wherein the laws of the government would be violated. The list of demands consisted the following: (1) prohibit intoxicants, (2) change the ratio between the rupee and the sterling, (3) reduce the rate of land revenue, (4) abolition of salt tax, (5) reduce the military expenditure, (6) reduce expenditure on civil administration, (7) impose custom duty on foreign cloth, (8) accept the Postal Reservation Bill, (9) abolish the CID department, (10) release all political prisoners, and (11) issue licences of arms to citizens for self-protection. Gandhi made it clear that if the 11 points are ignored, the only way out was civil disobedience.

Breaking the salt laws of the government non-violently was the basic activity of civil disobedience. Along with this activity, activities like no tax campaign, no revenue and no rent (land tax) campaign became very popular in different parts of India. After deciding to start the Dandi Salt Satyagraha, Gandhi addressed a letter to Lord Irwin on 2 March, 1930 intimating, "on the 11th day of this month, I shall proceed with such co-workers of the Ashram as I can take, to disregard the provisions of the salt laws. It is, I know, open to you to frustrate my design by arresting me, I hope that there will be tens of thousands ready, in a disciplined manner, to take up the work after me, and in the act of disobeying the Salt Act to lay themselves upon to the penalties of a law that should never have disfigured the statute book". Bipan Chandra et al. correctly point out "the deceptively innocuous move was to prove devastatingly effective", as later day events successfully proved. Gandhi started his march, staff in hand with a band of dedicated peaceful Satyagrahis and reached Dandi on 6 April, 1930 and inaugurated the civil disobedience movement, a movement that was to remain unsurpassed in the history of the Indian national movement for the country-wide mass participation it unleashed. Nearly 90,000 people belonging to all social groups spread over the whole of India participated wholeheartedly in this movement. Significantly, for

Indian women, the movement was the most liberating experience to date and the can be said to have marked their entry into public space. The British government resorted to cruel repression in spite of the total non-violent conduct of the movement by issuing more than a dozen ordinances. The Indian National Congress was declared an illegal body and Gandhi was arrested on 5 May, 1930. The arrest of Gandhi infuriated the masses and they voluntarily expressed their solidarity with the movement. The uncommon heroism exhibited by thousands of Satyagrahis throughout the breadth of India was really very commendable and exemplary as that of Thota Narasayya Naidu who held the flag in hand in spite of severe beating by the police of Machilipatnam. The national flag, the symbol of the new spirit, now became a common sight even in remote villages. While the civil disobedience was going on, the British government convened the Round Table Conferences. Gandhi did not attend the first one held in 1930. Gandhi agreed to attend the Second Round Table Conference of 1931 and in this background only Gandhi-Irwin pact was concluded, which was variously described as a 'truce' and a 'provisional settlement'. By this agreement it was agreed upon: (a) to withdraw all ordinances and pending prosecutions, (b) to release all political prisoners except those who were guilty of violence, (c) to restore the confiscated property of the Satyagrahis, (d) to permit peaceful picketing of liquor, opium and foreign cloth shops, and (e) to permit the collection or manufacture of salt, free of duty, by persons residing within a specific distance of the sea shore, (f) the Congress agreed not to press for investigation into police excess, (g) to suspend the civil disobedience movement, and (h) to stop boycott and to participate in the Second Round Table Conference. In 1931 certain events – coming to power of conservatives, replacement of the Viceroy, and execution of Bhagat Singh – created an atmosphere of dejection in Gandhi and other younger Indian leaders. The Congress decided to restart the movement in January 1932. As usual, the British government took stern steps to suppress the movement and in the meanwhile the British Prime Minister announced communal award in 1932. The civil disobedience movement continued upto 1934 and it was suspended in that year. Bipan Chandra et al. observe: "The civil disobedience movement of 1930–31, then marked a critically important stage in the progress of the anti-imperialist struggle". But Anil Seal, the Cambridge historian observes "Civil disobedience, the salt march to Dandi (an astute move by Gandhi to play for time and to test opinion), his programme tailored to achieve the widest appeal (whether temperance, Khadi, enlisting women or social uplift, especially of Harijans) and the 60,000 or more who went to jails not withstanding, failed to mobilize India's millions. Except here and there in Gujarat and the Godavari deltas and as a part of Midnapore, civil disobedience was not a mass movement. They had merely scratched a surface of Indian society. They had not shaken the British Raj and by 1933 they had in reality been defeated". This statement of Anil Seal has been disproved by Bipan Chandra and Sumit Sarkar.

The Quit India Movement (1942)

The Quit India movement or the Revolt of 1942 or 'August Revolution' of 1942 was the most popular and powerful mass movement in the series of agitations led by Gandhi in the course of freedom struggle. By the time this mass movement was planned, the Second World War was going on, the shadows of the Japanese invasion on India were making the sky dark and cloudy, the efforts of Cripps mission bore no fruit and the prices of essential commodities were soaring high and the day does not appear to be far off for the deliverance from the British imperialism. Sumit Sarkar writes "The summer of 1942 found Gandhi in a strange and uniquely militant mood, 'Leave India to God or to anarchy' he repeatedly urged the British – this orderly disciplined anarchy should go, and if as a result there is complete lawlessness I would risk it". These statements made, in May 1942 are indicative of the restlessness of the leader, who 'promised' Swaraj within one year and who is eager and anxious to see that his mission of gaining freedom for India is realized soon. Sumit Sarkar aptly observes "though the need for non-violence was always reiterated, Gandhi's mantra of *Do or Die* represents the militant mood of Gandhi".

In the working committee meeting held at Wardha on 14 July, 1942 the Congress first accepted the idea of a struggle. The All India Congress Committee that met in Bombay in August ratified this decision to go in for struggle. In his speech Gandhi made it very clear "I am not going to be satisfied with anything short of complete freedom. May be, he (the Viceroy) will propose the abolition of salt tax, the drink evil. But I will say nothing less than freedom". Gandhi then followed up with the now famous exhortation Do or Die. "Here is a Mantra, a short one, that I give you. You may imprint it on your hearts and let every breath of yours give expression to it. The mantra is *Do or Die*. We shall either free India or die in the attempt; we shall not live to see the perpetuation of slavery". Gandhi also gave a call to all sections of the people, the princes, the Jagirdars, the Zamindars, the propertied and moneyed classes, who derive their wealth and property from the workers in the fields and factories and elsewhere, to whom eventually power and authority belong. In the view of Sumit Sarkar, the above statement of Gandhi indicates his social radicalism and shift in the philosophy of the Congress, by now people with the goals of socialism and communism have become a part of the broad-based Congress organization; On the other hand, the British too were equally determined to crush any movement of the Congress. The then Viceroy Linlithgow in a letter dated 8 August, 1946 categorically made his mind very clear "I feel very strongly that the only possible answer to a declaration of war by any section of Congress in the present circumstances must be a declared determination to crush the organization as a whole". Thus, the two sides were ready to act and even before the formal launching of the movement, the government in a single sweep arrested all the top leaders of the Congress in the early hours of August 9, 1942. This led to spontaneous outburst of mass anger against the arrest of leaders. There was mass upsurge all over the country for six or seven weeks after the unexpected event of August 9, 1942. Bipan Chandra writes, "People devised a variety of ways of expressing their anger in some places, huge crowds attacked police stations, post offices, courts, railway stations and other symbols of government authority. National flags were forcibly hoisted on public buildings in defiance of the police". Cities, towns and villages witnessed the people's wrath. Peasants, workers and students actively participated in showing their resentment against the government. By following tactics of brutality, the government suppressed the movement. Gandhi who was arrested in the early hours of 9 August, started fast on 10 February by declaring that the fast would last for 21 days. One more feature to be noticed in this connection was the refusal of Gandhi to condemn the violence of the masses and held the government responsible for this violence. All over the country people responded positively and actively towards the fast of Gandhi. Gandhi was released on 6 May, 1944 on medical grounds. It is to be noted that the Quit India movement was the spontaneous participation of the masses compared to the earlier non-cooperation and civil disobedience movements. Bipan Chandra was of the view: "the great significance of this historic movement was that it placed the demand for independence on the immediate agenda of the national movement. After 'Quit India' there could be no retreat. Independence was no longer a matter of bargain. And this became amply clear after the war". The spirit unleashed was carried further by Indian National Army of Subhas Chandra Bose. An understanding of the process of the struggle for independence of India reveals its long drawn dynamics of the strategy adopted by the leaders of this movement. While the pre-Gandhian phase was one of creating conscious awareness of the evils of the colonial and imperialist among the masses, the Gandhian phase of 'struggle-truce-struggle' was one of sustaining the tempo of the movement through the stages of non-cooperation followed by civil disobedience, followed by the Quit India movement. Besides Gandhi's ideology of non-violence and technique of Satyagraha, it was the strategy of struggle-truce-struggle that accelerated and sustained the urge for freedom and enabled India to achieve freedom in 1947. We find a gradual and slow transition from mini-scale minority of freedom seekers to mass organization of freedom seekers during the time of Gandhi, and his most outstanding contribution was the successful strategy of struggle-truce-struggle in stages to sustain the tempo of the movement. Undoubtedly, Gandhi was a great strategist of the 20th century mass political mobilization process motivated by self-reliant rule of the masses through more of non-violent means.

Revolutionary Movements

It is an established fact that the Indian national movement was undoubtedly one of the biggest mass movements modern society has ever witnessed in the course of the human history. The general perception prevalent was that India's struggle for independence was mostly non-violent in nature and was the effort of the Indian National Congress and its moderate, extreme and Gandhian phases. But in the last forty years, new perceptions have come to light in consequence to the in-depth study of multiple factors that influenced the process of India's struggle for independence. "It is now agreed upon that the movement underwent transitions in the goal and method from time to time. In the evolution of the struggle of Indian independence, the Gandhian or the post-1920 phase was not only the period that witnessed mass movement but also the emergence of ideological impact on the process of the movement.

Bipan Chandra is of the view that the Indian national movement was open to the alternative hegemony of socialist ideas. Bipan Chandra further writes, "The national movement did, in fact, undergo constant ideological transformation. In the late 1920s and 1930s, Jawaharlal Nehru, Subhas Chandra Bose, the communists, the Congress socialists and other left minded socialist groups and individuals made an intense effort to give the movement and the National Congress a socialist direction. One aspect of this was the effort to organize the peasants in Kisan Sabhas, the workers in trade unions and the youth in youth leagues and student unions. The other was the effort to give the entire national movement a socialist ideological orientation, to make it adopt a socialist vision of free India. The effort did achieve a certain success and socialist ideas spread widely and rapidly. Almost all young intellectuals of the 1930s and 1940s belonged to some shade of pink or red. Kisan Sabhas and trade unions also tended to shift to the left. Thus, the movement for India's struggle for independence was a multi-stream movement which subscribed and coexisted with widely divergent political and ideological perspectives.

Sudden stoppage of the mass agitation of the non-violent non-cooperation movement in 1922 by Gandhi made the young participants like Jogesh Chandra Chatterjea, Suryasen, Jatin Das, Chandrasekhar Azad, Bhagat Singh, Sukh Dev, Shiv Varma, Bhagavati Charan Vohra and Jaidev Kapur to turn to the revolutionary terrorist politics. Slowly, two strands of revolutionary terrorism developed in Bengal and the Punjab, UP and Bihar under the impact of new social forces like working class trade unionism after the end of the First World War and the Russian revolution of 1917 and the newly emerging communist groups with their emphasis on Marxism, socialism and the proletariat. The Hindustan Republican Association (or Army) to organize an armed revolution to overthrow the colonial rule and to establish a Federal Republic of the United States of India based on adult franchise was established at Kanpur in 1924. In order to procure money, the revolutionaries resorted to the action of the Kakori robbery in 1925. Some of those involved in the Kakori robbery case were put behind bars and Ashfatapullah Khan, Ramprasad Bismil, Roshan Singh and Rajendra Lahiri were hanged. Influenced by the socialist ideas, a group of young revolutionaries like Bejoy Kumar Sinha, Shiv Varma, Bhagat Singh, Sukha Dev and Chandrasekhar Azad started a new group of Hindusthan Socialist Republican Association in 1928 and declared socialism as their official goal. This group wanted to take revenge on Saunders, a police official involved in the 'lathi charge' of Lala Lajpat Rai and killing him at Lahore on December 17,1928. Bhagat Singh and B.K. Dutt decided to show their antagonism against the Public Safety Bill and the Trade Disputes Bill by throwing a bomb in the Central Legislative Assembly. The motive behind this act was to utilize the court platform to convince the public about the atrocities of the government and to bring awareness in the minds of majority of silent Indians. Ultimately, their fearless exposure and open pleadings for martyrdom made Bhagat Singh a household name in the land. Bhagat Singh was hanged on 23 March, 1931 along with Sukh Dev and Rajguru. The Lahore conspiracy case, the Chittagong Army Raid and such revolutionary activities made young women participate in such revolutionary activities. One more effect of this revolutionary movement was the reduction of the religious appeal in the minds of the young revolutionaries and these activities helped spread of nationalist consciousness and socialist consciousness. Bipan Chandra aptly concludes that "the politics of the revolutionary terrorists had severe limitations above all, theirs was not the politics of a mass movement. They failed to politically activate the masses or move them into political action; they could not even establish contact with the masses. At the same time they made an abiding contribution to the national freedom movement. Their deep patriotism courage and determination, and sense of sacrifice stirred the Indian people". Rise of the left wing consciousness by 1920–1930, due to the spread of socialist consciousness and left wing ideology of world view, the goal of political independence acquired a clearer and sharper social and economic emancipation of the suppressed and exploited segments of Indian society. The youth in particular led by charismatic Nehru and Bose symbolized the socialist aspirations. In this background, they re-emerged as two powerful movements of the left – the Communist Party of India and the Congress Socialist Party. In the wake of the sudden suspension of the non-violent, non-cooperation movement by Gandhi, several socialist and communist groups came into operation throughout India. Newspapers and booklets began to appear spreading to left ideology. *Labour, Kissan Gazette* of Singaravelu founded at Madras, *Navyug* of Mazafar Ahmad, *The Socialist* of S.A. Dange, *Inquilab* of Ghulam Hussaini and the pamphlet of *Gandhi and Lenin* by S.A. Dange deserve to be noticed. During 1927, 1928 and 1929 hundreds of youth conferences were held, wherein capitalism, imperialism and landlordism were strongly condemned and socialism and communism were offered as alternative solutions to the ills of inequality and exploitation. Economic depression also made the situation worse and the world depression brought the capitalist system into disrepute and developed attention towards Marxism and socialism. The election of Nehru as Congress President for 1936 and 1937 and Bose for 1938 and 1939 and the formation of the Congress Socialist Party made people look towards socialism as panacea for all evils. As noted by S. Gopal, the biographer of Nehru, Nehru became a self-conscious revolutionary radical. Nehru joined with Subhas Chandra Bose in 1928 to organize the Independence for India League to fight for complete independence after which 'a socialist revision of the economic structure of society'. In 1929 he proclaimed, "I am a socialist and a republican and advocated India should have to adopt a full socialist programme if she was to end her poverty and inequality". By 1936 he proclaimed that the only key to the solution of the problems of the world and India was socialism, and he favoured to be within the Congress fold of Gandhi and the right wing by making the working class and the peasants more active participants in the mainstream of the national struggle.

In 1920 M.N. Roy set up a Communist Party of India and in 1925 all the communist groups joined and started the Communist Party of India. In the beginning the early communists worked among the peasants and workers. Along with Jawaharlal and Subhas Chandra Bose, the youth leagues and other Left forces, the Workers and Peasants Party also played an important role in creating a strong, left wing within the Congress and in giving "the Indian national movement a leftward direction". Alarmed at these developments, the British government arrested 32 radical political and trade union activists including some British. The Meerut conspiracy case was hatched by the British against the 32 radical political and trade union activists. The efforts of the government to isolate the communists failed but the communists themselves deviated from the mainstream by branding Gandhi and the Congress as 'the agents of the bourgeoisie'. In 1934, the government declared CPI illegal but the communists participated in Civil Disobedience movement and by the Dutt-Bradely thesis, it is recognized that the National Congress could play a great part and be the foremost in the work of realizing the anti-imperialist people's front. During 1936–1942, they built up powerful peasant movements in Kerala, Andhra, Bengal and Punjab. The idea of the formation of a socialist party took concrete shape in 1930–31 and 1932–34 in jails by the younger generation of Congressmen who were disenchanted by the Gandhian strategy of non-violent method to achieve independence. As a result of dialogue and discussion,, finally they founded Congress Socialist Party (CSP) at Bombay in October 1934 under the leadership of Jaya Prakash Narayan, Acharya Narendradev and Minoo Masani. They also decided to work within the Congress party. The CSP made it a policy to transform the Congress and strengthen it. But when it did not yield the desired result, they decided to go for composite leadership and this experiment too did not succeed. From the beginning, the CSP leaders were divided into three broad ideological groups: the Marxians, the Fabian and the Gandhian but they identified socialism with Marxian and in due course, positive appreciations of Gandhian ideals made CSP adopt them. The Left could not make deep impact on Indian polity and society because it failed to understand the Indian reality and also failed to grasp the Gandhian strategy of struggle.

Peasants and Workers' Movement

In British colonial India, the unrest of the peasants and the workers was a well-established common feature, as the colonial set-up was interested in gaining maximum revenue from the cultivator and wanted to obtain maximum profit by paying meagre wages to the workers. But by the time we come to the second decade of the 20th century, due to the ongoing Indian independence struggle and the Gandhian strategy of mass involvement in national struggle, the peasants and workers too became a part of the national movement.

Consequently, separate organizations representing the interests of the peasants and workers took shape in different parts of India. In 1918, the UP Kisan Sabha was set up by Gouri Shankar Misra and Indra Narain Dwivedi whose effort was blessed by Madan Mohan Malaviya. The Kisan Sabha played very active role in championing the cause of nationalism in 1919, 1920 and 1921 and we notice a change in the nature of the peasant activity towards violence and looting. In the region of Avadh, peasant discontentment surfaced again under the leadership of the EKA or unity movement but the relation between the EKA movement and the nationalist movement minimized due to the refusal of EKA leaders to follow the discipline of the nationalist movement. Kerala witnessed the peasant movement of the Mappilas in 1921. This movement was repressed by the local authorities. It was a violent movement and further communalization of the movement isolated the Mappilas in which nearly ten thousand people died. Besides UP and Malabar, Bardoli in Gujarat also witnessed an organized peasant rebellion in 1928, in which Vallabhai Patel played a crucial role. Gandhi spoke of Bardoli as follows: "whatever the Bardoli struggle may be, it clearly is not a struggle for the attainment of Swaraj. That every such awakening, every such effort as that of Bardoli will bring Swaraj nearer and may it bring it nearer even than any direct effort is undoubtedly true". Bipan Chandra observes, "the modern worker makes his appearance in India in the second half of the 19th century with the slow beginning of modern industry and the growth of the utilities like the railways, and the post and telegraph network". He further observes "the process of the desperate groups of workers in various parts of country emerging as an organized self-conscious, all India class is inextricably linked with the growth of the Indian national movement through the process of the Indian nation in the making because the notion of the Indian working class could not exist before the notion of the Indian people had begun to take root". Attempts were made in 1870–1880 to better the working conditions of the workers by legislation. Till the Swadeshi surge of 1903–8, there was no concerted effort to better the working conditions of the labour: Once again between 1915–1922, there was resurgence of workers' movement along with the Home Rule movement and the Non-cooperation movement. The most important development was undoubtedly, the formation of All-India Trade Union Congress under the leadership of Tilak and Lala Lajpat Rai. Since then the working class movement became strong and by 1930 onwards ideological tone was added to the movement. The last years of the colonial rule also saw a remarkable sharp increase in strikes on economic issues all over the country. The all-India strike of the Post and Telegraph Department employees being the most well known among them. The peasant organizations started in various parts of India could not effectively mobilize the peasants, so it was realized that there should be independent Kisan Sabhas. Consequently, Bihar Kisan Sabha in 1927, the Provincial Kisan Sabha in UP in 1935, the Madras Presidency Ryots Association in 1935, the Madras Presidency Agriculturists Association in 1937 and a Kisan School at Nidubrolu in 1938 were started to train the 'kisans' in organizational work. As a result of the pressure exerted by these organizations, the Debt Relief Act of UP of 1934, the Regulations of Accounts Act in 1934 in Punjab, the Moneylenders Act in 1939 and the Relief of Indebtedness Act of 1935 in Bengal were passed. The first All India Kisan Congress was founded in 1935. The Congress ministries between 1937–1939 passed certain acts to improve the conditions of the peasants. The Second World War for a short time put brakes in the peasant movements. The demand for abolition of Zamindaris was pressed with greater sense of urgency. In Andhra region there was a struggle for higher wages and use of standard measures for payment of wages in kind. The peasants of Punnapra-Vayalar in Travancore fought bloody bitter battles with the police. The famous Telangana armed struggle is an example of peasants' resistance against landlords oppression and it played a crucial role in the anti-Nizam struggle. One more peasant struggle that deserves our notice was the Tebhaga struggle in Bengal led by the sharecroppers in 1946. Bipan Chandra observes that the peasant movements of pre-independent India were not clearly aimed at the overthrow of the existing agrarian structure but towards alleviating its most oppressive aspects.

Depressed Class Movements

The rising tide of national and democratic aspirations, awareness and consciousness among the downtrodden and depressed classes to obtain more and more civil liberties based on liberty, equality and fraternity made them agitate for change in their lives and this was reflected in the anti-caste domination struggles launched by nationalists and others in different parts of India in pre-independent India. Bipan Chandra aptly observes, "the struggle to reform Indian society tendered to merge with the anti-imperialist struggle". Sumit Sarkar points out "As in earlier periods, the varied contradictions of Indian society often formed expression through caste associations and movements, which could be divisive and basically conservative, but at times also potentially quite radical". Of such movements, anti-Brahmin justice party in Madras Presidency, Dalit self-respect movement spearheaded by Babasahab Dr B.R. Ambedkar in Maharashtra, E.V. Ramaswami Naikar's anti-Brahmin priests and forcible temple entry, the burning of the Manusmriti and outright atheism in Tamil Nadu and the Vaikkom Satyagraha in Kerala for temple entry were very important movements that spread the concepts of social justice in a stratified traditional social set-up. Gandhi through his constructive programme in between the agitation tried to ameliorate the conditions of the depressed classes. Sumit Sarkar makes a pointed statement: "it is interesting that in all these regions, militant lower caste movements contributed to the emergence of Leftist trends". Of such leaders, Sahajananda, a leader of the peasant movement, the Congress, socialists and the communists, and Nana Patil, who was a participant in Satyasodhak Mandal's activities in 1919–1920, became by 1942 the best known. We may agree with the view of Bipan Chandra, "The main weakness of the temple entry movement and the Gandhian or nationalist approach in fighting caste oppression was that even while arousing the people against untouchability they lacked a strategy for ending the caste system itself". The rise of Left wing ideology along with peasant and workers participation movements and anti-caste domination movements stirred the consciousness of the common people and made them think of travelling on the path towards the egalitarian society where oppression and social injustice are absent in reality.

Government of India Act of 1935

In the evolution of the process of Indian constitutional development of pre-independent India, the Government of India Act of 1935 was a landmark, no doubt, but from the Indian perspective, it was an unwelcome landmark. Many factors like the appointment of Simon Commission with all white men to review the working of the Montague-Chelmsford Reforms, ignoring purposefully the Purnaswaraj demand of the Congress and callous and arrogant negative attitude of the British towards the aspirations of the Indians made the Indians dissatisfied. Further, the challenge of the British to evolve a consensus on constitutional reforms made the Indians appoint Nehru Committee to suggest constitutional reforms. The boycott of Simon Commission with black flags throughout India also strengthened the atmosphere of mistrust between the British and the Indians. In such vitiated environment, in March 1933, the British issued a small document known as the white paper. On the basis of the report of the joint select committee submitted in November 1934, a Bill was introduced in the House of Commons on 5 February, 1935 and House of Lords in June 1935 and was passed in July 1935. This bill received the Royal ascent on 2 August, 1935 as Government of India Act, 1935.

Provisions of the Act

1. The Act provided for an All India Federation. But at that time there were Indian states and provinces of British India. It stipulated that the Indian states were to send 125 members and the provinces were to send 250 members to the Federal Assembly. The Indian states were to send 104 members and 156 members to the council of the states. While the Indian states nominated members, the provinces elected their members on communal lines. Further, the Indian Federation as provided by this Act was different from the other federal systems. Instead of simple division of powers between the centre and the units, the Act provided three –Federal, Provincial and the Concurrent lists.
2. The Act provided for diarchy at the centre, where certain federal subjects were kept in the Governor General's control, who is to be assisted by 3 councillors appointed by him. Defence, External Affairs, Ecclesiastical Affairs and the administration of tribal areas were reserved for the Governor General. The other subjects are to be administered by council of ministers, who are to be; not more than 10, as advisors to the Governor General. The Act purposefully made the ministers weak and dependent.

3. The Act provided for bicameral legislature of Federal Assembly and the Council of States. The life of the Federal Assembly was fixed for 5 years and the life of the Council of States was fixed to be permanent, of which one third members were to retire for every three years. The powers of the Indian legislatures were severely restricted and the powers of the Governor General were enlarged.
4. The Act provided for the establishment of a Federal Court with jurisdiction over the states and the provinces. The Federal Court was provided with one Chief Justice and two judges and this Federal Court was given both original and appellate authority. Though this court was given power and authority to interpret the constitution, the final authority was the Privy Council sitting in London.
5. The Act of 1935 abolished the India Council of the Secretary of the State. Instead of the Council, he was provided with advisors, who may or may not be consulted. Both the Governor General and the Governors of the Provinces were made responsible to the Secretary of State. The Act provided for elaborate safeguards which acted as aberrations for responsible or self-government.
6. The Act provided for a rigid constitution and the constitution can be amended by the British Government alone.
7. The most important provision of this Act was the provision of provincial autonomy but this does not mean that this Act established full-fledged responsible government in the provinces as the Governors were given both discretional and individual powers. As such the provincial autonomy according to this Act was merely a sham criticism of the Act of 1935.

Nehru criticized this Act as one that made the Indian Constitution 'a machine with strong brakes and no engine'. C. Rajagopalachari was of the view: "The new constitutional is worse than diarchy". Percival Spear observes, "it (the Act) proposed a conservative framework for an independent India The obstinate British adherence to ideas of a one community state with its doctrine of parliamentary sovereignty and rule by majorities was an ill-wind which was to reap the whirl wind of post-partition masses … . It was India which had to pay for this following".

Indian Polity (1939–1945)

The period from 1939 to 1945 witnessed the Second World War that had a devastating effect on humanity and coming to India in particular, it was a prelude to the declaration of Indian independence and partition of India into India and Pakistan on communal grounds. This period brought to light primarily the fragile nature of the mosaic of Indian society and polity wherein the internal squabbles of the Congress organization surfaced openly defying the existing traditions in the form of conflict between Subhas Chandra Bose and Gandhi, and the sharpened teeth of extreme communalism hardened the Muslim League to opt for their desired sacred land of Pakistan. Further, as an indirect effect of the Second World War, the condition of the common people became extremely worse due to the soaring of prices of necessities in addition to the devastating famines. Unrest of labour and the peasants dominated the Indian scenario. Lord Linlithgow was the Governor General of India between 1936–1944 and he was followed by Lord Wavel, who was the Governor General till 1947. Thus when the Second World War started in 1939, Linlithgow was the Governor General and when the Second World War ended in 1945, Wavel was the Governor General. Before the war started, the Indian National Congress formed ministries with absolute majority in Madras, Bihar, Orissa, central provinces and united provinces and with a near majority in Bombay in 1937. Sumit Sarkar aptly observes: "For millions of Indians, particularly in the Hindu majority general constituencies, the "Vote for Gandhi and the Yellow Box signified appreciation of patriotic self-sacrifice, plus some hopes of socio-economic change". But as observed by Sumit Sarkar, we notice a steady shift to the right, occasionally veiled by 'left' rhetoric and increasingly characterized the functioning of the Congress ministries as well as of the party High Command between 1937 and 1939. The relations between the Muslim League and the Congress were so strained that Jinnah denounced 'congress fascism' in the Patna session of the League in 1938. Thus, throughout the 27 months of the Congress rule in provinces, the League continued its intense vicious propaganda against the Congress and by March 1940, the League adopted the 'Pakistan resolution', in spite of a compromise made by Congress working committee in 1937 to drop the closing stanzas of the Vandemataram recognizing the validity of the criticism of the League and the Muslim community. Hindu communalism championed by the Hindu Mahasabha also raised its voice against what it considered to be anti-Hindu sentiment and in 1938 V.D. Savarkar declared in the Nagpur session that we Hindus are a nation by ourselves, Hindu nationalists should not at all be apologetic to being called Hindu communalists. Thus, communal divide began to take deep roots in this period due to the, growth of militancy among the Hindus and the Muslims. During this period, the Congress ministries tried to implement Gandhian socio-economic reforms, yet Ambedkar and Jinnah joined together and celebrated 'the day of deliverance' when the Congress ministries resigned in 1939. Interestingly during this period only, there developed a honeymoon of durable alliance between the capitalists of India and the Congress as observed by Claude Markovitz and Sumit Sarkar. Besides communal militancy, the militancy of labour and Kisans become dominant between 1937–1939. During this period only, states Peoples' Movement strengthened in many princely states. The Left wing ideology also became a dominant force and tried to persuade the Congress leadership to adopt a more sympathetic attitude towards trade unions and Kisan Sabhas and to give open support to states people's movements. In such a bewildered maze, the Tripuri crisis or open conflict between Subhas Chandra Bose and Gandhi followers openly erupted, signifying opposition to the Gandhian policy of non-violence. Bose's action was not liked by Gandhi camp and Bose was debarred from holding any office. In such a situation, Linlithgow, the then Governor General, unilaterally associated India with the declaration of joining the Second World War against Germany on 3 September, 1939. Linlithgow never bothered to consult the leaders of the Congress ministries. Dissatisfied by the unilateral action of Linlithgow, the Congress ministries resigned on 29–30 October, 1939. The six-year period of war has been divided into two phases. The first phase was from 1939 to 1942 and the second phase 1942 to 1945. In the beginning it was felt that the war would affect very little of India and Indians but the collapse of France and the isolation of Britain caused a general feeling of anxiety and the success of Britain won the admiration of the Indians. The delay of granting dominion status until after the war created sourness and suspicion in the minds of the Indians. Gandhi very generously declared in 1940, 'we do not seek independence out of Britain's ruins'. Sensing the mood of the Indians, the government announced the August offer of 1940. In this offer, Linlithgow assured the Muslims that complete protection would be provided to them in case of any settlement taking place between Britain and India. The August offer held out the promise of dominion status for India with the assurance that after the end of the war a representative body would be set up to devise a framework of the new constitution. This offer of August 1940 was rejected by the Congress as well as the Muslim League. After rejecting the August offer, the Congress launched individual civil disobedience movement in which nearly 25,000 Satyagrahis courted arrest. In the midst of this civil disobedience movement, the Viceroy expanded the council and constituted a National Defence Council with 50 members belonging to provinces and princely states. In 1941 Japan and America entered the war. Percival Spear observes: "A new chapter began with the entry of Japan and America into the war in December 1941. On the one hand India was now intimately concerned with events, and on the other the British government was now subject to American suggestions and pressures which were not being applied". In 1942 on March 11, the British government announced the dispatch of Sir Stafford Cripps with proposals to India. This offer caused great excitement in India and everyone looked with great expectation for the arrival of the Cripps Mission. The appointment of the Mission was the result of the intervention of the American President Roosevelt with Churchill and also because of request of Sapru and Jayakar. Even Chang Kai Shek during his visit to India expressed sympathy for India's aspiration for freedom. Cripps persuaded the war cabinet to agree to his draft proposals. In this draft proposal he promised post-war dominion status with right of secession, a constitution making body elected by provincial legislatures, with individual provinces being given the right not to join it, and with states being invited to appoint representatives. Finally, Cripps proposals were rejected by the Congress and other sections. Gandhi launched Quit India movement which was opposed by the League. Even before the Quit India movement was formally launched, in the early hours of 9, August, the British government arrested all the worthwhile leaders of the movement. Strangely, Rajaji and the communists viewed that there should be an understanding with the League by agreeing to the right of the majority of Muslim provinces to secede through plebiscite after India becomes independent. Keeping aside these views, Nehru moved the resolution of Quit India movement which the communists opposed. Britain tried to win the world opinion by painting India as a 'fifth columnist conspirator' forgetting its earlier anti-fascist stance. Shifting fortunes of the war also decided the course to be followed by the Congress. By the end of 1942, by brutal suppression the movement was brought under control. Gandhi was kept in jail and was released in 1944. In the meanwhile, the Muslim League made rapid strides and by 1943, it formed ministries in Assam, Sind, Bengal and North Western Frontier provinces. The slogan of Pakistan gained momentum.

Subhas Chandra Bose, who left India during this period continued his efforts of achieving independence to India by starting Indian Legion in Berlin in 1941. But he left Germany in 1943 by giving his famous call 'Delhi Chalo' and formed Azad Hind Government and the Indian National Army on 21 October 1943. Subhas Chandra Bose sought the blessings of Mahatma for all his efforts. On July 6, 1944, Subhas Chandra Bose in a broadcast on Azad Hind Radio addressed Gandhi as follows: "India's last war of independence has begun Father of our nation! In this holy war of India's liberation we ask for your blessing and good wishes". Between March and June 1944, the INA was in action on Indian soil which ultimately ended in total failure. INA men surrendered to Britain in mid-1945 and became prisoners again. Till even today, we are not certainly sure of what happened to Bose. Some believed that Bose died in an air crash and some really believe that he is still alive. When the British government tried to try the INA men as prisoners of war, there was spontaneous outburst of anger against British in November 1945. Sumit Sarkar observes: "Even more significant was the probable link between the INA experience and the way of disaffection in the British Indian army during the winter of 1945–46, which culminated in the great Bombay naval strike of February 1946 and was quite possibly the single most decisive reason behind the British decision to make a quick withdrawal". The Second World War came to an end in 1945 and it was followed by Simla conference in June 1945. Unfortunately, the conference failed to arrive at any consensus due to determined policy of the Muslims and the Hindus.

As explained above, India passed through a most disturbing phase of agony and crisis due to the rigid stand of contending social and economic groups and the adamancy of the British in satisfying the nationalist aspirations of the Indians. By 1945, the realization of the dream of the Indians to attain independence was only a foot away with a certainty of the unhappy division of India on communal lines.

Subhas Chandra Bose and Indian National Army

One of the great freedom fighters produced by Mother India in the struggle for freedom, was Subhas Chandra Bose, regarded *Deshnayak* by Ravindranath

Tagore. He was a well-known social reformer, social activist and a reputed organizer and leader. Subhas was born in an educated and cultured Bengali family in 1897 and exhibited deep love towards India from his childhood. At the age of 15, he wrote to his mother 'India is God's beloved land'. Such was his deep conviction of the greatness of India and at the end of his life; he exhorted his fellow countrymen "Never for a moment falter in your faith in India's destiny. There is no power on earth that can keep India enslaved. India shall be free before long". Subhas was a product of the resurgent Bengali milieu of the 20th century. He had his collegiate education in Bengal and was qualified for Indian Civil Service but inspired by the sacrifices of the earlier leaders of Indian National Congress resigned the post of ICS and plunged into freedom struggle voluntarily. Chittaranjan Das was his political guru. His training as political activist committed to non-violent way of peaceful protest started with the non-cooperation movement launched by Gandhi in 1920. He also played a major role in the student, youth and labour movements. He was imprisoned more than ten times by the British government. Bose was a man of firm conviction of courage and had definite ideas about the destiny of India. He advocated that India should become an independent federal republic. His exhortation to the nationalists of India not to become a queer mixture of political democrats and social conservatives reflects his social and political ideals. He stood for the upliftment of women, depressed classes and labouring masses. In 1928 itself, at the Calcutta session, he demanded *Purnaswaraj* or complete independence instead of dominion status.

Bose had the courage of conviction to oppose the persons and the views he did not accept. This can be seen in opposing Gandhi followers and standing for the Presidency of the Indian National Congress. He himself resigned his post when they non-cooperated with him. The British government put him in prison on 2 July, 1940 and he was released on 5 December and was imprisoned again. On January 16–17, 1941 he planned an escape and finally reached Germany. Subhas left India and reached Germany to win over the Indian soldiers in the British Indian army who were held prisoners of war. From Germany, he reached South-East Asia. Subhas too was inspired by the goal of achieving total independence for India like Gandhi. The path chosen by Gandhi was non-violent, non-cooperation and civil disobedience through mass struggle in stages but the path chosen by Subhas was through military action with the support of the enemies of the Raj. Exasperated by waiting and delay, Subhas chose this path to reach the goal early.

Subhas assumed the leadership of INA as its supreme commander and gave a call for 'Delhi Chalo' and 'Jai Hind'. INA was not the idea of Subhas but was conceived by Mohan Singh, an Indian officer of the British Indian army in Malaya. With the help of Japan, Mohan Singh successfully recruited and organized INA and the outbreak of the 'August Revolution' gave fillip to the INA. Anti-British demonstrations were organized in Malaya expressing solidarity with Congress-led Quit India movement. Japan encouraged INA because it wanted INA to be a party to the planned invasion of India. But by December 1942, differences arose between Japan and INA over its role in future and Mohan Singh and Niranjan Singh Gill, the two important senior leaders of INA were arrested.

After the landing of Subhas in Singapore by July 1943, the next phase of INA began: Bose met Tozo, the Prime Minister of Japan and got assurance from him that Japan entertained no territorial ambition on India. Totally convinced of Japan's motives, Subhas returned to Singapore and set up the Provisional Government of Free India on 21 October, 1943. It is to be remembered that Bose sought the blessings of Gandhi in his operations of INA. It clearly indicates that Bose differed with Gandhi about the path but he has great respect and admiration towards Gandhi as leader of the masses. The self-proclaimed provisional Government of Free India declared war on the Britain and the USA. Axis powers and their satellites recognized the Government of Free India. Subhas set up two headquarters of INA at Rangoon and in Singapore. Subhas also created a women's regiment called Rani Jhansi Regiment. An army contingent of INA commanded by Shah Nawaj participated in the Imphal campaign along with the Japanese forces but the discrimination shown by the Japanese demoralized the INA. INA finally surrendered to the British by 1945. Though the experiment of INA failed, Subhas successfully proved that Hindus, Muslims, North Indians and South Indians, Sikhs and Pathans can be mobilized to move as one family in the realization of the liberation of the motherland. He also successfully proved by example how to achieve Hindu-Muslim unity and amity and make women the rightful claimants to their place of honour as equal partners along with men by giving them their due share in INA or Azad Fouz. Though Subhas and INA appear to have failed in their mission of achieving independence faster by military force, his alternative vision made him eternally admired for his courage of conviction and deep commitment in what he believed to be correct and appropriate. As hailed by Gandhi, Subhas is undoubtedly 'a Prince among Patriots' and certainly deserves the title of Netaji or the respected leader. It is because of this only, when the British tried to try INA as war prisoners, the whole country as one individual condemned their trial and praised them as heroes who stood for the liberation of the motherland.

Emergence of Communal Politics and Partition

An important feature of colonial India was the emergence of communalism as a force that guided the destiny of India into a blood bath and inevitable partition of the Indian subcontinent on communal lines. Though India was a land of multi-religions, creeds and faiths, pre-colonial India was never plagued by the worm of communalism. It was the purposeful colonial policy of divide and rule that laid the seeds of communalism which grew into a huge tree that disturbed the solidarity, of the age-old mosaic of India and it is still haunting to sap the vitality of the newly won independence. Communalism is thus a modern phenomenon which has gained currency as a negative concept in recent times.

Bipan Chandra observes: 'communalism is basically an ideology appears to be a simple and easily understood. Communalism or communal ideology consists of three basic elements or stages, one following the other. The three basic premises are: (1) belief that people who follow the same religion have common political, economic, cultural and social interests, (2) belief in a notion that in a multi-religious society like India, the common interests of the followers of one religion are dissimilar and divergent from the interests of the followers of another religion, and (3) belief that the interests of the followers of different religions or different communities are seen to be mutually incompatible, antagonistic and hostile". The practice of communalism based on the above principles leads to communal politics, communal violence and communal terrorism. We can trace stages in the growth of the trends of liberal and extreme communalism. Bipan Chandra is of the view that 1937 was the dividing landmark and pre 1937, was an era of liberal communalism and the post-1937 phase was that of extreme communalism.

We may agree with Bipan Chandra's perception that communalism emerged as consequence of the modern politics based on mass mobilization and politicization which has become evident in the Indian context from 1930 onwards. Nehru also notices "one must never forget that communalism in India is a latter day phenomenon which has grown up before our eyes". Thus, the communal consciousness arose as a result of the transformation of Indian society under colonialism and its results like administrative unification of regions, the formation of modern social classes and the spread of new ideas of nationalism based on cultural and linguistic development. Another factor was the economic stagnation, ruination of industries and crafts, stark unemployment and dwindling of resources and the growing number of people vying for the pie. Communalism does not mean social conflict or class conflict between the exploiter and the exploited. Communalism is thus a complex phenomenon where many factors real and unreal, contributed to the rise of consciousness of communalism. There is a considered, view advocated by Bipan Chandra and agreed upon by many, a strong contributory factor in the growth of communalism was the pronounced Hindu tinge in much of nationalist thought and propaganda in the beginning of the 20th century. Added to this, the communal approach adopted by James Mill, the British historian in dividing the periods of Indian history as the Hindu, the Muslim and the British showed considerable influence on the thought process of young and old mind in developing communal consciousness of superiority and inferiority. Some sections of the Hindu and the Muslim communalists used religion as the mobilizing factor for their selfish interests. We may say that religion by itself was not a major contributor to communalism as such but the narrow minded religiosity promoted by intolerant leaders led to extreme communalism with a political end.

In India, till 1880 communal consciousness as a driving force was absent both in the Hindus and the Muslims. Sir Sayyad Ahmad Khan, an outstanding intellectual of India announced in 1884, "Do you, not inhabit this land? Are you not buried in it or cremated on it? Surely, you live and die in the same land. Remember that Hindus and Muslims are religious terms. Otherwise Hindus, Muslims and Christians who live in this country are by virtue of this fact one *Qauam* (nation or community)". Till the founding of Indian National Congress, he believed in the oneness of Indians, i.e., Hindus and Muslims. The establishment of the Indian National Congress in 1885 sowed the seeds of uncertainty and made him view Congress as a Hindu body, whose major objectives were against the Muslim interest. The concept of elections and consequential power made him oppose the Congress and as desired by the government, the Muslims began to be loyal to the British. But some Muslims under the leadership of Badruddin Tyabji joined Congress and by the time of Swadeshi movement some more sided with the Congress. In such a situation, the Indian Muslim League was founded in 1907 by big landlords and Zamindars. This loyalist, communal and conservative political organization supported the partition of Bengal, demanded separate electorates and made its motto to oppose Congress but not colonial rule. Side by side, with Muslim communalism, Hindu communalism also began by demanding that Hindi language was the language of the Hindus and it should be protected. They also started a movement for banning cow slaughter in 1896. They also began to demand due share to the Hindus in legislature and government jobs. The Punjab Hindu Sabha founded in 1909 and the All India Hindu Mahasabha founded in 1915 spearheaded the activities of the Hindu communalists. But the younger generation of the Muslim League were dissatisfied with the loyalist approach and in 1916 there was an understanding between the League and Congress known as Lucknow Pact which led to the Khilafat and non-cooperation movement. Once again the communalists became active after the end of the non-cooperation movement in 1922. The nationalists made determined bid to frustrate the efforts of the communalists. But the Round Table Conference once again provided an opportunity to the communalists to stress, "the inherent impossibility of securing any merger of Hindu and Muslim, political or indeed social interests and the impracticability of ever governing India through anything but a British agency". The announcement of communal award of 1932 which included the demands embodied in 1927 Delhi proposals and Jinnah's 14 points of 1929 further bolstered the communalists.

Since 1937 began the extreme communalism of the Muslims and the Hindus. It was so because the Congress formed ministries in five provinces and the Congress refused to cooperate with Muslim League. In 1938, M.A. Jinnah, in his presidential address of the League announced "The High Command of the Congress is determined, absolutely determined to crush all other communities and cultures in this country and establish Hindu raj in the country". In 1940, he told the students of Aligarh, "Mr Gandhi's hope is to subjugate and vassalize the Muslims under a Hindu raj". By 1941, Jinnah announced that "Pakistan is not only a practical goal but the only goal if you want to save Islam from complete annihilation in this country". Finally, in 1946, while asking the Muslims to vote for the League, he declared if we fail to realize our duty today you will be reduced to the status of Sudras and Islam will be vanquished from India". Besides Jinnah, Z.A. Suleri, F.M. Durrani and M.A. Gazdar also propagated for the annihilation of the Hindus. Gazdar proclaimed "The Hindus will have to be eradicated like the Jews in Germany if they did not behave properly". The Muslim communalists launched a vicious campaign against Maulana Abdul Kalam Azad and Khan Abdul Gafar Khan as the stooges of the nationalist Hindus. While Muslim communalism was becoming extremely violent, Hindu communalism was lagging behind. By 1923, Lala Lajpat Rai was no more and by 1937 another liberal communalist Madan Mohan Malaviya also retired from active politics. V.D. Savarkar of the Hindu Mahasabha and M.S. Golwarkar of the RSS led the extreme communalists of the Hindus. In 1937, V.D. Savarkar announced that Muslims "want to brand the forehead of the Hindu down and other non-Muslim sections of the Hindustan with a stamp of self-humiliation and Muslim domination" and "to induce the Hindus to the position of helots in their own land". In 1938, he reiterated and affirmed "we Hindus are (already) reduced to the veritable helots throughout our land". M.S. Golwalkar in 1939 declared that if minority demands were accepted, Hindu national life runs the risk of being shattered and he attacked the nationalists for "hugging to our bosom our most inveterate enemies (Muslims) and thus endangering our very existence". Thus both the Hindu and Muslim extremists tried to play on the fears and suspicious of majority and minority and raised the cry of 'Hinduism in danger' and 'Islam in danger' or Hindu culture and Islamic culture in danger. This creation of hatred proved harmful to both the Hindus and the Muslims in the end and thousands lost their lives in the communal holocaust. In this atmosphere of extreme communalism preached and practised by the determined few from both sides, the British added fuel to the fire. When the Second World War began and the Viceroy without consulting the Indian leaders, admitted India into the Second World War, the Congress ministries resigned in 1939. The Muslim League celebrated that day as the day of deliverance. The British assured that they would grant Dominion status to India immediately after the war. This announcement made the Muslim League to press for a separate homeland for Muslims in 1940. By his August offer of 1940, Linlithgow, the Viceroy assured the Muslims that their interests would be protected. Dr B.R. Ambedkar, C. Rajagopalachari and the communists suggested that the demand of a separate homeland to the Muslims be accepted. The British appointed Cripps Mission in 1942 and the proposals of Cripps were rejected by both the League and Congress. When Congress launched Quit India movement in August 1942, the League opposed it and propagated its dream of separate homeland. The League took the help of Islam to spread its idea of Pakistan along with popular newspapers. In 1944, C. Rajagopalachari placed his compromise formula before Jinnah. Owing to the adamancy of the League, the Wavel plan and the Simla plan failed. When elections were held in 1946 as per the 1935 Act, the League rejected it and refused to participate in the interim government. In protest, the Muslim League observed

August 16, 1946 as the Direct Action Day which led to Hindu and Muslim riots throughout India. The League joined, the interim government formed under the leadership of Nehru. When Constituent Assembly was formed, the League refused to accept it. In the meanwhile communal riots flared up throughout the country in which both Hindus and Muslims suffered a lot. In February 1947, the British government announced that it would leave India certainly before June 1948. On March 27, 1947, the League celebrated 'Pakistan Day' in East Bengal and Punjab. It led to the worst fears of large scale massacre and the interim government remained helpless. Except Gandhi, the others agreed for the partition and V.P. Menon drafted the proposal for partition of India. It was put as June Plan or Mountbatten Plan before the League and Congress. This was accepted by both the League and Congress. The Independence Act of 1947 made the partition legal and real.

As the entire nation rejoiced, very disappointed and disillusioned Gandhi spent the first day of Indian independence in 24-hour fast. Later, he spent the rest of the time in healing the wounds of suspicion and hatred of communal frenzy. On 30 January, 1948 in an evening prayer Gandhi was shot by a fanatic; thus the cause so near and dear to him cost his life and plunged the nation into darkness.

26

India: 1947–1964

The protracted mass struggle of Indians successfully ended the two centuries of foreign yoke and resulted in the declaration of independence on 15 August, 1947. The first day of freedom was celebrated with mixed feelings of exuberance and elation on the one hand and by despair and agony on the other hand as the tasks ahead were of gigantic nature. But the first Prime Minister of India, Nehru in his memorable address 'Tryst with Destiny' to the Constituent Assembly declared his governments' commitment and dedication as follows: "Long years ago we made a tryst with destiny and now the time comes when we shall redeem our pledge. At the stroke of the midnight hour, when the world sleeps, India will awake to life and freedom. A moment comes, which comes but rarely in history, when we step out from the old to the new, when an age ends, and when the soul of a nation, long suppressed, finds utterance. It is fitting that at this solemn moment we take the pledge of dedication to the service of India and her people and to the still larger cause of humanity we end today a period of ill future and India discovers herself again". He further appropriately reminded, "The achievement we celebrate today is but a step, an opening of opportunity, to the greater type and achievements. That future is not one of ease and resting but of incessant striving so that we may fulfill the pledges we have so often taken".

The incipient Indian nation state had to tackle not one but multiple arduous tasks of immediate urgency like the territorial and administrative integration of princely states, the communal riots that followed the partition of India, the rehabilitation of nearly six million refugees who had migrated from Pakistan, the protection of Muslims threatened by communalists, the need to forestall war with Pakistan and the communist insurgency. Undaunted by these stupendous tasks ahead of the Indian government, Nehru rightly declared, "First things must come first and the first thing is the security and stability of India". W.H. Morris Jones observed that the task of the newly born state should be "to hold things together, to ensure survival, to get accustomed to the feel of being on the water, to see to it that the vessels kept afloat".

The most immediate problem that required the serious attention of the political set-up in the post-partition India was the urgency of unifying under one administration, the princely states. In pre-independent colonial India nearly 40 per cent of the territory was occupied by 56 small and large states by princes who experienced different degrees of autonomy under the system of British paramountcy which protected them from external aggression and internal insurgency. In the backdrop of the partition of India and Pakistan, the matter of princely states assumed significance as a matter of serious concern. It is so because larger princely native states toyed with the idea of becoming free and began to scheme and plan and they began that the paramount is non-transferable either to India or to Pakistan. The princely states developed such an ambition as Atlee, the Prime Minister of England announced on 20 February, 1947. "His Majesty's government does not intend to hand over their powers and obligations under paramountcy to any Government of British India". Banking on this pronouncement, many princely states felt that they could become independent principalities from August 15, 1947 joining neither India nor Pakistan. This idea was further strengthened by Jinnah's announcement of 18 June, 1947 that "the states would be independent sovereign states on the termination of paramountcy and "were free to remain independent if they so desired". Atlee changed his stand in his speech of the Independence of India Bill as follows: "It is the hope of His Majesty's government that all the states will in due course find their appropriate place with one or the other Dominion within the British Commonwealth". In the circumstances narrated above, the Government of India created States Department with V.P. Menon as its Secretary under the control of the Independent Home Minister of India, Sardar Vallabhai Patel, the Iron Man of India who also assumed the charge of the newly created states department. Patel was fully aware of the impending danger to the unit of India due to the possible intransigencies of the rulers of the states. Patel took V.P. Menon into confidence and informed, "the situation held dangerous possibilities and that if we did not handle it promptly and effectively, our hard earned freedom might disappear through the states door". The words 'promptly and effectively' used by Patel reveal his iron will to deal with the recalcitrant states expeditiously. Primarily, Patel implemented the carrot and stick policy by appealing to their good sense and see reason in joining India and also made it implicitly clear that they may have to face the wrath of the people of the native states for not joining India and he will not be in a position to stop or control the mounting anger of the multitude against them. Except the native states of Junagadh, Jammu & Kashmir and Hyderabad, the rest understood the message of Patel and coolly responded positively for Patel's implied threat and message. All the native states except those mentioned above acceded to India by 15 August, 1947.

Junagadh

The Nawab of Junagadh against the wish of majority of the people unilaterally decided to accede his state to Pakistan by 15 August, 1947. It was a tiny state on the coast of Saurashtra. It was surrounded by Indian territory on all sides. Added to the problem was that it was discontinuous to Pakistan, geographically. The Indian nationalist leaders wanted the people to decide by plebiscite to whom they wish to be acceded. But Pakistan without caring either for the wishes of the inhabitant of Junagadh accepted the accession declared by the Nawab. People, who opposed the move of the Nawab of Junagadh organized a massive protest movement against the Nawab and made him flee from Junagadh. At this critical juncture, the Diwan of Junagadh, Shah Nawaz Bhutto approached the Government of India to intervene and the Indian troops marched into the state. By February 1948, the people of Junagadh chose to join India through a plebiate. Thus, the opposition of the Nawab of Junagadh ended as a fiasco and people's wish became a reality, ultimately.

Jammu & Kashmir

The state of Jammu & Kashmir consisted of five main regions – Jammu region, the region of high mountains of Ladakh bordering Tibet, the tracts of Gilgit and Balistan and the Kashmir valley. All these disparate regions were moulded into a single state in the 19th century by Dogra Rajput family. It is culturally heterogeneous, it shares borders with Afghanistan, Chinese Sinkiang and Tibet. It is strategically located and its population is also divided between the Hindus, Muslims and Sikhs. In this background we have to trace and understand why India and Pakistan wanted to have it in their possession. It is to be noted that the battle for Kashmir was, and is, not merely or even mostly a battle for territory because it is a struggle of two ways of life, two concepts of political organization, two scales of values, two spiritual attitudes as observed by Joseph Korbel fifty years ago of danger in Kashmir. The state of Kashmir was on the border of both India and Pakistan. While the 75 per cent of the inhabitants were the Muslims, the ruler was a Hindu. Hari Singh, the ruler of Kashmir did not want to join either India or Pakistan for he suspected that because of the prevalence of democracy in India, he would be 'nobody' in India and he thought that it would not be safe for him in a theocratic state of Pakistan. Hari Singh preferred to be an independent sovereign power. Shaik Abdullah, the leader of the majority National Conference preferred to join India. Indian government and Indian leaders did not grab the opportunity provided by Shaik Abdullah and his party but Gandhi, Nehru and Patel wanted the people to exercise their option freely and join either India or Pakistan. But Pakistan 'short circuited' the policies of the people and led an unofficial invasion into Kashmir on 22 October 1947. The invaders pushed into Srinagar, the capital of Kashmir. In a situation of helplessness Raja Hari Singh appealed to India to intervene on 24 October. Nehru, the democrat did not insist an accession of Kashmir to India. India could not send its armies to Kashmir as it was not a part of India as per the international procedures. In this situation both Shaik Abdullah and Patel insisted on Kashmir's accession to India. On 26 October, Maharaja Hari Singh acceded to India and also agreed to put Shaik Abdullah as the head of the administration.

Both Maharaja and Shaik Abdullah insisted on permanent and firm accession to India but as a true democrat Nehru on the advice of Mountbatten announced that it would hold a referendum on the accession decision after peace and order was restored in Kashmir. With the approval of the cabinet and Gandhi's acceptance, on 27 October 100 planes air lifted men and ammunition to Srinagar to drive away the invaders. The Indian army partially succeeded in driving away the invaders and the armed conflict continued for some more months. The Indian government on the advice of Mountbatten took a fateful decision to refer the Kashmir issue to the Security Council of UNO asking for the vacation of the invaders of Pakistan from Kashmir. In the long run the decision of Nehru proved to be disadvantageous to India as Great Britain and USA aligned with Pakistan. In a frustrated mood, India agreed for ceasefire on 31 December, 1948 and the state was divided along the ceasefire line. Nehru expressed his anguish in a letter to Vijayalakshmi Pandit in February 1948 in the following lines: "I could not imagine that the Security Council could probably behave in the trivial and partisan manner in which it functioned. Those people are supposed to keep the world in order. It is not surprising that the world is going to pieces. The United States and Britain have played a dirty role, Britain probably being the chief actor behind the scenes".

The next step in the Kashmir issue was the passing of a resolution by UNO in 1951 for the referendum under UN supervision after Pakistan had withdrawn its troops from the part of Kashmir under its control. Unfortunately, the resolution had retained infractions as Pakistan forces adamantly remained in occupied Kashmir or Azad Kashmir. Thanks to the partisan attitude of great powers, toothless UNO, adamant attitude of Pakistan, the Kashmir problem is still a burning issue standing as an obstacle in the path of friendship between India and Pakistan. While India regards Kashmir accession as final and irrevocable and Kashmir as an integral part of India, Pakistan continues to stoutly deny this genuine claim and right of India. There is a view that Nehru should be blamed for taking up this issue to the Security Council of UNO. This criticism of Nehru appears to be too strong. A letter written by Nehru to Maharaja Hari Singh on 1 December, 1947 clearly reveals the mind of Nehru and his readiness to solve the problem. The letter reads as follows:

> It is of the most vital importance that Kashmir should remain within Indian union … but however much we may want this, it cannot be done ultimately except through the goodwill of the mass of the population. Even if military forces held Kashmir for a while a later consequence might be a strong reaction against this essentially, therefore, this is a problem of psychological approach to the mass of the people and of making them feel they will be benefited by being in the Indian Union. If the average Muslim feels that he has no safe or secure place in the union, then obviously he will look elsewhere. Our basic policy must keep this in view or else we fail.

Ramachandra Guha very aptly writes that this letter shows that contrary to received wisdom, the Indian prime minister was quite prepared to compromise on Kashmir. Indeed, the four opinions he outlined in December 1947 remain the four options being debated today. There is also a view that if Patel had been given a free hand, Kashmir problem would have been solved forever and we would have been free from the continuing headache.

Hyderabad

Hyderabad was the largest native state in India. It was ruled by the Nizams, who accepted the paramountcy of the British sovereign. Hyderabad too was surrounded by Indian territories on all sides. The Nizam of Hyderabad too like the Nawab of Junagadh and the ruler of Kashmir did not accede to India before the date of 15 August. Encouraged by Pakistan and Muslim natives, he desired to be an independent power by improving his armed forces. Patel made it clear to Nizam of Hyderabad that India would not tolerate "an isolated spot which would destroy the very union which we have built up with our blood and toil".

In November 1947, the Indian government signed a standstill agreement with the Nizam with a firm hope that he would introduce representative government in the Nizam's Hyderabad which would make the merger with India easy. Contrary to Government of India's views, the Nizam entertained different points of view. The Nizam engaged an experienced British lawyer Sir Walter Monckton, who was a friend of Mountbatten to negotiate with the Government of India on his behalf. The Nizam desired to prolong deliberations for a good length of time and wanted to utilize the time gap to build up his armed forces to deal with India with a strong strength or to accede to Pakistan in view of the tension building up over the issue of Kashmir. In this backdrop, three important developments took place in the state of Hyderabad: (a) rapid growth of Muslim communal organization, *Ittihad ul Muslim* and its para-military wing, the Razakars, (b) the mass struggle launched by Hyderabad State Congress on 7 August, 1947. There developed direct clashes between the Razakars and the State Congress Satyagrahis in which many were wounded and sacrificed their lives and many more fled from Hyderabad to neighbouring Indian territories for temporary stay, and (c) the peaceful State Congress opposition to Nizam took violent turn and they started armed resistance against the Nizam. Along with this movement, by then a powerful communist-led peasant movement in the shape of armed struggle had developed in the Telangana region of the state from the latter half of 1946. The communist *Dalams* or squads too attacked the Razakars by resorting to armed defence in their villages. Till June 1948, there was no light at the end of the tunnel for the Hyderabad problem. Impatient and exasperated Patel wrote from his sickbed to Nehru, "I feel very strongly that a stage has come when we should tell them quite frankly that nothing short of unqualified acceptance of accession and of introduction of undiluted responsible government would be acceptable to us". In spite of provocative and hostile attitude of defiance from the side of the Nizam and the Razakars, the Government of India patiently waited for some more time. As the Razakars activated dangerous proportions, finally the

Government of India took a hard decision of moving armies to Telangana on 13 September, 1948. On 16 September, the Nizam of Hyderabad surrendered and acceded to the Indian Union in November 1948. 17 September is celebrated as Hyderabad's liberation day, every year. The Government of India showed generosity towards the Nizam and did not punish him. The Nizam was retained as the head of the state or *Rajpramukh*. He was not only given a privy purse of 5 million rupees and was also permitted to retain his entire assets. Thus, with the accession of Hyderabad in November, 1948, the merger of princely states with the Indian union was accomplished and the Government of India became a sovereign power over the whole of geographical area of India. The success of Hyderabad episode clearly proves the victory of Indian secularism as most of the Muslims preferred to join hands with the Government of India. Thus by the year 1948, the first stage in the full integration of the princely states into Indian union was completed.

The second and the very difficult stage of the full integration of the princely states into the new Indian nation began in December 1947. In this phase too, Sardar Patel moved with speed and completed the process by merging small princely states with the neighbouring states or merged together to "form centrally administered areas. A large number were grouped together into five new unions – Madhya Bharat, Rajputana, Patiala and East Punjab Union (PEPSU). Saurashtra and Travancore-Cochin, Mysore, Hyderabad and Jammu & Kashmir retained their original form as separate states of the union.

The Government of India provided privy purses in perpetuity, free of all taxes to the rulers of the major states. The amount covered by the privy purse came to Rs 4.66 crores in 1949. Later on it was given constitutional validity. The Government of India satisfied their egos by allowing and retaining privileges like keeping their titles, flying their personal flags and gun salutes on ceremonial occasions. Though there was certain amount of harsh criticism against the privileges granted to the rulers of the native states, they received that type of treatment to suit their earlier status and statures in Indian society.

Two more trouble spots that deserved the attention of the Government of India in attaining total integration were the French and the Portuguese owned settlements on India's East and West Coasts with Pondicherry and Goa forming their centres of activities. The people living in these settlements too desired to join the Indian union like their brothers and sisters of the other regions. By 1954, the French agreed for peaceful transition of their territories into India. But Portugal backed by England and America defiantly decided to continue its sway over Indian territories and as Indian government did not want to be an aggressor, it patiently waited while the people started movement for liberation of their territories by the Portuguese. In 1961, sensing the mood of the Indians, Nehru reluctantly ordered troops to march into Goa. The Governor General of Goa surrendered without fight and by 1961 the territorial and the geographical integration of India was totally completed. By consistent and careful tactics, the Government of India completed smoothly and successfully the total political and geographical completion of the making of the Indian nation by the accession of native states and the Portuguese and the French settlements.

Along with the major native states, many minor states were merged into bigger states. The post-independent Government of India initiated a three-pronged strategy of integration, democratization and modernization as to make the people of these states citizens of a free and independent developing India. As announced in the white paper on the states, "The aim was the integration of all elements in the country of free, united and democratic India". In this process, the first to be merged were the native states of Orissa and Chattisgarh. There were 39 such states. Their population was estimated to be 70 lakh. Their territorial area was nearly 56,000 square miles. Sardar Patel initiated a dialogue for their merger on 14–15 December, 1947. The princes agreed to surrender their authority by 1 January, 1948 and by that day all those tiny native states became part of Orissa and central provinces. The next to be merged were the Deccan states numbering 17. All these were merged with Bombay in March 1948. Later on Kolhapur was merged with Bombay. In June 1948, Gujarats' 297 states were merged with Bombay presidency. In May 1949, Baroda was also merged. Further, some small states of Punjab, the state of Banaganapalli of Andhra Pradesh, Pudukottai and Sandur in Madras, Cooch Behar in West Bengal, the Khasi Hills states in Assam and Tehri Garhwal, Banaras and Rampur in UP were merged in the surrounding provinces by 1948 and 1949.

The other form of integration of states was the creation of centrally administered areas of Union of Himachal Pradesh on 15 April, 1948 by merging the areas of Himachal Pradesh, Vindhya Pradesh, Kutch, Bilaspur, Bhopal, Tripura and Manipur and 21 states of East Punjab. By January 1950, newly created Vindhya Pradesh was taken over by the Government of India. Bilaspur in 1948, Bhopal in June 1949 and Tripura on 15 October, 1949 were taken over by Government of India.

By forming states unions, like the united states of Kathiawar, united states of Matsya, the Patiala and East Punjab states union and the united states of Rajasthan, an attempt was made to merge the states into the Indian union. Of this, the united states of Kathiawar had 222 states, estates and talukas. The united states of Matsya consisted of Alwar and Bharatpur. The PEPSU consisted of 7 big states of Patiala, Nabha, Kapurtala among others. One of the greatest obstacles for national integration was linguistic chauvinism and in equal development of the states. The Government of India tackled these problems with foresight and wisdom. Demand for linguistic based division and creation of linguistic states was there for more than forty years in India. Bipan Chandra et al. observe: "The language problem was the most divisive issue in the first twenty years of independent India, and it created the apprehension among many that the political and cultural unity of the country was in danger". In order to appease this demand, the linguistic Province Committee or Dar Committee was set up in 1948. The Committee did not favour the idea of creation of linguistic states. But in order to meet the active demand for the creation of linguistic states, the Congress appointed a committee with Nehru, Patel and Pattabhi, popularly called JVP Committee in December 1948, to examine the question afresh. This committee also advised against the creation of linguistic states for the time being, emphasizing the unity, national security and economic development as the needs of the hour. Despite its recommendations, the popular movements for that reorganization of the states all over the country, which persisted with varying degree of intensity till 1960. In this movement, the most important development of significance was the fast unto death over the demand for a separate Andhra state by a popular freedom fighter Potti Sriramulu and his end on the 58th day. This sacrifice of Sriramulu triggered spontaneous opposition and violent events all over Andhra for three days. Nehru and the Indian government conceded the demand by creating the state of Andhra in October 1953 and Tamil Nadu also. The success of the movement encouraged other states also to demand for the creation of linguistic states. Nehru reluctantly agreed as pointed out by S. Gopal. He felt that it would be undemocratic to smother this sentiment which in general grounds, he did not find objectionable. Indeed, a linguistic mosaic might well provide a firmer base for national unity. What concerned him were the timing, the agitation and violence with which linguistic provinces were demanded and the harsh antagonism between various sections of the Indian people which underly these demands. He appointed in August 1953, the States Reorganization Commission (SRC) with Justice Fazl Ali, K.M. Panikkar and Hridayanath Kunjra as members to examine objectively and dispassionately this question of linguistic division demand. After two years of hard work and visiting different areas, the SRC submitted its report in 1955. It accepted in principle for the demand, except for the division of Bombay and Punjab. As per the recommendations of the committee, the States Reorganization Act was passed by parliament in November 1956. It provided for 14 states and 6 centrally administered territories. The Telengana area of the Hyderabad state was merged with Andhra and Andhra Pradesh came into existence on 1 November, 1956. A separate state of Kerala was created by merging the Malabar district of the old Madras Presidency with Travancore-Cochin. Some territories of Bombay, Madras, Hyderabad and Coorg were added to Mysore state and Karnataka state emerged. Bipan Chandra writes, "Thus, after more than ten years of continuous strife and popular struggles linguistic reorganization of India was largely completed, making room for greater political participation by the people". Bipan Chandra assures that "the federal structure of the union was not adversely affected or weakened or paralysed the centre as many had feared". W.H. Morris Jones also writes "the newly fashioned units, it is true, have a self-conscious coherence, but they are willing, thus equipped, to do business with the centre, to work as part of a whole that is India". We may agree with Bipan Chandra and Morris Jones but it is to be noted with caution that linguistic division demand is still lingering in the minds of the people yet, because of unequal economic development besides the urge for cohesion among the people speaking the same language. India is still passing through the birth pangs of a true nation because of the deep-rooted historical processes that influenced the course of India.

Making of the Indian Constitution

The day 26th of January, 1950 was a red-letter day in the history of India. On that day the written constitution of India came into operation. January 26th was purposefully chosen (as the date on which the constitution became operative) because since 1930, the day has been celebrated as the day of complete independence throughout India by millions of people. It is very befitting to declare such a historic day as the day of operation of the Constitution of Republic of India. The Constitution of India was the longest written constitution having the best elements of all the existing constitutions up to that date. The Constitution of India is the modern sacred text of the contemporary India. It reflects the new aspirations and values of the people of India and testifies how the people of India are the supreme masters in all matters concerning the welfare of Indians. The Constitution of India was not prepared in haste but the process of the evolution of the constitution began many decades before India became independent in 1947. The process continued unabated since it originated in the freedom struggle till a new constitution was drafted after prolonged debates and discussions in the Constituent Assembly. A galaxy of learned wise men interested in the longevity of the emerging nation of India framed the constitution in its present form after a thorough debate and discussion of each proposal. The nationalists consciously, popularized the concepts of parliamentary democracy, republicanism, civil liberties, social and economic justice which happen to be the most basic tenets of the constitution. Bipan Chandra rightly remarks, "when the constitution in 1950 adopted a parliamentary form of government, with a cabinet led by a prime minister it was not, as is commonly supposed, the British parliament that it was emulating. It was formalizing nationalist practices, which the people were already familiar with". Even the spirit of democracy was familiarized by the national movement. Bipan Chandra correctly points out, "this found expression in widespread mass participation. It ensured a place for adult franchise after independence".

A view is in circulation that the British initiated a modern responsible constitutional government in India and the constitution was merely the culmination of the series of constitutional initiatives made by them in 1861, 1892, 1909, 1919 and 1935. This view is not totally correct as the British government conceded reluctantly and belatedly only partially the demands of the leaders of the national movement and tried to reduce the intensity of the movement as a last resort from time to time. Gandhi's statement made in 1922 proves "Swaraj will not be a free gift of the British Parliament. It will be a declaration of India's full self-expression. That it will be expressed through an act of Parliament is true. Swaraj can never be a free gift by one nation to another. It is a treasure to be purchased with a nation's best blood. It will cease to be a gift when we have paid clearly for it". This statement of Gandhi clearly proves beyond doubt that the British did introduce constitutional reforms by their voluntary initiative is a myth. No doubt, the British introduced the principle of election in the 1892 Indian Council Act in partial response to a sustained struggle by the press and the Indian nationalists for more than two decades and while the nationalists demanded elections to the councils and elected majorities and greater powers to the non-official members, the British by the Act of 1892 provided for election principle but limited it to minority only. There was a see-saw battle between the demands of the national movement and the concessions granted through the Acts of 1909, 1919 and 1935. The leaders of the national movement started demanding for grant of responsible government in India from 1890 onwards and by 1916 they began to "espouse the doctrine of self-determination or the right of the Indians to frame their own constitution". Thus, the desire to have a constitution based on self-determination was as old as 1916. In response to the continuous demand of the national movement, the British government appointed all-white Simon Commission in November 1927 to recommend constitutional changes. The Secretary of State, Lord Borkenhead, challenged the Indians "Let them produce a constitution which carries behind it a fair measure of general agreement among the great peoples of India" in 1925 and reiterated the challenge again in 1927, moving a bill for the appointment of the Simon Commission. In response the national movement as one man boycotted the Simon Commission in all parts of India and appointed a committee with Motilal Nehru as the Chairman in 1928 "to determine the principles of the constitution for India". The Nehru report was submitted on 10 August, 1928. It was an outline of a draft constitution for India. Most of its features were later included in the Constitution of India. It visualized a parliamentary system with full responsible government and joint electorates with time bound reservation of seats for minorities. The Nehru's report laid special emphasis on securing fundamental human rights for the people of India. Of the nineteen rights listed in the Nehru report, ten were incorporated into the constitution. The Nehru report has recommended that "the redistribution of provinces should take place on a linguistic basis". This was followed by the declaration of complete independence as their objective and followed with the launching of mass civil disobedience movement in April 1930. In 1934, the Congress Working Committee rejected the white paper presented by the British government on further constitutional reforms and resolved that the "only satisfactory alternative to the white paper is a constitution drawn by a Constituent Assembly elected on the basis of adult suffrage or as near it as possible". After 1934 the demand for the Constituent Assembly became very frequent and they included it in the Congress manifesto for the year 1936–37 elections. The Congress won majority of states in 1937 elections and in its Faizpur session demanded the newly elected members of the assemblies to articulate the demand for a Constituent Assembly as soon as possible in the new legislatures. The demand for the Constituent Assembly become vociferous and in the meanwhile the

Second World War broke out in 1939 and in order to secure the cooperation of the Indians in the Second World War, the British for the first time announced in 1940 by August offer that the framing of the new constitution should be primarily the responsibility of the Indians themselves. It also offered to set up, after the end of the war, "a body representative of the principal elements in India's national life, in order to devise the framework of the new constitution". This offer, unfortunately, did not spell out, how the body is going to be constituted, and also the method to be followed in deciding the membership of the body to be constituted. This vague aspect proves that the British reluctantly agreed to this idea of Constituent Assembly and were not serious about its implementation. Consequently, this offer of 1940 was rejected by all the shades of nationalists and the Congress Party started the Individual Civil Disobedience movement to register their protest. In 1942, the British government appointed Cripps Mission. The Cripps proposals categorically stated that the constitution would be the sole responsibility of the Indians alone. The idea of the Constituent Assembly was also accepted and they spelt out its modalities and in other respects, it failed. Once again there was confrontation between the Congress and the British, which resulted in the Quit India movement of 9 August, 1942. For the first time openly and vehemently, the nationalists demanded the British to 'Quit India' and exhorted the Indians 'do or die' in this struggle. The Government of India took all measures to suppress this Quit India struggle and at the end of the war in 1945, they issued a white paper, which was followed by the abortive Simla Conference. The victory of the Labour Party in England and change in the guard enabled the British government to declare and promise to convene a constitution-making body as soon as possible. The Cabinet Mission was appointed to carry out this purpose and it visited India in 1946, on 24 March. After a lot of deliberation between the Congress and the Muslim League and the British, finally the Constituent Assembly came into existence.

The Constituent Assembly

In the year 1946, on 20 November a decision was taken to convene the first session of the Constituent Assembly on 9 December, 1946. The number of members was decided to be 389. It was also decided that out of that strength, 296 were to be from the British provinces and 93 to be from the princely Indian states. Elections to elect members from British India were held in July–August 1946. The Congress won 199 out of 210 general categories of seats. The Congress also won three seats out of four Sikh seats from the Punjab, and three out of 78 seats reserved for Muslims and three seats from Coorg, Ajmer, Mewar and Delhi. The total tally of the Congress was 208 and the Muslim League won 73 out of 78 Muslim seats. For these elections to the Constituent Assembly, only the Sikhs and the Muslims were reorganized as minorities and elections for the Constituent Assembly was not held on the basis of universal adult franchise. In order to make the Constituent Assembly, a wide representative body, the Congress Working Committee took special measures to include representatives of scheduled castes, Parsis, Indian Christians, Anglo-Indians, tribals and women in the Congress list for the general category. The Congress also took extra care to see that only the best intellectuals are chosen to be included in the list of the members of the Constituent Assembly. The Indian Muslim League tried its best to put hurdles in the smooth functioning of the Constituent Assembly, despite the best efforts of Nehru's conciliatory gestures. In this backdrop, the deliberations of the Constituent Assembly began on 9 December, 1946. Before the commencement of deliberations of the Constituent Assembly, Nehru announced, "the first task of this Assembly is to free India through a constitution, to feed the starving people, and to clothe the naked masses, and to give every Indian the fullest opportunity to develop himself according to his capacity". The oldest member, Dr Sachchidanand Sinha was made the Provisional President of the Assembly but, the invitations were dispatched by the secretary of the assembly and not by the Viceroy, though he desired to do so.

The first session was attended by 207 members. The Muslim League stayed away from the deliberations and the Congress Muslims attended the session. On 11 December, Dr Rajendra Prasad was chosen by election as the first permanent Chairman of the Assembly. Nehru moved the famous objectives resolution on 13 December and it was discussed for a week and they postponed the adoption of the objectives resolution as the members of the Muslim League were absent and the princely states were to join the Assembly. In the session which took place between January 20 and 22, 1947, the objectives resolution was passed. The third session of the Assembly took place from 28 April to 2 May 1947, and on 3 June the Mountbatten Plan was announced despite the absence of the Muslim League. The Mountbatten Plan clearly made the partition of India as India and Pakistan certain. After the declaration of Independence on 15 August, 1947, the Constituent Assembly became a sovereign body and also doubled as the legislature for the new state. It served as a constitution-making body as well as law-making organ. A number of committees were created and of such committees, one was headed by B.N. Rao and the other to draft the constitution was headed by Dr B.R. Ambedkar. In July 1946 itself a committee consisting of Nehru as the Chairman and Asaf Ali, K.T. Shah, D.R. Gadgil, K.M. Munshi, Humayun Kabir, R. Santhanam and N. Gopalaswamy Ayyangar as members was constituted to prepare material and proposals for the constitution. The Constituent Assembly as well as the Congress Working Committee thoroughly discussed all the points. This was made clear by Austin as follows: "The Congress Assembly Party was the unofficial, private forum that debated every provision of the constitution and in most cases decided the fate before it" reached the floor of the House. Every one elected to the Assembly on the Congress ticket could attend the meetings whether or not he was a member of the party or even close to it".

In the constitution-making process, both Nehru and Sardar Patel played a very important role by their keen involvement. Bipan Chandra rightly observes that it was Nehru who spelt out the philosophy and basic features of the constitution and Sardar Patel played the decisive role in bringing in the representatives of the erstwhile princely states into the Constituent Assembly, in seeing to it that separate electorates were eliminated and in scotching any move for reservation of seats for religious minorities. Bipan Chandra further adds "Rajendra Prasad won acclaim for his impartiality and dignity as President of the Assembly. Maulana Azad brought his formidable scholarship and philosophical mind to bear on many issues of grave importance". The credit also should be given to the Congress for its non-sectarian approach. It is pointed out by Austin, the chronicler of the history of constitution making in India as follows:

> The Constituent Assembly was a one party body in an essentially one party country. The Assembly was the Congress and the Congress was India. There was a third point that completed a tight triangle, the government (meaning the apparatus of elected government both provincial and national), for the Congress was the government too one might assume, aware of the character of the monolithic political systems in other countries, that a mass party in India would be rigid and narrow in outlook and that its powerful leadership would silence dissent and confine policy and decision making to the hands of the select few. In India reverse was the case. The membership of the Congress in the Constituent Assembly and outside held social, economic and political views ranging from the reactionary to the revolutionary, and it did not hesitate to voice them. The leaders of the Assembly, who played the same role in the Congress and in the union government, were national heroes and had almost unlimited power, yet decision making in the Assembly was democratic. The Indian constitution expresses the will of the many rather than the needs of the few.

The Constituent Assembly consisting of eminent Indians made the Constitution of India between the years 1946 to 1950, and it became operative from 26 January, 1950 by borrowing freely and unabashedly from other constitutions. Bipan Chandra observes, "the widsom of the US constitution and its Supreme Court, the innovations of the Irish constitution, the time tested conventions of the British Parliament, the administrative minutiae of the Government of India Act 1935, and much else, essence of their own people's struggle for freedom – all went into the design and content of the Indian Constitution". The unambiguous commitment to a democratic, secular, egalitarian and civil libertarian society by the framers of the constitution is a clear indication of the foresight of the learned makers of the constitution and their commitment for the welfare of all but not of the few.

Foreign Policy: The Nehru Era

The post-independent foreign policy initiated and implemented by Jawaharlal Nehru, the first Prime Minister of Independent India (1947–1964) was a product of its long history and recent past. The foreign policy marks a great deal of consistency and continuity. Its parameters were evolved during the freedom struggle. Nehru, the architect of the post-independent foreign policy categorically stated that in order to play a crucial role in international sphere, India with its age-old civilization and culture should preserve its identity and vitality by its imperative independent voice without identifying totally with either the Western or capitalist bloc, or the communist bloc of Russia, Eastern Europe and China. It was so because Nehru understood that the newly independent, poor countries of Asia and Africa need all their resources to promote the welfare of their people and the scarce resources should not be spent in war effort. Thus, the economic and social interests of the country decided the nature of the foreign policy. Nehru preferred 'Non-alignment' and declared, "So far as all these evil forces of fascism, colonialism and racialism or the nuclear bomb and aggression and suppression are concerned, we stand most emphatically and unequivocally committed against them. We are unaligned only in relation to the cold war with its military pacts. We object to all this business of forcing the new nations of Asia and Africa into their cold war machine. Otherwise, we are free to condemn any development which we consider wrong or harmful to the world or ourselves and we use that freedom every time the occasion arises". Bipan Chandra writes, "Non-alignment came to symbolize the struggle of India and other newly independent nations to retain and strengthen their independence from colonialism and imperialism. Non-alignment, thus, advanced the process of democratization of international relations. Non-alignment served the basic objective of Indian foreign policy of extending support to colonial and ex-colonial countries in their struggle against colonialism and facilitated the promotion of world peace. Further, Nehru played a positive role in placing the goal of peace, nuclear and general disarmament before the world and the need for peaceful coexistence of countries with different ideologies, differing system as necessity as believed that nobody had a monopoly on the truth and pluralism was a fact of life". Nehru further enunciated *Panchsheel* or the five principles of peaceful coexistence: (a) mutual respect for each other's territorial integrity and sovereignty, (b) non-aggression, (c) non-interference in each other's internal affairs, (d) equality and mutual benefit, and (e) peaceful coexistence. Nehru propagated his ideas continuously in all national and international platforms and conferences. Of such conferences, the important one was Bandung Conference held in 1955 and this was a precursor to the Belgrade Non-aligned Conference wherein Nehru, Nasser and Tito gave a call for nuclear disarmament and peace. Though India's foreign policy revolved around the concept of 'Non-alignment', India never preferred isolation but adopted a pragmatic approach and maintained friendly relations with both warring camps and all countries in the longer national interests. Bipan Chandra rightly notices, "Indian foreign policy sometimes linked with apparently irreconcilable goals. For example, the Soviet Union and India initiated in 1963 and signed in 1964, 1965 and November 1965, major arms deals by which the Soviet Union became the largest arms supplier to India and Indo-Soviet relations entered a qualitatively new phase. At the same time, India decided to adopt the Green Revolution technology for agricultural development, which was backed by the US. The arms deals with the Soviet Union and the Green Revolution which led India to become self-sufficient in food in a few years time increased India's capacity to stand on her own and take a more independent stand in world affairs". The basis of this type of foreign policy was to gain advantages for the nation, and with the same objective India projected an active profile in multinational bodies in the Commonwealth and UNO.

Korean War, Indo-China, Suez Canal, Hungary, and Congo provided India an opportunity to play active international role. India played her cards very judiciously keeping in mind the longer and the larger interests of the developing status of India. Instead of succumbing to western imperialism, India maintained its independent stand and took decisions it felt to be for the good of the country. Nehru's prescription of solutions became the basis of peace efforts, in Indo-China, though it became a major cold war theatre. The nationalization of the Suez Canal by Egypt led to war situation between Britain and France and Egypt. India under Nehru's leadership played active role in the London Conference of 1956 and openly declared the attack of Britain, France and Israel on Egypt as 'naked aggression' and ultimately the aggressors were made to leave Egypt. India valiantly withstood the pressure of the West in the issue of Hungary and India maintained the integrity and independence of Congo by its action of supporting UNO. "It is a well-known fact", Dags Hammerskjold is reported to have said, "Thank God, for India". Bipan Chandra writes "the praise was not undeserved. It was indeed one of the finest moments for policy of non-alignment, of help to newly independent countries of Africa and Asia, and strengthening of the role of multilateral bodies such as the UN". The success of the Nehruvian vision envisaged through non-alignment proves "that given the will, non-alignment could work and there was not just space but also the need for the non-aligned to assert themselves on the side of newly emerging nations".

Relations with Superpowers: USA and USSR

Non-alignment policy initiated, advocated and implemented by India in the Nehru era did not inhibit India from developing friendly relations with USA, a leading capitalist country in post-war world. India followed such a policy because it needed the support of America in critical areas of development but there were irritants like the perception of cold war, recognition of communist China by India, deep-rooted suspicion about India's reliability and stability that stood in the way of friendly relations between India and America, though there was no unremitting hostility between these two governments. However, people to people relations remained friendly. There were pro-Indian groups in America and there were pro-American groups in India too. Towards the end of fifties there was a considerable improvement in relations because of growth of economic ties and exchange of technology and machinery between India and America. The Kennedy administration through its ambassador John K. Galbraith made sincere effort to improve ties. In this situation only, the Chinese attack of India shocked Nehru to the core and made him turn towards the Kennedy administration. Thanks to the mediation of John K. Galbraith, the awkward situation was partially eased for Nehru.

Relations between India and USSR also started on a cool note and acquired great warmth in due course. USSR too suspected India as it wanted to be a member of Commonwealth and Stalin never gave audience to the Indian Ambassador Vijayalakshmi Pandit. But since 1951–52, the nature of relations began to change. Stalin met our Ambassador S. Radhakrishnan and even offered a treaty of friendship. USSR began to support India on the Kashmir issue in the UN and in 1954 USSR offered to give military equipment but India refused. Nehru visited USSR in 1955 and Kruschev and Bulganin visited India in 1956. The path of economic development through planning based on public sector brought the two countries still closer. While US hesitated to help, USSR expressed readiness to help us technologically and economically. By 1973–74, it was said that 50 per cent of India's steel, 35 per cent of oil, 20 per cent of the electrical power, 65 per cent of heavy electrical equipment and 85 per cent of our heavy machine-making machines are produced in projects set up with Soviet aid. When China invaded India in 1962, USSR maintained neutrality and in December 1962, Suslov, the important Soviet leader declared China as responsible for war in the meeting of the Supreme Soviet. USSR started military supplies since 1963 on a large scale and it is no exaggeration to suggest that the victory in 1971 war, was due to the important independent manufacturing base created in India with the assistance of USSR. Bipan Chandra writes, "the Soviet Union too gained from this link. India was an important entry point to the Afro-Asian world of newly independent countries that did not want to become US satellites and were open to Soviet friendship. This helped the USSR in the cold war as well. The Indo-Soviet friendship thus emerged as one of the most critical elements of Indian foreign policy".

Relations with Neighbours

There is a view that India has been behaving like a big brother towards her neighbours. Of all these neighbouring countries, India had strained relations with Pakistan and China and she had cordial relations with the rest of the countries. India signed a Treaty of Peace and Friendship in 1950, which provided Nepal unrestricted access for commercial transit through India. India too settled with Burma a long unguarded border and the problem of settlers amicably and successfully. India maintained with Sri Lanka, leaving aside the problem of settlers, amicable relations. India had to face the continuous hostility of Pakistan because of the unsolved Kashmir issue and with China, due to India's attitude towards Dalai Lama and for giving him asylum in India. In the following pages let us study in detail the relations between India and Pakistan and China.

Pakistan

The causes for friction between India and Pakistan are deep-rooted suspicion and dislike between the two communities – Hindus and Muslims – due to historical happenings of the early and later medieval period. British for their own selfish end of justifying and perpetuating their rule in India by pursuing the policy of "divide and rule" broadened and widened the gulf between the two communities and showed apparent partisan love towards the Muslims. The idea East is East and West is West propagated by the occidentalists created the seeds of "Two Nation Theory" which ultimately led to the demand of the partition of the Indian subcontinent. As the parties involved – the Hindus and the Muslims took extreme stand disagreeing to see reason, the emotionally charged minds persisted for bifurcation. All genuine India lovers expected the division of India would solve the problem forever and usher an era of peace, once their wish is fulfilled. But, contrary to expectations, what happened was that the acrimony was shifted from the internal arena to the international arena giving scope for mediation of the third party. The Kashmir issue added fuel to the existing fire and kindled widespread flames of communal strife. USA took advantage of this volatile situation and tried to integrate Pakistan into the fold of USA through CENTO, SEATO, The Baghdad Pact and a military pact with the US in 1954. In such a situation only, the USSR began to thwart all resolutions on Kashmir unacceptable to India. A new dimension was added by the Chinese attack on India in 1962 and Pakistan and China supported each other. The Indo-Pak war of 1965 ended in a futile attempt by Pakistan. Till the death of Nehru, the rancour that characterized the Indo-Pak relations, made him very unhappy and bitter and he died in 1964 with a broken heart and utmost sadness for the back-biting of China, whom Nehru believed to be a good friend of India and for his failure to end the Pakistani hatred towards India.

China

From time immemorial, India and China had fruitful contacts. In the modern times, India and China became were the victims of colonialism and imperialism, and both the countries with organized struggle against these succeeded in attaining freedom and liberation in 1947 and 1948 respectively. India pleaded for a permanent seat for China in the Security Council, having faith in the new regime. The occupation of Tibet by China in 1950 upset Nehru very much but in 1954 India and China signed a treaty in which India recognized the rights of China over Tibet. Both the countries became party to *Panchsheel* and in the Bandung Conference of 1959, Nehru took measures to project China and Chou Enlai. In 1959, a revolt took place in Tibet and Dalai Lama with his followers fled to India. Dalai Lama was given asylum in India and he was strictly warned not to carry out political activities on the Indian soil. Despite our efforts to stop the Dalai Lama from such activities, the Chinese were unhappy and in October 1959, the Chinese opened fire on Indian patrol near Kongalca pass in Ladakh. Since then relations were strained and on 8 September, 1962, the Chinese army attacked the Thagla ridge and dislodged Indian troops. A week later, the Chinese army launched a huge attack and overran Indian posts in the eastern sector of NEFA or the present day Arunachal Pradesh. The Indian army without resistance accepted defeat and fled. On 20 October, in the western sector, the Chinese captured 13 posts in the Galwan valley and threatened the Chausal airstrip. There was a great furore in India and on 9 November, Nehru sought a wide range military help describing the situation in India 'really desperate' and also sought British assistance. China unilaterally withdrew within 24 hours "leaving behind a heart broken friend and a confused and disoriented people". It is no exaggeration to suggest that Nehru's death in 1964 was hastened by this sudden blow on self-respect by one supposed to be a trust-worthy friend. Much was written about 'whose fault was it' and the aftermath of the Chinese attack. V.P. Dutt observes, "China had arrived at a new theoretical understanding of its own national interests. It had despaired of a peaceful solution to the outstanding problems with the United States and the fulfilment of its primary objectives, viz., the return of Taiwan acceptance of China as a great power, seat in the Security Council. It had now come to believe that the international balance of forces was shifting in favour of the socialist camp to view the Soviet advances in rocketry and ICBMs and that the time had come for the adoption of an uncompromising and militant line in order to compel the United States to make concessions". Bipan Chandra argues that "the Chinese attack on India had little to do with issues between India and China, but was a reaction to a feeling of isolation, abandonment and frustration. By attacking India, they may have wanted to topple Nehru or at least push India into the western camp so that the USSR could have no illusions about Indian non-alignment and would have to rethink its policy of peaceful coexistence, which, the Chinese figured was leading to their isolation". Bipan Chandra is of the view: "the causes of the Indian military humiliation could not be reduced to Indian foreign policy's failure". K. Subrahmanyam suggests that it could "only be characterized as one of the unforeseeable random events of history". Thus, the foreign policy initiated and implemented by Nehru, the first Prime Minister of India was based on the principle of non-alignment, which was not a blueprint for policy but was an approach, a method which the young nation consisting of hungry and illiterate millions was to journey on the dusty road to reach the goal of self-help and self-reliance which can make India a developed country. Though Nehru was a visionary and dreamer, his foreign policy based on non-alignment reflects his pragmatic approach to achieve the objective of a self-reliant independent sovereign republic.

Bibliography

Agarwal, D.P., *Archaeology in India*, London: Curzon Press, 1982.

Allchin, R. and Allchin, B., *The Birth of Indian Civilization,* London: Penguin, 1968.

Altekar, A.S., *The Rashtrakutas and Their Times*, 1934.

Bandyopadhyay, Sekhar, *From Plassey to Partition: A History of Modern India*, Hyderabad: Orient Longman, 2004.

Banerjee, N.R., *Iron Age in India*, New Delhi, 1965.

Basham, A.L., *The Wonder That Was India,* Bombay: Rupa, 1971.

Bhattacharya, N.N., *Ancient Indian History and Civilization: Trends and Perspectives*, Delhi: Manohar, 1988.

Chandra, Bipan et al., *India's Struggle for Independence (1857–1947)*, Delhi: Penguin, 1996.

——, *India After Independence, 1947-2000*, Delhi: Penguin, 2000.

Chandra, Satish, *Medieval India, From Sultanate to the Mughals*, Delhi: Har Anand Publication, 1997.

Chattopadhyaya, B.D., *Aspects of Rural Settlements and Rural Society in Early Medieval India*, Calcutta: K.P. Bagchi, 1990.

——, *The Making of Early Medieval India*, New Delhi: Oxford University Press, 1994.

Chopra, P.N., Puri, B.N. and Das, M.N., *A Social, Cultural, and Economic History of India*, Delhi: Macmillan, 1974.

Dhavalikar, M.K., *Historical Archeology of India*, New Delhi: Books & Books, 1999.

Dumont, Louis, *Homo Hierarchicus: The Caste System and Its Implications*, New Delhi: Vikas Publications, 1970.

Farquhar, J.N., *An Outline of the Religious Literature of India,* Delhi: Motilal Banarsidass, 1967.

Gordon, Stewart, *The Marathas, 1600–1818, The New Cambridge History of India 11,* Delhi: Foundation Books, 1994.

Guha, Ramachandra, *India after Gandhi*, Macmillan Company, 2007.

Habib, Irfan, *Essays on Indian History: Towards Marxist Perception*. New Delhi: Tulika, 1995.

Hazra, R.C., *Studies in the Puranic Records on Hindu Rites and Customs*, 2nd ed. New Delhi: Motilal Banarsidass,1975.

Jaiswal, Suvira, *Caste: Origin, Functions and Dimensions of Change*. New Delhi: Manohar, 1998.

Jha, D.N. (ed.), *Feudal Social Formation in Early India,* Delhi: Chanakya, 1988.

Kane, P.V., *History of Dharmasastras*, Vols. 1 to 5, Pune, 1975.

Khilnani, Sunil, *The Idea of India*, New York: Straus and Giores, 1977.

Kosambi, D.D., *An Introduction to the Study of Indian History,* Bombay: Popular Prakashan, 1975.

Majumdar, R.C., Raychaudhari, H.C. and Datta, K.K., *An Advanced History of India*, London: Macmillan, 1996.

Majumdar, R.C. et al. (eds.), *History and Culture of the Indian People*, Vols. I, II, III, Bombay, 1974.

Raychaudhari, H.C., *Political History of Ancient India,* Revised edition with commentary by B.N. Mukherjee, Delhi, 1996.

Richards, John F., *Mughal Empire, New Cambridge History of India*, I.S., Delhi: Cambridge 1993.

Rizvi, S.A.A., *The Wonder That Was India*, Vol. 2, London: 1987, 11.4, Delhi: Foundation Books 1993, Reprint Paperback, 1993.

Sarkar, Sumit, *Modern India (1885–1947),* Delhi: Macmillan, 1985.

Sastri, Nilakanta K.A., *A Comprehensive History of India*, Vols. I and II, Orient Longman, 1936.

——, *A History of South India*. New Delhi: Oxford University Press, 1955.

Sastry, P.V.P., *The Kakatiyas*, Hyderabad, 1978.

Sharma, R.S., *Aspects of Political Ideas and Institutions in Ancient India,* Delhi: Motilal Banarsidass, 1991.

Stein, Burton, *A History of India*, Oxford: Blackwell, 1998.

——, *Peasant State and Society in Medieval South India*, Delhi: Oxford University Press, 1980.

Talbot, Cynthia, *Pre-colonial India in Practice: Society, Religion and Identity in Medieval Andhra*, Oxford University Press, 2000.

Thapar, Romila (ed.), *Recent Perspectives of Early Indian History*, Bombay: Popular Prakashan, 1995.

——, *Ancient Indian Social History: Some Interpretations*, Delhi: Orient Longman, 1984.

——, *Asoka and the Decline of the Mauryas,* Delhi: Oxford University Press, 1997.

——, *Early India: From Origins to 1300 AD*, New Delhi: Penguin, 2002.

——, *From Lineage to State*, New Delhi: Oxford University Press, 1984.

Tirumalai, R., *Land Grants and Agrarian Reactions in Chola and Pandya Times*, Madras, 1987.

Tripathi, R.P., *Rise and Fall of the Mughal Empire*, Allahabad: Central Book Depot, 1963.

Wink, Andre, "Al Hind: The Making of Indo-Islamic World", Vol. 1, *Early Medieval India and the Expansion of Islam, 7–11 Century*, New Delhi: Oxford University Press, 1990.

Index